Lecture Notes in Computer Science 6538

Commenced Publication in 1973
Founding and Former Series Editors:
Gerhard Goos, Juris Hartmanis, and Jan van Leeuwen

Ranjit Jhala   David Schmidt (Eds.)

Verification,
Model Checking,
and Abstract Interpretation

12th International Conference, VMCAI 2011
Austin, TX, USA, January 23-25, 2011
Proceedings

 Springer

Volume Editors

Ranjit Jhala
University of California, San Diego, USA
E-mail: jhala@cs.ucsd.edu

David Schmidt
Kansas State University, Kansas City, USA
E-mail: das@ksu.edu

ISSN 0302-9743   e-ISSN 0302-9743
ISBN 978-3-642-18274-7   e-ISBN 978-3-642-18275-4
DOI 10.1007/978-3-642-18275-4
Springer Heidelberg Dordrecht London New York

Library of Congress Control Number: Applied for

CR Subject Classification (1998): F.3.1, F.3.2, D.2.4, F.4.1, D.1-3, D.3.4

LNCS Sublibrary: SL 1 – Theoretical Computer Science and General Issues

Typesetting: Camera-ready by author, data conversion by Scientific Publishing Services, Chennai, India

Printed on acid-free paper

Springer is part of Springer Science+Business Media (www.springer.com)

Preface

This volume contains the proceedings of the 12th International Conference on Verification, Model Checking, and Abstract Interpretation (VMCAI 2011), held in Austin, Texas, USA, during January 23-25, 2011. VMCAI 2011 was the 12th in a series of meetings; previous editions of the conference were held in Port Jefferson 1997, Pisa 1998, Venice 2002, New York 2003, Venice 2004, Paris 2005, Charleston 2006, Nice 2007, and San Francisco 2008, Savannah 2009, and Madrid 2010.

VMCAI provides a forum for researchers from the communities of verification, model checking, and abstract interpretation. The conference showcases state-of-the-art research in each of those areas and facilitates interaction, cross-fertilization, and advancement of hybrid methods that span multiple areas. The topics covered in the conference include program verification, model checking, abstract interpretation static analysis, deductive methods, program certification, debugging techniques, abstract domains, type systems, optimization. Papers may address any programming paradigm, including concurrent, constraint, functional, imperative, logic and object-oriented programming.

This year, 71 papers were submitted to VMCAI. Each submission was reviewed by at least three Program Committee members, and on average each paper was reviewed by 3.3 committee members. After carefully deliberating over the relevance and quality of each paper, the Program Committee chose to accept 24 papers for presentation at the conference.

This year's edition continued the VMCAI tradition of inviting distinguished speakers to give talks and tutorials. The program includes talks by:

- David Dill (Stanford University) on *Are Cells Asynchronous Circuits?*
- Ganesh Gopalakrishnan (University of Utah) and Stephen Siegel (University of Delaware) on *Formal Analysis of Message Passing*
- Francesco Logozzo (Microsoft Research, Redmond) on *Practical Verification for the Working Programmer with CodeContracts and Abstract Interpretation*
- Bernhard Steffen and Oliver Rüthing on *Quality Engineering Leveraging Heterogeneous Information*

The quality of the conference crucially depends on the hard work the Program Committee and subreviewers put into the paper selection process; we would like to profusely thank them for their efforts. Our thanks also go to the Steering Committee members for helpful advice, in particular to Lenore Zuck for her invaluable efforts in the conference organization. VMCAI 2011 was co-located with POPL 2011 and held in co-operation with ACM (Association for Computing

Machinery). We thank Matthew Might, who served as our interface to the POPL organizers and ACM for help with the local arrangements. Finally, we are grateful to Andrei Voronkov whose EasyChair system eased the submission and paper selection process, and greatly simplified the compilation of the proceedings.

January 2011   Ranjit Jhala
David Schmidt

Conference Organization

Program Chairs

Ranjit Jhala   David Schmidt

Program Committee

Josh Berdine   Orna Kupferman
Ahmed Bouajjani   Akash Lal
Swarat Chaudhuri   Kedar Namjoshi
Patrick Cousot   Corina Pasareanu
Dino Di Stefano   Ganesan Ramalingam
Azadeh Farzan   Andrey Rybalchenko
Cormac Flanagan   Sriram Sankaranarayanan
Aarti Gupta   Tachio Terauchi
Viktor Kuncak   Lenore Zuck

Steering Committee

Agostino Cortesi   Andreas Podelski
Patrick Cousot   Thomas W. Reps
E. Allen Emerson   David Schmidt
Giorgio Levi   Lenore Zuck

External Reviewers

Aws Albarghouthi   Christoph Csallner
Elvira Albert   Eva Darulova
Paolo Baldan   Giorgio Delzanno
Nick Benton   Isil Dillig
Frederic Besson   Thomas Dillig
Armin Biere   Cezara Dragoi
Sylvie Boldo   Constantin Enea
Aaron Bradley   Jérôme Feret
Arthur Charguéraud   Bernd Finkbeiner
Krishnendu Chatterjee   Robert Frohardt
Yannick Chevalier   Malay Ganai
Adam Chlipala   Vijay Ganesh
Arlen Cox   Pierre Ganty

Ganesh Gopalakrishnan
Alexey Gotsman
Radu Grigore
Arie Gurfinkel
Peter Habermehl
Chris Hawblitzel
Pieter Hooimeijer
Swen Jacobs
Radha Jagadeesan
Barbara Jobstmann
Vineet Kahlon
Nicholas Kidd
Zachary Kincaid
Johannes Kinder
Laura Kovacs
Sudipta Kundu
Shuvendu Lahiri
Arun Lakhotia
Vincent Laviron
Francesca Levi
Wenchao Li
Francesco Logozzo
Giuliano Losa
Roberto Lublinerman
Stephen Magill
Rupak Majumdar
Roman Manevich
Laurent Mauborgne
Alexandru Mereacre
Yasuhiko Minamide
Antoine Miné
Anders Möller
Michael Monerau
Madanlal Musuvathi
Aditya Nori

Gethin Norman
Madhusudan Parthasarathy
Rasmus Lerchedahl Petersen
Polyvios Pratikakis
Vishwanath Raman
Bernhard Reus
Noam Rinetzky
Xavier Rival
Neha Rungta
Yaniv Sa'ar
Mark Schellhase
Koushik Sen
Mihaela Sighireanu
Rishabh Singh
A. Prasad Sistla
Jeremy Sproston
Manu Sridharan
Saurabh Srivastava
Ofer Strichman
Philippe Suter
Serdar Tasiran
Aditya Thakur
Ashish Tiwari
Richard Trefler
Viktor Vafeiadis
Kapil Vaswani
Thomas Wahl
Andrzej Wasowski
Sam Weber
Westley Weimer
Herbert Wiklicky
Greta Yorsh
Fadi Zaraket
Florian Zuleger

Table of Contents

Are Cells Asynchronous Circuits?
(Invited Talk)

David L. Dill

Stanford University, Stanford, CA (USA)
dill@cs.stanford.edu

Cells do not seem to have "clocks" in the same sense as synchronous sequential digital circuits. But cells must operate extremely reliably in spite of large amounts of noise and environmental variations which would result in timing variation in a Boolean model of cellular control.

We define timing robustness as the ability of cells to function correctly when there are significant variations in the timing of internal events, and explore timing robustness in cellular control systems using symbolic model checking. For example, we started with an existing model of the control of the budding yeast cell cycle, which was originally evaluated using a completely synchronous model, and checked whether it had the same property in a completely speed-independent model. We found that there were a small number of hazards in the cell cycle control that would cause it to deadlock for some variations in timing, but that all deadlocks could be eliminated by changes in the model that could be justified from the biological literature. Furthermore, model checking with random mutations shows evidence for evolutionary pressure to maintain speed independence.

We then propose a less conservative timing model than speed independence that allows for "fast" and "slow" processes, which is more realistic biologically than complete speed independence and appears to yield reasonable results for more complex models of the cell cycle and some simple examples from developmental biology.

R. Jhala and D. Schmidt (Eds.): VMCAI 2011, LNCS 6538, p. 1, 2011.
© Springer-Verlag Berlin Heidelberg 2011

Formal Analysis of Message Passing
(Invited Talk)

Stephen F. Siegel[1],[*] and Ganesh Gopalakrishnan[2],[**]

[1] Verified Software Laboratory, Department of Computer and Information Sciences
University of Delaware, Newark, DE 19716, USA
siegel@cis.udel.edu
http://vsl.cis.udel.edu
[2] School of Computing, University of Utah, Salt Lake City, UT 84112, USA
ganesh@cs.utah.edu
http://www.cs.utah.edu/fv

Abstract. The message passing paradigm underlies many important families of programs—for instance programs in the area of high performance computing that support science and engineering research. Unfortunately, very few formal methods researchers are involved in developing formal analysis tools and techniques for message passing programs. This paper summarizes research being done in our groups in support of this area, specifically with respect to the Message Passing Interface. We emphasize the need for specialized varieties of many familiar notions such as deadlock detection, race analysis, symmetry analysis, partial order reduction, static analysis and symbolic reasoning support. Since these issues are harbingers of those being faced in multicore programming, the time is ripe to build a critical mass of researchers working in this area.

1   Introduction

Ever since Dijkstra introduced the notion of semaphores [10], shared memory concurrent programming has been a familiar research topic for computer scientists. Shared memory programming allows the deployment of parallel activities (threads or tasks) that access pieces of shared data. A variety of mechanisms, ranging from static scheduling to runtime schedule management using locks, ensure the integrity of shared data. The underlying hardware maintains the shared memory view by employing cache coherency protocols.

Shared memory concurrency now dominates the attention of computer science researchers—especially those interested in formal analysis methods for correctness [2,46]. The purpose of this article, however, is to bring focus sharply onto the predicament of application scientists who had long ago realized the need for parallelism. A fairly significant milestone was reached about seventeen years ago when these scientists and computer manufacturers interested in large scale scientific computing standardized parallel programming around the Message Passing

---

[*] Supported by the U.S. National Science Foundation grants CCF-0733035 and CCF-0953210, and the University of Delaware Research Foundation.
[**] Supported by Microsoft, and NSF CCF-0903408, 0935858.

R. Jhala and D. Schmidt (Eds.): VMCAI 2011, LNCS 6538, pp. 2–18, 2011.

Interface, which soon became the *de facto* standard in this area. Development of MPI has continued, with the latest edition of the MPI Standard, version 2.2, published in 2009 [26].

Message passing has long been realized as "the other dominant paradigm for parallel programming." As opposed to shared memory, message passing makes it the responsibility of programmers to explicitly move data between participant processes/threads. The semantics of message passing programs has been a popular research topic, with two notable publications being Hoare's theory of Communicating Sequential Processes [15] and Milner's Calculus of Communicating Systems [27]. However, the brand of message passing that has truly succeeded—namely MPI—is a far cry from notations such as CCS and CSP, and even their embellished programming language versions, Occam [18] and Erlang [1]. MPI 2.2 specifies over 300 primitives, including dozens of functions for *point-to-point* sending and receiving of messages, *collective* operations such as broadcast and reduce, and many other functions for structuring large-scale simulation codes using abstractions such as *communicators* and *topologies*.

It is without doubt that MPI has succeeded in a practical sense. It is the single notation that *all* application scientists around the world use for performing large-scale "experiments" on expensive supercomputers. It has enabled cutting-edge research on numerous fronts: how chemical reactions occur; how black holes evolve; how weather systems work; how new theories in physics are put to test; and how we may one day build efficient and safe nuclear reactors. This paper asks the following fair question: *what are formal methods researchers doing to help MPI programmers?* The answer unfortunately is *next to nothing!* We describe some of the research directions being pursued in our groups. We close by reiterating the importance of developing tools for message passing concurrency, both because MPI continues to be relevant for the coming decade and because other APIs and languages inspired by the message passing ideas incubated in MPI are becoming important in the upcoming era of concurrent and parallel computing.

2   An Overview of MPI and Its Correctness Issues

Structure of an MPI program. An MPI program comprises some number $n \geq 1$ of MPI processes. MPI does provide for dynamic process creation, but this feature is not widely used, and we will assume n is fixed for the runtime of the program. Each MPI process is specified as a C/C++ or Fortran program which uses the types, constants, and procedures defined in the MPI library. While there is no requirement that the processes are generated from the same source code, or even written in the same language, in practice one almost always writes and compiles a single generic program and specifies n when the program is executed. The MPI runtime system instantiates n processes from this code. Though generated from the same code, the processes can behave differently because each can obtain its unique PID and the code can contain branches on this value.

MPI provides an abstraction—the *communicator*—which represents an isolated communication universe. Almost every MPI function takes a communicator as an argument. Messages sent using one communicator can never be received or have any impact upon another communicator. A set of processes is associated to each communicator. If the size of this set is m, the processes are numbered from 0 to $m-1$; this number is the *rank* of the process with respect to the communicator. One process may take part in many communicators and have a different rank in each. MPI defines a type MPI_Comm for communicators, and a number of functions to create and manipulate them. The predefined communicator MPI_COMM_WORLD consists of all n processes; the rank of a process with respect to MPI_COMM_WORLD may be thought of as the process's unique PID. The function MPI_Comm_size is used to obtain the number of processes in a communicator and MPI_Comm_rank is used to obtain the rank of the calling process. For examples of these, see Fig. 2(b).

Point-to-point operations. MPI's *point-to-point* functions are used to send a message from one process to another. There are many variants, but the most basic are MPI_Send and MPI_Recv, and many useful MPI programs can be written with just these two communication operations. The sending process specifies the rank of the destination process as well as an integer *tag* which the receiver can use in selecting messages for reception. The receiving process may specify the rank of the source and the tag, but may instead use the *wildcard* values MPI_ANY_SOURCE and MPI_ANY_TAG for either or both of these arguments, indicating that a message from any source and/or with any tag can be received.

A message *matches* a receive if the communicators agree, the sources agree (or the receive uses MPI_ANY_SOURCE), and the tags agree (or the receive uses MPI_ANY_TAG). A receive cannot accept a message x from process i if there is an earlier matching message from process i that has not yet been received [26, §3.5]. This "non-overtaking" requirement means that point-to-point messaging may be modeled by a system of FIFO queues—one for each ordered pair of processes—with the exception that message tags may be used to pull a message from the middle of a queue. Early approaches to the verification of MPI programs used the model checker SPIN [16] and took exactly this approach; see [23, 39].

Neither the type nor the number of data elements is used to match messages with receives. It is up to the programmer to "get these right." If the types are incompatible or the receive buffer is not large enough to contain the incoming message, anything could happen: the Standard does not require the MPI implementation to report an error. Implementations might interpret floating-point numbers as integers, or overwrite the receive buffer (perhaps resulting in a segmentation fault). If error messages are issued, they are often cryptic.

What about buffering? Unlike standard channel models, which assign a fixed capacity to each channel, the MPI model makes no assumptions about the availability of buffer space. At any time, a message sent by MPI_Send *may* be buffered, so the sender can proceed even if the receiving process has not reached a corresponding receive, *or* the sender may be blocked until the receiver arrives at a matching receive and the message can be copied directly from the send buffer to the receive buffer. The Standard places no restrictions on how the MPI implementation makes this decision, though in practice most implementations will base the decision on factors such as the amount of buffering space available and the size of the message. A correct MPI program must behave as expected no matter how these decisions are made. In particular, a correct program should never reach a state in which progress is only possible if a message is buffered. Even though such an action may succeed, it is also possible that the program deadlocks, depending on the choices made by the MPI implementation. This undesirable state is known as *potential deadlock*, and much developer effort is expended on avoiding, detecting, and eliminating potential deadlocks.

A formal model of programs that use a subset of MPI (including the functions described above) is described in [39,40]. Using this model, several theorems facilitating formal verification can be proved. In particular, programs that do not use MPI_ANY_SOURCE exhibit a number of desirable deterministic properties. For example, absence of potential deadlocks can be established by examining only synchronous executions (those in which every send is forced to take place synchronously)—this is true even in the presence of local nondeterminism within a process. If in addition each process is deterministic, absence of potential deadlocks and in fact any property of the terminal state of the program can be verified by examining any single interleaving.

All of these theorems fail for programs that use MPI_ANY_SOURCE. Even for these programs, however, it is not necessary to explore every possible interleaving and behavior allowed by the MPI Standard in order to verify many desirable properties, such as absence of potential deadlock. MPI-specific *partial order reduction* approaches have been developed to determine precisely when it is safe to restrict attention to a smaller classes of behaviors. The *urgent* POR scheme, for example, defines a reduced state space in such a way that when control is away from an any-source receive only a single interleaving needs to be examined, but when at such a receive multiple interleavings might have to be explored [35]. This reduction is safe for any property of potentially halted states. MPI-specific *dynamic* POR schemes are another approach [47,48].

Collectives. MPI provides a number of higher-level communication operations that involve all processes in a communicator, rather than just two. These *collective* functions include barrier, broadcast, and reduction operations. The syntax follows an SPMD style. For example, to engage in a broadcast, all processes invoke the same function, MPI_Bcast, with the same value for argument root, the rank of the process that is sending. On the root process, argument buf is a pointer to the send buffer, while on a non-root process, it points to the buffer that will be used to receive the broadcast message. The MPI Standard requires that all processes in the communicator invoke the same collective operations on the communicator, in the same order, and that certain arguments (such as root) have the same value on every process. If these conditions are violated, the behavior of the MPI implementation is undefined.

The synchronization semantics of the collective operations are also loosely defined. Certain operations, such as MPI_Barrier or an MPI_Allreduce using addition, must necessarily create a synchronization barrier: no process can leave the operation until every process has entered it. Others do not *necessarily* impose a barrier: it is possible for the root to enter and leave a broadcast operation before any other process arrives at the broadcast, because the messages it sends out could be buffered. The MPI Standard allows the implementation to choose the degree of synchronization. As in the case with `MPI_Send`, the degree of synchronization can change dynamically and unpredictably during execution. A correct program cannot assume anything.

Every MPI collective operation is functionally equivalent to a routine that can be written using point-to-point operations. Indeed, in many places the Standard describes a collective operation by giving an equivalent sequence of point-to-point operations. One might wonder why MPI specifies the collectives, since the programmer could just implement them using the point-to-points. The answer is that the collective may be functionally equivalent, but is expected to give better performance in most cases than anything that could be expressed on top of point-to-points. In the IBM BlueGene series, for example, many collective operations are mapped directly to a tree-based network optimized for communication involving all nodes in a partition. Point-to-point operations use a separate 3d-torus network. However, if one is only interested in functional correctness, this does mean that many verification techniques can be extended to the collectives "for free." The theorems mentioned above, for example, all apply to programs using collectives. (Technically, this only holds for reduction operations for which the reduction operator is commutative and associative. Since floating-point addition and multiplication are not associative, it is possible for a reduction using either operator to return different values when invoked twice from the same state. This is because the Standard does not insist that the operation be applied to the processes in any particular order, such as by increasing rank. However, this is the only source of nondeterminism arising from the use of collectives.)

Nonblocking Operations. MPI provides ways for the programmer to specify how computational and communication actions associated to a process may take place concurrently. Modern high-performance architectures can take advantage of this information by mapping these actions to separate, concurrently executing hardware components. This capability is often credited with a significant share of the high level of performance obtained by state-of-the-art simulations.

The MPI mechanism for specifying such overlap is *nonblocking communication*. The idea is to decompose the *blocking* send and receive operations discussed above into two distinct phases: the first *posts* a communication request; the second *waits* until that request has completed. Between the posting and waiting, the programmer may include any code (including other communication operations) that does not modify (or, in the case of a nonblocking receive, read) the buffer associated to the communication.

The nonblocking function `MPI_Isend` posts a send request, creates a request object, and returns a handle to that object (a value of type `MPI_Request`). This call always returns immediately, before the data has necessarily been copied out of the send buffer. (The `I` in `MPI_Isend` stands for "immediate.") A subsequent call to `MPI_Wait` on that handle blocks until the send operation has completed, i.e., until the data has been completely copied from the send buffer—either into some temporary buffer (if the send is buffered) or directly into the matching receive buffer (if the send is executed synchronously). In particular, the return of `MPI_Wait` does not mean the message has been received, or even that a matching receive operation has been posted. The call to `MPI_Wait` also results in the request object being deallocated. After that call returns, it is again safe to modify, re-use, or deallocate the send buffer. `MPI_Irecv` posts a nonblocking receive request and behaves similarly. These functions generalize the blocking send and receive: `MPI_Send` is equivalent to an `MPI_Isend` followed immediately by an `MPI_Wait`; `MPI_Recv` to an `MPI_Irecv` followed immediately by `MPI_Wait`.

A formal model of the nonblocking semantics, as well as a description of their realization in a model checking tool, can be found in [36]. Extensions of the theorems discussed above to the nonblocking case are given in [41].

Nonblocking operations provide a powerful mechanism to the programmer, but also a number of dangers. For example, the programmer must take care to not write to a send buffer involved in a nonblocking operation until after the call to `MPI_Wait` returns. As with all the other pitfalls discussed above, the behavior of the MPI implementation in the case of a violation is undefined.

Properties. In Fig. 1, we summarize a number of correctness properties that any MPI program should satisfy. The programmer cannot count on the compiler or MPI runtime to check any of these, or even to report errors if they are violated. Violations can lead to erroneous results, or to a crash several days in to a long-running simulation on an expensive supercomputer. Given the stakes, the need for tools that can verify such properties before execution is clear.

In addition to these generic correctness properties, developers have expressed interest in a number of properties that may be applicable only in certain cases, or that bear more on performance than correctness. A sampling follows:

1. *The program contains no unnecessary barriers.* (Barriers can take a huge toll on performance, but it is often difficult to decide when a particular one is required for correctness.)

2. *The number of outstanding communication requests never exceeds some specified bound.* (With most MPI implementations, performance can degrade sharply when the number of such requests becomes excessive.)

3. *Every nonblocking communication request is issued as early as possible; the completion operation is issued as late as possible.* (The goal is to maximize the overlap to get the best performance from the runtime.)

4. *A specific receive operation is always issued before the corresponding send is issued.* (Dealing with "unexpected" messages can lead to expensive memory copies and other slow-downs.)

5. *The program is input-output deterministic.* (I.e., the final output is a function only of the input, and does not depend on the interleaving or any other choices made by a compliant MPI implementation.)

6. *The program is input-output equivalent to some other given (sequential or MPI) program.* (Often, a simple sequential program is used as the starting point and serves as the specification for the optimized MPI version.)

1. For each process, no MPI function is invoked before `MPI_Init`; if `MPI_Init` is invoked then `MPI_Finalize` will be invoked before termination; no MPI function will be invoked after `MPI_Finalize`.
2. Absence of potential deadlock.
3. In MPI functions involving "count" arguments, such arguments are always non-negative; if a "count" argument is positive, the corresponding buffer argument is a valid non-null pointer.
4. Any rank argument used in an MPI function call (e.g., `source`, `dest`, `root`) lies between 0 and $m - 1$ (inclusive), where m is the number of processes in the communicator used in that call. (Exceptions: `source` may be `MPI_ANY_SOURCE`, `source` or `dest` may be `MPI_PROC_NULL`.)
5. The element type of any message received is compatible with the type specified by the receive statement.
6. Assuming weak fairness, every message sent is eventually received.
7. Any message received does not overflow the specified receive buffer.
8. For any communicator, all processes belonging to the communicator issue the same sequence of collective calls on that communicator, in the same order, and with compatible arguments (`root`, `op`, etc.).
9. Every nonblocking communication request is eventually completed, by a call to `MPI_Wait` or similar function.
10. The receive buffer associated to a nonblocking receive request is never read or modified before the request completes; the send buffer associated to a nonblocking send request is never modified before the request completes.

Fig. 1. Generic correctness properties applicable to all MPI programs

3   Symbolic Execution and Reachability Analysis for MPI

Symbolic execution involves executing a program using symbolic expressions in place of ordinary concrete values [19]. It has been used for test generation, analysis and verification in many contexts. Its great advantage is that it may be used to reason about many possible input and parameter values at once. When combined with model checking techniques which reason about all possible interleavings and other nondeterministic behaviors, it can be a powerful tool in verifying properties of MPI programs such as those discussed above.

MPI-SPIN [36, 37, 38, 41, 42, 43] was one of the first tools to combine model checking and symbolic execution to verify MPI programs. An extension to SPIN, it adds to SPIN's input language many of the most commonly used MPI functions, types, and constants. It also adds a library of functions supporting symbolic arithmetic, including a simple but fast theorem-proving capability.

One of MPI-SPIN's most innovative features is the ability to establish that two programs are functionally equivalent. The idea is to form a model which is the sequential composition of the two programs and add an assertion at the final state that the outputs from the two programs agree. If the assertion can be shown to hold for all inputs and all possible behaviors of the MPI implementation, the property holds. Typically, bounds must be placed on certain inputs and parameters so that the model will have a finite number of states.

MPI-SPIN requires a Promela model. To extract such a model by hand is labor-intensive and error-prone. In contrast, its successor, the *Toolkit for Accurate Scientific Software* [34,44,45], works directly from C/MPI source code. The front end automatically extracts a TASS *model*. Many of the most challenging programming language constructs can be represented directly in the model and are supported by the TASS verification engine. These include functions and recursion, pointers and pointer arithmetic, multi-dimensional arrays, dynamically allocated data, and of course, a subset of MPI. TASS also supports many MPI-specific optimizations (such as the urgent POR scheme discussed in §2) that are not possible to implement on top of SPIN.

TASS performs two basic functions: (1) verification of a single program, in which properties such as those of Fig. 1 are checked, and (2) comparison of two programs for functional equivalence. In both cases, the user adds annotations to the program in the form of pragmas. These may be used to indicate which variables are to be considered the input or output, to place assumptions (such as bounds) on parameters or variables, or to specify special assertions [44]. To verify a program, TASS takes as input this annotated C code and a concrete value n for the number of processes. It constructs an internal model of an n-process instantiation of the program and performs an explicit, depth-first search of the model's state space, using symbolic expressions for all values. The symbolic module performs sophisticated simplifications of expressions and can also dispatch many of the queries. For those it cannot dispatch on its own, it invokes CVC3 [4]. In comparison mode, either, both, or none of the programs may use MPI, and the number of processes for each is specified separately.

Example: Matrix Multiplication. Consider the problem of multiplying two matrices. The straightforward sequential version is given in part (a) of Fig. 2 while part (b) presents a parallel MPI version adapted from [13].

The MPI version uses the manager-worker pattern. The problem is decomposed into a set of tasks. One process, the manager, is responsible for assigning tasks to workers and collecting and processing the results. As soon as a worker returns a result, the manager sends that worker a new task, and proceeds in this way until all tasks have been distributed. When there are many more tasks than processes, and the amount of time required to complete a task is unpredictable, this approach offers a practical solution to the load-balancing problem.

In our example, a task is the computation of one row of the product matrix. The manager is the process of rank 0, and begins by broadcasting the second matrix b to all workers. The manager then sends one task to each worker; the task is encoded as a message in which the data is the row of a and the tag is the index of that row. (A tag of 0 indicates that there are no more tasks, so the worker should terminate.) The manager waits for a response from any worker using a wildcard receive. In the message sent by the worker, the data contains the computed values for the row of the product matrix and the tag contains the index of the row. The identity of the worker whose result was received is obtained from the `MPI_SOURCE` field of the status object; this worker is sent the next task, if work remains. Finally, all workers are sent the termination signal.

```
void vecmat(double vector[L], double matrix[L][M], double result[M]) {
  int j, k;
  for (j = 0; j < M; j++)
    for (k = 0, result[j] = 0.0; k < L; k++) result[j] += vector[k]*matrix[k][j];
}
int main(int argc, char *argv[]) {
  int i, j, k; double a[N][L], b[L][M], c[N][M]; /* read a, b somehow */
  for (i = 0; i < N; i++) vecmat(a[i], b, c[i]);
  return 0;
}
```

(a) Sequential version

```
#define comm MPI_COMM_WORLD
int main(int argc, char *argv[]) {
  int rank, nprocs, i, j; MPI_Status status;
  MPI_Init(&argc, &argv); MPI_Comm_size(comm, &nprocs); MPI_Comm_rank(comm, &rank);
  if (rank == 0) {
    int count; double a[N][L], b[L][M], c[N][M], tmp[M]; /* read a, b somehow */
    MPI_Bcast(b, L*M, MPI_DOUBLE, 0, comm);
    for (count = 0; count < nprocs-1 && count < N; count++)
      MPI_Send(&a[count][0], L, MPI_DOUBLE, count+1, count+1, comm);
    for (i = 0; i < N; i++) {
      MPI_Recv(tmp, M, MPI_DOUBLE, MPI_ANY_SOURCE, MPI_ANY_TAG, comm, &status);
      for (j = 0; j < M; j++) c[status.MPI_TAG-1][j] = tmp[j];
      if (count < N) {
        MPI_Send(&a[count][0], L, MPI_DOUBLE, status.MPI_SOURCE, count+1, comm);
        count++;
      }
    }
    for (i = 1; i < nprocs; i++) MPI_Send(NULL, 0, MPI_INT, i, 0, comm);
  } else {
    double b[L][M], in[L], out[M];
    MPI_Bcast(b, L*M, MPI_DOUBLE, 0, comm);
    while (1) {
      MPI_Recv(in, L, MPI_DOUBLE, 0, MPI_ANY_TAG, comm, &status);
      if (status.MPI_TAG == 0) break;
      vecmat(in, b, out);
      MPI_Send(out, M, MPI_DOUBLE, 0, status.MPI_TAG, comm);
    }
  }
  MPI_Finalize();
  return 0;
}
```

(b) Parallel MPI version using manager-worker pattern

Fig. 2. Matrix multiplication

For many programs (especially those that avoid wildcards and other sources of nondeterminism), TASS can scale to very large configurations and process counts. But manager-worker programs are notorious for the combinatorial blow-up in the state space, and by their very nature, they must contain some non-deterministic construct, such as MPI_ANY_SOURCE. This example is therefore one of the most challenging for a tool such as TASS. Nevertheless, TASS is able to verify functional equivalence of the two versions over a region of the parameter space in which the number of tasks is bounded by 10, for up to 12 processes.

Fig. 3 shows various statistics arising from this use of TASS. Note that after a point, increasing n only reduces the state space: this is because a greater portion of the work is distributed in the initial deterministic phase of the program. After the number of workers exceeds the number of tasks (moving from $n = 11$ to $n = 12$), there is very little change in the number of states, since one is only

n	transitions	statesSeen	statesSaved	stateMatches	memory (MB)	time (s)
2	58537	58538	1110	0	85	3.3
3	547958	545943	20831	3249	85	14.8
4	4214154	4187479	125521	36279	196	109.9
5	24234538	23996300	561447	275823	522	1127.5
6	86671454	85436358	1545815	1304667	1353	6593.4
7	154537494	151752013	2167303	2841957	1982	8347.8
8	140695720	137779991	1605759	2938383	1242	3732.5
9	75252734	73553814	724211	1704339	699	1400.4
10	27706410	27048664	235531	658791	255	473.2
11	10801810	10543295	90147	258921	144	192.1
12	10819370	10560855	90815	258921	146	197.0

Fig. 3. TASS performance verifying equivalence of sequential and parallel matrix multiplication programs. For each number of processes n, equivalence is verified for all L, M, and N satisfying $0 \leq L, M \leq 2$ and $0 \leq N \leq 10$. The number of tasks is N. Run on a 2.8GHz quad-core Intel i7 iMac with 16GB RAM.

adding processes that never do any work. The number of states saved is only a small fraction of the number of states explored. This is because TASS never saves a state that has no chance of being seen again ("matched"), one of the keys to scalability. At the worst point, $n = 7$, more than 150 million states are explored, and over 2 million saved, taking 2.5 hours. Surely symmetry or some other reduction approach could be applied to examples such as this to reduce this computational effort, though so far no one has figured out how to do this.

4   Dynamic Analysis of MPI

It is widely acknowledged that static analysis methods for concurrent programs cannot be accurate, highly scalable, and highly automated—all at the same time. Therefore it is crucially important to have efficient dynamic verification methods for MPI programs—a trend already apparent in other areas of concurrent programming [11, 14, 29]. We first discuss some of the highly desirable attributes of a dynamic analyzer for MPI programs, illustrating them on a simple example (Figure 4 from [47]). We then describe our dynamic formal verifier ISP which has most of these attributes. In the past we have demonstrated [51] that nontrivial MPI programs (e.g., the 15KLOC hypergraph partitioner ParMETIS) can be analyzed using ISP even on modest computational platforms such as laptop computers. While the use of a small number of MPI processes helped in these demonstrations, it was the fact that these examples were *deterministic* that helped the most. Exploiting determinism, the MPI-specific dynamic partial order reduction algorithm used in ISP can analyze these examples in seconds, generating only one interleaving.

Unfortunately, MPI applications currently of interest to practitioners tend to be much larger, and generate many nondeterministic MPI calls. Such applications can quickly exhaust the computational as well as memory resources of ISP.

P_0	P_1	P_2
$Isend\ (to:1,22)$;	$Irecv\ (from:*,x)$	$Barrier$;
$Barrier$;	$Barrier$;	$Isend\ (to:1,33)$;
	$if\ (x==33)\ bug$;	

Fig. 4. MPI Example Illustrating Need for MPI-specific DPOR

Even if a scaled down model of these applications can be analyzed on modestly sized platforms, bugs can be missed because both the MPI algorithms as well as the MPI library algorithms involved while executing on larger data sets will be different from those used for executing on smaller data sets. More often than not, these examples cannot be scaled down meaningfully, or are poorly parameterized, thus preventing designers from downscaling them. To address the need for highly scalable dynamic analysis methods, we have built a preliminary tool called DAMPI (distributed analyzer for MPI programs) [50]. Already, DAMPI has analyzed many large Fortran and C applications[1]on a 1000 CPU supercomputer cluster with nearly the same level of coverage guarantees as obtainable through ISP. We now proceed to describe the basics of dynamic verification algorithms for MPI, followed by ISP and DAMPI.

Requirements of an MPI Dynamic Analyzer. An idealized MPI dynamic analyzer must possess (at least) the following features:

De-bias from the absolute speeds of the platform: Conventional execution based testing methods for MPI omit many important schedules, causing them to miss bugs even in short MPI programs [9]. This is mainly because of the fact that their executions get trapped into a narrow range of all feasible schedules [52]. To illustrate this issue, consider Figure 4. Here, a non-blocking send call is issued by P_0. The matching wait for this call is not shown, but assumed to come well after the *Barrier* call in P_0 (and similarly for *Irecv*, the non-blocking receive from P_1 and for *Isend* from P_2). Also note that *Irecv* can match any sender (its argument is `MPI_ANY_SOURCE`, denoted by $*$). Therefore, after starting P_0's *Isend* and P_1's *Irecv*, an MPI platform is actually allowed to execute the "*Barrier*" calls. This enables *Isend* of P_2 also to be executed, thus setting up a race between the two *Isend*s within "the MPI runtime" (a distributed system) to match *Irecv*. Ordinary testing methods for MPI programs cannot influence whether *Barrier* calls happens first or which *Isend* matches P_1's *Irecv*. They also cannot exert control over who wins races within MPI runtimes. ISP verifies an MPI program by dynamically reordering as well as dynamically rewriting MPI calls, as described under *forcing nondeterminism coverage* (below). These are done with the objective of discovering the maximal extent of nondeterminism at runtime. Approaches based on 'delay padding' are unreliable for MPI and very wasteful of testing resources.

---

[1] Thanks to excellent profiling support developed for MPI [31], it is possible to make dynamic analysis language agnostic—an important requirement in the MPI domain.

Force nondeterminism coverage: Schedule independent bugs (e.g., an allocated MPI object that is not freed) can often be caught through conventional testing. To detect schedule dependent bugs, ISP must explore the maximal extent of nondeterminism possible. Our approach will be to employ stateless model checking [11], set up a backtracking point around $Irecv(from : *)$, and *rewrite the call* to $Irecv(from : 0)$ and $Irecv(from : 2)$ in turn, pursuing these two courses. ISP can determine this set of *relevant executions* and it replays over them automatically, thus ensuring nondeterminism coverage.

Eliminate redundant tests: Ordinary schedule perturbation methods such as [52] may end up permuting the order of *Barrier* invocations over all the $n!$ equivalent cases. Such wastage is completely eliminated in ISP which does not permute the schedules of fully deterministic MPI operations.

However, ISP can still generate redundant tests when it comes to nondeterministic operations. Patterns such as in Figure 4 where the received data is decoded tend to be somewhat rare in MPI. However, building accurate static analysis methods to detect where data decoding occurs, and to maintain such static analyzers across multiple languages requires non-trivial effort (future work). For now, we use heuristics to limit schedule explosion due to nondeterministic calls used in succession.

Base tool operation on a theory of happens-before: The decision to execute *Barriers* before $Irecv(from : *)$ is not a one-off special case in the ISP scheduler. Special case based dynamic verification tools tend to be very brittle and formally impossible to characterize. Instead, this decision is a natural consequence of exploiting the *happens-before* order we have defined for MPI [47]. While MPI itself can be formalized in several ways (e.g., [22, 35]), we have found that it is this more "macroscopic" formal semantics of happens-before ordering that directly guides the construction of the ISP scheduler.

We conducted an *ad hoc* test of the generality of this approach by applying ISP on many simple (but fairly tricky) questions pertaining to MPI program behavior [3]. We observed that ISP's scheduler could determine program outcomes based on the happens-before relation alone.[2] The following additional analysis algorithms are based on ISP's happens-before:

- The consequences of MPI_Send not having adequate buffering (with respect to the message being sent) can be modeled through a happens-before edge connecting the underlying MPI_Isend and MPI_Wait.
- MPI programs can sometimes deadlock more if buffering is *increased*. We can precisely model and study whether a given MPI program has this vulnerability by analyzing the underlying happens-before structure [49].
- We include an algorithm to detect *functionally irrelevant barriers* in MPI programs [33] by analyzing the happens-before structure and seeing whether the presence of an MPI_Barrier alters this relation.

Cover the input-space: The bug "*bug*" in process P_1 will be hit only if P_0 and P_2 supply the right values in their $Isend$ operations. This may ultimately be a

---

[2] A few flaws in ISP were also found and fixed in the process.

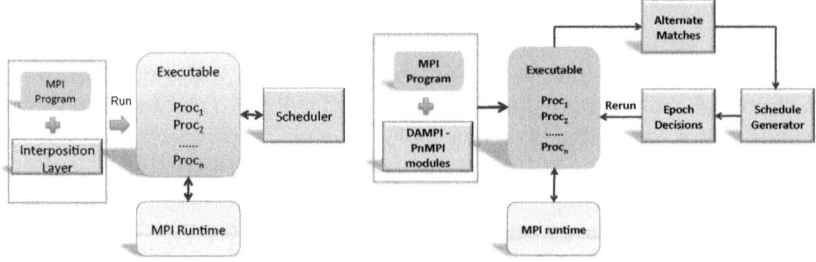

Fig. 5. ISP (left) and DAMPI (right)

function of the inputs to the whole program. Currently ISP does not have the ability to perform input selection; this is an important item of future work.

Provide a well engineered development environment: We have released a tool called Graphical Explorer of MPI programs (GEM, [17]). GEM is now an official part of the Eclipse Parallel Tools Platform (PTP, [28]) release 4.0. One can directly download GEM from the official Eclipse PTP site, and couple it with ISP which is released from our site. The availability of GEM makes it much easier to understand (and teach) MPI. One can use a rigorous approach in this teaching, as GEM is equipped with facilities for viewing the MPI program behavior through the happens-before relation. GEM can also display the MPI schedule from the programmers' perspective, but can also display the internally reordered schedule that ISP actually uses. The release of GEM through PTP is expected to encourage integration with other MPI tool efforts (e.g., conventional debuggers).

ISP and DAMPI. We have built two tools to carry out dynamic verification. The first is ISP (mentioned already) which exerts centralized scheduling control through a profiling layer. The ISP approach guarantees nondeterminism coverage [47] because of its dynamic MPI call reordering and rewriting already explained. ISP's dynamic verification algorithm is as follows:

  – It picks a process and runs it under the control of the verification scheduler.
  – ISP sends the intercepted MPI calls to the MPI runtime whenever the calls are deterministic. Nondeterministic MPI calls are delayed until after all processes are at a *fence*.
  – A process reaches a *fence* when all its further operations are happens-before ordered after its current operation. At this time, ISP switches processes.
  – When all processes are at a fence, ISP reaches a decision point. It can now exactly determine all the matches for an MPI nondeterministic operation. It replaces the nondeterministic calls by their determinized counterparts as explained before.

ISP's dynamic partial order reduction algorithm can be expressed as a prioritized transition system consisting of process transitions and MPI runtime transitions. The theory of ample sets [7] formalizes this algorithm.

Distributed Analyzer of MPI Programs (DAMPI). ISP uses a centralized scheduler. It ends up duplicating much of what an MPI runtime would do, but precisely with a view to obtain scheduling control that is important in order to guarantee coverage. ISP's usage of the MPI library—however advanced it might be—is to merely "finish up" message matches. All these result in many limitations: (i) it is very difficult to parallelize ISP's scheduler; (ii) we slow down the processing of an MPI application by intercepting at every juncture; (iii) a highly efficient MPI library may be underutilized; (iv) ISP's scheduler is very complex and difficult to maintain. DAMPI incorporates a few key innovations. First, it tracks happens-before in a distributed setting using logical clocks. While vector clocks will ensure full coverage, Lamport clocks [20] are a much cheaper alternative adequate for realistic MPI programs. Second, it only tracks the nondeterministic component of the happens-before relation. All other calls can be "fired and forgotten." Last but not least, DAMPI allows processes to run at full speed, with piggyback messages helping convey logical clocks. At the end of each execution run, DAMPI calculates which alternative matches were possible on that run for nondeterministic receives. It then generates these alternate run schedules, and enforces them through MPI call rewriting as before. This process is repeated until the space of nondeterminism is exhausted or bugs are located.

5   Concluding Remarks

MPI continues to be of central importance to programmers in high performance computing, and will continue to hold this position for the forseeable future. In addition, MPI's influence can be seen in recently proposed message passing notations such as the Multicore Communications API [25] and the RCCE library [24]. In [32], we show that many of the lessons learned from the design of ISP can be applied to some of these APIs.

But more research and new ideas are needed in order for formal methods to become a truly practical tool for HPC developers [12]. We have already seen the challenges certain nondeterministic MPI constructs pose to standard state enumeration techniques. Similar issues arise using dynamic model checking: in the example of Fig. 2, ISP generates 18 interleavings for 4×4 matrices using four processes. This shoots up to 54 interleavings for a 5×4 times 4×5 multiplication. Certainly many, if not all, of these executions could be considered "equivalent" under some suitable notion of equivalence. The goal is to find a notion of equivalence which obtains significant reductions in commonly-occuring coding patterns, while still preserving properties of interest. There is a large body of work on symmetry reduction in model checking, but it is not yet clear how this can be applied to programs such as those of Fig. 2.

Other interesting avenues of research include applications of static analysis and Abstract Interpretation to MPI or other message-passing systems. These approaches could potentially reason without bounds on parameters or process counts. Yet very little research has been done in this area. (Some exceptions are [5,8,53].) Parametrized model checking approaches might also be applicable.

There are many avenues for further research on symbolic execution support for MPI. For example, typical scientific programs perform many complex array operations. A significant portion of the verification time involves many element-by-element symbolic array operations. If instead these could be recognized as part of a single high level operation (such as copying one segment of an array to another), the analysis could scale much further, and perhaps even deal with arrays of arbitrary size.

References

1. Armstrong, J.: Programming in Erlang: Software for a Concurrent World. Pragmatic Bookshelf (July 2007)
2. Asanovic, K., Bodik, R., Demmel, J., Keaveny, T., Keutzer, K., Kubiatowicz, J., Morgan, N., Patterson, D., Sen, K., Wawrzynek, J., Wessel, D., Yelick, K.: A view of the parallel computing landscape. Comm. ACM 52(10), 56–67 (2009)
3. Atzeni, S.: ISP takes Steve's midterm exam, http://www.cs.utah.edu/~simone/Steve_Midterm_Exam/
4. Barrett, C., Tinelli, C.: CVC3. In: Damm, W., Hermanns, H. (eds.) CAV 2007. LNCS, vol. 4590, pp. 298–302. Springer, Heidelberg (2007)
5. Bronevetsky, G.: Communication-sensitive static dataflow for parallel message passing applications. In: Proceedings of The Seventh International Symposium on Code Generation and Optimization, pp. 1–12. IEEE Computer Society, Los Alamitos (2009)
6. Cappello, F., Hérault, T., Dongarra, J. (eds.): PVM/MPI 2007. LNCS, vol. 4757. Springer, Heidelberg (2007)
7. Clarke, E.M., Grumberg, O., Peled, D.A.: Model Checking. MIT Press, Cambridge (2000)
8. Cousot, P., Cousot, R.: Semantic analysis of communicating sequential processes. In: de Bakker, J.W., van Leeuwen, J. (eds.) ICALP 1980. LNCS, vol. 85, pp. 119–133. Springer, Heidelberg (1980)
9. DeLisi, M.: Test results comparing ISP, Marmot, and mpirun, http://www.cs.utah.edu/fv/ISP_Tests
10. Dijkstra, E.W.: Cooperating sequential processes. In: Genuys, F. (ed.) Programming Languages: NATO Advanced Study Inst., pp. 43–112. Academic Press, London (1968)
11. Godefroid, P.: Model checking for programming languages using VeriSoft. In: Proceedings of the 24th ACM SIGPLAN-SIGACT Symposium on Principles of Programming Languages, POPL 1997, pp. 174–186. ACM, New York (1997)
12. Gopalakrishnan, G.L., Kirby, R.M.: Top ten ways to make formal methods for HPC practical. In: 2010 FSE/SDP Workshop on the Future of Software Engineering Research. ACM, New York (to appear, 2010)
13. Gropp, W., Lusk, E., Skjellum, A.: Using MPI: portable parallel programming with the Message-Passing Interface. MIT Press, Cambridge (1999)
14. Havelund, K., Pressburger, T.: Model checking Java programs using Java PathFinder. Intl. J. on Software Tools for Technology Transfer 2(4) (April 2000)
15. Hoare, C.A.R.: Communicating Sequential Processes. Prentice Hall Intl., Englewood Cliffs (1985)
16. Holzmann, G.J.: The SPIN Model Checker. Addison-Wesley, Boston (2004)

17. Humphrey, A., Derrick, C., Gopalakrishnan, G., Tibbitts, B.R.: GEM: Graphical explorer for MPI programs. In: Parallel Software Tools and Tool Infrastructures, ICPP Workshop (2010), http://www.cs.utah.edu/fv/GEM
18. Jones, G., Goldsmith, M.: Programming in occam2. Prentice Hall Intl. Series in Computer Science (1988), http://www.comlab.ox.ac.uk/geraint.jones/publications/book/Pio2/
19. King, J.C.: Symbolic execution and program testing. Comm. ACM 19(7), 385–394 (1976)
20. Lamport, L.: Time, clocks, and the ordering of events in a distributed system. Commun. ACM 21(7), 558–565 (1978)
21. Lastovetsky, A., Kechadi, T., Dongarra, J. (eds.): EuroPVM/MPI 2008. LNCS, vol. 5205. Springer, Heidelberg (2008)
22. Li, G., Palmer, R., DeLisi, M., Gopalakrishnan, G., Kirby, R.M.: Formal specification of MPI 2.0: Case study in specifying a practical concurrent programming API. Science of Computer Programming (2010), http://dx.doi.org/10.1016/j.scico.2010.03.007
23. Matlin, O.S., Lusk, E., McCune, W.: SPINning parallel systems software. In: Bošnački, D., Leue, S. (eds.) SPIN 2002. LNCS, vol. 2318, pp. 213–220. Springer, Heidelberg (2002)
24. Mattson, T., Wijngaart, R.V.: The 48-core SCC processor: the programmers view. In: SC10 [30] (to appear)
25. Multicore association, http://www.multicore-association.org
26. Message Passing Interface Forum: MPI: A Message-Passing Interface Standard, version 2.2, September 4, (2009), http://www.mpi-forum.org/docs/
27. Milner, R.: Communication and Concurrency. Prentice-Hall, Inc., Upper Saddle River (1989)
28. The Eclipse Parallel Tools Platform, http://www.eclipse.org/ptp
29. Research, M.: CHESS: Find and reproduce Heisenbugs in concurrent programs, http://research.microsoft.com/en us/projects/chess (accessed 11/7/10)
30. SC 2010: The International Conference for High Performance Computing, Networking, Storage and Analysis, New Orleans, LA. ACM, New York (to appear, 2010)
31. Schulz, M., de Supinski, B.R.: P^NMPI tools: a whole lot greater than the sum of their parts. In: Proceedings of the 2007 ACM/IEEE Conference on Supercomputing, SC 2007, pp. 30:1–30:10. ACM, New York (2007)
32. Sharma, S., Gopalakrishnan, G., Mercer, E., Holt, J.: MCC - A runtime verification tool for MCAPI user applications. In: 9th International Conference Formal Methods in Computer Aided Design (FMCAD), pp. 41–44. IEEE, Los Alamitos (2009)
33. Sharma, S., Vakkalanka, S., Gopalakrishnan, G., Kirby, R.M., Thakur, R., Gropp, W.: A formal approach to detect functionally irrelevant barriers in MPI programs. In: Lastovetsky et al. [21], pp. 265–273
34. Siegel, S.F.: The Toolkit for Accurate Scientific Software web page (2010), http://vsl.cis.udel.edu/tass
35. Siegel, S.F.: Efficient verification of halting properties for MPI programs with wildcard receives. In: Cousot, R. (ed.) VMCAI 2005. LNCS, vol. 3385, pp. 413–429. Springer, Heidelberg (2005)
36. Siegel, S.F.: Model checking nonblocking MPI programs. In: Cook, B., Podelski, A. (eds.) VMCAI 2007. LNCS, vol. 4349, pp. 44–58. Springer, Heidelberg (2007)
37. Siegel, S.F.: Verifying parallel programs with MPI-Spin In: Cappello et al. [6], pp. 13–14

38. Siegel, S.F.: MPI-Spin web page (2008), http://vsl.cis.udel.edu/mpi-spin
39. Siegel, S.F., Avrunin, G.S.: Verification of MPI-based software for scientific computation. In: Graf, S., Mounier, L. (eds.) SPIN 2004. LNCS, vol. 2989, pp. 286–303. Springer, Heidelberg (2004)
40. Siegel, S.F., Avrunin, G.S.: Modeling wildcard-free MPI programs for verification. In: Proceedings of the 2005 ACM SIGPLAN Symposium on Principles and Practice of Parallel Programming (PPoPP 2005), pp. 95–106. ACM Press, New York (2005)
41. Siegel, S.F., Avrunin, G.S.: Verification of halting properties for MPI programs using nonblocking operations. In: Cappello et al. [6], pp. 326–334
42. Siegel, S.F., Mironova, A., Avrunin, G.S., Clarke, L.A.: Combining symbolic execution with model checking to verify parallel numerical programs. ACM Transactions on Software Engineering and Methodology 17, Article 10, 1–34 (2008)
43. Siegel, S.F., Rossi, L.F.: Analyzing BlobFlow: A case study using model checking to verify parallel scientific software. In: Lastovetsky et al. [21]
44. Siegel, S.F., Zirkel, T.K.: Collective assertions. In: Jhala, R., Schmidt, D. (eds.) VMCAI 2011. LNCS, vol. 6538, Springer, Heidelberg (2011)
45. Siegel, S.F., Zirkel, T.K.: Automatic formal verification of MPI-based parallel programs. In: Proceedings of the 2011 ACM SIGPLAN Symposium on Principles and Practice of Parallel Programming (PPoPP 2011). ACM Press, New York (to appear, 2011)
46. Sutter, H.: The free lunch is over: A fundamental turn toward concurrency in software. Dr. Dobb's Journal 30(3) (March 2005),
    http://www.drdobbs.com/architecture-and-design/184405990
47. Vakkalanka, S.: Efficient Dynamic Verification Algorithms for MPI Applications. Ph.D. thesis, University of Utah (2010),
    http://www.cs.utah.edu/formal_verification/pdf/sarvani_dissertation.pdf
48. Vakkalanka, S., Gopalakrishnan, G., Kirby, R.M.: Dynamic verification of MPI programs with reductions in presence of split operations and relaxed orderings. In: Gupta, A., Malik, S. (eds.) CAV 2008. LNCS, vol. 5123, pp. 66–79. Springer, Heidelberg (2008)
49. Vakkalanka, S., Vo, A., Gopalakrishnan, G., Kirby, R.: Precise dynamic analysis for slack elasticity: Adding buffering without adding bugs. In: Keller, R., Gabriel, E., Resch, M., Dongarra, J. (eds.) EuroMPI 2010. LNCS, vol. 6305, pp. 152–159. Springer, Heidelberg (2010)
50. Vo, A., Aananthakrishnan, S., Gopalakrishnan, G., de Supinski, B.R., Schulz, M., Bronevetsky, G.: A scalable and distributed dynamic formal verifier for MPI programs. In: SC10 [30] (to appear), http://www.cs.utah.edu/fv/DAMPI/sc10.pdf
51. Vo, A., Vakkalanka, S., DeLisi, M., Gopalakrishnan, G., Kirby, R.M., Thakur, R.: Formal verification of practical MPI programs. In: PPoPP, pp. 261–269 (2009)
52. Vuduc, R., Schulz, M., Quinlan, D., de Supinski, B., Sæbjørnsen, A.: Improving distributed memory applications testing by message perturbation. In: PADTAD 2006: Proceeding of the 2006 Workshop on Parallel and Distributed Systems: Testing and Debugging, pp. 27–36. ACM, New York (2006)
53. Zhang, Y., Duesterwald, E.: Barrier matching for programs with textually unaligned barriers. In: Proceedings of the 12th ACM SIGPLAN Symposium on Principles and Practice of Parallel Programming, PPoPP 2007, pp. 194–204. ACM, New York (2007)

Practical Verification for the Working Programmer with CodeContracts and Abstract Interpretation

(Invited Talk)

Francesco Logozzo

Microsoft Research, Redmond, WA (USA)
logozzo@microsoft.com

CodeContracts provide a language agnostic way to specify and check preconditions, postconditions and object invariants (collectively called contracts [17]). Specifications take the form of calls to static methods of a `Contract` library [7]. The authoring library is available out-of-the-box to all .NET programmers from $v4$.

An example of CodeContracts usage is reported in Fig. 1. The code illustrates the specification and the implementation of a simple string sanitizer, which filters only ASCII letters and converts all the upper cases into lower cases. The sanitizer also returns the number of lower case and upper case letters in the original string. Strings are represented as `char` arrays. The precondition requires the input string to be not null. The postcondition specifies that the counters are non-negative, that the total number of letters is no larger than the length of the original string and the length of returned string is exactly that size. Furthermore the postcondition also promises the caller that all the elements in the result string are lower case ASCII characters.

The implementation of the sanitizer is pretty straightforward. The original string is systematically traversed, and when an ASCII letter is encountered it is copied into a buffer as it is or if it is upper case, converted to a lower case and then stored into the buffer. A priori we do not know the number of non-ASCII characters, thus the temporary buffer is made as large as the original string. However, on loop exit, we exactly know the length of the sanitized string (it is `lower + upper`), so a buffer of the right size is allocated, all the sanitized elements are copied into it, and then it is returned.

The CodeContracts static checker (codename Clousot [9]), performs an abstract interpretation of `Sanitize` to verify that the implementation meets its contract (specification). Clousot analyzes methods in isolation using a classical assume/guarantee reasoning. Clousot directly analyzes bytecode, so it is independent of the particular source language [15]. As a matter of fact Clousot users include C# as well as VB programmers. All the internals of the analyzer are hidden to the user, to whom the Clousot is exposed as an extension of the usual development environment (Fig. 2).

From a high point of view, Clousot has three main phases: inference, checking and inter-module propagation. In the inference phase the program is analyzed to infer facts. In the checking phase the facts are used to discharge the proof

R. Jhala and D. Schmidt (Eds.): VMCAI 2011, LNCS 6538, pp. 19–22, 2011.

```
public char[] Sanitize(char[] str, ref int lower, ref int upper)
{
 Contract.Requires(str != null);

 Contract.Ensures(upper >= 0);
 Contract.Ensures(lower >= 0);
 Contract.Ensures(lower + upper <= str.Length);
 Contract.Ensures(lower + upper == Contract.Result<char[]>().Length);

 Contract.Ensures(
  Contract.ForAll(0, lower + upper, index => 'a' <= Contract.Result<char[]>()[index]));
 Contract.Ensures(
  Contract.ForAll(0, lower + upper, index => Contract.Result<char[]>()[index] <= 'z'));

 upper = lower = 0;

 var tmp = new char[str.Length];

 int j = 0;
 for (int i = 0; i < str.Length; i++)
 {
   var ch = str[i];

   if ('a' <= ch && ch <= 'z') { lower++; tmp[j++] = ch;}
   else if ('A' <= ch && ch<= 'Z'){ upper++; tmp[j++] = (char)(ch | ' ');}
 }

 var result = new char[j];
 for (int i = 0; i < j; i++) { result[i] = tmp[i]; }

 return result;
}
```

Fig. 1. A string sanitizer and its specification with CodeContracts. Clousot, the Code-Contracts static checker, proves that the postcondition holds at the end of the method and that no runtime exception is ever thrown. The verification is completely automatic, with Clousot inferring the right loop invariants with no user assistance.

obligations. There are two kinds of proof obligations: explicit (assertions from contracts) and implicit (assertions from the semantics of the language). If the checking phase is inconclusive, the analysis is refined by using a more precise abstract domain and/or a backward goal-directed reasoning. In the inter-module propagation, inferred contracts are propagated to the callers [5].

Unlike previous approaches based on weakest precondition calculus (*e.g.* [12,3,1,2,11]), Clousot is based on abstract interpretation [4]. This provides us several advantages. First, the analyzer is automatic: Loop invariants are automatically inferred, without requiring the programmer to provide (for instance) trivial loop invariants. In the example above *all* the invariants are inferred without user interaction. Similarly, the underlying abstract domains are of infinite height and width, providing a stronger expressivity than the domains used for instance in predicate abstraction. For instance in the example the non-trivial loop invariant $lower + upper == j$ is automatically discovered by the analysis. Second, the analyzer is performing: The trade-off cost/precision can be finely

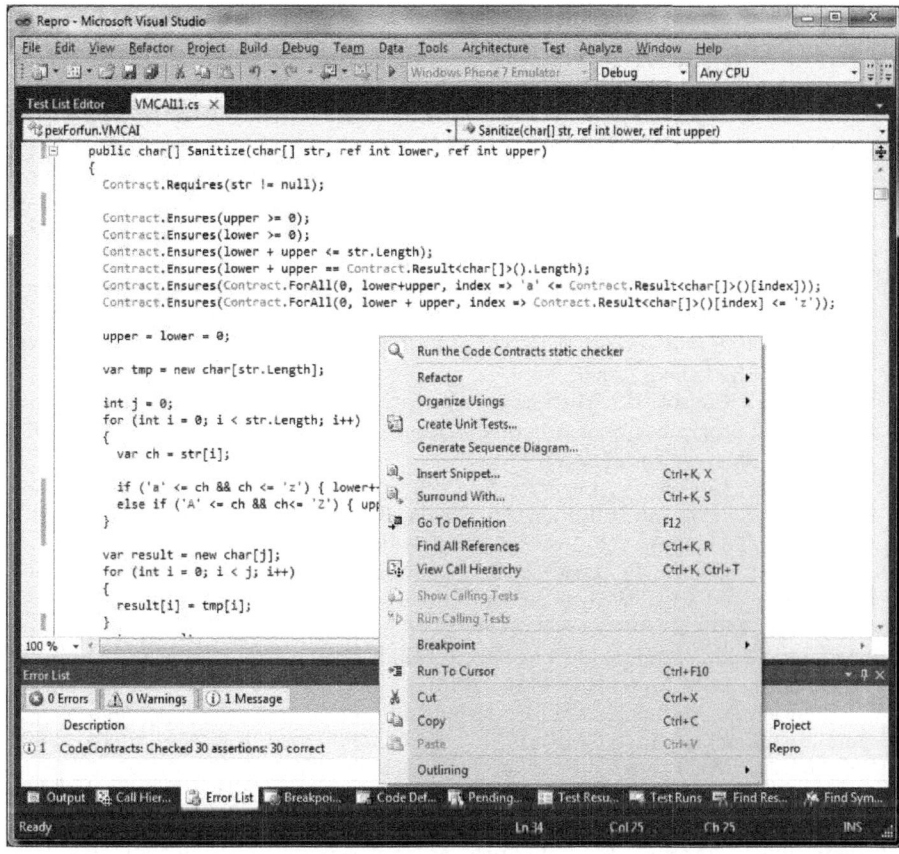

Fig. 2. A screenshot illustrating the user experience with Clousot in Visual Studio. The user can run the analyzer on the whole project, or she can opt for a selective method/class verification with a simple right click. The output is reported in the usual `ErrorList` window, the same where *e.g.* the compiler provides its output.

tuned by adjusting the precision of the underlying abstract domains. Third, the analysis is predictable: by performing chaotic iterations following the program structure, the analysis mimics the intentions of the programmer, so that causes of false positive can be (more) easily found. Furthermore, termination is guaranteed so that annoying causes of analysis non-determinism such as unlucky infinite quantifier instantiation are ruled out. There are some drawbacks though. The main one is that Clousot verification focuses only on a certain class of properties, forgetting for instance general universal quantified or existential quantifiers. Clousot instead contains abstract domains to check common contracts involving: non-nullness [8], linear arithmetic [16,14,13] and numerical properties in general [10], simple facts over arrays and containers [6] and un-interpreted facts.

References

1. Barnett, M., Chang, B.-Y.E., DeLine, R., Jacobs, B., Leino, K.R.M.: Boogie: A modular reusable verifier for object-oriented programs. In: de Boer, F.S., Bonsangue, M.M., Graf, S., de Roever, W.-P. (eds.) FMCO 2005. LNCS, vol. 4111, pp. 364–387. Springer, Heidelberg (2006)
2. Barthe, G., Burdy, L., Charles, J., Grégoire, B., Huisman, M., Lanet, J.-L., Pavlova, M., Requet, A.: JACK — A tool for validation of security and behaviour of Java applications. In: de Boer, F.S., Bonsangue, M.M., Graf, S., de Roever, W.-P. (eds.) FMCO 2006. LNCS, vol. 4709, pp. 152–174. Springer, Heidelberg (2007)
3. Chalin, P., Kiniry, J.R., Leavens, G.T., Poll, E.: Beyond assertions: Advanced specification and verification with JML and ESC/Java2. In: de Boer, F.S., Bonsangue, M.M., Graf, S., de Roever, W.-P. (eds.) FMCO 2005. LNCS, vol. 4111, pp. 77–101. Springer, Heidelberg (2006)
4. Cousot, P., Cousot, R.: Abstract interpretation: a unified lattice model for static analysis of programs by construction or approximation of fixpoints. In: ACM POPL 1977. ACM, New York (1977)
5. Cousot, P., Cousot, R., Logozzo, F.: Contract precondition inference from intermittent assertions on collections. In: Jhala, R., Schmidt, D. (eds.) VMCAI 2011. LNCS, vol. 6538, pp. 150–168. Springer, Heidelberg (2011)
6. Cousot, P., Cousot, R., Logozzo, F.: A parametric segmentation functor for fully automatic and scalable array content analysis. In: ACM POPL 2011. ACM Press, New York (2011)
7. Fähndrich, M., Barnett, M., Logozzo, F.: Embedded contract languages. In: ACM SAC 2010. ACM Press, New York (2010)
8. Fähndrich, M., Leino, K.R.M.: Declaring and checking non-null types in an object-oriented language. In: ACM OOPSLA 2003. ACM Press, New York (2003)
9. Fähndrich, M., Logozzo, F.: Static contract checking with abstract interpretation. In: Beckert, B. (ed.) FoVeOOS 2010. LNCS, vol. 6528, pp. 10–30. Springer, Heidelberg (2011)
10. Ferrara, P., Logozzo, F., Fähndrich, M.: Safer unsafe code in.NET. In: ACM OOPSLA 2008, ACM Press, New York (2008)
11. Filliâtre, J.-C., Marché, C.: The why/Krakatoa/Caduceus platform for deductive program verification. In: Damm, W., Hermanns, H. (eds.) CAV 2007. LNCS, vol. 4590, pp. 173–177. Springer, Heidelberg (2007)
12. Flanagan, C., Leino, K.R.M., Lillibridge, M., Nelson, G., Saxe, J.B., Stata, R.: Extended static checking for Java. In: ACM PLDI 2002. ACM Press, New York (2002)
13. Laviron, V., Logozzo, F.: Refining abstract interpretation-based static analyses with hints. In: Hu, Z. (ed.) APLAS 2009. LNCS, vol. 5904, pp. 343–358. Springer, Heidelberg (2009)
14. Laviron, V., Logozzo, F.: SubPolyhedra: A (More) scalable approach to infer linear inequalities. In: Jones, N.D., Müller-Olm, M. (eds.) VMCAI 2009. LNCS, vol. 5403, pp. 229–244. Springer, Heidelberg (2009)
15. Logozzo, F., Fähndrich, M.: On the relative completeness of bytecode analysis versus source code analysis. In: Hendren, L. (ed.) CC 2008. LNCS, vol. 4959, pp. 197–212. Springer, Heidelberg (2008)
16. Logozzo, F., Fähndrich, M.: Pentagons: a weakly relational abstract domain for the efficient validation of array accesses. In: ACM SAC 2008. ACM Press, New York (2008)
17. Meyer, B.: Eiffel: The Language. Prentice-Hall, Englewood Cliffs (1991)

Quality Engineering:
Leveraging Heterogeneous Information
(Invited Talk)

Bernhard Steffen and Oliver Rüthing

TU Dortmund University, Chair of Programming Systems,
Otto-Hahn-Str. 14, 44227 Dortmund, Germany
Tel.: ++49-231-755-5800; Fax: ++49-231-755-5802
{steffen,oliver.ruething}@cs.tu-dortmund.de

Abstract. In this paper we present a flexible framework for fine tuning the quality of program analysis based on variations, generalizations, and pragmatic extensions of Plotkin's *Structured Operational Semantics* (SOS). Key to these variations is the idea of *Property-Oriented Expansion*, here the non-standard use of the data component in SOS configurations, which ranges from simple abstract interpretations, over arbitrary data flow information, to e.g., temporal constraints. In its most general form, which is characterized by the notion of unifying models, this results in a framework not only for fine-tuning program analysis according to an aspect (quality) of choice, but also for synthesizing orchestrations for service-oriented applications based on loose temporal specifications. From an engineering perspective, the simple interface pattern underlying the unifying models approach was key for realizing our experimental platform. Our experimental results, in particular concerning the state explosion problem, indicate that, in practice, limiting the expansion to the previously determined areas of impact suffices to keep the code growth quite moderate.

1 Introduction

The ongoing dramatic changes of the IT infrastructure impose dramatic changes also on the conceptual landscape. In many settings, space and time are no longer rare resources, and the style of system development has changed form a team effort to a community effort, involving hundreds if not thousands of developers. From the verification point of view this observation has two very different implications. On the one hand new technologies, combined with the effects of Moore's law allow us to deal with increasingly complex systems. On the other hand, the pace of growth of realistic systems, often based on large public domain software libraries, is so high that we continue to fall more and more behind. This is the more so as most realistic systems underly continuous changes, which may easily invalidate most of the previous verification efforts. This situation suggests that besides more and more powerful individual techniques, we need more and more flexibility, in order to adapt to the particular needs of a certain setting. This does

R. Jhala and D. Schmidt (Eds.): VMCAI 2011, LNCS 6538, pp. 23–37, 2011.

not only mean adaptations to different application scenarios, but also different levels in certain design hierarchies. Indeed, it is possible to adapt many of the well-known analysis techniques also for the so-called orchestration level, in order to validate service-oriented applications. At this level, full verification down to the running code is impossible, but it is e.g. possible to considerably increase reliability and time-to-market by controlling the orchestration of the involved services via model checking [2]. In the corresponding project with Siemens the acceptance and impact of this method was very high, in particular, because of the low threshold: already the first temporal constraint had an effect, and this effect increased with every formula added to the constraint library [24]. Even better, this effect is inherited by the whole product line development, because variations of product lines typically require only very minor modifications of their corresponding constraint set. Of the about 200 constraints defined by Siemens in 1996 for their Intelligent Network Solution, most constraints were technical, expressing some aspects of service level agreements between the services and the platform, and only very few were product line specific. This shows the impact of minor adaptations – here the application of model checking at a very high, coarse granular level – and of thinking in terms of frameworks for the easy construction of scenario-specific solutions with their specific notion of *quality*.

This paper is intended to provide ideas on how to develop analysis frameworks flexible enough to capture varying application scenarios with their specific notion of quality. We choose Plotkin's structured operational semantics [17] as a well-known starting point, on which we can then elaborate in order to illustrate our intentions. More concretely, the rest of the paper will

- start with variations of Gordon Plotkin's well-known structured operational semantics [17] in Section 2, where we in particular characterize classical control flow analysis simply as a form of partial evaluation,
- transfer the established viewpoint to a setting for property-oriented system analysis in terms of *Property-Oriented Expansion* [20] in Section 3, which leads to a notion of 'meet/join'-free program analysis. This technique provided the first algorithm for eliminating *all* partial redundancies as illustrated in Section 3.1. In addition, we will present a novel corresponding algorithm for *virtual call resolution* (cf. Section 3.2), and
- sketch the engineering side of our approach in Section 4 by providing simple patterns for implementation, which do not only capture the above techniques, but also a powerful notion of software synthesis (at the orchestration level)[4,14,13,12].

The following development, which is characterized by generalizing the perspective beyond the original intents of the considered technologies, in particular blurs the classical distinction between control flow and data flow [5]: control (flow) is no longer defined by means of standard control operators, but can now be flexibly refined at need by adding (finite) aspects of the data flow in order to increase precision. These refinements may lead to an explosion in the size of the arising (generalized) control flow graphs. Our experimental experience indicates, however, that it is possible to control this size explosion by limiting the expansion to the previously determined areas of impact (see e.g., Table 1). This is due to the fact that the individual ranges of optimization are mostly comparatively local.

In the following we will illustrate how to fine tune the quality of data flow analysis by specifically refining the considered analysis models in order to better express a given aspect of interest.

2 Structured Operational Semantics

Structured operational semantics (SOS) [17] is an intuitive and elegant method for describing the semantics of programming languages. In this section we will see that the underlying 'design pattern' can be exploited much more generally, and that it can be combined nicely with abstract interpretation [3]: already the trivial abstraction to the one point domain resembles classical control flow analysis.

2.1 Standard SOS

Let us consider sequential programs from a simple imperative language:

$$S ::= x = a \mid \textbf{skip} \mid S; S \mid \textbf{if } (b) \ \{S\} \ \textbf{else} \ \{S\} \mid \textbf{while } (b) \ \{S\}$$

SOS assigns meaning to program in terms of partially defined state transformers[1] $\Sigma \xrightarrow{part} \Sigma$. States $\sigma \in \Sigma$ map variables to integer values. We inductively extend the notion of states to arithmetic expressions. For the sake of simplicity we further abuse 1 and 0 as Boolean values true and false.

The core of SOS is given in terms of syntax-oriented rules which define a small-step transition relation among configurations. Configurations are either pairs $\langle S, \sigma \rangle$ capturing a residual statement and a state which occurs during a program's execution or in case of final configurations states alone. For our model language the standard SOS-rules are as follows:

$$\frac{-}{\langle \textbf{skip}, \sigma \rangle \Rightarrow \sigma} \qquad\qquad \frac{-}{\langle x = a, \sigma \rangle \Rightarrow \sigma\{\sigma(a)/x\}}$$

$$\frac{\langle S_1, \sigma \rangle \Rightarrow \langle S_1', \sigma' \rangle}{\langle S_1; S_2, \sigma \rangle \Rightarrow \langle S_1'; S_2, \sigma' \rangle} \qquad\qquad \frac{\langle S_1, \sigma \rangle \Rightarrow \sigma'}{\langle S_1; S_2, \sigma \rangle \Rightarrow \langle S_2, \sigma' \rangle}$$

$$\frac{-}{\langle \textbf{if } (b) \ \{S_0\} \ \textbf{else} \ \{S_1\}, \sigma \rangle \Rightarrow \langle S_i, \sigma \rangle} \quad i = 1 - \sigma(b)$$

$$\frac{-}{\langle \textbf{while } (b) \ \{S\}, \sigma \rangle \Rightarrow \langle \textbf{if } (b) \ \{S; \textbf{while } (b) \ \{S\}\} \ \textbf{else} \ \{\textbf{skip}\}, \sigma \rangle}$$

---

[1] Please note that the meaning of 'state' in this section only concerns Σ, in contrast to the other sections, where 'state' denotes nodes of a transitions system.

Based on the above rules the standard SOS-semantics $[\![S]\!]$ of our model language is given by:

$$[\![S]\!](\sigma) = \begin{cases} \sigma' & \text{if } \langle S, \sigma \rangle \Rightarrow^* \sigma' \\ \text{undefined} & \text{otherwise} \end{cases}$$

Hence for a given state σ the program either reaches a final configuration σ' or diverges with an infinite sequence of non-final configurations.

Due to the infinite data domains, SOS's for realistic programming languages typically define infinite transitions systems, and are therefore more a concept than an actual tool. This may change, however, when considering finite abstract interpretations of Σ [3].

2.2   Control Flow Analysis: The One Point Domain

Collapsing Σ to just one point, $\bullet$, and adding the chosen elementary statement as transitions label, we obtain:

$$\frac{\overline{}}{\langle \mathbf{skip}, \bullet \rangle \overset{\mathbf{skip}}{\Longrightarrow} \bullet} \qquad\qquad \frac{\overline{}}{\langle x = \mathtt{a}, \bullet \rangle \overset{x = \mathtt{a}}{\Longrightarrow} \bullet}$$

$$\frac{\langle S_1, \bullet \rangle \overset{\alpha}{\Longrightarrow} \langle S_1', \bullet \rangle}{\langle S_1; S_2, \bullet \rangle \overset{\alpha}{\Longrightarrow} \langle S_1'; S_2, \bullet \rangle} \qquad\qquad \frac{\langle S_1, \bullet \rangle \overset{\alpha}{\Longrightarrow} \bullet}{\langle S_1; S_2, \bullet \rangle \overset{\alpha}{\Longrightarrow} \langle S_2, \bullet \rangle}$$

$$\frac{\overline{}}{\langle \mathbf{if}\ (b)\ \{S_0\}\ \mathbf{else}\ \{S_1\}, \bullet \rangle \overset{i}{\Longrightarrow} \langle S_i, \bullet \rangle}\ \ i \in \{0, 1\}$$

$$\frac{\overline{}}{\langle \mathbf{while}\ (b)\ \{S\}, \bullet \rangle \overset{\mathbf{skip}}{\Longrightarrow} \langle \mathbf{if}\ (b)\ \{S; \mathbf{while}\ (b)\ \{S\}\}\ \mathbf{else}\ \{\mathbf{skip}\}, \bullet \rangle}$$

This rule set can be used to automatically generate control flow graphs in transition system format, in our experience a format superior to the classical node-centric formats, where data flow information needs to be qualified as *pre* and *post*. We used this fact for our Fixpoint Analysis Machine [22] for front end generation. The effect can be nicely illustrated using the following simple sample program S_{fac} for computing the factorial of an argument variable n:

```
f = 1;
 while (n != 1){
   f = f * n;
   n = n-1
}
```

Using abbreviations S_1 = **while** (n != 1) {f = f*n; n=n-1}, S_2 = **if** (n != 1) {f = f*n; n = n-1; S_1} **else** skip, S_3 = (f = f*n; n = n-1; S_1) and S_4 = (n = n-1; S_1) we obtain the control flow graph depicted in Figure 1.

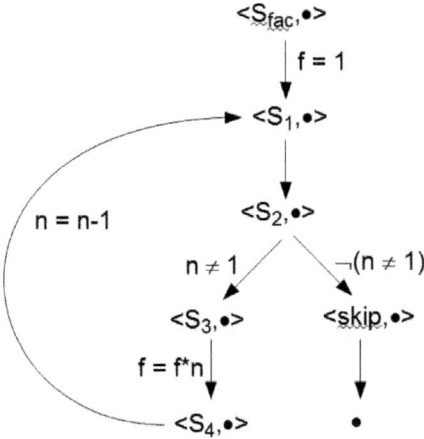

Fig. 1. Stateless SOS unrolls the control flow graph of the factorial program

2.3   SOS-Based Odd/Even Analysis

Of course, Σ can also be abstracted in an arbitrary fashion using appropriate abstract operations and relations. For Odd/Even analysis abstract addition and multiplication can be straightforwardly be defined as:

+	odd	even
odd	even	odd
even	odd	even

*	odd	even
odd	odd	even
even	even	even

The definition of the required $\neq$-operator shows the abstraction-caused loss of precision, as $odd \neq odd$ can evaluate to both true (e.g. $3 \neq 5$) and false (e.g. $3 \neq 3$).

$\neq$	odd	even
odd	$\{0, 1\}$	$\{1\}$
even	$\{1\}$	$\{0, 1\}$

Figure 2 displays the result of applying these rules under the assumption that the computations started with an even argument n. Here the second component of the configurations represent the abstract values of n and f, respectively. We observe that f has an even value whenever a final configuration is reached. Moreover, as this only happens for $n = 1$, the value of n's value is correctly determined odd.

3   Property Oriented Expansion

Recapitulating Section 2 it is worth noting that the graph related to the odd/even abstraction in Figure 2 can be regarded as an expanded model of the pure control flow graph of Figure 1, in the sense that nodes with different odd/even values are

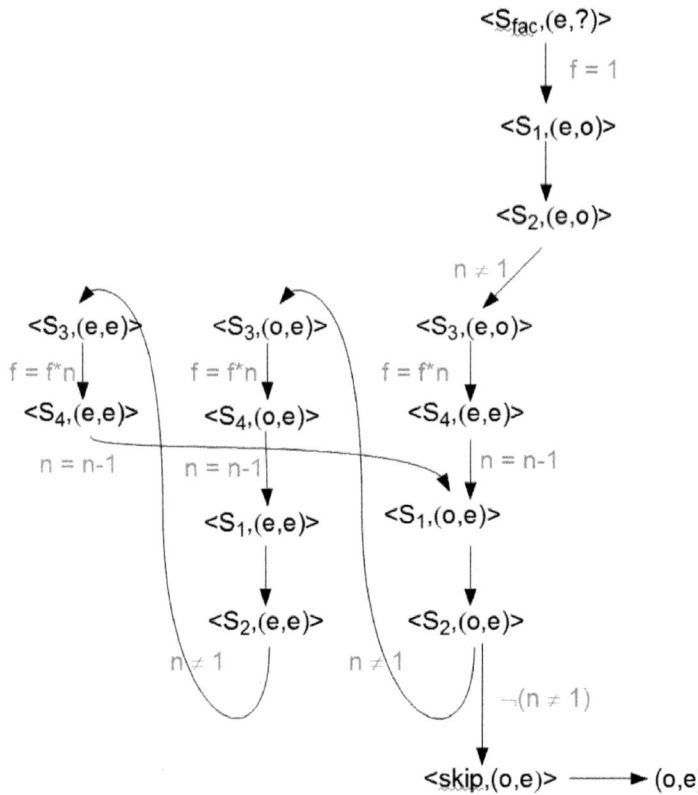

Fig. 2. SOS semantics wrt. odd/even analysis finitely unrolls the control flow graph of the factorial program

split into distinct copies. We call such a splitting procedure *Property-Oriented Expansion* (POE) [20]. POE applies to any (flow) graph structure and any (data flow) property. Indeed, classical SOS can be regarded as such an expansion of the control flow graph with the standard semantics taken as property. Moreover, any set of data flow properties together with its transfer functions defines a POE, which can be regarded as a *meet/join-free* data flow analysis, as no merging of information is required: Properties (e.g. data flow facts) are simply propagated along paths in the control flow graph, and whenever ambivalent information is propagated to a join point separate copies of the node annotated by their properties are created. This simple procedure has nice applications:

3.1 Eliminating All Partial Redundancies

An expression t occurring on an edge (u, v) of the control flow graph is called *redundant*, if there is a t-occurrence on every program path reaching u such that no operand of t is modified in between these occurrences. Redundant computations can be eliminated by storing the computed value into a temporary variable which is then accessed instead of recomputing the redundant expression. If in the above definition of redundancy a weaker requirement is considered where t-occurrences have to be present only on *some* paths reaching u, the t-occurrence on the edge (u, v) is called *partially redundant*.

Classically, partially redundant computations were eliminated by code motion [15,8,9,10], a technique based on the observation that moving computations against the direction of the control flow may move computations into positions where they are totally redundant and can thus be eliminated. Unfortunately, in a fixed control flow graph it is not possible to eliminate all partial redundancies as illustrated in Figure 3(a). Here all the computations of $a + b$ except the first one are partially redundant. However, the computations cannot be eliminated as the rightmost, yet $a + b$-free path prohibits any sound code movement.[2]

In contrast, POE has no problems with this worst-case pattern for partial redundancy elimination. One simply needs to exploit the corresponding redundancy information (typically just bit vectors indicating whether a certain computation is redundant or not) as a driver for the expansion, with the result that at each node of the expanded graph each computation is either totally redundant of fully required. All 'partiality' is automatically eliminated (the *quality* aimed for here)! Subsequently, one simply needs to eliminate the total redundancies as usual in order to arrive at 3(b). Applying classical automata minimization, as proposed in [20] together with the first solution for eliminating all partial redundancies results in 3(c).[3]

Perhaps even more illuminating than the worst-case pattern for partial redundancy elimination of Figure 3 is the treatment of the one state irreducible program graph of Figure 4(a) which our POE transforms into the optimal three state program graph of Figure 4(b) without any need of automata minimization.

POE straightforwardly applies to forward oriented program analyses with finite domains. However, in the original paper [20] the extension towards backwards oriented problems, like *partial dead code elimination* [9], is also addressed, and in [11] we extended POE based redundancy elimination towards the much more general notion of *semantic redundancies*, a problem with an infinite data domain [18,19].

In the following section we present a more recent application of POE to a challenging object-oriented scenario: Virtual Call Resolution. In this context, heuristics for taming complexity become a vital issue.

3.2 Case Study: Virtual Call Resolution

Traditionally, type systems of object oriented languages offer polymorphism with respect to the subclass hierarchy. Variables of a declared class type A can actually

---

[2] For the sake of simplicity we use a uniform assignment pattern $x = a + b$ in the example. This allows us to eliminate complete statements without keeping track on temporaries. A detailed discourse on the issue of assignment vs. expression motion can be found in [10].

[3] In a realistic setting minimization would take conditions of branching into account.

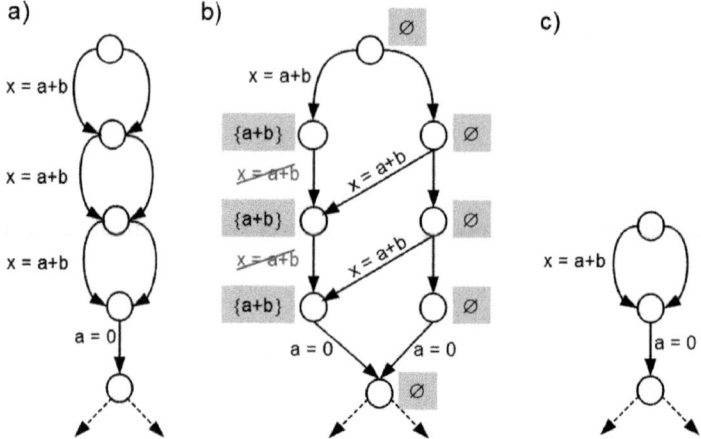

Fig. 3. a) Partially redundant computations that cannot be eliminated by standard techniques. b) Complete redundancy elimination by POE. Nodes are expanded according to the attached redundancy sets. c) Expanded model after minimization.

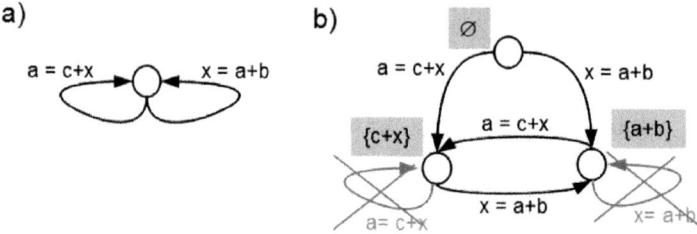

Fig. 4. a) Irreducible program loop with partially redundant computations. b) Optimal program due to POE.

be instantiated by objects of class B if B is a subclass of A. This is illustrated in the following Java code fragment:

```
A a;
  :
if (cond)
    a = new A();
else
    a = new B();
  :
a.m();    // virtual call of m
  :
```

Suppose that method m is implemented by class A and overwritten by the subclass B. Then the method that is actually addressed by the call a.m(); has to be determined at runtime. Traditionally, such method calls are denoted as *virtual calls*. Alternatively, the problem has also been addressed by the phrases *late binding* or *dynamic dispatch* [6,1,25].

Identifying those virtual calls where the called methods can be detected statically is an important optimization issue for object-oriented languages and known as *virtual call resolution (VCR)*. An obvious advantage of VCR is that one may replace virtual calls by less expensive calls that directly target their respective method code. Alternatively, the code of resolved virtual methods can also be inlined in certain cases. Considering the Java Virtual Machine (JVM) there are only two different instructions for methods calls: `invokevirtual` and `invokestatic`. While the latter one is exclusively used for translating calls of static methods, all other method calls are translated to `invokevirtual`. This instruction, however, is burdened by its run-time overhead caused by the intrinsic method search. Thus resolving `invokevirtual` instructions either requires to extend the Java virtual machine by a new invoke instruction or to employ inlining whenever this is possible. Besides the immediate simplification of virtual calls addressed above, the technique offers another benefit, which is at least as important. VCR has an undisputed role as a catalyst for other interprocedural analyses. Since resolving virtual calls narrows the set of potential callees, interprocedural analyses can proceed with less loss of precision.

Resolving virtual calls via POE. However, any traditional VCR method fails when dealing with method calls that are truly polymorphic. For instance, in the above code fragment it is not possible to resolve the virtual method call of m, as the types of the objects being referred by a differ depending on the traversed path. Fortunately, POE offers a means for disambiguating such situations. To this end, variables with a declared class type are annotated with their actual types. These type informations have their origin at program points where a variable is instantiated by a newly created object and can be propagated via assignments. Figure 5(b) shows how POE disambiguates the virtual call of m in our motivating example.

The idea to employ POE for enhancing virtual call resolution has been thoroughly examined within a master thesis of our research group [7]. As the domain of types, which is given by a program's class hierarchy, is more ambitious than the Boolean properties of the introductory example we were particularly interested in the questions of applicability and scalability. Unfortunately, a first implementation using a naive expansion strategy actually led to a tremendous degree of code growth. For instance, we applied the naive POE approach to the source code of the Eclipse project and reported an increase in the code size by a factor of 16 (See Table 1).

Optimizing Program Size Using Liveness. Inspecting the expanded programs more closely we noticed that in many cases nodes were unnecessarily expanded. The main cause for this phenomenon was the fact that splitting nodes according to type information is blind with regard to the actual points of interest, which are the call sites of methods. Thus we added a live variable analysis

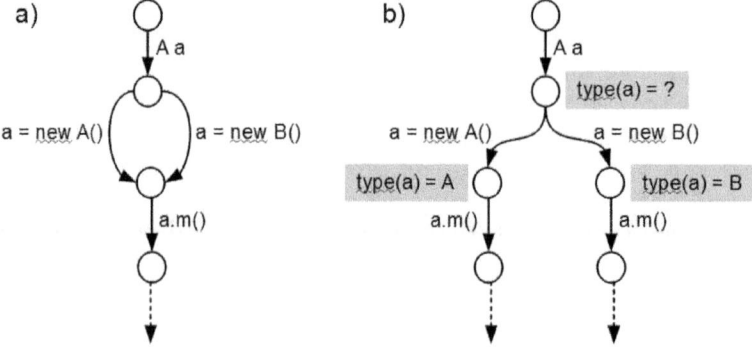

Fig. 5. a) A flow graph with polymorphic virtual method call. b) Virtual call resolution via POE. The type information for variable a is highlighted using grey boxes.

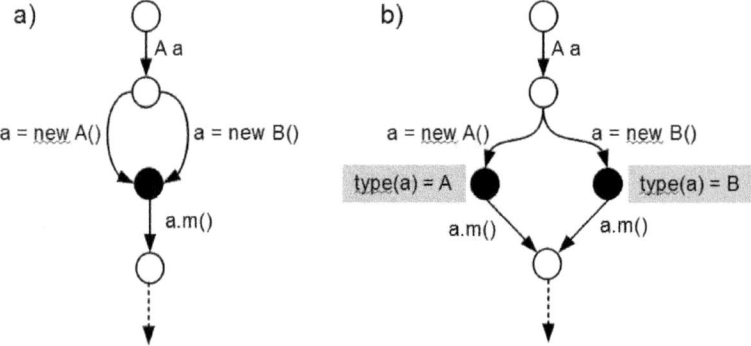

Fig. 6. a) Filled nodes indicate the liveness of a. b) Restricting the expansion process to properties of live variables limits code growth.

as a preprocess of POE which determines whether a variable is actually later accessed by a method call.

Figure 6 illustrates this idea in the context of our example. Assuming that there are no further method calls in which variable a is involved the type information is only relevant at nodes where a is live, i.e. a refers to an object for which one of its methods is called later without passing another assignment to a. In fact, restricting the POE technique to live variables tremendously reduces code replication. In fact, for all examined programs including Eclipse the code growth of our POE based VCR with liveness analysis is well below 5%.

Limitations and future directions. As Table 1 shows all sample programs exhibit a significant amount of virtual calls. Unfortunately, even with support of POE only a small fragment can actually be resolved. The reason for this is

Table 1. Code growth and eliminated virtual calls for sample programs

Program	Code Growth in %		Portion of	Portion of
	Naive	+ Liveness	virtual calls	resolved calls
Antlr	90.2	1.5	63.5	8.4
Bloat	186.5	1.8	57.3	5.1
Chart	302	2.5	55.8	5.3
Eclipse	1590.4	3.4	61.6	11.8
Hsqldb	243	2.7	62.4	7.3
Jython	121.5	0.9	60.8	5
Luindex	69	3.9	75.3	13.9
Pmd	82	1.5	53.3	7.1
Xalan	16.2	2	58.9	12.8

that in our initial solution only top-level objects have been considered as viable variable references. Hence objects that are created as components of arrays or dynamic objects are beyond the scope of our analysis.

The moderate code growth of the basic technique leaves some room for detecting resolvable calls that are beyond this basic scenario. Since in the presence of dynamic data structures the number of objects is unbounded, however, it is not possible to resolve all virtual calls. In particular, subclass polymorphism allows to have data structures with inhomogeneous component types. For instance, consider Java lists with elements of type `Object`. It should be noted that such data structures are quite frequent in real-life Java programs, where generic classes are translated to byte code by using type erasure, a mechanism that eliminates unconstrained type parameters by falling back to `Object` references. In the light of this situation, we investigate to generalize our approach by integrating heuristics that statically determine dynamic data structures with homogeneous component types. In this case, references to such objects can be fully incorporated in the type analysis.

At least to some extent also components of potentially inhomogeneous data structures can be taken into account. As a simple heuristics one may consider to keep track of the types of all objects that can be reached from variables by no more than k references, where k is a small predefined constant.

4   Unifying Models

Unifying Models [21] have been proposed to serve as a conceptual framework for consistency of descriptions of different type from an operational perspective. Basic idea is the existence of a common unifying model structure, in our case in terms of Kripke Transition System KTS [16], i.e. directed graphs whose edges are labeled with action names and whose states are labeled with names reflecting propositions. As example consider Figure 2, where the action names are the atomic statements and conditions of the while language, and the propositions the tuples describing the parity of n and f. Another example is given in Figure 3(b), where again the edges are labeled with statements of the while language, whereas the nodes are labeled with redundancy predicates, and, similarly, Figures 5 and 6 capture type knowledge in an object-oriented setting.

Precondition for this approach are agreed common underlying alphabets for action labels (e.g. the while language) and node labels (e.g. odd/even predicates or redundancy information). The individual descriptions themselves are simply considered as constraints on possible KTS labeled with these alphabet symbols. For obtaining the result of Figure 2 we had two descriptions, the while program for the factorial, which is interpreted via the corresponding SOS, and the lattice of Boolean pairs, here interpreted as parity of n and f, respectively. Figure 2 shows the corresponding smallest consistent KTS, and similarly, Figure 3(b) shows the smallest consistent KTS for the left-hand side graph with a labeling in terms of redundancy information.

This idea of operational consistency is quite general. In particular it works quite well also with constraints written in temporal logics, a setting which can nicely be exploited for high-level software synthesis [4,14,13]. In this case, one of the descriptions may comprise typing constraints, whereas a second could consist of goal descriptions in temporal logics. The algorithm proposed in [4] computed the set of all/all smallest KTS that satisfy both descriptions, i.e. that are type correct and satisfy the goal description in temporal logics. This has been exploited in the ETI environment for automated tool composition [23]. More recently we generalized this approach for supporting a quite flexible notion of *loose programming*, where orchestrations are allowed to contain loose edges which are then automatically expanded to concrete realizations by means of the synthesis algorithm [12].

All these scenarios can nicely be captured using a quite simple design pattern:

- Constraint descriptions are given in term of *black boxes* which support a very simple interface;
  - *commit*, characterizing the actions allowed next in a certain state,
  - *effect*, changing the internal state of the black box according to some chosen action, and
  - *known?*, exposing whether a certain target state is already known.
- The unifying model, which is simply the synchronous product of the KTS of the individual descriptions, can then be easily generated on the fly.

From a (quality) engineering perspective, this pattern is very powerful. It allows one 1) to combine heterogeneous descriptions, 2) to experiment with strategies, e.g. different orders in which to combine or to evaluate constraints, and 3) to add new aspects simply by providing a corresponding black box. This has been exploited in our loose programming approach [12], which comprises loose (control) flow graph specifications, type and data flow information, as well as temporal constraints.

5   Conclusions and Perspectives

We have seen how variations of Plotkin's SOS allowed us to fine tune program analysis in an aspect (or quality) driven way. Depending on the chosen abstract domain for modeling the second component of SOS configurations, we were able to mimic control flow analysis or other kinds of finite abstract interpretations. In its essence, this approach is reminiscent of partial evaluation: the classical starting point is the sole interpretation of the control operators, here realized by a trivial second component of SOS configurations. This interpretation can now incrementally be refined by enhancing the interpretation with more detail about the data part in order to strengthen the precision. In this guise POE can be seen as a simple relaxation of the syntax-oriented SOS approach for 'merging' any computational structure with property information, and the unifying models approach as a further generalization capturing arbitrary operational descriptions, as long as they agree on a certain interface. This engineering perspective leads to an implementation framework, which does not only capture program analysis, but also high-level program synthesis in a uniform and very flexible fashion.

Our experimental results, in particular concerning the state explosion problem, indicate that, in practice, limiting the expansion to the previously determined areas of impact suffices to keep the code growth quite moderate. In fact, it turned out that the individual ranges of optimization are mostly comparatively local, meaning that conceptually involved structures are mostly local too. This observation brings us back to the question of Moore's law and the still growing gap between analyzable models and realistic systems. Just looking at numbers (e.g. of lines), the impression that the gap grows is correct. However, if one considers the situation more carefully, one observes that the conceptual complexity typically does not grow. Rather, huge systems can be seen as a combination of a number of moderate size conceptually complex structures, perhaps organized at different levels in some abstraction hierarchy. Thus it is possible to deal with such systems as soon as one understands this inherent structure. Or, one can control huge systems, as long as they are built in a sufficiently compositional fashion. Service orientations aims at such a kind of high-level compositionality. We are convinced that if service-orientation is taken seriously, we will be able to close the above-mentioned gap with adequate combinations of tailored analysis methods managing the interplay of service-level agreements and local functionality in a high-level assume-guarantee fashion.

Acknowledgement

We would like to thank Norman Karsch for his contributions to the work on POE-based virtual call resolution, and Anna-Lena Lamprecht and Tiziana Margaria for their constructive comments.

References

1. Bacon, D.F., Sweeney, P.F.: Fast static analysis of c++ virtual function calls. In: OOPSLA 1996: Proceedings of the 11th ACM SIGPLAN Conference on Object-oriented Programming, Systems, Languages, and Applications. ACM, New York (1996)

2. Clarke, E.M., Grumberg, O., Peled, D.: Model Checking. MIT Press, Cambridge (2000)
3. Cousot, P., Cousot, R.: Abstract interpretation: A unified lattice model for static analysis of programs by construction or approximation of fixpoints. In: Conf. Record of the 4th ACM Symposium on Principles of Programming Languages, POPL, Los Angeles, CA, pp. 238–252 (1977)
4. Freitag, B., Margaria, T., Steffen, B.: A pragmatic approach to software synthesis. In: Workshop on Interface Definition Languages, pp. 46–58 (1994)
5. Hecht, M.S.: Flow Analysis of Computer Programs. Elsevier, North-Holland (1977)
6. Hölzle, U., Ungar, D.: Optimizing dynamically-dispatched calls with run-time type feedback. In: PLDI 1994: Proceedings of the ACM SIGPLAN 1994 Conference on Programming Language Design and Implementation, pp. 326–336. ACM, New York (1994)
7. Karsch, N.: Virtual call resolution basierend auf property oriented expansion. Master's thesis, Department of Computer Science, Technical University of Dortmund (2009)
8. Knoop, J., Rüthing, O., Steffen, B.: Lazy code motion. In: Proc. ACM SIGPLAN Conference on Programming Language Design and Implementation, PLDI 1992, San Francisco, CA, June 1992. ACM SIGPLAN Notices, vol. 27(7), pp. 224–234 (1992)
9. Knoop, J., Rüthing, O., Steffen, B.: Partial dead code elimination. In: Proc. ACM SIGPLAN Conference on Programming Language Design and Implementation, PLDI 1994, Orlando, FL, June 1994. ACM SIGPLAN Notices, vol. 29(6), pp. 147–158 (1994)
10. Knoop, J., Rüthing, O., Steffen, B.: The power of assignment motion. In: Proc. ACM SIGPLAN Conference on Programming Language Design and Implementation, PLDI 1995, La Jolla, CA, June 1995. ACM SIGPLAN Notices, vol. 30(6), pp. 233–245 (1995)
11. Knoop, J., Rüthing, O., Steffen, B.: Expansion-based removal of semantic partial redundancies. In: Jähnichen, S. (ed.) CC 1999. LNCS, vol. 1575, pp. 91–107. Springer, Heidelberg (1999)
12. Lamprecht, A.-L., Naujokat, S., Margaria, T., Steffen, B.: Synthesis-Based Loose Programming. In: Proceedings of the 7th International Conference on the Quality of Information and Communications Technology, QUATIC (2010)
13. Margaria, T., Meyer, D., Kubczak, C., Isberner, M., Steffen, B.: Synthesizing semantic web service compositions with jMosel and golog. In: Bernstein, A., Karger, D.R., Heath, T., Feigenbaum, L., Maynard, D., Motta, E., Thirunarayan, K. (eds.) ISWC 2009. LNCS, vol. 5823, pp. 392–407. Springer, Heidelberg (2009)
14. Margaria, T., Steffen, B.: Backtracking-free design planning by automatic synthesis in METAFrame. In: Astesiano, E. (ed.) ETAPS 1998 and FASE 1998. LNCS, vol. 1382, pp. 188–204. Springer, Heidelberg (1998)
15. Morel, E., Renvoise, C.: Global optimization by suppression of partial redundancies. Communications of the ACM 22(2), 96–103 (1979)
16. Müller-Olm, M., Schmidt, D.A., Steffen, B.: Model-checking. In: Cortesi, A., Filé, G. (eds.) SAS 1999. LNCS, vol. 1694, pp. 330–354. Springer, Heidelberg (1999)
17. Plotkin, G.: A structural approach to operational semantics. Technical report, Aarhus Univ., Computer Science Dept., Denmark, DAIMI FN-19 (1981)
18. Rüthing, O., Knoop, J., Steffen, B.: Detecting equalities of variables: Combining efficiency with precision. In: Cortesi, A., Filé, G. (eds.) SAS 1999. LNCS, vol. 1694, p. 232. Springer, Heidelberg (1999)

19. Steffen, B., Knoop, J., Rüthing, O.: The value flow graph: A program representation for optimal program transformations. In: Jones, N.D. (ed.) ESOP 1990. LNCS, vol. 432, pp. 389–405. Springer, Heidelberg (1990)

20. Steffen, B.: Property-oriented expansion. In: Cousot, R., Schmidt, D.A. (eds.) SAS 1996. LNCS, vol. 1145, pp. 22–41. Springer, Heidelberg (1996)

21. Steffen, B.: Unifying models. In: Reischuk, R., Morvan, M. (eds.) STACS 1997. LNCS, vol. 1200, pp. 1–20. Springer, Heidelberg (1997)

22. Steffen, B., Claßen, A., Klein, M., Knoop, J., Margaria, T.: The fixpoint-analysis machine. In: Lee, I., Smolka, S.A. (eds.) CONCUR 1995. LNCS, vol. 962, pp. 72–87. Springer, Heidelberg (1995)

23. Steffen, B., Margaria, T., Braun, V.: The electronic tool integration platform: Concepts and design. STTT 1(1-2), 9–30 (1997)

24. Steffen, B., Margaria, T., Claßen, A., Braun, V.: Incremental formalization: A key to industrial success. Software - Concepts and Tools 17(2), 78–91 (1996)

25. Sundaresan, V., Hendren, L., Razafimahefa, C., Vallée-Rai, R., Lam, P., Gagnon, E., Godin, C.: Practical virtual method call resolution for Java. In: OOPSLA 2000: Proceedings of the 15th ACM SIGPLAN Conference on Object-oriented Programming, Systems, Languages, and Applications, pp. 264–280. ACM, New York (2000)

More Precise Yet Widely Applicable Cost Analysis

Elvira Albert[1], Samir Genaim[1], and Abu Naser Masud[2]

[1] DSIC, Complutense University of Madrid (UCM), Spain
[2] DLSIIS, Technical University of Madrid (UPM), Spain

Abstract. Cost analysis aims at determining the amount of resources required to run a program in terms of its input data sizes. Automatically inferring *precise* bounds, while at the same time being able to handle a *wide* class of programs, is a main challenge in cost analysis. (1) Existing methods which rely on computer algebra systems (*CAS*) to solve the obtained *cost recurrence equations* (*CR*) are very precise when applicable, but handle a very restricted class of *CR*. (2) Specific solvers developed for *CR* tend to sacrifice accuracy for wider applicability. In this paper, we present a novel approach to inferring precise *upper* and *lower* bounds on *CR* which, when compared to (1), is strictly more widely applicable while precision is kept and when compared to (2), is in practice more precise (obtaining even tighter complexity orders), keeps wide applicability and, besides, can be applied to obtain useful lower bounds as well. The main novelty is that we are able to accurately bound the worst-case/best-case cost of each iteration of the program loops and, then, by summing the resulting sequences, we achieve very precise upper/lower bounds.

1 Introduction

Static cost analysis [13] aims at automatically inferring the resource consumption (or cost) of executing a program as a function of its input data sizes. The classical approach to cost analysis consists of two phases. First, given a program and a *cost model*, the analysis produces *cost relations* (*CRs*), i.e., a system of recursive equations which capture the cost of the program in terms of the size of its input data. Let us motivate our work on the contrived example depicted in Fig. 1a. The example is sufficiently simple to explain the main technical parts of the paper, but still interesting to understand the challenges and precision gains. For this program and the *memory consumption* cost model, the cost analysis of [3] generates the *CR* which appears in Fig. 1b. This cost model estimates the number of objects allocated in the memory. Cost analyzers are usually parametric on the cost model, e.g., cost models widely used are the number of executed bytecode instructions, number of calls to methods, etc. Observe that the structure of the Java program and its corresponding *CR* match. The equations for C correspond to the `for` loop, those of B to the inner `while` loop and those of A to the outer `while` loop. The recursive equation for C states that the memory consumption of executing the inner loop with $\langle k, j, n \rangle$ such that $k < n+j$ is 1 (one object) plus

R. Jhala and D. Schmidt (Eds.): VMCAI 2011, LNCS 6538, pp. 38–53, 2011.

```
void f(int n) {
  List l = null;
  int i=0;
  while (i<n) {
    int j=0;
    while ( j<i ) {
      for(int k=0;k<n+j;k++)
        l=new List(i*k*j,l);
      j=j+random()?1:3;}
    i=i+random()?2:4;
  } }
```

$$
\begin{aligned}
F(n) &= A(0,n) \quad \{\} \\
A(i,n) &= 0 \quad \{i \geq n\} \\
A(i,n) &= B(0,i,n) + A(i',n) \\
&\quad \{\, i < n, i+2 \leq i' \leq i+4\} \\
B(j,i,n) &= 0 \quad \{j \geq i\} \\
B(j,i,n) &= C(0,j,n) + B(j',i,n) \\
&\quad \{j < i, j+1 \leq j' \leq j+3\} \\
C(k,j,n) &= 0 \quad \{k \geq n+j\} \\
C(k,j,n) &= 1 + C(k',j,n) \\
&\quad \{k' = k+1, k < n+j\}
\end{aligned}
$$

(a) Running Example   (b) *CRs* for Memory Consumption

Fig. 1. Running Example and its Cost Relation System

that of executing the loop with $\langle k', j, n \rangle$ where $k'=k+1$. The recursive equation for B states that executing the loop with $\langle j, i, n \rangle$ costs as executing $C(0, j, n)$ plus executing the same loop with $\langle j', i, n \rangle$ where $j+1 \leq j' \leq j+3$. While, in the Java program, j' can be either $j+1$ or $j+3$, due to the static analysis, the case for $j+2$ is added in order to have a convex shape [7]. The process of generating *CRs* heavily depends on the programming language and, thus, multiple analyses have been developed for different paradigms. However, the resulting *CRs* are a common target of cost analyzers.

Our work focuses on the second phase of cost analysis: once *CRs* are generated, analyzers try to compute *closed-forms* for them, i.e., cost expressions which are not in recursive form. Two main approaches exist: (1) Since cost relations are syntactically quite close to *recurrence relations*, most cost analysis frameworks rely on existing *Computer Algebra Systems* (*CAS*) for finding closed-forms. Unfortunately, only a restricted class of *CRs* can be solved using *CAS*, namely only some of those which have an exact solution. In practice, this seldom happens. For instance, in the cost relation B, variable j' can increase by one, by two or by three at each iteration, so an exact cost function which captures the cost of any possible execution does not exist. (2) Instead, specific upper-bound solvers developed for *CRs* try to reason on the worst-case cost and obtain sound *upper-bounds* (UBs) of the resource consumption. As regards *lower-bounds* (LBs), due in part to the difficulty of inferring under-approximations, general solvers for *CRs* able to obtain useful approximations of the best-case cost have not been developed yet. As regards the number of iterations, for B, the worst-case (resp. best-case) cost must assume that j' increases by one (resp. three) at each iteration. Besides, there is the problem of bounding the cost of each of the iterations. For UBs, the approach of [2] assumes the worst-case cost for all loop iterations. E.g., an UB on the cost of any iteration of B is n_0+i_0-1, where n_0 and i_0 are respectively the initial values for n and i. This corresponds to the memory allocation of the last iteration of the corresponding while loop. This approximation, though often imprecise, makes it possible to obtain UBs for most *CRs* (and thus programs). Observe that it is not useful to obtain LBs since by assuming the best-case cost for all iterations, the obtained LB would be in most cases zero.

Needless to say, precision is fundamental for most applications of cost analysis. For instance, UBs are widely used to estimate the space and time requirements of programs execution and provide resource guarantees [8]. Lack of precision can make the system fail to prove the resource usage requirements imposed by the software client. LBs are used to scheduling the distribution of tasks in parallel execution. Likewise, precision will be essential to achieve a satisfactory scheduling. A main achievement in this paper is the seamless integration of both approaches so that we get the best of both worlds: precision as (1), whenever possible, while applicability as close to (2) as possible. Intuitively, the precision gain stems from the fact that, instead of assuming the worst-case cost for all iterations, we infer tighter bounds on each of them in an automatic way and then approximate the summation of the sequence. For UBs, we do so by taking advantage of existing automatic techniques, which are able to infer UBs on the number of loop iterations and the worst-case cost of all of them, in order to generate a novel form of *(worst-case) recurrence relations* which can be solved by *CAS*. The exact solution of such recurrence relation (*RR*) is guaranteed to be a precise UB of the original *CR*. As another contribution, we present a new technique for inferring LBs on the number of iterations. Then, the problem of inferring LBs on the cost becomes dual to the UBs.

To the best of our knowledge, this is the first general approach to inferring LBs from *CRs* and, as regards UBs, the one that achieves a better precision vs. applicability balance. Importantly, when *CRs* originate from nested loops in which the cost of the inner loop depends on the outer loop, our approach obtains more precise bounds than [9,2]. Moreover, as our experiments show, we are able to produce upper bounds with a tighter complexity order than those inferred by [9,2], e.g., improving from $O(n * log(n))$ to $O(n)$. On the other hand, when compared to [10], our approach is of wider applicability in the sense that it can infer general polynomial, exponential and logarithmic bounds, not only univariate polynomial bounds as [10]. Since *CRs* obtained from different programming languages have the same features, our work is applicable to cost analysis of any language. Preliminary experiments on Java (bytecode) programs confirm the good balance between the accuracy and applicability of our analysis.

2   Preliminaries

The sets of natural, integer, real, non-zero natural and non-negative real values are denoted respectively by $\mathbb{N}$, $\mathbb{Z}$, $\mathbb{R}$, $\mathbb{N}^+$ and $\mathbb{R}^+$. We write x, y, z to denote variables which range over $\mathbb{Z}$. A *linear expression* has the form $v_0+v_1x_1+\ldots+v_nx_n$, where $v_i \in \mathbb{Z}$. A *linear constraint* (over $\mathbb{Z}$) has the form $l_1 \leq l_2$, where l_1 and l_2 are linear expressions. We write $l_1=l_2$ instead of $l_1 \leq l_2 \wedge l_2 \leq l_1$, and $l_1 < l_2$ instead of $l_1+1 \leq l_2$. We use $\bar{t}$ to denote a sequence of entities $t_1, \ldots, t_n$. We use φ or Ψ to denote a set (conjunction) of linear constraints and $\varphi_1 \models \varphi_2$ to indicate that φ_1 implies φ_2. A mapping from a set of variables to integers is denoted by σ.

2.1   Cost Relations: The Common Target of Cost Analyzers

Let us now recall the general notion of *cost relation* (*CR*) as defined in [2] which generalizes the *CRs* yield by most analyzers. The basic building blocks of *CRs* are the so-called *cost expressions* e which are generated using this grammar:

$$e ::= r \mid \mathsf{nat}(\ell) \mid e + e \mid e * e \mid e^r \mid \log(\mathsf{nat}(\ell)) \mid n^{\mathsf{nat}(l)} \mid \max(S)$$

where $r \in \mathbb{R}^+$, $n \in \mathbb{N}^+$, l is a linear expression, S is a non empty set of cost expressions and $\mathsf{nat} : \mathbb{Z} \to \mathbb{N}$ is defined as $\mathsf{nat}(v) = \max(\{v, 0\})$. Importantly, linear expressions are always wrapped by nat in order to avoid negative evaluations. For instance, as we will see later, an UB for $C(k, j, n)$ is $\mathsf{nat}(n + j - k)$. Without the use of nat, the evaluation of $C(5, 5, 11)$ results in the negative cost -1 which must be evaluated to zero, since they correspond to executions in which the `for` loop is not entered (i.e., $k \geq n + j$).

Definition 1 (Cost Relation). *A cost relation C is defined by a set of equations of the form $\mathcal{E} \equiv \langle C(\bar{x}) = e + \sum_{i=1}^{k} D_i(\bar{y}_i) + \sum_{j=1}^{n} C(\bar{z}_j), \varphi \rangle$ with $k, n \geq 0$, where C and D_i are cost relation symbols with $D_i \neq C$; all variables $\bar{x}$, $\bar{y}_i$ and $\bar{z}_j$ are distinct; e is a cost expression; and φ is a set of linear constraints over $vars(\mathcal{E})$.*

The evaluation of a *CR* C for a given valuation $\bar{v}$, denoted $C(\bar{v})$, is like a constraint logic program [11] and consists of the next steps: (1) first a matching equation of the form $\langle C(\bar{x}) = e + \sum_{i=1}^{k} D_i(\bar{y}_i) + \sum_{j=1}^{n} C(\bar{z}_j), \varphi \rangle$ is chosen; (2) then, we need to choose an assignment σ s.t. $\sigma \models \bar{v} = \bar{x} \wedge \varphi$; (3) then, evaluate e w.r.t. σ and accumulate it to the result; and (4) evaluate each call $D_i(\bar{v}_i)$ where $\bar{v}_i = \sigma(\bar{y}_i)$ and $C(\bar{v}_j)$ where $\bar{v}_j = \sigma(\bar{z}_j)$. The result (i.e., the cost of the execution) of the evaluation is the sum of all cost expressions accumulated in step (3). Even if the original program is deterministic, due to the abstractions performed during the generation of the *CR*, it might happen that several results can be obtained for a given $C(\bar{v})$. Correctness of the underlying analysis used to obtain the *CR* must ensure that the actual cost is one of such solutions (see [2]). This makes it possible to use *CR* to infer both UBs and LBs from them.

Example 1. Let us evaluate $B(0, 3, 3)$. The only matching equation is the second one for B. In step (2), we choose an assignment σ. Here we have a non-deterministic choice for selecting the value of j' which can be 1, 2 or 3. In step (4), we evaluate the cost of $C(0, 0, 3)$. Finally, one of the recursive calls of $B(1, 3, 3)$, $B(2, 3, 3)$ or $B(3, 3, 3)$ will be made, depending on the chosen value for j'. If we continue executing all possible derivations until reaching the base cases, the final result for $B(0, 3, 3)$ is any of $\{9, 10, 13, 14, 15, 18\}$. The actual cost is guaranteed to be one of such values.

W.l.o.g., we formalize our method by making two simplifications: (1) *Direct recursion:* we assume that all recursions are *direct* (i.e., cycles in the call graph are of length one). Direct recursion can be automatically achieved by applying partial evaluation as described in [2]. (2) *Standalone cost relations:* we assume that *CRs* do not depend on any other *CR*, i.e., the equations do not contain external calls and thus have this simplified form $\langle C(\bar{x}) = e + \sum_{j=1}^{n} C(\bar{z}_j), \varphi \rangle$. This can be assumed because our approach is compositional. We start by computing bounds for the CRs which do not depend on any other CRs, e.g., C in Fig. 1b is solved by providing the UB $\mathsf{nat}(n + j - k)$. Then, we continue by replacing the computed bounds on the equations which call such relation, which in turn become standalone. For instance, replacing the above solution in the relation B results in the equation $B(j, i, n) = \mathsf{nat}(n + j) + B(j', i, n), \{j < i, j + 1 \leq j' \leq j + 3\}$. This operation is repeated until no more CR need to be solved. In what follows, CR refers to standalone CRs in direct recursive form.

2.2   Single-Argument Recurrence Relations

It is fundamental for this paper to understand the differences between CRs and RRs. The following features have been identified in [2] as main differences, which in turn justify the need to develop specific solvers to bound CRs:

1. CRs often have *multiple arguments* that increase or decrease over the relation (e.g., in A variable i' increases). The number of evaluation steps (i.e., recursive calls performed) is often a function of such several arguments.
2. CRs often contain *inexact size relations*, e.g., variables range over an interval $[a, b]$ (e.g., variable j' in B). Thus, given a valuation, we might have several solutions which perform a different number of evaluation steps.
3. Even if the original programs are deterministic, due to the loss of precision in the first stage of the static analysis, CRs often involve several *non-deterministic equations*. This will be further explained in Sec. 4.3.

As a consequence of 2 and 3, an exact solution often does not exist and hence CAS just cannot be used in such cases. But, even if a solution exists, due to such three additional features, CAS do not accept CRs as a valid input. Below, we define a class of recurrence equations that CAS can handle.

Definition 2 (single-argument RR). *A single-argument recurrence relation C is defined by at most one recursive equation $\langle C(x) = E + \sum_{i=1}^{n} C(x-1) \rangle$ where E is a function on x (and might have constant symbols), and a base case $\langle C(0) = \kappa \rangle$ where κ is a symbol representing the value of the base case.*

Depending on the number of recursive calls in the recursive equation and the expression E, such solution can be of different complexity classes (exponential, polynomial, etc.). A closed-form solution for $C(x)$, if exists, is an arithmetic expression that depends only on the variable x, the base-case symbol κ, and might include constant symbols that appear in E. W.l.o.g., in what follows, we assume that $\kappa = 0$. In the implementation, we replace κ in the closed-form UB (resp. LB) by the maximum (resp. minimum) value that it can take, as done in [2].

3   An Informal Account of Our Approach

This section informally explains the approximation we want to achieve and compares it to the actual cost and the approximation of [2]. Consider a CR in its simplest form with a base case $\langle C(\bar{x})=0, \varphi_0 \rangle$ and a recursive case with a single recursive call $\langle C(\bar{x})=e+C(\bar{x}'), \varphi_1 \rangle$. The challenge is to accurately estimate the cost of $C(\bar{x})$ for any input. *CAS* aim at obtaining the exact cost function. As we have discussed in Sec. 2.2, this is often not possible since even a single evaluation has multiple solutions. Thus, the goal of static cost analysis is to infer closed-form UBs/LBs for C. Our starting point is the general approximation for UBs proposed by [2] which has two dimensions. (1) *Number of applications of the recursive case:* The first dimension is to infer an UB on the number of times the recursive equations can be applied (which, for loops, corresponds to the number of iterations). This is done by inferring an UB $\hat{n}$ on the length of chains of recursive calls; (2) *Cost of applications:* The second dimension is to infer an UB $\hat{e}$ for all e_i. Then, for a relation with a single recursive call, $\hat{n} * \hat{e}$ is guaranteed to be an UB for C. If the relation C had two recursive calls, the solution would be an exponential function of the form $2^{\hat{n}} * \hat{e}$. Programming-languages techniques of wide applicability have been proposed by [2] in order to solve the two dimensions, as detailed below.

Ranking functions. A ranking function is a function f such that for any recursive equation $\langle C(\bar{x})=e+C(\bar{x}_1)+\cdots+C(\bar{x}_k), \varphi \rangle$ in the *CR*, it holds that $\forall 1 \le i \le k. \varphi \models f(\bar{x}) > f(\bar{x}_i) \wedge f(\bar{x}) > 0$. This guarantees that when evaluating $C(\bar{v})$, the length of any chain of recursive calls to C cannot exceed $f(\bar{v})$. Thus, f is used to bound the length of these chains [2,5,6]. We rely on [2] for automatically inferring a ranking function $\hat{f}_C(\bar{x}_0)$ for C (variables $\bar{x}_0$ denote the initial values).

Maximization. In [2] the second dimension is solved by first inferring an *invariant* $\langle C(\bar{x}_0) \rightsquigarrow C(\bar{x}), \Psi \rangle$, where Ψ is a set of linear constraints, which describes the relation between the values that $\bar{x}$ can take in any recursive call and the initial values $\bar{x}_0$. Then in order to generate $\hat{e}$ each $\mathsf{nat}(l) \in e$ is replaced by $\mathsf{nat}(\hat{l})$ where $\hat{l}$ is a linear expression (over $\bar{x}_0$) which is an UB for any valuation of l. We rely on the techniques of [2] in order to automatically obtain $\mathsf{nat}(\hat{l})$ for $\mathsf{nat}(l)$.

Our challenge is to improve precision of [2] while keeping a similar applicability for UBs and, besides, be able to apply our approach to infer useful LBs. The fundamental idea is to generate a sequence of (different) elements $u_1, \ldots, u_{\hat{n}}$ such that for any concrete evaluation $e_1, \ldots, e_n$ it holds $\forall 0 \le i \le n-1. u_{\hat{n}-i} \ge e_{n-i}$. Note that it is ensured that the last n elements of the u sequence are larger than (or equal to) the n elements of the e sequence, but it is not guaranteed that $u_i \ge e_i$. This guarantees that $u_1 + \cdots + u_{\hat{n}}$ is an UB for $e_1 + \cdots + e_n$. Our UB is potentially more precise than $\hat{n} * \hat{e}$, since each e_i is approximated more tightly by a corresponding u_j. Technically, we do this by transforming the *CR* into a (worst-case) *RR* (as in Def. 2) whose closed-form solution is $u_1 + \cdots + u_{\hat{n}}$. The novel idea is to view $u_1, \cdots, u_{\hat{n}}$ as an arithmetic sequence that starts from $u_{\hat{n}} \equiv \hat{e}$ and each time decreases by $\check{d}$ where $\check{d}$ is an under approximation of all $d_i = e_{i+1} - e_i$, i.e., $u_i = u_{i-1} + \check{d}$. In our approach the problem of inferring LBs is dual, namely we can infer a LB $\check{n}$ on the length of chains of recursive calls, the minimum value $\check{e}$ to which e_i can be evaluated, and then sum the sequence $\ell_1, \ldots, \ell_{\check{n}}$ where $\ell_i = \ell_{i-1} + \check{d}$ and $\ell_1 = \check{e}$.

4   Inference of Precise Upper Bounds

In this section, we present our approach to accurately infer UBs on the resource consumption in three steps: first in Sec. 4.1, we handle a subclass of *CRs* which accumulate a constant cost, then we handle *CRs* which accumulate non-constant costs in Sec. 4.2 and *CRs* with multiple overlapping equations in Sec. 4.3.

4.1   Constant Cost Relations

We consider *CRs* defined by a single recursive equation with constant cost:

$$\langle C(\bar{x}) = 0, \varphi_1 \rangle \mid \langle C(\bar{x}) = e + C(\bar{x}_1) + \cdots + C(\bar{x}_k), \varphi_2 \rangle \tag{1}$$

where e contributes a *constant cost*, i.e., it is a constant number or an expression that always evaluates to the same value. As explained in Sec. 3, any chain of recursive calls in C is at most of length $\hat{f}_C(\bar{x}_0)$ (when starting from $C(\bar{x}_0)$). We aim at obtaining an UB for C by solving a *RR* P_C in which all chains of recursive calls are of length $\hat{f}_C(\bar{x}_0)$. Intuitively, $P_C(x)$ can be seen as a special case of a *RR* with the same number of recursive calls as in C, where all chains of recursive calls are of length x, and each application accumulates the constant cost e. Its solution can be then instantiated for the case of C by replacing x by $\hat{f}_C(\bar{x}_0)$.

Definition 3. *The worst-case RR of C is $\langle P_C(x) = e + P_C(x - 1) + \cdots + P_C(x-1) \rangle$.*

The main achievement of the above transformation is that, for constant *CRs*, we get rid of their problematic features described in Sec. 2.2 which prevented us from relying on *CAS* to obtain a precise solution. The following theorem explains how the closed-form solution of the *RR* P_C can be transformed into an UB for the *CR* C.

Theorem 1. *If E is a solution for $P_C(x)$ then $E[x/\hat{f}_C(\bar{x}_0)]$ is an UB for $C(\bar{x}_0)$.*

Example 2. The worst-case *RR* of the *CR* C of Fig. 1b is $\langle P_C(x) = 1 + P_C(x-1) \rangle$, which is solved using *CAS* to $P_C(x) = x$ for any $x \geq 0$. The UB for C is obtained by replacing x by $\hat{f}_C(k_0, j_0, n_0) = \mathsf{nat}(j_0 + n_0 - k_0)$.

4.2   Non-constant Cost Relations

During cost analysis, in many cases we obtain *CRs* like the one of Eq. 1, but with a non-constant expression e which is evaluated to different values e_i in different applications of the recursive equation. The transformation in Def. 3 would not be correct since in these cases e must be appropriately related to x. In particular, the main difficulty is to simulate the accumulation of the non-constant expressions e_i at the level of the *RR*. As we have illustrated in Sec. 3, the novel idea is to simulate this behavior with an arithmetic sequence that starts from the maximum value that e can take, and in each step decreases by the minimum distance $\breve{d}$ between two consecutive expressions e_i and e_{i+1}.

Since the expression e might have a complex form (e.g., exponential, polynomial, etc), inferring a precise LB on the distance $\check{d}$ is usually impractical. A key observation in our approach is that, since variables are wrapped by nat, it is enough to reason on the behavior of its nat sub-expressions, i.e., we only need to understand how each $\mathsf{nat}(l)$ of e (denoted $\mathsf{nat}(l) \in e$) changes along a sequence of recursive calls.

Definition 4 (nat with linear behaviour). *Consider the CR C of Eq. 1 with e a (possibly) non-constant expression. We say that a given $\mathsf{nat}(l) \in e$ is linearly increasing (resp. decreasing) if there exists a non-negative integer $\check{d}$, such that for a given renamed apart instance of the recursive equation $\langle C(\bar{y}) = e' + C(\bar{y}_1) + \cdots + C(\bar{y}_k), \varphi'_2 \rangle$, it holds that $\varphi_2 \wedge \varphi'_2 \wedge \bar{x}_i = \bar{y} \models l' - l \geq \check{d}$ (resp. $\varphi_2 \wedge \varphi'_2 \wedge \bar{x}_i = \bar{y} \models l - l' \geq \check{d}$) for any $\bar{x}_i$, where $\mathsf{nat}(l') \in e'$ is the renaming of $\mathsf{nat}(l)$.*

In practice, computing $\check{d}$ for a given $\mathsf{nat}(l) \in e$ can be done using integer programming tools. In what follows, when the conditions of Def. 4 hold for a given $\mathsf{nat}(l) \in e$, we say that it has a linear behavior. Moreover, when all $\mathsf{nat}(l) \in e$ have the same linear behavior (i.e., all increasing or all decreasing), we say that e has a linear behavior.

Example 3. For B, replacing $C(0, j, n)$ by the UB $\mathsf{nat}(n+j)$ computed in Ex. 2 results in $\langle B(j, i, n) = \mathsf{nat}(n+j) + B(j', i, n), \varphi_1 \rangle$, where $\varphi_1 = \{j < i, j+1 \leq j' \leq j+3\}$. Its renamed apart instance is $\langle B(j_r, i_r, n_r) = \mathsf{nat}(n_r + j_r) + B(j'_r, i_r, n_r), \varphi_2 \rangle$ where $\varphi_2 = \{j_r < i_r, j_r + 1 \leq j'_r \leq j_r + 3\}$. Then, the formula $\varphi_1 \wedge \varphi_2 \wedge \{j' = j_r, i = i_r, n = n_r\} \models (n_r + j_r) - (n+j) \geq \check{d}$ holds for $\check{d} = 1$. Therefore, $\mathsf{nat}(n+j)$ increases linearly.

Let us intuitively explain how our method works by focusing on a single $\mathsf{nat}(l) \in e$ within the relation C. Assume that during the evaluation of an initial query $C(\bar{x}_0)$, $\mathsf{nat}(l)$ is evaluated to $\mathsf{nat}(l_1), \ldots, \mathsf{nat}(l_n)$ in n consecutive recursive calls, and suppose that it is linearly increasing at least by $\check{d}$, i.e., $l_{i+1} - l_i \geq \check{d}$ for all $1 \leq i \leq n-1$. As explained in Sec. 3, we can infer an expression $\mathsf{nat}(\hat{l})$ which is an UB for all $\mathsf{nat}(l_i)$, and a ranking function $\hat{f}_C$ such that $n \leq \hat{f}_C(\bar{x}_0)$. A tight approximation is the arithmetic sequence which starts from $\mathsf{nat}(\hat{l})$ and each time decreases by $\check{d}$. Clearly, the first element of this sequence is greater than $\mathsf{nat}(l_n)$, the second is greater than $\mathsf{nat}(l_{n-1})$, and so on.

However, a main problem is that, since $\hat{f}_C$ provides an over-approximation of the actual number of iterations, the sequence might go to negative values. This is because an imprecise (too large) $\hat{f}_C$ would lead to a too large decrease $\check{d} * \hat{f}_C(\bar{x}_0)$ and the smallest element $\mathsf{nat}(\hat{l}) - \check{d} * \hat{f}_C(\bar{x}_0)$ (and possibly other subsequent ones) could be negative. Hence, the approximation would be unsound since the actual evaluations of such negative values are zero. We avoid this problem by viewing this sequence in a dual way: we start from the smallest value and in each step increase it by $\check{d}$. Since still the smallest values could be negative, we start from $\mathsf{nat}(\hat{l} - \check{d} * \hat{f}_C(\bar{x}_0))$ which is guaranteed to be positive and greater than or equal to $\mathsf{nat}(\hat{l}) - \check{d} * \hat{f}_C(\bar{x}_0)$. The next definition uses this intuition to replace each nat by an expression that generates its corresponding sequence at the level of RR.

Definition 5. *Consider the CR C of Eq. 1 where e has a linear behavior. Let $\hat{f}_C(\bar{x}_0) = \mathsf{nat}(l')$ be its corresponding ranking function. We define its associated worst-case RR as $\langle P_C(x) = E_e + P_C(x-1) + \cdots + P_C(x-1) \rangle$ where E_e is obtained from e by replacing each $\mathsf{nat}(l) \in e$ by $\mathsf{nat}(\hat{l} - \check{d} * l') + x * \check{d}$.*

Definition 5 generalizes Def. 3 and an equivalent theorem to Theorem 1 holds.

Theorem 2. *If E is a solution for $P_C(x)$ then $E[x/\hat{f}_C(\bar{x}_0)]$ is an UB for $C(\bar{x}_0)$.*

Example 4. Following Ex. 3, we have that $\check{d}=1$. Since $\mathsf{nat}(n_0+i_0-1)$ is an UB of the cost $\mathsf{nat}(n+j)$ accumulated in B, and $\hat{f}_B(j_0, i_0, n_0)=\mathsf{nat}(i_0-j_0)$, according to Def. 5, we have $\langle P_B(x)=\mathsf{nat}(n_0+i_0-1-(i_0-j_0)*1)+x*1+P_B(x-1)\rangle$ which is solved by CAS to $P_B(x)=\mathsf{nat}(n_0+j_0-1)*x+x*(x+1)/2$. Thus, $B(j_0, i_0, n_0) = P_B(x)[x/\mathsf{nat}(i_0-j_0)]$. Similarly, for A we obtain the RR $P_A(x) = (q+2x)(q/2+x)+r(q+2x)+q/2+x+P_A(x-1)$ where $q = \mathsf{nat}(i_0-2)$ and $r = \mathsf{nat}(n_0-1)$, which is solved to $P_A(x) = qx^2+qrx+rx+2/3x^3+rx^2+3/2x^2+5/6x+1/2q^2x+3/2qx$. Thus, $A(i_0, n_0) = P_A(x)[x/\mathsf{nat}((n_0 - i_0)/2)]$. Finally, for F, we obtain the UB $F(n_0) = y(4y^2+6zy+9y+6z+5)/6$, whereas [2] provides $2*\mathsf{nat}(n_0/2+1/2)*z^2$, where $y = \mathsf{nat}(n_0/2)$ and $z = \mathsf{nat}(n_0 - 1)$, which is much less precise.

Our approach can be also applied when nat expressions are increasing or decreasing geometrically, i.e., when $\mathsf{nat}(l_{i+1}) \leq k * \mathsf{nat}(l_i)$ for some positive rational k called common ratio. This is the case in a CR like $\langle C(n)=\mathsf{nat}(n)+C(n/2), \{n \geq 1\}\rangle$, which is similar to what we obtain when analyzing the recursive implementation of merge-sort algorithm (mergesort has two recursive calls). In such geometric case, the counterpart condition to Def. 4 checks if there exists a minimum ratio $\check{k}$ such that $\varphi_2 \wedge \varphi_2' \wedge \bar{x}_i = \bar{y} \models l \geq \check{k} * l'$. Then, in a counterpart definition to Def. 5, we replace such $\mathsf{nat}(l) \in e$ by $\mathsf{nat}(\hat{l}) * \check{k}^{m-x} \in E_e$ where $m = \hat{f}_C(\bar{x}_0)$. Intuitively, we accumulate $\mathsf{nat}(\hat{l})$ when $x = \hat{f}_C(\bar{x}_0)$, and, at each subsequent step, the expression is geometrically reduced by the ratio. For the above CR, we obtain a linear UB $C(n_0) = 2 * \mathsf{nat}(n_0)$, whereas techniques described in [2,9] would obtain $C(n_0) = \mathsf{nat}(n_0) * log_2(\mathsf{nat}(n_0 + 1))$. Note that here our approach improves even the complexity order. Using a similar construction, for merge-sort (see experiments), we are able to infer the upper bound $63\mathsf{nat}(a + 1)log_2(\mathsf{nat}(2a - 1) + 1) + 50\mathsf{nat}(2a - 1)$ on the number of executed instructions. For conciseness, rest of the paper formalizes the arithmetic case, but all results are directly applicable to geometric progressions as described above.

4.3   Non-deterministic Non-constant Cost Relations

Any approach for solving CRs that aims at being practical has to consider CRs with several recursive equations as shown in equation 2. This kind of CRs is very common during cost analysis and they mainly originate from conditional statements inside loops.

$$\langle C(\bar{x}) = e_0, \varphi_0 \rangle$$
$$\langle C(\bar{x}) = e_1 + C(\bar{x}_1) + \cdots + C(\bar{x}_{k_1}), \varphi_1 \rangle$$
$$\vdots$$
$$\langle C(\bar{x}) = e_h + C(\bar{x}_1) + \cdots + C(\bar{x}_{k_h}), \varphi_h \rangle \tag{2}$$

For instance, the instruction if (x[i]>0) {A;} else {B;}, may lead to two non-deterministic equations which accumulate the costs of A and B. This is because arrays are typically abstracted to their length and, hence, the guard x[i]>0 is abstracted to true, i.e., we do not keep this information on the CR. Thus, $\varphi_0, \ldots, \varphi_h$ are not necessarily mutually exclusive. W.l.o.g., we assume that $k_1 \geq \cdots \geq k_h$, i.e., the first (resp. last) recursive equation has the maximum (resp. minimum) number of recursive calls among all equations. We also assume that $\hat{f}_C(\bar{x}_0) = \text{nat}(l')$ is a *global* ranking function for this CR, i.e., a ranking function for all equations.

In non-deterministic CRs, the costs contributed by a chain of recursive calls might not be instances of the same cost expression, but rather of different expressions $e_1, \ldots, e_h$, i.e., the equations might interleave. Namely, we might apply one equation and for another call another different equation. The worst-case cost might originate from such interleaving sequences (see [2]). Thus, when inferring how a given $\text{nat}(l) \in e_i$ changes, we have to consider subsequent instances of $\text{nat}(l)$ which are not necessarily consecutive. For this, we infer an invariant that holds between two subsequent (not necessarily consecutive) applications of the same equation, similar to what [2] does, and then we compute the distance $\check{d}$ between its subsequent instances as in Def. 4 but considering this invariant.

As a first solution, similarly to Def. 5, for each expression e_i, we can generate a corresponding F_i by replacing each $\text{nat}(l)$ by $\text{nat}(\hat{l} - \check{d}*l') + x*\check{d}$ where $\check{d}$ is the distance for $\text{nat}(l)$. Clearly, if e is a closed-form solution for the RR $P_C(x) = \max(E_1, \ldots, E_h) \mid P_C(x-1) \mid \ldots \mid P_C(x-1)$ with k_1 recursive calls, then $e[x/\hat{f}_C(\bar{x}_0)]$ is an UB for C (because in each application we take the worst-case). Unfortunately, CAS fail to solve RRs which involve (non-constant) max expressions. Therefore, this approach is not practical. Clearly, in the case that one of $e_1, \ldots, e_h$ is provable to be the maximum, this approach works since we can eliminate the max operator. Unfortunately, even comparing simple cost expressions is difficult and in many cases not feasible [1]. In what follows, we describe a practical solution to this problem, which is based on finding an expression E which does not include max and is always larger than or equal to $\max(E_1, \ldots, E_h)$. This way, we can replace the max by E and still get an UB for C.

First, observe that any cost expression (which does not include max) can be normalized to the form $\Sigma_{i=1}^n \Pi_{j=1}^{m_i} b_{ij}$ (i.e., sum of multiplications) where each b_{ij} is a *basic element* of the following form $\{r, \text{nat}(l), n^{\text{nat}(l)}, \log(\text{nat}(l))\}$. We assume that all $e_1, \ldots, e_h$ of Eq. 2 are given in this form. For simplicity, we assume that all expressions have the same number of multiplicands, and all multiplicands have the same number of basic expressions (if not, we just add 1 in multiplication and 0 for sum). Now since e_i is in a normal form, the corresponding E_i will be also in a corresponding normal form. Given two cost expressions e_1 and e_2, and their corresponding E_1 and E_2, the following definition describes how to generate an expression E such that it is larger than (or equal to) both E_1 and E_2.

Definition 6. *Given two expressions $E_i = a_{11} \cdots a_{1m_1} + \cdots + a_{n1} \cdots a_{1m_n}$ and $E_j = b_{11} \cdots b_{1m_1} + \cdots + b_{n1} \cdots b_{1m_n}$. We define the generalization of E_i and E_j as $E_i \sqcup E_j = c_{11} \cdots c_{1m_1} + \cdots + c_{n1} \cdots c_{1m_n}$ where $c_{ij} = b_{ij}$ if we can prove that $b_{ij} \geq a_{ij}$, $c_{ij} = a_{ij}$ if we can prove that $a_{ij} \geq b_{ij}$, otherwise $c_{ij} = a_{ij} + b_{ij}$.*

Although we need to compare expressions when constructing $E_i \sqcup E_j$ (namely b_{ij} to a_{ij}), this comparison is on the basic elements rather than on the whole expression and hence it is far simpler. By construction, we guarantee that $E_i \sqcup E_j$ is always greater than or equal to both E_i and E_j. Clearly, the quality of $E_i \sqcup E_j$ (i.e., how tight it is) depends on the ordering of the summands and the elements of each summand (i.e., multiplicands) in both E_i and E_j. In order to obtain tighter bounds, we use some heuristics like ordering the elements inside each multiplication in increasing complexity in such a way that we always try to compare basic elements of the same complexity order. Besides, we try to compare basic elements that involve the same variable.

Definition 7. *Let C be the CR of Eq. 2, $\hat{f}_C(\bar{x}_0) = \mathsf{nat}(l')$ its corresponding ranking function, and E_i generated from e_i by replacing each $\mathsf{nat}(l) \in e_i$ by $\mathsf{nat}(\hat{l} - d * l') + x * \check{d}$ where $\check{d}$ is the distance of $\mathsf{nat}(l)$. The corresponding worst-case RR is $\langle P_C(x) = E_1 \sqcup \cdots \sqcup E_h + P_C(x-1) + \cdots + P_C(x-1) \rangle$ with k_1 recursive calls.*

Theorem 3. *If E is a solution for $P_C(x)$ then $E[x/\hat{f}_C(\bar{x}_0)]$ is an UB for $C(\bar{x}_0)$.*

Example 5. Let us add the contrived recursive equation $B(j, i, n) = \mathsf{nat}(n+15) + B(j', i, n) + B(j'', i, n)$ $\{j < i, j' = j+1, j'' = j+2\}$ to the CR B. It has two recursive calls and a non-deterministic choice for accumulating either $e_1 = \mathsf{nat}(n + j)$ or $e_2 = \mathsf{nat}(n + 15)$. The function $f_B(j_0, i_0, n_0) = \mathsf{nat}(i_0 - j_0)$ is a ranking function for all equations. Next, we compute $E_1 \sqcup E_2$ where $E_1 = \mathsf{nat}(n_0 + i_0 - 1 - (i_0 - j_0)) + x$ and $E_2 = \mathsf{nat}(n_0 + 15 - (i_0 - j_0)) + x$. A naive generalization results in $\mathsf{nat}(n_0 + i_0 - 1 - (i_0 - j_0)) + \mathsf{nat}(n_0 + 15 - (i_0 - j_0)) + x$, but syntactically analyzing the expressions and employing the above heuristics, we automatically obtain a tighter bound $\mathsf{nat}(n_0 + j_0 + 15) + x$. Now we generate $\langle P_B(x) = \mathsf{nat}(n_0 + j_0 + 15) + x + P_B(x - 1) + P_B(x - 1) \rangle$ which can be solved to $\langle P_B(x) = 2^x(q + 2) - q - x - 2 \rangle$ for $q = \mathsf{nat}(n_0 + j_0 + 15)$ and therefore $B(j_0, i_0, n_0) = P_B(x)[x/\mathsf{nat}(i_0 - j_0)]$.

5   The Dual Problem: Lower Bounds

We now aim at applying the approach from Sec. 4 in order to infer *lower bounds*, i.e., under-approximations of the best-case cost. Such LBs are typically useful in granularity analysis to decide if tasks should be executed in parallel. This is because the parallel execution of a task incurs various overheads, and therefore the LB cost of the task can be useful to decide if it is worth executing it concurrently as a separate task. Due in part to the difficulty of inferring under-approximations, a general framework for inferring LBs from CR does not exist.

When trying to adapt the UB framework of [2] to LB, we only obtain trivial bounds. This is because the minimization of the cost expression accumulated along the execution is in most cases zero and, hence, by assuming it for all executions we would obtain a trivial (zero) LB. In our framework, even if the minimal cost could be zero, since we do not assume it for all iterations, but rather only for the first one, the resulting LB is non-trivial.

Existing approaches typically assume that the length of chains of recursive calls depends on a single decreasing argument. We first propose a new technique to inferring LBs on the length of such chains, which does not have this restriction. Essentially, we add a counter to the equations in the CR and infer an invariant which involves this counter. The invariant is indeed the same one used later to obtain $\check{l}$. The minimum value of this counter when we enter a non-recursive case is a LB on the length of those chains.

Definition 8. *Given the CR of Eq. 2, we compute $\check{f}_C(\bar{x}_0) = \mathsf{nat}(l)$ which is a lower bound on the length of any chain of recursive calls when starting from $C(\bar{x}_0)$ in three steps: (1) Replace each head $C(\bar{x})$ by $C(\bar{x}, lb)$ and each recursive call $C(\bar{x}_j)$ by $C(\bar{x}_j, lb+1)$; (2) Infer an invariant $\langle C(\bar{x}_0, 0) \rightsquigarrow C(\bar{x}, lb), \Psi \rangle$ for the new CR; (3) Syntactically look for $lb \geq l$ in $\Psi \wedge \varphi_0$ (projected on $\bar{x}_0$ and lb).*

Example 6. Applying step (1) on the CR B results in $\langle B(j, i, n, lb) = 0, \{j \leq i\} \rangle$ and $\langle B(j, i, n, lb) = \mathsf{nat}(n+j) + B(j', i, n, lb+1), \{j<i, j+1\leq j'\leq j+3\} \rangle$. The invariant Ψ for this CR is $\{j-j_0-lb\geq 0, j_0+3lb-j\geq 0, i=i_0, n=n_0\}$. Projecting $\Psi \wedge \{j \geq i\}$ on $\langle j_0, i_0, n_0, lb \rangle$ results in $\{lb\geq 0, j_0+3lb-i_0\geq 0\}$ which implies $lb \geq (i_0 - j_0)/3$. Similarly $\check{f}_C(k_0, j_0, n_0) = \mathsf{nat}(n_0+j_0 - k_0)$ and $A(i_0, n_0) = \mathsf{nat}(\frac{n_0-i_0}{4})$.

We present the approach directly for the non-deterministic CR of Eq. 2. As in Def. 6, we can reduce the expressions $E_1, \ldots, E_h$ in order to get an expression which is guaranteed to be smaller than or equal to $\min(E_1, \ldots, E_h)$.

Definition 9. *Given the expressions E_i and E_j in Def. 6, we define their reduction as $E_i \sqcap E_j = c_{11} \cdots c_{1m_1} + \cdots + c_{n1} \cdots c_{1m_n}$ where $c_{ij} = b_{ij}$ if we can prove that $b_{ij} \leq a_{ij}$, $c_{ij} = a_{ij}$ if we can prove that $a_{ij} \leq b_{ij}$, otherwise $c_{ij} = 0$.*

The case of $c_{ij} = 0$ can be improved to obtain a tighter LB by relying on heuristics, similarly to what we have discussed in Sec. 4.3. As intuitively explained in Sec. 3, the main idea is to simulate each $\mathsf{nat}(l)$ by a sequence that starts from $\mathsf{nat}(\check{l})$ and increases in each iteration by the minimal distance $\check{d}$.

Definition 10. *Let C be the CR of Eq. 2 such that for each $\mathsf{nat}(l) \in e_i$ it holds that $\check{l} \geq 0$, and let E_i be the expression generated from e_i by replacing each $\mathsf{nat}(l)$ by $\mathsf{nat}(\check{l}) + (x - 1) * \check{d}$. The corresponding best-case RR is $\langle P_C(x) = E_1 \sqcap \cdots \sqcap E_h + P_C(x - 1) + \cdots + P_C(x - 1) \rangle$ with k_h recursive calls.*

In the above definition, it can be observed that, for the sake of soundness, we require that for each $\mathsf{nat}(l)$ it holds that $\check{l} \geq 0$. Intuitively, when such expressions take negative values, by definition of nat, they evaluate to zero and there can be a sequence of zeros until the evaluation becomes positive. Our under-approximation would be unsound in this case, because it assumes as minimum value zero and then starts to increase it by the minimum distance. Thus, for some values, the approximation could be actually bigger than the actual value.

Theorem 4. *If E is a solution for $P_C(x)$, then $E[x/\check{f}_C(\bar{x}_0)]$ is a LB for $C(\bar{x}_0)$.*

Example 7. Consider the LBs on iterations of Ex. 6. Since $C(k_0, j_0, n_0)$ accumulates a constant cost 1, its LB cost is $\mathsf{nat}(n_0+j_0-k_0)$. We now replace the call $C(0, j, n)$ in B by its LB $\mathsf{nat}(n+j)$ and obtain the equation: $B(j, i, n) = \mathsf{nat}(n+j) + B(j', i, n)$ $\{j<i, j+1\leq j'\leq j+3\}$. Notice the need of the soundness requirement in Th. 3, i.e., $\mathsf{nat}(n+j)\geq 0$. E.g., when evaluating $B(-5, 5, 0)$ the first 4 instances of $\mathsf{nat}(n+j)$ are zero since they correspond to $\mathsf{nat}(-5), \ldots, \mathsf{nat}(-1)$. Therefore, it would be incorrect to start accumulating from 0 with a difference 1 at each iteration. After solving A and B in the same way, the computed final LB for $F(n)$ is: $\frac{1}{3}\mathsf{nat}(n)\mathsf{nat}(\frac{n}{4}-1)+\frac{1}{18}\mathsf{nat}(\frac{n}{4}-1)\mathsf{nat}(\frac{n}{4}-1)+\frac{1}{6}\mathsf{nat}(\frac{n}{4}-1)$.

6   Experiments and Conclusions

We have implemented our approach in COSTA, a COSt and Termination Analyzer for Java bytecode. The obtained *RRs* are solved using MAXIMA [12] or PURRS [4]. As benchmarks, we use classical examples from complexity analysis and numerical methods: DetEval evaluates the determinant of a matrix; LinEq-Solve solves a set of linear equations; MatrixInverse computes the inverse of an input matrix; MatrixSort sorts the rows in the upper triangle of a matrix; InsertSort, SelectSort, BubbleSort, and MergeSort implement sorting algorithms; PascalTriangle computes and prints Pascal's Triangle; NestedRecIter is an interesting programming pattern we found in the Java libraries with a spacial form of nested loops that uses recursion and a simple iteration for loop. Our implementation (and examples) can be tried out at `http://costa.ls.fi.upm.es` by enabling the option `series` in the manual configuration.

Table 1 illustrates the accuracy and efficiency on the above benchmarks using the cost model *"number of executed (bytecode) instructions"*. We abbreviate $\mathsf{nat}(x)$ as $\eta(x)$. The second column shows: in the top row the UB obtained by [2], next the UB obtained by us and at the bottom our LB. Unfortunately, there are no other cost analysis tools for imperative languages available to compare experimentally to (e.g., SPEED [9]). As regards UBs, we improve the precision over [2] in all benchmarks. This improvement, in all benchmarks except MergeSort and NestedRecIter, is due to nested loops were the inner loops bounds depend on the outer loops counters. In these cases, we accurately bound the cost of each iteration of the inner loops, rather than assuming the worst-case cost. For MergeSort, we obtain a tight bound in the order of $a*log(a)$. Note that [2] could obtain $a*log(a)$ only for simple cost models that count the visits to a specific program point but not for number of instructions, while ours works with any cost model. For NestedRecIter, we improve the complexity order over [2] from $a*2^a$ to 2^a. As regards LBs, it can be observed from the last row of each benchmark that we

Table 1. 1. DetEval(a) 2. LinEqSolve(a,b,c) 3. MatrixInv(a) 4. MatrixSort(a,b,c) 5. InsertSort(a) 6. MergeSort(a) 7. SelectSort(a) 8. PascalTriangle(a) 9. BubbleSort(a) 10. NestedRecIter(a).

#	UBs and LBs	T
	$24\eta(a-1)^3+36\eta(a-1)^2+27\eta(a)^2+39\eta(a)\eta(a-1)+35\eta(a-1)+72\eta(a)+54$	1240
1	$8\eta(a-1)^3+27\eta(a)^2+\frac{99}{2}\eta(a-1)^2+\frac{231}{2}\eta(a-1)+72\eta(a)+54$	1395
	$8\eta(a-2)^3+46\eta(a-2)^2+105\eta(a-2)+55\eta(a-1)+54$	204
	$24\eta(c-1)^3+36\eta(c-1)^2+28\eta(c)^2+\eta(c-1)(40\eta(c)+35)+25\eta(c)+48\eta(b-1)^2+46\eta(b-1)+74$	1270
2	$8\eta(c-1)^3+28\eta(c)^2+50\eta(c-1)^2+25\eta(c)+117\eta(c-1)+24\eta(b-1)^2+70\eta(b-1)+74$	1425
	$8\eta(c-2)^3+48\eta(c-2)^2+25\eta(c-1)+111\eta(c-2)+24\eta(b-2)^2+70\eta(b-2)+74$	247
	$24\eta(a-1)^3+56\eta(a)\eta(a-1)^2+27\eta(a)^2+46\eta(a-1)^2+75\eta(a)+77\eta(a)\eta(a-1)+49\eta(a-1)+62$	3617
3	$8\eta(a-1)^3+28\eta(a)\eta(a-1)^2+27\eta(a)^2+\frac{109}{2}\eta(a-1)^2+75\eta(a)+66\eta(a)\eta(a-1)+\frac{269}{2}\eta(a-1)+62$	3890
	$18\eta(a-2)^3+81\eta(a-2)^2+75\eta(a-1)+144\eta(a-2)+62$	415
	$25\eta(b)\eta(c)\eta(c-1)+30\eta(b)\eta(c)+16\eta(b)+6$	130
4	$25/2\eta(b)\eta(c-b)^2+25\eta(b)^2\eta(c-b)+25/2\eta(b)^3+40\eta(b)^2+135/2\eta(b)\eta(c-b)+87/2\eta(b)+6$	200
	$21/2\eta(b-1)^2+21\eta(b-1)\eta(c-b)+53/2\eta(b-1)+6$	60

#	UBs and LBs	T	#	UBs and LBs	T
	$19\eta(a-1)^2+25\eta(a-1)+7$	44		$43\eta(a)\eta(2a-3)+53\eta(2a-3)+17$	2127
5	$19/2\eta(a-1)^2+69/2\eta(a-1)+7$	63	6	$63\eta(a+1)log_2(\eta(2a-1)+1)+50\eta(2a-1)$	2100
	$18\eta(a-2)+7$	10		0	40
	$27\eta(a-1)^2+16\eta(a-1)+9$	103		$16\eta(a)^2+27\eta(a-1)^2+31\eta(a)+10\eta(a-1)+25$	200
7	$27/2\eta(a-1)^2+59/2\eta(a-1)+9$	120	8	$27/2\eta(a)^2+27\eta(a-1)^2+10\eta(a-1)+67/2\eta(a)+25$	247
	$13/2\eta(a-2)^2+45/2\eta(a-2)+9$	25		$5/2\eta(a-1)^2+10\eta(a-2)+67/2\eta(a)+25$	60
	$34\eta(a)\eta(a-1)+12\eta(a)+8$	174		$2^{\eta(a-1)}(5\eta(a-1)+21)+5\eta(a)-5\eta(a-1)-7$	104
9	$17\eta(a)^2+29\eta(a)+8$	197	10	$31*2^{\eta(a-1)}+5\eta(a)-5\eta(a-1)-17$	144
	$8\eta(a-1)^2+20\eta(a-1)+8$	24		$31*2^{\eta(a-2)}+5\eta(a-1)-5\eta(a-2)-17$	34

have been able to prove the positive nat condition and obtain non-trivial LBs in all cases except MergeSort. For MergeSort, the lower bound on loop iterations is a logarithmic which cannot be inferred by our linear invariant generation tool and hence we get trivial bound 0. Note that for InsertSort we infer a linear LB which happens when the array is sorted. Column T shows the time (in milliseconds) to compute the bounds from the generated CR. Our approach is slightly slower than [2] mainly due to the overhead of connecting COSTA to the external CAS.

7   Conclusions

When comparing our approach (for UBs) to [9], since the underlying cost analysis framework is fundamentally different from ours, it is not possible to formally compare the resulting upper bounds in all cases. However, by looking at small examples, we can see why our approach can be more precise. For instance, in [9] the worst-case time usage $\sum_{i=1}^{n} i$ is over-approximated by n^2, while our series-based approach is able to obtain the precise solution. For such polynomial cases, the approach of [10] can compute also the exact solution. However, this approach is restricted to univariate polynomial bounds, while ours can be applied to obtain general polynomial, exponential and logarithmic bounds as well.

Finally, to conclude, we have proposed a novel approach to infer precise upper/lower bounds of *CRs* which, as our experiments show, achieves a very good balance between the accuracy of our analysis and its applicability. The main idea is to automatically transform *CRs* into a simple form of worst-case/best-case *RRs* that *CAS* can accurately solve to obtain upper/lower bounds on the resource consumption. The required transformation is far from trivial since it requires transforming non-deterministic equations involving multiple increasing/decreasing arguments into deterministic equations with a single decreasing argument.

Acknowledgements. This work was funded in part by the Information & Communication Technologies program of the European Commission, Future and Emerging Technologies (FET), under the ICT-231620 *HATS* project, by the Spanish Ministry of Science and Innovation (MICINN) under the TIN-2008-05624 *DOVES* project, the HI2008-0153 (Acción Integrada) project, the UCM-BSCH-GR58/08-910502 Research Group and by the Madrid Regional Government under the S2009TIC-1465 *PROMETIDOS* project.

References

1. Albert, E., Arenas, P., Genaim, S., Herraiz, I., Puebla, G.: Comparing cost functions in resource analysis. In: van Eekelen, M., Shkaravska, O. (eds.) FOPARA 2009. LNCS, vol. 6324, pp. 1–17. Springer, Heidelberg (2010)
2. Albert, E., Arenas, P., Genaim, S., Puebla, G.: Closed-Form Upper Bounds in Static Cost Analysis. Journal of Automated Reasoning (to appear, 2010)
3. Albert, E., Arenas, P., Genaim, S., Puebla, G., Zanardini, D.: Cost Analysis of Java Bytecode. In: De Nicola, R. (ed.) ESOP 2007. LNCS, vol. 4421, pp. 157–172. Springer, Heidelberg (2007)
4. Bagnara, R., Pescetti, A., Zaccagnini, A., Zaffanella, E.: PURRS: Towards Computer Algebra Support for Fully Automatic Worst-Case Complexity Analysis. Technical report (2005), arXiv:cs/0512056, http://arxiv.org/
5. Ben-Amram, A.M.: Size-change termination, monotonicity constraints and ranking functions. In: Bouajjani, A., Maler, O. (eds.) CAV 2009. LNCS, vol. 5643, pp. 109–123. Springer, Heidelberg (2009)
6. Feautrier, P., Alias, C., Darte, A., Gonnord, L.: Multi-dimensional rankings, program termination, and complexity bounds of flowchart programs. In: Cousot, R., Martel, M. (eds.) SAS 2010. LNCS, vol. 6337, pp. 117–133. Springer, Heidelberg (2010)
7. Cousot, P., Halbwachs, N.: Automatic discovery of linear restraints among variables of a program. In: Proc. POPL. ACM, New York (1978)
8. Crary, K., Weirich, S.: Resource bound certification. In: POPL 2000. ACM Press, New York (2000)

9. Gulwani, S., Mehra, K.K., Chilimbi, T.M.: Speed: precise and efficient static estimation of program computational complexity. In: POPL, pp. 127–139. ACM, New
   York (2009)
10. Hoffmann, J., Hofmann, M.: Amortized resource analysis with polynomial poten-
    tial. In: Gordon, A.D. (ed.) ESOP 2010. LNCS, vol. 6012, pp. 287–306. Springer,
    Heidelberg (2010)
11. Marriot, K., Stuckey, P.: Programming with Constraints: An Introduction. The
    MIT Press, Cambridge (1998)
12. Maxima.sourceforge.net. Maxima, a Computer Algebra System. Version 5.21.1
    (2009), http://maxima.sourceforge.net/
13. Wegbreit, B.: Mechanical Program Analysis. Communications of the ACM 18(9)
    (1975)

Refinement-Based CFG Reconstruction from Unstructured Programs*

Sébastien Bardin, Philippe Herrmann, and Franck Védrine

CEA, LIST,
Gif-sur-Yvette CEDEX, 91191 France
first.name@cea.fr

Abstract. This paper addresses the issue of recovering a both safe and precise approximation of the Control Flow Graph (CFG) of an unstructured program, typically an executable file. The problem is tackled in an original way, with a refinement-based static analysis working over finite sets of constant values. Requirement propagation allows the analysis to automatically adjust the domain precision only where it is needed, resulting in precise CFG recovery at moderate cost. First experiments, including an industrial case study, show that the method outperforms standard analyses in terms of precision, efficiency or robustness.

1 Introduction

Motivation. Automatic analysis of programs from their executable files has many potential applications in safety and security, for example: automatic analysis of mobile code and malware, security testing or worst case execution time estimation. This paper addresses the problem of (safe) CFG reconstruction, i.e. constructing a both safe and precise approximation of the Control Flow Graph (CFG) of an unstructured program (typically: an executable file). CFG reconstruction is a cornerstone of safe unstructured program analysis: if the recovery is unsafe, subsequent analyses will be unsafe too; if it is too rough, they will be blurred by too many unfeasible branches and instructions.

Challenges. Such an approximation is difficult to obtain because of dynamic jumps, i.e. jump instructions whose target expression is resolved at run-time and may vary from one execution to the other, leading to vicious circles between value analysis and CFG reconstruction. Unfortunately, dynamic jumps are ubiquitous in native code programs: they may be introduced at compile-time either for efficiency (switch in C) or by necessity (return statements, function pointers in C, virtual methods in C++, etc.). Two reasons make CFG reconstruction even more challenging. First, real-life unstructured programs (executable files) contain many junk instructions, i.e. unreachable but well-defined instructions. Since junk instructions cannot be easily recognised when encountered, a small loss of precision on jump targets will often result in an unbearable noise propagation in the analysis. Second, there is no reason why all valid targets of a dynamic jump should follow a nice regular pattern. Indeed they are just addresses in the executable code, often arbitrarily assigned by a compiler. Hence any analysis based on

---

* Work partially funded by ANR (grants ANR-05-RNTL-02606 and ANR-08-SEGI-006).

R. Jhala and D. Schmidt (Eds.): VMCAI 2011, LNCS 6538, pp. 54–69, 2011.

popular domains (i.e. convex domains possibly enhanced with congruence information) will introduce many false targets. For example, consider an instruction cgoto(x) with $x \in \{1355, 1356, 2126\}$: such an analysis cannot recover better than $x \in [1355..2126]$, reporting 99% of false targets.

Related approaches. Many works have been developed since the 80's for the CFG reconstruction of *structured programs* (cf. Control Flow Analysis [22]), focusing on control mechanisms such as high-order functions, dynamic methods or function pointers. Moreover, many static analysers targeting programs written in Java or C commonly face the CFG reconstruction issue. However, there are a few significant differences with the case of unstructured programs: the "jump" information is clearly identified and separated from data information (syntactically or through types), it cannot be arbitrarily manipulated (syntactic restrictions or clean encapsulation) and the set of all possible jump targets is statically known and usually small. Thus, in Java or C a safe approximation of the CFG can often be recovered with an abstract propagation based on finite sets of constants (k-sets) limited to a few relevant and easy-to-find variables. Unfortunately none of these restrictions hold on unstructured programs.

Only very few works address the CFG reconstruction of *unstructured programs* (simply referred to as CFG reconstruction in the rest of the paper). Reps *et al.* [5,7,8] develop dedicated heuristics based on strided intervals, affine relationships discovery and local variable identification to avoid rough abstraction of jump targets. Their results are implemented in CODESURFER/X86 [1]. The tool JAKSTAB [18] developed by Kinder and Veith is based on k-set propagation [19]. Experiments reported by the authors show that while each approach performs much better than current industrial tools, like IDA PRO [24], both techniques still recover many false targets. Especially, strided intervals cannot capture precisely sets of jump targets, and k-sets are too sensitive to their cardinality bound, potentially leading to either imprecise or expensive analyses.

Our approach. We make the following observations. First, while k-sets are considered as a crude and/or costly domain in most static analysis settings, we think that it is the only abstract domain well-suited for representing sets of dynamic targets, as long as the cardinality bound is large enough. Second, CFG reconstruction seems really well-suited to lazy reasoning: on the one hand, target expressions must be tracked very precisely since a small precision loss there may have a dramatic impact on the whole analysis, on the other hand, we claim that in most realistic settings only a few facts need to be tracked to solve dynamic jumps. The last point may be exploited to reduce the cost of k-set propagation without affecting preciseness.

Contribution. The main results of this paper are twofold. First, we introduce a new framework of Value Analysis with Precision Requirements (VAPR) and show how precise CFG reconstruction fits this framework. We then propose an original refinement-based procedure to solve this problem. The procedure is built on two main steps: a forward k-set propagation with local cardinality bounds (ranging from 0 up to a given parameter $Kmax$), and a refinement step controling these cardinality bounds, driven by backward requirement propagation. The procedure is sound and terminates, moreover it is complete relative to standard k-set propagation on a class of non-trivial programs.

Second, this framework has been implemented in a prototype and first experiments demonstrate a very precise and efficient CFG reconstruction, with great robustness to the initial parameter $Kmax$. The approach performs better than other straightforward analyses, demonstrating that it is really the combination of local refinement and k-sets which leads to precision and efficiency. The prototype has also been successfully tested against an industrial case study, proving the scalability of the approach.

Outline. The rest of the paper is structured as follows. Section 2 presents notations and background. Section 3 describes the Value Analysis with Precision Requirements (VAPR) problem and the Propagate-and-Refine (PaR) procedure to solve it. Section 4 studies the relative completeness of the approach. Section 5 describes a prototype implementation and experiments. Finally, Section 6 discusses related work and Section 7 provides a conclusion and directions for future works.

2   Preliminaries

Unstructured programs. An unstructured program P is a tuple (L, V, A, T, l_0) where: $L \subseteq \mathbb{N}$ is the finite set of code addresses, V is the finite set of program variables, A is the finite set of arrays, $T : L \mapsto I$ is a partial function mapping code addresses to program instructions $i \in I$, and l_0 is the initial code address. Arrays have a statically known size. For the sake of simplicity, all variables and arrays range over the set of natural numbers $\mathbb{N}$, however all results of the paper are easy to adapt to any basic data type. The set of extended variables, i.e. either variables $v \in V$ or array elements $a[k]$ with $a \in A$ and $k \in \mathbb{N}$, is denoted by $V^{\#}$. Program instructions are composed of: assignments $v:=e$, static jumps goto l, branching instructions ite($cond,l_1,l_2$), dynamic jumps cgoto(v) and halting instruction stop, where $l \in L$, $v \in V^{\#}$, $cond$ and e are predicates and expressions built over $\mathbb{N}$, V and A.

The concrete domain of P is $Dom = \mathbb{N}^{|V^{\#}|}$. The operational semantics of P is given in a standard way by a transition system whose configurations are either pairs $(l, \sigma) \in L \times Dom$ or an error configuration $Undef$. Considering a valuation $\sigma \in Dom$, the value of $v \in V^{\#}$ in σ is denoted by $\sigma(v)$. The successor (l', σ') of (l, σ) through instruction $(l, T(l)) \in L \times I$ is defined straightforwardly for assignments, static jumps and conditional branchings. If $T(l)$ is of the form cgoto(v) then $(l', \sigma') = (\sigma(v), \sigma)$. If $T(l)$ is undefined the successor is $Undef$, which has no successor itself. An instruction at address l is well-defined if $T(l)$ is defined. A valid instruction is a well-defined and reachable instruction, a junk instruction is a well-defined but unreachable instruction.

The k-set domains. We follow the basic concepts of abstract interpretation [9]. The abstract domains considered in this paper are based on k-sets, i.e. finite sets of constant values (in $\mathbb{N}$). The lattice (or domain) of all k-sets of cardinality at most k (extended with $\top = \mathbb{N}$, and $\bot$ denotes $\emptyset$) is denoted by $KSET(k)$. An abstract value $\hat{d} \in KSET(k)$ is either a k-set with at most k values or $\top$. For example, $KSET(1)$ is the lattice of constant propagation and $KSET(0)$ is $\{\bot, \top\}$. By convention $KSET(\infty)$ will denote the set of all k-sets (no cardinality bound) extended with $\top$. A pair $(l, v) \in L \times V^{\#}$ is called a *location*. A memory state is a map M from locations to k-sets.

Running example. Here is a small example illustrating the "chicken-or-egg" issue between value analysis and CFG reconstruction of unstructured programs. Because of the mod operation at line 1, possible values of x at the beginning of line 2 are $\{0, 1, 2\}$, then possible targets of the dynamic jump at line 3 are $\{10, 20, 30\}$. Let us also suppose that code address 11 contains a junk instruction goto 2. We consider a CFG recovery performed with intervals and standard widening (denoted $\triangledown$). Starting from $(1, x) = \top$, abstract value $(2, x) = [0..2]$ is propagated, yielding the potential targets $[10..30]$ at line 3. Values are propagated to valid instructions at line 10, 20 and 30. The $Undef$ configuration is propagated for all other potential targets but 11. However, the abstract value at line 3 is also propagated to the junk instruction at line 11 (carrying $x = 11$), and

```
1 : assign x := x mod 3 ; goto 2
2 : assign x := 10(x+1) ; goto 3
3 : cgoto(x)
10 : stop
11 : goto 2    /* junk */
20 : stop
30 : stop
```

Fig. 1. Running example Foo

propagated back to line 2. Then $(2, x)$ becomes $[0..2] \triangledown [11] = \top$ and target jump $(3, x)$ becomes $\top$, leading to a very imprecise CFG reconstruction.

Moreover, the best possible abstract value for the target expression using any convex domain is $x \in [10..30]$, still yielding 18 false targets out of 21 recovered values.

3   The Propagate and Refine Procedure

3.1   Value Analysis with Precision Requirements (VAPR)

Given a program P, an atomic precision requirement is a pair $(l, v) \in L \times V^{\#}$, denoted by $\varphi\langle l, v \rangle$. A memory state M satisfies $\varphi\langle l, v \rangle$ if $M(l, v) \neq \top$, denoted by $M \models \varphi\langle l, v \rangle$. The definition is extended to any set C of precision requirements: $M \models C$ iff M satisfies every $\varphi\langle l, v \rangle \in C$. A location (l, v) is faulty for (M, C) whenever $M(l, v) = \top$ and $\varphi\langle l, v \rangle \in C$. Given a program P and a set of precision requirements C, the problem of *Value Analysis with Precision Requirements* (VAPR) on (P, C) consists in computing an over-approximation M of the collecting semantics of P such that $M \models C$.

Precise CFG reconstruction can be achieved through VAPR as follows: an unstructured program P is transformed into a VAPR problem by adding a requirement $\varphi\langle l, v \rangle$ for each instruction $(l, cgoto\ v)$ in P, ensuring at least that no jump target will evaluate to $\top$. It turns out that this simple kind of requirements combined with k-sets leads to precise results in practice (cf. Section 5).

3.2   Basic Intuitions on the Propagate and Refine Procedure

A refinement-based procedure for VAPR is sketched here, a detailed description is given in Section 3.3. The procedure returns either an invariant of the program or a FAIL message. It follows a "propagate-and-refine" scheme: a domain precision is attached to each location ; abstract values are forward-propagated almost as usual; when a precision requirement is violated, a backward refinement mechanism takes place from faulty locations to remove the violation by increasing the precision of some (hopefully relevant) domains; if at least one domain is improved, the refinement succeeds and propagation is restarted with the new domains and the initial memory state, otherwise the procedure returns FAIL. The procedure is sound, in the sense that in case of success the invariant respects the precision requirements, and terminates (cf. Section 3.3). The main ingredients of the procedure are the following:

1- Each location (l, v) is associated with a $KSET$ domain, whose size (denoted by $D(l, v)$) is bounded by a global parameter $Kmax$. Implicit casts are performed during propagation between locations with different domains: computation is first done with maximal precision, then adjusted to the cardinality bound of the destination (the cast function returns identity if the k-set size matches the new bound, $\top$ otherwise). Casts allow to loosen precision on some (hopefully irrelevant) locations and gain efficiency.

2- During propagation, $\top$ values are tagged with labels (namely, $\top$-labels) recording their origins. Especially, the labelled value $\top_{init}$ denotes initial $\top$ values, while $\top_{\langle d_1,...,d_q \rangle}$ indicates a $\top$ value coming from the abstraction of a k-set $\{d_1, \ldots, d_q\}$ to $\top$ (called a $\top$-abstraction). $\top$-abstractions are very important in the procedure: these sources of precision loss could have been avoided with a domain bound large enough if $Kmax \geq q$. Values $\top_{\langle d_1,...,d_q \rangle}$ allow the analysis to pinpoint such $\top$-abstraction and indicate the minimal domain bound required. Finally, $\top_*$ denotes $\top$ values coming from propagation of $\top_{init}$ or $\top_{\langle d_1,...,d_q \rangle}$.

3- Refinement starts from faulty locations and follows backward data-dependencies to find all ancestors (l, v) evaluating to some $\top_{\langle d_1,...,d_q \rangle}$ with $q \leq Kmax$. In that case, $D(l, v)$ is increased to q (we say that it is *corrected*). The propagation chain stops on $\top_{init}$ and $\top_{\langle d_1,...,d_q \rangle}$ with $q > Kmax$ since they cannot be corrected. Refinement fails when no domain has been increased.

4- A journal logs which target jumps, conditional branches and array indexes have been used for each instruction during value propagation. This information allows to prune requirement propagation, playing a major role in refinement accuracy.

Refinement. The refinement step is the crucial point of the procedure: if too many location domains are refined the procedure will be inefficient, if not enough location domains are refined the procedure will often fail while standard propagation over $KSET(Kmax)$ would have succeeded. In a sense, we would like to discover along the propagation trace where the relevant loss of precision occurs first, correct the domain precision accordingly, and restart the propagation from that point. However, this temporal reasoning is not practical since it would imply to log huge traces of (large) memory states. Instead, the standard propagation mechanism is enriched with a little additional information ($\top$-labels, journal) so that the costly temporal reasoning on traces is replaced by a lighter spatial reasoning on the current memory state (cf. Figure 2). This reduction is not perfect and some information is lost in the general case, however it appears to be very precise and efficient in practice (cf. Section 5), and the reduction is perfect for certain classes of unstructured programs (cf. Section 4).

Figure 2 exemplifies the refinement mechanism in a simple case. Each code address L_1 to L_5 is annotated with the domain bound and abstract value of the relevant variable for the next instruction. Domain bounds are written Dx, Da and Db. At step 1 of the propagation, value $\top_{\langle 1,2 \rangle}$ is propagated to (L_3, x) by incoming transitions from L_1 and L_2 because Dx < 2. This $\top$-abstraction leads to (L_5, b) evaluating to $\top$ at step 3. Let us assume that this is a requirement violation. Then a temporal reasoning would amount to go back along the execution trace to find the source of precision loss, at location (L_3, x) in step 1. Thanks to additional information, a simple backward propagation on data-dependencies on the local memory state (step 3) allows to detect that the requirement violation comes from (L_3, x), whose domain bound should be at least 2.

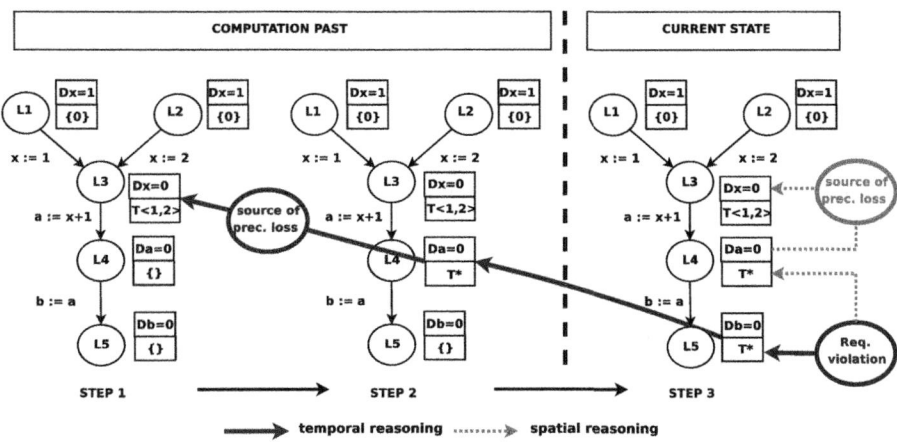

Fig. 2. Temporal reasoning (along the execution trace) vs spatial (local) reasoning

Running example. The program Foo of Figure 1 is turned into a VAPR problem by adding a single precision requirement $C = \{\varphi\langle 3, x\rangle\}$. Let M be the memory state built during the analysis, and D the function which maps each location to its domain cardinality bound. At the beginning of the procedure, $M(1, x) = \top_{init}$ and all other locations evaluate to $\bot$. Moreover, all domain bounds are set to 0. A first propagation step takes place, ending with the following memory state : $M = \{(1, x) \mapsto \top_{init}, (2, x) \mapsto \top_{\{0,1,2\}}, (3, x) \mapsto \top_*,\}$ ($\bot$ values are omitted), and a requirement violation is detected for $(3, x)$. The refinement step takes place from $(3, x)$. Since $(3, x)$ cannot be corrected (it is only a simple $\top_*$), the requirement is propagated to its unique predecessor $(2, x)$. The abstract value is $\top_{\{0,1,2\}}$ and $D(2, x) = 0$. If $Kmax < 3$ then $(2, x)$ cannot be corrected and the procedure fails since no location has been corrected. Note that it is indeed impossible to satisfy the requirement with $Kmax$ strictly less than 3. Otherwise ($Kmax \geq 3$) $D(2, x)$ is set to 3 and the propagation is restarted, leading to $M = \{(1, x) \mapsto \top_{init}, (2, x) \mapsto \{0, 1, 2\}, (3, x) \mapsto \top_{\{10,20,30\}}\}$, and a requirement violation is again detected for $(3, x)$. The refinement step goes on and $(3, x)$ is directly corrected, $D(3, x)$ is set to 3 and the propagation is restarted. The memory state obtained is $M = \{(1, x) \mapsto \top_{init}, (2, x) \mapsto \{0, 1, 2\}, (3, x) \mapsto \{10, 20, 30\}, (10, x) \mapsto \top_*, (20, x) \mapsto \top_*, (30, x) \mapsto \top_*\}$. No violation is reported, the procedure succeeds.

3.3   The PaR Procedure for VAPR

The Propagate and Refine procedure (PaR) for VAPR is described precisely hereafter. Procedure 1 is the top-level procedure, based on the propagation step (Procedure 2) and the refinement step (Procedure 3), built itself on requirement propagation (Procedure 4). In the following procedures, P is an unstructured program (type $\mathcal{P}$), C is a set of requirements (type $\mathcal{R}$), $S \subseteq L \times V^{\#}$ is a set of locations (type $\mathcal{S}$), $D : L \times V^{\#} \mapsto \mathbb{N}$ is a domain map (type $\mathcal{D}$), $M : (l, v) \in L \times V^{\#} \mapsto KSET(D(l, v))$ is a memory state (type $\mathcal{M}$), and e is a program expression (type $\mathcal{E}$). Expressions are built on integer values, variables, array-reads and unary / binary operators. The notation $?Type$ indicates that a procedure returns either a value of type $Type$ or a special value $FAIL$.

Propagation (see Procedure 2). The forward (flow-sensitive) value propagation (PROP-AGATE*) differs from a standard one on a few points: (1) faulty locations are systematically discarded and recorded (in output S), (2) implicit casts are performed during propagation between locations with different domains, (3) $\top$-labels are propagated as explained hereafter, (4) value propagation also updates the journal.

Journal. The journal is updated in procedure PROPAGATE* (Procedure 2) and read in requirement propagation (Procedure 4) to prune valid but irrelevant data-dependencies. For the sake of clarity, the journal is split into two different maps $H_1 : L \times I \times \mathcal{E} \to KSET(\infty)$ (type $\mathcal{H}_1$) and $H_2 : L \times I \times \mathbb{B} \to \mathbb{B}$ (type $\mathcal{H}_2$), where $\mathbb{B}$ is the set of boolean values. An instruction is *fired* when it is used in value propagation. The value $H_1(l, i, e)$ stores the maximal k-set at which expression e has been evaluated when instruction (l, i) was fired. This is used to record relevant jump targets and array indexes. The value $H_2(l, i, b)$ stores whether or not the conditional instruction (l, i) has been fired with condition evaluating to b.

$\top$-labels. The set F of $\top$-labels has four kind of elements: f_{init} for initial $\top$ values, $f_{\langle d_1, d_2, \dots \rangle}$ for the $\top$-abstraction of $\{d_1, d_2, \dots\}$, f_* for other $\top$-values, and $f_\perp$ to denote the absence of $\top$-value. Hence each location is associated to a pair in $KSET(\infty) \times F$. F is equipped with the following order: $f_\perp$ is the minimal element, all other elements are incomparable. Propagation rules for $\top$-labels are the following: f_{init} and $f_{\langle \dots \rangle}$ are kept in place (never overwritten), and they are propagated as f_*. Strictly speaking, F is not a lattice. However, since $\top$-labels are not considered for concretization, k-set propagation or inclusion testing, they can be seen as an additional information not affecting the main k-set propagation. From a theoretical point of view, there are now several minimal fixpoints of the program only diverging on their $\top$-labels. In the following $f_\perp$ is always omitted, and for other $f_\# \in F$, $(\top, f_\#)$ is written $\top_\#$.

Theorem 1. *Procedure PaR(P,C) terminates and is sound, i.e. it returns either FAIL or a safe approximation M of the collecting semantics of P such that $M \models C$.*

Proof. The proof for soundness is straightforward since all requirements are checked to hold before procedure PaR returns an invariant of the program. For termination, note first that procedures PROPAGATE* and REFINE terminate: for PROPAGATE*, lattices based on cartesian products of k-sets satisfy the Ascending Chain Condition, and $\top$-label propagation terminates because a $\top_{\langle \dots \rangle}$ cannot be overwritten ; for REFINE, each $(l, v) \in L \times V^\#$ is processed at most once in the procedure. Moreover, PaR can go through label `restart` only when a domain refinement occurs, which can happen at most $|L| \times |V^\#| \times Kmax$ times, ensuring termination. $\qquad\square$

The procedure runs in polynomial-time: there are at most $|L| \times |V^\#| \times Kmax$ domain refinements, hence there are at most $|L| \times |V^\#| \times Kmax$ steps of propagation-refinement, and both propagation and refinement are polynomial-time procedures.

PaR : $(P : \mathcal{P}) \times (C : \mathcal{R}) \mapsto ?\mathcal{M}$
  parameter: a maximal bound for k-sets $Kmax$
  input: a program $P = (L, V, A, T, l_0)$ and a set of precision requirements C
  output: an invariant M of P covering $(l_0, \top^{|V|^{\#}})$ such that $M \models C$, or FAIL

  $D := \mathrm{map}((l, v) \mapsto 0)$ /* $D : L \times V \mapsto \mathbb{N}$ maps (l, v) to a size of k-set */
  label restart
  $M := \mathrm{map}((l, v) \mapsto \; if \; l = l_0 \; then \; \top_{init} \; else \; \bot \;)$
    /* M : memory map, $M(l, v)$ is a k-set whose size is bounded by $KSET(D(l, v))$ */
  $(H_1, H_2) :=$ empty-journal /* H_1 always evaluates to $\bot$, H_2 always evaluates to $false$ */
  $S := \emptyset$ /* set of faulty locations */
  $(M, H_1, H_2, S) :=$ PROPAGATE*(P, C, M, D)
  if $S \neq \emptyset$ **then**
    case REFINE(P, D, M, H_1, H_2, S) **of**
     | FAIL : return FAIL
     | RES(D') : $D := D'$; goto restart   /* domain is refined */
    end case
  end if
  return M

Procedure 1. PaR, global scheme

PROPAGATE* : $(P : \mathcal{P}) \times (C : \mathcal{R}) \times (M : \mathcal{M}) \times (D : \mathcal{D}) \mapsto \mathcal{M} \times \mathcal{H}_1 \times \mathcal{H}_2 \times \mathcal{S}$
  input: a program $P = (L, V, A, T, l_0)$, a domain map D, a memory state M,
    a set of precision requirements C
  output: updated version of M, a journal (H_1, H_2) and the set of faulty locations for (M, C)

  $S := \emptyset$; $(H_1, H_2) :=$ empty-journal
  While M not a fixpoint of P **do**
    forall $(l, T(l)) \in L \times I$ of P **do**
      if for all $\varphi \langle l, v \rangle \in C$, $M(l, v) \models \varphi \langle l, v \rangle$ **then**
        $M' :=$ **eval**$((l, i), M, D)$ /* D is needed for cast between domains */
        $(H_1, H_2) :=$ **update-journal**$((l, i), M, D, H_1, H_2)$
        $M := M \sqcup M'$
      end if
    end forall
  end while
  $S := \{(l, v) \in L \times V^{\#} | M(l, v) \not\models C\}$
  return (M, H_1, H_2, S)

---

journal updates : H_1 and H_2 are updated according to the following events
  – when instruction $(l, i) = (l, cgoto\; v)$ is fired, then $H_1(l, i, v) := M(l, v)$
  – when $(l, i) = (l, ite(p, l_1, l_2))$ is fired for p evaluating to b, then $H_2(l, i, b) := true$
  – when $(l, i) = (l, a[e] := ...)$ is fired, then $H_1(l, i, e) := M(l, e)$
  – when $(l, i) = (l, ... := f(a[e], v_1, ..., v_n))$ is fired, then $H_1(l, i, e) := M(l, e)$

Procedure 2. Value propagation

REFINE : $(P : \mathcal{P}) \times (D : \mathcal{D}) \times (M : \mathcal{M}) \times (H_1 : \mathcal{H}_1) \times (H_2 : \mathcal{H}_2) \times (S : \mathcal{S}) \mapsto ?\mathcal{D}$
parameter: a maximal bound for k-sets $Kmax$
input: a program $P = (L, V, A, T, l_0)$, a domain map D, a memory state M,
      a journal (H_1, H_2), a set of locations $S = \{(l_i, v_i)\}$ such that $M(l_i, v_i) = \top$
output: return updated version of D, or FAIL

---

success := false
SET := **propagate-req**$^*(P, S, M, H_1, H_2)$
For all $(l, v) \in$ SET such that $M(l, v) = \top_{\langle d_1, \ldots, d_q \rangle}$ **do**   /* *clearly $D(l, v) < q$* */
   if $q \leq Kmax$ **then** $D(l, v) := q$, success := true **end if**
end for
if success **return** RES(D) **else return** FAIL **end if**

Procedure 3. Refinement

---

propagate-req* : $(P : \mathcal{P}) \times (S : \mathcal{S}) \times (M : \mathcal{M}) \times (H_1 : \mathcal{H}_1) \times (H_2 : \mathcal{H}_2) \mapsto \mathcal{S}$
input: a program P, a memory state M, a journal (H_1, H_2), a set of faulty locations S
output: set of locations influencing the value of locations in S, with pruning based on (H_1, H_2)

---

return lfp of **prop-req-instr** starting from locations in S and using all $(l, i) \in L \times I$ of P

---

prop-req-instr : $((l_0, i) : L \times I) \times ((l, v) : L \times V^\#) \times (M : \mathcal{M}) \times (H_1 : \mathcal{H}_1) \times (H_2 : \mathcal{H}_2) \mapsto \mathcal{S}$
/* *backward propagation from faulty location (l, v) for instruction (l_0, i)* */
if $M(l, v) = \top_{init}$ or $M(l, v) = \top_{\langle \ldots \rangle}$ **then** return $\emptyset$
else if $M(l, v) \neq \top_*$ **then** return $\emptyset$
else case l_0, i **of**   /* *we sketch only the most representative cases* */
   | $l_0, cgoto(x)$: **if** $l \in H_1(l_0, i, x)$ return $\{(l_0, v)\}$ **else** return $\emptyset$
   | $l_0, ite(p, l_1, l_2)$ with $l = l_1$: **if** $H_2(l_0, i, true) = true$ **then** return $\{(l_0, v)\}$ **else** return $\emptyset$
   | $l_0, ite(p, l_1, l_2)$ with $l = l_2$: **if** $H_2(l_0, i, false) = true$ **then** return $\{(l_0, v)\}$ **else** return $\emptyset$
   | $l_0, a[e'] := e, l$ and $v = a[k]$:
      if $\{k\} = H_1(l_0, i, e')$ **then** return $\{l_0\} \times$**prop-req-expr**(e, H_1, l, i)
      else if $k \notin H_1(l_0, i, e')$ **then** return (l_0, v)
      else return $(\{l_0\} \times$**prop-req-expr**$(e, H_1, l, i)) \bigcup \{(l_0, v)\}$
      end if
end case
end if

---

prop-req-expr : $(e : \mathcal{E}) \times (H_1 : \mathcal{H}_1) \times (l : L) \times (i : I) \mapsto 2^{V^\#}$
case e **of**   /* *we sketch only the most representative cases* */
   | $k \in \mathbb{N}$: return $\emptyset$ | $v \in V$: return $\{v\}$ | $a[k], k \in \mathbb{N}$: return $\{a[k]\}$
   | $op(e_1, e_2)$: return **prop-req-expr**$(e_1, H_1, l, i) \cup$ **prop-req-expr**(e_2, H_1, l, i)
   | $a[e]$: **if** $H_1(l, i, e) = \top$ **then** return **prop-req-expr**(e, H_1, l, i)
      else return $\{a[k] | k \in H_1(l, i, e)\}$
      end if
end case

Procedure 4. Requirement propagation

4 Relative Completeness

Let $(P, \mathcal{C})$ be a VAPR problem. We denote by $KSET(k)$-PROP the standard forward value propagation built over $KSET(k)$, and by $lfp_{\langle kset(k) \rangle}(P)$ the best abstraction of the collecting semantics of P using $KSET(k)$. PaR is relatively complete if PaR$(P, \mathcal{C})$ with parameter $Kmax$ returns successfully when $KSET(Kmax)$-PROP$(P) \models \mathcal{C}$. Relative completeness indicates how precise the refinement is.

No relative completeness in the general case. Here is a small example demonstrating that PaR is not relatively complete. Let us consider the Foo2 program in Figure 3 with precision requirement $\mathcal{C} = \{\varphi\langle 5, t \rangle\}$ and $Kmax = 1$. Procedure $KSET(1)$-PROP returns M with $M(l_5, t) = \{100\}$, thus the result satisfies $\mathcal{C}$. However, PaR fails on that program. The first value propagation computes a memory state such that $\{(1, x) \mapsto \top_{init}; (2, x) \mapsto \top_{\langle 1 \rangle}; (5, t) \mapsto \top_{\langle 100 \rangle}\}$ or $\{(1, x) \mapsto \top_{init}; (2, x) \mapsto \top_{\langle 1 \rangle}; (5, t) \mapsto \top_{\langle 200 \rangle}\}$, depending on the order of propagation steps in PROPAGATE*. $\mathcal{C}$ is violated, and a refinement is launched. $D(5, t)$ is increased to 1, and the forward propagation goes on. Note that

1. x:=1, goto 2
2. if x=1 then goto 3 else goto 4
3. t := 100, goto 5
4. t := 200, goto 5
5. cgoto t

Fig. 3. The Foo2 program

$D(2, x)$ still equals 0. The result satisfies $M(5, t) = \top_{\langle 100, 200 \rangle}$, again violating $\mathcal{C}$. However, this time $D(5, t)$ cannot be corrected ($Kmax$ is too low), and the backward refinement propagation stops (only constant assignments to $(5, t)$). The refinement procedure fails, causing PaR to fail.

Relative completeness on SVAPR. We consider relations $R \subseteq 2^{Dom} \times 2^{Dom}$ over sets of valuations, variables of the relation being partitioned into input variables (x_i)'s and output variables (x_i')'s. A relation $R(x_1, \ldots, x_n, x_1', \ldots, x_n')$ is *simple* if for all $i \in [1..n]$, there exists $J_i \subseteq [1..n]$ such that (a) the value of x_i' depends only of $\{x_j | j \in J_i\}$, and (b) $card(x_i') = +\infty$ iff $\bigvee_{j \in J_i} card(x_j) = +\infty$. A function from 2^{Dom} to 2^{Dom} is simple if its associated relation is simple. The class of simple functions comprises operations such as $+, -, abs, \times k$. The $\times$ operation is not simple, since $\mathbb{N} \times \{0\} = \{0\}$.

The class of SVAPRs comprises all VAPRs $(P, \mathcal{C})$ such that there are no conditional branching (only non-deterministic choice), all functions in expressions are simple, and $\mathcal{C}$ comprises a requirement $\varphi\langle l, v \rangle$ for each instruction $(l, cgoto\ v)$ and each array expression $a[v]$ at code address l. Jumps and array expressions are said to be *guarded*.

Theorem 2 (Relative completeness). *PaR is relatively complete on SVAPR.*

The proof is sketched hereafter. In the following, a value $\top_{\langle d_1, \ldots, d_q \rangle}$ is said to be rectifiable if $q \leq Kmax$, the symbol $\top$ is used to denote any special $\top$ value regardless its $\top$-label and a proper k-set denotes a k-set different from $\top$. The general scheme of the proof is to consider an arbitrary execution ρ of PaR leading to a failure (let us imagine that $\varphi\langle l_n, v_n \rangle \in \mathcal{C}$ is violated), and build from it a sequence of propagations in $KSET(Kmax)$ demonstrating that $lfp_{\langle kset(kmax) \rangle}(P)(l_n, v_n) = \top$. It then follows that any safe analysis of P based on $KSET(Kmax)$ cannot satisfy $\mathcal{C}$.

Let $\pi = t_1 \ldots t_n$ be the part of ρ representing the last call to PROPAGATE*. Let us denote by $M_1, \ldots, M_n$ the sequence of successive memory states obtained from

M_0 (initial state) following π. We suppose that $M_n(l_n, v_n) = \top$ while $\varphi\langle l_n, v_n\rangle \in \mathcal{C}$. By definition of π, there is no requirement violation when t_k is applied to M_k, and no predecessor of (l_n, v_n) (by requirement propagation) can be corrected since refinement fails. Let us denote by (M'_i)'s the memory states obtained from $M_0 = M'_0$ by a $KSET(Kmax)$ propagation following π. The proof consists in showing that $M'_n(l_n, v_n) = \top$. We first suppose that there are no array expressions nor dynamic jumps along π. The main steps of the proof are the following.

(L1) We can always find (s, l_s, v_s) such that $M_s(l_s, v_s)$ is a non-rectifiable source of the requirement violation, i.e.: (l_s, v_s) is a predecessor of (l_n, v_n), and $M_s(l_s, v_s)$ either evaluates to $\top_{\langle d_1, \ldots, d_q\rangle}$ with $q > Kmax$ and the direct predecessors of (l_s, v_s) in M_{s-1} being proper k-sets, or evaluates to $\top_{init}$. In the first case, the inequality $q > Kmax$ is deduced from the failure of the refinement.

(L2) Proper k-sets computed in PaR along π are conserved in $KSET(Kmax)$, i.e. if $M_i(l_i, v_i)$ is a proper k-set then $M'_i(l_i, v_i) = M_i(l_i, v_i)$. This result comes from a specific property of k-sets: the same computations on $KSET(k_1)$ and $KSET(k_2)$ with $k_1 \le k_2$ either output the same results, or a pair made of $\top$ and a proper k-set.

(L3) It can be shown that if $M'_s(l_s, v_s) = \top$ then $M'_n(l_n, v_n) = \top$. Indeed, the same data dependencies hold in the (M_i)'s and in the (M'_i)'s, and simple functions ensure that $\top$'s are systematically propagated in every instruction from input to output.

(L4) Finally, it is easy to prove that $M'_s(l_s, v_s) = \top$ because either $M_s(l_s, v_s)$ is an initial $\top$ value independent of the domain precision, or the predecessors of $M'_s(l_s, v_s)$ are the same proper k-sets than for $M_s(l_s, v_s)$ (by L1 and L2), hence $M'_s(l_s, v_s) = cast_{Kmax}(\{d_1, \ldots, d_q\})$ with $q > Kmax$, which evaluates to $\top$. The conclusion follows as explained previously.

In the general case, both the journal and guards are necessary to handle array expressions and dynamic jumps. The main problem is that $KSET(Kmax)$ propagation could compute more precise k-sets on array expressions / jump targets, involving less value propagation and breaking lemmas L2 and L3. Guards ensure that intermediate array expressions and jumps evaluate to proper k-sets in the (M_i)'s. Result L2 can still be proved, and intermediate array expressions and jumps have even the same values in (M_i)'s and (M'_i)'s. L3 is also satisfied thanks to both lemma L2 and the restriction of backward propagation (through the journal) to effectively observed jump targets / array indexes. The rest of the proof remains the same.

5   Experiments

Implementation. Procedure PaR has been implemented into a prototype performing CFG reconstruction from 32-bit PowerPC (PPC) executable files (ELF format). The prototype is about 29 kloc of C++. The forward propagation follows a standard flow-sensitive scheme, enhanced with standard efficient data structures [21] to represent memory states. Procedures are inlined, calls and returns being identified syntactically. Array writes and dynamic jumps are guarded, while array reads are not. CFG reconstruction and instruction decoding are interleaved, i.e. the analysis can discover new instructions on-the-fly. This feature requires only slight modifications of the procedure and theoretical framework presented so far (cf. [19]) with no incidence on the main results. The tool can handle low-level features such as instruction overlapping and call stack overwriting, but self-modifying code is not addressed. Note that dealing with other instruction sets such as x86 is only a matter of front-end.

Goal. We are interested in evaluating the four following properties of PaR: (P1) absolute performance, both in terms of (a) precision and (b) efficiency, (P2) relative performance compared to standard approaches based on k-sets or intervals, (P3) locality of the refinement, (P4) scalability, and (P5) robustness to $Kmax$.

Test benches. Two test benches T1 and T2 are considered (cf. Table 1). T1 is a set of 12 small hand-written C programs compiled with gcc. They are intended to represent common situations where dynamic jumps arise from C code, like switch and function pointers. T2 is a single industrial case study (aircraft) taken from a safety-critical embedded software for aeronautics (developed by the SAGEM company). The functionalities of the program are not relevant for CFG reconstruction, details can be found in [2]. The source code size is about 21 kloc of C, compiled with WindRiver. The executable counts 32405 instructions and 51 dynamic jumps. All dynamic jumps have between 8 and 16 valid jump targets, for a total of 461 valid jump targets[1]. The program does not use dynamic memory allocation.

Protocol and results. To evaluate P1, we report: (a) the number of dynamic jumps for which precision requirements are met and the number of recovered invalid targets (∞ if a target evaluates to $\top$); (b) the computation time. To evaluate P2, PaR is compared to other straightforward flow-sensitive propagation procedures (with inlining): value analysis based on k-sets for different k, and global and undirected refinement of k-set propagation (start with k=1, when a target expression evaluates to $\top$, increase k by 5 - up to $Kmax$ - and restart the computation). Precision and efficiency are compared with the metrics of P1. We also perform a "mind experiment" (on T1 only) to compare the precision of PaR to the best possible precision of any convex domain-based analysis and strided interval-based analysis. To do so, results of PaR are compared to the best abstractions of each set of targets of each dynamic jump. Best abstractions are deduced through manual inspection. For P3, the minimal, maximal and average k-set sizes used by PaR are reported. T2 is used to evaluate P4. Finally, for P5 procedure PaR is launched with different $Kmax$ and we observe metrics of P1. Experiments were performed on a PC Intel 2Ghz equipped with 2 GBytes of RAM. Results are reported in Tables 2 to 4.

Comments. Results from Table 2 and Table 4 show that PaR is both reasonably efficient and very precise. Indeed, *no target expression evaluates to* $\top$ and very few false targets are recovered: 9 false targets for 123 valid targets on T1, 42 false targets for 461 valid targets on T2. Results from Table 3 and Table 4 shows that PaR exhibits very good locality : on each example, the maximal k-set employed is very close to the optimal one (max #T), and the average cardinality of k-sets is very low (< 1.2). Hence, precise computation is performed only on a small portion of the program. Moreover, as expected, the computation time is independent from $Kmax$ (Table 2 and Table 4) as long as $Kmax$ is large enough. These results also hold on T2, demonstrating the scalability of the approach. According to Table 2 and Table 4, PaR performs better than the other approaches considered here in at least precision, performance or robustness.

---

[1] This information was retrieved from WindRiver output for validation only, the prototype does not make any advantage of it.

Table 1. Test benches T1 and T2

	program	lines of C	#I	#DJ	#T	max#T
	test0	29	66	1	2	2
	test1	56	207	1	6	6
	test2	60	192	1	2	2
	test3	114	504	2	14	8
	test4	143	351	1	2	2
T1	test5	164	654	3	19	9
	test6	170	496	1	6	6
	test7	199	619	1	6	6
	test8	234	795	2	14	8
	test9	258	909	2	14	8
	test10	280	945	3	19	9
	test11	290	1006	3	19	9
T2	aircraft	21562	32405	51	461	16

#I: native code instructions
#DJ: dynamic jumps
#T: feasible targets
max#T: max. #T for a jump

Table 2. T1: Summarised results

	# SDJ	#FT	Time (s)
1-set propagation	0/21	∞/123	2
5-set propagation	6/21	∞/123	7
10-set propagation	13/21	∞/123	8
15-set propagation	21/21	9/123	12
50-set propagation	21/21	9/123	35
k-set iter ($Kmax = 50$)	21/21	9/123	29
PaR ($Kmax = 15$)	21/21	9/123	11
PaR ($Kmax = 50$)	21/21	9/123	11
PaR ($Kmax = 100$)	21/21	9/123	11
perfect Convex	21/21	5337/123	NA
perfect Strided Interval	21/21	498/123	NA

SDJ: DJ with target $\neq \top$ w.r.t. total #DJ
FT: recovered false targets w.r.t. total #T

Table 3. T1: locality of PaR ($Kmax = 50$)

program	max #T	min-k	max-k	avg-k
test0	2	0	3	1.08
test1	6	0	6	1.17
test2	2	0	3	1.18
test3	8	0	11	1.16
test4	2	0	3	1.12
test5	9	0	11	1.17
test6	6	0	6	1.11
test7	6	0	6	1.10
test8	8	0	12	1.12
test9	8	0	11	1.08
test10	9	0	13	1.12
test11	9	0	12	1.08

Table 4. Results on T2

	#SDJ	#FT	max-k	avg-k	Time (mn)
1-set propagation	0/51	∞/461	NA	NA	1
5-set propagation	0/51	∞/461	NA	NA	7
10-set propagation	33/51	∞/461	NA	NA	24
15-set propagation	45/51	∞/461	NA	NA	26
20-set propagation	51/51	6/461	NA	NA	44
30-set propagation	51/51	6/461	NA	NA	44
50-set propagation	51/51	6/461	NA	NA	44
k-set iter ($Kmax = 50$)	51/51	6/461	NA	NA	103
PaR ($Kmax = 20$)	51/51	42/461	16	1.18	18
PaR ($Kmax = 30$)	51/51	42/461	16	1.18	18
PaR ($Kmax = 50$)	51/51	42/461	16	1.18	18

The k-set propagation is very sensitive to $Kmax$, too coarse or/and too expensive when the bound is not well tuned. However, precision is very good when the bound is large enough. On T2, the recovery is slightly better than the one achieved by PaR, illustrating that the refinement process is not perfect. The naive k-set refinement method is also slightly more precise than PaR, but much more expensive. Finally, on these examples, PaR outperforms largely in terms of precision any value analysis based on convex domains (at least 5337 false targets) or strided intervals (at least 498 false targets).

These experiments show that PaR is a very precise and robust approach to CFG reconstruction with very moderate cost. PaR outperforms standard approaches in terms of preciseness (convex-based domains, k-set with small bound), cost (k-set with large bound or global refinement) or robustness (k-set with manual setting).

6   Related Work

The recent work of Thakur *et al.* [23] describes a refinement-based safety analysis on unstructured programs. A refined CFG reconstruction is performed, but the preciseness of the recovery is driven by the needs of the safety property to check, while the present work targets a precise recovery prior to any other analysis. Noticeably, the technique can cope with self-modifying code. CFA analysis and CFG reconstruction for structured programs have already been discussed in the introduction.

CFG reconstruction for unstructured programs. Industrial tools like IDA PRO [24] or AIT [12] usually rely on linear sweep decoding (brute force decoding of all code addresses) or recursive traversal (recursive decoding until a dynamic jump is encountered), enhanced with limited constant propagation, pattern matching techniques based on the knowledge of the compiling chain process and user annotations. These techniques are unsafe on general programs, missing many legal targets and branches (see experiments with IDA PRO in [4,18]). The only safe techniques we are aware of are those by Reps *et al.* [5,7,8] and Kinder and Veith [18,19], already presented in the introduction. None of these approaches rely on refinement. Note that the line of work presented in [5,7,8] addresses more issues than CFG reconstruction, like variable recovery and type reconstruction. Finally, some recent tools are able to generate test data from executable files [3,4,14], but they do not propose any safe CFG reconstruction.

Refinement-based software analysis. Since a decade, many refinement-based software verification techniques have been developed, either in static analysis [11,13,16,17,20] or in software model checking [6,15]. In client-driven analysis [13], precision requirements are given by an external client and refinement is directed by data-dependencies. However, the precision of the analysis depends on the query to solve, precision is increased through adjusting the degree of flow/context-sensitiveness, and backward data-dependencies are not pruned by a journal mechanism. Other standard refinements [11,16,17,20] include various kinds of "CFG refinements" (node splitting, trace partitioning) and enriching common domains with non-mergeable boolean values. These techniques are orthogonal to the domain refinement proposed here.

CEGAR [6,10,15] offers a systematic way of refining predicate domains through error trace analysis. However, it requires a very precise and expensive symbolic execution on abstract traces, as well as a clear and effective notion of (concrete) error trace, which is lacking for CFG recovery because of junk instructions.

7   Conclusion

This paper introduces the problem of Value Analysis with Precision Requirements (VAPR) and show how CFG reconstruction can be performed within VAPR. We then describe a refinement-based static analysis for VAPR, working over finite sets of constant values. Requirement propagation allows to automatically adjust the domain precision only where it is needed, resulting in a very precise CFG recovery at moderate cost. The procedure is sound, terminates and is relatively complete on a class of nontrivial programs. First experiments, including an industrial case study, show that the method does scale to realistic problems and outperforms standard analyses in terms of precision, efficiency or robustness. Future works comprise improving performance, conducting wider experiments and exploring other applications of the VAPR framework.

Acknowledgements. We are very grateful to Jérôme Leroux, Éric Goubault and the anonymous referees for their insightful comments, and to Philippe Baufreton and SAGEM for the case-study.

References

1. Balakrishnan, G., Gruian, R., Reps, T.W., Teitelbaum, T.: CodeSurfer/x86—A platform for analyzing x86 executables. In: Bodik, R. (ed.) CC 2005. LNCS, vol. 3443, pp. 250–254. Springer, Heidelberg (2005)
2. Baufreton, P., Heckmann, R.: Reliable and precise wcet and stack size determination for a real-life embedded application. In: ISoLA, Workshop On Leveraging Applications of Formal Methods, Verification and Validation, Poitiers-Futuroscope, France, December 12-14 (2007)
3. Bardin, S., Herrmann, P.: Structural Testing of Executables. In: IEEE ICST 2008. IEEE Computer Society, Los Alamitos (2008)
4. Bardin, S., Herrmann, P.: OSMOSE: Automatic Structural Testing of Executables. International Journal of Software Testing, Verification and Reliability (STVR), doi 10.1002/stvr.423
5. Balakrishnan, G., Reps, T.W.: Analyzing memory accesses in x86 executables. In: Duesterwald, E. (ed.) CC 2004. LNCS, vol. 2985, pp. 5–23. Springer, Heidelberg (2004)
6. Ball, T., Rajamani, S.: The SLAM project: Debugging system software via static analysis. In: POPL 2002. ACM, New York (2002)
7. Balakrishnan, G., Reps, T.W.: DIVINE: DIscovering Variables IN Executables. In: Cook, B., Podelski, A. (eds.) VMCAI 2007. LNCS, vol. 4349, pp. 1–28. Springer, Heidelberg (2007)
8. Balakrishnan, G., Reps, T.W.: Analyzing Stripped Device-Driver Executables. In: Ramakrishnan, C.R., Rehof, J. (eds.) TACAS 2008. LNCS, vol. 4963, pp. 124–140. Springer, Heidelberg (2008)
9. Cousot, P., Cousot, R.: Abstract Interpretation: A Unified Lattice Model for Static Analysis of Programs by Construction or Approximation of Fixpoints. In: POPL 1977. ACM, New York (1977)
10. Clarke, E.M., Grumberg, O., Jha, S., Lu, Y., Veith, H.: Counter Example-Guided Abstraction Refinement for Symbolic Model Checking. Journal of the ACM 50(5) (2003)
11. Dhurjati, D., Das, M., Yang, Y.: Path-Sensitive Dataflow Analysis with Iterative Refinement. In: Yi, K. (ed.) SAS 2006. LNCS, vol. 4134, pp. 425–442. Springer, Heidelberg (2006)
12. Ferdinand, C., Heckmann, R.: aiT: worst case execution time prediction by static program analysis. In: IFIP Congress Topical Sessions 2004. Kluwer, Dordrecht (2004)
13. Guyer, S.Z., Lin, C.: Client-driven pointer analysis. In: Cousot, R. (ed.) SAS 2003. LNCS, vol. 2694. Springer, Heidelberg (2003)
14. Godefroid, P., Levin, M.Y., Molnar, D.: Automated Whitebox Fuzz Testing. In: NDSS 2008. The Internet Society, San Diego (2008)
15. Henzinger, T.A., Jhala, R., Majumbar, R., Sutre, G.: Lazy Abstraction. In: POPL 2002. ACM, New York (2002)
16. Handjieva, M., Tzolovski, S.: Refining static analyses by trace-based partitioning using control flow. In: Levi, G. (ed.) SAS 1998. LNCS, vol. 1503, pp. 200–214. Springer, Heidelberg (1998)
17. Jeannet, B., Halbwachs, N., Raymond, P.: Dynamic partitioning in analyses of numerical properties. In: Cortesi, A., Filé, G. (eds.) SAS 1999. LNCS, vol. 1694, p. 39. Springer, Heidelberg (1999)

18. Kinder, J., Veith, H.: Jakstab: A Static Analysis Platform for Binaries. In: Gupta, A., Malik, S. (eds.) CAV 2008. LNCS, vol. 5123, pp. 423–427. Springer, Heidelberg (2008)
19. Kinder, J., Zuleger, F., Veith, H.: An Abstract Interpretation-Based Framework for Control Flow Reconstruction from Binaries. In: Logozzo, F., Peled, D.A., Zuck, L.D. (eds.) VMCAI 2008. LNCS, vol. 4905. Springer, Heidelberg (2008)
20. Mauborgne, L., Rival, X.: Trace Partitioning in Abstract Interpretation Based Static Analyzers. In: Sagiv, M. (ed.) ESOP 2005. LNCS, vol. 3444, pp. 5–20. Springer, Heidelberg (2005)
21. Myers, E.W.: Efficient Applicative Data Types. In: POPL 1984. ACM, New York (1984)
22. Shivers, O.: Control-Flow Analysis in Scheme. In: PLDI 1988. ACM, New York (1988)
23. Thakur, A.V., Lim, J., Lal, A., Burton, A., Driscoll, E., Elder, M., Andersen, T., Reps, T.W.: Directed Proof Generation for Machine Code. In: Touili, T., Cook, B., Jackson, P. (eds.) CAV 2010. LNCS, vol. 6174, pp. 288–305. Springer, Heidelberg (2010)
24. IDA Pro homepage, `http://www.hex-rays.com/idapro`

SAT-Based Model Checking without Unrolling

Aaron R. Bradley

Dept. of Electrical, Computer & Energy Engineering
University of Colorado at Boulder
Boulder, CO 80309
bradleya@colorado.edu

Abstract. A new form of SAT-based symbolic model checking is described. Instead of unrolling the transition relation, it incrementally generates clauses that are inductive relative to (and augment) stepwise approximate reachability information. In this way, the algorithm gradually refines the property, eventually producing either an inductive strengthening of the property or a counterexample trace. Our experimental studies show that induction is a powerful tool for generalizing the unreachability of given error states: it can refine away many states at once, and it is effective at focusing the proof search on aspects of the transition system relevant to the property. Furthermore, the incremental structure of the algorithm lends itself to a parallel implementation.

1 Introduction

Modern SAT-based model checkers unroll the transition relation and thus present the SAT solver with large problems [2,24,21,23]. We describe a new SAT-based model checking algorithm that does not unroll the transition relation, that is nevertheless complete, that is competitive with the best available model checkers [3], and that can be implemented to take advantage of parallel computing environments. The fundamental idea is to generate clauses that are inductive relative to stepwise reachability information.

When humans analyze systems, they produce a set of lemmas — typically inductive properties — that together imply the desired property. Each lemma holds *relative to* some subset of previously proved lemmas in that this prior knowledge is invoked in proving the new lemma [19]. A given lemma usually focuses on just one aspect of the system. Typically, early lemmas discuss variable domains, properties about module-local data structures, and so on, while later lemmas address more global aspects of the system. Yet even the later lemmas are fairly easy to prove since prior information heavily constrains the state space. When a lemma is too difficult to prove directly, a skilled human verifier typically searches for additional supporting lemmas.

In contrast, standard model checkers employ monolithic strategies. Many iteratively compute pre- or post-images precisely [7,20] or approximately [21]; others unroll the transition relation [2,24,23]. Section 5 provides further discussion of related work.

R. Jhala and D. Schmidt (Eds.): VMCAI 2011, LNCS 6538, pp. 70–87, 2011.

This paper describes a model checking algorithm for safety properties whose strategy is not monolithic but rather closer to that of a human, albeit a particularly industrious one. It produces lemmas in the form of clauses that are inductive *relative to* previous lemmas and stepwise assumptions. At convergence, a subset of the generated lemmas comprise a 1-step inductive strengthening of the given property. Humans construct lemmas of a more general form than clauses, and in this respect, the analogy breaks down; but the incremental construction of lemmas to form a proof is similar. Section 3 covers induction in further depth, reviews previous work on generating inductive clauses [6], and motivates the use of stepwise assumptions. Sections 4 and 6 discuss the algorithm in detail.

The implementation of the algorithm, ic3 ("Incremental Construction of Inductive Clauses for Indubitable Correctness"), has certain runtime characteristics that support the comparison to a human strategy (see Table 1 of Section 7). A typical run of ic3 on a nontrivial problem executes many tens of thousands of SAT queries that test whether various formulas are 1-step inductive, and it produces hundreds or thousands of intermediate lemmas. Each SAT query is trivial compared to the queries made in other techniques [20,2,24,23]: ic3 successfully employs ZChaff [22], a decidedly non-state-of-the-art solver, yet one that provides efficient incremental support. While a human would likely produce fewer but higher-level lemmas, the overall pattern of applying relatively low reasoning power to produce many lemmas is familiar to the experienced human verifier. In HWMCC'10, ic3 ranked third, placing it among sophisticated, multi-engine model checkers. It is available for download at the author's website [3].

The human verifier analogy can be taken one step further. Just as large verification problems benefit from the attention of several humans, they also benefit from the attention of multiple cooperating ic3 instances. In particular, because the *relative to* relation among lemmas is a partial order and typically not a linear order, ic3 can take advantage of multi-core and distributed computing environments. Each instance shares only its lemmas and not the work that went into producing them, and it incorporates the lemmas that the other processes generate. Section 8 demonstrates empirically that this parallel implementation is effective and that, in particular, processes do not duplicate work too frequently.

2 Definitions

A *finite-state transition system* $S : (\bar{i}, \bar{x}, I, T)$ is described by a pair of propositional logic formulas: an initial condition $I(\bar{x})$ and a transition relation $T(\bar{i}, \bar{x}, \bar{x}')$ over a set of input variables $\bar{i}$, internal state variables $\bar{x}$, and the next-state primed forms $\bar{x}'$ of the internal variables [9]. Applying prime to a formula, F', is the same as priming all of its variables.

A state of the system is an assignment of Boolean values to all variables $\bar{x}$ and is described by a *cube* over $\bar{x}$, which, generally, is a conjunction of literals, each *literal* a variable or its negation. An assignment s to all variables of a formula F either satisfies the formula, $s \models F$, or falsifies it, $s \not\models F$. If s is interpreted as a state and $s \models F$, we say that s is an F-state. A formula F *implies* another formula G, written $F \Rightarrow G$, if every satisfying assignment of F satisfies G.

A *clause* is a disjunction of literals. A subclause $d \subseteq c$ is a clause d whose literals are a subset of c's literals.

A *trace* $s_0, s_1, s_2, \ldots$, which may be finite or infinite in length, of a transition system S is a sequence of states such that $s_0 \models I$ and for each adjacent pair (s_i, s_{i+1}) in the sequence, $s_i, s'_{i+1} \models T$. That is, a trace is the sequence of assignments in an execution of the transition system. A state that appears in some trace of the system is *reachable*.

A safety property $P(\bar{x})$ asserts that only P-states are reachable. P is *invariant* for the system S (that is, S-invariant) if indeed only P-states are reachable. If P is not invariant, then there exists a finite *counterexample* trace $s_0, s_1, \ldots, s_k$ such that $s_k \not\models P$.

3   Applying Induction Incrementally

For a transition system $S : (\bar{i}, \bar{x}, I, T)$, an *inductive* assertion $F(\bar{x})$ describes a set of states that (1) includes all initial states: $I \Rightarrow F$, and that (2) is closed under the transition relation: $F \wedge T \Rightarrow F'$. The two conditions are sometimes called *initiation* and *consecution*, respectively. An inductive *strengthening* of a safety property P is a formula F such that $F \wedge P$ is inductive. Standard symbolic model checkers [7,20] and interpolation-based model checkers [21] compute inductive strengthenings of a given safety property P. Upon convergence, iterative post-image, respectively pre-image, computation yields the strongest, respectively weakest, inductive strengthening of P, while approximate methods yield strengthenings of intermediate strength.

Induction need not be applied in a monolithic way, however. One can construct a sequence of inductive assertions, each inductive *relative to* (a subset of) the previous assertions [19]. An assertion F is inductive *relative to* another assertion G if condition (1) holds unchanged: $I \Rightarrow F$, and a modified version of (2) holds: $G \wedge F \wedge T \Rightarrow F'$. The assertion G reduces the set of states that must be considered so that an assertion F that is not inductive on its own (because $F \wedge T \not\Rightarrow F'$) may be inductive relative to G.

The value of using induction in an incremental fashion is that constructing a sequence of simple lemmas is often easier than constructing a strengthening all at once. Of course, translating human intuition into a model checking algorithm is difficult if not impossible, so one typically fixes a domain of assertions [10].

In previous work, we introduced a technique for discovering relatively inductive clauses [6]. We review it here as motivation for the algorithm that we subsequently introduce. The main idea is to augment the following naive model checker: enumerate states that can reach a violation of the asserted property P and conjoin their negations to P until an inductive assertion is produced. For each such state s, the method searches for an *inductive generalization* $c \subseteq \neg s$ to conjoin to P instead. Such a subclause (1) is inductive relative to known or assumed reachability information (P, previous inductive generalizations, and the negations of considered states without inductive generalizations) and (2) is minimal in that it does not contain any strict subclauses that are also inductive.

In practice, such a *minimal inductive subclause* is substantially smaller than $\neg s$ and excludes states that are not necessarily related to s by T.

While the method succeeds on some hard benchmarks [4], it sometimes enters long searches for the next relatively inductive clause, for a state may not have an inductive generalization even if it is unreachable. It is this problem of search that motivated investigation into a more effective way to use inductive clause generation. The new approach de-emphasizes global information that is sometimes hard to discover in favor of stepwise information that is easy to discover. In particular, stepwise assumptions guarantee that an unreachable state always has a *stepwise-relative inductive generalization*, one that asserts that s and many similar states are unreachable for some number of steps. Because we consider finite state systems, these stepwise-relative inductive generalizations eventually become truly inductive.

Since finding minimal inductive subclauses remains a core subprocedure in the new approach, an informal description of it is in order. To find a subclause $d \subseteq c = c_0$ that is inductive relative to G, if such a clause exists, first consider consecution: $G \wedge c_0 \wedge T \Rightarrow c_0'$. If both this implication and initiation hold, c_0 is itself inductive. Otherwise, a counterexample state s exists. Form the clause $c_1 = c_0 \cap \neg s$ by keeping only the literals that c_0 and $\neg s$ share. Iterate this process until it converges to some clause c_i. If c_i satisfies initiation, then let $d = c_i$; otherwise, c_0 does not have an inductive subclause. This process is called the down algorithm [6].

Now $d \subseteq c_0$ is inductive, but it is not necessarily minimal — and in practice it is large. Form d_1 by dropping some literal of d, and apply down to d_1. If down succeeds, the result is a smaller inductive subclause; if it fails, try again with a different literal. Continue until no literal can be dropped from the current inductive subclause. The result is a minimal inductive subclause of c_0. This process is called the MIC algorithm; it can be accelerated using the up algorithm [6]. Section 7 discusses optimizations to these procedures.

4   Informal Description

Consider a transition system $S : (\bar{i}, \bar{x}, I, T)$ and a safety property P. The algorithm decides whether P is S-invariant, producing an inductive strengthening if so or a counterexample trace if not.

Let us first establish the core logical data structure. The algorithm incrementally refines and extends a sequence of formulas $F_0 = I, F_1, F_2, \ldots, F_k$ that are over-approximations of the sets of states reachable in at most $0, 1, 2, \ldots, k$ steps. While major iterations of the algorithm increase k, minor iterations can refine any i-step approximation F_i, $0 < i \leq k$. Each minor iteration conjoins one new clause to each of $F_0, \ldots, F_j$ for some $0 < j \leq k$, unless a counterexample is discovered. (Adding a clause to $F_0 = I$ is useless, but it simplifies the exposition.)

Assuming that any clause conjoined to $F_0, \ldots, F_j$ over-approximates j-step reachability, this simple description implies that the sequence always obeys the following properties: (1) $I \Rightarrow F_0$ and (2) $F_i \Rightarrow F_{i+1}$ for $0 \leq i < k$. Actually, letting clauses(F_i) be the set of clauses that comprise F_i, (2) can be more strongly expressed as (2') clauses(F_{i+1}) $\subseteq$ clauses(F_i) for $0 \leq i < k$. The algorithm guarantees two other relationships: (3) $F_i \Rightarrow P$ for $0 \leq i \leq k$, and (4) $F_i \wedge T \Rightarrow F'_{i+1}$ for $0 \leq i < k$. If ever clauses(F_i) = clauses(F_{i+1}), then these properties imply that F_i is an inductive strengthening of P.

With this logical data structure and its intended invariants in mind, we now turn to the workings of the algorithm. Initially the satisfiability of $I \wedge \neg P$ and $I \wedge T \wedge \neg P'$ are checked to detect 0- and 1-step counterexamples. If none exist, F_1 is set to P.

Now let us suppose that we are in major iteration $k > 0$, so that sequence $F_0, F_1, \ldots, F_k$ satisfies properties (1)-(4). Is it the case that $F_k \wedge T \Rightarrow P'$?

Suppose so. Then the extended sequence $F_0, F_1, \ldots, F_k, P = F_{k+1}$ satisfies properties (1)-(4). We can move onto major iteration $k+1$. Additionally, for any clause $c \in F_i$, $0 \leq i \leq k$, if $F_i \wedge T \Rightarrow c'$ and $c \notin$ clauses(F_{i+1}), then c is conjoined to F_{i+1}. If during the process of propagating clauses forward it is discovered that clauses(F_i) = clauses(F_{i+1})[1] for some i, the proof is complete: P is invariant.

Now suppose not: $F_k \wedge T \not\Rightarrow P'$. There must exist an F_k-state s that is one transition away from violating P. What is the maximum F_i (that is, the weakest stepwise assumption), $0 \leq i \leq k$, such that $\neg s$ is inductive relative to it? If $\neg s$ is not even inductive relative to F_0, then P is not invariant, for s has an I-state predecessor. But if P is invariant, then $\neg s$ must be inductive relative to some F_i.[2] We then apply inductive generalization to s: a minimal subclause $c \subseteq \neg s$ that is *inductive relative to* F_i is extracted as described in Section 3. Because the inductive generalization is performed relative to F_i, this process must succeed. After all, $\neg s$ is itself inductive relative to F_i. The clause c is conjoined to each of $F_0, \ldots, F_{i+1}$. (Why to F_{i+1}? Because $F_i \wedge c \wedge T \Rightarrow c'$ holds.)[3]

If $i = k - 1$ or $i = k$, then c was conjoined to F_k, eliminating s as an F_k-state. Subsequent queries of $F_k \wedge T \Rightarrow P'$ must either indicate that the implication holds or produce different counterexample states than s. But it is possible that $i < k - 1$. In this case, s is still an F_k-state.

Consider this question: Why is $\neg s$ inductive relative to F_i but not relative to F_{i+1}? There must be a predecessor, t, of s that is an F_{i+1}-state but not an F_i-state. Now if $i = 0$, t may have an I-state as a predecessor, in which case P would not be invariant. But if $i > 0$, then because of property (4), $\neg t$ must be inductive relative to at least F_{i-1}. And even if $i = 0$, $\neg t$ may nevertheless be inductive relative to some F_j.

---

[1] Notice that this syntactic check avoids checking semantic equivalence of potentially complex formulas.

[2] In fact, $\neg s$ is inductive relative to F_{k-2}, if not a later stepwise approximation. For suppose not; then there would exist an F_{k-2}-state t that is a predecessor to s, so that by (4), s would be a F_{k-1}-state. But then an F_{k-1}-state could reach a violation in one transition, contradicting (3) and (4).

[3] In practice, because c may actually be inductive relative to F_j for some $j > i$ even though $\neg s$ is not, we attempt to push it forward as far as possible, that is, until $F_j \wedge c \wedge T \Rightarrow c'$ but $F_{j+1} \wedge c \wedge T \not\Rightarrow c'$. However, this variation complicates the discussion, so we do not consider it further.

Hence we recur on t. The new subgoal is to produce a subclause of $\neg t$ that is inductive relative to F_i, eliminating t at F_{i+1}. Unless P is not invariant, such a clause is eventually added to F_{i+1}, possibly after considering one or more predecessors of t. Then s can be considered with respect to the strengthened over-approximation F_{i+1}. This process of considering predecessors recursively continues until $\neg s$ is finally inductive relative to F_k (unless a counterexample trace is discovered first). In practice, it is worthwhile to find subclauses inductive relative to F_k for every other state considered during the recursion, as the resulting clauses may be mutually inductive but not independently inductive.

With s no longer an F_k-state, $F_k \wedge T \Rightarrow P'$ can be considered again.

5   Related Work

SAT-based unbounded model checking constructs clauses via quantifier elimination; for a safety property P, it computes the weakest inductive strengthening of P [20]. In our algorithm, induction is a means not only to construct clauses by generalizing from states, but also to abstract the system based on the property.

Our algorithm can be viewed from the perspective of predicate abstraction/refinement [17,8]: the minor iterations generate new predicates (clauses) while the major iterations propagate them forward through the stepwise approximations (that is, add $c \in F_i$ to F_{i+1} if $F_i \wedge T \Rightarrow c'$). If the current clauses are insufficient for convergence to an inductive strengthening of P, the next sequence of minor iterations generates new clauses that enable propagation to continue at least one additional step.

The stepwise over-approximation structure of $F_0, F_1, F_2, \ldots, F_k$ is similar to that of interpolation-based model checking (ITP), which uses an interpolant from an unsatisfiable K-step BMC query to compute the post-image approximately [21]. All states in the image are at least $K - 1$ steps away from violating the property. A larger K refines the image by increasing the minimum distance to violating states. In our algorithm, if the frontier is at level k, then F_i, for $0 \leq i \leq k$, contains only states that are at least $k - i + 1$ steps from violating the property. As k increases, the minimum number of steps from F_i-states to violating states increases. In both cases, increasing k (in ours) or K (in ITP) sufficiently for a correct system yields an inductive assertion. However, the algorithms differ in their underlying "technology": ITP computes interpolants from K-step BMC queries, while our algorithm uses inductive generalization of cubes, which requires only 1-step induction queries for arbitrarily large k.

Our work could in principle be applied as a method of strengthening k-induction [24,23,1,25]. However, k-induction would simply eliminate the states that are easiest to inductively generalize — since they have short predecessor chains — so we do not recommend this combination.

The method described in this paper first appeared in a technical report [5].

Listing 1.1. The main function

```
{ @post:  rv  iff  P  is  S-invariant }                          1
bool  prove ():                                                  2
    if  sat(I ∧ ¬P)  or  sat(I ∧ T ∧ ¬P'):                       3
      return  false                                              4
    F₀ := I,   clauses(F₀) := ∅                                  5
    Fᵢ := P,   clauses(Fᵢ) := ∅  for  all  i > 0                 6
    for  k := 1  to  ...:                                        7
        { @rank:  2^|x̄| + 1                                      8
          @assert  (A):                                          9
            (1)  ∀ i ≥ 0,  I ⇒ Fᵢ                                10
            (2)  ∀ i ≥ 0,  Fᵢ ⇒ P                                11
            (3)  ∀ i > 0,  clauses(Fᵢ₊₁) ⊆ clauses(Fᵢ)          12
            (4)  ∀ 0 ≤ i < k,  Fᵢ ∧ T ⇒ F'ᵢ₊₁                    13
            (5)  ∀ i > k,  |clauses(Fᵢ)| = 0  }                  14
        if  not  strengthen (k):                                 15
          return  false                                          16
        propagateClauses (k)                                     17
        if  clauses(Fᵢ) = clauses(Fᵢ₊₁)  for  some  1 ≤ i ≤ k:   18
          return  true                                           19
```

6   Formal Presentation and Analysis

We present the algorithm and its proof of correctness simultaneously with annotated pseudocode in Listings 1.1-1.5 using the classic approach to program verification [16,18]. In the program text, *@pre* and *@post* introduce a function's pre- and post-condition, respectively; *@assert* indicates an invariant at a location; and *@rank* indicates a ranking function represented as the maximum number of times that the loop may iterate. As usual, a function's pre-condition is over its parameters while its post-condition is over its parameters and its return value, rv. For convenience, the system $S : (\bar{i}, \bar{x}, I, T)$ and property P are assumed to be in scope everywhere. Also, some assertions are labeled and subsequently referenced in annotations. All assertions are inductive, but establishing the ranking functions requires additional reasoning, which we provide below.

Listing 1.1 presents the top-level function prove, which returns true if and only if P is S-invariant. First it looks for 0-step and 1-step counterexample traces. If none are found, $F_0, F_1, F_2, \ldots$ are initialized to assume that P is invariant, while their clause sets are initialized to empty. As a formula, each F_i for $i > 0$ is interpreted as $P \wedge \bigwedge \text{clauses}(F_i)$. Then it constructs the sequence of k-step over-approximations starting with $k = 1$. On each iteration, it first calls strengthen(k) (Listing 1.2), which strengthens F_i for $1 \leq i \leq k$ so that F_i-states are at least $k - i + 1$ steps away from violating P, by assertions $A(2)$ and strengthen's $post(2)$. Next it calls propagateClauses(k) (Listing 1.3) to propagate clauses forward through $F_1, F_2, \ldots, F_{k+1}$. If this propagation yields

Listing 1.2. The strengthen function

```
{ @pre :                                                              20
   (1)  A                                                             21
   (2)  k ≥ 1                                                         22
  @post :                                                             23
   (1)  A.1−3                                                         24
   (2)  if  rv  then  ∀ 0 ≤ i ≤ k, Fᵢ ∧ T ⇒ F'ᵢ₊₁                     25
   (3)  ∀ i > k + 1, |clauses(Fᵢ)| = 0                                26
   (4)  if ¬rv then  there  exists  a  counterexample  trace }        27
bool  strengthen (k  :  level ):                                      28
  try :                                                               29
    while  sat (Fₖ ∧ T ∧ ¬P' ):                                       30
      { @rank :  2^|x̄|                                                31
        @assert  (B ):                                                32
         (1)  A.1−4                                                   33
         (2)  ∀ c ∈ clauses(Fₖ₊₁), Fₖ ∧ T ⇒ c'                        34
         (3)  ∀ i > k + 1, |clauses(Fᵢ)| = 0  }                       35
      s  :=  the predecessor extracted from the witness               36
      n  :=  inductivelyGeneralize(s , k − 2, k)                      37
      pushGeneralization ({(n + 1, s)}, k)                           38
      { @assert  (C ):  s ⊭ Fₖ }                                      39
    return  true                                                      40
  except  Counterexample :                                            41
    return  false                                                     42
```

Listing 1.3. The propagateClauses function

```
{ @pre :                                                              43
   (1)  A.1−3                                                         44
   (2)  ∀ 0 ≤ i ≤ k, Fᵢ ∧ T ⇒ F'ᵢ₊₁                                   45
   (3)  ∀ i > k + 1, |clauses(Fᵢ)| = 0                                46
  @post :                                                             47
   (1)  pre                                                           48
   (2)  ∀ 0 ≤ i ≤ k,∀c ∈ clauses(Fᵢ),  if  Fᵢ ∧ T ⇒ c'  then  c ∈ Fᵢ₊₁ } 49
void  propagateClauses (k  :  level ):                                50
for  i  :=  1  to  k :                                                51
  { @assert :  ∀ 0 ≤ j < i,∀c ∈ clauses(Fⱼ),  if  Fⱼ ∧ T ⇒ c'  then  c ∈ Fⱼ₊₁ } 52
    for  each  c ∈ clauses(Fᵢ):                                       53
      { @assert :  pre }                                              54
      if  not  sat (Fᵢ ∧ T ∧ ¬c' ):                                   55
        clauses(Fᵢ₊₁)  :=  clauses(Fᵢ₊₁) ∪ {c}                       56
```

any adjacent levels F_i and F_{i+1} that share all clauses, then F_i is an inductive strengthening of P, proving P's invariance.

While the assertions are inductive, an argument needs to be made to justify the ranking function. By $A(3)$, the state sets represented by $F_0, F_1, \ldots, F_k$ are nondecreasing with level. Given propagateClauses's $post(2)$, avoiding termination at line 19 requires that they be strictly increasing with level, which is

Listing 1.4. Stepwise-relative inductive generalization

```
{ @pre :                                                                     57
  (1)  B                                                                     58
  (2)  min ≥ −1                                                              59
  (3)  if min ≥ 0 then  ¬s  is  inductive  relative  to  Fmin               60
  (4)  there  is  a  trace  from  s  to  a  ¬P−state                        61
  @post :                                                                    62
  (1)  B                                                                     63
  (2)  min ≤ rv ≤ k ,  rv ≥ 0                                               64
  (3)  s ⊭ Frv+1                                                            65
  (4)  ¬s  is  inductive  relative  to  Frv }                               66
level inductivelyGeneralize(s : state , min : level , k : level)           67
  if min < 0 and sat(F0 ∧ T ∧ ¬s ∧ s′):                                    68
    raise  Counterexample                                                    69
  for  i := max(1 , min + 1)  to  k :                                       70
    { @assert :                                                             71
      (1)  B                                                                 72
      (2)  min < i ≤ k                                                       73
      (3)  ∀ 0 ≤ j < i ,  ¬s  is  inductive  relative  to  Fj }            74
    if sat(Fi ∧ T ∧ ¬s ∧ s′):                                              75
      generateClause(s , i − 1 , k)                                         76
      return i − 1                                                          77
  generateClause(s , k , k)                                                 78
  return k                                                                  79
                                                                            80
{ @pre :                                                                    81
  (1)  B                                                                     82
  (2)  i ≥ 0                                                                 83
  (3)  ¬s  is  inductive  relative  to  Fi                                  84
  @post :  (1)  B ,  (2)  s ⊭ Fi+1 }                                        85
void generateClause(s : state , i : level , k : level ):                   86
  c := subclause of  ¬s  that is inductive relative to  Fi                  87
  for  j := 1  to  i + 1:                                                   88
    { @assert :  B }                                                        89
    clauses(Fj) :=  clauses(Fj) ∪ {c}                                       90
```

impossible when k exceeds the number of possible states. Hence, k is bounded by $2^{|\bar{x}|} + 1$, and, assuming that the called functions always terminate, prove always terminates.

For level k, strengthen(k) (Listing 1.2) iterates until F_k excludes all states that lead to a violation of P in one step. Suppose s is one such state. It is eliminated by, first, inductively generalizing $\neg s$ relative to some F_i through a call to inductivelyGeneralize($s, k - 2, k$)[4] (Listing 1.4) and, second, pushing for a generalization at level k through a call to pushGeneralization($\{(n+1, s)\}$, k) (Listing 1.5). At the end of the iteration, F_k excludes s (assertion C). This

---

[4] Note that $\neg s$ is inductive relative to F_{k-2} by $A(2)$ and $A(4)$.

Listing 1.5. The pushGeneralization function

```
{ @pre :                                                                      91
    (1)  B                                                                    92
    (2)  ∀ (i, q) ∈ states, 0 < i ≤ k + 1                                     93
    (3)  ∀ (i, q) ∈ states, q ⊭ Fᵢ                                           94
    (4)  ∀ (i, q) ∈ states, ¬q is inductive relative to Fᵢ₋₁                 95
    (5)  ∀ (i, q) ∈ states , there is a trace from q to a ¬P−state            96
  @post :                                                                     97
    (1)  B                                                                    98
    (2)  ∀ (i, q) ∈ states, q ⊭ Fₖ }                                         99
void pushGeneralization (states : (level , state) set , k : level )         100
  while true:                                                                101
      { @rank : (k + 1)2^|x̄|                                                 102
        @assert (D):                                                         103
          (1)  pre                                                            104
          (2)  ∀ (i, q) ∈ states_prev, ∃j ≥ i, (j, q) ∈ states }             105
      (n, s) := choose from states , minimizing n                            106
      if n > k : return                                                      107
      if sat (Fₙ ∧ T ∧ s'):                                                  108
          p := the predecessor extracted from the witness                    109
          { @assert (E): ∀ (i, q) ∈ states, p ≠ q }                         110
          m := inductivelyGeneralize(p, n − 2, k)                            111
          states := states ∪ {(m + 1, p)}                                   112
      else :                                                                 113
          m := inductivelyGeneralize(s, n, k)                               114
          { @assert (F): m + 1 > n }                                        115
          states := states \ {(n, s)} ∪ {(m + 1, s)}                        116
```

progress implies that the loop can iterate at most as many times as there are possible states, yielding strengthen's ranking function.

The functions in Listing 1.4 perform inductive generalization relative to some F_i. If $min < 0$, s might have an I-state predecessor, which is checked at line 68.

The pushGeneralization algorithm (Listing 1.5) is the key to "pushing" inductive generalization to higher levels. The insight is simple: if a state s is not inductive relative to F_i, apply inductive generalization to its F_i-state predecessors. The complication is that this recursive analysis must proceed in a manner that terminates despite the presence of cycles in the system's state graph. To achieve termination, a set $states$ of pairs (i, s) is maintained such that each pair $(i, s) \in states$ represents the knowledge that (1) s is inductive relative to F_{i-1}, and (2) F_i excludes s. The loop in pushGeneralization always selects a pair (n, s) from $states$ such that n is minimal over the set. Hence, none of the states already represented in $states$ can be a predecessor of s at level n.

Formally, termination of pushGeneralization is established by the inductive assertions $D(2)$, which asserts that the set of states represented in $states$ does not decrease ($states_{prev}$ represents $states$'s value on the previous iteration or, during the first iteration, upon entering the function); E, which asserts that the new state p is not yet represented in $states$; and F, which asserts that the level associated with a state can only increase. Given that each iteration either adds a new state to *states* or increases a level for some state already in *states* and that levels peak at $k + 1$, the number of iterations is bounded by the product of $k + 1$ and the size of the state space.

Listings 1.1-1.5 and the termination arguments yield total correctness:

Theorem 1. *For finite transition system $S : (\bar{i}, \bar{x}, I, T)$ and safety property P, the algorithm terminates, and it returns* **true** *if and only if P is S-invariant.*

A variation exists that is perhaps more satisfying conceptually. Recall that `inductivelyGeneralize` and `generateClause` (Listing 1.4) together generate a subclause of $\neg s$ that is inductive relative to F_i, where F_i is the weakest stepwise assumption relative to which $\neg s$ is inductive. It is possible to find the highest level $j \geq i$ for which $\neg s$ has a subclause that is inductive relative to F_j even if $\neg s$ is not itself inductive relative to F_j (in which case $j > i$). However, in practice, this variation requires more time on designs with many latches. Whereas the unsatisfiable core of the query $F_{i-1} \wedge T \wedge \neg s \wedge s'$ at line 75 can be used to reduce s, often significantly, before applying inductive generalization (see Section 7), no such optimization is possible for the variation.

7   Single-Core Implementation

Our submission to HWMCC'10, `ic3`, placed third in the "unsatisfiable" category, third overall, and solved 37 more benchmarks than the 2008 winner [3].[5] We discuss the implementation details of `ic3` in this section.

We implemented the algorithm, AIG sweeping [11], and conversion of the transition relation to CNF based on technology mapping [13] in OCaml. The preprocessor of MiniSAT 2.0 is applied to further simplify the transition relation [12,13]. The time spent in preprocessing the transition relation is amortized over thousands to millions of 1-induction SAT instances in a typical analysis.

One implementation choice that may seem peculiar is that we used a modified version of ZChaff for SAT-solving [22]. The most significant modification was to change the main data structure and algorithm for BCP to be like Min-iSAT [14]. We chose ZChaff, which is considered to be outdated, because it offers efficient incremental functionality: clauses can be pushed and popped, which is necessary for finding an inductive subclause. While this functionality can be simulated in more recent solvers [15], each push/pop iteration requires a new literal. Given that hundreds to thousands of push/pop cycles occur *per second* in our analysis, each involving clauses, it seems that the amount of garbage that would accumulate in the simulated approach would be prohibitive. Thus we elected to use a library with built-in incremental capability. The consequence is that ZChaff caused timeouts on the following benchmarks during HWMCC'10:

---

[5] The data are available at `http://fmv.jku.at/hwmcc10`. The competition binary and an open source version of `ic3` are available at `http://ecee.colorado.edu/~bradleya`

`bobaesdinvdmit`, `bobsmfpu`, `bobpcihm`, and `bobsmminiuart`. Otherwise, the percentage of time spent in SAT solving varies from as low as 20% to as high as 85%. Benchmarks on which SAT solving time dominates could benefit from a faster solver.

We highlight important implementation decisions. The most significant optimization is to extract the unit clauses of an unsatisfiable core whenever possible. Consider the unsatisfiable query $F \wedge c \wedge T \wedge \neg c'$; the unsatisfiable core can reveal a clause $d \subset c$ such that $F \wedge c \wedge T \wedge \neg d'$ is also unsatisfiable. The clause d is an inductive subclause if it satisfies initiation. If the initial state is defined such that all latches are 0 (as in HWMCC'10) and d does not satisfy initiation, `ic3` simply restores a negative literal from c. This optimization applies in the following contexts: (1) in the `inductivelyGeneralize` algorithm, from the unsatisfiable query that indicates that $\neg s$ is inductive relative to F_i when $\neg s$ is not inductive relative to F_{i+1} (Listing 1.4, line 75); (2) in the `down` algorithm [6], from the (final) unsatisfiable query indicating an inductive subclause; (3) in the `up` algorithm; and (4) in `propagateClauses`, during propagation of clauses between major iterations (Listing 1.3, line 55).

In the implementation of inductive generalization (algorithm MIC [6]), we use a threshold to end the search for a minimal inductive subclause. If `down` is applied unsuccessfully to three subclauses of c, each formed by removing one randomly chosen literal, then c is returned. While c may not be minimal — that is, some $d \subset c$ may also be (relatively) inductive — it is typically sufficiently strong; and the search is significantly faster.

We use a stepwise cone of influence (COI) [2] to reduce cubes: if a state s is i transitions away from violating P, the initial clause $c \subseteq \neg s$ is set to contain only state variables of the i-step COI; the transition relation is unchanged for practical reasons. The generated clause is more relevant with respect to P in explaining why states similar to s are unreachable, although c may only be inductive relative to a stronger stepwise assumption than $\neg s$.

Subsumption reduces clause sets across levels between major iterations: if clause c at level i subsumes clause d at level $j \leq i$, then d is removed.

For memory efficiency, one SAT manager is used for computing consecution at all levels. A level-specific literal is added to each generated clause. Clauses at and above level i are activated when computing consecution relative to F_i.

An initial set of simulation runs yields candidate equivalences between latches. These candidate equivalences are then logically propagated across the stepwise approximations between major iterations. Some benchmarks are easily solved once key equivalences are discovered, and while the pure analysis is poor at discovering them, propagation easily finds them. Simulation make this analysis inexpensive even when it is not effective. This binary clause analysis fits well with the overall philosophy of generating stepwise-relative inductive clauses.

When searching for inductive subclauses, using an arbitrary static ordering of literals to consider for removal yields poor results. We tried various heuristics for dynamically ordering the literals, but none were particularly effective. The competition version of `ic3` prefers the negations of literals that appear frequently

Table 1. Runtime data for selected benchmarks from HWMCC'10 [3]

Benchmark	Result	Time (s)	# queries	|proof|	k
bjrb07amba10andenv	unsat	260	12238	262	7
bob3	unsat	10	44058	865	7
boblivea	unsat	5	34884	652	14
boblivear	unsat	4	34547	668	14
bobsmnut1	unsat	9	20530	554	15
intel007	unsat	30	31250	1382	6
intel044	sat	303	578982	92	57
intel045	sat	316	596539	124	49
intel046	sat	223	431123	78	44
intel047	sat	293	561304	82	52
intel054	unsat	56	147986	1459	19
intel055	unsat	9	28302	385	15
intel056	unsat	15	63877	649	19
intel057	unsat	21	72925	731	18
intel059	unsat	11	47840	558	17
intel062	unsat	301	389065	3372	26
nusmvbrp	unsat	5	55281	306	27
nusmvreactorp2	unsat	51	308627	779	116
nusmvreactorp6	unsat	178	753335	1723	119
pdtvisns3p00	unsat	11	4428	465	12
pdtvisns3p01	unsat	27	104750	1109	10
pdtvisns3p02	unsat	21	85812	680	12
pdtvisns3p03	unsat	21	80810	745	12
pdtvisns3p04	unsat	115	281812	1783	14
pdtvisns3p05	unsat	135	326604	2033	13
pdtvisns3p06	unsat	13	55016	631	9
pdtvisns3p07	unsat	84	228175	1631	11
pj2017	unsat	233	74417	685	27

in the *states* set of `pushGeneralization`. A clause with such literals is relevant to many of the states in *states*. However, the only definite claim is that changing the variable ordering is superior to using an arbitrary static ordering. We have not investigated whether well-chosen static orderings might yield better performance.

While time and memory data for HWMCC'10 are already publicly available, Table 1 provides data particular to `ic3` for the benchmarks that `ic3` and at most two other entries solved. The table indicates the number of executed SAT queries (**# queries**); the size of the proof (**\|proof\|**), which is the number of clauses for unsatisfiable benchmarks and the length of the counterexample for satisfiable benchmarks; and the maximum value of k. Notice how widely the maximum k value varies. The benefit of the work described in this paper over previous work [6] is particularly apparent for benchmarks with large k, as such benchmarks require generalizing the many states of long sequences simultaneously. Notice also the rate at which SAT queries are solved — several thousand per second — indicating that these queries are trivial compared to those posed by other SAT-based model checkers.

A variant of this algorithm emphasizes speed over quality in inductive clause generation. Rather than using "strong" induction to compute a minimal inductive subclause $c \subseteq d$ relative to F_i, it computes a prime implicate $\hat{c}$ of $F_i \wedge d \wedge T$, that is, a minimal subclause $\hat{c} \subseteq d$ such that $F_i \wedge d \wedge T \Rightarrow \hat{c}'$ holds. On the HWMCC'10 benchmark set, this variation solves 28 fewer unsatisfiable benchmarks and three fewer satisfiable benchmarks. Quality matters.

8   Parallel Implementation

Converting the implementation from sequential to parallel is straightforward. The overall model is of independent model checkers sharing information. Each time a process generates a clause c at level i, it sends the tuple (c, i) to a central server and receives in return a list of clause-level tuples generated since its last communication. To avoid one source of duplicated effort, it uses the new information to syntactically prune its *states* set. During `propagateClauses` calls, each process propagates a subset of the clauses based on hashing modulo the number of total processes, and the processes proceed in lockstep, level by level. Additional communications handle exceptional situations such as the discovery of a counterexample. Processes attempt to avoid discovering the same information simultaneously simply through exploiting the randomness in the ZChaff implementation, although co-discovery occurs in practice early and late in each major iteration.

How well does the parallel implementation scale with available cores? To investigate this question, we selected eight benchmarks from the competition that are difficult but possible for the non-parallel version: Intel benchmarks 20, 21, 22, 23, 24, 29, 31, and 34. We ran the non-parallel and parallel implementations on four Quad Core i5-750/2.66GHz/8MB-cache machines with 8GB, DDR3 non-ECC SDRAM at 1333MHz, running 64-bit Ubuntu 9.10. One process was arranged as a single process on an otherwise mostly idle machine; four processes were arranged as one process per machine; eight processes were arranged as two processes per machine; and twelve processes were arranged as three processes per machine. Unfortunately, (shared) memory latency increased significantly with the number of processes per machine so that the twelve-process configuration was not necessarily an improvement on the eight-process configuration in terms of the system-wide number of SAT problems solved per second.

Each benchmark was analyzed eight times by each configuration, with a timeout of two hours (7200 seconds). Figure 1 presents the results in eight graphs that plot running times against the number of processes. The numbers adjacent to dots at 7200 indicate the number of timeouts.

Every benchmark benefits from additional cores. One possible explanation, however, is simply that parallelism reduces variance. The high variability of the single-process implementation may be a result of "lucky" discoveries of certain clauses that yield major progress toward proofs. Runs that fail to make these discoveries early can take significantly longer than those that do. To explore this possibility, we set up the following configuration: eight non-communicating processes, where the first to finish causes the others to terminate. In other words, the minimum time is taken from eight independent runs, except that all are executed simultaneously, thus experiencing the memory latency of the eight-process communicating configuration. The results are shown in Figure 2(**a**).

The data show that some performance gain can indeed be attributed to a reduction in variance. However, comparing Figures 1 and 2 for each benchmark indicates that this reduction in variance cannot explain all of the performance gain. In particular, the standard eight-process parallel version is significantly

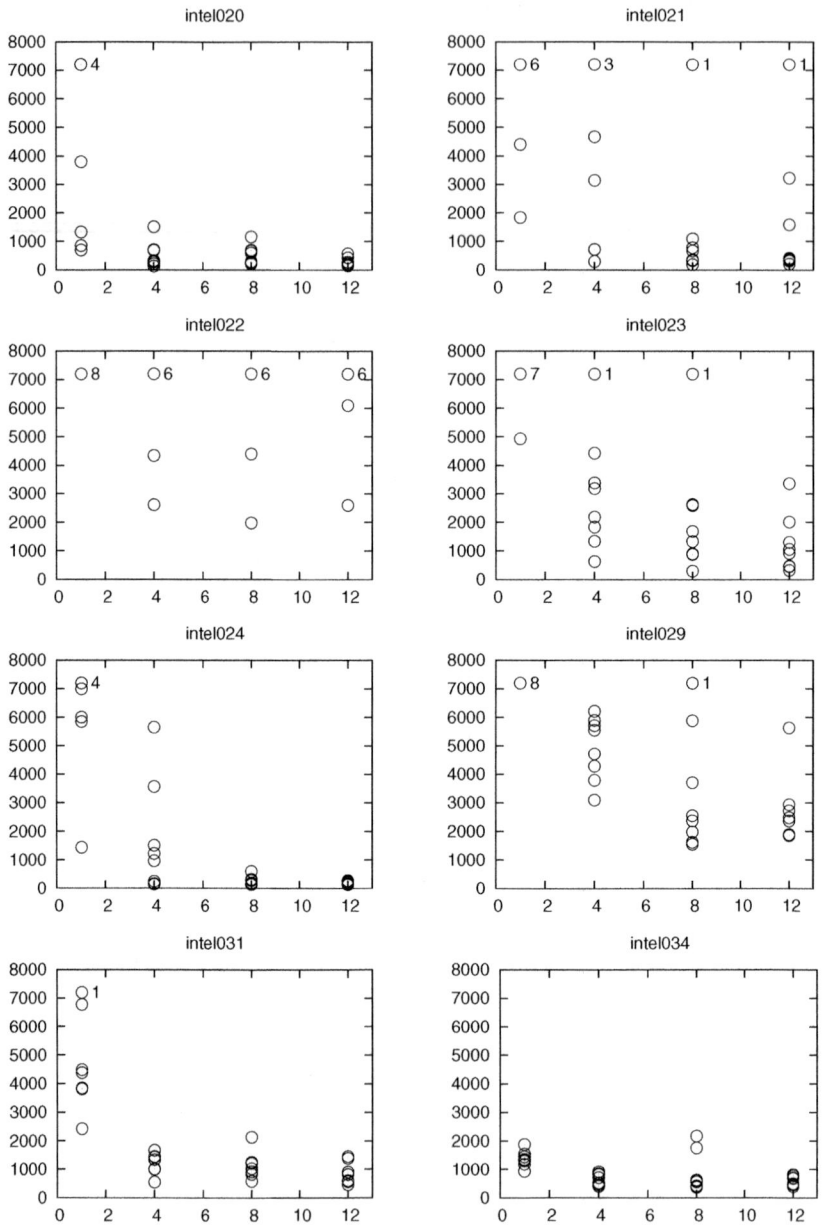

Fig. 1. Number of communicating processes *vs.* time (in seconds)

faster on benchmarks 23, 24, and 29. Except on benchmark 22, for which the data are inconclusive, it is faster on the other benchmarks as well. Therefore, communication is a significant factor in explaining superior performance.

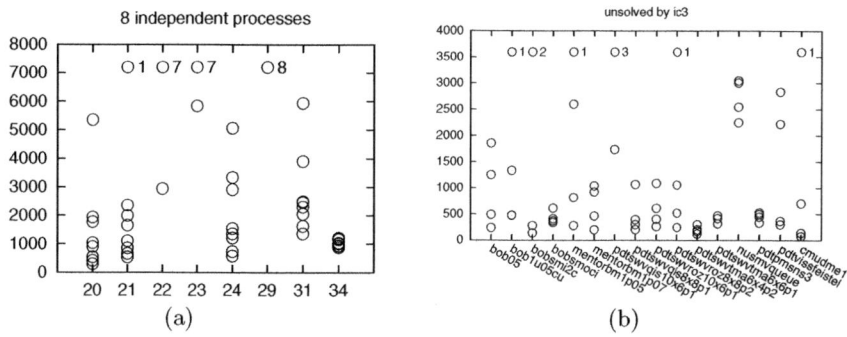

Fig. 2. Benchmarks *vs.* time

Unfortunately, saturation is also possible: at some number of processes, the rate of co-discovery of information is such that additional processes do not improve runtime. For example, the performance that benchmarks 31 and 34 gain from the four-process configuration is not improved upon with additional processes. However, the data do not indicate degrading performance, either.

Having established that communicating processes are superior to independent processes, we next tested if parallel ic3 is superior to serial ic3 in numbers of benchmarks solved in a given time, in particular the 900 seconds per benchmark allotted in HWMCC'10. We ran the twelve-process communicating configuration for one hour on each of the 105 benchmarks that ic3 failed to solve during HWMCC'10 and then extracted the 16 benchmarks that were proved to be unsatisfiable, excluding the intel set of Figure 1. Analyzing these 16 benchmarks four times each with a timeout of one hour produced the data in Figure 2(**b**). Figures 1 and 2(**b**) indicate that the twelve-process configuration would yield at least twelve additional proofs within 900 seconds.

9 Conclusion

The performance of ic3 in HWMCC'10 shows that the incremental generation of stepwise-relative inductive clauses is a promising new approach to symbolic model checking. Furthermore, it is amenable to simple yet effective parallelization, a crucial characteristic given modern architectures.

Why does this algorithm work so well? Consider a clause c. Predecessors to c-states are likely to be or to look similar to c-states, to the extent that dropping a few literals from c may yield an inductive clause d. This reasoning motivates the inductive generalization algorithm (Section 3). However, systems violate this observation to a varying extent. The stepwise sets $F_0, ..., F_k$ offer a new possibility: c, if invariant, is inductive relative to a stepwise assumption F_i. Subsequent discovery of additional clauses can yield a set of mutually (relatively) inductive clauses that are propagated forward together.

Ongoing research includes designing a thread-safe incremental SAT solver, in which threads share a common set of core constraints but have thread-local temporary constraints; investigating how inductive clause generation can accelerate finding counterexamples; and exploring how stepwise-relative inductive generalization can apply to the analysis of infinite-state systems.

Acknowledgments. I am grateful to Fabio Somenzi for many fruitful discussions. Arlen Cox provided the initial implementation of technology mapping-based CNF translation. This work was supported by NSF grant CCF 0952617.

References

1. Awedh, M., Somenzi, F.: Automatic invariant strengthening to prove properties in bounded model checking. In: DAC, pp. 1073–1076. ACM Press, New York (2006)
2. Biere, A., Cimatti, A., Clarke, E.M., Zhu, Y.: Symbolic model checking without BDDs. In: Cleaveland, W.R. (ed.) TACAS 1999. LNCS, vol. 1579, pp. 193–207. Springer, Heidelberg (1999)
3. Biere, A., Claessen, K.: Hardware model checking competition. In: Hardware Verification Workshop (2010)
4. Bradley, A.R.: Safety Analysis of Systems. PhD thesis, Stanford University (May 2007)
5. Bradley, A.R.: k-step relative inductive generalization. Tech. Rep., CU Boulder (March 2010), http://arxiv.org/abs/1003.3649
6. Bradley, A.R., Manna, Z.: Checking safety by inductive generalization of counterexamples to induction. In: FMCAD (2007)
7. Burch, J.R., Clarke, E.M., McMillan, K.L., Dill, D.L., Hwang, L.J.: Symbolic model checking: 10^20 states and beyond. Inf. Comput. 98(2), 142–170 (1992)
8. Clarke, E., Grumberg, O., Jha, S., Lu, Y., Veith, H.: Counterexample-guided abstraction refinement for symbolic model checking. J. ACM 50(5) (2003)
9. Clarke, E., Grumberg, O., Peled, D.: Model Checking. MIT Press, Cambridge (2000)
10. Cousot, P., Cousot, R.: Abstract interpretation: A unified lattice model for static analysis of programs by construction or approximation of fixpoints. In: POPL, pp. 238–252. ACM Press, New York (1977)
11. Eén, N.: Cut sweeping. Tech. rep., Cadence (2007)
12. Eén, N., Biere, A.: Effective preprocessing in SAT through variable and clause elimination. In: Bacchus, F., Walsh, T. (eds.) SAT 2005. LNCS, vol. 3569, pp. 61–75. Springer, Heidelberg (2005)
13. Eén, N., Mishchenko, A., Sörensson, N.: Applying logic synthesis for speeding up SAT. In: Marques-Silva, J., Sakallah, K.A. (eds.) SAT 2007. LNCS, vol. 4501, pp. 272–286. Springer, Heidelberg (2007)
14. Eén, N., Sörensson, N.: An extensible SAT-solver. In: Giunchiglia, E., Tacchella, A. (eds.) SAT 2003. LNCS, vol. 2919, pp. 502–518. Springer, Heidelberg (2004)
15. Eén, N., Sörensson, N.: Temporal induction by incremental SAT solving. In: BMC (2003)
16. Floyd, R.W.: Assigning meanings to programs. In: Symposia in Applied Mathematics, vol. 19, pp. 19–32. American Mathematical Society, Providence (1967)
17. Graf, S., Saidi, H.: Construction of abstract state graphs with PVS. In: Grumberg, O. (ed.) CAV 1997. LNCS, vol. 1254, pp. 72–83. Springer, Heidelberg (1997)

18. Hoare, C.A.R.: An axiomatic basis for computer programming. Communications of the ACM 12(10), 576–580 (1969)
19. Manna, Z., Pnueli, A.: Temporal Verification of Reactive Systems: Safety. Springer, New York (1995)
20. McMillan, K.L.: Applying SAT methods in unbounded symbolic model checking. In: Brinksma, E., Larsen, K.G. (eds.) CAV 2002. LNCS, vol. 2404, pp. 250–264. Springer, Heidelberg (2002)
21. McMillan, K.L.: Interpolation and SAT-based model checking. In: Hunt Jr., W.A., Somenzi, F. (eds.) CAV 2003. LNCS, vol. 2725, pp. 1–13. Springer, Heidelberg (2003)
22. Moskewicz, M.W., Madigan, C.F., Zhao, Y., Zhang, L., Malik, S.: Chaff: Engineering an Efficient SAT Solver. In: DAC (2001)
23. de Moura, L., Rueß, H., Sorea, M.: Bounded model checking and induction: From refutation to verification. In: Hunt Jr., W.A., Somenzi, F. (eds.) CAV 2003. LNCS, vol. 2725, pp. 14–26. Springer, Heidelberg (2003)
24. Sheeran, M., Singh, S., Stålmarck, G.: Checking safety properties using induction and a SAT-solver. In: Johnson, S.D., Hunt Jr., W.A. (eds.) FMCAD 2000. LNCS, vol. 1954, pp. 108–125. Springer, Heidelberg (2000)
25. Vimjam, V.C., Hsiao, M.S.: Fast illegal state identification for improving SAT-based induction. In: DAC, pp. 241–246. ACM Press, New York (2006)

Beyond Quantifier-Free Interpolation
in Extensions of Presburger Arithmetic[*]

Angelo Brillout[1], Daniel Kroening[2], Philipp Rümmer[2],
and Thomas Wahl[2]

[1] ETH Zurich, Switzerland
[2] Oxford University Computing Laboratory, United Kingdom

Abstract. Craig interpolation has emerged as an effective means of
generating candidate program invariants. We present interpolation procedures for the theories of Presburger arithmetic combined with (i) uninterpreted predicates (QPA+UP), (ii) uninterpreted functions (QPA+UF)
and (iii) extensional arrays (QPA+AR). We prove that none of these
combinations can be effectively interpolated without the use of quantifiers, even if the input formulae are quantifier-free. We go on to identify
fragments of QPA+UP and QPA+UF with restricted forms of *guarded
quantification* that are closed under interpolation. Formulae in these fragments can easily be mapped to quantifier-free expressions with integer
division. For QPA+AR, we formulate a sound interpolation procedure
that potentially produces interpolants with unrestricted quantifiers.

1 Introduction

Given two first-order logic formulae A and C such that A implies C, written
$A \Rightarrow C$, *Craig interpolation* determines a formula I such that the implications $A \Rightarrow I$ and $I \Rightarrow C$ hold, and I contains only non-logical symbols occurring
in both A and C [1]. Interpolation has emerged as a practical approximation
method in computing and has found many uses in formal verification, ranging
from efficient image computations in SAT-based model checking, to computing
candidate invariants in automated program analysis.

In software verification, interpolation is applied to formulae encoding the
transition relation of a model underlying the program. In order to support a
wide variety of programming language constructs, much effort has been invested
in the design of algorithms that compute interpolants for formulae of various
first-order theories. For example, interpolating integer arithmetic solvers have
been reported for fragments such as difference-bound logic, linear equalities,
and constant-divisibility predicates.

The goal of this paper is an interpolation procedure that is instrumental in
analysing programs manipulating integer variables. We therefore consider the
first-order theory of *quantified Presburger arithmetic* (quantified linear integer

---

[*] This research is supported by the EPSRC project EP/G026254/1, by the EU FP7
STREP MOGENTES, and by the EU ARTEMIS CESAR project.

R. Jhala and D. Schmidt (Eds.): VMCAI 2011, LNCS 6538, pp. 88–102, 2011.
© Springer-Verlag Berlin Heidelberg 2011

arithmetic), denoted QPA. Combined with *uninterpreted predicates* (UP) and *uninterpreted functions* (UF), this allows us to encode the theory of *extensional arrays* (AR), using uninterpreted function symbols for read and write operations. Our interpolation procedure extracts an interpolant directly from a proof of $A \Rightarrow C$. Starting from a sound and complete proof system based on a sequent calculus, the proof rules are extended by labelled formulae and annotations that reduce, at the root of a closed proof, to interpolants. In earlier work, we presented a similar procedure for quantifier-free Presburger arithmetic [2].

In program verification, an interpolating theorem prover often interacts tightly with various decision procedures. It is therefore advantageous for the interpolants computed by the prover to be expressible in simple logic fragments. Unfortunately, interpolation procedures for expressive first-order fragments, such as integer arithmetic with uninterpreted predicates, often generate interpolants with *quantifiers*, which makes subsequent calls to decision procedures involving these interpolants expensive. This is not by accident. In fact, in this paper we first show that interpolation of QPA+UP in general requires the use of quantifiers, *even if the input formulae are themselves free of quantifiers.*

In order to solve this problem, we study fragments of QPA+UP that are *closed under interpolation*: fragments such that interpolants for input formulae can again be expressed in the theory. By the result above, such fragments must allow at least a limited form of quantification. Our second contribution is to show that the theory PAID+UP of Presburger arithmetic with uninterpreted predicates and a restricted form of *guarded quantifiers* indeed has the closure property. A similar fragment, PAID+UF, can be identified for the combination of Presburger arithmetic with uninterpreted functions. Moreover, by allowing *integer divisibility* (ID) predicates, the guarded quantifiers can be rewritten into quantifier-free form, facilitating further processing of the interpolants.

In summary, we present in this paper an interpolating calculus for the first-order theory of Presburger arithmetic and uninterpreted predicates, QPA+UP. We show that, for some quantifier-free input formulae, quantifiers in interpolants cannot be avoided, and suggest a restriction of QPA+UP that is closed under interpolation, yet permits quantifier-free interpolants conveniently expressible in standard logics. We extend these results to Presburger theories with uninterpreted functions and, specifically, to quantified array theory, resulting in the first sound interpolating decision procedure for Presburger arithmetic and arrays.

2 Background

2.1 Presburger Arithmetic with Predicates and Functions

Presburger arithmetic. We assume familiarity with classical first-order logic (e.g., [3]). Let x range over an infinite set X of variables, c over an infinite set C of constants, p over a set P of uninterpreted predicates with fixed arity, f over a set F of uninterpreted functions with fixed arity, and α over the set $\mathbb{Z}$ of integers. (Note the distinction between constant *symbols*, such as c, and integer *literals*, such as 42.) The syntax of terms and formulae considered in this paper is defined by the following grammar:

$$\phi \ ::= \ t \doteq 0 \ \big| \ t \leq 0 \ \big| \ \alpha \mid t \ \big| \ p(t, \ldots, t) \ \big| \ \phi \wedge \phi \ \big| \ \phi \vee \phi \ \big| \ \neg\phi \ \big| \ \forall x.\phi \ \big| \ \exists x.\phi$$

$$t \ ::= \ \alpha \ \big| \ c \ \big| \ x \ \big| \ \alpha t + \cdots + \alpha t \ \big| \ f(t, \ldots, t)$$

The symbol t denotes terms of linear arithmetic. Divisibility atoms $\alpha \mid t$ are equivalent to formulae $\exists s. \ \alpha s - t \doteq 0$, but are required for quantifier-free interpolation. Simultaneous substitution of a vector of terms $\bar{t} = (t_1, \ldots, t_n)$ for variables $\bar{x} = (x_1, \ldots, x_n)$ in ϕ is denoted by $[\bar{x}/\bar{t}]\phi$; we assume that variable capture is avoided by renaming bound variables as necessary. For simplicity, we sometimes write $s \doteq t$ as a shorthand of $s - t \doteq 0$, and $\forall c.\phi$ as a shorthand of $\forall x.[c/x]\phi$ if c is a constant. The abbreviation *true* (*false*) stands for the equality $0 \doteq 0$ ($1 \doteq 0$), and the formula $\phi \rightarrow \psi$ abbreviates $\neg\phi \vee \psi$. Semantic notions such as structures, models, satisfiability, and validity are defined as is common over the universe $\mathbb{Z}$ of integers (e.g., [3]).

Full *quantified Presburger arithmetic* (QPA) consists of the formulae that do not contain uninterpreted predicates or functions; *(quantifier-free) Presburger arithmetic* (PA) is the quantifier-free fragment of QPA. The logic QPA+UP (QPA+UF) extends QPA to formulae with uninterpreted predicates (functions), according to the above grammar.

2.2   An Interpolating Sequent Calculus

Interpolating sequents. To extract interpolants from unsatisfiability proofs of $A \wedge B$, formulae are labelled either with the letter L ("left") to indicate that they are derived from A or with R ("right") for formulae derived from B (as in [2]). More formally, if ϕ is a formula without free variables, then $\lfloor\phi\rfloor_L$ and $\lfloor\phi\rfloor_R$ are L/R-labelled formulae. If Γ, Δ are finite sets of labelled formulae and I is an unlabelled formula without free variables, then $\Gamma \vdash \Delta \blacktriangleright I$ is an *interpolating sequent*. Similarly, if Γ, Δ are sets of unlabelled formulae without free variables, then $\Gamma \vdash \Delta$ is an (ordinary) *sequent*. An ordinary sequent is *valid* if the formula $\bigwedge \Gamma \rightarrow \bigvee \Delta$ is valid.

The semantics of interpolating sequents is defined using the projections $\Gamma_L =_{\text{def}} \{\phi \mid \lfloor\phi\rfloor_L \in \Gamma\}$ and $\Gamma_R =_{\text{def}} \{\phi \mid \lfloor\phi\rfloor_R \in \Gamma\}$, which extract the L/R-parts of a set Γ of labelled formulae. A sequent $\Gamma \vdash \Delta \blacktriangleright I$ is *valid* if (i) the sequent $\Gamma_L \vdash \Delta_L, I$ is valid, (ii) the sequent $\Gamma_R, I \vdash \Delta_R$ is valid, and (iii) the constants and uninterpreted predicate/functions in I occur in both $\Gamma_L \cup \Delta_L$ and $\Gamma_R \cup \Delta_R$. As special cases, $\lfloor A \rfloor_L \vdash \lfloor C \rfloor_R \blacktriangleright I$ reduces to I being an interpolant of the implication $A \Rightarrow C$, while $\lfloor A \rfloor_L, \lfloor B \rfloor_R \vdash \emptyset \blacktriangleright I$ captures the concept of interpolants for unsatisfiable conjunctions $A \wedge B$ common in formal verification.

Interpolating sequent calculi. An *interpolating rule* is a binary relation between a finite set of interpolating sequents, called the premises, and a sequent called the conclusion:

$$\frac{\Gamma_1 \vdash \Delta_1 \blacktriangleright I_1 \quad \cdots \quad \Gamma_n \vdash \Delta_n \blacktriangleright I_n}{\Gamma \vdash \Delta \blacktriangleright I}$$

$$\frac{\Gamma, \lfloor \phi \rfloor_L \vdash \Delta \; \blacktriangleright \; I \quad}{\Gamma, \lfloor \phi \vee \psi \rfloor_L \vdash \Delta \; \blacktriangleright \; I \vee J} \; \text{OR-LEFT-L} \qquad \frac{\Gamma, \lfloor \phi \rfloor_R \vdash \Delta \; \blacktriangleright \; I \quad}{\Gamma, \lfloor \phi \vee \psi \rfloor_R \vdash \Delta \; \blacktriangleright \; I \wedge J} \; \text{OR-LEFT-R}$$

with premises $\Gamma, \lfloor \psi \rfloor_L \vdash \Delta \; \blacktriangleright \; J$ and $\Gamma, \lfloor \psi \rfloor_R \vdash \Delta \; \blacktriangleright \; J$ respectively.

$$\frac{\Gamma, \lfloor \phi \rfloor_D, \lfloor \psi \rfloor_D \vdash \Delta \; \blacktriangleright \; I}{\Gamma, \lfloor \phi \wedge \psi \rfloor_D \vdash \Delta \; \blacktriangleright \; I} \; \text{AND-LEFT} \qquad \frac{\Gamma \vdash \lfloor \phi \rfloor_D, \Delta \; \blacktriangleright \; I}{\Gamma, \lfloor \neg \phi \rfloor_D \vdash \Delta \; \blacktriangleright \; I} \; \text{NOT-LEFT}$$

$$\frac{*}{\Gamma, \lfloor \phi \rfloor_L \vdash \lfloor \phi \rfloor_L, \Delta \; \blacktriangleright \; false} \; \text{CLOSE-LL} \qquad \frac{*}{\Gamma, \lfloor \phi \rfloor_R \vdash \lfloor \phi \rfloor_R, \Delta \; \blacktriangleright \; true} \; \text{CLOSE-RR}$$

$$\frac{*}{\Gamma, \lfloor \phi \rfloor_L \vdash \lfloor \phi \rfloor_R, \Delta \; \blacktriangleright \; \phi} \; \text{CLOSE-LR} \qquad \frac{*}{\Gamma, \lfloor \phi \rfloor_R \vdash \lfloor \phi \rfloor_L, \Delta \; \blacktriangleright \; \neg \phi} \; \text{CLOSE-RL}$$

$$\frac{\Gamma, \lfloor [x/t]\phi \rfloor_L, \lfloor \forall x.\phi \rfloor_L \vdash \Delta \; \blacktriangleright \; I}{\Gamma, \lfloor \forall x.\phi \rfloor_L \vdash \Delta \; \blacktriangleright \; \forall_{Rt} \, I} \; \substack{\text{ALL-}\\\text{LEFT-L}} \qquad \frac{\Gamma, \lfloor [x/t]\phi \rfloor_R, \lfloor \forall x.\phi \rfloor_R \vdash \Delta \; \blacktriangleright \; I}{\Gamma, \lfloor \forall x.\phi \rfloor_R \vdash \Delta \; \blacktriangleright \; \exists_{Lt} \, I} \; \substack{\text{ALL-}\\\text{LEFT-R}}$$

$$\frac{\Gamma, \lfloor [x/c]\phi \rfloor_D \vdash \Delta \; \blacktriangleright \; I}{\Gamma, \lfloor \exists x.\phi \rfloor_D \vdash \Delta \; \blacktriangleright \; I} \; \substack{\text{EX-}\\\text{LEFT}} \qquad \frac{\Gamma \vdash \lfloor [x/c]\phi \rfloor_D, \Delta \; \blacktriangleright \; I}{\Gamma \vdash \lfloor \forall x.\phi \rfloor_D, \Delta \; \blacktriangleright \; I} \; \substack{\text{ALL-}\\\text{RIGHT}}$$

Fig. 1. The upper box presents a selection of interpolating rules for propositional logic, while the lower box shows the interpolating rules to handle quantifiers. Parameter D stands for either L or R. The quantifier $\forall_{Rt}$ denotes universal quantification over all constants occurring in t but not in $\Gamma_L \cup \Delta_L$; likewise, $\exists_{Lt}$ denotes existential quantification over all constants occurring in t but not in $\Gamma_R \cup \Delta_R$. In the rules EX-LEFT and ALL-RIGHT, c is a constant that does not occur in the conclusion.

An interpolating rule is *sound* if, for all instances whose premises $\Gamma_1 \vdash \Delta_1 \; \blacktriangleright \; I_1$, $\dots$, $\Gamma_n \vdash \Delta_n \; \blacktriangleright \; I_n$ are valid, the conclusion $\Gamma \vdash \Delta \; \blacktriangleright \; I$ is valid, too. Fig. 1 presents a selection of interpolating rules (used throughout the paper) for predicate logic. An exhaustive list of rules is given in [2].

Interpolating proofs are trees growing upwards, in which each node is labelled with an interpolating sequent, and each non-leaf node is related to the node(s) directly above it through an instance of a calculus rule. A proof is *closed* if it is finite and all leaves are justified by an instance of a rule without premises.

To construct a proof for an interpolation problem, we build a proof tree starting from the root $\Gamma \vdash \Delta \; \blacktriangleright \; I$ with unknown interpolant I, i.e., I acts as a place holder. For example, to solve an interpolation problem $A \wedge B$, we start with the sequent $\lfloor A \rfloor_L, \lfloor B \rfloor_R \vdash \emptyset \; \blacktriangleright \; I$. Rules are then applied successively to decompose and simplify the sequent. Once all branches are closed, i.e., a proof is found, an interpolant can be extracted from the proof. Starting from the leaves, intermediate interpolants are computed and propagated back to the root leading to an interpolant I. An example of this procedure is given in the next section.

3 Interpolation for Uninterpreted Predicates

3.1 Presburger Arithmetic and Uninterpreted Predicates

We begin by studying the interpolation problem for Presburger arithmetic extended with uninterpreted predicates (QPA+UP), which forms a simple yet expressive base logic in which functions and arrays can be elegantly encoded. The case of predicates is instructive, since essentially the same phenomena occur under interpolation as with uninterpreted functions.

Example 1. We illustrate the construction of an interpolating proof by deriving an interpolant for $A \Rightarrow C$, with $A = (\neg p(c) \vee p(d)) \wedge p(c)$ and $C = p(d)$. A complete interpolating proof of this implication looks as follows:

$$
\cfrac{
  \cfrac{
    \cfrac{
      \cfrac{*}{\lfloor p(c) \rfloor_L \ \vdash\ \lfloor p(d) \rfloor_R, \lfloor p(c) \rfloor_L \ \blacktriangleright\ false}\ \text{\scriptsize CLOSE-LL}
    }{\lfloor \neg p(c) \rfloor_L, \lfloor p(c) \rfloor_L \ \vdash\ \lfloor p(d) \rfloor_R \ \blacktriangleright\ false}\ \text{\scriptsize NOT-LEFT}
    \quad
    \cfrac{*}{\lfloor p(d) \rfloor_L, \lfloor p(c) \rfloor_L \ \vdash\ \lfloor p(d) \rfloor_R \ \blacktriangleright\ p(d)}\ \text{\scriptsize CLOSE-LR}
  }{\lfloor \neg p(c) \vee p(d) \rfloor_L, \lfloor p(c) \rfloor_L \ \vdash\ \lfloor p(d) \rfloor_R \ \blacktriangleright\ false \vee p(d)}\ \text{\scriptsize OR-LEFT-L}
}{\lfloor (\neg p(c) \vee p(d)) \wedge p(c) \rfloor_L \ \vdash\ \lfloor p(d) \rfloor_R \ \blacktriangleright\ false \vee p(d)}\ \text{\scriptsize AND-LEFT}
$$

The shaded regions indicate the parts of the formula being matched against the rules in Fig. 1. The sequent $\lfloor (p(c) \vee p(d)) \wedge p(c) \rfloor_L \ \vdash\ \lfloor p(d) \rfloor_R \ \blacktriangleright\ I$ is the root of the proof, where $I = \ false \vee p(d)$ has been filled in once the proof was closed. The AND-LEFT rule propagates the L-label to the subformulae of the antecedent of the first sequent. By applying OR-LEFT-L to the disjunction $p(c) \vee p(d)$, the proof splits into two branches. The right branch can immediately be closed using CLOSE-LR. The left branch requires an application of NOT-LEFT before it can be closed with CLOSE-LL. We compute an interpolant by propagating (intermediate) interpolants from the leaves back to root of the proof. As specified by CLOSE-LR, the interpolant of the right branch is $p(d)$. On the left branch, the CLOSE-LL rule yields the interpolant *false*, which is carried through by NOT-LEFT. The rule OR-LEFT-L takes the interpolants of its two subproofs and generates $false \vee p(d)$. This is the final interpolant, since the last rule AND-LEFT propagates interpolants without applying modifications.   □

In this example, the arguments of occurrences of uninterpreted predicates literally matched up, which need not be the case. The rules presented so far are insufficient to prove more complex theorems, such as $p(c) \wedge c \doteq d \rightarrow p(d)$, in which arithmetic and predicate calculus interact. To fully integrate uninterpreted predicates, we use an explicit *predicate consistency* axiom

$$PC_p = \quad \forall \bar{x}, \bar{y}.\ \big((p(\bar{x}) \ \wedge\ \bar{x} - \bar{y} \doteq 0) \ \rightarrow\ p(\bar{y})\big) \tag{1}$$

which can be viewed as an L- or R-labelled formula that is implicitly present in every sequent. The label L/R is chosen depending on whether p occurs in $\Gamma_L \cup \Delta_L$, in $\Gamma_R \cup \Delta_R$, or in both.

To make use of (1) in a proof, we need additional proof rules to instantiate quantifiers, which are given in the bottom part of Fig. 1. Formula (1) can be instantiated with techniques similar to the e-matching in SMT solvers [4]: it suffices to generate a ground instance of (1) by applying ALL-LEFT-L/R whenever literals $p(\bar{s})$ and $p(\bar{t})$ occur in the antecedent and succedent [5]:

$$
\cfrac{\Gamma, \lfloor p(\bar{s}) \rfloor_D, \lfloor (p(\bar{s}) \ \wedge\ \bar{s} - \bar{t} \doteq 0) \ \rightarrow\ p(\bar{t}) \rfloor_L \ \vdash\ \lfloor p(\bar{t}) \rfloor_E, \Delta \ \blacktriangleright\ I}{\Gamma, \lfloor p(\bar{s}) \rfloor_D \ \vdash\ \lfloor p(\bar{t}) \rfloor_E, \Delta \ \blacktriangleright\ \forall_{R\bar{s}\bar{t}}\ I}\ \text{\scriptsize ALL-LEFT-L}^+
$$

where $D, E \in \{L, R\}$ are arbitrary labels, and $\forall_{R\bar{s}\bar{t}}$ denotes universal quantification over all constants occurring in the terms $\bar{s}, \bar{t}$ but not in the set of left formulae $(\Gamma, \lfloor p(\bar{s}) \rfloor_D)_L \cup (\Delta, \lfloor p(\bar{t}) \rfloor_E)_L$ (like in Fig. 1). Similarly, instances of (1) labelled with R can be generated using ALL-LEFT-R. To improve efficiency, refinements can be formulated that drastically reduce the number of generated instances [6].

Correctness. The calculus consisting of the rules in Fig. 1, the arithmetic rules of [2], and axiom (1) generates correct interpolants. That is, whenever a sequent $\lfloor A \rfloor_L \vdash \lfloor C \rfloor_R \blacktriangleright I$ is derived, the implications $A \Rightarrow I$ and $I \Rightarrow C$ are valid, and the constants and predicates in I occur in both A and C. More precisely:

Lemma 2 (Soundness). *If an interpolating QPA+UP sequent $\Gamma \vdash \Delta \blacktriangleright I$ is provable in the calculus, then it is valid.*

In particular, the sequent $\Gamma_L, \Gamma_R \vdash \Delta_L, \Delta_R$ is valid in this case. As shown in [2], Lem. 2 holds for the calculus consisting of the arithmetic and propositional rules. It is easy to see that the additional rules presented in this paper are sound, too.

Concerning completeness, we observe that the logic of quantified Presburger arithmetic with predicates is Π_1^1-complete, which means that no complete calculi exist [7]. On the next pages, we therefore discuss how to restrict the quantification allowed in formulae to achieve completeness, while retaining the ability to extract interpolants from proofs.

3.2 Quantifiers in QPA+UP Interpolants

We first consider the quantifier-free fragment PA+UP. With the help of results in [5,2], it is easy to see that our calculus is sound and complete for PA+UP, and can in fact be turned into a decision procedure. There is a caveat, however: although formulae in PA+UP are quantifier-free, generated interpolants may still contain quantifiers and thus lie outside of PA+UP. The source of quantifiers are the rules ALL-LEFT-L/R in Fig. 1, which can be used to instantiate L/R-labelled quantified formulae with terms containing alien symbols. Such symbols have to be eliminated from resulting interpolants through quantifiers. The following example illustrates this situation.

Example 3. Fig. 2 shows the derivation of an interpolant for the unsatisfiable conjunction $(2c - y \doteq 0 \wedge p(c)) \wedge (2d - y \doteq 0 \wedge \neg p(d))$. After propositional reductions, we instantiate PC_p with the predicate arguments c and d, due to the occurrences of the literals $p(c)$ and $p(d)$ in the sequent. The proof can then be closed using propositional rules, complementary literals, and arithmetic reasoning [2]. The final interpolant is the formula $I = \forall x. (y - 2x \not\doteq 0 \vee p(x))$, in which a quantifier has been introduced via ALL-LEFT-L to eliminate the constant d. □

In fact, as we formally prove in [8], quantifier-free interpolants for the inconsistent PA+UP formulae $2c - y \doteq 0 \wedge p(c)$ and $2d - y \doteq 0 \wedge \neg p(d)$ do not exist. Abstracting from this example, we obtain:

$$\cfrac{\cfrac{*}{\ldots, \lfloor 2c - y \doteq 0 \rfloor_L, \lfloor 2d - y \doteq 0 \rfloor_R \vdash \lfloor c - d \doteq 0 \rfloor_L, \ldots \blacktriangleright y - 2d \not\equiv 0}}{\mathcal{D}}$$

$$\cfrac{\cfrac{\cfrac{\cfrac{\cfrac{\cfrac{\cfrac{\cfrac{*}{\ldots, \lfloor p(c) \rfloor_L \vdash \lfloor p(c) \rfloor_L \blacktriangleright false} \quad \mathcal{D} \quad \cfrac{*}{\ldots, \lfloor p(d) \rfloor_L \vdash \lfloor p(d) \rfloor_R \blacktriangleright p(d)}}{\ldots, \lfloor (p(c) \land c - d \doteq 0) \rightarrow p(d) \rfloor_L \vdash \ldots \blacktriangleright y - 2d \not\equiv 0 \lor p(d)}}{\lfloor PC_p \rfloor_L, \lfloor PC_p \rfloor_R, \lfloor p(c) \rfloor_L, \lfloor 2c - y \doteq 0 \rfloor_L, \lfloor 2d - y \doteq 0 \rfloor_R \vdash \lfloor p(d) \rfloor_R \blacktriangleright I}}{\lfloor PC_p \rfloor_L, \lfloor PC_p \rfloor_R, \lfloor p(c) \rfloor_L, \lfloor 2c - y \doteq 0 \rfloor_L, \lfloor 2d - y \doteq 0 \rfloor_R, \lfloor \neg p(d) \rfloor_R \vdash \blacktriangleright I}}{\lfloor PC_p \rfloor_L, \lfloor PC_p \rfloor_R, \lfloor p(c) \rfloor_L, \lfloor 2c - y \doteq 0 \rfloor_L, \lfloor 2d - y \doteq 0 \land \neg p(d) \rfloor_R \vdash \blacktriangleright I}}{\lfloor PC_p \rfloor_L, \lfloor PC_p \rfloor_R, \lfloor 2c - y \doteq 0 \land p(c) \rfloor_L, \lfloor 2d - y \doteq 0 \land \neg p(d) \rfloor_R \vdash \blacktriangleright I}}$$

with labels OR-LEFT-L$^+$, ALL-LEFT-L, NOT-LEFT, AND-LEFT, AND-LEFT

Fig. 2. Example proof involving uninterpreted predicates

Theorem 4. *PA+UP is not closed under interpolation.*

Intuitively, Theorem 4 holds because the logic PA does not provide an integer division operator. Divisibility predicates $\alpha \mid t$ are insufficient in the presence of uninterpreted predicates, because they cannot be used within terms: no quantifier-free formula can express the statement $\forall x. \ (y - 2x \not\equiv 0 \lor p(x))$, which is equivalent to $2 \mid y \rightarrow p(\frac{y}{2})$.

Adding integer division is sufficient to close PA+UP under interpolation. More formally, we define the logic PAID ("PA with Integer Divisibility"), extending PA by *guarded* quantified expressions

$$\forall x. \ (\alpha x + t \not\equiv 0 \lor \phi), \qquad \exists x. \ (\alpha x + t \doteq 0 \land \phi) \qquad (2)$$

where $x \in X$ ranges over variables, $\alpha \in \mathbb{N} \setminus \{0\}$ over non-zero integers, t over terms not containing x, and ϕ over PAID formulae (possibly containing x as a free variable). The logic PAID+UP is obtained by adding uninterpreted predicates to PAID. Note that the interpolant I computed in Example 3 is in PAID+UP.

It is easy to extend our interpolating calculus to a sound and complete calculus for PAID+UP; the only necessary additional rules are

$$\cfrac{\Gamma, \lfloor (\alpha \nmid t) \lor \exists x. \ (\alpha x + t \doteq 0 \land \phi) \rfloor_D \vdash \Delta \blacktriangleright I}{\Gamma, \lfloor \forall x. \ (\alpha x + t \not\equiv 0 \lor \phi) \rfloor_D \vdash \Delta \blacktriangleright I} \quad \text{ALL-LEFT-GRD}$$

$$\cfrac{\Gamma \vdash \lfloor (\alpha \mid t) \land \forall x. \ (\alpha x + t \not\equiv 0 \lor \phi) \rfloor_D, \Delta \blacktriangleright I}{\Gamma \vdash \lfloor \exists x. \ (\alpha x + t \doteq 0 \land \phi) \rfloor_D, \Delta \blacktriangleright I} \quad \text{EX-RIGHT-GRD}$$

with the side conditions that $\alpha \neq 0$, and that x does not occur in t.

Theorem 5 (Completeness). *Suppose Γ, Δ are sets of labelled PAID+UP formulae. If the sequent $\Gamma_L, \Gamma_R \vdash \Delta_L, \Delta_R$ is valid, then there is a formula I such that (i) the sequent $\Gamma \vdash \Delta \blacktriangleright I$ is provable in the calculus of Sect. 3.1, enriched with the rules ALL-LEFT-GRD and EX-RIGHT-GRD, and (ii) I is a PAID+UP formula up to normalisation of guards to obtain expressions of the form (2).*

Guard normalisation is necessary in general, because interpolants generated by proofs can take the shape $\forall \bar{x}.\ (t_1 \not\doteq 0 \vee \cdots \vee t_k \not\doteq 0 \vee \phi)$, grouping together multiple quantifiers and guards. We show in [8] that such formulae can effectively be transformed to the form (2). To prove the theorem, we first argue that sequent proofs of a certain restricted form are guaranteed to result in PAID+UP interpolants, up to normalisation of guards:

Lemma 6. *Suppose that every instantiation of the axiom* (1) *in a proof* $\mathcal{P}$ *of the PAID+UP sequent* $\Gamma \vdash \Delta \; \blacktriangleright \; I$ *has the form*

$$
\frac{
\begin{array}{c}
\vdots \\
\dfrac{\ldots, \lfloor p(\bar{s}) \rfloor_D \;\vdash\; \lfloor \bar{s} - \bar{t} \doteq 0 \rfloor_F, \lfloor p(\bar{t}) \rfloor_E, \ldots \; \blacktriangleright \; J_2}{\mathcal{Q}}
\end{array}
}{
\dfrac{
\dfrac{\overset{*}{\ldots, \lfloor p(\bar{s}) \rfloor_D \vdash \lfloor p(\bar{s}) \rfloor_F, \ldots \; \blacktriangleright \; J_1} \quad \mathcal{Q} \quad \overset{*}{\ldots, \lfloor p(\bar{t}) \rfloor_F \vdash \lfloor p(\bar{t}) \rfloor_E, \ldots \; \blacktriangleright \; J_3}}{\ldots, \lfloor (p(\bar{s}) \wedge \bar{s} - \bar{t} \doteq 0) \to p(\bar{t}) \rfloor_F \vdash \ldots \; \blacktriangleright \; J_4}\ \text{OR-LEFT}^+
}{
\ldots, \lfloor p(\bar{s}) \rfloor_D \vdash \lfloor p(\bar{t}) \rfloor_E, \ldots \; \blacktriangleright \; J_5
}\ \text{ALL-LEFT}^+
}
$$

where (i) $D, E \in \{L, R\}$ *and* $F \in \{D, E\}$ *are arbitrary labels, (ii) the proof* $\mathcal{Q}$ *only uses the rules* RED-RIGHT, MUL-RIGHT, IPI-RIGHT, AND-RIGHT-L, *and* CLOSE-EQ-RIGHT *applied to an equality derived from* $\bar{s} - \bar{t} \doteq 0$ *(see [2] for definitions of the rules), and (iii)* ALL-LEFT *and* EX-RIGHT *are not applied in any other places in* $\mathcal{P}$. *Then* I *is a PAID+UP formula up to normalisation of guards.*

A proof of this lemma is contained in [8]. Intuitively, the conditions in the lemma enable the application of (1) to atoms $p(\bar{s})$ and $p(\bar{t})$ only if the equations present in a sequent entail that the arguments $\bar{s}$ and $\bar{t}$ match up. There are various ways of relaxing this restriction: most importantly, the applications of axiom (1) only has to be constrained when unifying literals $\lfloor p(\bar{s}) \rfloor_D$ and $\lfloor p(\bar{t}) \rfloor_E$ with *distinct* labels $D \neq E$. Applications of the axiom to literals with the same label are uncritical, because they never introduce quantifiers in interpolants. In fact, practical experience with our theorem prover PRINCESS shows that generated interpolants are often naturally in the PAID+UP fragment, even when not imposing any restrictions on the proof generation process.

The second ingredient in proving the completeness theorem Thm. 5 is to show that the calculus with the restrictions imposed in Lem. 6 is still complete. We describe a proof procedure abiding by these restrictions in [8]. As a corollary of the completeness, we obtain:

Corollary 7. *PAID+UP is closed under interpolation.*

Despite this closure property, some proofs may result in interpolants outside PAID+UP, by applying "wrong" rules in the sub-proof $\mathcal{Q}$ of Lem. 6:

Example 8. Starting from PAID+UP input formulae, the following proof generates the interpolant $\forall c.\, p(c)$, which is not equivalent to any PAID+UP formula:

$$
\frac{
\dfrac{\overset{*}{\lfloor p(0) \rfloor_L \vdash \lfloor p(0) \rfloor_L \; \blacktriangleright \; false} \quad \dfrac{\overset{*}{\lfloor q \rfloor_L \vdash \lfloor c \doteq 0 \rfloor_L, \lfloor q \rfloor_L \; \blacktriangleright \; false} \quad \overset{*}{\lfloor p(c) \rfloor_L \vdash \lfloor p(c) \rfloor_R \; \blacktriangleright \; p(c)}}{\ldots, \lfloor p(0) \rfloor_L, \lfloor q \rfloor_L, \lfloor (p(0) \wedge c \doteq 0) \to p(c) \rfloor_L \vdash \lfloor c \rfloor_R, \lfloor q \rfloor_L \; \blacktriangleright \; p(c)}}{\lfloor PC_p \rfloor_L, \lfloor PC_p \rfloor_R, \lfloor p(0) \rfloor_L, \lfloor q \rfloor_L \vdash \lfloor p(c) \rfloor_R, \lfloor q \rfloor_L \; \blacktriangleright \; \forall c.\, p(c)}
}{}\ \text{ALL-LEFT-L}
$$

The first step in the proof is to instantiate axiom (1), in an attempt to unify the formula $\lfloor p(0) \rfloor_L$ and $\lfloor p(c) \rfloor_R$; this instantiation later introduces the unguarded quantifier $\forall c$ in the interpolant. The proof violates the conditions in Lem. 6, because the middle sub-proof is closed using the atoms $\lfloor q \rfloor_L$ instead of the equa-tion $\lfloor c \doteq 0 \rfloor_L$. A correct PAID+UP interpolant for this example is *false*.   □

PAID and integer division. Despite the presence of guarded quantifiers, PAID is close to simple quantifier-free assertion languages found in programming lan-guages like Java or C, making PAID expressions convenient to pass on to decision procedures. Specifically, the following equivalences hold:

$$\forall x. \, (\alpha x + t \not\equiv 0 \vee \phi) \equiv (\alpha \nmid t) \vee [x/(t \div \alpha)]\phi, \qquad (\alpha \mid t) \equiv \alpha(t \div \alpha) \doteq t$$

where $\div$ denotes integer division. Vice versa, an expression $c \doteq t \div \alpha$ can be encoded in PAID using axioms like $\alpha c \leq t \,\wedge\, (t < \alpha c + \alpha \vee t < \alpha c - \alpha)$.

4 Interpolation for Uninterpreted Functions

4.1 A Relational Encoding of Uninterpreted Functions

For practical verification and interpolation problems, uninterpreted functions are more common and often more important than uninterpreted predicates. In the context of interpolation, functions share many properties with predicates; in particular, the quantifier-free fragment PA+UF is again not closed under interpolation, in analogy to Theorem 4.

Similar to the previous section, the interpolation property can be restored by adding means of integer division. To this end, we define the logic PAID+UF like PAID, but allowing arbitrary occurrences of uninterpreted functions in terms. For reasoning and interpolation purposes, we represent functions via an encod-ing into uninterpreted predicates. The resulting calculus strongly resembles the congruence closure approach used in SMT solvers (e.g., [4]). To formalise the encoding, we introduce a further logic, PAID+UF$_p$. Recall that P and F denote the vocabularies of uninterpreted predicates and functions. We assume that a fresh $(n + 1)$-ary uninterpreted predicate $f_p \in P$ exists for every n-ary unin-terpreted function $f \in F$. The logic PAID+UF$_p$ is then derived from PAID by incorporating occurrences of predicates f_p of the following form:

$$\exists x. \, \big(f_p(t_1, \ldots, t_n, x) \wedge \phi\big) \qquad (3)$$

where $x \in X$ ranges over variables, $t_1, \ldots, t_n$ over terms that do not contain x, and ϕ over PAID+UF$_p$ formulae (possibly containing x). In order to avoid uni-versal quantifiers, we do not allow expressions (3) underneath negations.

Formulae in PAID+UF can uniformly be mapped to PAID+UF$_p$ by rewriting:

$$\phi[f(t_1, \ldots, t_n)] \quad \rightsquigarrow \quad \exists x. \, (f_p(t_1, \ldots, t_n, x) \wedge \phi[x]) \qquad (4)$$

provided that the terms $t_1, \ldots, t_n$ do not contain variables bound in ϕ. To stay within PAID+UF$_p$, application of the rule underneath negations has to be avoided, which can be done by transformation to negation normal form. We write ϕ_{Rel} for the function-free PAID+UF$_p$ formula derived from a PAID+UF formula ϕ by exhaustive application of (4). Vice versa, ϕ can be obtained from ϕ_{Rel} by applying (4) in the opposite direction. Assuming *functional consistency*, the formulae ϕ and ϕ_{Rel} are satisfiability-equivalent:

Lemma 9. *Let FC_f denote the functional consistency axiom:* [1]

$$FC_f = \quad \forall \bar{x}_1, \bar{x}_2, y_1, y_2. \left((f_p(\bar{x}_1, y_1) \wedge f_p(\bar{x}_2, y_2) \wedge \bar{x}_1 \doteq \bar{x}_2) \rightarrow y_1 \doteq y_2 \right) \quad (5)$$

A PAID+UF formula ϕ is satisfiable exactly if $\phi_{Rel} \wedge \bigwedge_{f \in F} FC_f$ is satisfiable.

By the lemma, it is sufficient to construct a proof of $\neg(\phi_{Rel} \wedge \bigwedge_{f \in F} FC_f)$ in order to show that ϕ is unsatisfiable.[2] The axioms FC_f can be handled by ground instantiation, just like the predicate consistency axiom (1): whenever atoms $f_p(\bar{s}_1, t_1)$ and $f_p(\bar{s}_2, t_2)$ occur in the antecedent of a sequent, an instance of FC_f can be generated using the rules ALL-LEFT-L/R and the substitution $[\bar{x}_1/\bar{s}_1, \bar{x}_2/\bar{s}_2, y_1/t_1, y_2/t_2]$. This form of instantiation is sufficient, because predicates f_p only occur in positive positions in ϕ_{Rel}, and therefore only turn up in antecedents. As before, the number of required instances can be kept under control by formulating suitable refinements [6].

4.2   Interpolation for PAID+UF

PAID+UF conjunctions $A \wedge B$ can be interpolated by constructing a proof of

$$\lfloor A_{Rel} \rfloor_L, \lfloor B_{Rel} \rfloor_R, \{\lfloor FC_f \rfloor_L\}_{f \in F_A}, \{\lfloor FC_f \rfloor_R\}_{f \in F_B} \vdash \emptyset \blacktriangleright I \quad (6)$$

where F_A/F_B are the uninterpreted functions occurring in A/B. Due to the soundness of the calculus, the existence of a proof guarantees that I is an interpolant. Vice versa, a completeness result corresponding to Thm. 5 also holds for PAID+UF$_p$. Because PAID+UF$_p$ interpolants can be translated back to PAID+UF by virtue of (4), we also have a closure result:

Theorem 10. *The logic PAID+UF is closed under interpolation.*

Example 11. We consider the PAID+UF interpolation problem $A \wedge B$ with

$$A = \quad b \doteq f(2) \wedge f(a+1) \doteq c \wedge d \doteq 1, \qquad B = \quad a \doteq 1 \wedge f(b) \doteq f(c) + d .$$

The corresponding PAID+UF$_p$ formulae are:

$$A_{Rel} = \quad \exists x_1. \left(f_p(2, x_1) \wedge \exists x_2. \left(f_p(a+1, x_2) \wedge b \doteq x_1 \wedge x_2 \doteq c \wedge d \doteq 1 \right) \right)$$
$$B_{Rel} = \quad \exists y_1. \left(f_p(b, y_1) \wedge \exists y_2. \left(f_p(c, y_2) \wedge a \doteq 1 \wedge y_1 \doteq y_2 + d \right) \right) .$$

---

[1] Axiom (5) can also be formulated as $\forall \bar{x}_1, y_1, y_2. \ (f_p(x, y_1) \wedge f_p(\bar{x}, y_2) \rightarrow y_1 \doteq y_2)$, assuming the predicate consistency axiom (1). We chose (5) to avoid having to consider the auxiliary axiom (1) at this point, which simplifies presentation.

[2] Note that this formulation fails to work if arbitrary quantifiers are allowed in ϕ; this case would require axioms for totality of functions as well.

$$
\cfrac{
  \cfrac{
    \cfrac{
      \cfrac{*}{\dots, \lfloor b \doteq x_1 \rfloor_L, \lfloor x_2 \doteq c \rfloor_L \vdash \lfloor b \doteq c \rfloor_R \;\blacktriangleright\; b \doteq c}{\lfloor x_1 \doteq x_2 \rfloor_L} \qquad
      \cfrac{*}{\dots, \lfloor y_1 \doteq y_2 \rfloor_R, \lfloor d \doteq 1 \rfloor_L \vdash \emptyset \;\blacktriangleright\; d \doteq 1}{\lfloor y_1 \doteq y_2 + d \rfloor_R}
    }{\dots, \lfloor (f_p(b, y_1) \wedge f_p(c, y_2) \wedge b \doteq c) \;\rightarrow\; y_1 \doteq y_2 \rfloor_R \vdash \emptyset \;\blacktriangleright\; b \doteq c \wedge d \doteq 1}
  }{\dots, \lfloor f_p(b, y_1) \rfloor_R, \lfloor f_p(c, y_2) \rfloor_R, \lfloor FC_f \rfloor_R, \lfloor x_1 \doteq x_2 \rfloor_L \vdash \emptyset \;\blacktriangleright\; b \doteq c \wedge d \doteq 1} \;\; \text{(ii)}
}{\mathcal{D}}
$$

$$
\cfrac{
  \cfrac{
    \dots \qquad
    \cfrac{*}{\dots, \lfloor a \doteq 1 \rfloor_R \vdash \lfloor 2 \doteq a + 1 \rfloor_L \;\blacktriangleright\; a \not\doteq 1} \qquad \mathcal{D}
  }{
    \cfrac{\dots, \lfloor (f_p(2, x_1) \wedge f_p(a + 1, x_2) \wedge 2 \doteq a + 1) \;\rightarrow\; x_1 \doteq x_2 \rfloor_L \vdash \emptyset \;\blacktriangleright\; I_1}{\dots, \lfloor f_p(2, x_1) \rfloor_L, \lfloor f_p(a + 1, x_2) \rfloor_L, \lfloor FC_f \rfloor_L \vdash \emptyset \;\blacktriangleright\; I_1} \;\; \text{(i)}
  } \text{ OR-LEFT-L}^+
}{
  \cfrac{\vdots}{\lfloor A_{Rel} \rfloor_L, \lfloor B_{Rel} \rfloor_R, \lfloor FC_f \rfloor_L, \lfloor FC_f \rfloor_R \vdash \emptyset \;\blacktriangleright\; I_1} \text{ AND-LEFT}^+, \text{ EX-LEFT}^+
}
$$

Fig. 3. Interpolating proof of Example 11. Parts of the proof concerned with arithmetic reasoning or application of the CLOSE-* rules are not shown.

The unsatisfiability of $A_{Rel} \wedge B_{Rel}$ is proven in Fig. 3, requiring two applications of FC_f: (i) for the pair $f(2), f(a + 1)$, and (ii) for $f(b), f(c)$. The resulting interpolant is $I_1 = \; a \not\doteq 1 \vee (b \doteq c \wedge d \doteq 1)$ and contains a disjunction due to splitting over an L-formula (i), and a conjunction due to (ii). □

As in Lem. 6, a sufficient condition for PAID+UF$_p$ interpolants can be given by restricting applications of the functional consistency axiom:

Lemma 12. *Suppose that every instantiation of an axiom FC_f in a proof $\mathcal{P}$ of (6) has the form*

$$
\cfrac{
  \cfrac{
    \cfrac{
      \cfrac{\vdots}{\dots \vdash \lfloor \bar{s}_1 \doteq \bar{s}_2 \rfloor_F, \dots \;\blacktriangleright\; J_3}{\mathcal{Q}} \qquad
      \cfrac{\vdots}{\dots, \lfloor t_1 \doteq t_2 \rfloor_F \vdash \dots \;\blacktriangleright\; J_4}{\mathcal{R}}
    }{}
  }{}
}{}
$$

$$
\cfrac{
  \cfrac{*}{\lfloor f_p(\bar{s}_1, t_1) \rfloor_D \vdash \lfloor f_p(\bar{s}_1, t_1) \rfloor_F \;\blacktriangleright\; J_1} \quad
  \cfrac{*}{\lfloor f_p(\bar{s}_2, t_2) \rfloor_E \vdash \lfloor f_p(\bar{s}_2, t_2) \rfloor_F \;\blacktriangleright\; J_2} \quad \mathcal{Q} \quad \mathcal{R}
}{
  \cfrac{\dots, \lfloor (f_p(\bar{s}_1, t_1) \wedge f_p(\bar{s}_2, t_2) \wedge \bar{s}_1 \doteq \bar{s}_2) \;\rightarrow\; t_1 \doteq t_2 \rfloor_F \vdash \dots \;\blacktriangleright\; J_5}{\dots, \lfloor f_p(\bar{s}_1, t_1) \rfloor_D, \lfloor f_p(\bar{s}_2, t_2) \rfloor_E \vdash \dots \;\blacktriangleright\; J_6} \text{ ALL-LEFT}^+
}
$$

where (i) $D, E \in \{L, R\}$ and $F \in \{D, E\}$ are arbitrary labels, (ii) $R \in \{D, E\}$ implies $F = R$, (iii) the proof $\mathcal{Q}$ only uses the rules RED-RIGHT, MUL-RIGHT, IPI-RIGHT, AND-RIGHT-L, *and* CLOSE-EQ-RIGHT *applied to an equality derived from $\bar{s}_1 \doteq \bar{s}_2$ (see [2]), (iv)* ALL-LEFT *and* EX-RIGHT *are not applied in any other places in $\mathcal{P}$. Then I is a PAID+UF$_p$ formula up to normalisation of guards.*

Proofs of this shape closely correspond to the reasoning of congruence closure procedures (e.g., [4]): two terms/nodes $f(\bar{s}_1)$ and $f(\bar{s}_2)$ are collapsed only once the equations $\bar{s}_1 \doteq \bar{s}_2$ have been derived. Congruence closure can therefore be used to efficiently generate proofs satisfying the conditions of the lemma (abstracting from the additional reasoning necessary to handle the integers).

As in Sect. 3.2, it is also possible to relax the conditions of the lemma; in particular, there is no need to restrict FC_f applications with $D = E$. The resulting interpolation procedure is very flexible, in the sense that many different interpolants can be generated from essentially the same proof. Reordering FC_f applications, for instance, changes the propositional structure of interpolants:

Example 13. In Example 11, the interpolant $I_1 = a \not\doteq 1 \lor (b \doteq c \land d \doteq 1)$ is derived using two FC_f applications (i) and (ii). Reordering the applications, so as to perform (ii) before (i), yields the interpolant $I_2 = (a \not\doteq 1 \lor b \doteq c) \land d \doteq 1$. □

4.3 Interpolation for the Theory of Extensional Arrays

The first-order theory of arrays [9] is typically encoded using uninterpreted function symbols *select* and *store* by means of the following axioms:

$$\forall x, y, z.\ select(store(x, y, z), y) \doteq z \tag{7}$$

$$\forall x, y_1, y_2, z.\ \big(y_1 \doteq y_2 \lor select(store(x, y_1, z), y_2) \doteq select(x, y_2)\big) \tag{8}$$

Intuitively, $select(x, y)$ retrieves the element of array x stored at position y, while $store(x, y, z)$ denotes the array that is identical to x, except that position y stores value z. The *extensional* theory of arrays additionally supports equalities between arrays and is encoded using the following axiom:

$$\forall x_1, x_2.\ (x_1 \doteq x_2 \leftrightarrow (\forall y.\ select(x_1, y) \doteq select(x_2, y))) \tag{9}$$

The quantifier-free theory of arrays is again not closed under interpolation, even without arithmetic, as was already noted in [10,11]. A classical example is given by the following inconsistent formulae:

$$\begin{aligned} A = &\ M' \doteq store(M, a, d) \\ B = &\ b \not\doteq c \land\ select(M', b) \not\doteq select(M, b)\ \land\ select(M', c) \not\doteq select(M, c)\,, \end{aligned}$$

which only permit quantified interpolants, of the form

$$\forall y_1, y_2.\ \big(y_1 \doteq y_2 \lor\ select(M, y_1) \doteq select(M', y_1) \lor\ select(M, y_2) \doteq select(M', y_2)\big).$$

Naturally, combining array theory with quantifier-free Presburger arithmetic only exacerbates the problem. As we have shown in previous sections, extending PA+UP by guarded integer divisibility predicates results in a theory that is closed under interpolation. We can extend this solution to the theory of arrays, but still only obtain closure under interpolation for small fragments of the logic (like for formulae that do not contain the *store* symbol). The resulting interpolation procedure is similar in flavour to the procedures in [12,13] and works by explicit instantiation of the array axioms. As in Sect. 3, axioms are handled lazily using the rules ALL-LEFT-L/R, which introduce quantifiers in interpolants as needed.

Array interpolation via relational encoding. To reduce array expressions to expressions involving uninterpreted predicates, we use the same relational encoding as in Sect. 4. We first lift the axioms (7), (8), and (9) to the relational encoding:

$$AR_1 = \forall x_1, x_2, y, z_1, z_2. \left(store_p(x_1, y, z_1, x_2) \wedge select_p(x_2, y, z_2) \; \rightarrow \; z_1 \doteq z_2 \right)$$

$$AR_2 = \forall x_1, x_2, y_1, y_2, z, z_1, z_2. \left(\begin{array}{l} store_p(x_1, y_1, z, x_2) \\ \wedge \; select_p(x_1, y_2, z_1) \\ \wedge \; select_p(x_2, y_2, z_2) \end{array} \; \rightarrow \; y_1 \doteq y_2 \vee z_1 \doteq z_2 \right)$$

$$AR_3 = \forall x_1, x_2. \left(\begin{array}{c} \forall y, z_1, z_2. \; (select_p(x_1, y, z_1) \wedge select_p(x_2, y, z_2) \rightarrow z_1 \doteq z_2) \\ \rightarrow x_1 \doteq x_2 \end{array} \right)$$

As in the previous sections, these axioms can be used in proofs by ground instantiation based on literals that occur in antecedents of sequents; in the case
of AR_3, it is also necessary to perform instantiation based on equations occurring in the succedent. This yields an interpolating (though incomplete) calculus for the full logic QPA+AR, and an interpolating decision procedure for
the combined theory PAID+AR of Presburger arithmetic with integer division
and arrays. Interpolants expressed via the relational encodings of the functions
select and *store* can be translated into interpolants over array expressions via
re-substitution rules.

Array properties. The *array property fragment*, introduced by Bradley et al. [14],
comprises Presburger arithmetic and the theory of extensional arrays parame-
terised by suitable element theories. In array property formulae, integer variables
may be quantified universally, provided that the matrix of the resulting quantified formula is *guarded* by a Boolean combination of equalities and non-strict
inequalities. Using such formulae, one can express properties like equality and
sortedness of arrays, as they commonly occur in formulae extracted from programs. Despite its expressiveness, satisfiability for this fragment was shown to
be decidable by providing an effective decision procedure [14].

Although Bradley et al. did not consider interpolation for the theory of array properties, we observe that the decision procedure given in [14] can easily
be made interpolating using the calculus for QPA+AR provided in this paper.
The decision procedure proceeds by reducing, in a sequence of 5 steps, array
property formulae to formulae in the combined theory of Presburger arithmetic
with uninterpreted functions and the element theories. These 5 steps essentially
correspond to instantiation of the array axioms and of quantified parts of the
input formulae, which can be implemented using the interpolating rules provided
in Fig. 1. The final step is a call to an interpolating decision procedure for Presburger arithmetic and uninterpreted functions combined with suitable element
theories; we have presented such a procedure in this paper.

We remark that the array property fragment is not subsumed by the restriction of QPA+AR to Presburger arithmetic and array theory with guarded
quantification as allowed in PAID+UF.

5   Related Work and Conclusion

Related work. For work on interpolation in pure quantifier-free Presburger
arithmetic, see [2]. Yorsh et al. [15] present a combination method to generate interpolants using interpolation procedures for individual theories. To be

applicable, the method requires individual theories to be *equality interpolating*; this is neither the case for Presburger arithmetic nor for arrays. To the best of our knowledge, it is unknown whether quantifier-free Presburger arithmetic with the integer division operator $\div$ is equality interpolating.

Interpolation procedures for uninterpreted functions are given by McMillan [10] and Fuchs et al. [16]. The former approach uses an interpolating calculus with rules for transitivity, congruence, etc.; the latter is based on congruence closure algorithms. Our calculus in Sect. 4 has similarities with [16], but is more flexible concerning the order in which congruence rules are applied. A more systematic comparison is planned as future work, including estimating the cost of interpolating uninterpreted functions via a reduction to predicates, rather than via some direct procedure. The papers [10,16] do not consider the combination with full Presburger arithmetic.

Kapur et al. [11] present an interpolation method for arrays that works by reduction to the theory of uninterpreted functions. To some degree, the interpolation procedure of Sect. 4.3 can be considered as a lazy version of the procedure in [11], performing the reduction to uninterpreted functions only on demand.

In [12], Jhala et al. define a *split prover* that computes quantifier-free interpolants in a fragment of the theory of arrays, among others. The main objective of [12] is to derive interpolants in restricted languages, which makes it possible to guarantee convergence and a certain form of completeness in model checking. While our procedure is more general in that the full combined theory of PA with arrays can be handled, we consider it as important future work to integrate techniques to restrict interpolant languages into our procedure.

McMillan provides a complete procedure to generate (potentially) quantified interpolants for the full theory of arrays [13] by means of explicit array axioms. Our interpolation method resembles McMillan's in that explicit array axioms are given to a theorem prover, but our procedure is also complete in combination with Presburger arithmetic.

Bradley et al. introduce the concept of constrained universal quantification in array theory [14], which essentially allows a single universal array index quantifier, possibly restricted to an index subrange, e.g. all indices in some range $[l, u]$. Unlike full quantified array theory, satisfiability is decidable in Bradley's fragment; interpolation is not considered in this work. We have discussed the relationship of this fragment to QPA+AR in Section 4.3.

Conclusion. We have presented interpolating calculi for the theories of Presburger arithmetic combined with uninterpreted predicates (QPA+UP), uninterpreted functions (QPA+UF), and extensional arrays (QPA+AR). We have demonstrated that these extensions require the use of quantifiers in interpolants. Adding notions of *guarded quantification*, we therefore identified fragments of the full first-order theories that are closed under interpolation, yet are expressible in assertion languages present in standard programming languages.

As future work, we plan to extend our results to interpolating SMT solvers, particularly aiming at procedures that can be used in model checkers based on the *lazy abstraction with interpolants* paradigm. On the theoretical side, we will study the relationship between the logics discussed in this paper, and architectures for combining interpolating procedures, e.g., [15]. We also plan to investigate, possibly along the lines of [17], how our interpolation procedure for uninterpreted functions relates to existing methods [10,16], and how it affects the strength of computed interpolants. Finally, we plan to investigate a combination of our calculus with the Split-Prover approach in [12].

References

1. Craig, W.: Linear reasoning. A new form of the Herbrand-Gentzen theorem. The Journal of Symbolic Logic 22(3), 250–268 (1957)
2. Brillout, A., Kroening, D., Rümmer, P., Wahl, T.: An Interpolating Sequent Calculus for Quantifier-Free Presburger Arithmetic. In: Giesl, J., Hähnle, R. (eds.) IJCAR 2010. LNCS, vol. 6173, pp. 384–399. Springer, Heidelberg (2010)
3. Fitting, M.C.: First-Order Logic and Automated Theorem Proving, 2nd edn. Springer, Heidelberg (1996)
4. Detlefs, D., Nelson, G., Saxe, J.B.: Simplify: A theorem prover for program checking. Journal of the ACM 52, 365–473 (2005)
5. Rümmer, P.: A constraint sequent calculus for first-order logic with linear integer arithmetic. In: Cervesato, I., Veith, H., Voronkov, A. (eds.) LPAR 2008. LNCS (LNAI), vol. 5330, pp. 274–289. Springer, Heidelberg (2008)
6. Rümmer, P.: Calculi for Program Incorrectness and Arithmetic. PhD thesis, University of Gothenburg (2008)
7. Halpern, J.Y.: Presburger arithmetic with unary predicates is Π_1^1 complete. Journal of Symbolic Logic 56 (1991)
8. Brillout, A., Kroening, D., Rümmer, P., Wahl, T.: Beyond quantifier-free interpolation in extensions of Presburger arithmetic (extended Technical Report). Technical report, CoRR abs/1011.1036 (2010)
9. McCarthy, J.: Towards a mathematical science of computation. In: Information Processing 1962: Proceedings IFIP Congress 1962, North-Holland, Amsterdam (1963)
10. McMillan, K.L.: An interpolating theorem prover. Theor. Comput. Sci. 345 (2005)
11. Kapur, D., Majumdar, R., Zarba, C.G.: Interpolation for data structures. In: SIGSOFT 2006/FSE-14, pp. 105–116. ACM, New York (2006)
12. Jhala, R., McMillan, K.L.: A practical and complete approach to predicate refinement. In: Hermanns, H. (ed.) TACAS 2006. LNCS, vol. 3920, pp. 459–473. Springer, Heidelberg (2006)
13. McMillan, K.L.: Quantified invariant generation using an interpolating saturation prover. In: Ramakrishnan, C.R., Rehof, J. (eds.) TACAS 2008. LNCS, vol. 4963, pp. 413–427. Springer, Heidelberg (2008)
14. Bradley, A.R., Manna, Z., Sipma, H.B.: What's decidable about arrays? In: Emerson, E.A., Namjoshi, K.S. (eds.) VMCAI 2006. LNCS, vol. 3855, pp. 427–442. Springer, Heidelberg (2005)
15. Yorsh, G., Musuvathi, M.: A combination method for generating interpolants. In: Nieuwenhuis, R. (ed.) CADE 2005. LNCS (LNAI), vol. 3632, pp. 353–368. Springer, Heidelberg (2005)
16. Fuchs, A., Goel, A., Grundy, J., Krstić, S., Tinelli, C.: Ground interpolation for the theory of equality. In: Kowalewski, S., Philippou, A. (eds.) TACAS 2009. LNCS, vol. 5505, pp. 413–427. Springer, Heidelberg (2009)
17. D'Silva, V., Purandare, M., Weissenbacher, G., Kroening, D.: Interpolant Strength. In: Barthe, G., Hermenegildo, M. (eds.) VMCAI 2010. LNCS, vol. 5944, pp. 129–145. Springer, Heidelberg (2010)

Probabilistic Büchi Automata with Non-extremal Acceptance Thresholds

Rohit Chadha[1], A. Prasad Sistla[2], and Mahesh Viswanathan[3]

[1] LSV, ENS Cachan & CNRS & INRIA Saclay, France
[2] Univ. of Illinois, Chicago, USA
[3] Univ. of Illinois, Urbana-Champaign, USA

Abstract. This paper investigates the power of Probabilistic Büchi Automata (PBA) when the threshold probability of acceptance is non-extremal, i.e., is a value strictly between 0 and 1. Many practical randomized algorithms are designed to work under non-extremal threshold probabilities and thus it is important to study power of PBAs for such cases.

The paper presents a number of surprising expressiveness and decidability results for PBAs when the threshold probability is non-extremal. Some of these results sharply contrast with the results for extremal threshold probabilities. The paper also presents results for Hierarchical PBAs and for an interesting subclass of them called simple PBAs.

1 Introduction

Probabilistic Büchi Automata (PBA), introduced in [?] to model *open, reactive* probabilistic systems, are finite state machines that process input strings of infinite length like Büchi automata. However, unlike Büchi automata, they have probabilistic transitions. The semantics of such machines is defined as follows. A run on an input word is considered to be *accepting* if it satisfies the Büchi acceptance condition. The collection of all accepting runs on any input is known to be measurable [14,2]. For any given acceptance threshold x, the language $\mathcal{L}_{>x}(\mathcal{B})$ $(\mathcal{L}_{\geq x}(\mathcal{B}))$ of a PBA $\mathcal{B}$ is defined to be the set of all inputs for which the above measure is $> x$ $(\geq x)$.

In a series of papers [2,1,9,4], researchers have studied the behavior of PBAs when the acceptance threshold x is either 0 or 1, delineating the expressive power of such machines and establishing the precise complexity of various decision problems. While extremal thresholds (of 0 and 1) are important for studying randomized algorithms and protocols, in many practical scenarios only algorithms with non-extremal thresholds can solve the problem — consensus in synchronized distributed systems [15], and semantic security [8], being a couple of examples. Thus, studying PBAs under non-extremal thresholds, which is the focus of this paper, is important.

We begin by observing that for non-extremal thresholds $x \in (0, 1)$, the actual value of x itself is not important: for every PBA $\mathcal{B}$, one can efficiently construct another PBA $\mathcal{B}'$ such that $\mathcal{L}_{>x}(\mathcal{B}) = \mathcal{L}_{>\frac{1}{2}}(\mathcal{B}')$ (or $\mathcal{L}_{\geq x}(\mathcal{B}) = \mathcal{L}_{\geq \frac{1}{2}}(\mathcal{B}')$). Thus, we consider the acceptance threshold to be always $\frac{1}{2}$. Our results on the decidability of the emptiness and universality decision problems are summarized in Figure 1.

R. Jhala and D. Schmidt (Eds.): VMCAI 2011, LNCS 6538, pp. 103–117, 2011.
© Springer-Verlag Berlin Heidelberg 2011

A few salient points about our results on decision problems are as follows. Typically, solving decision problems for automata with non-extremal thresholds is harder than for those with extremal thresholds, as is borne out by similar results for probabilistic finite automata [11,6] and for finite state probabilistic monitors [3]. Interestingly, this observation does not hold for checking emptiness of $\mathcal{L}_{>0}(\mathcal{B})$ for a given PBA $\mathcal{B}$, but holds for other problems. More specifically, for a given PBA $\mathcal{B}$, the problems of checking emptiness of $\mathcal{L}_{>\frac{1}{2}}(\mathcal{B})$ and emptiness of $\mathcal{L}_{>0}(\mathcal{B})$ have the same level of undecidability; both of them are Σ_2^0-complete. On the other hand, the problems of checking emptiness and universality of $\mathcal{L}_{\geq\frac{1}{2}}(\mathcal{B})$ are Π_1^1-complete and **co-R.E.**-complete, respectively, as opposed to both being **PSPACE**-complete for $\mathcal{L}_{=1}(\mathcal{B})$. The universality problem for $\mathcal{L}_{>\frac{1}{2}}(\mathcal{B})$ is Π_1^1-complete as opposed to being Σ_2^0-complete for $\mathcal{L}_{>0}(\mathcal{B})$.

Previously, we [4] had introduced a syntactic subclass of PBAs called *hierarchical* PBAs (HPBA) as an expressively less powerful, but computationally more tractable fragment of PBAs. With extremal thresholds, the emptiness and universality problems are efficiently decidable — emptiness and universality of $\mathcal{L}_{>0}(\mathcal{B})$ are **NL**-complete and **PSPACE**-complete, respectively, while for $\mathcal{L}_{=1}(\mathcal{B})$ they are **PSPACE**-complete and **NL**-complete, when $\mathcal{B}$ is an HPBA. Considering non-extremal acceptance thresholds, these decision problems not only become undecidable, but are *as difficult as* in the case general PBAs. The only exception to this is the case of checking emptiness of $\mathcal{L}_{>\frac{1}{2}}(\mathcal{B})$ which is **co-R.E.**-complete when $\mathcal{B}$ is an HPBA and is Σ_2^0-complete for general PBAs. This upper bound of **co-R.E.** in this case is established by observing that for an HPBA $\mathcal{B}$, $\mathcal{L}_{>\frac{1}{2}}(\mathcal{B})$ is non-empty if and only if there is an ultimately periodic word in $\mathcal{L}_{>\frac{1}{2}}(\mathcal{B})$; this observation may be of independent interest.

Next, our undecidability proofs for these various decision problems rely on Condon and Lipton's [6] ideas, used to show the undecidability of the emptiness problem of probabilistic finite automata. However, in order to obtain lower bounds for HPBAs and obtain "hierarchical" machines, we modify the original reduction by Condon and Lipton, and we believe our modification yields a conceptually simpler proof of the undecidability of the emptiness problem for probabilistic finite automata. In order, to prove the undecidability result, Condon and Lipton do the following. Given a 2-counter machine M, they construct a probabilistic finite automata $\mathcal{A}_M$ whose inputs are computations of M, such that a correct halting computation of M, repeated sufficiently many times, is accepted by $\mathcal{A}_M$ with high probability ($> \frac{1}{2}$) and all other inputs are rejected with high probability. Thus, $\mathcal{L}_{>\frac{1}{2}}(\mathcal{A}_M)$ is non-empty iff M has a halting computation. Now, in order to carry out this reduction, the automaton $\mathcal{A}_M$ "checks" every pair of successive configurations in the input for correctness, and maintains a variety of bounded counters to ensure that the asymptotic probability of acceptance has the desired properties. We observe that if the automaton only "checks" one pair of successive configurations (where the pair to be checked is chosen randomly) the reduction still works, yielding a "simpler" automaton construction and a simpler analysis of the assymptotics. However, one casualty of our simpler proof is the following — while we can show that the emptiness problem of probabilistic finite automata is undecidable, the Condon-Lipton proof establishes a stronger fact, namely, that the problem remains undecidable even under the promise that the acceptance probability of every input is bounded away from $\frac{1}{2}$.

Our next set of results pertain to the expressiveness of PBAs and HPBAs with non-extremal acceptance thresholds. Let $\mathbb{L}(\text{PBA}^{>0})$ be the collection of all languages recognized by PBAs with threshold 0, $\mathbb{L}(\text{PBA}^{=1})$ be those recognized with threshold 1, $\mathbb{L}(\text{PBA}^{>\frac{1}{2}})$ be those recognized with a strict threshold of $\frac{1}{2}$, and $\mathbb{L}(\text{PBA}^{\geq\frac{1}{2}})$ be those recognized with a non-strict threshold of $\frac{1}{2}$. Results in [1,4] establish that $\mathbb{L}(\text{PBA}^{>0})$ is closed under complementation, $\mathbb{L}(\text{PBA}^{=1})$ is not closed under complementation, and $\mathbb{L}(\text{PBA}^{>0})$ is the Boolean closure of $\mathbb{L}(\text{PBA}^{=1})$. Observations in [4] already imply that $\mathbb{L}(\text{PBA}^{\geq\frac{1}{2}})$ is not closed under complementation. Moreover, the complexity results of the decision problems in Theorem 1 imply that if $\mathbb{L}(\text{PBA}^{>\frac{1}{2}})$ were complementable, the procedure would not be recursive. We establish that, in fact, $\mathbb{L}(\text{PBA}^{>\frac{1}{2}})$ is not closed under complementation, and therefore cannot be the Boolean closure of $\mathbb{L}(\text{PBA}^{\geq\frac{1}{2}})$. We also show that even though $\mathbb{L}(\text{PBA}^{\geq\frac{1}{2}})$ is a topologically simpler class of languages than $\mathbb{L}(\text{PBA}^{>\frac{1}{2}})$, it is not contained in $\mathbb{L}(\text{PBA}^{>\frac{1}{2}})$; in fact, the two sets $\mathbb{L}(\text{PBA}^{>\frac{1}{2}})$ and $\mathbb{L}(\text{PBA}^{\geq\frac{1}{2}})$ are incomparable. The classes $\mathbb{L}(\text{HPBA}^{>0})$, $\mathbb{L}(\text{HPBA}^{=1})$, $\mathbb{L}(\text{HPBA}^{>\frac{1}{2}})$, and $\mathbb{L}(\text{HPBA}^{\geq\frac{1}{2}})$ can be analogously defined for HPBAs. It was shown in [4] that HPBAs with extremal thresholds correspond to regular languages — $\mathbb{L}(\text{HPBA}^{=1})$ is exactly the set of deterministic ω-regular languages, while $\mathbb{L}(\text{HPBA}^{>0})$ is exactly the set of ω-regular languages. With non-extremal thresholds, HPBAs can recognize non-regular languages. In addition, the observations about PBA expressiveness extend to HPBAs: $\mathbb{L}(\text{HPBA}^{>\frac{1}{2}})$ and $\mathbb{L}(\text{HPBA}^{\geq\frac{1}{2}})$ are not closed under complementation and they are incomparable.

Our motivation in considering HPBAs in [4] was that with extremal thresholds, they were a "regular", tractable subclass of PBAs. However, as observed in the preceding paragraphs, many of these nice properties of HPBAs are lost when considering non-extremal thresholds. Therefore we consider a syntactic subclass of HPBAs that we call *simple* PBAs (SPBA). In simple PBAs, the states are partitioned into two sets. The initial and final states belong to the first partition, and the transitions out of states in the first partition are such that at most one successor belongs to the first partition. Transitions from states in the second partition all remain within the second partition. We show that emptiness and universality problems for such machines is tractable, and that the collection of languages recognized by simple PBAs with strict and non-strict thresholds is exactly the class of deterministic ω-regular languages.

The rest of the paper is organized as follows. Section 2 contains some preliminaries. Section 3 contains some examples motivating HPBAs. Section 4 contains the undecidability results for emptiness and universality of of PBAs and HPBAs. Section 5 contains our expressiveness results. Section 6 contains our results on simple PBAs and we conclude in Section 7. The missing proofs can be found in [5].

2   Preliminaries

We assume that the reader is familiar with arithmetical and analytical hierarchies. We also assume that the reader is familiar with Büchi automata and ω-regular languages.

The set of natural numbers will be denoted by $\mathbb{N}$, the closed unit interval by $[0,1]$ and the open unit interval by $(0,1)$. The power-set of a set X will be denoted by 2^X.

Sequences. Given a finite set S, $|S|$ denotes the cardinality of S. Given a sequence (finite or infinite) $\kappa = s_0 s_1 \ldots$ over S, $|\kappa|$ will denote the length of the sequence (for infinite sequence $|\kappa|$ will be ω), and $\kappa[i]$ will denote the ith element s_i of the sequence. As usual S^* will denote the set of all finite sequences/strings/words over S, S^+ will denote the set of all finite non-empty sequences/strings/words over S and S^ω will denote the set of all infinite sequences/strings/words over S. Given $\eta \in S^*$ and $\kappa \in S^* \cup S^\omega$, $\eta\kappa$ is the sequence obtained by concatenating the two sequences in order. Given $L_1 \subseteq \Sigma^*$ and $L_2 \subseteq \Sigma^\omega$, the set $L_1 L_2$ is defined to be $\{\eta\kappa \mid \eta \in L_1 \text{ and } \kappa \in L_2\}$. Given natural numbers $i, j \leq |\kappa|$, $\kappa[i : j]$ is the finite sequence $s_i, \ldots s_j$ and $\kappa[i : \infty]$ is the infinite sequence $s_i, s_{i+1} \ldots$, where $s_k = \kappa[k]$. The set of *finite prefixes* of κ is the set $Pref(\kappa) = \{\kappa[0, j] \mid j \in \mathbb{N}, j \leq |\kappa|\}$.

Languages of infinite words. A language L of infinite words over a finite alphabet Σ is a subset of Σ^ω. (Please note we restrict only to finite alphabets.) A language L is said to be a *safety language* if L is *prefix-closed*, i.e., if for every infinite string α, if every prefix of α is a prefix of some string in L, then α itself is in L.

Probabilistic Büchi Automaton (PBA). We recall the definition of PBA given in [2]. Informally, a PBA is like a finite-state deterministic Büchi automaton except that the transition function from a state on a given input is described as a probability distribution which determines the probability of the next state. PBAs generalize the probabilistic finite automata (PFAs) [12,13,11] on finite input strings to infinite input strings.

Definition 1. A *finite state probabilistic Büchi automata* (PBA) over a finite alphabet Σ is a tuple $\mathcal{B} = (Q, q_s, Q_f, \delta)$ where Q is a finite set of *states*, $q_s \in Q$ is the *initial state*, $Q_f \subseteq Q$ is the set of *accepting/final states*, and $\delta : Q \times \Sigma \times Q \rightarrow [0, 1]$ is the *transition relation* such that for all $q \in Q$ and $a \in \Sigma$, $\delta(q, a, q')$ is a rational number and $\sum_{q' \in Q} \delta(q, a, q') = 1$.

Notation: The transition function δ of PBA $\mathcal{B}$ on input a can be seen as a square matrix δ_a of order $|Q|$ with the rows labeled by "current" state, columns labeled by "next state" and the entry $\delta_a(q, q')$ equal to $\delta(q, a, q')$. Given a word $u = a_0 a_1 \ldots a_n \in \Sigma^+$, δ_u is the matrix product $\delta_{a_0} \delta_{a_1} \ldots \delta_{a_n}$. For an empty word $\epsilon \in \Sigma^*$ we take δ_ϵ to be the identity matrix. Finally for any $Q_0 \subseteq Q$, we say that $\delta_u(q, Q_0) = \sum_{q' \in Q_0} \delta_u(q, q')$. Given a state $q \in Q$ and a word $u \in \Sigma^+$, $\text{post}(q, u) = \{q' \mid \delta_u(q, q') > 0\}$.

Intuitively, the PBA starts in the initial state q_s and if after reading $a_0, a_1 \ldots, a_i$ results in state q, then it moves to state q' with probability $\delta_{a_{i+1}}(q, q')$ on symbol a_{i+1}. Given a word $\alpha \in \Sigma^\omega$, the PBA $\mathcal{B}$ can be thought of as an infinite state Markov chain which gives rise to the standard σ-algebra on Q^ω defined using cylinders and the standard probability measure on Markov chains [14,10]. We shall henceforth denote the σ-algebra as $\mathcal{F}_{\mathcal{B}, \alpha}$ and the probability measure as $\mu_{\mathcal{B}, \alpha}$.

A *run* of the PBA $\mathcal{B}$ is an infinite sequence $\rho \in Q^\omega$. A run ρ is *accepting* if $\rho[i] \in Q_f$ for infinitely many i. A run ρ is said to be *rejecting* if it is not accepting. The set of accepting runs and the set of rejecting runs are measurable [14]. Given a word α, the measure of the set of accepting runs is said to be the *probability of accepting* α and is henceforth denoted by $\mu_{\mathcal{B}, \alpha}^{acc}$; and the measure of the set of rejecting runs is said to be the *probability of rejecting* α and is henceforth denoted by $\mu_{\mathcal{B}, \alpha}^{rej}$.

Hierarchical PBA. Intuitively, a hierarchical PBA is a PBA such that the set of its states can be stratified into (totally) ordered levels. From a state q, for each letter a, the machine can transition with non-zero probability to at most one state in the same level as q, and all other probabilistic successors belong to a higher level.

Definition 2. Given a natural number k, a PBA $\mathcal{B} = (Q, q_s, Q, \delta)$ over an alphabet Σ is said to be a *k-level hierarchical PBA* (*k*-PBA) if there is a function $\mathsf{rk} : Q \to \{0, 1, \ldots, k\}$ such that the following holds.

Given $j \in \{0, 1, \ldots, k\}$, let $Q_j = \{q \in Q \mid \mathsf{rk}(Q) = j\}$. For every $q \in Q$ and $a \in \Sigma$, if $j_0 = \mathsf{rk}(q)$ then $\mathsf{post}(q, a) \subseteq \cup_{j_0 \leq \ell \leq k} Q_\ell$ and $|\mathsf{post}(q, a) \cap Q_{j_0}| \leq 1$.

The function rk is said to be a *compatible ranking function* of $\mathcal{B}$ and for $q \in Q$ the natural number $\mathsf{rk}(q)$ is said to be the *rank* or *level* of q. $\mathcal{B}$ is said to be a *hierarchical PBA (HPBA)* if $\mathcal{B}$ is k-hierarchical for some k.

Language recognized by a PBA. Given rational $x \in [0, 1]$ and a PBA $\mathcal{B}$ on alphabet Σ, we can define two *languages*:[1]

- $\mathcal{L}_{>x}(\mathcal{B}) = \{\alpha \in \Sigma^\omega \mid \mu_{\mathcal{B}, \alpha}^{acc} > x\}$, and
- $\mathcal{L}_{\geq x}(\mathcal{B}) = \{\alpha \in \Sigma^\omega \mid \mu_{\mathcal{B}, \alpha}^{acc} \geq x\}$.

The exact value of x is not important thanks to the following proposition.

Proposition 1. For any PBA (respectively, HPBA) $\mathcal{B}$, rational $x \in [0, 1)$ and rational $y \in (0, 1)$, there is a PBA (respectively, HPBA) $\mathcal{B}'$ constructible in polynomial time such that $\mathcal{L}_{>x}(\mathcal{B}) = \mathcal{L}_{>y}(\mathcal{B}')$. Furthermore, for any rational $r \in (0, 1]$ and rational $s \in (0, 1)$, there is a PBA (respectively, HPBA) $\mathcal{B}'$ constructible in polynomial time such that $\mathcal{L}_{\geq r}(\mathcal{B}) = \mathcal{L}_{\geq s}(\mathcal{B}')$.

This gives rise to the following classes of languages of infinite words.

Definition 3. Given a finite alphabet Σ, $\mathbb{L}(\mathrm{PBA}^{>0}) = \{L \subseteq \Sigma^\omega \mid \exists \mathrm{PBA}\ \mathcal{B}.\ L = \mathcal{L}_{>0}(\mathcal{B})\}$, $\mathbb{L}(\mathrm{PBA}^{=1}) = \{L \subseteq \Sigma^\omega \mid \exists \mathrm{PBA}\ \mathcal{B}.\ L = \mathcal{L}_{=1}(\mathcal{B})\}$, $\mathbb{L}(\mathrm{PBA}^{>\frac{1}{2}}) = \{L \subseteq \Sigma^\omega \mid \exists \mathrm{PBA}\ \mathcal{B}.\ L = \mathcal{L}_{>\frac{1}{2}}(\mathcal{B})\}$ and $\mathbb{L}(\mathrm{PBA}^{\geq \frac{1}{2}}) = \{L \subseteq \Sigma^\omega \mid \exists \mathrm{PBA}\ \mathcal{B}.\ L = \mathcal{L}_{\geq \frac{1}{2}}(\mathcal{B})\}$.

The classes $\mathbb{L}(\mathrm{PBA}^{>0})$ and $\mathbb{L}(\mathrm{PBA}^{=1})$ have been studied extensively in [2,1,9,4]. We restrict our attention here to the classes $\mathbb{L}(\mathrm{PBA}^{>\frac{1}{2}})$ and $\mathbb{L}(\mathrm{PBA}^{\geq \frac{1}{2}})$. For hierarchical PBAs we can define classes analogous to $\mathbb{L}(\mathrm{PBA}^{>0})$, $\mathbb{L}(\mathrm{PBA}^{=1})$, $\mathbb{L}(\mathrm{PBA}^{>\frac{1}{2}})$ and $\mathbb{L}(\mathrm{PBA}^{\geq \frac{1}{2}})$; and we will call them $\mathbb{L}(\mathrm{HPBA}^{>0})$, $\mathbb{L}(\mathrm{HPBA}^{=1})$, $\mathbb{L}(\mathrm{HPBA}^{>\frac{1}{2}})$ and $\mathbb{L}(\mathrm{HPBA}^{\geq \frac{1}{2}})$ respectively.

Freivalds' game. Freivalds' game is a probabilistic game first presented in [7] and later used in [6] to show that checking emptiness of a PFA with non-extremal thresholds is undecidable. The game allows one to check using finite bounded memory whether two input sequences a^i and b^j, where $i, j > 0$, are of equal length.

---

[1] One does not need to explicitly consider $\mathcal{L}_{<x}(\mathcal{B})$ and $\mathcal{L}_{\leq x}(\mathcal{B})$ since $\mathcal{L}_{<x}(\mathcal{B}) = \Sigma^\omega \setminus \mathcal{L}_{\geq x}(\mathcal{B})$ and $\mathcal{L}_{\leq x}(\mathcal{B}) = \Sigma^\omega \setminus \mathcal{L}_{>x}(\mathcal{B})$.

108   R. Chadha, A. Prasad Sistla, and M. Viswanathan

The game on input a^i, b^j is as follows. While processing a^i, (a.1) Toss $2i$ fair coins and note if all of them turned heads. (a.2) Toss a separate set of i fair coins and note if all of them turned heads. (a.3) Toss yet another set of i fair coins and note if all of them turned heads.

While processing b^j, (b.1) Toss $2j$ fair coins and note if all of them turned heads. (b.2) Toss a separate set of j fair coins and note if all of them turned heads. (b.3) Toss yet another set of j fair coins and note if all of them turned heads.

Let A be the event that either all coins in (a.1) or (b.1) turns up heads, and B be the event that either all coins in (a.2) and (b.2) turn up heads or all coins in (a.3) and (b.3) turn up heads. The outcome of the game is said to be (a) *Acc* if B happens and A does not, (b) *Rej* if A happens and B does not, (c) *AllHeads* if all the coins tosses (in (a.1),(a.2),(a.3),(b.1),(b.2), and (b.3)) all result in heads, and (d) *neither* if none of the above cases hold.[2] The following observation holds about the probability of these outcomes.

Proposition 2. $Pr(Acc) \geq Pr(AllHeads)$. If $i = j$ then $Pr(Rej) = Pr(Acc)$. If $i \neq j$, $Pr(Rej) - Pr(Acc) > 3Pr(AllHeads)$.

Remark 1. In order to play the game on input a^k, b^ℓ, we need to keep track of the following pieces of information. While processing the as we need to remember 3 bits, r_1, r_2, and r_3, where r_i records whether any of the coins tossed in $(a.i)$ resulted in tails. Then while processing the bs we need to 6 bits of information — the first 3 bits to remember the results of the experiments conducted while processing the as, and the second set of 3 bits s_1, s_2, and s_3 to remember if any of the coins tossed in $(b.i)$ resulted in tails. Thus, implementing it as a finite state machine requires $2^3 + 2^6 = 72$ states. Initially, all the bits being recorded are 0, denoting that we have not seen any tails in any of the trials. Next observe that once one of these bits (say r_i) changes to 1, it will never switch back to 0. While processing the sequence of as, we will first (possibly) change the settings for the $r_i s$ and then change the $s_i s$ when processing the bs. Thus, this game can be played using a finite state machine with a hierarchical structure, where the rank of a state, records the number of $r_i s$ that are 1 and the number of $s_i s$ that are 1, giving us 8 levels.

3   Examples

Example 1. (**Recognizing non-ω-regular languages**). Several examples of PBAs recognizing non-ω-regular languages with non-extremal thresholds have been constructed in literature [2,1,9,4,4]. Herein, we give yet another example, which exploits the Freivalds' game [7] described in Section 2.

Let $\Sigma = \{0, 1, \#\}$ and consider the language $L = \{0^n 1^n \# \alpha \mid n > 0, \alpha \in \Sigma^\omega\}$. L is a standard example of a non-ω-regular language. We will construct a PBA $\mathcal{B}$ such that $\mathcal{L}_{>\frac{1}{2}}(\mathcal{B}) = L$.

$\mathcal{B}$ is constructed as follows. It has two special absorbing states q_a and q_r. q_a is also the only accepting state of $\mathcal{B}$. $\mathcal{B}$ proceeds as follows. When the first letter is input, $\mathcal{B}$

---
[2] The original Freivalds' game only considers the outcomes *Acc* and *Rej*. However, for our purposes the outcome *AllHeads* shall prove to be useful.

checks if it is **0** or not. If the letter is not **0**, *i.e.*, it is either **1** or **#**, then $\mathcal{B}$ moves to q_r with probability 1 and thus the input is rejected with probability 1. If the input is **0**, then $\mathcal{B}$ starts playing the Freivalds' game in order to check if the rest of the input contains a finite sequence of **0**s followed by a sequence of **1**s of the same length and which is followed by **#**. As long as $\mathcal{B}$ continues seeing input **0**, $\mathcal{B}$ tosses coins according to (a.1), (a.2) and (a.3) of the Freivalds' game. If $\mathcal{B}$ encounters an input different from **0**, then it proceeds as follows. If the input is **#** then $\mathcal{B}$ transitions to q_r with probability 1. If the input is **1**, then $\mathcal{B}$ tosses coins according (b.1), (b.2) and (b.3) of the Freivalds' game as long as $\mathcal{B}$ continues seeing **1**. If $\mathcal{B}$ encounters input **0** then $\mathcal{B}$ transitions to q_r with probability 1. If $\mathcal{B}$ encounters input **#**; then the transition is defined according to result of Freivalds' game as follows.

- Freivalds' game results in event Acc: $\mathcal{B}$ transitions to q_a with probability 1.
- Freivalds' game results in event Rej: $\mathcal{B}$ transitions to q_r with probability 1.
- Freivalds' game results in event $AllHeads$: $\mathcal{B}$ transitions to q_a with probability 1.
- In all other cases, $\mathcal{B}$ transitions to q_a and q_r with probability $\frac{1}{2}$.

It is easy to see that $\mathcal{B}$ is the required PBA. Infact, observations in Remark 1 imply that $\mathcal{B}$ can be taken to be a HPBA.

Example 2. (**Multi-threaded systems and bounded context switching**). Consider a system consisting of k finite state processes. The system takes inputs and changes states. At each point, one and only one process is *active*. At each point, the system may probabilistically *context switch* making a new process *active*. Otherwise, the behavior of the system is deterministic. One may want to check that on every input, the system satisfies a property specified by a deterministic Büchi automaton with probability $\geq$ threshold value. If the system is modeled as probabilistic automata $\mathcal{A}$ and the specification by Spec, then by taking the synchronous cross-product of the automaton and specification, we can obtain a PBA $\mathcal{B}$ such that the probability of system satisfying the specification on input α is exactly the probability of $\mathcal{B}$ accepting α, thus turning the verification question into a problem of deciding universality of a PBA with a non-extremal threshold. If we bound the number of context switches, then the PBA can be taken to be a HPBA.

Remark 2. Bounding the number of context switches is a technique used to make analysis of multithreaded recursive programs tractable. Our results in [4] imply that this technique will also be useful for verification of probabilistic systems with extremal thresholds. However, our results in this paper would mean that bounding context switches might not be sufficient for non-extremal thresholds.

4 Decision Problems

Given a PBA $\mathcal{B}$, the problem of checking whether $\mathcal{L}_{>0}(\mathcal{B})$ is empty (or universal) was shown to be undecidable in [1] and was later proved to be Σ_2^0 complete in [4]. The problem of checking whether $\mathcal{L}_{=1}(\mathcal{B})$ is empty (or universal) was shown to be **PSPACE**-complete in [4] (the emptiness problem was shown to be in **EXPTIME** in [1]). All the above problems become decidable when we restrict $\mathcal{B}$ to be hierarchical.

	Emptiness	Universality
$\mathbb{L}(\text{PBA}^{>\frac{1}{2}})$	Σ_2^0-complete	$\mathbf{\Pi}_1^1$-complete
$\mathbb{L}(\text{HPBA}^{>\frac{1}{2}})$	**co-R.E.**-complete	$\mathbf{\Pi}_1^1$-complete
$\mathbb{L}(\text{PBA}^{\geq\frac{1}{2}})$	$\mathbf{\Pi}_1^1$-complete	**co-R.E.**-complete
$\mathbb{L}(\text{HPBA}^{\geq\frac{1}{2}})$	$\mathbf{\Pi}_1^1$-complete	**co-R.E.**-complete

Fig. 1. Hardness of decision problems

Although the decidability of checking whether $\mathcal{L}_{>\frac{1}{2}}(\mathcal{B})$ is empty (or universal) has not been studied explicitly in literature, undecidability of the emptiness (and universality) problems for PFAs when the acceptance threshold is $\frac{1}{2}$ implies the undecidability of checking the emptiness (and universality) of $\mathcal{L}_{>\frac{1}{2}}(\mathcal{B})$. Similarly, checking emptiness/universality of the language $\mathcal{L}_{\geq\frac{1}{2}}(\mathcal{B})$ is also undecidable. Rather surprisingly, the undecidability result continues to hold even if $\mathcal{B}$ is hierarchical. Our results on hardness of decidability are summarized in Figure 1. We begin by establishing the lower bounds.

Lemma 1. Given a hierarchical PBA $\mathcal{B}$ on alphabet Σ, the problem of checking $\mathcal{L}_{>\frac{1}{2}}(\mathcal{B}) = \emptyset$ is **co-R.E.**-hard, checking $\mathcal{L}_{>\frac{1}{2}}(\mathcal{B}) = \Sigma^\omega$ is $\mathbf{\Pi}_1^1$-hard, checking $\mathcal{L}_{\geq\frac{1}{2}}(\mathcal{B}) = \emptyset$ is $\mathbf{\Pi}_1^1$-hard and checking $\mathcal{L}_{\geq\frac{1}{2}}(\mathcal{B}) = \Sigma^\omega$ is **co-R.E.**-hard.

Proof. We prove the **co-R.E.**-hardness of checking the emptiness of $\mathcal{L}_{>\frac{1}{2}}(\mathcal{B})$. The other lower bound proofs are obtained by modifying this construction and can be found in [5].

The hardness result will reduce the halting problem of deterministic 2-counter machines to the non-emptiness problem of HPBAs with strict acceptance thresholds. We begin by outlining the broad ideas behind the construction. Let T be deterministic 2-counter machine with control states Q and a special halting state q_h. We will also assume, without loss of generality, that each transition of T changes at most one counter and the initial counter values are 0. Recall that a configuration of such a machine is of the form (q, a^{i+1}, b^{j+1}), where $q \in Q$ is the current control state, and a^i (b^j) is the unary representation of the value stored in the first counter (second counter, respectively). The input alphabet of the HPBA $\mathcal{B}_T$ that we will construct will consist of the set Q as well as 5 symbols- ",", "(", ")", a and b. The HPBA $\mathcal{B}_T$ will have the following property: if $\rho = \sigma_1\sigma_2\cdots\sigma_n$ is a halting computation of T then $\mathcal{B}$ will accept the word $\rho\sigma_n^\omega$ with probability $> \frac{1}{2}$; if $\rho = \sigma_1\sigma_2\cdots$ is a non-halting computation of T then $\mathcal{B}_T$ will accept ρ with probability $\frac{1}{2}$; and if $\rho \in \Sigma^\omega$ is an encoding of an invalid computation (i.e., if ρ is not of the right format or has incorrect transitions) and no prefix of ρ is a valid halting computation of T then $\mathcal{B}_T$ will accept ρ with probability $< \frac{1}{2}$. Given this property we will be able to conclude that T halts iff $\mathcal{L}_{>\frac{1}{2}}(\mathcal{B}_T)$ is non-empty, thus demonstrating the **co-R.E.**-hardness of the emptiness problem.

In order to construct a HPBA $\mathcal{B}_T$ with the above properties, $\mathcal{B}_T$ must be able to check if there is a finite prefix α of input $\rho \in \Sigma^\omega$ that encodes a valid halting computation of T. This requires checking the following properties. (1) α is of the right format, i.e., it is a sequence of tuples of the form (q, a^i, b^j). (2) The first configuration is the initial configuration. (3) Successive configurations in the sequence follow because of a valid transition of T. (4) In the last configuration, T is in the halting state q_h.

Observe that checking properties (1), (2) and (4) can be easily accomplished using only finite memory. On the other hand checking (3) requires checking that the counters are updated correctly which cannot be done deterministically using finite memory. Instead it will be checked using Freivalds game described in Section 2. This check will indeed be similar to the one used in the construction of Example 1, where it is used to check that every valid input must start with a number of 0s followed an equal number of 1s followed by a #. In order to check properties (1), (2), (3), and (4) above for an input ρ, $\mathcal{B}_T$ proceeds in "phases" that are informally outlined here.

- $\mathcal{B}_T$ reads the first symbol of ρ. If this first symbol is not "(", then ρ is not of the right format and so $\mathcal{B}_T$ will move to the "reject" phase. Otherwise, $\mathcal{B}_T$ will choose (probabilistically) to do one of the following: (a) Move to "check initial" phase to check if the first few symbol encode the initial configuration; (b) Move to "check transition" phase to check if the second configuration follows from the first; (c) Move to "continue" phase to ignore the first configuration and possibly check some subsequent configuration.
- *Check initial phase:* Check if the first few symbols encode the initial configuration. If they do move to "accept" phase, and if not move to "reject" phase.
- *Continue phase:* Probabilistically choose to (a) ignore input and move to accept phase; (b) ignore input and move to reject phase; (c) ignore input and stay in continue phase; or (d) if current symbol is the beginning of a configuration (i.e., "(") then move to check transition phase to check if the next two configurations correspond to a valid transition.
- *Check Transition phase:* Check if there is a prefix of the form (q_1, a^{i_1}, b^{j_1}) (q_2, a^{i_2}, b^{j_2}) and if the configurations encoded correspond to a valid transition by playing the Freivalds game. Also check if q_2 is a halting state. Based on these checks move (probabilistically) to accept phase or reject phase.
- *Accept phase:* Ignore the input as it has been deemed to be accepted.
- *Reject phase:* Ignore the input as it has been deemed to be rejected.

Observe that the above phases can be linearly ordered and so can be implemented using a hierarchical control structure. When we spell out the details of each phase, it will also be clear that each of the checks within a phase can be implemented within a hierarchical PBA. The probability with which different options are chosen within a phase will be set to ensure that on a prefix α of ρ the following properties hold: (a) if α is the prefix of a valid computation that has not yet reached the halting state, then the probability of reaching the accept phase is the same as the probability of reaching the reject phase, (b) if α is not a valid computation (and no prefix of alpha is a valid halting computation) then the probability of reaching the reject phase is greater than the probability of reaching the accept phase, and (c) if α is a valid halting computation then the probability of reaching the accept phase is greater than the probability of reaching the reject phase. Observe that these conditions will ensure the correctness of our reduction.

Having outlined the intuitions behind the reduction, we now give the details including the probability of the various transitions. From the initial state, $\mathcal{B}_T$ on input "(" will move to check initial phase with probability $\frac{2}{3}$, move to check transition phase with probability $\frac{1}{6}$ and move to continue phase with probability $\frac{1}{6}$. On all other inputs, $\mathcal{B}_T$ moves to the reject phase with probability 1 from the initial state.

Check initial phase. Observe that the check initial phase can be carried out by a deterministic finite state machine. If an error is discovered, the $\mathcal{B}_T$ moves to the reject phase with probability 1. On the other hand, if no error is found, then $\mathcal{B}_T$ moves to accept phase and reject phase with probability $\frac{1}{2}$.

Continue phase. The continue phase is implemented by a single state q_{cont}. On input symbol "(" (denoting the start of a configuration), $\mathcal{B}_T$ stays in continue phase with probability $\frac{1}{4}$, moves to accept phase with probability $\frac{1}{4}$, moves to reject phase with probability $\frac{1}{4}$, and moves to check transition phase with probability $\frac{1}{4}$. On all other input symbols, it moves to accept phase (and reject phase) with probability $\frac{15}{32}$, and stays in q_{cont} with probability $\frac{1}{16}$.

Accept and Reject phases. Since in these phases the input is ignored, the accept phase consists of a single absorbing state q_a, and the reject state consists of a single absorbing state q_r. The state q_a (for the accept phase) is the unique accepting state of the machine.

Check transition phase. This is the most interesting part of $\mathcal{B}_T$ that requires checking if there is a prefix of the remaining input of the form $(q_1, a^{i_1}, b^{j_1})(q_2, a^{i_2}, b^{j_2})$, where (q_1, a^{i_1}, b^{j_1}) and (q_2, a^{i_2}, b^{j_2}) are successive configurations of correct computational step of T. $\mathcal{B}_T$ must check for "formatting" errors and that q_2 is right next control state — these can be accomplished by a deterministic finite state machine. The difficulty is in checking that the counter values are correct. For this, $\mathcal{B}_T$ plays the Freivalds game (see Section 2) that checks if $i = j$ in an input a^i, a^j. So to check the correctness of counter values, $\mathcal{B}_T$ plays two Freivalds games; if i_2 (j_2) is supposed to be the increment of i_1 (j_1) then we play on a^{i_1+1}, a^{i_2} (b^{j_1+1}, b^{j_2}); if it follows by a decrement then the game is played on a^{i_1}, a^{i_2+1} (b^{j_1}, b^{j_2+1}) and if the counter values are unchanged then the game is played on a^{i_1}, a^{i_2} (b^{j_1}, b^{j_2}). The Freivalds game has 4 possible outcomes: *Acc*, *Rej*, *AllHeads*, and *neither*. After playing the two games, if both result in *Acc* then $\mathcal{B}_T$ moves to accept phase with probability 1, and if both result in *Rej* then move to reject phase with probability 1. If neither of the above cases hold then $\mathcal{B}_T$'s transitions depend on whether q_2 is the halting state. If q_2 is the halting state and if both games have outcome *AllHeads*, $\mathcal{B}_T$ moves to accept phase with probability 1. In all other cases, $\mathcal{B}_T$ moves to accept and reject phase with probability $\frac{1}{2}$.

From the construction of $\mathcal{B}_T$ it is easy to see that it is an HPBA. Furthermore, it is easy to see that if T has a halting computation $\sigma_1\sigma_2...\sigma_n$ then $\mathcal{B}_T$ will accept the word $\sigma_1\sigma_2...\sigma_n\sigma_n^\omega$ with probability $> \frac{1}{2}$. If T has a non-halting computation $\sigma_1\sigma....$ then the word $\sigma_1\sigma_2...$ is accepted with probability $= \frac{1}{2}$. Now the **co-R.E.**-hardness of emptiness checking follows from the observation below.

Claim. If $\alpha \in \Sigma^w$ does not represent a valid computation of T and no prefix of α is a valid halting computation then $\mathcal{B}_T$ accepts α with probability $< \frac{1}{2}$.

Proof of the claim: If α satisfies the premise of the above claim then one the following things must happen — (1) The initial configuration is not correct, (2) α has a prefix $\sigma_0\sigma_1 \ldots \sigma_n u$ where σ_i is of the form $(q, a^{\ell_i}, b^{\ell'_i})$ and u is incorrectly formatted, *i.e.* either $u = w_1)w_2$ where w_1 does not contain ")" and w_1 in not contained in the set $\{(q, a^r, b^s \mid q$ is a control state of $T, r, s \geq 1\}$ or u has a prefix w that does not contain ")" and w itself is not contained in $Pref\{(q, a^r, b^s \mid q$ is a control state of $T, r, s \geq 1\}$,

(3) α has a finite prefix $\sigma_0 \sigma_1 \ldots \sigma_n$ where σ_i is of the form $(q, a^{\ell_i}, b^{\ell'_i})$ and one of the following happens: a) control states in two consecutive configurations σ_j, σ_{j+1} are not in accordance with the transition function of T, or b) counter values in two consecutive configurations σ_j, σ_{j+1} are not in accordance with the transition function of T, (4) $\alpha \in \Sigma^* a^\omega$ or $\alpha \in \Sigma^* b^\omega$.

We consider here the most interesting case when α has a finite prefix $\sigma_0 \sigma_1 \ldots \sigma_n$ where σ_i is of the form $(q, a^{\ell_i}, b^{\ell_i})$ and the first *error* in α is that the counter values in two consecutive configurations σ_j, σ_{j+1} are not in accordance with the transition function of T. Let j_0 be the first j such that the counter values in $\sigma_{j_0}, \sigma_{j_0+1}$ are not in accordance with the transition function of T. We will assume that j_0 is > 0. The case when j_0 is 0 is similarly handled. Let σ_{j_0} be (q_1, a^{r_1}, b^{s_1}) and σ_{j_0+1} be (q_2, a^{r_2}, b^{s_2}). Consider the event $CheckBefore_{j_0}$ in which $\mathcal{B}_T$ either moves to the check initial phase or moves to the check transition phase before σ_{j_0}. Note that the probability of $\mathcal{B}_T$ accepting α given that $CheckBefore_{j_0}$ happens is exactly $\frac{1}{2}$.

Let $Check_{j_0}$ be the event that $\mathcal{B}_T$ moves to the check transition phase upon encountering σ_{j_0}, $Check_{j_0+1}$ be the event that $\mathcal{B}_T$ moves to the check transition phase on encountering σ_{j_0+1} and $CheckAfter_{j_0+1}$ be the event that $\mathcal{B}_T$ moves to the check transition phase sometime after σ_{j_0+1}. The claim follows from the following observations.

- Given the event $Check_{j_0}$ happens, the probability of $\mathcal{B}_T$ transitioning to q_r is bounded away from the probability of $\mathcal{B}_T$ transitioning to q_a by at least $\frac{2}{2^{4r_1+4s_1+4r_2+4s_2+4}}$. This follows from Proposition 2.
- Given the event $Check_{j_0+1}$ happens, the difference in probability of $\mathcal{B}_T$ transitioning to q_a and the probability of $\mathcal{B}_T$ transitioning to q_r is $\leq \frac{1}{2^{4r_2+4s_2}}$.
- This implies that given that the event $CheckBefore_{j_0}$ does not happen, the difference in the probability of $\mathcal{B}_T$ transitioning to q_r and probability of $\mathcal{B}_T$ transitioning to q_a is $> \frac{1}{4}\big(\frac{2}{2^{4r_1+4s_1+4r_1+4s_2+4}} - \frac{1}{2^{4r_1+4s_1+17}} \frac{1}{2^{4r_2+4s_2}} - \frac{1}{2^{4r_1+2^{4s_1}+2^{4r_2}+2^{4s_2}+33}} \big) > 0$.

$\sqcap$

Observe that since HPBAs are special PBAs, the lower bounds in Lemma 1 established for HPBAs apply also to general PBAs. In addition, for general PBA, the Σ_2^0-hardness of checking emptiness of $\mathcal{L}_{>0}(\mathcal{B})$ [4] coupled with Proposition 1, establishes the Σ_2^0-hardness of checking the emptiness of $\mathcal{L}_{>\frac{1}{2}}(\mathcal{B})$. The lower bounds implied by Lemma 1 and the preceding arguments in this paragraph are in fact tight. The most interesting case is the **co-R.E.** decision procedure for checking the emptiness of $\mathcal{L}_{>\frac{1}{2}}(\mathcal{B})$ for HPBAs $\mathcal{B}$, which is a consequence of the proof of the fact that for a HPBA $\mathcal{B}$, $\mathcal{L}_{>\frac{1}{2}}(\mathcal{B}) \neq \emptyset$ iff $\mathcal{L}_{>\frac{1}{2}}(\mathcal{B})$ contains an ultimately periodic word. This property is not true for general PBAs (see [1]). This property is also not true for the case $\mathcal{L}_{\geq\frac{1}{2}}(\mathcal{B})$ even if we take $\mathcal{B}$ to be hierarchical. However, we can show that if $\mathcal{L}_{\geq\frac{1}{2}}$ is not universal, then its complement $\Sigma^\omega \setminus \mathcal{L}_{\geq\frac{1}{2}}(\mathcal{B})$ must contain an ultimately periodic word (even in the case $\mathcal{B}$ is not hierarchical).

Lemma 2. If $\mathcal{B}$ is a HPBA on Σ and $\mathcal{L}_{>\frac{1}{2}}(\mathcal{B}) \neq \emptyset$ then $\mathcal{L}_{>\frac{1}{2}}(\mathcal{B})$ contains an ultimately periodic word. If $\mathcal{B}$ is a PBA (not necessarily hierarchical) on Σ and $\mathcal{L}_{\geq\frac{1}{2}}(\mathcal{B}) \neq \Sigma^\omega$ then $\Sigma^\omega \setminus \mathcal{L}_{\geq\frac{1}{2}}(\mathcal{B})$ contains an ultimately periodic word.

We are ready to establish the upper bounds of the decision problems.

Theorem 1. Given a PBA $\mathcal{B}$ on alphabet Σ,

- the problem of checking whether $\mathcal{L}_{>\frac{1}{2}}(\mathcal{B}) = \emptyset$ is Σ_2^0-complete. If $\mathcal{B}$ is hierarchical, the problem of checking whether $\mathcal{L}_{>\frac{1}{2}}(\mathcal{B}) = \emptyset$ is **co-R.E.**-complete.
- The problem of checking whether $\mathcal{L}_{>\frac{1}{2}}(\mathcal{B}) = \Sigma^\omega$ is $\mathbf{\Pi}_1^1$-complete. The problem continues to $\mathbf{\Pi}_1^1$-complete even if we restrict $\mathcal{B}$ to the class of hierarchical PBAs.
- The problem of checking whether $\mathcal{L}_{\geq\frac{1}{2}}(\mathcal{B}) = \emptyset$ is $\mathbf{\Pi}_1^1$-complete. The problem continues to $\mathbf{\Pi}_1^1$-complete even if we restrict $\mathcal{B}$ to the class of hierarchical PBAs.
- The problem of checking whether $\mathcal{L}_{\geq\frac{1}{2}}(\mathcal{B}) = \Sigma^\omega$ is **co-R.E.**-complete. The problem continues to be **co-R.E.**-complete even if we restrict $\mathcal{B}$ to the class of hierarchical PBAs.

5 Expressiveness

Language properties of classes $\mathbb{L}(\text{PBA}^{>0})$ and $\mathbb{L}(\text{PBA}^{=1})$ have been extensively studied in [1,4,9]. The main results established therein are the following.

- The class $\mathbb{L}(\text{PBA}^{=1})$ strictly contains the class of all deterministic ω-regular languages [1,9] and is a strict subset of all languages recognized by a deterministic Büchi automata (with possibly infinite states) [4]. Therefore, $\mathbb{L}(\text{PBA}^{=1})$ is not closed under complementation [1,4,9].
- The class $\mathbb{L}(\text{PBA}^{>0})$ strictly contains the class of all ω-regular languages [1,9] and is the Boolean closure of the class $\mathbb{L}(\text{PBA}^{=1})$ [4]. Boolean closure of a class of languages $\mathcal{C}$ is the smallest class of languages which contains $\mathcal{C}$ and is closed under finite unions, finite intersections and complementation. This implies that $\mathbb{L}(\text{PBA}^{>0})$ is closed under complementation, a fact that was established in [1]. Indeed, [1] shows that the complementation is recursive.

Results of [4] immediately imply that the class $\mathbb{L}(\text{PBA}^{\geq\frac{1}{2}})$ is also a subset of all languages recognized by a deterministic Büchi automata (with possibly infinite states) [4] and the containment can be shown to be strict. The classes $\mathbb{L}(\text{PBA}^{\geq\frac{1}{2}})$ and $\mathbb{L}(\text{PBA}^{>\frac{1}{2}})$ were also shown to contain strictly the classes $\mathbb{L}(\text{PBA}^{=1})$ and $\mathbb{L}(\text{PBA}^{>0})$ respectively [9]. Since $\mathbb{L}(\text{PBA}^{>\frac{1}{2}})$ contains all ω-regular languages (even those not recognized by deterministic Büchi automata), $\mathbb{L}(\text{PBA}^{>\frac{1}{2}})$ cannot be a subset of $\mathbb{L}(\text{PBA}^{\geq\frac{1}{2}})$.

The natural question that arises is whether the class $\mathbb{L}(\text{PBA}^{>\frac{1}{2}})$ is a Boolean closure of the class $\mathbb{L}(\text{PBA}^{\geq\frac{1}{2}})$. Observe that Theorem 1 already implies that if $\mathbb{L}(\text{PBA}^{>\frac{1}{2}})$ were to be closed under complementation, the complementation cannot be recursive. We will establish that $\mathbb{L}(\text{PBA}^{>\frac{1}{2}})$ is not closed under complementation thus answering the above question in the negative. Further, we will also show that the class $\mathbb{L}(\text{PBA}^{\geq\frac{1}{2}})$ is not even contained in $\mathbb{L}(\text{PBA}^{>\frac{1}{2}})$. In order to establish these results, we shall need the concept of **robust** PBAs.

Robust PBAs. In the context of probabilistic automata on finite strings (PFAs), [12] introduced the notion of isolated cutpoints. A real number x is said to be an isolated cutpoint for a PFA A if there is an ϵ such that for every finite word u, the probability of A accepting u is at least ϵ away from x. We extend this notion to PBAs.

Definition 4. A PBA, $\mathcal{B}$ on Σ, is said to be *x-robust* for some $x \in (0,1)$ if there is an $\epsilon > 0$ such that for any $\alpha \in \Sigma^\omega$, $|\mu_{\mathcal{B},\alpha}^{acc} - x| > \epsilon$.

Observe first that if $\mathcal{B}$ is x-robust then $\mathcal{L}_{>x}(\mathcal{B}) = \mathcal{L}_{\geq x}(\mathcal{B})$. It was shown in [12] that the languages recognized by robust PFAs are regular languages over finite words. We had extended this result for finite probabilistic monitors (FPMs) in [3]. A FPM is a PBA in which all states except one absorbing state, called *reject state*, are final states. We will demonstrate a similar result for PBAs and show that if $\mathcal{B}$ is x-robust and $\mathcal{L}_{>x}(\mathcal{B})$ is a safety language then $\mathcal{B}$ is ω-regular. The same result also holds if complement of $\mathcal{L}_{>x}(\mathcal{B})$ is a safety language. The proof essentially follows the proof of [12] except that it depends on the assumed topological properties of $\mathcal{L}_{>x}(\mathcal{B})$.

Proposition 3. Let $\mathcal{B}$ be x-robust for some $x \in (0,1)$. If either $\mathcal{L}_{>x}(\mathcal{B})$ a safety language or $\Sigma^\omega \setminus \mathcal{L}_{>x}(\mathcal{B})$ is a safety language, then $\mathcal{L}_{>x}(\mathcal{B})$ is ω-regular.

Lemma 3. There is a language $\mathsf{L} \in \mathbb{L}(\mathrm{PBA}^{\geq \frac{1}{2}})$ such that $\mathsf{L} \notin \mathbb{L}(\mathrm{PBA}^{>\frac{1}{2}})$. Furthermore, $\mathbb{L}(\mathrm{PBA}^{>\frac{1}{2}})$ is not closed under complementation.

Proof. Let $\Sigma = \{0, 1\}$. Let $\mathrm{num}(0)$ be the natural number 0 and $\mathrm{num}(1)$ be the natural number 1. For any word $\alpha = a_0 a_1 \ldots \in \Sigma^\omega$ let $\mathrm{bin}(\alpha)$ be the real number $\sum_{i \in \mathbb{N}, i > 0} \frac{\mathrm{num}(a_i)}{2^{i+1}}$. Let $\mathrm{wrd}(\frac{1}{\sqrt{2}})$ be the unique α such that $\mathrm{bin}(\alpha) = \frac{1}{\sqrt{2}}$. We had shown in [3] that there is a FPM $\mathcal{M}$ such that $\mathcal{L}_{\geq \frac{1}{16}}(\mathcal{M}) = \{\mathrm{wrd}(\frac{1}{\sqrt{2}})\}$ Let $\mathsf{L}_0 = \{\mathrm{wrd}(\frac{1}{\sqrt{2}})\}$. L_0 is a safety language but not ω-regular.

We claim that L_0 is not in $\mathbb{L}(\mathrm{PBA}^{>\frac{1}{2}})$. We proceed by contradiction. If there is a PBA $\mathcal{B}$ such that $\mathcal{L}_{>\frac{1}{2}}(\mathcal{B}) = \mathsf{L}_0$ then $\mu_{\mathcal{B},\mathrm{wrd}(\frac{1}{\sqrt{2}})}^{acc} > \frac{1}{2}$ and for any word $\beta \neq \mathrm{wrd}(\frac{1}{\sqrt{2}})$, $\mu_{\mathcal{B},\beta}^{acc} \leq \frac{1}{2}$. Clearly $\mathcal{B}$ is $\frac{1}{2} + \frac{\mu_{\mathcal{B},\alpha}^{acc} - \frac{1}{2}}{2}$-robust. Thus, L_0 should be ω-regular by Proposition 3 which contradicts the fact that L_0 is not ω-regular.

In order to see that $\mathbb{L}(\mathrm{PBA}^{>\frac{1}{2}})$ is not closed under complementation, consider the PBA $\mathcal{B}$ obtained from $\mathcal{M}$ by taking the reject state of the FPM $\mathcal{M}$ above as the only accept state. It is easy to see that $\mathcal{L}_{>\frac{15}{16}}(\mathcal{B})$ is the language $\Sigma^\omega \setminus \mathsf{L}_0$. But the complement of $\mathcal{L}_{>\frac{15}{16}}(\mathcal{B})$ is L_0 which as already observed above is not in $\mathbb{L}(\mathrm{PBA}^{>\frac{1}{2}})$.   □

Remark 3. Note that the FPM $\mathcal{M}$ built in the proof above to show that $\mathbb{L}(\mathrm{PBA}^{\geq \frac{1}{2}})$ is not contained in $\mathbb{L}(\mathrm{PBA}^{>\frac{1}{2}})$ is also a HPBA. Therefore, $\mathbb{L}(\mathrm{HPBA}^{\geq \frac{1}{2}}) \not\subseteq \mathbb{L}(\mathrm{HPBA}^{>\frac{1}{2}})$ and the class $\mathbb{L}(\mathrm{HPBA}^{>\frac{1}{2}})$ is also not closed under complementation.

6   Simple PBAs

Unlike the case of extremal thresholds, as the results in the previous sections demonstrate, HPBAs under non-extremal thresholds lose their "regularity" and "tractability"

properties. In this section we introduce a special class of HPBAs that we call *simple*
PBAs that have many nice tractable properties even under non-extremal thresholds.

We begin by formally defining *simple* PBAs (SPBA). A HPBA $\mathcal{B}$ is called simple if it
is a 1-level HPBA and all its accepting states are at level 0, i.e., the lowest level. Recall
that in a 1-level HPBA, the level of each state is either 0 or 1. Analogous to the class
$\mathbb{L}(\mathrm{HPBA}^{>\frac{1}{2}})$ and $\mathbb{L}(\mathrm{HPBA}^{\geq\frac{1}{2}})$, we can define the corresponding classes for simple
PBAs, namely, $\mathbb{L}(\mathrm{SPBA}^{>\frac{1}{2}})$ and $\mathbb{L}(\mathrm{SPBA}^{\geq\frac{1}{2}})$.[3]

Theorem 2. $\mathbb{L}(\mathrm{SPBA}^{>\frac{1}{2}}) = \mathbb{L}(\mathrm{SPBA}^{\geq\frac{1}{2}}) = \mathrm{DetReg}$, where DetReg is the collection
of ω-regular languages recognized by deterministic finite state Büchi automata.

Proof. Observe that every deterministic Büchi automata is a simple PBA; the language
remains the same no matter what threshold (> 0) we choose and whether we interpret
the threshold to be strict or non-strict. Thus, one direction of the above theorem is trivial.
We now prove the other direction.

Let $\mathcal{B} = (Q, q_s, Q_f, \delta)$ be a simple PBA and let $x \in (0, 1)$. For a state $q \in Q$, let
$\mathrm{rk}(q) \in \{0, 1\}$ denote the level of q.

We show that the language $\mathcal{L}_{\geq x}(\mathcal{B})$ is a deterministic ω-regular language by constructing a deterministic Büchi automaton $\mathcal{A}$ that accepts exactly $\mathcal{L}_{\geq x}(\mathcal{B})$. The construction is based upon the observation that for a finite input u, there is at most one
level 0 state q of $\mathcal{B}$ such that $\delta_u(q_s, q) > 0$. Essentially, each state of the automaton
$\mathcal{A}$ is either a pair of the form (q, y) where $y \in [x, 1]$ and q is a level 0 state of $\mathcal{B}$ (i.e.,
$\mathrm{rk}(q) = 0$), or is the error state *error*. $\mathcal{A}$ is constructed to satisfy the following properties. If u is a finite input and q is a level 0 state such that $\delta_u(q_s, q) = y$ and $y \geq x$, then
the automaton $\mathcal{A}$ goes to state (q, y) on the input u. If there is no such state q, then $\mathcal{A}$
goes to state *error* on the input u.

Now, we give a formal definition of $\mathcal{A}$. Let $X = \{\delta_a(q, q') : a \in \Sigma, 0 < \delta_a(q, q') <$
$1, \mathrm{rk}(q) = \mathrm{rk}(q') = 0\}$. Essentially, X is the set of non-zero probabilities less than 1,
associated with transitions of $\mathcal{B}$ between level 0 states. Let $Y = \{y \geq x : y =$
$1 \text{ or } y = p_1 \times p_2 \times ... \times p_m, p_1, ..., p_m \in X\}$. The set Y is finite. To see this, let
$p = \max(X)$. Note that $p < 1$. Now, let l be the maximum integer such that $p^l \geq x$.
It should be easy to see that each element in Y is a product of at most l numbers from
X and hence Y is bounded. Let $\mathcal{A} = (Q', (q_s, 1), F', \delta')$ be a deterministic Büchi
automaton where $Q' = (Q \times Y) \cup \{error\}$, $F' = Q_f \times Y$ and δ' is as given
below: $\delta' = \{((q, y), a, (q', y')) \mid a \in \Sigma, \mathrm{rk}(q) = \mathrm{rk}(q') = 0, y, y' \in Y, y' =$
$y \times \delta_a(q, q')\} \cup \{((q, y), a, error) \mid a \in \Sigma, y \in Y \text{ and there is no } q' \text{ such that } rk(q') =$
$0 \text{ and } y \times \delta_a(q, q') \in Y\} \cup \{(error, a, error) \mid a \in \Sigma\}$. It is not difficult to see that
$L(\mathcal{A}) = \mathcal{L}_{\geq x}(\mathcal{B})$. Clearly, $\mathcal{A}$ is a deterministic Büchi automaton. To show that the
language $\mathcal{L}_{>x}(\mathcal{B})$ is a deterministic ω-regular language, we simply modify the above
construction by defining Y to be all $y > x$ which are products of members of X. □

Theorem 3. Given a simple PBA $\mathcal{B}$ and rational $x \in (0, 1)$, the following problems are
all decidable in polynomial time: determining if (a) $\mathcal{L}_{>x}(\mathcal{B}) = \emptyset$, (b) $\mathcal{L}_{\geq x}(\mathcal{B}) = \emptyset$, (c)
$\mathcal{L}_{>x}(\mathcal{B}) = \Sigma^\omega$, and (d) $\mathcal{L}_{\geq x}(\mathcal{B}) = \Sigma^\omega$.

---

[3] The construction in Proposition 1 which allows one to change thresholds does not yield simple
PBAs. However, the proof of Theorem 2 allows one to switch thresholds. Theorem 3 shows
that emptiness and universality are polynomial-time decidable for every threshold value.

7 Conclusions and Further Work

In this paper, we presented a number of expressiveness and decidability results for PBAs and HPBAs when the acceptance thresholds are non-extremal. We contrasted these results with the cases when the threshold probabilities are extremal. We also considered a subclass of HPBAs, called *simple* PBAs. We showed that the class of languages accepted by them under non-extremal threshold probabilities is exactly the class of deterministic ω-regular languages.

For an HPBA $\mathcal{B}$, checking the emptiness (and universality) of $\mathcal{L}_{>\frac{1}{2}}(\mathcal{B})$ is undecidable. In contrast the same problems are decidable if $\mathcal{B}$ is a simple PBA. Simple PBAs are a special class of 1-level HPBA. It would be interesting to see if the decidability result can be extended to all 1-level HPBAs. It will also be interesting to investigate use of simple PBAs for modeling practical systems that may fail. Investigation of other interesting subclasses of PBAs and HPBAs, for which the emptiness and universality problems are decidable for non-extremal threshold probabilities, are also interesting future work.

Acknowledgements. The authors would like to thank anonymous referees for their valuable comments. A. Prasad Sistla was supported by NSF-0720525, NSF CCF-0916438, NSF CNS-1035914 and Mahesh Viswanathan was supported by NSF CCF 0448178, NSF CCF 1016989, and NSF CNS 1016791.

References

1. Baier, C., Bertrand, N., Größer, M.: On decision problems for probabilistic büchi automata. In: Amadio, R.M. (ed.) FOSSACS 2008. LNCS, vol. 4962, pp. 287–301. Springer, Heidelberg (2008)
2. Baier, C., Größer, M.: Recognizing ω-regular languages with probabilistic automata. In: Proceedings of LICS, pp. 137–146 (2005)
3. Chadha, R., Sistla, A.P., Viswanathan, M.: On the expressiveness and complexity of randomization in finite state monitors. J. of the ACM 56(5) (2009)
4. Chadha, R., Sistla, A.P., Viswanathan, M.: Power of randomization in automata on infinite strings. In: Bravetti, M., Zavattaro, G. (eds.) CONCUR 2009. LNCS, vol. 5710, pp. 229–243. Springer, Heidelberg (2009)
5. Chadha, R., Sistla, A.P., Viswanathan, M.: Probabilistic Büchi automata with non-extremal acceptance thresholds. Technical Report LSV-10-19, LSV, ENS Cachan, France (2010)
6. Condon, A., Lipton, R.J.: On the complexity of space bounded interactive proofs (extended abstract). In: Proceedings of FOCS, pp. 462–467 (1989)
7. Freivalds, R.: Probabilistic two-way machines. In: Gruska, J., Chytil, M.P. (eds.) MFCS 1981. LNCS, vol. 118, pp. 33–45. Springer, Heidelberg (1981)
8. Goldwasser, S., Micali, S.: Probabilistic encryption and how to play mental poker keeping secret all partial information. In: STOC, pp. 365–377 (1982)
9. Größer, M.: Reduction Methods for Probabilistic Model Checking. PhD thesis, TU Dresden (2008)
10. Kemeny, J., Snell, J.: Denumerable Markov Chains. Springer, Heidelberg (1976)
11. Paz, A.: Introduction to Probabilistic Automata. Academic Press, London (1971)
12. Rabin, M.O.: Probabilistic automata. Inf. and Control 6(3), 230–245 (1963)
13. Salomaa, A.: Formal Languages. Academic Press, London (1973)
14. Vardi, M.: Automatic verification of probabilistic concurrent systems. In: Proceedings of FOCS, pp. 327–338 (1985)
15. Varghese, G., Lynch, N.: A tradeoff between safety and liveness for randomized coordinated attack protocols. In: Proceedings of PODC, pp. 241–250 (1992)

Synthesis of Fault-Tolerant Embedded Systems Using Games: From Theory to Practice

Chih-Hong Cheng[1], Harald Rueß[2], Alois Knoll[1], and Christian Buckl[2]

[1] Department of Informatics, Technische Universität München
Boltzmann Str. 3, Garching D-85748, Germany
[2] Fortiss GmbH, Guerickestr. 25, D-80805 München, Germany
{chengch,knoll}@in.tum.de, {ruess,buckl}@fortiss.org

Abstract. In this paper, we present an approach for fault-tolerant synthesis by combining predefined patterns for fault-tolerance with algorithmic game solving. A non-fault-tolerant system, together with the relevant fault hypothesis and fault-tolerant mechanism templates in a pool are translated into a distributed game, and we perform an incomplete search of strategies to cope with undecidability. The result of the game is translated back to executable code concretizing fault-tolerant mechanisms using constraint solving. The overall approach is implemented to a prototype tool chain and is illustrated using examples.

1 Introduction

Given a distributed straight-line program with hard real-time constraints together with a fault model we are considering the problem of synthesizing a corresponding program that tolerates the specified faults. Solving this problem is challenging as it involves complexities along several dimensions arising from interleaving, timing constraints, and non-deterministic fault appearance. In fact, already the synthesis of (untimed) distributed systems is undecidable in general.

In a first step we augment the problem description with pre-defined fault tolerance patterns such as fail-resend or voting mechanisms in order to guide synthesis. Thus our synthesis method emphasizes automated selection and instantiation of predefined FT patterns, and it includes synthesis of tedious and error-prone implementation details such as timing constraints. Given such a problem statement including a distributed program, a fault hypothesis, and a finite set of FT patterns, we translate the problem into a corresponding distributed game [10].

Solving distributed games is undecidable in general [10]. As we are mainly interested in synthesizing embedded programs with bounded resources, it is natural to restrict ourselves to the problem of searching for, say, positional strategies. It turns out that the problem of finding a positional strategy of a distributed game (for control) is NP-Complete. This result motivates our approach of translating the problem of finding positional strategies of distributed games into a corresponding SAT problem.

The final step in our synthesis approach is to transform these strategies such obtained to a executable problem. The main problem here is that these strategies only incorporate restrictions on the partial order of executions but they may not obey the given timing

R. Jhala and D. Schmidt (Eds.): VMCAI 2011, LNCS 6538, pp. 118–133, 2011.

requirements. Based on our modeling framework, this problem is translated to a linear constraint system.

Due to lack of space we do not include complete algorithms and proofs; these can be found in [4].

2 Motivating Scenario

2.1 Adding FT Mechanisms to Resist Message Loss

We give a motivating scenario in embedded systems to facilitate our mathematical definitions. The simple system described in Figure 1 contains two *processes* $\mathcal{A}$, $\mathcal{B}$ and one bidirectional *network* $\mathcal{N}$. Processes $\mathcal{A}$ and $\mathcal{B}$ start executing sequential actions together with a looping period of $100ms$. In each period, $\mathcal{A}$ first reads an input using a sensor to variable m, followed by sending the result to the network $\mathcal{N}$ using the action MsgSend(m), and outputing the value (e.g., to a log).

In process $\mathcal{A}$, for the action MsgSend(m), a message containing value of m is forwarded to $\mathcal{N}$, and $\mathcal{N}$ broadcasts the value to all other processes which contain a variable named m, and set the variable m_v in $\mathcal{B}$ as $\top$ (indicating that the content is valid). However, $\mathcal{A}$ is unaware whether the message has been sent successfully: the network component $\mathcal{N}$ is unreliable, which has a faulty behavior of *message loss*. The fault type and the frequency of the faulty behavior are specified in the *fault model*: in this example for every complete period ($100ms$), at most one message loss can occur.

In $\mathcal{B}$, its first action RecvMsg(m) has a property describing an interval $[60, 100)$, which specifies the *release time* and *deadline* of this action to be $60ms$ and $100ms$, respectively. By posing the release time and the deadline, in this example, $\mathcal{B}$ can finalize its decision whether it has received the message m successfully using the equality constraint ($m_v = \perp$), provided that the time interval $[40, 60)$ between (a) deadline of MsgSend(m) and (b) release time of RecvMsg(m) overestimates the *worst case transmission time* for a message to travel from $\mathcal{A}$ to $\mathcal{B}$. After RecvMsg(m), it outputs the received value (e.g., to an actuator).

Due to the unreliable network, it is easy to observe that two output values may not be the same. Thus the *fault-tolerant synthesis* problem in this example is to perform suitable modification on $\mathcal{A}$ and $\mathcal{B}$, such that two output values from $\mathcal{A}$ and $\mathcal{B}$ are the same at the end of the period, regardless of the disturbance from the network.

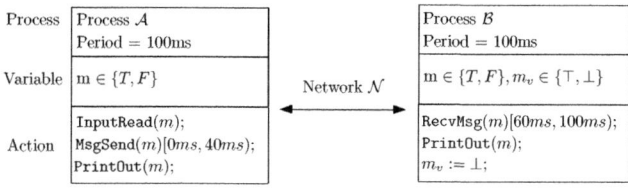

Process	Process $\mathcal{A}$ Period = 100ms		Process $\mathcal{B}$ Period = 100ms
Variable	$m \in \{T, F\}$	Network $\mathcal{N}$	$m \in \{T, F\}, m_v \in \{\top, \perp\}$
Action	InputRead(m); MsgSend(m)[$0ms, 40ms$); PrintOut(m);		RecvMsg(m)[$60ms, 100ms$); PrintOut(m); $m_v := \perp$;

Fig. 1. An example for two processes communicating over an unreliable network

2.2   Solving Fault-Tolerant Synthesis by Instrumenting Primitives

To perform FT synthesis in the example above, our method is to introduce several slots (the size of slots are fixed by the designer) between actions originally specified in the system. For each slot, an atomic operation can be instrumented, and these actions are among the pool of predefined *fault-tolerant primitives*, consisting of message sending, message receiving, local variable modifications, or null-ops. Under this setting we have created a game, as the original transitions in the fault-intolerant system combined with all FT primitives available constitute the controller (player-0) moves, and the triggering of faults and the networking can be modeled as environment (player-1) moves.

3   System Modeling

3.1   Platform Independent System Execution Model

We first define the execution model where timing information is included; it is used for specifying embedded systems and is linked to our code-generation framework. In the definition, for ease of understanding we also give each term intuitive explanations.

Definition 1. *Define the syntax of the **Platform-Independent System Execution Model** (PISEM) be $\mathcal{S} = (\mathcal{A}, \mathcal{N}, \mathcal{T})$.*

- $\mathcal{T} \in \mathbb{Q}$ *is the replication period of the system.*
- $\mathcal{A} = \bigcup_{i=1...n_A} \mathcal{A}_i$ *is the set of processes, where in $\mathcal{A}_i = (V_i \cup V_{env_i}, \overline{\sigma_i})$,*
  - V_i *is the set of variables, and V_{env_i} is the set of environment variables. For simplicity assume that V_i and V_{env_i} are of integer domain.*
  - $\overline{\sigma_i} := \sigma_1[\alpha_1, \beta_1); \ldots; \sigma_j[\alpha_j, \beta_j); \ldots; \sigma_{k_i}[\alpha_{k_i}, \beta_{k_i})$ *is a sequence of actions.*
    - $\sigma_j := \text{send}(pre, index, n, s, d, v, c) \mid a \leftarrow e \mid \text{receive}(pre, c)$ *is an atomic action (action pattern), where $a, c \in V_i$, e is function from $V_{env_i} \cup V_i$ to V_i (this includes null-op), pre is a conjunction of over equalities/inequalities of variables, $s, d \in \{1, \ldots, n_A\}$ represents the source and destination, $v \in V_d$ is the variable which is expected to be updated in process d, $n \in \{1, \ldots, n_N\}$ is the network used for sending, and $index \in \{1, \ldots, size_n\}$ is the index of the message used in the network.*
    - $[\alpha_j, \beta_j)$ *is the execution interval, where $\alpha_j \in \mathbb{Q}$ is the release time and $\beta_j \in \mathbb{Q}$ is the deadline.*
- $\mathcal{N} = \bigcup_{i=1...n_N} \mathcal{N}_i, \mathcal{N}_i = (\mathcal{T}_i, size_i)$ *is the set of network.*
  - $\mathcal{T}_i : \mathbb{N} \to \mathbb{Q}$ *is a function which maps the index (or priority) of a message to the worst case transmission time.*
  - $size_i$ *is the number of messages used in $\mathcal{N}_i$.*

[Example] Based on the above definitions, the system under execution in section 2.1 can be easily modeled by PISEM: let $\mathcal{A}$, $\mathcal{B}$, and $\mathcal{N}$ in section 2.1 be renamed in a PISEM as $\mathcal{A}_1$, $\mathcal{A}_2$, and $\mathcal{N}_1$. For simplicity, we use $\mathcal{A}.j$ to represent the variable j in process $\mathcal{A}$, assume that the network transmission time is 0, and let v_{env} contain only one variable v in $\mathcal{A}_1$. Then in the modeled PISEM, we have $\mathcal{N}_1 = (f : \mathbb{N} \to 0, 1)$, $\mathcal{T} = 100$, and the action sequence of process $\mathcal{A}_1$ is

$$m \leftarrow \text{InputRead}(v)[0, 40); \text{send}(true, 1, 1, 1, 2, m, \mathcal{A}_1.m)[0, 40); v \leftarrow \text{PrintOut}(m)[40, 100);$$

For convenience, we use $|\overline{\sigma}_i|$ to represent the length of the action sequence $\overline{\sigma}_i$, σ_j. *deadline* to represent the deadline of σ_j, and $iSet(\overline{\sigma}_i)$ to represent a set containing (a) the set of subscript numbers in $\overline{\sigma}_i$ and (b) $|\overline{\sigma}_i| + 1$, i.e., $\{1, \ldots, k_i, k_i + 1\}$.

Definition 2. *The configuration of S is* $(\bigwedge_{i=1 \ldots n_A}(v_i, v_{env_i}, \Delta_{next_i}), \bigwedge_{j=1 \ldots n_N}(occu_j,$ $s_j, d_j, var_j, c_j, t_j, ind_j), t)$, *where v_i is the set of the current values for the variable set V_i, v_{env_i} is the set of the current values for the variable set V_{env_i}, $\Delta_{next_i} \in [1, |\overline{\sigma}_i| + 1]$ is the next atomic action index taken in $\overline{\sigma}_i$[1], $occu_j \in \{\texttt{false}, \texttt{true}\}$ is for indicating whether the network is busy, $s_j, d_j \in \{1, \ldots, n_A\}$, $var_j \in \bigcup_{i=1,\ldots,n_A}(V_i \cup V_{env_i})$, $c_j \in \mathbb{Z}$ is the content of the message, $ind_j \in \{1, \ldots, size_j\}$ is the index of the message occupied in the network, t_j is the reading of the clock used to estimate the time required for transmission, t is the current reading of the global clock.*

The change of configuration is caused by the following operations.

1. (*Execute local action*) For machine i, let s and j be the current configuration for var and Δ_{next_i}, and v_i, v_{env_i} are current values of V_i and V_{env_i}. If $j = |\overline{\sigma}_i| + 1$ then do nothing (all actions in $\overline{\sigma}_i$ have been executed in this cycle); else the action $\sigma_j := var \leftarrow \texttt{e}[\alpha_j, \beta_j)$ updates var from s to $\texttt{e}(v_i, v_{env_i})$, and changes Δ_{next_i} to $min\{x|x \in iSet(\overline{\sigma}_i), x > j\}$. This action should be executed between the time interval $t \in [\alpha_j, \beta_j)$.
2. (*Send to network*) For machine i, let s and j be the current configuration for var and Δ_{next_i}. If $j = |\overline{\sigma}_i| + 1$ then do nothing; else the action $\sigma_j := \texttt{send}(pre, index, n, s, d, v, c)[\alpha_j, \beta_j)$ should be processed between the time interval $t \in [\alpha_j, \beta_j)$, and changes Δ_{next_i} to $min\{x|x \in iSet(\overline{\sigma}_i), x > j\}$.
   - When pre is evaluated to true (it can be viewed as an $\texttt{if}$ statement), it then checks the condition $occu_n = false$: if the condition holds, it updates network n with value $(occu_n, s_n, d_n, var_n, c_n, t_n, ind_n) := (true, i, d, v, c, 0, index)$. Otherwise it blocks until the condition holds.
   - When pre is evaluated to false, it skips the sending.
3. (*Process message*) For network j, for configuration $(occu_j, s_j, d_j, var, c_j, t_j, ind_j)$ if $occu_j = true$, then during $t_j < T_j(ind_j)$, a transmission occurs, which updates $occu_j$ to $\texttt{false}$, $A_{d_j}.var$ to c_j, and $A_{d_j}.var_v$ to $\texttt{true}$.
4. (*Receive*) For machine i, let s and j be the current configuration for c and Δ_{next_i}. If $j = |\overline{\sigma}_i| + 1$ then do nothing; else for $\texttt{receive}(pre, c)[\alpha_j, \beta_j)$ in machine i, it is processed between the time interval $t \in [\alpha_j, \beta_j)$ and changes Δ_{next_i} to $min\{x|x \in iSet(\overline{\sigma}_i), x > j\}$[2].
5. (*Repeat Cycle*) When $t = T$, t is reset to 0, and for all $x \in \{1, \ldots, n_A\}$, Δ_{next_x} are reset to 1.

Notice that by using this model to represent the embedded system under analysis, we make the following assumptions:

---

[1] Here an interval $[1, |\overline{\sigma}_i| + 1]$ is used for the introduction of FT mechanisms described later.

[2] In our formulation, the $\texttt{receive}(pre, c)$ action can be viewed as a syntactic sugar of $\texttt{null-op}$; its purpose is to facilitate the matching of send-receive pair with variable c.

– *All processes and networks in S share a globally synchronized clock.*
– For all actions σ, $\sigma.deadline < \mathcal{T}$; for all send actions $\sigma := \mathsf{send}(pre, index, n,$
  $s, d, v, c)$, $\sigma.deadline + \mathcal{T}_n(index) < \mathcal{T}$, i.e., all processes and networks should
  finish its work within one complete cycle.

3.2   Interleaving Model (IM)

Next, we establish the idea of interleaving model (IM) which is used to offer an intermediate representation to bridge PISEM and game solving, such that (a) it captures the
execution semantics of PISEM without explicit statements of timing, and (b) by using
this model it is easier to connect to the standard representation of games.

Definition 3. *Define the syntax of the **Interleaving Model (IM)** be $S_{IM} = (A, N)$.*
- $A = \bigcup_{i=1...n_A} A_i$ *is the set of processes, where in* $A_i = (V_i \cup V_{env_i}, \overline{\sigma_i})$,
  – V_i *is the set of variables, and* V_{env_i} *is the set of environment variables.*
  – $\overline{\sigma_i} := \sigma_1[\wedge_{m=1...n_A}[pc_{1,m_{low}}, pc_{1,m_{up}}]]; \ldots; \sigma_j[\wedge_{m=1...n_A}[pc_{j,m_{low}}, pc_{j,m_{up}}]];$
    $\ldots; \sigma_{k_i}[\wedge_{m=1...n_A}[pc_{k_i,m_{low}}, pc_{k_i,m_{up}}]]$ *is a fixed sequence of actions.*
    - $\sigma_j := \mathsf{send}(pre, index, n, s, d, v, c) \mid \mathsf{receive}(pre, c) \mid a \leftarrow e$ *is an*
      action, where a, c, e, pre, v, n, s, d *are defined similarly as in PISEM.*
    - *For* $\sigma_j, \forall m \in \{1, \ldots, n_A\}$, $pc_{j,m_{low}}, pc_{j,m_{up}} \in \{1, \ldots, |\overline{\sigma_m}| + 2\}$ *is the*
      lower and the upper bound (PC-precondition interval) concerning
      1. precondition of program counter in machine k, when $m \neq i$.
      2. precondition of program counter for itself, when $m = i$.
- $N = \bigcup_{i=1...n_N} N_i$, $N_i = (\mathcal{T}_i, size_i)$ *is the set of network.*
  – $\mathcal{T}_i : \mathbb{N} \to \wedge_{m=1...n_A} (\{1, \ldots, |\overline{\sigma_m}|+2\}, \{1, \ldots, |\overline{\sigma_m}|+2\})$ *is a function which*
    maps the index (or priority) of a message to the PC-precondition interval of
    other processes.
  – $size_i$ *is the number of messages used in* $\mathcal{N}_i$.

Definition 4. *The configuration of S_{IM} is* $(\wedge_i(v_i, v_{env_i}, \Delta_{next_i}), \wedge_j(occu_j, s_j, d_j, c_j))$,
where $v_i, v_{env_i}, \Delta_{next_i}, occu_j, s_j, d_j, c_j$ *are defined similarly as in PISEM.*

The change of configurations in IM can be interpreted analogously to PISEM; we omit
details here but mention three differences:

- For an action σ_j having the precondition $[\wedge_{m=1...n_A}[pc_{j,m_{low}}, pc_{j,m_{up}}]]$, it should
  be executed between $pc_{j,m_{low}} \leq \Delta_{next_m} < pc_{j,m_{up}}$, for all m.
- For processing a message, constraints concerning the timing of transmission in
  PISEM are replaced by referencing the PC-precondition interval of other processes
  in IM, similar to 1.
- The system repeats the cycle when $\forall x \in \{1, \ldots, n_A\}$, $\Delta_{next_x} = |\overline{\sigma_x}| + 1$ and
  $\forall x \in \{1, \ldots, n_N\}$, $occu_x = \mathsf{false}$.

3.3   Games

For the proof of complexity results, we use similar notations in [10] to define a distributed game, which are games formulating multiple processes with no interactions
among themselves but only with the environment. For details we refer readers to [10,4].

A *local game graph* is a directed graph $G = (V_0 \uplus V_1, E)$ whose nodes are partitioned into two classes V_0 (player-0 or control) and V_1 (player-1 or environment), and E is the set of edges. A *distributed game graph* $\mathcal{G} := (\mathcal{V}_0 \uplus \mathcal{V}_1, \mathcal{E})$ can be viewed as a combination of n local games $G_1, \ldots, G_n$: during the execution player-1 can execute a global move (the translation is explicitly specified but does not need to respect the local game graph), while player-0 executes a move for all local games i which is in the player-0 vertex using his strategy f_i from his strategy set $\langle f_1, \ldots, f_n \rangle$. Notice that f_i is local, i.e., it is insensitive of contents in other subgames G_j, for all $j \neq i$.

4 Step A: Front-End Translation from Models to Games

4.1 Step A.1: From PISEM to IM

To translate from PISEM to IM, the key is to generate abstractions from the release time and the deadline information specified in PISEM. As in our formulation, the system is equipped with a globally synchronized clock, the execution of actions respecting the release time and the deadline can be translated into a partial order. Algorithm 1 concretizes this idea[3].

Starting from the initialization where no PC is constrained, the algorithm performs a restriction process using four if-statements $\{(1), (2), (3), (4)\}$ listed.

- In (1), if $\sigma_m.releaseTime > \sigma_n.deadline$, then before σ_m is executed, σ_n should have been executed.
- In (2), if $\sigma_m.deadline < \sigma_n.releaseTime$, then σ_n should not be executed before executing σ_m.
- Similar analysis is done with (3) and (4). However, we need to consider the combined effect together with the network transmission time: we use 0 to represent the best case, and $\mathcal{T}_n(ind)$ for the worst case.

[Example] For the example in sec. 2, consider the action $\sigma_1 = m \leftarrow \texttt{InputRead}(v)[0, 40)$ in $\mathcal{A}_1$ of a PISEM. Algorithm 1 returns $mapLB(\sigma)$ and $mapUB(\sigma)$ with two arrays $[1, 1]$ and $[2, 2]$, indicated in Figure 2a. Based on the definition of IM, σ_1 should be executed with the temporal precondition that no action in $\mathcal{A}_2$ is executed, satisfying the semantics originally specified in PISEM. For the analysis of message sending time, two cases are listed in Figure 2b and Figure 2c, where the WCMTT is estimated as 15ms and 30ms, respectively.

4.2 Step A.2: From IM to Distributed Game

Here we give main concepts how a game is created after step A.1 is executed. To create a distributed game from a given interleaving model $S_{IM} = (A, N)$, we need to proceed with the following three steps:

---

[3] Here we assume that in each period, for all $\mathcal{N}_j$, each message of type $ind \in \{1, \ldots, size_j\}$ is sent at most once. In this way, the algorithm can assign an unique PC-precondition interval for every message type.

Algorithm 1. GeneratePreconditionPC

Data: PISEM model $\mathcal{S} = (\mathcal{A}, \mathcal{N}, \mathcal{T})$
Result: Two maps $mapLB, mapUB$ which map from an action σ (or a msg processing
        by network) to two integer arrays $lower[1 \ldots n_A], upper[1 \ldots n_A]$
begin

    /* Initial the map for recording the lower and upper bound for action */
    for *action σ_k in $\mathcal{A}_i$ of $\mathcal{A}$* **do**
        $mapLB.put(\sigma_k, \textbf{new int}[1 \ldots n_A](1))$ /* Initialize to 1 */
        $mapUB.put(\sigma_k, \textbf{new int}[1 \ldots n_A])$
        for $\mathcal{A}_j \in \mathcal{A}$ **do** $mapUB.get(\sigma_k)[j] := |\overline{\sigma_j}| + 2$ /* Initialize to upperbound */
        $mapLB.get(\sigma_k)[i] = k; mapUB.get(\sigma)[i] = k+1;$ /* self PC */

    for *action σ_m in $\mathcal{A}_i$ of $\mathcal{A}, m = 1, \ldots, |\overline{\sigma_i}|$* **do**
        for *action σ_n in $\mathcal{A}_j$ of $\mathcal{A}, n = 1, \ldots, |\overline{\sigma_j}|, j \neq i$* **do**
1   **if** $\sigma_m.releaseTime > \sigma_n.deadline$ **then**
               $mapLB.get(\sigma_m)[j] := \max\{mapLB.get(\sigma_m)[j], n+1\}$
2   **if** $\sigma_m.deadline < \sigma_n.releaseTime$ **then**
               $mapUB.get(\sigma_m)[j] := \min\{mapUB.get(\sigma_m)[j], n+1\};$

    /* Initialize the map for recording the lower and upper bound for msg transmission */
    for *action $\sigma_k = send(pre, ind, n, s, d, v, c)$ in $\mathcal{A}_i$ of $\mathcal{A}$* **do**
        $mapLB.put(n.ind, \textbf{new int}[1 \ldots n_A](1))$ /* Initialize to 1 */
        $mapLB.get(n.ind)[i] := k+1$ /* Strictly later than executing send() */
        $mapUB.put(n.ind, \textbf{new int}[1 \ldots n_A])$
        for $\mathcal{A}_j \in \mathcal{A}$ **do** $mapUB.get(n.ind)[j] := |\overline{\sigma_j}| + 2$ /* Initialize to upperbound */

    for *action $\sigma_k = send(pre, ind, n, s, d, v, c)$ in $\mathcal{A}_i$ of $\mathcal{A}$* **do**
        for *action σ_m in $\mathcal{A}_j$ of $\mathcal{A}, n = 1, \ldots, |\overline{\sigma_j}|$* **do**
3   **if** $\sigma_k.releaseTime + 0 > \sigma_m.deadline$ **then**
               $mapLB.get(n.ind)[j] := \max\{mapLB.get(n.ind)[j], m+1\}$
4   **if** $\sigma_k.deadline + \mathcal{T}_n(ind) < \sigma_m.releaseTime$ **then**
               $mapUB.get(n.ind)[j] := \min\{mapUB.get(n.ind)[j], m+1\};$

end

Step A.2.1: Creating non-deterministic timing choices for existing actions. During the translation from a PISEM $\mathcal{S} = (\mathcal{A}, \mathcal{N}, \mathcal{T})$ to its corresponding IM $\mathcal{S}_{IM} = (A, N)$, for all process $\mathcal{A}_i$ in $\mathcal{A}$, for every action $\sigma[\alpha, \beta]$ where $\sigma[\alpha, \beta] \in \overline{\sigma_i}$, algorithm 1 creates the PC-precondition interval $[\wedge_{m=1 \ldots n_A}[pc_{m_{low}}, pc_{m_{up}}]]$ of other processes. Thus in the corresponding game, for $\sigma[\wedge_{m=1 \ldots n_A}[pc_{m_{low}}, pc_{m_{up}}]]$, each element $\sigma[\wedge_{m=1 \ldots n_A}(pc_m)]$, where $pc_{m_{low}} \leq pc_m < pc_{m_{up}}$, is a nondeterministic transition choice which can be selected separately by the game engine.

Step A.2.2: Introducing fault-tolerant choices as $\sigma_{\frac{a}{b}}$. In our framework, fault-tolerant mechanisms are similar to actions, which consist of two parts: *action pattern* σ and *timing precondition* $[\wedge_{m=1 \ldots n_A}[pc_{m_{low}}, pc_{m_{up}}]]$. Compared to existing actions where nondeterminism comes from timing choices, for fault-tolerance transition choices include all combinations from (1) timing precondition and (2) action patterns available from a predefined pool.

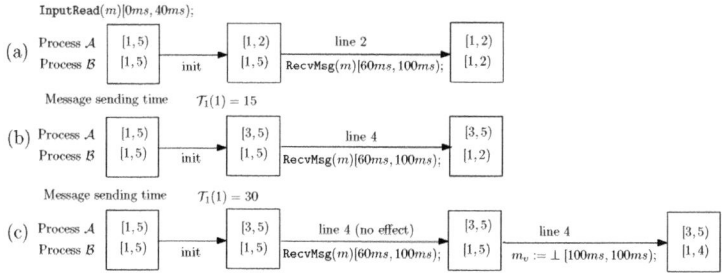

Fig. 2. An illustration for Algorithm 1

Algorithm 2. DecideInsertedFTTemplateTiming

Data: $\sigma_c[\wedge_{m=1...n_A}[pc_{c,m_{low}}, pc_{c,m_{up}}]]$, $\sigma_d[\wedge_{m=1...n_A}[pc_{d,m_{low}}, pc_{d,m_{up}}]]$, which are consecutive actions in $\overline{\sigma_i}$ of A_i of $S_{IM} = (A, N)$, and one newly added action pattern $\sigma_{\frac{a}{b}}$ to be inserted between

Result: Temporal preconditions for action pattern $\sigma_{\frac{a}{b}}$: $[\wedge_{m=1...n_A}[pc_{\frac{a}{b},m_{low}}, pc_{\frac{a}{b},m_{up}}]]$

begin

    for $m = 1, \ldots, n_A$ **do**

        if $m \neq i$ **then**

            $pc_{\frac{a}{b},m_{low}} := pc_{c,m_{low}}$ /* Use the lower bound of c for its lower bound */

            $pc_{\frac{a}{b},m_{up}} := pc_{d,m_{up}}$ /* Use the upper bound of d for its upper bound */

        else

            $pc_{\frac{a}{b},m_{low}} := \frac{a}{b}; pc_{\frac{a}{b},m_{up}} := d$

end

We use the notation $\sigma_{\frac{a}{b}}$, where $\frac{a}{b} \subset \mathbb{Q}\backslash\mathbb{N}$, to represent an inserted action pattern between $\sigma_{\lfloor \frac{a}{b} \rfloor}$ and $\sigma_{\lceil \frac{a}{b} \rceil}$. With this formulation, multiple FT mechanisms can be inserted within two consecutive actions σ_i, σ_{i+1} originally in the system, and the execution semantic follows what has been defined previously: as executing an action updates Δ_{next_i} to $min\{x|x \in iSet(\overline{\sigma_i}), x > j\}$, updating to a rational value is possible. Note that as $\sigma_{\frac{a}{b}}$ is only a fragment without temporal preconditions, we use algorithm 2 to generate all possible temporal preconditions satisfying the semantics of the original interleaving model: after the synthesis only temporal conditions satisfying the acceptance condition will be chosen.

Step A.2.3: Game Creation by Introducing Faults. In our implementation, we do not generate the primitive form of distributed games (DG), as the definition of DG is too primitive to manipulate. Instead, algorithms in our implementations are based on the variant called **symbolic distributed games (SDG)**:

Definition 5. *Define a symbolic distributed game* $\mathcal{G}_{ABS} = (V_f \uplus V_{CTR} \uplus V_{ENV}, A, N, \sigma_f, pred)$.

- V_f, V_{CTR}, V_{ENV} *are disjoint sets of (fault, control, environment) variables.*
- $pred : V_f \times V_{CTR} \times V_{ENV} \rightarrow \{\texttt{true}, \texttt{false}\}$ *is the partition condition.*

	DG	SDG
State space	product of all vertices in local games	product of all variables (including variables used in local games)
Vertex partition (V_0 and V_1)	explicit partition	use $pred$ to perform partition
Player-0 transitions	defined in local games	defined in $\overline{\sigma_i}$ of A_i, for all $i \in \{1, \ldots, n_A\}$
Player-1 transitions	explicitly specified in the global game	defined in N and σ_f

Fig. 3. Comparison between DG and SDG

- $A = \bigcup_{i=1 \ldots n_A} A_i$ is the set of **symbolic local games (processes)**, where in $A_i = (V_i \cup V_{env_i}, \overline{\sigma_i})$,
  - V_i is the set of variables, and $V_{env_i} \subseteq V_{ENV}$.
  - $\overline{\sigma_i} := \bigcup \sigma_{i_1} \langle \wedge_{m=1, \ldots, n_A} pc_{i_{1_m}} \rangle; \ldots; \bigcup \sigma_{i_k} \langle \wedge_{m=1, \ldots, n_A} pc_{i_{k_m}} \rangle$ is a sequence, where $\forall j = 1, \ldots, k$, $\bigcup \sigma_{i_j} \langle \wedge_{m=1, \ldots, n_A} pc_{i_{j_m}} \rangle$ is a set of choice actions for player-0 in A_i.
    - σ_{i_j} is defined similarly as in IM.
    - $\forall m = \{1, \ldots, n_A\}, pc_{i_{j_m}} \in [pc_{i_j, m_{low}}, pc_{i_j, m_{up}}), pc_{i_j, m_{low}}, pc_{i_j, m_{up}} \in iSet(\overline{\sigma_m})$.
  - $V_{CTR} = \bigcup_{i=1 \ldots n_A} V_i$.
- $N = \bigcup_{i=1 \ldots n_N} N_i$, $N_i = (T_i, size_i, tran_i)$ is the set of network processes.
  - T_i and $size_i$ are defined similarly as in IM.
  - $tran_i : V_f \times \{\text{true}, \text{false}\} \times \{1, \ldots, n_A\}^2 \times \bigcup_{i=1, \ldots, n_A} (V_i \cup V_{env_i}) \times \mathbb{Z} \times \{1, \ldots, size_i\} \to V_f \times \{\text{true}, \text{false}\} \times \{1, \ldots, n_A\}^2 \times \bigcup_{i=1, \ldots, n_A} (V_i \cup V_{env_i}) \times \mathbb{Z} \times \{1, \ldots, size_i\}$ is the network transition relation for processing messages (see sec. 3.1 for meaning), but can be influenced by variables in V_f.
- $\sigma_f : V_f \times V_{CTR} \times V_{ENV} \times \bigwedge_{i=1 \ldots n_A} iSet(\overline{\sigma_i}) \to V_{ENV} \times V_f \times \bigwedge_{i=1 \ldots n_A} iSet(\overline{\sigma_i})$ is the environment update relation.

We establish an analogy between SDG and DG using Figure 3.

1. The configuration v of a SDG is defined as the product of all variables used.
2. A play for a SDG starting from state v_0 is a maximal path $\pi = v_0 v_1 \ldots$, where
   - In v_k, player-1 determines the move $(v_k, v_{k+1}) \in E$ when $pred(v_k)$ is evaluated to true (false for player-0); the partition of vertices V_0 and V_1 in SDG is implicitly defined based on this, rather than specified explicitly as in DG.
   - A move (v_k, v_{k+1}) is a selection of executable transitions defined in N, σ_f, or A; in our formulation, transitions in N and σ_f are all environment moves[4], while transitions in A are control moves[5].
3. Lastly, a distributed positional strategy for player-0 in a SDG can be defined analogously as to uniquely select an action from the set $\bigcup \sigma_{\alpha_j} \langle \wedge_{m=1, \ldots, n_A}, pc_{\alpha_{j_m}} \rangle$, for all A_i and for all program counter j defined in $\overline{\sigma_i}$. Each strategy should be insensitive of contents in other symbolic local games.

---

[4] As the definition of distributed games features multiple processes having no interactions among themselves but only with the environment, a SDG is also a distributed game. In the following section, our proof of results and algorithms are all based on DG.

[5] This constraint can be released such that transitions in A can either be control (normal) or environment (induced by faults) moves; here we leave the formulation as future work.

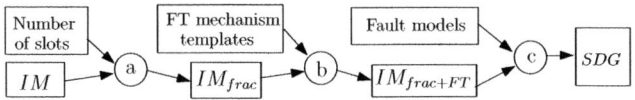

Fig. 4. Creating the SDG from IM, FT mechanisms, and faults

We now summarize the logical flow of game creation using Figure 4.

- (a) Based on the fixed number of slots (for FT mechanisms) specified by the user, extend IM to IM_{frac} to contain fractional PC-values induced by the slot.
- (b) Create $IM_{frac+FT}$, including the sequence of choice actions (for the SDG) by
  - Extracting action sequences defined in IM_{frac} to choices (step A.2.1).
  - Inserting FT choices (step A.2.2).
- (c) Introduce faults and partition player-0 and player-1 vertices: In engineering, a *fault model* specifies potential undesired behavior of a piece of equipment, such that engineers can predict the consequences of system behavior. Thus, a *fault* can be formulated with three tuples: (1) the fault type (an unique identifier, e.g., MsgLoss, SensorError), (2) the maximum number of occurrences in each period, and (3) additional transitions not included in the original specification of the system (*fault effects*). We perform the translation into a game using the following steps.
  - For (1), introduce variables to control the triggering of faults.
  - For (2), introduce counters to constrain the maximum number of fault occurrences in each period.
  - For (3), for each transition used in the component influenced by the fault, create a corresponding fault transition which is triggered by the variable and the counter; similarly create a transition with normal behavior (also triggered by the variable and the counter). Notice that our framework is able to model faults actuating on the FT mechanisms, for instance, the behavior of network loss on the newly introduced FT messages.

[Example] We outline how a game (focusing on fault modeling) is created with the example in sec. 2; similar approaches can be applied for input errors or message corruption; here the modeling of input (for InputRead(m)) is skipped.

- Create the predicate *pred*: *pred* is evaluated to false in all cases except (a) when the boolean variable *occu* (representing the network occupance) is evaluated to true and (b) when for all $i \in \{1, \ldots, n_A\}$, $\Delta_{next_i} = |\overline{\sigma_i}| + 1$ (end of period); the predicate partitions player-0 and player-1 vertices.
- For all process i and program counter j, the set of choice actions $\bigcup \sigma_{\alpha_j}$ $\langle \wedge_{m=1,\ldots,n_A} pc_{\alpha_{j_m}} \rangle$ are generated based on the approach described previously.
- Create variable $v_f \in V_f$, which is used to indicate whether the fault has been activated in this period.
- For each message sending transition t in the network, create two normal transitions $(v_f = \text{true} \wedge v_f' = \text{true}) \wedge t$ and $(v_f = \text{false} \wedge v_f' = \text{false}) \wedge t$ in the game.
- For each message sending transition t in the network, generate a transition t' where the message is sent, but the value is not updated in the destination. Create a fault transition $(v_f = \text{false} \wedge v_f' = \text{true}) \wedge t'$ in the game.

- Define σ_f to control v_f: if for all $i \in \{1, \ldots, n_A\}$, $\Delta_{next_i} = |\overline{\sigma_i}| + 1$, then update v_f to `false` as Δ_{next_i} updates to 1 (reset the fault counter at the end of the period).

5   Step B: Solving Distributed Games

We summarize the result from [10] as a general property of distributed games.

Theorem 1. *There exists distributed games with global winning strategy but (a) without distributed memoryless strategies, or (b) all distributed strategies require memory. In general, for a finite distributed game, it is undecidable to check whether a distributed strategy exists from a given position [10].*

As the problem is undecidable in general, we restrict our interest in finding a distributed positional strategy for player 0, if there exists one. We also focus on games with reachability winning conditions. By posing the restriction, the problem is NP-Complete.

Theorem 2. *[PositionalDG$_0$] Given a distributed game $\mathcal{G} = (\mathcal{V}_0 \uplus \mathcal{V}_1, \mathcal{E})$, an initial state $x = (x_1, \ldots, x_n)$ and a target state $t = (t_1, \ldots, t_n)$, deciding whether there exists a positional (memoryless) distributed strategy for player-0 from x to t is NP-Complete.*

Proof. The proof can be found in the extended version [4].

With the NP-completeness proof, finding a distributed reachability strategy amounts to the process of searching. For searching, we consider (a) bounded forward searching which combines the nodes in the search tree with BDDs, and (b) distributed version of the witness algorithm using SAT unrolling[6].

6   Conversion from Strategies to Concrete Implementations

Once when the distributed game has returned a positive result, and assume that the result is represented as an IM, the remaining problem is to check whether the synthesized result can be translated to PISEM and thus further to concrete implementation. If for each existing action or newly generated FT mechanism, the worst case execution time is known (with available WCET tools), then we can always answer whether the system is implementable by a full system rescheduling, which can be complicated. Nevertheless, based on our system modeling (assumption with a globally synchronized clock), perform modification on the release time and the deadline from the synthesized IM can be translated to a linear constraint system, as in IM every action contains a timing precondition based on program counters. Here we give a simplified algorithm which performs *local timing modification (LTM)*. Intuitively, LTM means to perform partitions on either

1. the interval d between the deadline of action $\sigma_{\lfloor \frac{a}{b} \rfloor}$ and release time of $\sigma_{\lceil \frac{a}{b} \rceil}$, if (a) $\sigma_{\frac{a}{b}}$ exists and (b) $d \neq 0$, or
2. the execution interval of action $\sigma_{\lfloor \frac{a}{b} \rfloor}$, if $\sigma_{\frac{a}{b}}$ exists.

---

[6] A sketch of the algorithm can be found in the appendix.

In the algorithm, we assume that for every action σ_d, $d \in \mathbb{N}$ where FT mechanisms are not introduced between σ_d and σ_{d+1} during synthesis, its release-time and deadline should not change; this assumption can be checked later or added explicitly to the constraint system under solving (but it is not listed here for simplicity reasons). Then we solve a constraint system to derive the release time and deadline of all FT actions introduced. Algorithm 3 performs such execution[7]: for simplicity at most one FT action exists between two actions σ_i, σ_{i+1}; in implementation this assumption is released:

- Item (1) performs a interval split between $\sigma_{\lfloor \frac{a}{b} \rfloor}$ and $\sigma_{\frac{a}{b}}$.
- Item (3) assigns the deadline of $\sigma_{\lfloor \frac{a}{b} \rfloor}$ to be the original deadline of $\sigma_{\frac{a}{b}}$.
- Item (4), (5) ensure that the reserved time interval is greater than the WCET.
- Item (6) to (11) introduce constraints from other processes:
  - Item (6) (7) (8) consider existing actions which do not change the deadline and release time; for these fetch the timing information from PISEM.
  - Item (9) (10) (11) consider newly introduced actions or existing actions which change their deadline and release time; for these actions use variables to construct the constraint.
- Item (12) is a conservative dependency constraint between $\sigma_{\frac{a}{b}}$ and a send σ_d.

7   Implementation and Case Studies

For implementation, we have created our prototype software as an Eclipse-plugin, called GECKO, targeting to offer an open-platform based on the model-based approach for the design, synthesis, and code generation for fault-tolerant embedded systems.

To evaluate our approach, here we reuse the example in sec. 2 and perform automatic tuning synthesis for the selected FT mechanisms[8]. The user now selects a set of FT mechanism templates with the intention to implement a *fail-then-resend* operation, which is shown in Figure 5a. The selected patterns introduce two additional messages in the system, and the goal is to orchestrate multiple synchronization points introduced by the FT mechanisms between $\mathcal{A}$ and $\mathcal{B}$ (the timing in FT mechanisms is unknown). The fault model assumes that in each period at most one message loss occurs.

Once when GECKO receives the system description (including the fault model) and the reachability specification, it translates the system into a distributed game. In Figure 5b, the set of possible control transitions are listed[9]; the solver generates an appropriate PC-precondition for each action to satisfy the specification. In Figure 5b, bold numbers (e.g., $\langle \mathbf{0000} \rangle$) indicate the synthesized result. The time line of the execution (the synthesized result) is explained as follows:

- Process $\mathcal{A}$ reads the input, sends MsgSend(m), and waits.
- Process $\mathcal{B}$ first waits until it is allowed to execute (RecvMsg(m)). Then it performs a conditional send MsgSend(req) and waits.

---

[7] Here we list case 2 only; for case 1 similar analysis can be applied.

[8] The complete of the case study (including the implementability analysis via constraint solving and the screenshots) can be found in the extended version.

[9] In our implementation, the PC starts from 0 rather than 1; which is different from the formulation in IM and PISEM.

Algorithm 3. LocalTimingModification

Data: Original PISEM $\mathcal{S} = (\mathcal{A}, \mathcal{N}, \mathcal{T})$, synthesized IM $S = (A, N)$

Result: For each $\sigma_{\frac{a}{b}}$ and $\sigma_{\lfloor\frac{a}{b}\rfloor}$, their execution interval $[\alpha_{\frac{a}{b}}, \beta_{\frac{a}{b}})$, $[\alpha_{\lfloor\frac{a}{b}\rfloor}, \beta_{\lfloor\frac{a}{b}\rfloor})$

For convenience, use $(X \ in \ \mathcal{S})$ to represent the retrieved value X from PISEM $\mathcal{S}$.

begin

   for $\sigma_{\frac{a}{b}}[\wedge_{m=1...n_A}[pc_{\frac{a}{b},m_{low}}, pc_{\frac{a}{b},m_{up}}]]$ *in* $\overline{\sigma_i}$ *of* A_i **do**

      let $\alpha_{\frac{a}{b}}, \beta_{\frac{a}{b}}, \alpha_{\lfloor\frac{a}{b}\rfloor}, \beta_{\lfloor\frac{a}{b}\rfloor}$ // Create a new variable for the constraint system

      /* Type A constraint: causalities within the process */

1        $constraints.add(\alpha_{\frac{a}{b}} = \beta_{\lfloor\frac{a}{b}\rfloor})$

2        $constraints.add(\alpha_{\lfloor\frac{a}{b}\rfloor} = (\alpha_{\lfloor\frac{a}{b}\rfloor} in \ \mathcal{S}))$

3        $constraints.add(\beta_{\frac{a}{b}} = (\beta_{\lfloor\frac{a}{b}\rfloor} in \ \mathcal{S}))$

4        $constraints.add(\beta_{\frac{a}{b}} - \alpha_{\frac{a}{b}} > WCET(\sigma_{\frac{a}{b}}))$

5        $constraints.add(\beta_{\lfloor\frac{a}{b}\rfloor} - \alpha_{\lfloor\frac{a}{b}\rfloor} > WCET(\sigma_{\lfloor\frac{a}{b}\rfloor}))$

      /* Type B constraint: causalities crossing different processes */

      for $\sigma_{\frac{a}{b}}[\wedge_{m=1...n_A}[pc_{\frac{a}{b},m_{low}}, pc_{\frac{a}{b},m_{up}}]]$ *in* $\overline{\sigma_i}$ *of* A_i **do**

         for $\sigma_d[\wedge_{m=1...n_A}[pc_{d,m_{low}}, pc_{d,m_{up}}]]$ *in* $\overline{\sigma_j}$ *of* A_j **do**

           if $d \in \mathbb{N}$ *and not exists* $\sigma_{\frac{x}{y}} \in \overline{\sigma_j}$ *where* $\lfloor\frac{x}{y}\rfloor = d$ **then**

6   **if** $pc_{d,j_{up}} < pc_{\frac{a}{b},j_{low}}$ **then** $constraints.add((\beta_d \ in \ \mathcal{S}) < \alpha_{\frac{a}{b}})$

7   **if** $pc_{d,j_{low}} > pc_{\frac{a}{b},j_{up}}$ **then** $constraints.add((\alpha_d \ in \ \mathcal{S}) > \beta_{\frac{a}{b}})$

              if $\sigma_{\frac{a}{b}} := send(pre, ind, n, dest, v, c) \wedge pc_{d,j_{low}} > pc_{\frac{a}{b},j_{up}}$ **then**

8                 $constraints.add((\alpha_d \ in \ \mathcal{S}) > \beta_{\frac{a}{b}} + WCMTT(n, ind))$

           else

9   **if** $pc_{d,j_{up}} < pc_{\frac{a}{b},j_{low}}$ **then** $constraints.add(\beta_d < \alpha_{\frac{a}{b}})$

10   **if** $pc_{d,j_{low}} > pc_{\frac{a}{b},j_{up}}$ **then** $constraints.add(\alpha_d > \beta_{\frac{a}{b}})$

              if $\sigma_{\frac{a}{b}} := send(pre, ind, n, dest, v, c) \wedge pc_{d,j_{low}} > pc_{\frac{a}{b},j_{up}}$ **then**

11               $constraints.add(\alpha_d > \beta_{\frac{a}{b}} + WCMTT(n, ind))$

      /* Type C constraint: conservative data dependency constraints */

      for $\sigma_{\frac{a}{b}}[\wedge_{m=1...n_A}[pc_{\frac{a}{b},m_{low}}, pc_{\frac{a}{b},m_{up}}]]$ *in* $\overline{\sigma_i}$ *of* A_i **do**

         for $\sigma_d[\wedge_{m=1...n_A}(pc_{d,m_{low}}, pc_{d,m_{up}})]$ *in* $\overline{\sigma_j}$ *of* A_j **do**

           if $\sigma_d := send(pre, ind, n, dest, v, c) \wedge pc_{d,j_{up}} < pc_{\frac{a}{b},j_{low}} \wedge \sigma_{\frac{a}{b}}$ *reads*

           variable c **then**

12             $constraints.add((\beta_d \ in \ \mathcal{S}) + WCMTT(n, ind) < \alpha_{\frac{a}{b}})$

   solve $constraints$ using (linear) constraint solvers.

end

- Process $\mathcal{A}$ performs RecvMsg(req), following a conditional send MsgSend(rsp).
- Process $\mathcal{B}$ performs conditional assignment, which assigns the value of rsp to m, if m_v is empty.

Concerning the running time of the above example, the engine (based on forward searching + BDD for intermediate image storing) is able to report the result in 3 seconds, while constraint solving is also relatively fast (within 1 second). Our engine offers a translation scheme to dump the BDD to mechanisms in textual form; this process occupies most of the execution time. Note that the NP-completeness result does not bring

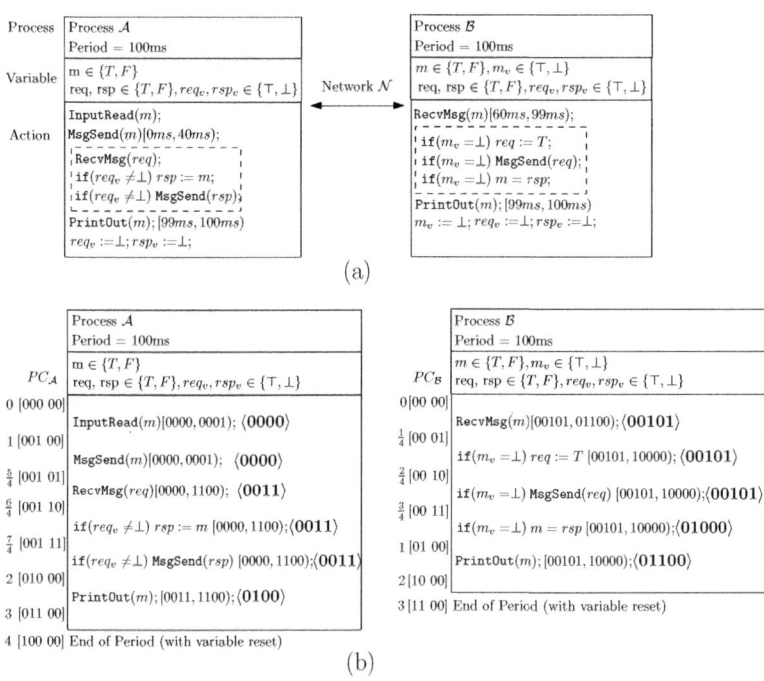

Fig. 5. An example where FT primitives are introduced for synthesis (a), and concept illustration for the control choices in the generated game (b)

huge benefits, as another exponential blow-up caused by the translation from variables to states is also unavoidable.

8   Related Work

Recently there has been an increasing interest in applying games for synthesis, including work by Bloem and Jobstmann et al. (the program repair framework [7]), Henzinger and Chatterjee et al. (Alpaga and the interface synthesis [3,5]), and David and Larson et al. (Uppaal TIGA [2]); these approaches are usually based on non-distributed settings. Our starting model of distributed and timed straight-line programs is based on commonly used paradigms from the real-time community [8].

The work that is closest to ours is by Kulkarni et.al. [9] and Girault et al. [6]. Their work is on protocol synthesis based on synthesizing finite state machines (FSMs) from non-fault tolerant FSMs and pre-specified fault models. In contrast to the work mentioned above we do not address the complete synthesis of FT mechanisms such as voting; instead we are synthesizing the FT mechanisms based on the application of pre-defined FT patterns, thereby considerably restricting the space of possible solutions. Our approach is based on standard notions of distributed games and game-theoretic algorithms for solving these games. As we are mainly interested in synthesizing distributed embedded programs, we naturally restrict ourselves to finding positional strategies; this problem turns out to be NP-complete. The synthesis algorithm we describe in this paper works in several steps from distributed embedded timed programs to interleaving semantics and the formulation of distributed games. Solutions for these game-theoretic problems are obtained by translation to a corresponding Boolean SAT problem (although our implementation, Gecko, is currently still based on specialized search strategies). This formulation of solving distributed games based on SAT closely follows the main steps as provided by [1].

9   Concluding Remarks

This paper presents a comprehensive approach (see Figure 6 for concept illustration) for augmenting fault-tolerance in real-time distributed systems under a game-theoretic framework. These mechanisms may have interesting applications in distributed process control and robotics. We plan to further validate our approach using our prototype implementation Gecko. To handle the complexity in practice it will also be necessary to partition systems into subsystems in a compositional way.

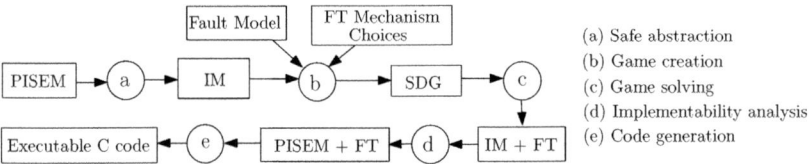

Fig. 6. Concept illustration of the overall approach for fault-tolerant synthesis; IM+FT means that an IM model is equipped with FT mechanisms

References

1. Alur, R., Madhusudan, P., Nam, W.: Symbolic computational techniques for solving games. International Journal on Software Tools for Technology Transfer (STTT) 7(2), 118–128 (2005)
2. Behrmann, G., Cougnard, A., David, A., Fleury, E., Larsen, K.G., Lime, D.: UPPAAL-tiga: Time for playing games! In: Damm, W., Hermanns, H. (eds.) CAV 2007. LNCS, vol. 4590, pp. 121–125. Springer, Heidelberg (2007)
3. Berwanger, D., Chatterjee, K., De Wulf, M., Doyen, L., Henzinger, T.: Alpaga: A tool for solving parity games with imperfect information. In: Esparza, J., Majumdar, R. (eds.) TACAS 2010. LNCS, vol. 6015, pp. 58–61. Springer, Heidelberg (2010)
4. Cheng, C.-H., Ruess, H., Knoll, A., Buckl, C.: A game-theoretic approach for synthesizing fault-tolerant embedded systems (extended version). In: arXiv:1011.0268 [cs.GT] (2010)
5. Doyen, L., Henzinger, T., Jobstmann, B., Petrov, T.: Interface theories with component reuse. In: EMSOFT 2008, pp. 79–88. ACM, New York (2008)
6. Girault, A., Rutten, É.: Automating the addition of fault folerance with discrete controller synthesis. Formal Methods in System Design 35(2), 190–225 (2009)
7. Jobstmann, B., Griesmayer, A., Bloem, R.: Program repair as a game. In: Etessami, K., Rajamani, S.K. (eds.) CAV 2005. LNCS, vol. 3576, pp. 226–238. Springer, Heidelberg (2005)

8. Kshemkalyani, A., Singhal, M.: Dirstributed computing: principles, algorithms, and systems. Cambridge University Press, Cambridge (2008)
9. Kulkarni, S., Arora, A.: Automating the addition of fault-tolerance. In: Joseph, M. (ed.) FTRTFT 2000. LNCS, vol. 1926, pp. 82–359. Springer, Heidelberg (2000)
10. Mohalik, S., Walukiewicz, I.: Distributed games. In: Pandya, P.K., Radhakrishnan, J. (eds.) FSTTCS 2003. LNCS, vol. 2914, pp. 338–351. Springer, Heidelberg (2003)

Appendix: Sketch of the SAT Witness Algorithm for Distributed Games

Madhusudan, Nam, and Alur [1] designed the *bounded witness algorithm* for solving reachability games using SAT. Although based on their experiments, the witness algorithm is not as efficient as the BDD-based approach in centralized games, with some modifications, we find it potentially useful for distributed games.

We first paraphrase the concept of *witness* defined in [1], a set of states which witnesses the fact that player 0 wins. In [1], consider the generated SAT problem from a local game $G = (V_0 \uplus V_1, E)$ trying to reach from V_{init} to V_{goal}: for $i = 1, \ldots, d$ and vertex $v \in V_0 \uplus V_1$, variable $\langle v \rangle_i = \texttt{true}$ when one of the following holds:

- $v \in V_{init}$ and $i = 1$ (if $v \notin V_{init} \wedge i = 1$ then $\langle v \rangle_i = \texttt{false}$).
- $v \in V_{goal}$ (if $v \notin V_{goal} \wedge i = d$ then $\langle v \rangle_i = \texttt{false}$).
- $v \in V_0 \setminus V_{goal}$ and $\exists v' \in V_0 \uplus V_1$. $\exists e \in E$. $\exists j > i$. $(e = (v, v') \wedge \langle v' \rangle_j = \texttt{true})$
- $v \in V_1 \setminus V_{goal}$ and $\forall e = (v, v') \in E$. $\exists j > i$. $\langle v' \rangle_j = \texttt{true}$

This recursive definition implies that if $v \in V_0$ (resp. $v \in V_1$) is not the goal but in the witness set, then its successor (resp. all of its successors) v' should either be (i) in a goal state or (ii) also in the witness: note that for (ii), the number of allowable steps to reach the goal is decreased by one.

In general, our algorithm creates SAT problems based on the above concept but contains modifications to ensure (1) the unique selection of local edges and (2) the progress of a global move is a combination of local moves (see Algorithm 4 for fragments)[10].

Algorithm 4. PositionalDistributedStrategy_BoundedSAT_0 (fragment only)

. . .

1 **for** *local control transition* $e = (x_i, x_i') \in E_i, x_i \in V_{0_i}$ **do**

    for *local transition* $e_1 = (x_i, x_{i_1}'), \ldots, e_k = (x_i, x_{i_k}') \in E_i, e_1 \ldots e_k \neq e$ **do**

        clauses.add([$\langle e \rangle \Rightarrow (\neg \langle e_1 \rangle \wedge \ldots \wedge \neg \langle e_k \rangle)$])

2 **for** $v = (v_1, \ldots, v_m) \in \mathcal{V}_0$ **do**

    for $(e_1, \ldots, e_m)$: $e_i = (v_i, v_i') \in E_i$ *if* $v_i \in V_{0_i}$ *or* $e_i = (v_i, v_i)$ *if* $x_i \in V_{1_i}$ **do**

        // $e_i = (v_i, v_i)$ when $x_i \in V_{1_i}$ are dummy edges for ease of formulation

        for $j = 1, \ldots, d - 1$ **do**

            clauses.add([$\langle v_1, \ldots, v_m \rangle_j \Rightarrow ((\bigwedge_{\{i | v_i \in V_{0_i}\}} \langle e_i \rangle) \Rightarrow (\langle v_1', \ldots, v_m' \rangle_{j+1})$])

---

[10] The complete algorithm can be found in the full version [4].

Proving Stabilization of Biological Systems

Byron Cook[1,2], Jasmin Fisher[1], Elzbieta Krepska[1,3], and Nir Piterman[4]

[1] Microsoft Research
[2] Queen Mary, University of London
[3] VU University Amsterdam
[4] University of Leicester

Abstract. We describe an efficient procedure for proving stabilization of biological systems modeled as qualitative networks or genetic regulatory networks. For scalability, our procedure uses modular proof techniques, where state-space exploration is applied only locally to small pieces of the system rather than the entire system as a whole. Our procedure exploits the observation that, in practice, the form of modular proofs can be restricted to a very limited set. For completeness, our technique falls back on a non-compositional counterexample search. Using our new procedure, we have solved a number of challenging published examples, including: a 3-D model of the mammalian epidermis; a model of metabolic networks operating in type-2 diabetes; a model of fate determination of vulval precursor cells in the *C. elegans* worm; and a model of *pair-rule* regulation during segmentation in the *Drosophila* embryo. Our results show many orders of magnitude speedup in cases where previous stabilization proving techniques were known to succeed, and new results in cases where tools had previously failed.

1 Introduction

Biologists are increasingly turning to computer-science techniques in the quest to understand and predict the behavior of complex biological systems [1, 2, 3]. In particular, application of formal verification tools to models of biological processes is gaining impetus among biologists. In some cases known formal verification techniques work well (*e.g.* [4, 5, 6, 7]). Unfortunately in other cases—such as proving stabilization [8]—we find existing abstractions and heuristics to be ineffective.

In this paper we address the open challenge to find scalable algorithms for proving stabilization of biological systems. A proof of stabilization elucidates system robustness with respect to time, while stabilization counterexamples give insight into system homeostasis – in both cases the result is useful to biologists. In computer science terms, stabilization means the existence of a *unique* fixpoint state that is always eventually reached. We are trying to prove this property of large parallel systems, where the size of these systems forces us to use some form of modular reasoning. Since stabilization is formally a liveness property, we must be careful when using the powerful cyclic modular proof rules (*e.g.* [9, 10]), as they are only sound in the context of safety [11]. Furthermore, we

R. Jhala and D. Schmidt (Eds.): VMCAI 2011, LNCS 6538, pp. 134–149, 2011.

find that the complex temporal interactions between the modules are crucial to the stabilization of the system as a whole; meaning that we cannot use scalable techniques that simply abstract away the interactions altogether.

In this paper we present a procedure for proving stabilization of biological systems modeled as communicating components in the qualitative networks formalism [12] with synchronous updates of variables, or a genetic regulatory networks [13], where updates are asynchronous. We compose these stabilization proofs out of small lemmas that can be solved using quick local proof techniques on the components. The key to our tool's performance is the observation that it suffices to take the lemmas only of a very limited form: $[FG(p_1) \wedge \ldots \wedge FG(p_k)] \Rightarrow FG(q)$, where $p_1 \ldots p_k$ are atomic formulae over inputs of a small component that we want to reason about, q is a atomic formula about this component's output, F denotes "eventually" in LTL [16], and G denotes "always". We compute the set of all provable lemmas of this form by iterative strengthening. After this procedure, if for each component v its lemma implies $FG(v = k_v)$ for some constant k_v, that means that we have proved stabilization. If some component is left unfixed, then we use the lemmas to restrict the counterexample search space.

Our stabilization proving procedure is sound and complete. We experimentally confirm that it is scalable. We find that our lemma generation procedure accelerates both the proving as well as the disproving of stabilization. Section 4 demonstrates with experimental evidence how our lemma generation procedure leads to many orders of magnitude speedup in cases where known previous techniques work, and new results in cases where known techniques fail. These include challenging published examples such as: a 3-D model of the mammalian epidermis based on [12]; a model of metabolic networks operating in type-2 diabetes [17]; a model of fate determination of vulval precursor cells in *C. elegans* [18]; and a model of *pair-rule* cross-regulation during segmentation in *Drosophila* fly embryo [19]. Applying our procedure to the multidimensional model of epidermis revealed a bug in the model from [12], as we proved the system non-stabilizing. Consulting the biological papers corroborated that the model was, in fact, in disagreement with the biological evidence. After fixing the bug we could then prove the system stabilizing (see Section 2).

Related work. With the exception of [12], no tools have been previously reported that are directly tailored to the problem of proving stabilization or other liveness properties of large biological systems modeled as discrete systems (*e.g.* qualitative networks). Classic theory of stability of differential equations is applied to continuous systems, *e.g.* in [20]. Recent work is known on the stability of hybrid systems, *e.g.* [21,22,23]. In the context of stabilization for discrete systems, [12] uses the compositional structure of a system modeled as qualitative network to accelerate the computation of a fixpoint-based computation of the reachable states. However, the final check is not modular, and thus is less scalable than our approach. Genetic regulatory networks [13] have been extensively studied, *e.g.* in [13,19], but the analysis relies on state space enumeration, which is not scalable, or stable states computation that does not account for reachability [14].

The current state-of-the-art amongst biologists interested in stabilization is to use either techniques from [12] or other off-the-shelf model checking tools for finite-state systems. Recently developed tools for proving liveness of infinite-state systems (*e.g.* [24]) could also be used. As we show in Section 4, our procedure is many orders of magnitude faster than previously known approaches. The challenge is that biological models are very large, causing timeouts and out-of-memory failures for most tools not based on modular proof strategies. Note also that stabilization is not directly expressible in popular temporal logics, *e.g.* CTL or LTL, unless support for quantifiers is added, making the encoding of stabilization tricky in most formal verification tools. Qualitative networks could be implemented in Lustre [15], which however supports checking only safety properties.

We are not the first to attempt to address the difficulty of modular reasoning for liveness. For example, several previous papers have reported on heuristics tailored to the problem of proving liveness of non-blocking concurrent programs [25,24]. Their motivation is the same as here, but the approaches used differ as they are tailored to different problems. Another technique, as found in [26], is to use induction over time to facilitate the modular proving of liveness properties of finite-state models. In [26] the modular decomposition is given manually, whereas in our work we use the structure of the biological system to our advantage when automating the search for the modular decomposition. To show that our proofs are non-circular we use an argument similar to that of [26].

Our algorithm depends on a domain $\mathcal{L}$ over which lemmas range. When handling qualitative networks and genetic regulatory networks all variables range over domains of the form $\{0, \ldots, n\}$. Furthermore, the updates of variables are always in increments or decrements of 1. As our aim is to prove stabilization, lemmas that restrict variables to *one* subrange of their domain turn out to be sufficient. This insight is the basis for an optimization of the lemma generation algorithm, which works extremely fast in practice. When considering this optimization, our technique can be thought of as analyzing the system using abstract interpretation over the interval domain [27]. A similar usage of abstract interpretation to produce *tail invariants* used for termination proofs appears in [28].

Limitations and advantages. Our technique is geared towards the efficient proving of stabilization where the proof can be teased out by examining the system's compositional structure. This lemma-generation strategy comes with an overhead that can potentially hinder rather than help performance in some cases. In Section 4 we demonstrate an example of this.

An advantage of our procedure is compositionality: the local stabilization lemmas give a specification that, when established for new components, implies the whole system's stabilization without re-running the entire procedure. This can lead to experimenting with alternative components (*e.g.* testing modified components during a search for new drugs). This observation also leads to a practical advantage, as we check lemmas in parallel during the proof search.

2   Example: Skin Cells

Figure 1 contains a pictorial view of a simplified model of mammalian epidermis (outermost skin layer) that consists of five stacked cells [12]. Each cell represents a single skin layer and communicates with neighboring cells. The bottommost cells proliferate, migrate upwards and eventually decide to die and thus contribute to the cornified skin surface. It is this balance between proliferation and cell death that makes the system interesting to biologists: too much death is detriment to the skin, too little is cancerous. The original model is expressed as a qualitative network [12]. Formal definitions of qualitative and regulatory networks are given later, here we describe the epidermis model only informally.

The example model includes a few executing components, each updating a single variable. See, e.g., $\mathtt{wnt_3}$ or $\mathtt{NotchIC_3}$ in Fig. 1. Each variable holds a value, which is a number in $\{0, 1 \ldots N\}$, where $N + 1$ is a predefined, globally-fixed *granularity*. A *target function*, T_v, associated with each variable, v, determines how the variable is updated: if $v < T_v$ then $v' = v + 1$, if $v > T_v$ then $v' = v - 1$, else $v' = v$. In a qualitative network all variables are updated synchronously in parallel and in a genetic regulatory network they are updated asynchronously.

Intuitively, the update function of each variable is designed such that the value of the variable follows its target, which depends on other variables. In the biological setting, the typical target of a variable, v, combines positive influence of variables $w_1, w_2, \ldots w_s$ with negative influence of variables $w_{s+1}, w_{s+2}, \ldots w_{s+r}$ and ignores all other variables in the network:

$$T_v(w_1, w_2, \ldots w_{s+r}) = \max\left(0, \left\lfloor \frac{1}{s}\sum_{k-1}^{s} w_k - \frac{1}{r}\sum_{k-1}^{r} w_{s+k} \right\rfloor\right)$$

Graphically, this is often represented as an *influence graph* with $\rightarrow$ edges between each of $w_1, w_2, \ldots, w_s$ and v and $\relbar\blacksquare$ edges between each of $w_{s+1}, w_{s+2}, \ldots, w_{s+r}$ and v. In this section we discuss only several target functions used in the skin example. Refer to papers [12,17,18,19] for target functions used to model a large spectrum of aspects of signaling pathways, metabolic and genetic regulatory networks. In the skin example, the target of $\mathtt{wnt_3}$ is $T_{\mathtt{wnt_3}} = N - \mathtt{NotchIC_3}$, which means that $\mathtt{NotchIC_3}$ inhibits $\mathtt{wnt_3}$ (in Fig. 1 this fact is indicated by a 'blocking' arrow from $\mathtt{NotchIC_3}$ to $\mathtt{wnt_3}$). The target of $\mathtt{NotchIC_3}$ is $T_{\mathtt{NotchIC_3}} = \min(3, \mathtt{deltaext_3})$ and is indicated by an underline. The targets of the ext-variables round averaged cell inputs, which effectively requires at least one of the components to be present for some event to take place:

$$T_{\mathtt{deltaext_1}} = \left\lceil \frac{\mathtt{delta_0} + \mathtt{delta_2}}{2} \right\rceil, \qquad T_{\mathtt{wntext_1}} = \left\lfloor \frac{\mathtt{wnt_0} + \mathtt{wnt_2}}{2} \right\rfloor.$$

Figure 1 shows behavior of four selected variables, based on their target function.

Stabilization. If all executions end in *the same* cycle, and that cycle has length 1, then we say the network *stabilizes*. Note that both qualitative and regulatory networks are finite-state systems with only infinite executions. Thus, every execution must eventually end in *some type* of cycle. Stabilization guarantees

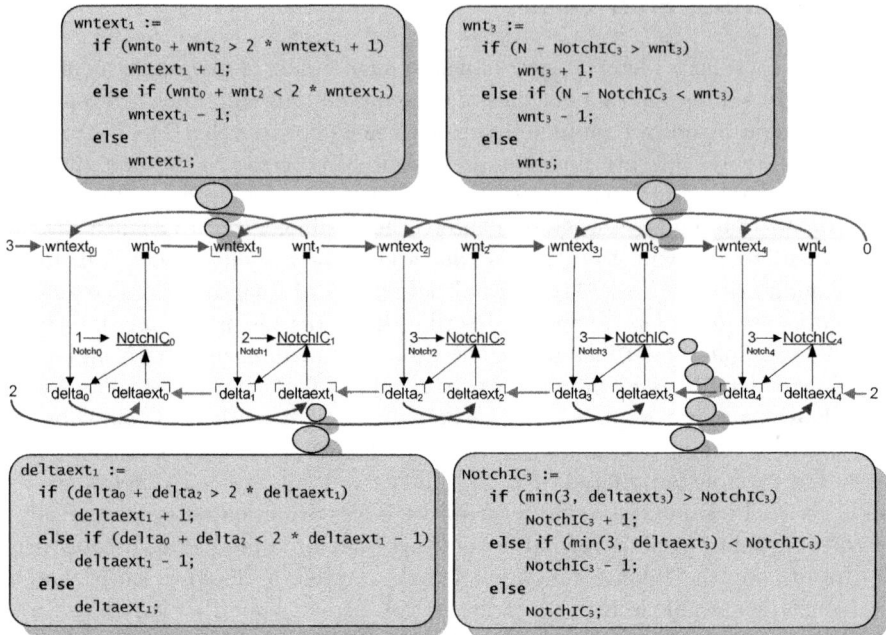

Fig. 1. Pictorial view of the skin model (rightmost cell is at skin surface). The bubbles show the underlying update functions for several of the variables in the model.

both that the system has only a single fixpoint and that the fixpoint is always eventually reached—a violation of this property is the existence of two fixpoints or a cycle of length greater than 1. Biologists are often interested to see what this fixpoint is when it exists, and to see a counterexample when it does not.

When applied to the skin example, our tool incrementally finds a modular proof of stabilization, as depicted in Fig. 2. The tool starts by guessing simple facts with the form $FG(p)$ about variables that can be proved locally, *i.e.* using the update function of only one variable with the definitions of the other variables abstracted away, see Fig. 2(a). In this case, we can infer locally the lemma $FG(\texttt{deltaext}_4 > 0)$ in the top cell. This property is provable using only local reasoning because the $\texttt{deltaext}_4$ variable follows a target $\lceil (2 + \texttt{delta}_3)/2 \rceil$, which is always a positive number, independently of the value of $\texttt{delta}_3$.

In the next step, we iteratively use proved facts to guide the search for additional facts to conclude. We search for locally provable facts of the form $FG(p) \Rightarrow FG(q)$, where we only try proving $FG(p) \Rightarrow FG(q)$ if $FG(p)$ is a consequent in a previous iteration. In our example, we can locally infer that $FG(\texttt{deltaext}_4 > 0) \Rightarrow FG(\texttt{NotchIC}_4 > 0)$, see Fig. 2(b). This implication holds because $\texttt{NotchIC}_4$ in the top cell follows a target, which effectively equals $\texttt{deltaext}_4$. Since $\texttt{deltaext}_4$ is eventually always positive, so is $\texttt{NotchIC}_4$.

In the next round, we can prove $FG(\texttt{NotchIC}_4 > 0) \Rightarrow FG(\texttt{wnt}_4 < N)$ in the top cell, see Fig. 2(c). This property holds locally, because the target of $\texttt{wnt}_4$ is $N - \texttt{NotchIC}_4$. Figure 2(c) contains also several subsequent stages of the proof.

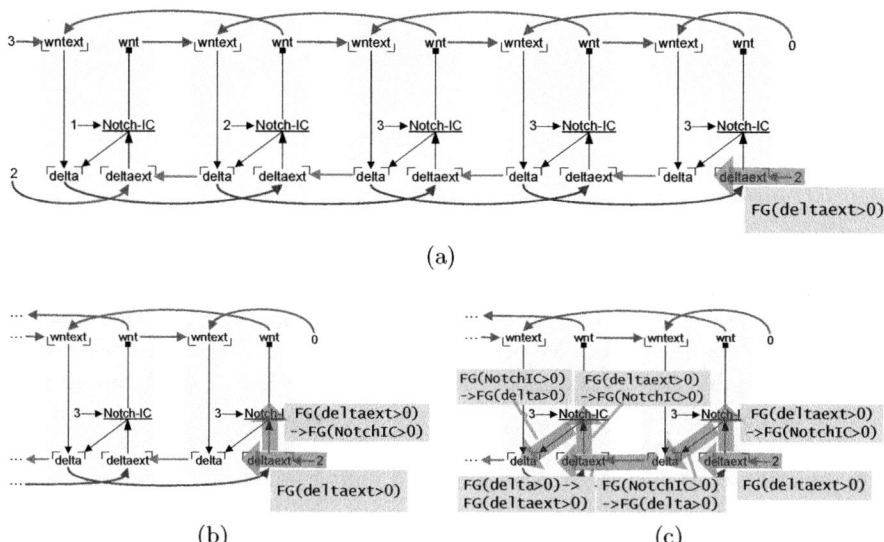

(a)

(b)   (c)

Fig. 2. Proof steps of skin model stabilization. Each arrow denotes a lemma.

We continue such reasoning until no new implications can be deduced. At that point, if we conclude $\dots FG(v = k_v)$ for some $k_v \in \{0, 1 \dots N\}$ for each variable v, then we have found a global stable state and proved that the model stabilizes.

A bug in the skin model. Applying our tool to the 1-D skin model described above proved the model stabilizing. Contrastingly, applying the tool to the 2-D skin model built out of several interconnected such 1-D models, revealed that the 2-D model is *not* stabilizing. This result was biologically surprising, so we suspected a bug in the original [12] model. After consulting biological literature [29], we discovered that the bug was real, *i.e.* the original model was in disagreement with biological evidence. The fix proposed was to change the value of the Notch protein (constant input of $NotchIC_0$ in the bottommost skin layer) from 0 to 1. By doing so we effectively introduced a low level of Notch protein into the basal layer of epidermis. With the bug fixed, we proved the multidimensional model stabilizing. While this finding offered no new biological insight, it helped to repair the existing model and confirmed usefulness of the method to biologists.

3   Stabilization Algorithm

We now describe our algorithm, which attempts to efficiently prove stabilization of systems using the modular strategy exemplified in the previous section.

Preliminaries. Following [12], a *qualitative network* (QN), $Q(V, T, N, n)$, of granularity $N + 1$ consists of n variables: $V = (v_1, v_2 \dots v_n)$. The state of the system is a finite map $s : V \to \{0, 1, \dots N\}$. The initial state is random. Each variable $v_i \in V$ has a *target function* $T_i \in T$ associated with it: $T_i : \{0, 1, \dots N\}^n \to \{0, 1, \dots N\}$. Qualitative networks update the variables using synchronous parallelism.

Target functions in qualitative networks direct the execution of the network: from state $v = (v_1, v_2 \ldots v_n)$, the *next state* $v' = (v'_1, v'_2 \ldots v'_n)$ is computed by:

$$v'_i = \begin{cases} v_i + 1 & v_i < T_i(v), \\ v_i & v_i = T_i(v), \\ v_i - 1 & v_i > T_i(v). \end{cases} \tag{1}$$

A *genetic regulatory network* (GRN) [13], $G(V, M, T, n)$, consists of n discrete variables: $V = (v_1, v_2 \ldots v_n)$ bounded individually by $M : V \to \{1, \ldots, N\}$. Nodes have target functions from T associated with them that govern updates of variables as in (1). The updates are asynchronous, which is the major difference between GRNs and QNs. We additionally assume that the updates are fair, *i.e.* each variable that is not equal to its target value is eventually updated.

Qualitative networks and genetic regulatory networks, as such, prove to be a suitable formalism to model some biological systems [12, 13, 17, 18, 19]. A target function of a variable v is typically a simple algebraic function, such as sum, over several other variables $w_1, w_2 \ldots w_m$. We often say that v *depends* on $w_1, w_2 \ldots w_m$ or that $w_1, w_2 \ldots w_m$ are *inputs* of v. $Q|_v$ denotes the restriction of Q to the variable v and its inputs, where the inputs behave arbitrarily. In the following, we use the term *network* to refer to both QNs and GRNs.

We say that a network is *stabilizing* if there exists a unique state s, that is eventually reached in all executions, such that $T(s) = s$. Intuitively, this means that starting from an arbitrary state, we always end up in a fixpoint and always the same one. Formally, we are attempting to prove the existence of a unique state $(k_1, k_2, \ldots k_n)$ such that $FG(\forall v_i \in V. \ v_i = k_i)$. Note that the stabilization property is not expressible in LTL unless we add support for both existential and universal quantification over states.

We define $\mathcal{L}$ to be a finite set of predicates that range over the simple inequalities of the form $m \le v \le M$, where m and M are constants in $\{0, 1, \ldots, N\}$.

We use the term *local lemma* over a variable v to represent proved assertions of the form $FG(p_1) \wedge FG(p_2) \wedge \cdots \wedge FG(p_m) \Rightarrow FG(q)$ where $q \in \mathcal{L}$ restricts v and p_1 through p_m are predicates about variables in the network proved previously.

Algorithm. Since networks considered are finite and all executions are infinite, each execution of the system must end in a cycle. We consider all possible executions of a network and note the trichotomy: (a) all executions end in the same fixpoint (the network stabilizes); or (b) there exists an execution that ends in a cycle of length greater than 1 (the network cycles); or (c) all executions end in a fixpoint and there exist at least two different fixpoints (the network bifurcates). As described later in this section, our algorithm covers all of these cases, and is therefore complete. We note that completeness depends on the finiteness of networks considered and on the fact that the algorithm falls back on the non-compositional SEARCH routine.

Our procedure is displayed in Alg. 1. It first applies a local lemma generation procedure GENLEMMAS (Alg. 2) that we explain next in this section. In all practical cases we find that the lemmas found during this phase directly imply stabilization in cases where the model does stabilize. If no proof has been found, the strategy is reversed: our procedure searches for one of two types of counterexamples: *multiple fixpoints* and *non-trivial cycles*. Both counterexample finding procedures are complete; therefore, in the instance that GENLEMMAS does not prove stabilization and yet no counterexample is found, we have still proved stabilization. The procedure SEARCH($V^{\min}, V^{\max}, Q$) is used by Alg. 1 to look for existence of a counterexample in a network Q. SEARCH uses the proved variable constraints $V^{\min}$ and $V^{\max}$ to reduce the state space in which it needs to explore. If SEARCH is unable to find a counterexample, no counterexample exists. Thus, in this case, we know that we need only find a single trivial cycle. This is easily done using a decision procedure as is done in SEARCH.

Lemma generation (Alg. 2). The key idea behind our approach is to first find *local lemmas* about the update functions for specific variables in the network. That is, if a variable v locally depends on variables $w_1, w_2, \ldots w_m$, we compute lemmas about interactions between v and w_i's of the following form:

$$FG(p_1) \wedge FG(p_2) \wedge \cdots \wedge FG(p_m) \Rightarrow FG(q)$$

where p_i's are predicates in $\mathcal{L}$ about variables w_j's and q is a predicate about v. We compute the local lemmas until no new ones can be deduced. If for each variable $v \in V$ we can use the lemmas to prove that $FG(v = k)$ for some constant k, then we can report that the system is stabilizing.

The procedure GENLEMMAS, Alg. 2, iteratively computes a set of lemmas, $\mathcal{P}$. During the iterative search it maintains a set of frontier variables, $\mathcal{F}$, for which new facts have been proved, but not used yet. Initially, $\mathcal{F}$ contains all unfixed variables in the network. The procedure repeatedly picks $w \in \mathcal{F}$ and generates new local lemmas about variables that depend on w. The lemmas are used to update $V^{\min}$ and $V^{\max}$, which overapproximate the least and upper bounds of values of variables; namely, for each $v \in V$ we have $FG\left(V^{\min}(v) \leq v \leq V^{\max}(v)\right)$. Alg. 2 terminates because the variable's bounds can be updated at most N times, so each variable can be enqueued at most N times. From this also follows that GENLEMMAS performs no exponential explorations. Generation of the local lemmas NEWLEMMAS is shown in Alg. 3. It proceeds via a search over the language of base inequalities $\mathcal{L}$: the predicates over v that improve current approximation and that are proven to hold, are returned. Termination of Alg. 3 follows from finiteness of $|\mathcal{L}| = \mathcal{O}(nN)$. The worst-case complexity of Alg. 2 is thus $\mathcal{O}(n^2 N|\mathcal{L}|)$ assuming constant cost of PROVE (see the following discussion).

Recall that with $Q|_v$ we denote the restriction of Q to a variable v and its inputs. The call PROVE($\phi, Q|_v$) is the application of model checking techniques to prove that $Q|_v$ respects the property ϕ. The key to the performance of our implementation is that checking ϕ *locally* is extremely fast. Since we are able to prove stabilization of the entire system while only ever applying PROVE to small parts of the system, our procedure is very efficient. That, coupled with the fact that PROVE calls can be executed in batches and thus in parallel on as many processors as are available, makes the method scalable.

Theorem 1 [36] establishes the soundness and completeness of our method.

Alg. 1. Stabilization proving procedure

input Q : QualitativeNetwork(N)
output fixpoint or counterexample
  $(V^{\min}, V^{\max}) := \text{GenLemmas}(Q)$
  if $\left(\forall v \in V . V^{\min}(v) = V^{\max}(v)\right)$ **then**
    return stabilizing at fixpoint $V^{\min}$
  else if $\text{Search}(V^{\min}, V^{\max}, Q)$ finds a counter-example π **then**
    return non-stabilizing with counterexample π
  else
    find single trivial fixpoint V
    return stabilizing at fixpoint V

Alg. 2. Lemma generation procedure GenLemmas

input Q : QualitativeNetwork(N)
output $V^{\min}, V^{\max} : V \to \{0, 1, \dots N\}$
  $\mathcal{F} := \varnothing; \quad \mathcal{P} := \varnothing$
  $\forall v \in V, v$ constant   . $V^{\min}(v) := v \wedge V^{\max}(v) := v$
  $\forall v \in V, v$ non-constant . $V^{\min}(v) := 0 \wedge V^{\max}(v) := N$
  for all non-constant variable $v \in Q$ **do**
    $\mathcal{F} := \mathcal{F} \cup \{v\}$
  while $\mathcal{F} \neq \varnothing$ **do**
    $w :=$ pick a variable from $\mathcal{F}$
    for all variable $v \in$ outputs(w) **do**
      for all lemma $l \in \text{NewLemmas}(v, V^{\min}, V^{\max})$ **do**
        $\mathcal{F} := \mathcal{F} \cup \{v\}$
        $\mathcal{P} := \mathcal{P} \cup \{l\}$
        update $V^{\min}(v), V^{\max}(v)$ with respect to l
  return $(V^{\min}, V^{\max})$

Alg. 3. Lemmas generation procedure NewLemmas

input v : variable
input $V^{\min}, V^{\max} : V \to \{0, 1, \dots N\}$
output S - lemmas
  $S := \varnothing$
  $(w_1, w_2, \dots, w_m) := \text{inputs}(v)$
  $p := \left(\bigwedge_i V^{\min}(w_i) \leq w_i \leq V^{\max}(w_i)\right)$
  for all predicate $q \in \mathcal{L}$ over v that strengthen $V^{\min}(v)$ or $V^{\max}(v)$ **do**
    $l := (FG(p) \Rightarrow FG(q))$
    if PROVE($l, Q|_v$) **then**
      $S := S \cup \{l\}$
  return S

Alg. 4. Domain-specific fast lemma generation F-NewLemmas

input v : variable
input $V^{\min}, V^{\max} : V \to \{0, 1, \dots N\}$
  $(w_1, w_2, \dots, w_m) := \text{inputs}(v)$
  $p := \left(\bigwedge_i V^{\min}(w_i) \leq w_i \leq V^{\max}(w_i)\right)$
  $T := T_v(\times_i [V^{\min}(w_i), V^{\max}(w_i)])$
  return $\{FG(p) \Rightarrow FG(\min(T) \leq v \leq \max(T))\}$

Domain specific optimization. Until now we have presented a general procedure that works with most models of concurrent update, and all possible update relations (not just those defined per variable to follow the target functions). However, due to specific target functions used in biological networks, we can reimplement the lemma generation routine in a way that PROVE is never needed, leading to significant performance improvements. Our alternative procedure F-NEWLEMMAS is shown in Alg. 4. We consider a variable v and its inputs $w_1, w_2 \ldots w_m$. Instead of guessing the influence of inputs under the constraints $V^{\min}$ and $V^{\max}$ on the output v, we compute it *exactly*. Namely, we compute the set T of values of target function T_v applied to all possible input combinations:

$$T = T_v([V^{\min}(w_1), V^{\max}(w_1)] \times [V^{\min}(w_2), V^{\max}(w_2)] \times \cdots \times [V^{\min}(w_m), V^{\max}(w_m)]),$$

thus obtaining a new approximation for v: $\min(T) \leq v \leq \max(T)$. In Theorem 2 [36] we prove that the lemmas generated by F-NEWLEMMAS indeed hold.

The worst-case cost of the stabilization proving procedure using F-NEW-LEMMAS is $\mathcal{O}(n^2 N^{d+1})$ where the network has n variables, of maximal indegree d (N^d results from generating input combinations). Since in all of our examples N is small, this procedure works exceptionally fast (see experimental results in Section 4). If N were larger, the procedure with NEWLEMMAS could be in principle more efficient than F-NEWLEMMAS.

Search for counterexamples. In Alg. 1, if the lemmas do not imply stabilization then the procedure SEARCH is called to search for a counterexample, or exhaustively show that no counterexample exists. SEARCH uses the bounds $V^{\min}$ and $V^{\max}$ computed earlier to limit the search space that is exhaustively explored.

SEARCH is designed to find one of two types of counterexamples: multiple trivial fixpoints and non trivial cycles. In the case of multiple fixpoints, SEARCH encodes the problem of existence of at least two fixpoints of the system of length 1 as an instance of a formula satisfiability problem. A decision procedure is used to search for the existence of two different states: $(v_1, \ldots v_n)$ and $(w_1, \ldots, w_n)$ such that each of them is a fixpoint: $\forall i \in \{1 \ldots n\} \,.\, (v_i' = v_i \wedge w_i' = w_i) \quad \wedge$ $\exists i \in \{1 \ldots n\} \,.\, (v_i \neq w_i)$, where the next state, v', is determined from v's inputs by (1). We can ignore reachability here because the set of initial states is equal to the set of all possible state configurations. Note also that, for efficiency, we conjoin the system with extra constraints using $V^{\min}$ and $V^{\max}$: $\forall v \in \{v_1 \ldots v_n, w_1, w_n\} \,.\, V^{\min}(v) \leq v \leq V^{\max}(v)$. Experimentally we find that the information from the proved lemmas leads to tremendous speedups when searching for multiple fixpoints. Satisfiability of the query proves the existence of at least two different fixpoints. If it is unsatisfiable, the system is cyclic or terminating. In the next phase we search for a non-trivial cycle counterexample.

To find a non-trivial cycle we use bounded model-checking [30] together with the encoding of liveness to safety found in [31]. For efficiency, as we unroll the system Q during bounded model checking, we conjoin the system with constraints on the values of the variables that come from the proven lemmas. Again we find that the information from the proved lemmas leads to tremendous speedups when searching for non-trivial cycles. Termination of the unrolling uses a naive diameter check [30], leading to a sound and complete technique. Fortunately we know only of toy examples where a search to the system's diameter is necessary.

4 Experimental Results

We have implemented Alg. 1 in a tool called BIOCHECK, using CADENCE SMV [32] as the implementation of PROVE and Z3 [33] as the decision procedure. The NEWLEMMAS procedure is easily parallelized: the local lemmas are proved in batches rather than one-by-one. All experiments were performed on a PC equipped with 4GB memory and a quad-core Intel processor with hyperthreading.

Biological systems tested. Information about the examples used during our experimental evaluation can be found in Tab. 1. These models are variations on four base systems: skin, diabetes, VPC and pair-rule genes.

The mammalian epidermis model [12], SKINFXD, consists of 5 cells, each containing 12 variables. We tested a simplified version, SSKINFXD, where only 5 variables per cell directly relevant to stabilization were considered (Fig. 1). We also built elongated variants of this model: ones that consist of more than 5 cells, ESKIN6-8FXD, and ones that emulate multidimensional skin tissue. SKIN2DFXD contains 4×5 cells (240 variables) and represents skin cross-section. SKIN3DFXD consists of $4 \times 5 \times 5 (= 100)$ 3-D mesh of cells (1200 variables). Note that, using our tool, we are the first to find a bug in the skin model from [12] (Section 2).

The model of several molecular pathways operating in type-2 diabetes and chronic obesity [17], DIABETES, exists in two variants that differ in constants: a variant after 8 days or 15 weeks after mice started being fed a fatty diet.

The vulval precursor cells (VPC) model [18], is a model of cell fate determination in the formation of *C. elegans* vulva. The model VPC4 includes 4 cells. In nature, there are 6 precursor cells, but the model was reduced by its author to 4 cells to make analysis by other tools tractable. Our tool easily handles the extended model VPC6, which includes 6 cells.

We also tested a genetic regulatory network, PAIRRULE, that models genes operating during segmentation in the *Drosophila* embryo [19], and a mutant of this network, PAIRRULEECTOEVE, with ectopic expression of the *even-skipped* gene. Sanchez *et al.* [19] report the former model non-stabilizing and the latter stabilizing, which is confirmed by our results. As the *pair-rule* model is very small, the time to analyze it is negligible and is not included in the performance comparison.

Results.   The comparison between our tool and existing tools is presented in Tab. 2. In this table we have compared the following tools:
- BC is our tool BIOCHECKimplementing Alg. 1 and 3 (NEWLEMMAS).
- FBC is BIOCHECK using F-NEWLEMMAS (Alg. 4) instead of NEWLEMMAS.
- NAIVE is an implementation of bounded model checking using a diameter check as the termination condition, *i.e.* $\text{NAIVE}(Q) = \text{SEARCH}(\varnothing, \varnothing, Q)$.
- TRM$^\alpha$ is the application of TERMINATOR [24] to solve a slightly different problem than stabilization (as stabilization itself is not encodable using LTL). For all the models that do stabilize, we test if the provided fixpoint

Table 1. Biological examples tested. $N + 1$ indicates the granularity of the network; #variables and #edges represent the number of variables (nodes) and the number of interactions between variables (edges), respectfully, in the model. The skin models SKIN2D and SKIN3D contain bugs that our tool found for the first time. The repaired versions are suffixed with FXD.

Model	N+1	#variables	#edges	Model	N+1	#variables	#edges
SSKINFXD	4	25	45	SKIN3DFXD	4	1200	2420
SKINFXD	4	60	90	SKIN3D	4	1200	2420
ESKIN6FXD	4	72	108	DIABETES8DAYS	3	75	148
ESKIN7FXD	4	84	126	DIABETES15WEEKS	3	75	148
ESKIN8FXD	4	96	144	VPC4	3	48	92
SKIN2DFXD	4	300	530	VPC6	3	72	138
SKIN2D	4	300	530	PAIRRULE(ECTOEVE)	4	7	23

Table 2. Comparison of our approach with other tools. BC is found in Alg. 1 in Section 3. FBC is the domain-specific version of BC using F-NEWLEMMAS instead of NEWLEMMAS. Runtimes are given in seconds. T indicates a timeout, where the threshold was set to 20mins. M represents an out-of-memory exception. The memory threshold was set to 4GB. V indicates tool failure after reporting too many variables.

Model	Result	BC	FBC	NAIVE	TRM$^\alpha$	SMV$_1^\alpha$	SMV$_2^\alpha$	QNB	SPN$^\alpha$	VIS
SSKINFXD	proved	3.8	0.0	T	T	M	T	M	T	T
SKINFXD	proved	9.0	0.0	T	T	M	T	M	T	T
ESKIN6FXD	proved	10.6	0.0	T	T	M	T	M	T	T
ESKIN7FXD	proved	12.9	0.0	T	T	M	T	M	T	T
ESKIN8FXD	dispr.	12.3	1.0	2.1	T	M	M	M	T	T
SKIN2DFXD	proved	50.3	0.0	T	T	M	M	M	T	T
SKIN2D	dispr.	56.5	13.1	T	T	M	M	M	M	T
SKIN3DFXD	proved	257.3	0.1	T	T	V	M	V	M	T
SKIN3D	dispr.	396.8	182.8	T	T	V	M	V	M	T
DIABETES8DAYS	proved	4.9	0.0	T	T	M	T	M	T	T
DIABETES15WEEKS	proved	5.2	0.0	T	T	M	T	M	T	T
VPC4	proved	4.6	0.0	T	T	T	T	M	T	T
VPC6	proved	7.0	0.0	T	T	M	T	M	T	T

is eventually reached. For those that do not guarantee stabilization we look for a non-trivial cycle. We use the symbol α to remind the reader that this application is not solving quite the same problem as stabilization.

- SMV$_1^\alpha$ and SMV$_2^\alpha$ are applications of Cadence SMV and NUSMV [34] respectively to the same problem as is used in TRM$^\alpha$.
- QNB is a tool from [12] that computes infinitely-often visited states in a network. For the comparison in Tab. 2, we could only use the tool that treats a system as a whole, rather than the version using the system's hierarchical structure to accelerate the whole-system reachable states computation. This acceleration-based technique has not been implemented. When applied manually to the example SKIN, on similar hardware, the acceleration-based technique took 21 mins. (see [12]). With some help by the author of the tool,

we have established that the acceleration-based technique still would not be able to handle our larger examples.

- SPN$^\alpha$ is the application of Spin [35] on the same formulas as in TRM$^\alpha$.
- VIS is used in our experiments to symbolically compute the model's reachable state spaces, from which we look for a stable state.

Table 3. Experimental details of application of our tool to the examples. Proof size is given as the number of implications in the proof, if the stabilization was proved. Otherwise counterexample size is given as "CEX size", which is cycle length and number of variables involved in the cycle. All times are given in seconds.

Model	GEN-LEMMAS	Opt. GEN-LEM.	SE-ARCH	Proof / CEX Size	Model	GEN-LEMMAS	Opt. GEN-LEM.	Proof Size
SKINFXD	9.0	0.0		177	ESKIN6FXD	10.6	0.0	212
ESKIN8FXD	11.3	0.0	1.0	2 / 74	ESKIN7FXD	12.9	0.0	251
SKIN2D	43.4	0.0	13.1	2 / 215	SKIN2DFXD	50.3	0.0	926
SKIN3D	214.1	0.1	182.7	2 / 860	SKIN3DFXD	257.3	0.1	3896
VPC4	4.6	0.0		75	DIABETES8DAYS	4.9	0.0	132
VPC6	7.0	0.0		107	DIABETES15WEEKS	5.2	0.0	132
PAIRRULE	4.8	0.0	1.6	2 / 4	PAIRRULEECTOEVE	1.7	0.0	8

Table 4. Performance of our tool FBC on scaled-up variants of the SKIN3DFXD model. M represents an out-of-memory exception.

Mesh (#cells)	#Variables	Optimized GENLEMMAS [s]	Mesh (#cells)	#Variables	Optimized GENLEMMAS [s]
$10 \times 10 \times 5$	$6.0 \cdot 10^3$	0.8	$75 \times 75 \times 5$	$3.4 \cdot 10^5$	57.4
$10 \times 20 \times 5$	$1.2 \cdot 10^4$	1.6	$100 \times 100 \times 5$	$6.0 \cdot 10^5$	103.8
$20 \times 20 \times 5$	$2.4 \cdot 10^4$	3.6	$100 \times 200 \times 5$	$1.2 \cdot 10^6$	208.5
$10 \times 50 \times 5$	$3.0 \cdot 10^4$	4.5	$200 \times 200 \times 5$	$2.4 \cdot 10^6$	423.0
$20 \times 50 \times 5$	$6.0 \cdot 10^4$	9.8	$100 \times 500 \times 5$	$3.0 \cdot 10^6$	544.3
$50 \times 50 \times 5$	$1.5 \cdot 10^5$	25.0	$200 \times 500 \times 5$	$6.0 \cdot 10^6$	M

Note that all previously known approaches fail to scale to the larger examples. For example, in the column TRM$^\alpha$ the encoding creates a program that, in essence, forces the liveness prover to find termination arguments for each possible path through the loop, which is a *very* large set (*e.g.* SKINFXD contains 3^{60} such paths). For this reason, TERMINATOR times out. In the case of SMV$^\alpha$, the SKINFXD has 4^{60} reachable states, which exceeds the typical limits of symbolic model checking tools. Note that unlike NAIVE, our implementation of SEARCH with range restrictions does scale. This shows how the range restrictions that come from the lemmas help reduce the state space significantly.

Note that in the case of the non-stabilizing ESKIN8FXD algorithm, our lemma generation procedure performs worse than the naive method. This demonstrates (as mentioned in Section 1) that our lemma generation procedure could in cases hinder rather than help performance.

Table 3 contains more statistics about the results of our tool during the experimental evaluation. The optimized lemma generation procedure performs an order of magnitude faster than the one that uses a model checker. The size of the counterexamples found corresponds to the number of nodes in the network that haven't been fixed by the proof procedure (not shown); meaning that the proof procedure comes close to a counterexample.

In Tab. 4 we check how our proof procedure scales to larger examples. We run them on models containing up to 10^4 cells (with or without bug) with a 10min timeout. The NEWLEMMAS-based implementation does not time out on exactly one of these examples, In contrast, the F-NEWLEMMAS-based implementation successfully verifies all but the 200×500 mesh model.

Release. We provide a *preliminary* packaging of the tool and benchmarks used at: `http://www.cs.vu.nl/~ekr/BioCheck` .

5   Conclusions

This paper reports on new advances in the area of formal analysis for biological models. We have addressed the open problem of scalable stabilization proving with a new sound and complete modular proof procedure. Our procedure takes advantage of the fact that, in practice, we can limit the set of possible modular proofs from which we search to those where the local lemmas are of a very restricted form. This leads to tremendous speedups, both for proving as well as disproving stabilization. It seems that it is the inherent robustness of the biological systems that makes our technique work so well—evolutionary developed systems remain naturally stable in the presence of timing and concentration variations.

Future work. While stabilization is a liveness property, safety techniques can in principle be used when checking finite-state systems. In future we might find useful adaptations of the circular proof rules (*e.g.* [9,10]) for the purpose of proving stabilization. Furthermore, it might be interesting to adapt our procedure to prove additional liveness properties beyond stabilization, and fair concurrent execution. Finally, the models that we have examined do not model certain important aspects, such as probabilities, aging or cell cycle which should fit in well with our current framework.

Acknowledgments. We thank M. Schaub for discussions about QNBuilder; C. Chaouiya for Drosophila models; S. Sankaranarayanan for clarifying the relation to tail invariants; and all the reviewers for their insightful comments.

References

1. Fisher, J., Henzinger, T.A.: Executable biology. In: Proc. WSC, pp. 1675–1682 (2006)
2. Bonzanni, N., Feenstra, A.K., Fokkink, W., Krepska, E.: What can formal methods bring to systems biology? In: Cavalcanti, A., Dams, D.R. (eds.) FM 2009. LNCS, vol. 5850, pp. 16–22. Springer, Heidelberg (2009)

3. Heath, J.: The equivalence between biology and computation. In: Degano, P., Gorrieri, R. (eds.) CMSB 2009. LNCS (LNBI), vol. 5688, pp. 18–25. Springer, Heidelberg (2009)

4. Fisher, J., et al.: Predictive modeling of signaling crosstalk during C. elegans Vulval Development. PLoS CB 3(5), e92 (2007)

5. Heath, J., Kwiatkowska, M., Norman, G., Parker, G., Tymchyshyn, O.: Probabilistic model checking of complex biological pathways. In: Priami, C. (ed.) CMSB 2006. LNCS (LNBI), vol. 4210, pp. 32–47. Springer, Heidelberg (2006)

6. Clarke, E., Faeder, J., Langmead, C., Harris, L., Jha, S., Legay, A.: Statistical model checking in BioLab: Applications to the automated analysis of T-Cell receptor signaling pathway. In: Heiner, M., Uhrmacher, A.M. (eds.) CMSB 2008. LNCS (LNBI), vol. 5307, pp. 231–250. Springer, Heidelberg (2008)

7. Chabrier-Rivier, N., Chiaverini, M., Danos, V., Fages, F., Schächter, V.: Modeling and querying biomolecular interaction networks. Theo. Comp. Sci. 325(1), 25–44 (2004)

8. Zotin, A.I.: The stable state of organisms in thermodynamic bases of biological processes: Physiological Reactions and Adaptations. De Gruyter, Berlin (1990)

9. Jones, C.: Specification and design of (parallel) programs. In: IFIP Congr. 1983, pp. 321–332 (1983)

10. Pnueli, A.: In transition from global to modular temporal reasoning about programs. In: Logics and Models of Concurrent Systems, pp. 123–144 (1985)

11. Abadi, M., Lamport, L.: Composing specifications. TOPLAS 15(1), 73–132 (1993)

12. Schaub, M., et al.: Qualitative networks: A symbolic approach to analyze biological signaling networks. BMC Systems Biology 1, 4 (2007)

13. Thomas, R., Thieffry, D., Kaufman, M.: Dynamical behaviour of biological regulatory networks—I. Biological role of feedback loops and practical use of the concept of the loop-characteristic state. Bullet. of Math. Bio. 55(2), 247–276 (1995)

14. Naldi, A., Thieffry, D., Chaouiya, C.: Decision diagrams for the representation and analysis of logical models of genetic networks. In: Calder, M., Gilmore, S. (eds.) CMSB 2007. LNCS (LNBI), vol. 4695, pp. 233–247. Springer, Heidelberg (2007)

15. Halbwachs, N., Lagnier, F., Ratel, C.: Programming and verifying critical systems by means of the synchronous data-flow programming language LUSTRE. IEEE Transactions on Software Engineering 18(9), 785–793 (1992)

16. Pnueli, A.: The temporal logic of programs. In: Proc. FOCS, pp. 46–57 (1977)

17. Beyer, A., Fisher, J.: Unpublished results (2009)

18. Beyer, A., et al.: Mechanistic insights into metabolic disturbance during type-2 diabetes and obesity using qualitative networks. In: Priami, C., Breitling, R., Gilbert, D., Heiner, M., Uhrmacher, A.M. (eds.) Transactions on Computational Systems Biology XII. LNCS (LNBI), vol. 5945, pp. 146–162. Springer, Heidelberg (2010)

19. Sanchez, L., Thieffry, D.: Segmenting the fly embryo: a logical analysis fo the pair-rule cross-regulatory module. Journal of Theoretical Biology 224, 517–537 (2003)

20. Ropers, D., Baldazzi, V., de Jong, H.: Model reduction using piecewise-linear approximations preserves dynamic properties of the carbon starvation response in E. coli. IEEE/ACM Trans. on Comp. Bio. and Bioinf. 99 (2009) (preprint)

21. Ghosh, R., Tomlin, C.: Symbolic reachable set computation of piecewise affine hybrid automata and its application to biological modelling: Delta-Notch protein signalling. IEE Systems Biology 1(1), 170–183 (2004)

22. Podelski, A., Wagner, S.: A sound and complete proof rule for region stability of hybrid systems. In: Bemporad, A., Bicchi, A., Buttazzo, G. (eds.) HSCC 2007. LNCS, vol. 4416, pp. 750–753. Springer, Heidelberg (2007)

23. Oehlerking, J., Theel, O.: Decompositional construction of Lyapunov functions for hybrid systems. In: Majumdar, R., Tabuada, P. (eds.) HSCC 2009. LNCS, vol. 5469, pp. 276–290. Springer, Heidelberg (2009)
24. Cook, B., Gotsman, A., Podelski, A., Rybalchenko, A., Vardi, M.Y.: Proving that programs eventually do something good. In: Proc. POPL, pp. 265–276 (2007)
25. Moore, J.S.: A mechanically checked proof of a multiprocessor result via a uniprocessor view. FMSD 14(2), 213–228 (1999)
26. McMillan, K.: Circular compositional reasoning about liveness. In: Pierre, L., Kropf, T. (eds.) CHARME 1999. LNCS, vol. 1703, pp. 342–345. Springer, Heidelberg (1999)
27. Cousot, P., Cousot, R.: Abstract Interpretation: A Unified Lattice Model for Static Analysis of Programs by Construction or Approximation of Fixpoints. In: Proc. POPL, pp. 238–252 (1977)
28. Colón, M.A., Sipma, H.B.: Practical Methods for Proving Program Termination. In: Brinksma, E., Larsen, K.G. (eds.) CAV 2002. LNCS, vol. 2404, pp. 442–454. Springer, Heidelberg (2002)
29. Lowell, S., et al.: Stimulation of human epidermal differentiation by delta-notch signalling at the boundaries of stem-cell clusters. Curr. Biol. 4, 10(9), 491–500 (2000)
30. Clarke, E., Biere, A., Raimi, R., Zhu, Y.: Bounded model checking using satisfiability solving. In: Proc. FMSD, vol. 19(1), pp. 7–34 (2001)
31. Biere, A., Artho, C., Schuppan, V.: Liveness checking as safety checking. In: Proc. FMICS. ENTCS, vol. 66(2), pp. 160–177 (2002)
32. McMillan, K.: Symbolic model checking (PhD thesis). Kluwer (1993)
33. De Moura, L., Bjørner, N.: Z3: An efficient SMT solver. In: Ramakrishnan, C.R., Rehof, J. (eds.) TACAS 2008. LNCS, vol. 4963, pp. 337–340. Springer, Heidelberg (2008)
34. Cimatti, A., et al.: NuSMV 2: An openSource tool for symbolic model checking. In: Brinksma, E., Larsen, K.G. (eds.) CAV 2002. LNCS, vol. 2404, p. 359. Springer, Heidelberg (2002)
35. Holzmann, G.: The SPIN model checker: Primer and ref. manual. Wesley (2003)
36. Cook, B., Fisher, J., Krepska, E., Piterman, N.: Proving stabilization of biological systems: Appendix. Technical Teport IR-CS-63

Precondition Inference from Intermittent Assertions and Application to Contracts on Collections

Patrick Cousot[2,3], Radhia Cousot[1,3,4], and Francesco Logozzo[4]

[1] Centre National de la Recherche Scientifique, Paris
[2] Courant Institute of Mathematical Sciences, New York University
[3] École Normale Supérieure, Paris
[4] Microsoft Research, Redmond

Abstract. Programmers often insert assertions in their code to be optionally checked at runtime, at least during the debugging phase. In the context of design by contracts, these assertions would better be given as a precondition of the method/procedure which can detect that a caller has violated the procedure's contract in a way which definitely leads to an assertion violation (*e.g.*, for separate static analysis). We define precisely and formally the contract inference problem from intermittent assertions inserted in the code by the programmer. Our definition excludes no good run even when a non-deterministic choice (e.g., an interactive input) could lead to a bad one (so this is not the weakest precondition, nor its strengthening by abduction, since a terminating successful execution is not guaranteed). We then introduce new abstract interpretation-based methods to automatically infer both the static contract precondition of a method/procedure and the code to check it at runtime on scalar and collection variables.

1 Introduction

In the context of compositional/structural static program analysis for design by contract [23, 24], it is quite frequent that preconditions for the code (*i.e.* a program/module/method/procedure/function/assembly/etc) have been only partially specified by the programmer (or even not at all for legacy code) and need to be automatically strengthened or inferred by taking into account the implicit *language assertions* (*e.g.*, runtime errors) and the explicit *programmer assertions* (*e.g.*, assertions and contracts of called methods/procedures). Besides the methodological advantage of anticipating future inevitable requirements when running a code, precise contracts are necessary in the context of a separate program analysis as *e.g.*, in Clousot, an abstract interpretation-based static contract checker for .NET [18]. We work in the context of contracts embedded in the program code [4] so that specification conditions are expressed in the programming language itself (and extracted by the compiler for use in contract related tools). The precondition inference problem for a code is twofold [4]:

R. Jhala and D. Schmidt (Eds.): VMCAI 2011, LNCS 6538, pp. 150–168, 2011.

- *Static analysis problem:* infer the entry semantic precondition from control flow dependent language and programmer assertions embedded in the code to guard, whenever possible, against inevitable errors;
- *Code synthesis problem:* generate visible side-effect free code checking for that precondition. This checking code must be separable from the checked code and should only involve elements visible to all callers of the checked code.

Example 1. The problem is illustrated by the following `AllNotNull` procedure where the precondition that the array `A` and all array elements should not be null $A \neq null \wedge \forall i \in [0, A.length) : A[i] \neq null$ is checked by the implicit language assertions while iterating over the array.

```
              void AllNotNull(Ptr[] A) {
/* 1: */   int i = 0;
/* 2: */   while /* 3: */
              (assert(A != null); i < A.length) {
/* 4: */   assert((A != null) && (A[i] != null));
/* 5: */   A[i].f = new Object();
/* 6: */   i++;
/* 7: */   }
/* 8: */ }
```

The language assertion `A[i] != null` for a *given* value of i is *intermittent* at program point 4: but not *invariant* since the array content is modified at program point 5:.

$\square$

On one hand, a solution to the contract inference problem could be to infer the precondition as a set of states, logical formula, or abstract property ensuring proper termination without any language or programmer assertion failure (as proposed *e.g.*, in [10, Sect. 10-4.6]) or [9, Sect. 3.4.5]). But this does not guarantee the precondition to be easily understandable and that efficient code can be generated to check it. Moreover this is stronger than strictly required (*e.g.*, the code `x = random(); assert(x ==0)` is not guaranteed to terminate properly, but has at least one execution without failure, so should not be rejected). On the other hand, the precondition checking code could be a copy of the method body where all code with random or visible side effect (including input) as well as all further dependent code is removed.

Example 2. Continuing Ex. 1, we get the straw man

```
bool CheckAllNotNull(Ptr[] A) {
    int i = 0;
    while (if (A == null) { return false }; i < A.length) {
        if ((A == null) || (0 > i) || (i >= A.length) || (A[i] == null))
            { return false };
        i++ }
    return true }
```

Modifications of i have no visible side effects while those of elements of A do have, so the assignment `A[i].f` is dropped. There is no code that depends on this value, so no other code needs to be removed. $\square$

However, these simple solutions may not provide a simple precondition both easily understandable by the programmer, easily reusable for separate modular static analysis, and efficiently checkable at runtime, if necessary.

Example 3. Continuing Ex. 1 and 2, we would like to automatically infer the precondition ForAll(0,A.length,i => A[i] != null) using ForAll quantifiers [4] over integer ranges and collections. Iterative checking code is then easy to generate.   □

The semantics of code is formalized in Sect. 2 and that of specifications by run-time assertions in Sect. 3. The contract precondition inference problem is defined in Sect. 4 and compared with weakest preconditions computation. Elements of abstract interpretation are recalled in Sect. 5 and used in Sect. 6 to provide a fixpoint solution to the contract precondition inference problem. Several effective contract precondition inference are then proposed, by data flow analysis in Sect. 7, for scalar variables both by forward symbolic analysis in Sect. 8 and by backward symbolic analysis in Sect. 9, for collections by forward analysis in Sect. 10. Sect. 11 has a comparison with related work, suggestions for future work, and conclusions.

2   Program Semantics

Small-step operational semantics. Following [9], the small-step operational semantics of code is assumed to be given by a *transition system* $\langle \Sigma, \tau, \Im \rangle$ where Σ is a set of *states*, $\tau \in \wp(\Sigma \times \Sigma)$ is a non-deterministic *transition relation* between a state and its possible successors, and $\Im \in \wp(\Sigma)$ is the set of *initial states* (on code entry, assuming the precondition, if any, to be true). We write $\tau(s, s')$ for $\langle s, s' \rangle \in \tau$. The *final or blocking states* without any possible successor (on code exit or violation of a language assertion with unpredictable consequences) are $\mathfrak{B} \triangleq \{ s \in \Sigma \mid \forall s' : \neg \tau(s, s') \}$. If the code must satisfy a *global invariant* $\mathfrak{G} \in \wp(\Sigma)$ (*e.g.*, class invariant for a method), we assume this to be included in the definition of the transition relation τ (*e.g.*, $\tau \subseteq \mathfrak{G} \times \mathfrak{G}$). We use a map $\pi \in \Sigma \to \Gamma$ of states of Σ into *control points* in Γ which is assumed to be of finite cardinality. The program has *scalar variables* $x \in \mathrm{x}$, *collection variables* $X \in \mathbb{X}$ and visible side effect free expressions $e \in \mathbb{E}$, including *Boolean expressions* $b \in \mathbb{B} \subseteq \mathbb{E}$. Collection variables X have elements $X[i]$ ranging from 0 to $X.\mathrm{count} - 1$ ($A.\mathrm{length} - 1$ for arrays A). The value of $e \in \mathbb{E}$ in state $s \in \Sigma$ is $[\![e]\!]s \in \mathcal{V}$. The *values* $\mathcal{V}$ include the Booleans $\mathcal{B} \triangleq \{true, false\}$ where the complete Boolean algebra $\langle \mathcal{B}, \Rightarrow \rangle$ is ordered by $false \Rightarrow true$. The value $[\![X]\!]s$ of a collection X in a state $s \in \Sigma$ is a pair $[\![X]\!]s = \langle n, X \rangle$ where $n = [\![X.\mathrm{count}]\!]s \geqslant 0$ is a non-negative integer and $X \in [0, n) \to \mathcal{V}$ denotes the value $X(i)$ of i-th element, $i \in [0, n)$, in the collection. When $i \in [0, n)$, we define $[\![X]\!]s[i] \triangleq X(i) (= [\![X[e]]\!]s$ where $[\![e]\!]s = i)$ to denote the i-th element in the collection.

Traces. We let traces be sequences of states in Σ. $\vec{\Sigma}^n$ is the set of non-empty *finite traces* $\vec{s} = \vec{s}_0 \dots \vec{s}_{n-1}$ of *length* $|\vec{s}| \triangleq n \geqslant 0$ including the *empty trace* $\vec{\epsilon}$ of length $|\vec{\epsilon}| \triangleq 0$. $\vec{\Sigma}^+ \triangleq \bigcup_{n \geqslant 1} \vec{\Sigma}^n$ is the set of *non-empty finite traces* and $\vec{\Sigma}^* \triangleq \vec{\Sigma}^+ \cup \{\vec{\epsilon}\}$. As usual, *concatenation* is denoted by juxtaposition and extended to sets of traces. Moreover, the *sequential composition* of traces is $\vec{s}s \circ s\vec{s}' \triangleq \vec{s}s\vec{s}'$

when $\vec{s}, \vec{s}' \in \vec{\Sigma}^*$ and $s \in \Sigma$, and is otherwise undefined. $\vec{S} \circ \vec{S}' \triangleq \{\vec{s}s\vec{s}' \mid \vec{s}s \in \vec{S} \cap \vec{\Sigma}^+ \wedge s\vec{s}' \in \vec{S}'\}$. The *partial execution traces* or *runs* of $\langle \Sigma, \tau, \mathfrak{I} \rangle$ are prefix traces generated by transitions, as follows

$$\vec{\tau}^n \triangleq \{\vec{s} \in \vec{\Sigma}^n \mid \forall i \in [0, n-1) : \tau(\vec{s}_i, \vec{s}_{i+1})\} \quad partial\ runs\ of\ length\ n \geqslant 0$$

$$\vec{\tau}^+ \triangleq \bigcup_{n \geqslant 1} \vec{\tau}^n \quad non\text{-}empty\ finite\ partial\ runs$$

$$\vec{\tau}^n \triangleq \{\vec{s} \in \vec{\tau}^n \mid \vec{s}_{n-1} \in \mathfrak{B}\} \quad complete\ runs\ of\ length\ n \geqslant 0$$

$$\vec{\tau}^+ \triangleq \bigcup_{n \geqslant 1} \vec{\tau}^n \quad non\text{-}empty\ finite\ complete\ runs.$$

The partial (resp. complete/maximal) runs starting from an initial state are $\vec{\tau}_{\mathfrak{I}}^+ \triangleq \{\vec{s} \in \vec{\tau}^+ \mid \vec{s}_0 \in \mathfrak{I}\}$ (resp. $\vec{\tau}_{\mathfrak{I}}^+ \triangleq \{\vec{s} \in \vec{\tau}^+ \mid \vec{s}_0 \in \mathfrak{I}\}$). Given $\mathfrak{S} \subseteq \Sigma$, we let $\vec{\mathfrak{S}}^n \triangleq \{\vec{s} \in \vec{\Sigma}^n \mid \vec{s}_0 \in \mathfrak{S}\}$, $n \geqslant 1$. Partial and maximal finite runs have the following fixpoint characterization [11]

$$\vec{\tau}_{\mathfrak{I}}^+ = \mathsf{lfp}_{\emptyset}^{\subseteq} \lambda \vec{T} \cdot \vec{\mathfrak{I}}^1 \cup \vec{T} \circ \vec{\tau}^2$$

$$\vec{\tau}^+ = \mathsf{lfp}_{\emptyset}^{\subseteq} \lambda \vec{T} \cdot \vec{\mathfrak{B}}^1 \cup \vec{\tau}^2 \circ \vec{T} = \mathsf{gfp}_{\vec{\Sigma}^+}^{\subseteq} \lambda \vec{T} \cdot \vec{\mathfrak{B}}^1 \cup \vec{\tau}^2 \circ \vec{T}. \quad \text{(1-a,1-b)}$$

3   Specification Semantics

The *specification* includes the existing precondition and postcondition, if any, the language and programmer assertions, made explicit in the form

$$\mathbb{A} = \{\langle \mathsf{c}_j, \mathsf{b}_j \rangle \mid j \in \Delta\}$$

whenever a runtime check $\mathsf{assert}(\mathsf{b}_j)$ is attached to a control point $\mathsf{c}_j \in \Gamma$, $j \in \Delta$. $\mathbb{A}$ is computed by a syntactic pre-analysis of the code. The Boolean expressions b_j are assumed to be both visible side effect free and always well-defined when evaluated in a shortcut manner, which may have to be checked by a prior assert (*e.g.*, $\mathsf{assert((A!= null)}$ && $\mathsf{(A[i] == 0)))}$. For simplicity, we assume that b_j either refers to a scalar variable (written $\mathsf{b}_j(\mathsf{x})$) or to an element of a collection (written $\mathsf{b}_j(\mathsf{X, i})$). This defines

$$\mathfrak{C}_{\mathbb{A}} \triangleq \{s \in \Sigma \mid \exists \langle c, b \rangle \in \mathbb{A} : \pi s = c \wedge \neg[\![b]\!]s\} \quad erroneous\ or\ bad\ states$$

$$\vec{\mathfrak{C}}_{\mathbb{A}} \triangleq \{\vec{s} \in \vec{\Sigma}^+ \mid \exists i < |\vec{s}| : \vec{s}_i \in \mathfrak{C}_{\mathbb{A}}\} \quad erroneous\ or\ bad\ runs.$$

As part of the implicit specification, and for the sake of brevity, we consider that program executions should terminate. Otherwise the results are similar after revisiting (1-a,1-b) for infinite runs as considered in [11].

4   The Contract Precondition Inference Problem

Definition 4. *Given a transition system $\langle \Sigma, \tau, \mathfrak{I} \rangle$ and a specification $\mathbb{A}$, the contract precondition inference problem consists in computing $P_{\mathbb{A}} \in \wp(\Sigma)$ such that when replacing the initial states $\mathfrak{I}$ by $P_{\mathbb{A}} \cap \mathfrak{I}$, we have*

$$\vec{\tau}^+_{P_{\mathbb{A}} \cap \mathbb{J}} \subseteq \vec{\tau}^+_{\mathbb{J}} \qquad \textit{(no new run is introduced)} \qquad (2)$$

$$\vec{\tau}^+_{\mathbb{J} \setminus P_{\mathbb{A}}} = \vec{\tau}^+_{\mathbb{J}} \setminus \vec{\tau}^+_{P_{\mathbb{A}}} \subseteq \vec{\mathcal{E}}_A \qquad \textit{(all eliminated runs are bad runs).} \qquad (3)$$

□

The following lemma shows that, according to Def. 4, no finite maximal good run is ever eliminated.

Lemma 5. (3) *implies* $\vec{\tau}^+_{\mathbb{J}} \cap \neg \vec{\mathcal{E}}_A \subseteq \vec{\tau}^+_{P_{\mathbb{A}}}$.

Choosing $P_{\mathbb{A}} = \mathbb{J}$ so that $\mathbb{J} \setminus P_{\mathbb{A}} = \emptyset$ hence $\vec{\tau}^+_{\mathbb{J} \setminus P_{\mathbb{A}}} = \emptyset$ is a trivial solution, so we would like $P_{\mathbb{A}}$ to be minimal, whenever possible (so that $\vec{\tau}^+_{\mathbb{J} \setminus P_{\mathbb{A}}}$ is maximal). Please note that this is **not** the weakest (liberal) precondition [17], which yields the weakest condition under which the code (either does not terminate or) terminates without assertion failure, whichever non-deterministic choice is chosen. So this is not either the problem of strengthening a precondition to a weaker one by abduction for specification synthesis [7].

Theorem 6. *The strongest*[1] *solution to the precondition inference problem in Def. 4 is*

$$\mathfrak{P}_{\mathbb{A}} \triangleq \{s \mid \exists s\vec{s} \in \vec{\tau}^+ \cap \neg \vec{\mathcal{E}}_A\}. \qquad (4)$$

□

Instead of reasoning on the set $\mathfrak{P}_{\mathbb{A}}$ of states from which there exists a good run without any error, we can reason on the complement $\overline{\mathfrak{P}}_A$ that is the set of states from which all runs are bad in that they always lead to an error. Define $\overline{\mathfrak{P}}_{\mathbb{A}}$ to be the set of states from which any complete run in $\vec{\tau}^+$ does fail.

$$\overline{\mathfrak{P}}_{\mathbb{A}} \triangleq \neg \mathfrak{P}_{\mathbb{A}} = \{s \mid \forall s\vec{s} \in \vec{\tau}^+ : s\vec{s} \in \vec{\mathcal{E}}_A\}.$$

5   Basic Elements of Abstract Interpretation

Galois connections. A *Galois connection* $\langle L, \leqslant \rangle \xrightarrow[\alpha]{\gamma} \langle \overline{L}, \sqsubseteq \rangle$ consists of posets $\langle L, \leqslant \rangle$, $\langle \overline{L}, \sqsubseteq \rangle$ and maps $\alpha \in L \to \overline{L}$, $\gamma \in \overline{L} \to L$ such that $\forall x \in L, y \in \overline{L}$: $\alpha(x) \sqsubseteq y \Leftrightarrow x \leqslant \gamma(y)$. The dual is $\langle \overline{L}, \sqsupseteq \rangle \xrightarrow[\gamma]{\alpha} \langle L, \geqslant \rangle$. In a Galois connection, the *abstraction* α preserves existing least upper bounds (lubs) hence is monotonically increasing so, by duality, the *concretization* γ preserves existing greatest lower bounds (glbs) and is monotonically increasing. If $\langle L, \leqslant \rangle$ is a complete Boolean lattice with unique complement $\neg$ then the self-dual *complement isomorphism* is $\langle L, \leqslant \rangle \xrightarrow[\neg]{\neg} \langle L, \geqslant \rangle$ (since $\neg x \leqslant y \Leftrightarrow x \geqslant \neg y$).

Fixpoint abstraction. Recall from [13, 7.1.0.4] that

---

[1] Following [17], P is said to be *stronger* than Q and Q *weaker* than P if and only if $P \subseteq Q$.

Lemma 7. *If $\langle L, \leqslant, \bot \rangle$ is a complete lattice or a cpo, $F \in L \to L$ is monotonically increasing, $\langle \overline{L}, \sqsubseteq \rangle$ is a poset, $\alpha \in L \to \overline{L}$ is continuous[2,3], $\overline{F} \in \overline{L} \to \overline{L}$ commutes (resp. semi-commutes) with F that is $\alpha \circ F = \overline{F} \circ \alpha$ (resp. $\alpha \circ F \sqsubseteq \overline{F} \circ \alpha$) then $\alpha(\mathsf{lfp}_{\bot}^{\leqslant} F) = \mathsf{lfp}_{\alpha(\bot)}^{\sqsubseteq} \overline{F}$ (resp. $\alpha(\mathsf{lfp}_{\bot}^{\leqslant} F) \sqsubseteq \mathsf{lfp}_{\alpha(\bot)}^{\sqsubseteq} \overline{F}$).*

Applying Lem. 7 to $\langle L, \leqslant \rangle \xleftrightarrow{\;\neg\;} \langle L, \geqslant \rangle$, we get Cor. 8 and by duality Cor. 9 below.

Corollary 8 (David Park [26, Sect. 2.3]). *If $F \in L \to L$ is monotonically increasing on a complete Boolean lattice $\langle L, \leqslant, \bot, \neg \rangle$ then $\neg\, \mathsf{lfp}_{\bot}^{\leqslant} F = \mathsf{gfp}_{\neg\bot}^{\leqslant} \neg \circ F \circ \neg$.*

Corollary 9. *If $\langle \overline{L}, \sqsubseteq, \top \rangle$ is a complete lattice or a dcpo, $\overline{F} \in \overline{L} \to \overline{L}$ is monotonically increasing, $\gamma \in \overline{L} \to L$ is co-continuous[4], $F \in L \to L$ commutes with F that is $\gamma \circ \overline{F} = F \circ \gamma$ then $\gamma(\mathsf{gfp}_{\top}^{\sqsubseteq} \overline{F}) = \mathsf{gfp}_{\gamma(\top)}^{\leqslant} F$.*

6   Fixpoint Strongest Contract Precondition

Following [11], let us define the abstraction generalizing [17] to traces

$$\mathsf{wlp}[\vec{T}] \triangleq \lambda \vec{Q} \cdot \{ s \mid \forall s\vec{s} \in \vec{T} : s\vec{s} \in \vec{Q} \}$$
$$\mathsf{wlp}^{-1}[\vec{Q}] \triangleq \lambda P \cdot \{ s\vec{s} \in \vec{\Sigma}^{+} \mid (s \in P) \Rightarrow (s\vec{s} \in \vec{Q}) \}$$

such that $\langle \wp(\vec{\Sigma}^{+}), \subseteq \rangle \xleftrightarrow[\lambda \vec{T} \cdot \mathsf{wlp}[\vec{T}]\vec{Q}]{\mathsf{wlp}^{-1}[\vec{Q}]} \langle \wp(\Sigma), \supseteq \rangle$ and $\overline{\mathfrak{P}}_{\mathbb{A}} = \mathsf{wlp}[\vec{\tau}^{+}](\vec{\mathfrak{C}}_{\mathbb{A}})$. By fixpoint abstraction, it follows from (1-a) and Cor. 8 that

Theorem 10. $\overline{\mathfrak{P}}_{\mathbb{A}} = \mathsf{gfp}_{\Sigma}^{\subseteq} \lambda P \cdot \mathfrak{C}_{\mathbb{A}} \cup (\neg \mathfrak{B} \cap \widetilde{\mathsf{pre}}[\tau]P)$ *and* $\mathfrak{P}_{\mathbb{A}} = \mathsf{lfp}_{\emptyset}^{\subseteq} \lambda P \cdot \neg \mathfrak{C}_{\mathbb{A}} \cap (\mathfrak{B} \cup \mathsf{pre}[\tau]P)$ *where* $\mathsf{pre}[\tau]Q \triangleq \{ s \mid \exists s' \in Q : \langle s, s' \rangle \in \tau \}$ *and* $\widetilde{\mathsf{pre}}[\tau]Q \triangleq \neg\mathsf{pre}[\tau](\neg Q) = \{ s \mid \forall s' : \langle s, s' \rangle \in \tau \Rightarrow s' \in Q \}$. □

If the set Σ of states is finite, as assumed in model-checking [2], the fixpoint definition of $\mathfrak{P}_{\mathbb{A}}$ in Th. 10 is computable iteratively, up to combinatorial explosion. The code to check the precondition $s \in \mathfrak{P}_{\mathbb{A}}$ can proceed by exhaustive enumeration. In case this does not scale up or for infinite state systems, bounded model-checking [5] is an alternative using $\bigcup_{i=0}^{k} \vec{\tau}^{i}$ instead of $\vec{\tau}^{+}$ but, by Th. 6, the bounded prefix abstraction $\alpha_{k}(\vec{T}) \triangleq \{ \vec{s}_0 \dots \vec{s}_{\min(k,|\vec{s}|)-1} \mid \vec{s} \in \vec{T} \}$ is unsound for approximating both $\mathfrak{P}_{\mathbb{A}}$ and $\overline{\mathfrak{P}}_{\mathbb{A}}$.

---

[2] α is *continuous* if and only if it preserves existing lubs of increasing chains.

[3] The continuity hypothesis for α can be restricted to the iterates $F^0 \triangleq \bot$, $F^{n+1} \triangleq F(F^n)$, $F^\omega \triangleq \bigsqcup_{n \geqslant} F^n$ of the least fixpoint of F.

[4] γ is *co-continuous* if and only if it preserves existing glbs of decreasing chains.

7 Contract Precondition Inference by Symbolic Flow Analysis

Instead of state-based reasonings, as in Sect. 4 and 6, we can consider symbolic (or even syntactic) reasonings moving the code assertions to the code entry, when the effect is the same. This can be done by a sound data flow analysis [21] when

1. the value of the visible side effect free Boolean expression on scalar or collection variables in the `assert` is exactly the same as the value of this expression when evaluated on entry;
2. the value of the expression checked on program entry is checked in an `assert` on all paths that can be taken from the program entry.

We propose a backward data flow analysis to check for both sufficient conditions 1 and 2.

Backward expression propagation. Let $c \in \Gamma$ be a control point and b be a Boolean expression. For example b can contain `ForAll` or `Exists` assertions on unmodified collections without free scalar variables and no visible side effect (see Sect. 10 otherwise). $P(c, b)$ holds at program point c when Boolean expression b will definitely be checked in an `assert`(b) on all paths from c without being changed up to this check. $P = \mathrm{gfp}^{\overset{\Rightarrow}{}} B[\![\tau]\!]$ is the $\Rightarrow$-greatest solution of the backward system of equations[5,6]

$$\begin{cases} P(c, b) = B[\![\tau]\!](P)(c, b) \\ c \in \Gamma, \quad b \in \mathbb{A}_\mathrm{b} \end{cases}$$

where the expressions of asserts are $\mathbb{A}_\mathrm{b} \triangleq \{b \mid \exists c : \langle c, b \rangle \in \mathbb{A}\}$ and the transformer $B \in (\Gamma \times \mathbb{A}_\mathrm{b} \to \mathcal{B}) \to (\Gamma \times \mathbb{A}_\mathrm{b} \to \mathcal{B})$ is

$$B[\![\tau]\!](P)(c, b) = true \quad \text{when} \quad \langle c, b \rangle \in \mathbb{A} \qquad \qquad (\mathtt{assert}(b) \text{ at } c)$$

$$B[\![\tau]\!](P)(c, b) = false \quad \text{when} \quad \exists s \in \mathcal{B} : \pi s = c \wedge \langle c, b \rangle \notin \mathbb{A} \qquad (\text{exit at } c)$$

$$B[\![\tau]\!](P)(c, b) = \bigwedge_{c' \in \mathsf{succ}[\![\tau]\!](c)} \mathsf{unchanged}[\![\tau]\!](c, c', b) \wedge P(c', b) \qquad (\text{otherwise})$$

the set $\mathsf{succ}[\![\tau]\!](c)$ of successors of the program point $c \in \Gamma$ satisfies

$$\mathsf{succ}[\![\tau]\!](c) \supseteq \{c' \in \Gamma \mid \exists s, s' : \pi s = c \wedge \tau(s, s') \wedge \pi s' = c'\}$$

$(\mathsf{succ}[\![\tau]\!](c) \triangleq \Gamma$ yields a flow-insensitive analysis) and $\mathsf{unchanged}[\![\tau]\!](c, c', b)$ implies than a transition by τ from program point c to program point c' can never change the value of Boolean expression b

$$\mathsf{unchanged}[\![\tau]\!](c, c', b) \Rightarrow \forall s, s' : (\pi s = c \wedge \tau(s, s') \wedge \pi s' = c') \Rightarrow ([\![b]\!]s = [\![b]\!]s').$$

---

[5] $\Rightarrow$ is the pointwise extension of logical implication $\Rightarrow$.
[6] The system of equations $\vec{X} = \vec{F}(\vec{X})$ where $\vec{X} = X_1, \ldots, X_n$ is written $\begin{cases} X_i = F_i(X_1, \ldots, X_n) . \\ i = 1, \ldots, n \end{cases}$

unchanged$[\![\tau]\!](c, c', b)$ can be a syntactic underapproximation of its semantic definition [3]. Define

$$\mathfrak{R}_\mathbb{A} \triangleq \lambda b \cdot \{\langle s,\ s'\rangle \mid \langle \pi s',\ b\rangle \in \mathbb{A} \wedge [\![b]\!]s = [\![b]\!]s'\}$$
$$\vec{\mathfrak{R}}_\mathbb{A} \triangleq \lambda b \cdot \{\vec{s} \in \vec{\Sigma}^+ \mid \exists i < |\vec{s}| : \langle \vec{s}_0,\ \vec{s}_i\rangle \in \mathfrak{R}_\mathbb{A}(b)\}$$

and the abstraction

$$\vec{\alpha}_D(\vec{T})(c, b) \triangleq \forall \vec{s} \in \vec{T} : \pi \vec{s}_0 = c \Rightarrow \vec{s} \in \vec{\mathfrak{R}}_\mathbb{A}(b)$$
$$\vec{\gamma}_D(P) \triangleq \{\vec{s} \mid \forall b \in \mathbb{A}_\mathbf{b} : P(\pi \vec{s}_0, b) \Rightarrow \vec{s} \in \vec{\mathfrak{R}}_\mathbb{A}(b)\}$$

such that $\langle \vec{\Sigma}^+,\ \subseteq\rangle \xleftarrow[\vec{\alpha}_D]{\vec{\gamma}_D} \langle \Gamma \times \mathbb{A}_\mathbf{b} \to \mathcal{B},\ \Leftarrow\rangle$. By (1-a) and Lem. 7, we have

Theorem 11. $\vec{\alpha}_D(\vec{\tau}^+) \Leftarrow \mathsf{lfp}^{\Leftarrow} B[\![\tau]\!] = \mathsf{gfp}^{\Rightarrow} B[\![\tau]\!] \triangleq P.$ □

Precondition generation. The syntactic precondition generated at entry control point $i \in \mathfrak{I}_\pi \triangleq \{i \in \Gamma \mid \exists s \in \mathfrak{I} : \pi s = i\}$ is (assuming $\&\& \emptyset \triangleq \mathbf{true}$)

$$\mathrm{P}_i \triangleq \underset{b \in \mathbb{A}_\mathbf{b},\ P(i,b)}{\&\&}\ b$$

The set of states for which the syntactic precondition P_i is evaluated to *true* at program point $i \in \Gamma$ is $P_i \triangleq \{s \in \Sigma \mid \pi s = i \wedge [\![\mathrm{P}_i]\!]s\}$ and so for all program entry points (in case there is more than one) $P_\mathfrak{I} \triangleq \{s \in \Sigma \mid \exists i \in \mathfrak{I}_\pi : s \in P_i\}$. We have

Theorem 12. $\mathfrak{P}_\mathbb{A} \cap \mathfrak{I} \subseteq P_\mathfrak{I}.$ □

By Th. 6 and 12, the precondition generation is sound: a rejected initial state would inevitably have lead to an assertion failure.

Example 13. Continuing Ex. 1, the assertion A != null is checked on all paths and A is not changed (only its elements are), so the data flow analysis is able to move the assertion as a precondition. □

However, the data flow abstraction considered in this Sect. 7 is rather imprecise because a precondition is checked on code entry only if

1. the exact same precondition is checked in an assert (since scalar and collection variable modifications are not taken into account, other than by annihilating the backward propagation);
2. and this, whichever execution path is taken (conditions are not taken into account).

We propose remedies to 1 and 2 in the following Sect. 8 and 9.

8 Contract Precondition Inference for Scalar Variables by Forward Symbolic Analysis

Let us define the cmd, succ and pred functions mapping control points to their command, successors and predecessors ($\forall c, c' \in \Gamma : c' \in \mathsf{pred}(c) \Leftrightarrow c \in \mathsf{succ}(c')$).

- c: x:=e; c':... $\mathsf{cmd}(c,c') \triangleq$ x:=e $\mathsf{succ}(c) \triangleq \{c'\}$ $\mathsf{pred}(c') \triangleq \{c\}$
- c: assert(b); c':... $\mathsf{cmd}(c,c') \triangleq$ b $\mathsf{succ}(c) \triangleq \{c'\}$ $\mathsf{pred}(c') \triangleq \{c\}$
- c: if b then $\mathsf{cmd}(c,c_t') \triangleq$ b $\mathsf{succ}(c) \triangleq \{c_t',c_f'\}$
  $\quad c_t':\ldots c_t'':$ $\mathsf{cmd}(c,c_f') \triangleq \neg$b $\mathsf{pred}(c_t') \triangleq \{c\}$
  else $\mathsf{cmd}(c_t'',c') \triangleq$ skip $\mathsf{succ}(c_t'') \triangleq \{c'\}$
  $\quad c_f':\ldots c_f'':$ $\mathsf{cmd}(c_f'',c') \triangleq$ skip $\mathsf{succ}(c_f'') \triangleq \{c'\}$ $\mathsf{pred}(c_f') \triangleq \{c\}$
  fi; c'... $\mathsf{pred}(c') \triangleq \{c_t'',c_f''\}$
- c :while c': b do $\mathsf{cmd}(c,c') \triangleq$ skip $\mathsf{succ}(c) \triangleq \{c'\}$ $\mathsf{pred}(c') \triangleq \{c,c_b''\}$
  $\quad c_b':\ldots c_b'':$ $\mathsf{cmd}(c',c_b') \triangleq$ b $\mathsf{succ}(c') \triangleq \{c_b',c''\}$ $\mathsf{pred}(c_b') \triangleq \{c'\}$
  od; c''... $\mathsf{cmd}(c',c'') \triangleq \neg$b $\mathsf{succ}(c_b'') \triangleq \{c'\}$ $\mathsf{pred}(c'') \triangleq \{c'\}$
                       $\mathsf{cmd}(c_b'',c) \triangleq$ skip

For programs with scalar variables $\vec{x}$, we denote by $\vec{\underline{x}}$ (or $\overrightarrow{x0}$) their initial values and by $\vec{x}$ their current values. Following [9, Sect. 3.4.5], the symbolic execution [22] attaches invariants $\Phi(c)$ to program points $c \in \Gamma$ defined as the pointwise $\overset{\Rightarrow}{\Rightarrow}$-least fixpoint of the system of equations $\Phi = F(\Phi)$ with

$$
\begin{cases}
F(\Phi)c = \bigvee_{c' \in \mathsf{pred}(c)} \mathcal{F}(\mathsf{cmd}(c',c),\Phi(c')) \vee \bigvee_{c \in \mathfrak{I}_\pi} (\vec{x} = \vec{\underline{x}}) \\
c \in \Gamma
\end{cases}
$$

where $\mathsf{pred}(c) = \emptyset$ for program entry points $c \in \mathfrak{I}_\pi$ and the forward transformers are in Floyd's style (the predicates ϕ depends only on the symbolic initial $\vec{\underline{x}}$ and current $\vec{x}$ values of the program variables $\vec{x}$)

$$\mathcal{F}(\mathsf{skip}, \phi) \triangleq \phi$$
$$\mathcal{F}(\mathsf{x:=e}, \phi) \triangleq \exists \vec{x}' : \phi[\vec{x} := \vec{x}'] \wedge \mathsf{dom}(e, \vec{x}') \wedge \vec{x} = \vec{x}'[x := e[\vec{x} := \vec{x}']]$$
$$\mathcal{F}(\mathsf{b}, \phi) \triangleq \phi \wedge \mathsf{dom}(b, \vec{x}) \wedge b[\vec{x} := \vec{x}]$$

where $\mathsf{dom}(e, \vec{x})$ is the condition on $\vec{x}$ for evaluating e as a function of $\vec{x}$ without runtime error. By allowing infinitary disjunctions, we have [9, Sect. 3.4.5]

Theorem 14. $\Phi = \mathsf{lfp}^{\overset{\Rightarrow}{}} F$ has the form $\Phi(c) = \bigvee_{i \in \Delta_c} p_{c,i}(\vec{\underline{x}}) \wedge \vec{x} = \vec{e}_{c,i}(\vec{\underline{x}})$ where $p_{c,i}(\vec{\underline{x}})$ is a Boolean expression defining the condition for control to reach the current program point c as a function of the initial values $\vec{\underline{x}}$ of the scalar variables $\vec{x}$ and $\vec{e}_i(\vec{\underline{x}})$ defines the current values $\vec{x}$ of the scalar variables $\vec{x}$ as a function of their initial values $\vec{\underline{x}}$ when reaching program point c with path condition $p_{c,i}(\vec{\underline{x}})$ true. □

The soundness follows from $\forall \vec{s} \in \vec{\tau}^+ : \forall j < |\vec{s}| : \phi(c)[\vec{\underline{x}} := [\![\vec{x}]\!]\vec{s}_0][\vec{x} := [\![\vec{x}]\!]\vec{s}_j] = \forall \vec{s} \in \vec{\tau}^+ : \forall j < |\vec{s}| : \forall i \in \Delta_{\pi\vec{s}_j} : p_{\pi\vec{s}_j,i}[\vec{\underline{x}} := [\![\vec{x}]\!]\vec{s}_0] \Rightarrow [\![\vec{x}]\!]\vec{s}_j = \vec{e}_{\pi\vec{s}_j,i}[\vec{\underline{x}} := [\![\vec{x}]\!]\vec{s}_0]$ where $[\![\vec{x}]\!]s$ is the value of the vector $\vec{x}$ of scalar variables in state s.

This suggests a method for calculating the precondition by adding for each assertion c:assert(b) the condition $\bigwedge_{i \in \Delta_c} p_{c,i}[\vec{\underline{x}} := \vec{x}] \Rightarrow b[\vec{x} := \vec{e}_{c,i}[\vec{\underline{x}} := \vec{x}]]$ which is checked on the initial values of variables.

Example 15. For the program

```
/* 1: x=x0 & y=y0 */          if (x == 0 ) {
/* 2: x0=0 & x=x0 & y=y0 */       x++;
/* 3: x0=0 & x=x0+1 & y=y0 */     assert(x==y);
                              }
```

the precondition at program point 1: is `(!(x==0)||(x+1==y))`. ☐

Of course the iterative computation of $\mathsf{lfp}^{\stackrel{.}{\Rightarrow}} F$ will in general not terminate so that a widening [12] is needed. A simple one would bound the number of iterations and widen $\bigvee_{i\in\Delta_c} p_{c,i}(\vec{\underline{x}}) \wedge \vec{x} = \vec{e}_{c,i}(\vec{\underline{x}})$ to $\bigwedge_{i\in\Delta_c} p_{c,i}(\vec{\underline{x}}) \Rightarrow \vec{x} = \vec{e}_{c,i}(\vec{\underline{x}})$.

9 Contract Precondition Inference by Backward Symbolic Analysis

Backward symbolic precondition analysis of simple assertions. The symbolic relation between entry and `assert` conditions can be also established backwards, starting from the `assert` conditions and propagating towards the entry points taking assignments and tests into account with widening around unbounded loops. We first consider simple assertions involving only scalar variables (including *e.g.*, the size of collections as needed in Sect. 10 where the case of collections is considered).

Abstract domain. Given the set $\mathbb{B}$ of visible side effect free Boolean expressions on scalar variables, we consider the abstract domain $\mathbb{B}/_{\equiv}$ containing the infimum `false` (unreachable), the supremum `true` (unknown) and equivalence classes of expressions $[\mathsf{b}]/_=$ for the abstract equivalence of expressions $=$ abstracting semantic equality that is $\mathsf{b} \equiv \mathsf{b}' \Rightarrow \forall s \in \Sigma : [\![\mathsf{b}]\!]s = [\![\mathsf{b}']\!]s$. The equivalence classes are encoded by choosing an arbitrary representative $\mathsf{b}' \in [\mathsf{b}]/_{\equiv}$. The abstract equivalence $\equiv$ can be chosen within a wide range of possibilities, from syntactic equality, to the use of a simplifier, of abstract domains, or that of a SMT solver. This provides an abstract implication $\mathsf{b} \mapsto \mathsf{b}'$ underapproximating the concrete implication $\Rightarrow$ in that $\mathsf{b} \mapsto \mathsf{b}'$ implies that $\forall s \in \Sigma : [\![\mathsf{b}]\!]s \Rightarrow [\![\mathsf{b}']\!]s$. The equivalence is defined as $\mathsf{b} \equiv \mathsf{b}' \triangleq \mathsf{b} \mapsto \mathsf{b}' \wedge \mathsf{b}' \mapsto \mathsf{b}$. The basic abstract domain is therefore $\langle \mathbb{B}/_{\equiv}, \mapsto \rangle$.

We now define the abstract domain functor

$$\overline{\mathbb{B}}^2 \triangleq \{ \mathsf{b}_p \rightsquigarrow \mathsf{b}_a \mid \mathsf{b}_p \in \mathbb{B} \wedge \mathsf{b}_a \in \mathbb{B} \wedge \mathsf{b}_p \not\mapsto \mathsf{b}_a \}$$

Notice that $\mathsf{b}_p \rightsquigarrow \mathsf{b}_a$ denotes the pair $\langle [\mathsf{b}_p]/_{\equiv}, [\mathsf{b}_a]/_{\equiv} \rangle$ of $\mathbb{B}/_{\equiv} \times \mathbb{B}/_{\equiv}$. The interpretation of $\mathsf{b}_p \rightsquigarrow \mathsf{b}_a$ is that when the path condition b_p holds, an execution path will be followed to some `assert(b)` and checking b_a at the beginning of the path is the same as checking this b later in the path when reaching the assertion. We exclude the elements such that $\mathsf{b}_p \mapsto \mathsf{b}_a$ which implies $\mathsf{b}_p \Rightarrow \mathsf{b}_a$ so that no precondition is needed. An example is `if (b_p) { assert(b_a) }` where the assertion has already been checked on the paths leading to that assertion. The abstract ordering on $\langle \overline{\mathbb{B}}^2, \mapsto \rangle$ is $\mathsf{b}_p \rightsquigarrow \mathsf{b}_a \mapsto \mathsf{b}'_p \rightsquigarrow \mathsf{b}'_a \triangleq \mathsf{b}'_p \mapsto \mathsf{b}_p \wedge \mathsf{b}_a \mapsto \mathsf{b}'_a$.

Different paths to different assertions are abstracted by elements of $\langle \wp(\overline{\mathbb{B}}^2),$ $\subseteq\rangle$, each $b_p \leadsto b_a$ corresponding to a different path to an assertion. The number of paths can grow indefinitely so $\langle \wp(\overline{\mathbb{B}}^2), \subseteq\rangle$ must be equipped with a widening.

Finally our abstract domain will be $\langle \Gamma \to \wp(\overline{\mathbb{B}}^2), \dot{\subseteq}\rangle$ ordered pointwise so as to attach an abstract property $\rho(c) \in \wp(\overline{\mathbb{B}}^2)$ to each program point $c \in \Gamma$.

Example 16. The program on the left has abstract properties given on the right.

```
/* 1: */   if ( odd(x) ) {
/* 2: */       y++;
/* 3: */       assert(y > 0);
           } else {
/* 4: */       assert(y < 0); }
/* 5: */
```

$\rho(1) = \{\texttt{odd(x)} \leadsto \texttt{y >= 0}, \neg\texttt{odd(x)} \leadsto \texttt{y < 0}\}$
$\rho(2) = \{\texttt{true} \leadsto \texttt{y >= 0}\}$
$\rho(3) = \{\texttt{true} \leadsto \texttt{y > 0}\}$
$\rho(4) = \{\texttt{true} \leadsto \texttt{y < 0}\}$
$\rho(5) = \emptyset$ □

Because the abstraction is syntactic, there may be no best abstraction, so we define the concretization (recall that $\mathbb{A}$ is the set of pairs $\langle c, b\rangle$ such that $\texttt{assert(b)}$ is checked at program point c and define $\mathbb{A}(c) \triangleq \bigwedge_{\langle c, b\rangle \in \mathbb{A}} b$)

$$\dot{\gamma} \in (\Gamma \to \wp(\overline{\mathbb{B}}^2)) \to \wp(\vec{\Sigma}^+), \qquad \dot{\gamma}(\rho) \triangleq \bigcup_{c \in \Gamma} \{\vec{s} \in \overline{\gamma}_c(\rho(c)) \mid \pi\vec{s}_0 = c\}$$

$$\overline{\gamma}_c \in \wp(\overline{\mathbb{B}}^2) \to \wp(\{\vec{s} \in \vec{\Sigma}^+ \mid \pi\vec{s}_0 = c\}), \qquad \overline{\gamma}_c(C) \triangleq \bigcap_{b_p \leadsto b_a \in C} \gamma_c(b_p \leadsto b_a)$$

$$\gamma_c \in \overline{\mathbb{B}}^2 \to \wp(\{\vec{s} \in \vec{\Sigma}^+ \mid \pi\vec{s}_0 = c\})$$

$$\gamma_c(b_p \leadsto b_a) \triangleq \{\vec{s} \in \vec{\Sigma}^+ \mid \pi\vec{s}_0 = c \wedge [\![b_p]\!]\vec{s}_0 \Rightarrow (\exists j < |\vec{s}| : [\![b_a]\!]\vec{s}_0 = [\![\mathbb{A}(\pi\vec{s}_j)]\!]\vec{s}_j)\}.$$

Observe that $\dot{\gamma}$ is decreasing which corresponds to the intuition that an analysis finding no path precondition $b_p \leadsto b_a$ defines all possible executions in $\vec{\Sigma}^+$.

Backward path condition and checked expression propagation. The system of backward equations $\rho = B(\rho)$ is (recall that $\bigcup \emptyset = \emptyset$)

$$\begin{cases} B(\rho)c = \displaystyle\bigcup_{c' \in \text{succ}(c),\, b \leadsto b' \in \rho(c')} B(\text{cmd}(c, c'), b \leadsto b') \cup \{\texttt{true} \leadsto b \mid \langle c, b\rangle \in \mathbb{A}\} \\ c \in \Gamma \end{cases}$$

where (writing $e[x := e']$ for the substitution of e' for x in e)

$B(\texttt{skip}, b_p \leadsto b_a) \triangleq \{b_p \leadsto b_a\}$
$B(\texttt{x:=e}, b_p \leadsto b_a) \triangleq \{b_p[x := e] \leadsto b_a[x := e]\}$ if $b_p[x := e] \in \mathbb{B} \wedge b_a[x := e] \in \mathbb{B}$
$\qquad\qquad\qquad\qquad\qquad\qquad\qquad\qquad \wedge\, b_p[x := e] \not\Rightarrow b_c[x := e]$
$\qquad\qquad \triangleq \emptyset \qquad\qquad\qquad\qquad\qquad$ otherwise
$B(\texttt{b}, b_p \leadsto b_a) \triangleq \{\texttt{b \&\& } b_p \leadsto b_a\} \qquad$ if $\texttt{b \&\& } b_p \in \mathbb{B} \wedge \texttt{b \&\& } b_p \not\Rightarrow b_a$
$\qquad\qquad \triangleq \emptyset \qquad\qquad\qquad\qquad\qquad$ otherwise

By Cor. 9 and (1-b), the analysis is sound, *i.e.*

Theorem 17. *If $\rho \dot{\subseteq} \text{lfp}^{\dot{\subseteq}} B$ then $\vec{\tau}^+ \subseteq \dot{\gamma}(\rho)$.*   □

Observe that B can be $\Rrightarrow$-overapproximated (*e.g.*, to allow for simplifications of the Boolean expressions).

Example 18. The analysis of the following program

```
/* 1: */    while (x != 0) {
/* 2: */        assert(x > 0);
/* 3: */        x--;
/* 4: */    }    /* 5: */
```

leads to the following iterates at program point 1: $\rho^0(1) = \emptyset$, $\rho^1(1) = \{x \neq 0 \rightsquigarrow x > 0\}$, which is stable since the next iterate is $(x \neq 0 \wedge x > 0 \wedge x - 1 \neq 0) \rightsquigarrow (x - 1 > 0) \equiv x > 1 \rightsquigarrow x > 1$, which is trivially satisfied hence not added to $\rho^2(1) = \rho^1(1)$. □

Example 19. The backward symbolic analysis of Ex. 1 moves the checks (A != null) to the precondition. □

A simple widening to enforce convergence would limit the size of the elements of $\wp(\overline{\mathbb{B}}^2)$, which is sound since eliminating a pair $b_p \rightsquigarrow b_a$ would just lead to ignore some assertion in the precondition, which is always correct.

Precondition generation. Given an analysis $\rho \stackrel{.}{\subseteq} \mathsf{lfp}^{\subseteq} B$, the syntactic precondition generated at entry control point $i \in \mathcal{I}_\pi \stackrel{\triangle}{=} \{i \in \Gamma \mid \exists s \in \mathcal{I} : \pi s = i\}$ is

$$ \mathrm{P}_i \stackrel{\triangle}{=} \underset{b_p \rightsquigarrow b_a \in \rho(i)}{\&\&} (!(b_p) \mid\mid (b_a)) \qquad \text{(again, assuming \&\& } \emptyset \stackrel{\triangle}{=} \textit{true)} $$

Example 20. For Ex. 18, the precondition generated at program point 1 will be !(x != 0) || (x > 0) since the static analysis was able to show that only the first assert in the loop does matter because when passed successfully it implies all the following ones. □

The set of states for which the syntactic precondition P_i is evaluated to *true* at program point $i \in \Gamma$ is $P_i \stackrel{\triangle}{=} \{s \in \Sigma \mid \pi s = i \wedge [\![\mathrm{P}_i]\!]s\}$ and so for all program entry points (in case there is more than one) $P_{\mathcal{I}} \stackrel{\triangle}{=} \{s \in \Sigma \mid \exists i \in \mathcal{I}_\pi : s \in P_i\}$.

Theorem 21. $\mathfrak{P}_A \cap \mathcal{I} \subseteq P_{\mathcal{I}}$. □

So, by Th. 6, the data flow analysis is sound, a rejected initial state would inevitably have lead to an assertion failure.

10   Contract Precondition Inference for Collections by Forward Static Analysis

Symbolic execution as considered in Sect. 8 and 9 for scalars is harder for data structures since all the elements of the data structure must be handled individually without loss of precision. We propose a simple solution for collections (including arrays). The idea is to move to the precondition the assertions on elements of the collection which can be proved to be unmodified before reaching the condition.

Abstract domain for scalar variables. For scalar variables $x \in \mathbb{x}$, we assume that we are given abstract properties in $\eta \in \Gamma \to \mathcal{R}$ with concretization $\gamma_x(\eta) \in \wp(\Sigma)$. Moreover, we consider a dataflow analysis with abstract properties $\zeta \in \Gamma \to \mathbb{x} \to \overline{\mathcal{A}}$ and pointwise extension of the order $0 \preceq 0 \prec 1 \preceq 1$ on $\overline{\mathcal{A}} \triangleq \{0, 1\}$ where 0 means "unmodified" and 1 "unknown". The concretization is

$$\gamma(\eta, \zeta) \triangleq \{\vec{s} \in \Sigma^+ \mid \forall j < |\vec{s}| : \vec{s}_j \in \gamma_x(\eta) \wedge$$
$$\forall x \in \mathbb{x} : \zeta(\pi \vec{s}_j)(x) = 0 \Rightarrow [\![x]\!]\vec{s}_0 = [\![x]\!]\vec{s}_j\}$$

Segmentation abstract domain. For collections $X \in \mathbb{X}$, we propose to use segmentation as introduced by [16]. A segmentation abstract property in $\overline{\mathcal{S}}(\overline{\mathcal{A}})$ depends on abstract properties in $\overline{\mathcal{A}}$ holding for elements of segments. So

$$\overline{\mathcal{S}}(\overline{\mathcal{A}}) \triangleq \{((\overline{\mathcal{B}} \times \overline{\mathcal{A}}) \times (\overline{\mathcal{B}} \times \overline{\mathcal{A}} \times \{\lrcorner, ?\})^k \times (\overline{\mathcal{B}} \times \{\lrcorner, ?\}) \mid k \geqslant 0\} \cup \{\bot\}$$

and the segmentation abstract properties have the form

$$\{e_1^1 \ldots e_{m_1}^1\} A_1 \{e_1^2 \ldots e_{m_2}^2\}[?^2] A_2 \ldots A_{n-1} \{e_1^n \ldots e_{m_n}^n\}[?^n]$$

where

- We let $\overline{\mathcal{E}}$ be a set of symbolic expressions in normal form depending on variables. Here, the abstract expressions $\overline{\mathcal{E}}$ are restricted to the normal form $v + k$ where $v \in \mathbb{x} \cup \{v_0\}$ is an integer variable plus an integer constant $k \in \mathbb{Z}$ (an auxiliary variable $v_0 \notin \mathbb{x}$ is assumed to be always 0 and is used to represent the integer constant k as $v_0 + k$);
- the segment bounds $\{e_1^i \ldots e_{m^i}^i\} \in \overline{\mathcal{B}}$, $i \in [1, n]$, $n > 1$, are finite non-empty sets of symbolic expressions in normal form $e_j^i \in \overline{\mathcal{E}}$, $j = 1, \ldots, m^i$;
- the abstract predicates $A_i \in \overline{\mathcal{A}}$ denote properties that are valid for all the elements in the collection between the bounds; and
- the optional question mark $[?^i]$ follows the upper bound of a segment. Its presence ? means that the segment might be empty. Its absence $\lrcorner$ means that the segment cannot be empty. Because this information is attached to the segment upper bound (which is also the lower bound of the next segment), the lower bound $\{e_1^1 \ldots e_{m_1}^1\}$ of the first segment never has a question mark. $\langle\{\lrcorner, ?\}, \preccurlyeq, \curlyvee, \curlywedge\rangle$ is a complete lattice with $\lrcorner \prec ?$.

Segmentation modification and checking analyses. We consider a *segmentation modification analysis* with abstract domain $\overline{\mathcal{S}}(\mathcal{M})$ where $\mathcal{M} \triangleq \{\mathfrak{e}, \eth\}$ with $\mathfrak{e} \sqsubseteq \mathfrak{e} \sqsubseteq \eth \sqsubseteq \eth$. The abstract property $\mathfrak{e}$ states that all the elements in the segment must be equal to their initial value (so $\gamma_{\mathcal{M}}(\mathfrak{e}) \triangleq \{\langle v, v\rangle \mid v \in \mathcal{V}\}$) and the abstract property $\eth$ means that some element in the segment might have been modified hence might be different from its initial value (in which case we define $\gamma_{\mathcal{M}}(\eth) \triangleq \mathcal{V} \times \mathcal{V}$).

For each `assert` in the program, we also use a *segmentation checking analysis* with abstract domain $\overline{\mathcal{C}} \triangleq \{\bot, \mathfrak{n}, \mathfrak{c}. \top\}$ where $\bot \sqsubseteq \mathfrak{n} \sqsubseteq \top$ and $\bot \sqsubseteq \mathfrak{c} \sqsubseteq \top$ to collect the set of elements of a collection that have been checked by this `assert`. The abstract property $\perp$ is unreachability, c states that all the elements in the segment have definitely been checked by the relevant `assert`, n when none of the elements in the segment have been checked, and $\top$ is unknown.

Example 22. The analysis of Ex. 1 proceeds as follows (the first segmentation in $\overline{S}(\mathcal{M})$ collects element modifications for A while the second in segmentation $\overline{S}(\overline{C})$ collects the set of elements `A[i]` of A checked by the assertion at program point 4: while equal to its initial value. The classical analyses for A (not `null` whenever used) and `i` are not shown.).

(a) 1: {0}e{A.length}? - {0}n{A.length}?
  no element yet modified (e) and none checked (n), array may be empty
(b) 2: {0,i}e{A.length}? - {0,i}n{A.length}? $i = 0$
(c) 3: $\perp \sqcup$ ({0,i}e{A.length}? - {0,i}n{A.length}?)   join
  = {0,i}e{A.length}? - {0,i}n{A.length}?
(d) 4: {0,i}e{A.length} - {0,i}n{A.length}
  last and only segment hence array not empty (since A.length $> i = 0$)
(e) 5: {0,i}e{A.length} - {0,i}c{1,i+1}n{A.length}?
                    A[i] checked while unmodified
(f) 6: {0,i}∂{1,i+1}e{A.length}? - {0,i}c{1,i+1}n{A.length}?
A[i] appears on the left handside of an assignment, hence is potentially modified
(g) 7: {0,i-1}∂{1,i}e{A.length}? - {0,i-1}c{1,i}n{A.length}?
                    invertible assignment $i_{old} = i_{new} - 1$
(h) 3: {0,i}e{A.length}? $\sqcup$ {0,i-1}∂{1,i}e{A.length}? -   join
    {0,i}n{A.length}? $\sqcup$ {0,i-1}c{1,i}n{A.length}?
  = {0}e{i}?e{A.length}? $\sqcup$ {0}∂{i}e{A.length}? - segment unification
    {0}⊥{i}?n{A.length}? $\sqcup$ {0}c{i}n{A.length}?
  = {0}∂{i}?e{A.length}? - {0}c{i}?n{A.length}?
          segmentwise join $e \sqcup ∂ = ∂$, $e \sqcup e = e$, $\perp \sqcup c = c$, $n \sqcup n = n$
(i) 4: {0}∂{i}?e{A.length} - {0}c{i}?n{A.length}last segment not empty
(j) 5: {0}∂{i}?e{A.length} - {0}c{i}?c{i+1}n{A.length}?
                    A[i] checked while unmodified
(k) 6: {0}∂{i}?∂{i+1}e{A.length}? - {0}c{i}?c{i+1}n{A.length}?
                    A[i] potentially modified
(l) 7: {0}∂{i-1}?∂{i}e{A.length}? - {0}c{i-1}?c{i}n{A.length}?
                    invertible assignment $i_{old} = i_{new} - 1$
(m) 3: {0}∂{i}?e{A.length}? $\sqcup$ {0}∂{i-1}∂{i}e{A.length}? -   join
    {0}c{i}?n{A.length}? $\sqcup$ {0}c{i-1}c{i}n{A.length}?
  = {0}∂{i}?e{A.length}? $\sqcup$ {0}∂{i}?e{A.length}? –segment unification
    {0}c{i}?n{A.length}? $\sqcup$ {0}c{i}?n{A.length}?
  = {0}∂{i}?e{A.length}? - {0}c{i}?n{A.length}?
                    segmentwise join, convergence
(n) 8: {0}∂{i,A.length}? - {0}c{i,A.length}?
  $i \leqslant$ A.length in segmentation and $\geqslant$ in test negation so $i =$ A.length.

To generate code for the precondition, the information ${0}c{i,A.length}$? in (n) is valid at program 8: dominating the end of the program, so assert(A[i] != null) has been checked on all the elements of the array before they where changed in the program. Hence the generated precondition is Forall(0,A.length,k => A[k] != null) where k is a dummy variable from which iterative code follows immediately.

Notice that the size of a collection can change and that the values of the symbolic bounds in a collection can change from one program point to another. So these expressions in the final segmentation must be expressed in terms of values on entry, a problem solved in Sect. 8.   □

Abstract domain for collections. The abstract properties are

$$\xi \in \Gamma \to \mathtt{X} \in \mathbb{X} \mapsto \overline{\mathcal{S}}(\overline{\mathcal{M}}) \times \mathbb{A}(\mathtt{X}) \to \overline{\mathcal{S}}(\overline{\mathcal{C}})$$

At program point $c \in \Gamma$, the collection $\mathtt{X} \in \mathbb{X}$ has the collection segmentation abstract property $\xi(c)(\mathtt{X})$ which is a pair $\langle \xi(c)(\mathtt{X})_{\overline{\mathcal{M}}}, \xi(c)(\mathtt{X})_{\overline{\mathcal{C}}} \rangle$. The abstract relational invariance property $\xi(c)(\mathtt{X})_{\overline{\mathcal{M}}}$ specifies which elements of the collection are for sure equal to their initial values. For each assertion in $\langle \mathtt{c}, \mathtt{b(X,i)} \rangle \in \mathbb{A}(\mathtt{X})$ (where c is a program point designating an assert(b) and b(X,i) is a side effect free Boolean expression checking a property of element X[i] of collection X [7]), the abstract trace-based property $\xi(c)(\mathtt{X})_{\overline{\mathcal{C}}}\langle \mathtt{c}, \mathtt{b(X,i)} \rangle$ specifies which elements of the collection have been checked for sure by b at point c while equal to their initial values.

Collection segmentation concretization. (a) The concretization $\gamma_S^{\mathtt{X}}$ of a segmentation $B_1 A_1 B_2[?^2] A_2 \ldots A_{n-1} B_n[?^n] \in \overline{\mathcal{S}}(\overline{\mathcal{A}})$ for a collection $\mathtt{X}$ is the set of prefixes $\vec{s} = \vec{s}_0 \ldots \vec{s}_\ell$ of the program run describing how the elements A[k], $k \in [0, \mathtt{A.count})$ of the collection X have been organized into consecutive, non-overlapping segments, covering the whole collection.

(b) All the elements of the collection in each segment $B_k A_k B_{k+1}[?^k]$ have the property described by A_k. The values of expressions in segment bounds $B_1, \ldots, B_n$ should be understood as evaluated in this last state $\vec{s}_\ell$ while the properties A_k may refer to some or all of the states $\vec{s}_0, \ldots, \vec{s}_\ell$.

(c) The segmentation should fully cover all the elements of the collection X. So all the expressions in B_1 should be equal and have value 0, $\forall \mathtt{e}_1 \in B_1 : [\![\mathtt{e}_1]\!]\vec{s}_\ell = 0$ while all the expressions in B_n should be equal to the number $[\![\mathtt{X.count}]\!]\vec{s}_\ell$ of the elements in the collection, so $\forall \mathtt{e}_n \in B_n : [\![\mathtt{e}_n]\!]\vec{s}_\ell = [\![\mathtt{X.count}]\!]\vec{s}_\ell$.

(d) The segment bounds B_k, $k \in [0, n]$ are sets of equal expressions when evaluated in the last state $\vec{s}_\ell$ of the prefix trace, so $\forall \mathtt{e}_1, \mathtt{e}_2 \in B_k : [\![\mathtt{e}_1]\!]\vec{s}_\ell = [\![\mathtt{e}_2]\!]\vec{s}_\ell$.

(e) In a segment segment $B_k[?^k] M_k B_{k+1}[?^{k+1}]$, $k \in [0, n)$, the marker $[?^k]$, $k \in [1, n)$ is relevant to the previous segment, if any. $[?^{k+1}]$ specifies the possible

---

[7] If more than one index is used, like in assert(A[i]<A[i+1]) or assert(A[i]<A[A.length-i]), the modification analysis must check that the array A has not been modified for all these indexes.

emptiness of the segment. If $[?^{k+1}] = \,?$ then the segment is possibly empty (in which case $<?$ stands for $\leqslant$). If $[?^{k+1}] = \,\_$ then the segment is definitely not empty (in which case there is no question mark and $<\_$ stands for $<$). The upper bound h of the segment is therefore greater (for non-empty segments) or greater or equal (for possibly empty segments) than its lower bound l and within the limit of the collection size so $\forall e_1, e_2 \in B_k$, $\forall e'_1, e'_2 \in B_{k+1}$, $0 \leq l = [\![e_1]\!]\vec{s}_\ell = [\![e_2]\!]\vec{s}_\ell <[?^{k+1}] \ [\![e'_1]\!]\vec{s}_\ell = [\![e'_2]\!]\vec{s}_\ell = h < [\![X.\mathtt{count}]\!]\vec{s}_\ell$. (a—e) explains the following definition of segmentation concretization.

$$\gamma_S^X(B_1 A_1 B_2[?^2]A_2 \ldots A_{n-1}B_n[?^n]) \triangleq \{\vec{s} \mid \ell = |\vec{s}| - 1 : \forall e_1 \in B_1 : [\![e_1]\!]\vec{s}_\ell = 0 \land$$
$$\forall e_n \in B_n : [\![e_n]\!]\vec{s}_\ell = [\![X.\mathtt{count}]\!]\vec{s}_\ell \land \forall k \in [0, n) : \forall e_1, e_2 \in B_k : \forall e'_1, e'_2 \in B_{k+1} :$$
$$0 \leq l = [\![e_1]\!]\vec{s}_\ell = [\![e_2]\!]\vec{s}_\ell <[?^{k+1}] \ [\![e'_1]\!]\vec{s}_\ell = [\![e'_2]\!]\vec{s}_\ell = h < [\![X.\mathtt{count}]\!]\vec{s}_\ell\}$$
and $\gamma_S^X(\bot) = \emptyset$.

Segmented modification analysis concretization. The concretization γ_M^X of a segmentation $B_1 M_1 B_2[?^2]M_2 \ldots M_{n-1}B_n[?^n] \in \overline{S}(\mathcal{M})$ for a collection X is the set of prefixes $\vec{s} = \vec{s}_0 \ldots \vec{s}_\ell$ of the program run describing how the collection X has been modified in the last state $\vec{s}_\ell$ compared to the initial state $\vec{s}_0$.

The abstract value $M_k = \eth$ of segment $B_k[?^k]M_k B_{k+1}[?^{k+1}]$ provides no information while $M_k = \mathfrak{e}$ states that the values of the all the elements $X[i]$ of the collection X have not changed between the initial state $\vec{s}_0$ and the current state $\vec{s}_\ell$ (which is the last of the prefix trace). So $\forall i \in [\ell, h) : [\![X]\!]\vec{s}_0[i] = [\![X]\!]\vec{s}_j[i]$.

The size of the collections may change monotonically. If the collection size only decreased, then all the elements $X[i]$, $i \in [\ell, h)$ did exist in the initial collection. If the collection size only increased, its current size $[\![X.\mathtt{count}]\!]\vec{s}_\ell$ is larger than the initial size $[\![X.\mathtt{count}]\!]\vec{s}_0$ so the comparison of elements can only be done for the elements $X[i]$, $i \in \min(h, [\![X.\mathtt{count}]\!]\vec{s}_0)$ existing in both in the initial and current states.

$$\gamma_M^X(B_1 M_1 B_2[?^2]M_2 \ldots M_{n-1}B_n[?^n]) \triangleq \{\vec{s} \in \gamma_S^X(B_1 M_1 B_2[?^2]M_2 \ldots M_{n-1}B_n[?^n]) \mid$$
$$\ell = |\vec{s}| - 1 \land \forall k \in [0, n) : \exists e \in B_k, l : l = [\![e]\!]\vec{s}_\ell \land \exists e' \in B_{k+1}, h : h = [\![e']\!]\vec{s}_\ell \land$$
$$\forall i \in [l, \min(h, [\![X.\mathtt{count}]\!]\vec{s}_0)) : \langle [\![X]\!]\vec{s}_0[i], [\![X]\!]\vec{s}_j[i] \rangle \in \gamma_{\mathcal{M}}(M_k)\}.$$

Segmented checking analysis concretization. The concretization γ_C^X of a segmentation $B_1 C_1 B_2[?^2]C_2 \ldots C_{n-1}B_n[?^n] \in \overline{S}(\overline{C})$ of a collection X for an assertion check $\langle c, \mathtt{b(X,i)} \rangle \in \mathbb{A}(X)$ is the set of prefixes of traces such that, at the end of the prefix, the elements of the collection in all segments $[B_k, B_{k+1})$, $k = 1, \ldots, n-1$ with $C_k = \mathfrak{c}$ have been submitted to the check $\langle c, \mathtt{b(X,i)} \rangle \in \mathbb{A}(X)$ while the situation is unknown when $C_k = \mathfrak{n}$.

$$\gamma_C^X(B_1 C_1 B_2[?^2]C_2 \ldots C_{n-1}B_n[?^n])(\langle c, \mathtt{b(X,i)} \rangle) \triangleq \{\vec{s} \in \gamma_S^X(B_1 C_1 B_2[?^2]C_2 \ldots B_n[?^n]) \mid$$
$$\ell = |\vec{s}| - 1 \land \forall k \in [0, n) : \exists e \in B_k, l : l = [\![e]\!]\vec{s}_\ell \land \exists e' \in B_{k+1}, h : h = [\![e']\!]\vec{s}_\ell \land$$
$$(C_k = \mathfrak{c}) \Rightarrow (\forall i \in [l, \min(h, [\![X.\mathtt{count}]\!]\vec{s}_0)) : \exists j \leqslant \ell :$$
$$\pi\vec{s}_j = c \land [\![\mathtt{i}]\!]\vec{s}_j = i \land [\![X]\!]\vec{s}_0[i] = [\![X]\!]\vec{s}_j[i])\}.$$

The modification analysis must be used to determine that $[\![X]\!]\vec{s}_0[i] = [\![X]\!]\vec{s}_j[i]$.

Segmented modification and checking analysis concretization. The concretization is

$$\gamma \in (\Gamma \to \mathbb{X} \in \mathbb{X} \mapsto \overline{\mathcal{S}}(\overline{\mathcal{M}}) \times \mathbb{A}(\mathbb{X}) \to \overline{\mathcal{S}}(\overline{\mathcal{C}})) \mapsto \vec{\Sigma}^+$$

$$\gamma(\xi) \triangleq \big\{ \vec{s} \in \vec{\Sigma}^+ \;\big|\; \forall j < |\vec{s}| : \forall \mathbb{X} \in \mathbb{X} : \forall \langle \mathtt{c}, \mathtt{b(X,i)} \rangle \in \mathbb{A}(\mathbb{X}) :$$

$$\vec{s}_0 \ldots \in \vec{s}_j \in \gamma_C^{\mathbb{X}}\big(\xi(\pi \vec{s}_j)(\mathbb{X})_{\overline{C}}(\langle \mathtt{c}, \mathtt{b(X,i)} \rangle) \big) \big\}$$

The soundness of the result $\xi \in \Gamma \to \mathbb{X} \in \mathbb{X} \mapsto \overline{\mathcal{S}}(\overline{\mathcal{M}}) \times \mathbb{A}(\mathbb{X}) \to \overline{\mathcal{S}}(\overline{\mathcal{C}})$ of collection segmentation modification and checking static analysis is stated by $\vec{\tau}^+ \subseteq \gamma(\xi)$. The details of the segmentation analysis are those of [16] for the specific abstract domains $\overline{\mathcal{M}}$ and $\overline{\mathcal{C}}$.

Precondition generation. Let $\mathtt{f}$ be the exit program point (assumed to be unique for simplicity and corresponding to a blocking state $\forall s \in \Sigma : \pi s = \mathtt{f} \Rightarrow s \in \mathfrak{B}$). Let $\mathbb{X} \in \mathbb{X}$ be any of the collection variables in the program. Let $\langle \mathtt{c}, \mathtt{b(X,i)} \rangle \in \mathbb{A}(\mathbb{X})$ by any assertion check for element $\mathtt{X[i]}$ of collection $\mathtt{X}$. let $\xi(\mathtt{f})(\mathbb{X})_{\overline{C}}(\langle \mathtt{c}, \mathtt{b(X,i)} \rangle) = B_1 C_1 B_2[?^2] C_2 \ldots C_{n-1} B_n[?^n] \in \overline{\mathcal{S}}(\overline{\mathcal{C}})$ be the information collected by the checking analysis (using the modification analysis no longer useful for the precondition generation). Let $\Delta \subseteq [1, n]$ be the set of indices $k \in \Delta$ for which $C_k = \mathfrak{c}$. The precondition code is

$$\underset{\mathtt{X} \in \mathbb{X}}{\&\&} \quad \underset{\langle \mathtt{c}, \mathtt{b(X,i)} \rangle \in \mathbb{A}(\mathbb{X})}{\&\&} \quad \underset{k \in \Delta}{\&\&} \quad \mathtt{ForAll(l}_k, \mathtt{h}_k, \mathtt{i} => \mathtt{b(X,i))} \tag{4}$$

where $\exists e_k \in B_k, e'_k \in B_{k+1}$ such that the value of e_k (resp. e'_k) at program point $\mathtt{f}$ is always equal to that of $\mathtt{l}_k$ (resp. $\mathtt{h}_k$) on program entry and is less that the size of the collection on program entry.

Theorem 23. *The precondition (4) based on a sound modification and checking static analysis ξ is sound.*

11   Related Work, Future Work, and Conclusions

The problem of calculating (weakest)-preconditions has been intensively studied since [17] e.g., [19] using assisted theorem proving. In the context of static analysis by abstract interpretation, the problem can be handled by backward analysis [13, Sect. 3.2] including in symbolic form [15, 8], a combination of forward and backward analyzes [9] (see also [14]), and overapproximation of negated properties to get underapproximations [10] followed by [6, 27]. Most often the precondition inference problem is considered in the context of partial or total correctness, including for procedure summary [7, 12, 20], contract inference [1] or specification abduction [7], where no bad behavior is allowed at all [17] so one has to consider under-approximations to ensure that any assertion that exists in the code holds when reached [25, 28]. Our point of view for non-deterministic programs is different and, to our knowledge, our formalization of the precondition inference problem is the first in the context of design by contracts. The derived precondition never excludes a bad run when a non-deterministic choice could alternatively yield a good run. So the program is not checked for partial/-total correctness, but the intentions of the programmer, as only expressed by his code and assertions within this code, are preserved, since only definite failures are prohibited. Future work includes the implementation, the combination of Sect. 10 with path-conditions as in Sect. 8, the study of the relation between forward and backward analyzes (using [10, Th. 10.13]), of infinite behaviors and of expressive abstract domains than segmentation to express relations between values of components of data structures in asserts and on code entry while preserving scalability.

References

[1] Arnout, K., Meyer, B.: Uncovering hidden contracts: The. NET example. IEEE Computer 36(11), 48–55 (2003)

[2] Baier, C., Katoen, J.-P.: Principles of Model Checking. MIT Press, Cambridge (2008)

[3] Barnett, M., Fähndrich, M., Garbervetsky, D., Logozzo, F.: Annotations for (more) precise points-to analysis. In: IWACO 2007, Stockholm U. and KTH (2007)

[4] Barnett, M., Fähndrich, M., Logozzo, F.: Embedded contract languages. In: SAC 2010, pp. 2103–2110. ACM, New York (2010)

[5] Biere, A., Cimatti, A., Clarke, E., Strichman, O., Zhu, Y.: Bounded model checking. Advances in Computers 58, 118–149 (2003)

[6] Bourdoncle, F.: Abstract debugging of higher-order imperative languages. In: PLDI 1993, pp. 46–55. ACM, New York (1993)

[7] Calcagno, C., Distefano, D., O'Hearn, P., Yang, H.: Compositional shape analysis by means of bi-abduction. In: 36th POPL, pp. 289–300. ACM, New York (2009)

[8] Chandra, S., Fink, S., Sridharan, M.: Snugglebug: a powerful approach to weakest preconditions. In: PLDI, pp. 363–374. ACM, New York (2009)

[9] Cousot, P.: Méthodes itératives de construction et d'approximation de points fixes d'opérateurs monotones sur un treillis, analyse sémantique de programmes (in French). Thèse d'État ès sciences mathématiques, Université scientifique et médicale de Grenoble (1978)

[10] Cousot, P.: Semantic foundations of program analysis. In: Muchnick, S., Jones, N. (eds.) Program Flow Analysis: Theory and Applications, ch. 10, pp. 303–342. Prentice-Hall, Englewood Cliffs (1981)

[11] Cousot, P.: Constructive design of a hierarchy of semantics of a transition system by abstract interpretation. TCS 277(1-2), 47–103 (2002)

[12] Cousot, P., Cousot, R.: Static determination of dynamic properties of recursive procedures. In: Neuhold, E. (ed.) IFIP Conf. on Formal Description of Programming Concepts, pp. 237–277. North-Holland, Amsterdam (1977)

[13] Cousot, P., Cousot, R.: Systematic design of program analysis frameworks. In: 6th POPL, pp. 269–282. ACM, New York (1979)

[14] Cousot, P., Cousot, R.: Abstract interpretation and application to logic programs. Journal of Logic Programming 13(2-3), 103–179 (1992)

[15] Cousot, P., Cousot, R.: Modular static program analysis. In: CC 2002. LNCS, vol. 2304, pp. 159–178. Springer, Heidelberg (2002)

[16] Cousot, P., Cousot, R., Logozzo, F.: A parametric segmentation functor for fully automatic and scalable array content analysis. In: POPL 2011. ACM, New York (2011)

[17] Dijkstra, E.: Guarded commands, nondeterminacy and formal derivation of programs. CACM 18(8), 453–457 (1975)

[18] Fähndrich, M., Logozzo, F.: Clousot: Static contract checking with abstract interpretation. In: FoVeOOS. Springer, Heidelberg (2010)

[19] Flanagan, C., Leino, K., Lillibridge, M., Nelson, G., Saxe, J., Stata, R.: Extended Static Checking for Java. In: PLDI, pp. 234–245. ACM, New York (2002)

[20] Gulwani, S., Tiwari, A.: Computing procedure summaries for interprocedural analysis. In: De Nicola, R. (ed.) ESOP 2007. LNCS, vol. 4421, pp. 253–267. Springer, Heidelberg (2007)

[21] Hecht, M.: Flow Analysis of Computer Programs. Elsevier, North-Holland (1977)

[22] King, J.: Symbolic execution and program testing. CACM 19(7), 385–394 (1976)

[23] Meyer, B.: Eiffel: The Language. Prentice-Hall, Englewood Cliffs (1991)

[24] Meyer, B.: Applying "Design by Contract". IEEE Computer 25(10), 40–51 (1992)

[25] Moy, Y.: Sufficient preconditions for modular assertion checking. In: Logozzo, F., Peled, D.A., Zuck, L.D. (eds.) VMCAI 2008. LNCS, vol. 4905, pp. 188–202. Springer, Heidelberg (2008)

[26] Park, D.: Fixpoint induction and proofs of program properties. In: Meltzer, B., Michie, D. (eds.) Machine Intelligences, vol. 5, pp. 59–78. Edinburgh University Press, Edinburgh (1969)

[27] Rival, X.: Understanding the origin of alarms in ASTRÉE. In: Hankin, C., Siveroni, I. (eds.) SAS 2005. LNCS, vol. 3672, pp. 303–319. Springer, Heidelberg (2005)

[28] Lev-Ami, T., Sagiv, M., Reps, T., Gulwani, S.: Backward analysis for inferring quantified preconditions. Tr-2007-12-01, Tel Aviv University (2007)

Strengthening Induction-Based Race Checking with Lightweight Static Analysis*

Alastair F. Donaldson, Leopold Haller, and Daniel Kroening

Oxford University Computing Laboratory, Oxford, UK

Abstract. Direct Memory Access (DMA) is key to achieving high performance in system-level software for multicore processors such as the Cell Broadband Engine. Incorrectly orchestrated DMAs cause *DMA races*, leading to subtle bugs that are hard to reproduce and fix. In previous work, we have shown that k-induction yields an effective method for proving absence of a restricted class of DMA races. We extend this work to handle a larger class of DMA races. We show that the applicability of k-induction can be significantly improved when combined with three inexpensive static analyses: 1) abstract-interpretation-based static analysis; 2) *chunking*, a domain-specific invariant generation technique; and 3) code transformations based on statement independence. Our techniques are implemented in the SCRATCH tool. We evaluate our work on industrial benchmarks.

1 Introduction

Many modern multicore architectures such as the Cell Broadband Engine (BE) [14] include cores equipped with small, local "scratch-pad" memories, whose management is under software control. It is the programmer's responsibility to orchestrate data movement between main memory and scratch-pad memory using Direct Memory Access (DMA) operations. The use of scratch-pad memory alleviates the *memory wall problem*, where multiple cores contend for access to a single shared memory. Through use of double- and triple-buffering techniques, the latency associated with DMA operations can be hidden, leading to high performance. The increase in performance comes at the expense of programmability: the asynchronous nature of DMA operations makes them difficult to schedule correctly. *DMA races*, where data associated with a pending DMA operation is accessed simultaneously, either by another DMA or a regular memory access, lead to nondeterministic bugs that are hard to diagnose and fix.

In previous work [7] we have shown that SAT-based bounded model checking [2,4] combined with k-induction [18] shows promise for DMA race analysis. The approach of [7] is restricted to *inter-DMA races* on scratch-pad memory: races between distinct DMA operations. This restriction allows loops that do not involve DMA operations to be removed from an input program via static slicing [19], often leaving just a *single* DMA processing loop to which k-induction can be applied. For increasing values of k, starting, *e.g.*, with $k = 1$, *base case* and *step case* programs are constructed. A

---

* This research is supported by the the Toyota Motor Corporation, by the EU FP7 STREP MOGENTES (project ID ICT-216679), and by EPSRC grant EP/G051100.

successful check of the base case ensures that no DMA races occur during the first k loop iterations. By checking the step case, it is ensured that, from an arbitrary state, if k loop iterations can be executed without a DMA race occurring, then executing a further iteration will not lead to a DMA race. The base and step case programs are loop-free, and can be checked using bounded model checking. If both succeed, for some k, the input program has been shown to be race-free. If the base case fails, a counterexample leading to a DMA race is reported. Otherwise, a larger value of k must be tried.

In this paper, we remove the restriction to inter-DMA races, extending our analysis to detect races between DMA operations and regular memory accesses. In this setting, it is *not* possible to slice away loops that access buffers with which DMA operations are associated. As a result, k-induction alone is usually too weak to enable verification.

We show that this problem can be solved when k-induction is combined with static analysis. Lightweight static analysis is used to compute an inductive invariant of the input program. Then, k-induction is applied, but the step case is restricted to consider only states which satisfy the inductive invariant. By tailoring the static analysis to the domain of DMA race analysis, we are able to compute sufficiently strong inductive invariants to allow verification of DMA race freedom, on practical examples, for small values of k. We use three distinct static analyses: 1) abstract interpretation, to generate simple strengthening invariants; 2) *chunking*, a domain-specific invariant generation technique; and 3) *code motion*, a code transformation based on statement independence, to compute DMA-related invariants for inner loops.

Our techniques have been implemented in the SCRATCH tool for DMA race analysis [7], and we present an experimental evaluation using a set of benchmarks from the IBM Cell SDK.

2   Guiding k-Induction with Invariants: An Overview

We begin with a high-level overview of our method for strengthening k-induction using static analysis, at the level of transition systems.

Consider a transition system $M = (S, T, I, E)$ where S is a set of states, $T \subseteq S \times S$ a transition relation, $I \subseteq S$ a set of initial states, and $E \subseteq S$ a set of error states. The successor function $post : 2^S \rightarrow 2^S$ is defined by: $post(Q) = \{\, q' \mid \exists q \in Q.\, T(q, q')\,\}$. We define reachability in the usual way. A set of states $Q \subseteq S$ is *safe*, written $safe(Q)$, if no state of E is reachable from any state in Q. The system M is safe if its initial states I are safe.

To prove that M is safe, it suffices to find a set Q which (i) contains the initial states ($I \subseteq Q$), (ii) is inductive ($post(Q) \subseteq Q$), and (iii) does not contain error states ($Q \cap E = \emptyset$). This can be stated as a proof rule as follows:

$$\frac{\text{(i) } I \subseteq Q \qquad \text{(ii) } post(Q) \subseteq Q \qquad \text{(iii) } Q \cap E = \emptyset}{safe(I)}$$

To implement this proof-rule as a procedure, a means for generating candidates for Q is required. One possibility is the use of some sound static analysis. Such a technique produces an invariant Q that fulfills (i) and (ii), but the results might be too weak to guarantee (iii).

The k-induction technique [18] provides another way to inductively prove correctness of transition systems by splitting the proof obligation into (a) a *base case*, showing that the transition system will not reach an error in k steps, and (b) a *step case*, showing that when no error can be reached in k steps from some arbitrary state s, no error can be reached from s in $k + 1$ steps. Writing $safe^k(Q)$ to denote that no error state is reachable from a set Q in at most k steps, the k-induction proof rule for transition systems is as follows:

$$\frac{k \geq 0 \quad \text{(a) } safe^k(I) \quad \text{(b) } \forall Q. \, safe^k(Q) \Rightarrow safe^{k+1}(Q)}{safe(I)}$$

For finite-state transition systems, the premises can be checked using a SAT solver, and the method can be made complete by adding additional restrictions, detailed in [18]. In order to succeed, k-induction can require large values of k, or in the case of infinite state transition systems, may fail for every value of k. When k-induction fails to succeed for feasible values of k, the problem is often that the induction hypothesis, *i.e.*, the antecedent of premise (b), is too weak.

In order to amend this, the above proof rules can be combined into the approach we use in this paper:

$$\frac{k \geq 0 \quad \text{(i) } I \subseteq Q \quad \text{(ii) } post(Q) \subseteq Q \quad \text{(a) } safe^k(I) \quad \text{(b) } safe^k(Q) \Rightarrow safe^{k+1}(Q)}{safe(I)}$$

To implement this rule as a procedure, we first use static analysis to obtain an inductive invariant Q fulfilling premises (i) and (ii). We do not require this invariant to be strong enough to prove the target property. We then perform a k-induction check. Base case (a) is as before, but in step case (b), we strengthen the induction hypothesis by our generated invariant.

3 DMA Race Analysis

We consider DMA primitives **get**, **put** and **wait**. Operation **get**(l,h,s,t), where l is a pointer to local memory, h a pointer to host memory, and s and t unsigned integers, issues a request for s bytes to be copied from host memory region $[h, h + s)$ to local memory region $[l, l+s)$. The operation is identified by a *tag*, t. The **put** primitive is dual to **get**. Execution of a **get/put** operation is asynchronous: the thread issuing the operation may continue to execute while the memory transfer takes place. However, access to the regions $[l, l+s)$ and $[h, h+s)$ before completion of the operation leads to undefined behaviour.[1] Before accessing these regions, the operation must be synchronized via a **wait** operation of the form **wait**(t), where t is the tag used to identify the DMA. This causes execution to block until *all* DMAs identified by tag t have completed.

In the example C program of Figure 1, adapted from an example provided with the IBM Cell SDK [14], function double_buffer will be executed by a Synergistic Processor

---

[1] Actually, read access to $[h, h+s)$ or $[l, l+s)$ is allowed in the case of **get** or **put** respectively.

```
1    #define SZ 4096
2    float bufs[2][SZ];
3
4    void process(float* b) {
5        for(unsigned int j = 0; j < SZ; j++) { b[j] = b[j] + 1.0f; }
6    }
7
8    void double_buffer(float* in_buf, float* out_buf, unsigned int num_chunks) {
9        unsigned int cur_buf = 0, next_buf, tags[2] = { 0, 1 };
10       get(bufs[cur_buf], in_buf, SZ*sizeof(float), tags[cur_buf]); in_buf += SZ;
11       for (unsigned int i = 1; i < num_chunks; i++) {
12           next_buf = cur_buf^1;
13           wait(tags[next_buf]);
14           get(bufs[next_buf], in_buf, SZ*sizeof(float), tags[next_buf]); in_buf += SZ;
15           wait(tags[cur_buf]);
16           process(bufs[cur_buf]);
17           put(bufs[cur_buf], out_buf, SZ*sizeof(float), tags[cur_buf]); out_buf += SZ;
18           cur_buf = next_buf;
19       }
20       wait(tags[cur_buf]);
21       process(bufs[cur_buf], SZ);
22       put(bufs[cur_buf], out_buf, SZ*sizeof(float), tags[cur_buf]);
23       wait(tags[cur_buf]);
24   }
```

Fig. 1. Using asynchronous DMA to achieve double-buffered data movement

Element core of the Cell processor, which is equipped with scratch-pad memory. Array in_buf is processed by adding 1 to each element, storing the result in out_buf. The arrays in_buf and out_buf reside in host memory. Chunks of data are copied via DMA from in_buf to local store, processed, then copied back to out_buf. *Double buffering* is used to hide the latency associated with DMAs: bufs consists of two local buffers which are used simultaneously for processing and fetching of data. In the main program loop (lines 11–19 of Figure 1), the **get** operation at line 14 requests data which will be processed in the *next* loop iteration. While this request is in progress, processing of the currently available data buffer can be performed. At the start of each loop iteration, the roles of the current and next buffer are exchanged.

A DMA *race* occurs when an attempt is made to access a region of memory that is associated with a pending DMA. Suppose we remove the **wait** at line 15 of Figure 1. Then the **put** at line 17 potentially causes a DMA race: in the first iteration of the loop, this operation accesses memory region [bufs[0] , bufs[0] + SZ*sizeof(float)), which is also accessed by the **get** operation at line 10. Without the intervening **wait**, there is no guarantee that the **get** will have completed. This is an example of an *inter-DMA* race. For similar reasons, the array access at line 5, in function process, may cause a DMA race, since it accesses elements of b, which is an alias for bufs[0] when process is invoked from line 16 during the first loop iteration. This is a race between a DMA and a regular memory access.

Statement	Instrumented version
start of program	tracker.l = 0; tracker.s = 0; tracker.t = $*$;
put/get(l, h, s, t);	**assert**(l != 0 && s < 16K && t < 32 &&
	$\quad$ **disjoint**(l, s, tracker.l, tracker.s));
	if($*$) { tracker.l = l; tracker.s = s; tracker.t = t }
wait(t);	**assume**(tracker.t != t);
$A[e]$ = ... / ... = ...$A[e]$...	**assert**(**disjoint**(&$A[e]$, **sizeof**(T), tracker.l, tracker.s));
	$A[e]$ = ... / ... = ...$A[e]$...$\quad$ (where T is the element type of A)

Fig. 2. Translating DMA operations into statements over instrumentation variables

Encoding DMA operations. To detect, or prove absence of, local memory DMA races, we instrument a C program with additional assertions and assignments to auxiliary variables. We use the encoding of [6], which improves on that of [7], facilitating analysis of races between DMA operations and local memory accesses.

Our encoding uses an instrumentation record, tracker, which tracks a single DMA. The tracker variable has three fields: l, s and t, recording the local memory address, size and tag of the tracked DMA respectively. Figure 2 shows how program statements relevant to DMA races are translated. At the start of the program, tracker does not track any DMA.

Operation **get/put**(l, h, s, t) is translated into an assertion, and a nondeterministically executed assignment. The assertion checks that the pointer parameter l is non-null. The assertion also checks that the memory region accessed by the new DMA is disjoint from the region accessed by the currently tracked DMA. In Figure 2, we use the predicate **disjoint**(l_1, s_1, l_2, s_2) as shorthand for ($l_1 + s_1 \leq l_2 \mid\mid l_2 + s_2 \leq l_2$). The nondeterministically executed assignment either updates tracker to track the new DMA operation or leaves it unchanged. Any statement involving an array access is prepended by an assertion checking that the accessed element is not part of the memory region associated with the tracked DMA. Operation **wait**(t) is translated into an assumption that the currently tracked DMA is not identified by tag t. This rules out the possibility that the last DMA nondeterministically chosen to be tracked also had tag t. The combination of non-deterministic assignments and assumptions ensures that tracker contains details of an *arbitrary* pending DMA. As a result, the assertions associated with DMA operations and array accesses *implicitly* check for races with *all* pending DMAs.

In the rules of Figure 2, and in our experiments (§6), we do not model the effect of a **get** operation on the associated region of local memory. This is sound for programs, including our benchmarks, where data fetched by DMA cannot affect control-flow. Otherwise, analysis may be unsound. To ensure soundness, an implementation could over-approximate the effect of a **get** operation by assigning nondeterministic values to the associated local memory region, which can lead to spurious reports of DMA races during analysis.

Figure 3 shows the main loop of the double buffering example of Figure 1 after instrumentation. The call to process has been inlined, and redundant assignments to in_buf and out_buf removed. The lines marked '!' are *not* generated by instrumentation, and will be explained in §5.1 and §5.2.

```
1    for (i = 1; i < num_chunks; i++) {
2        next_buf = cur_buf^1;
3        assume(tracker.t != tags[next_buf]);
4        assert(dma_cond(bufs[next_buf], SZ*sizeof(float), tags[next_buf]));
5        if(*) { tracker = ( bufs[next_buf], SZ*sizeof(float), tags[next_buf]); }
6        assume(tracker.t != tags[cur_buf]);
7        for(j = 0; j < SZ; j++) {
8 !          assume(0 <= cur_buf && cur_buf <= 1 && 0 <= next_buf && next_buf <= 1 &&
9 !              cur_buf != next_buf && tags[0] == 0 && tags[1] == 1);
10 !         assert(disjoint(&bufs[cur_buf][0], SZ*sizeof}(float}), tracker.l, tracker.s));
11          assert(disjoint(&bufs[cur_buf][j], sizeof(float), tracker.l, tracker.s));
12          bufs[cur_buf][j] = bufs[cur_buf][j] + 1.0f;
13      }
14      assert(dma_cond(bufs[cur_buf], SZ*sizeof(float), tags[cur_buf]));
15      if(*) { tracker = ( bufs[cur_buf], SZ*sizeof(float), tags[cur_buf]); }
16      cur_buf = next_buf;
17  }
```

Fig. 3. Instrumented version of main loop of Figure 1 after inlining. We write **dma_cond**(l, s, t) for the condition of the assertion associated with **put/get** operations (*cf.* column 2 of Figure 2), and tracker=(l, s, t) as shorthand for tracker.l=l; tracker.s=s;tracker.t=t. Statements marked '!' are not part of the instrumentation, and will be explained in sections §5.1 and §5.2.

4 k-Induction for Loops: Promise, and Problems

In [7], we proposed a formulation of k-induction for non-recursive programs with loops, based on the following rule, where correctness denotes partial correctness, characterised by assertions appearing in the program:

Base case

$$s_\alpha;$$

$$\overbrace{\textbf{if}(\phi) \{ s_\beta \} \ldots \textbf{if}(\phi) \{ s_\beta \}}^{k \text{ times}}$$
$$\textbf{if}(\neg\phi) \{ s_\gamma \} \text{ is correct}$$

Step case

$$\overbrace{\textbf{assume}(\phi); s_\beta^{assume}; \ldots; \textbf{assume}(\phi); s_\beta^{assume};}^{k \text{ times}}$$
$$\textbf{if}(\phi) \{ s_\beta \} \textbf{ else } \{ s_\gamma \} \text{ is correct}$$

$$s_\alpha; \textbf{while}(\phi) \{ s_\beta \}; s_\gamma \text{ is correct}$$

where s_β^{assume} is identical to s_β, except that every statement of the form **assert**(ψ) appearing in s_β is replaced with **assume**(ψ) in s_β^{assume}.

Let P be the program in the conclusion of the rule. The base case checks that there are no erroneous traces from the start of P that execute up to k loop iterations. The step case checks that any trace beginning in an arbitrary state and executing k loop iterations successfully can be extended to either safely execute a further loop iteration (if ϕ holds), or safely execute the tail of P (if $\neg\phi$ holds). Combining these two facts ensures that P admits no erroneous traces. Soundness of the rule is proved formally in [7]. The base case and step case correspond to the antecedents (a) and (b) of the rules for transition systems presented in section §2.

If the statements s_α, s_β and s_γ of P are loop-free, the base and step cases generated by the k-induction rule do not contain any loops. As a result, they can be checked exhaustively using bounded model checking. Starting with a small value of k, we attempt to verify P by checking a base and step case, increasing k until either a base case fails, revealing a bug in P, both base and step case succeed, indicating that P is correct, or a "give up" value for k is reached, in which case the verification attempt is abandoned.

If s_α, s_β or s_γ are not loop free, *i.e.* the program contains sequences and/or nests of loops, P can be transformed (using standard techniques) into an equivalent program P' containing a *single*, "monolithic" while loop, to which k-induction can be applied.

If we restrict our attention to inter-DMA race checking, as in [7], it is often possible to significantly simplify input programs before verification, through program slicing. For example, the process function of Figure 1 does not involve any DMA operations, and does not influence control-flow in double_buffer. Thus, for the purposes of inter-DMA race checking, we can slice away both calls to process in double_buffer. Applying the translation of §3 to the sliced program yields an instrumented program which can be verified successfully using k-induction: verification succeeds with $k = 2$. Experimental results show that, combined with program slicing, k-induction is effective for analysis of inter-DMA races [7].

Suppose we do not wish to restrict our attention to inter-DMA races when verifying the program of Figure 1, and want to check in addition that the array accesses in process do not race with pending DMAs. In this more complex scenario, k-inductive reasoning is more likely to fail. To illustrate this on our example, consider the inner loop of Figure 3 (excluding the lines marked '!', which should be ignored until §5). For any $k <$ SZ, attempts at proving the example program using k-induction will fail. To see this, consider the following partial state σ, which illustrates three problems that we encounter when attempting to prove our example program correct using k-induction:
$$\sigma = [\dots, \text{tracker.l} \mapsto \text{bufs}[0], \text{tracker.s} \mapsto 1, \text{cur\_buf} \mapsto 0, j \mapsto x, \text{tags} \mapsto \{40, 41\}]$$
where $1 \leq x \leq$ SZ.

Problem 1. *The step case fails to establish information about the contents of the* tags *array.* For any $k <$ SZ, the assertion at line 14 immediately following the loop (and corresponding to the **put** operation at line 17 of Figure 1) will fail because tags[cur_buf] is not less than 32 at state σ. By assuming successful execution of k iterations of the loop, for $k <$ SZ, we do not establish that tags[cur_buf] is within the permitted range.

Problem 2. *The step case fails to establish information about pending DMAs (I).* Let $k = $ SZ $- x$. The step case for k-induction will fail: it is possible to successfully execute k iterations of the inner loop from any state of the form σ: the values assigned to tracker ensure that the assertion at line 11 cannot fail for j > 0. However, the assertion at line 14 is guaranteed to fail, since tracker.l=bufs[0]=bufs[cur_buf].

To illustrate a further problem, we consider another partial state, σ':
$$\sigma' = [\dots, \text{tracker.l} \mapsto \text{bufs}[1], \text{tracker.s} \mapsto 1, \text{tracker.t} \mapsto 2, \text{cur\_buf} \mapsto 0,$$
$$\text{next\_buf} \mapsto 1, j \mapsto x, \text{tags} \mapsto \{0, 1\}, i \mapsto 1, \text{num\_chunks} \mapsto 1000]$$
where $0 \leq x \leq$ SZ.

Problem 3. *The step case fails to establish information about pending DMAs (II).* Let $k = $ SZ $- x + 1$. The k-inductive step case assumes k successful loop iterations. From state σ' it is possible to successfully execute SZ $- x$ iterations of the inner loop:

the assertion at line 11 repeatedly succeeds because tracker.l targets bufs[1] which is disjoint from bufs[cur_buf] = bufs[0]. Statements 14–16 and 2–6 of the outer loop can also be executed successfully; with the monolithic approach to k-induction for multiple loops, this counts as one further loop iteration. Control is now at the start of the inner loop, and we have tracker.l = bufs[1], size.s = 1, and cur_buf = 1. As a result, the assertion at line 11 is guaranteed to fail.

The crucial point common to Problems 1–3 is that the inner loop has too many iterations to be fully unwound, and does not contain sufficiently useful assertions to prove the assertion that follows (in the case of Problems 1 and 2), or assertions in the next outer loop iteration (in the case of Problem 3). In the remainder of the paper we show that we can overcome this problem, and achieve full DMA race analysis, by strengthening k-induction using static analysis techniques, as outlined in §2.

5   Strengthening k-Induction for DMA Race Analysis

To overcome the problems discussed in §4, we use a combination of three lightweight static analysis techniques: a simple abstract interpreter, which allows us to infer generic program invariants, and two techniques for inferring program properties specifically related towards DMA races. While none of these techniques can be used in isolation to prove DMA race freedom, their combination allows us to strengthen the inductive hypothesis sufficiently for successful verification using k-induction.

5.1   Abstract Interpretation-Based Static Analysis

In our experience, straightforward analysis with general-purpose abstract domains fails to establish program invariants strong enough to establish DMA race freedom of realistic examples. The properties we are interested in depend on precise interrelations between variable values over multiple, possibly nested loop iterations. General-purpose numeric abstract domains can typically not accurately handle such situations.

Instead of designing an abstract domain specifically for DMA race analysis, with potentially little reuse value, we use lightweight, general-purpose abstract domains together with k-induction. From the analysis result of an abstract interpreter, we extract a mapping inv from statements to local program invariants. We then construct a program P' which is identical to P, except that every statement s appearing in P is prepended with **assume**($inv(s)$). If the computed invariants are strong enough, it may now be possible to prove P' correct using k-induction.

Consider the code of Figure 3. As discussed in §4, this program fragment, without the lines marked '!', cannot be verified using k-induction due to the lack of useful invariants for the inner loop. The condition of the **assume** statement marked '!' (lines 8–9) is the relevant part of the invariant computed by our abstract interpreter. Merely assuming this invariant does not allow k-induction to succeed, but *does* rule out many of the conditions under which the step case for k-induction fails. For example, the inferred loop invariant establishes that tags[cur_buf] is in the range $\{0, 1\}$, which eliminates Problem 1 discussed in §4.

We now discuss details of our abstract interpreter.

Analysis with interval and (dis)equality domains. We have found invariants generated by the classical *interval domain* to be useful for our purposes. In addition, we have implemented a simple domain that keeps track of *equalities and disequalities* between variables. We use a reduced product [5] of these two domains, which yields an analysis that is more precise than applying the components in isolation.

Trace partitioning. We have found that, for some practical examples, it is necessary to increase the precision of generated invariants. In each of these cases, we are able to sufficiently increase the precision of the invariant by manually applying *trace partitioning* [16], a refinement technique for abstract domains that enables inference of disjunctive invariants using non-disjunctive domains. We performed *value-based trace partitioning*. This involves identifying a critical section of code α, a variable var and a set of distinct values $\{v_1, v2, \ldots, v_k\}$, and applying the following code transformation:

$$\alpha \longrightarrow \mathbf{if}(\text{var} == v_1) \; \{\; \alpha \;\} \; \mathbf{else} \; \mathbf{if}(\text{var} == v_2) \; \{\; \alpha \;\} \ldots \mathbf{else} \; \mathbf{if}(\text{var} == v_k) \; \{\; \alpha \;\} \; \mathbf{else} \; \{\; \alpha \;\}$$

Given a partitioning heuristic, trace partitioning can be automated. For our purposes, a simple heuristic that splits on the value of a variable, whenever this variable is in a very small range, would suffice.

5.2 Chunking

The invariants inferred by our abstract interpreter do not solve Problem 2 of §4: unless we choose $k \geq$ SZ, assuming k successful iterations of the inner loop does not rule out the possibility that a pending DMA is accessing bufs[cur_buf].

Iteration j of the inner loop accesses array element bufs[cur_buf][j] (line 12 of Figure 3), and DMA race checking instrumentation generates an assertion that no DMA is targeting this location (line 11). We describe how, from the assertion **assert**(ϕ) at line 11 of Figure 3, where:

$$\phi = \mathbf{disjoint}(\&\text{bufs[cur\_buf][j]}, \mathbf{sizeof(float)}, \text{tracker.l, tracker.s})$$

we can derive the assertion **assert**(ψ) marked '!' at line 10, where:

$$\psi = \mathbf{disjoint}(\&\text{bufs[cur\_buf][0]}, \text{SZ} * \mathbf{sizeof(float)}, \text{tracker.l, tracker.s})$$

A standard loop analysis (*cf.* [1]) establishes that j is an induction variable (a variable whose value increases linearly with the number of loop iterations) for the inner loop, j is used to access contiguous elements of bufs[cur_buf], and j ranges between 0 and constant value SZ, which are both loop-invariant expressions. It is clear that if a pending DMA operation can write to some portion of array bufs[cur_buf] starting at index a, where $0 \leq a <$ SZ, then the assertion at line 11 will fail when j $= a$. Because j is an induction variable and the loop has SZ iterations, we can deduce that either ψ is a loop invariant, or ϕ must be false in some loop iteration. Thus condition ψ is a *required* invariant for the loop, and can be added as an assertion: a program trace violating ψ on entry to the loop can be extended by at most SZ iterations to a trace violating ϕ.

We term this process of deriving assertions stating required loop invariants as *chunking*, since it involves gluing together many assertions about small, contiguous regions of memory to form a single summarizing assertion about a larger chunk of memory. We have implemented a chunking analysis for regularly structured loops such as the loop in our example. Such regularly structured loops are a common feature in streaming applications for architectures such as the Cell BE.

5.3   Code Motion to Ease Analysis of Inner Loops

Recall Problem 3 of §4. We illustrated the issue that, for certain potential states such as σ' on page 175, assuming successful iterations of the inner loop in Figure 3 does not eliminate failing assertions then the inner loop is entered on the next iteration of the outer loop. Unfortunately, neither abstract interpretation nor chunking alleviate this problem.

```
1       ...; assert(dma_cond(bufs[next_buf], SZ*sizeof(float), tags[next_buf]));
2       assume(tracker.t != tags[cur_buf]);
3       for(j = 0; j < SZ; j++) {
4   !     assume(dma_cond(bufs[next_buf], SZ*sizeof(float), tags[next_buf]));
5         assume(0 <= cur_buf && cur_buf <= 1 && 0 <= next_buf && next_buf <= 1 &&
6              cur_buf != next_buf && tags[0] == 0 && tags[1] == 1);
7         assert(disjoint(&bufs[cur_buf][0], SZ*sizeof(float), tracker.l, tracker.s));
8         assert(disjoint(&bufs[cur_buf][j], sizeof(float), tracker.l, tracker.s));
9         bufs[cur_buf][j] = bufs[cur_buf][j] + 1.0f;
10      }
11  !   if(*) { tracker = bufs[next_buf], SZ*sizeof(float), tags[next_buf]); }
12      assert(dma_cond(bufs[cur_buf], SZ*sizeof(float), tags[cur_buf])); ...
```

Fig. 4. Part of the fragment of Figure 3 after application of code motion, indicated by '!'

We overcome this issue through a sound program transformation which we term *code motion* (from *loop-invariant code motion* in compilers [1]). We first illustrate how code motion works using the running example.

Recall from Figure 2 that the instrumentation corresponding to a DMA operation consists of two parts: an assertion **assert**(ϕ) over the tracker record, and a nondeterministic conditional statement **if**($*$) { s }, where s is an assignment to tracker. For the **get** operation at line 14 of Figure 1, these appear at lines 4 and 5 of Figure 3, respectively.

For each instrumented DMA, code motion aims to push **if**($*$) { s } as late in the execution schedule as possible, within the confines of the lexical scope in which the statement appears. After this transformation, statements of the form **assume**(ϕ) are inserted into the headers of all loops lying between the **assert**(ϕ) and **if**($*$) { s }.

Returning to our running example, suppose abstract interpretation and chunking have already been applied to obtain the highlighted statements of Figure 3. Let s_{assign} denote the nondeterministically guarded assignment statement of line 5. Observe that s_{assign} is independent from the **assume** statement at line 8. Observe further that, if the assignment of s_{assign} *is* executed, then the guards of the **assume** and **assert** statements of lines 6, 10 and 11 are guaranteed to evaluate to *true*. This follows because, from the analysis result of the abstract interpreter, we know that cur_buf $\neq$ next_buf. Finally, note that s_{assign} refers to disjoint variables from the loop control statements j = 0 and j++, and modifies no variable appearing in the loop guard j < SZ.

As a result of these observations, we can move s_{assign} after the inner loop without affecting correctness of the program. In Figure 4, this transformation has been applied: s_{assign} now appears at line 11. To complete code motion for this example, observe that the assertion **assert(dma_cond**(...)**)** at line 1 of Figure 4 is guaranteed to be executed before the inner loop is entered, and we can statically deduce that no statement following this assertion until the end of the inner loop can affect the truth value of **dma_cond**(...). Hence, we can insert at line 4 of Figure 4 the statement **assume(dma_cond**(...)**)** without changing correctness of the program.

Code motion eliminates Problem 3 of §4: the **assume** at line 4 of Figure 4 ensures that the assertions at lines 7 and 8 will not fail when the inner loop is executed in the subsequent outer loop iteration. Code motion is frequently applicable to DMA programs: to overlap communication with computation, a DMA operation is often issued long before its results are needed; there is often an intervening processing loop, as in Figure 3. Code motion reverses this optimization, for the purposes of verification.

Formal details of code motion. To make precise the conditions under which code motion can be applied, we regard a program as a sequence of statements defined by the following grammar:

$$Stmt ::= x = Expr \mid \textbf{assert}(Expr) \mid \textbf{assume}(Expr) \mid$$
$$\textbf{if}(Expr) \{ \ Stmt \ \} \ \textbf{else} \ \{ \ Stmt \ \} \mid \textbf{while}(Expr) \{ \ Stmt \ \} \mid Stmt; \ Stmt$$

where $Expr$ denotes a side-effect free expression over a set of variables, which may involve the nondeterministic expression $*$, and the **else** branch of a conditional statement may be omitted. We assume standard trace semantics for programs.

Definition 1. *Statements s_1 and s_2 are* independent *if one of the following holds:*

1. *No variable assigned to by s_1 is referenced (in an assignment or expression) in s_2, and vice-versa*
2. *s_1 is '**if**(*) { $x = \phi_1$ }', s_2 is '**assert/assume**(ϕ_2)', and $\phi_2[x/\phi_1] \equiv true$*
3. *s_2 is '$s; s''$' or '**if**(ϕ) { s } **else** { s' }' or '**while**(ϕ) { s }', s_1 and s are independent, s_1 and s' are independent, and s_1 does not assign to any variable referenced in ϕ*

Essentially, independent statements can be re-ordered without affecting program correctness. In this context, the purpose of condition 1 in Definition 1 is obvious. Condition 2 is domain specific, allowing the nondeterministically executed assignment associated with a DMA operation to be moved. Condition 3 allows independence of compound statements to be established via independence of their components.

A statement s of P is *simple* if s is not a loop, assertion or assumption, and contains no loops, assertions or assumptions as sub-statements.

Lemma 1. *Let '$s_1; s_2$' be a statement sequence appearing in program P. Suppose s_1, s_2 are independent, and s_1 is simple. Let P' be identical to P, except that '$s_1; s_2$' in P is replaced with '$s_2; s_1$' in P'. Then P is correct if and only if P' is correct.*

Lemma 2. *Let $s =$ '$s_1; s_2; \ldots; s_n$' be a statement of program P, where $s_1 =$ '**assert**(ϕ)' and s_1, s_i are independent ($2 \leq i \leq n$). Let $s' =$ '$s_1, s_2'; \ldots; s_n'$', where for $2 \leq i \leq n$, s_i' is identical to s_i, except that any statement t appearing in s_i may be replaced with* '**assume**(ϕ); t' in s_i'. Let P' be identical to P, except that statement s is replaced with s'. Then P is correct if and only if P' is correct.

Lemma 1 (suitably extended to support record variables) allows the nondeterministically executed assignment associated with a DMA to be scheduled later in program execution. Lemma 2 establishes correctness of the strategy described above for placing **assume** statements of the form **assume**(ϕ) at program points dominated by **assert**(ϕ), where ϕ is the race checking condition associated with a DMA.

We omit the straightforward proofs of Lemmas 1 and 2, noting only that the loop-, assertion- and assumption-free conditions of Lemma 1 are necessary to ensure that code motion does not lose error traces, or introduce spurious error traces.

6   Experimental Evaluation

We have incorporated analyses based on abstract interpretation, chunking and code motion, into SCRATCH, a tool for DMA race analysis in Cell BE programs, first presented in [7]. SCRATCH performs instrumentation of DMA operations using the encoding of §3. Abstract interpretation and chunking are then applied, after which code motion is attempted for each DMA operation in an input program. In the context of C, independence of statements is determined using a SAT solver, incorporating information obtained via abstract interpretation and pointer alias analysis. SCRATCH attempts to verify the resulting program via k-induction, using the CBMC tool [4] for bounded model checking, equipped with MiniSat 2.0 as a back-end SAT solver.

Our focus is on using k-induction and static analysis to prove DMA race freedom of programs that are suspected to be correct. Bounded model checking, or runtime race analysis (e.g. with the IBM Race Check library [13]) are more effective for detecting DMA races in buggy programs. A comparison of SCRATCH with the IBM Race Check library is presented in [7].

Figure 5 shows experimental results applying SCRATCH to a set of benchmark programs provided with the IBM Cell SDK [14], on a 3.2GHz Intel Xeon machine with 48GB RAM, running Ubuntu. The benchmarks consist of six distinct data programs,

Benchmark	Lines of code	Time	of which AI	k	Max base case	Max step case
single buffer	152	1.70	9.86%	2	5873	178305
single buffer IO	160	4.25	5.21%	3	6781	334915
double buffer	270	8.52	9.06%	2	67418	386705
double buffer IO	284	24.74	3.49%	3	132266	726512
triple buffer	379	44.32	6.46%	3	9208	650404
triple buffer IO	420	54.80	3.96%	3	9224	707592
double buffer TP	359	9.13	15.65%	2	109783	206434
double buffer IO TP	390	42.47	7.18%	3	215385	854164
triple buffer TP	611	138.10	7.13%	3	8813	958183
triple buffer IO TP	1813	422.45	3.39%	3	8824	3377134

Fig. 5. Experimental results for verification of benchmarks from the IBM Cell SDK

using single, double or triple buffering for data-movement. For each buffering strategy there are two program variants, one where processing is performed in-place on a local buffer, and one where processing copies results from an input buffer to an output buffer. The latter variant are marked *IO* in Figure 5. In addition, for the double and triple buffering examples, we present semantically equivalent variants where trace partitioning has been manually applied as discussed in section §5.1. These benchmarks are marked *TP* in Figure 5. For the double and triple buffering examples without trace partitioning, a simple strengthening invariant was added manually.

Simplified versions of these benchmarks, where inner loops are manually sliced away, were studied in [7]. The techniques of [7], where k-induction is applied without strengthening, are unable to handle the full versions of the benchmarks which we consider here. Thus an experimental comparison with [7] is not meaningful.

For each benchmark, Figure 5 shows the number of lines of code, after DMA instrumentation and inlining, the total time (in seconds, averaged over multiple runs) taken for k-inductive verification with SCRATCH, the percentage of this time dedicated to abstract interpretation, and the value of k required for verification to succeed. The cost of the chunking and code motion analyses was negligible in all cases. In all cases, verification is performed with an initial k of 1, and increasing k by 1 until both the k-induction base and step case succeed. Our abstract domain is a prototype, and could be made significantly more efficient with a dedicated implementation. Verification of *triple buffer IO TP* takes significantly longer than for *triple buffer in out*. This is due to code blowup: value-based trace-partitioning leads to nine variations of a function call, repeated at three distinct points in the program.

We also show the number of variables for the largest SAT problems which had to be solved when checking base and step cases. The step case SAT problems are significantly larger than their associated base cases. The reason for this is that all benchmarks have a similar form to Figure 1, consisting of a main outer loop, and a series of calls to a process function containing a loop with SZ iterations, where SZ = 4096. Because of the loop in process, the base case *never* reaches the end of the first iteration of the main loop. As a result, the vast majority of verification work is undertaken in the step case.

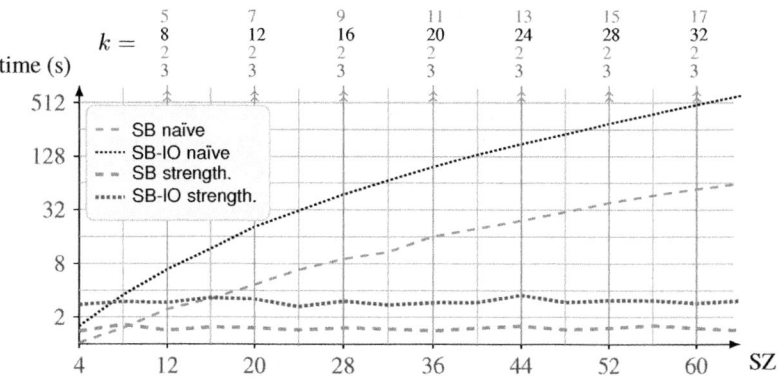

Fig. 6. Verification times for single buffer examples, with and without strengthening

The single buffer benchmarks do not require use of code motion. Verification of the double and triple buffering benchmarks requires all three of our static analysis techniques, and even then requires a non-trivial value of k to succeed. This shows that the mixture of techniques discussed in the paper really are working in tandem.

For the *single buffer* and *single buffer IO* benchmarks, verification by straightforward k-induction is possible if inner loops with SZ iterations are unrolled. This is infeasible when SZ is set to 4096. Therefore, we compare our strengthened k-induction procedure with the naïve approach by replacing SZ with small values. Results are shown in Figure 6, which also indicates the value of k required for verification in each case. The figure illustrates the benefits of strengthened induction: for the largest value of SZ considered, 64, the *single buffer IO* benchmark is verified 170 times faster when strengthening is employed.

7   Related Work

Inductive reasoning has played a key role in proofs of program correctness for many years [11]. The k-induction method was introduced in [18]. Variations and applications of k-induction have been extensively studied (see *e.g.* [7,8,12]).

The problem of strengthening induction is considered in [3]. A counterexample-driven technique is used to iteratively strengthen the property under consideration in an attempt to make it inductive. The work is primarily concerned with standard induction (1-induction), though experimental results for k-induction are also presented. In contrast, our approach to induction strengthening uses separate static analysis techniques—abstract interpretation, chunking and code motion—to process a program *before* inductive reasoning is applied. We believe our method is complementary to that of [3], and it may be beneficial to combine the approaches.

Techniques for detecting data races in shared memory multithreaded applications have been extensively studied, see *e.g.* [10,9,15,17]. However, none of these methods are applicable to DMA race detection for multicore architectures such as the Cell BE.

8   Summary

The k-induction method is a promising technique for SAT-based verification of programs with loops, and has shown merit in this area in the context of DMA race analysis. The main weakness of k-induction is its sensitivity to inner loops, which may contain insufficiently strong assertions to build up an inductive invariant that implies program correctness. We have addressed this weakness by using three kinds of static analysis: abstract interpretation, chunking, and code motion. We have incorporated these techniques into SCRATCH, a DMA race analysis tool for the Cell BE architecture, and shown experimentally that the combination of static analysis and k-induction takes a large step towards the goal of fully automated verification of programs in this application domain.

We believe there is potential for generalizing our chunking and code motion analyses to aid inductive verification of programs in other application domains. We also intend to achieve 100% automation through an implementation of trace partitioning. A key challenge will be to design heuristics to automatically decide where trace partitioning can be usefully applied.

References

1. Aho, A., Lam, M., Sethi, R., Ullman, J.: Compilers: Principles, Techniques and Tools. Addison-Wesley, Reading (2006)
2. Biere, A., Cimatti, A., Clarke, E.M., Strichman, O., Zhu, Y.: Bounded model checking. Advances in Computers 58, 118–149 (2003)
3. Bradley, A.R., Manna, Z.: Property-directed incremental invariant generation. Formal Asp. Comput. 20(4-5), 379–405 (2008)
4. Clarke, E., Kröning, D., Lerda, F.: A Tool for Checking ANSI-C Programs. In: Jensen, K., Podelski, A. (eds.) TACAS 2004. LNCS, vol. 2988, pp. 168–176. Springer, Heidelberg (2004)
5. Cousot, P., Cousot, R.: Systematic design of program analysis frameworks. In: POPL, pp. 269–282 (1979)
6. Donaldson, A.F., Kroening, D., Rümmer, P.: Scratch: a tool for automatic analysis of DMA races. In: PPoPP (to appear, 2011)
7. Donaldson, A.F., Kroening, D., Rümmer, P.: Automatic analysis of scratch-pad memory code for heterogeneous multicore processors. In: Esparza, J., Majumdar, R. (eds.) TACAS 2010. LNCS, vol. 6015, pp. 280–295. Springer, Heidelberg (2010)
8. Eén, N., Sörensson, N.: Temporal induction by incremental SAT solving. Electr. Notes Theor. Comput. Sci. 89(4) (2003)
9. Engler, D., Ashcraft, K.: RacerX: Effective, static detection of race conditions and deadlocks. In: SOSP, pp. 237–252. ACM, New York (2003)
10. Flanagan, C., Freund, S.N.: Type-based race detection for Java. In: PLDI, pp. 219–232. ACM, New York (2000)
11. Floyd, R.W.: Assigning meanings to programs. Mathematical aspects of computer science. In: Proceedings of Symposia in Applied Mathematics pp. 19–32 (1967)
12. Hagen, G., Tinelli, C.: Scaling up the formal verification of Lustre programs with SMT-based techniques. In: FMCAD, pp. 109–117. IEEE, Los Alamitos (2008)
13. IBM: Example Library API Reference, version 3.1 (July 2008)
14. IBM: Cell BE resource center (2009),
    http://www.ibm.com/developerworks/power/cell/
15. Naik, M., Aiken, A., Whaley, J.: Effective static race detection for Java. In: PLDI, pp. 308–319. ACM, New York (2006)
16. Rival, X., Mauborgne, L.: The trace partitioning abstract domain. ACM Trans. Program. Lang. Syst. 29(5) (2007)
17. Savage, S., Burrows, M., Nelson, G., Sobalvarro, P., Anderson, T.: Eraser: A dynamic data race detector for multithreaded programs. ACM Trans. Comput. Syst. 15(4), 391–411 (1997)
18. Sheeran, M., Singh, S., Stålmarck, G.: Checking safety properties using induction and a SAT-solver. In: Johnson, S.D., Hunt Jr., W.A. (eds.) FMCAD 2000. LNCS, vol. 1954, pp. 108–125. Springer, Heidelberg (2000)
19. Tip, F.: A survey of program slicing techniques. J. Prog. Lang. 3(3) (1995)

Access Nets: Modeling Access to Physical Spaces

Robert Frohardt, Bor-Yuh Evan Chang, and Sriram Sankaranarayanan

University of Colorado, Boulder, Colorado, USA
{frohardt,bec,srirams}@cs.colorado.edu

Abstract. Electronic, software-managed mechanisms using, for example, radio-frequency identification (RFID) cards, enable great flexibility in specifying access control policies to physical spaces. For example, access rights may vary based on time of day or could differ in normal versus emergency situations. With such fine-grained control, understanding and reasoning about what a policy permits becomes surprisingly difficult requiring knowledge of permission levels, spatial layout, and time. In this paper, we present a formal modeling framework, called ACCESS NETS, suitable for describing a combination of access permissions, physical spaces, and temporal constraints. Furthermore, we provide evidence that model checking techniques are effective in reasoning about physical access control policies. We describe our results from a tool that uses reachability analysis to validate security policies.

1 Introduction

Access to physical spaces such as buildings, museums, airports, and chemical plants is increasingly mediated by electronic, software-controlled mechanisms. These mechanisms combine traditional human mediation, mechanical lock-and-keys, as well as electronic technologies such as radio-frequency identification (RFID) cards. The use of computerized access control in these systems is on the rise, as they enable highly flexible policies. Computerized access control policies enable administrators to add or remove access to key personnel or specify policies that may vary depending on the time of the day (working hours versus evenings), day of the week (weekdays versus weekends), and months in the year (summer versus fall). These policies can even be automatically changed in response to emergencies such as a fire in the building—in contrast to access policies mediated using only mechanical lock-and-key.

In this paper, we address formal modeling and verification of access control policies for physical spaces. Our approach combines dynamic models of access control policies in physical spaces with an application of model-checking techniques. In particular, we make the following contributions:

- We present a formal framework ACCESS NETS for the modeling of access control in physical spaces, such as offices or buildings (Sect. 3). Our framework models the topology of the physical space, as well as the movement of personnel with various access levels in this space. Our model of access control accommodates rich specifications, including those that depend on time.
- We demonstrate a new and compelling application of formal verification techniques, like model checking. While software-managed access control systems may

R. Jhala and D. Schmidt (Eds.): VMCAI 2011, LNCS 6538, pp. 184–198, 2011.

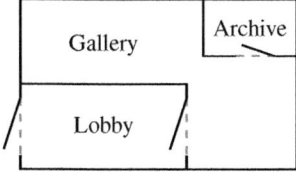

P1	The visitors may only be in the museum between 9:00 a.m. and 5:00 p.m.
P2	The visitors may only enter the archive with guard escort during museum hours.
P3	The curators may enter the museum and the archive at any time.

Fig. 1. A floor plan, access control roles (top) and access control policy (bottom) for a museum

be large and complex, we see that well-known state-space reduction techniques are surprisingly effective in reducing the size of the model. Thus, we identify a new domain where model checking techniques are particularly apt (Sect. 4).

– We provide evidence for the applicability of our techniques through an initial case study (Sect. 5). In particular, we observe that our ACCESS NET-specific reduction techniques are quite effective in reducing the state space.

Motivating Example. Figure 1 outlines a simple floor plan and an access control policy for a fictitious museum. The museum has a main entrance leading into a lobby. The lobby in turn leads into a gallery, which is connected to an archive. The main entrance and the entrance to the archive have key card readers. The archive entrance is staffed by a guard during opening hours. The access control policies are also described in Fig. 1.

Given such a policy specification, we wish to verify that the access control mechanisms support it. For example, is it possible for a visitor to be in the archive after hours? Can curators access the archive at any time? In general, it is hard to manually consider all the relevant scenarios, especially for larger buildings with more complex access control policies. Therefore, we desire a formal framework that captures the relevant details of such systems and enables automatic verification.

2   Overview

In this section, we present an overview of the main features in the ACCESS NETS model, using the museum example shown in Fig. 1. Note that we are not interested in details like the precise spatial layout of the building (e.g., coordinates). Thus, we seek a graph-like model that captures connectivity but abstracts spatial layout.

Drawing inspiration from Petri nets [19], we use tokens to model persons and transitions to capture the movement of persons from one place to another. Each transition has at least one incoming and one outgoing arc. Transitions move tokens *one-way* from their input places to their output places. This captures common situations wherein, a key is needed to enter a room but not needed to exit. The ACCESS NET model for the museum example has the graph structure shown in Fig. 2.

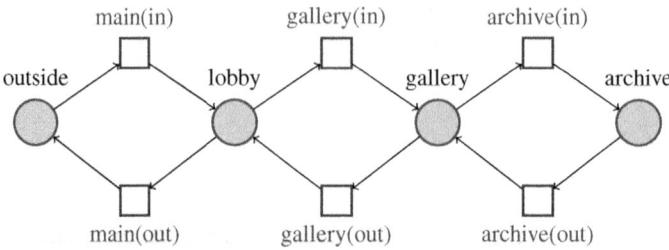

Fig. 2. The graph structure of the ACCESS NETS model for the example in Fig. 1

Token Types. Each token in our model has an associated type that represents its access level (e.g., visitor, guard, curator, administrator, or supervisor). Transitions are enabled based on the number of tokens of each type from each of their input places. For example, the rule that a visitor may only enter the archive under guard escort (rule P2 in Fig. 1) is shown in Fig. 3. Both the incoming and outgoing arcs of the archive(in) transition are annotated with 1 guard and 1 visitor. These labels specify the enabling condition that there must be a guard and a visitor present in the gallery.

Transition Firings. Transitions whose input conditions are satisfied may fire non-deterministically to yield a next state based on the output conditions of the transition. Thus, for example, to capture that a curator may enter the archive herself without guard escort (rule P3), we can simply add a separate transition with arcs from the gallery and to the archive each labeled with 1 curator.

Time. Some transition rules depend on the time of day. For example, anyone may enter the museum between 9:00 a.m. and 5:00 p.m. To model time, we add a global clock to an ACCESS NET state and a set of time intervals to the enabling condition of each transition. For instance, we can associate a set of times $[9, 17]$ with the main(in) transition in Fig. 3, so that it is enabled between 9:00 a.m. and 5:00 p.m.

Mandatory Transitions. Recall that visitors may be in the museum only between 9:00 a.m. and 5:00 p.m. (rule P1), so not only do we allow visitors to enter during those hours, but we must require visitors to leave when the museum closes at 5:00 p.m. To do so, we introduce the notion of a *mandatory transition*. At any state, if any mandatory transition is enabled, one of them must be taken next (see Sect. 3). In this scenario, we add mandatory transitions from the archive, gallery, and lobby to the outside requiring the visitors to leave during the time range $[17, 17.5]$ (i.e., 5:00 p.m. to 5:30 p.m.).

3   Access Nets

In this section, we provide a formalization of ACCESS NETS. The formal model provides a basis for verification techniques (Sect. 4) and the case studies (Sect. 5).

Topology. The topology of a building is modeled using a directed graph, whose nodes include a set of *places* P and a set of *transitions* T. The *arcs*, $F \subseteq (P \times T) \cup (T \times P)$, connect places to transitions, and transitions back to places. The

places	$p \in P$
transitions	$t \in T$
arcs	$f \in F$

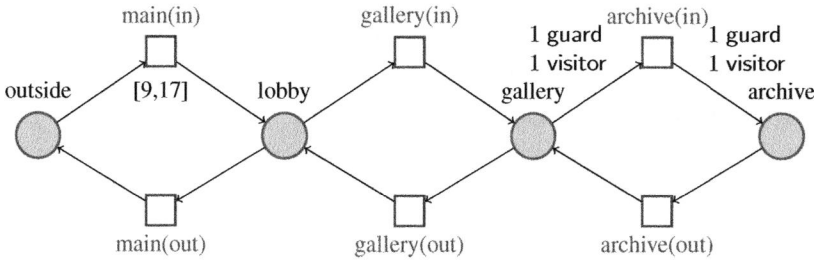

Fig. 3. The ACCESS NET model from Fig. 2 with access controls specified

inset box to the right summarizes the notation used. The incoming arcs for a transition t indicate the places from which t removes tokens, and the outgoing arcs indicate the places to which t adds tokens (cf. Definition 3). Pictorially, places are denoted as circles and transitions as rectangles (cf. Fig. 2).

State: Access Types, Markings, and Time. To model various access control roles, each token is annotated with a *type* drawn from a set S. For example, in the museum example discussed previously, the set S is $\{visitor, guard, curator\}$, represent-

$$
\begin{array}{rl}
\text{types} & s \in S \\
\text{markings} & m \ : (P \times S) \to \mathbb{N} \\
\text{global time} & \tau \in [\tau_{\min}, \tau_{\max}] \\
\text{enabled times} & H \ : T \to \mathcal{P}([\tau_{\min}, \tau_{\max}]) \\
\text{state} & \sigma = (m, \tau)
\end{array}
$$

ing various roles. Persons are represented by *tokens* of particular types (i.e., with particular access roles). As part of the state, we describe where people are with a *marking*.

Definition 1 (Marking). *A marking m is a function $m : (P \times S) \to \mathbb{N}$ that represents the number of tokens of type s in place p.*

Pictorially, a marking is denoted by drawing $m(p, s)$ dots labeled s at place p.

To model temporal access control rules, we introduce a global clock τ that is a value in a fixed range $[\tau_{\min}, \tau_{\max}]$. For example, we may choose $\tau_{\min} = 0$ and $\tau_{\max} = 24$ representing the hours of day. The framework is agnostic to translation of these values to "real time." Therefore, time can be modeled at the appropriate granularity (e.g., seconds, minutes, hours, and days). Time is updated in the ACCESS NET model by using a special *tick* transition. For each transition t, we define the "hours" function $H : T \to \mathcal{P}([\tau_{\min}, \tau_{\max}])$. For simplicity, $H(t)$ is assumed to be the union of finitely many disjoint intervals for each transition t, specifying the time instants during which the transition t can be *enabled* (cf. Definition 2). Diagrammatically, $H(t)$ is denoted by writing a range next to the transition (e.g., $[9, 17]$ in Fig. 3). The absence of such an annotation indicates that the transition is time independent (i.e., $H(t)$ is $[\tau_{\min}, \tau_{\max}]$).

A state σ of an ACCESS NET is then the pair (m, τ) consisting of its current marking and its current time.

State Transitions. The execution of an ACCESS NET models the movement of people throughout the building and the progression of time. Recall from Sect. 2 that our model contains *mandatory transitions* $M \subseteq T$ that are taken whenever enabled. Definition 2 describes the enforcement of mandatory transitions.

State transitions $\sigma \longrightarrow \sigma'$ denote a move from current state σ to a next state σ'. There are two main types of state transitions: (1) *token transitions* model the movement of people, and (2) *tick transitions* model the progression of time.

Token Transitions. An ACCESS NET has a *weight* function $W : (F \times S) \to \mathbb{N}$ that gives the number of tokens of a type s that move along each arc f during a transition.

Definition 2 (Enabled Transition). *Transition t is* enabled *in state $\sigma = (m, \tau)$ iff*

1. *The current time belongs to the permissible range:* $\tau \in H(t)$.
2. *There are sufficiently many tokens in the input places:* $W(f, s) \leq m(p, s)$ *for all $f : (p, t) \in$ in(t) and for all $s \in S$.*
3. *If $t \notin M$, then every mandatory transition $t_m \in M$ is not enabled.*

where in$(t) \overset{\text{def}}{=} \{(p, t) \in F \mid p \in P\}$ *and* out$(t) \overset{\text{def}}{=} \{(t, p) \in F \mid p \in P\}$ *(i.e., the incoming and outgoing arcs of transition t, respectively).*

An enabled transition can move tokens from its input places to its output places.

Definition 3 (Token Transition). *Given state $\sigma = (m, \tau)$ and enabled transition t, a token transition results in a new marking m', such that*

$$m'(p, s) = m(p, s) - W(f, s), \, \forall \, s \in S, \, f : (p, t) \in \text{in}(t).$$
$$m'(p, s) = m(p, s) + W(f, s), \, \forall \, s \in S, \, f : (t, p) \in \text{out}(t).$$

For simplicity in presentation, in(t) and out(t) are assumed disjoint, that is, there are no self-loops. Self-loops can be eliminated by the introduction of dummy transitions and places [19]. We write such a token transition as $(m, \tau) \overset{t}{\longrightarrow} (m', \tau)$.

Tick Transitions. Tick transitions model the elapse of time. For any state $\sigma = (m, \tau)$ such that $\tau \in [\tau_{\min}, \tau_{\max})$, and *no mandatory transitions are enabled*, the global time may progress to any time in $(\tau, \tau']$ where $\tau' = \min(\tau_M, \tau_{\max})$ where $\tau_M > \tau$ is the next time when some mandatory transition could be enabled. We write a time transition from τ to τ' as follows: $(m, \tau) \overset{\text{tick}}{\longrightarrow} (m, \tau')$. When checking the model, not all times values τ need to be considered. Instead, time is abstracted using a region construction along the lines of Alur and Dill [1]. To simplify some of formalization, we also define idling transitions that do not change the state, which we write as $\sigma \overset{\varepsilon}{\longrightarrow} \sigma$.

Execution. An *execution* of an ACCESS NET consists of a finite sequence of states $\sigma_0, \sigma_1, \dots, \sigma_n$ wherein each state σ_{i+1} is obtained from the previous state σ_i by a legal state transition as described above. For example, we write a sample execution as follows: $\sigma_0 \overset{t_1}{\longrightarrow} \sigma_1 \overset{\varepsilon}{\longrightarrow} \cdots \overset{\text{tick}}{\longrightarrow} \sigma_{n-1} \overset{t_2}{\longrightarrow} \sigma_n$. We consider finite sequences of states since we are interested in executions in which time remains within $[\tau_{\min}, \tau_{\max}]$. However, temporal logics are interpreted over infinite state sequences (or trees) [5]. We extend our finite sequences to infinite ones by adding infinitely many *idling transitions*.

Conservation. Since tokens represent people, there is a physical constraint that all state transitions $\sigma \longrightarrow \sigma'$ conserve the number and type of tokens. We enforce this by requiring that all transitions t are *conservative*. Conservative transitions is not an inherent limitation to our approach but rather a check for more faithful models.

Definition 4 (Conservative Transitions). *A transition* t *is* conservative *iff for every access type, the sum of tokens of that type on incoming edges to* t *is equal to the sum of that type on outgoing edges, that is, for all* $s \in S$,

$$\sum_{f \in \mathrm{in}(t)} W(f, s) = \sum_{f \in \mathrm{out}(t)} W(f, s) .$$

If all transitions are conservative, then any execution is also conservative capturing the desired physical constraint (see our companion technical report [10] for a proof).

For reference, we gather all of the pieces of an ACCESS NET as described above in our companion technical report [10]. There are related Petri net models, e.g., with typed tokens [16] and with predicates on transitions [11]. Here, we have incorporated the aspects that are critically necessary to capture access control policies.

4   Verification of Access Properties

In this section, we consider verifying properties of ACCESS NETS. Our primary goal is to check whether tokens of a certain type can be present in a certain room in a certain time range; for example, a property of interest could say, "There is never a visitor in the archive before 9:00 a.m. or after 5:30 p.m." This restricted class of reachability properties enables us to perform aggressive state-space reduction. It is possible to extend our reductions to verify ACTL* properties, following Clarke et al. [6].

Given an ACCESS NET A with a place p and a token type s, we say p is *token reachable* for s at time τ if and only if $\sigma_0 \longrightarrow^* \sigma_n$ where $\rightarrow^*$ is the transitive closure of the transition relation, state σ_0 is the initial state, and if $\sigma_n = (m_n, \tau_n)$ then $m_n(p, s) > 0$ and $\tau_n = \tau$. As expected, we can verify such properties using model checking.

The state space of an ACCESS NET blows up quickly as we increase the number of places, transitions, and token types, as we see in our case study (Sect. 5). Fortunately, there are several natural reductions that can be performed that respect the token reachability property of interest. Our reductions generate a new ACCESS NET that *abstracts* the original in the sense that it is sound with respect to token reachability. Stated more precisely, let A' be a reduced ACCESS NET of A, and let π be the function mapping each place of A to its corresponding place in A'. Then, the reduction is *sound* with respect to token reachability if whenever $\pi(p)$ is not reachable for s at time τ in A', then p is not reachable for s at time τ in A. In other words, reduction preserves safety. Furthermore, two of our three reductions, namely the unlocked doors and redundant transition reductions, are complete with respect to token reachability.

The two most interesting reductions use the following procedure(cf. Clarke et al. [6]): (1) we define an equivalence relation $\overset{\mathrm{pl}}{\sim}$ over places; (2) we define a new ACCESS NET A' as the quotient of A with respect to $\overset{\mathrm{pl}}{\sim}$.

Definition 5 (Access Net Reduction). *Let A be an* ACCESS NET *and let $\overset{\mathrm{pl}}{\sim}$ be an equivalence relation over places. This equivalence relation induces the following equivalence relation over arcs:*

$$f_1 \overset{\mathrm{ar}}{\sim} f_2 \quad \textit{iff} \quad p_1 \overset{\mathrm{pl}}{\sim} p_2 \textit{ and } t_1 = t_2, \textit{ and}$$
$$\textit{either } f_1 = (p_1, t_1) \textit{ and } f_2 = (p_2, t_2)$$
$$\textit{or } f_1 = (t_1, p_1) \textit{ and } f_2 = (t_2, p_2)$$

Let π map a place or arc in $A = (P, T, \ldots)$ to its respective equivalence class (under $\overset{pl}{\sim}$ or $\overset{ar}{\sim}$). We also write π^{-1} for the pre-image of this mapping. Then, $A' = (P', T', \ldots)$ is a reduced ACCESS NET *under equivalence relation $\overset{pl}{\sim}$:*

$$P' = \pi(P) \qquad F' = \pi(F)$$

$$T' = T \qquad M' = M \qquad S' = S$$

$$\tau_0' = \tau_0 \qquad \tau_{min}' = \tau_{min} \qquad \tau_{max}' = \tau_{max} \qquad H' = H$$

$$W' : (f', s) \mapsto \sum_{f \in \pi^{-1}(\{f'\})} W(f, s) \qquad m_0' : (p', s) \mapsto \sum_{p \in \pi^{-1}(\{p'\})} m_0(p, s)$$

where $\pi(P)$ is the image of P under π and $\pi(F)$ is the image of F under π. That is, we map all places and arcs to their equivalence classes (first line); transitions, mandatory transitions, token types, time constraints and the clock stay the same; weights on arcs and the initial marking are combined by summing the number of tokens of each type.

It remains to be shown that A' as defined above is actually an ACCESS NET. In particular, the main property that must be checked is that conservation is preserved, which is shown in our companion technical report [10]. We now define several reductions on ACCESS NETS that use this idea of defining equivalence relations over places.

Unlocked Doors Reduction. If the only barrier between two rooms is an unlocked door, then for the purpose of checking reachability, the two rooms can be merged into a single room.

Definition 6 (Equivalent up to Unlocked Doors). *A room p_2 can be reached through one unlocked door from a room $p_1 \neq p_2$, written* unlocked(p_1, p_2), *if and only if for every security role s, there is some transition t such that*

1. *We have $H(t) = [\tau_{min}, \tau_{max}]$, that is, the transition is enabled at all times.*
2. *We have* pred$(t) = \{p_1\}$ *and* succ$(t) = \{p_2\}$ *where* pred *and* succ *are the functions mapping a place to its sets of predecessor and successor places, respectively. In other words, t is a transition from p_1 to p_2 and does not take tokens from or send tokens to any places other than p_1 and p_2.*

Two rooms p_1 and p_2 are equivalent up to unlocked doors in one-step, *written $p_1 \overset{pl}{\sim}_1 p_2$, if and only if* unlocked(p_1, p_2) *and* unlocked(p_2, p_1). *The equivalence relation for unlocked doors is simply the reflexive-transitive closure of $\overset{pl}{\sim}_1$.*

Figure 4(a) shows a simplified ACCESS NET of the office building (ECOT) used in our case study (see Sect. 5) with two token types s and f (to represent students and faculty, respectively). Figure 4(b) shows the result of applying the unlocked doors reduction to Fig. 4(a). We see that the two places hall 1 and hall 2 have been merged into a place [hall 1], as the two places allow free passage of both s and f in both directions. After the unlocked doors reduction, the reduced model technically would have unnecessary self-loop transitions between each new representative and itself. These transitions can be deleted from the model.

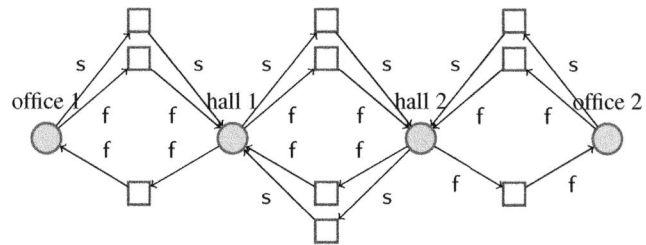

(a) Simplified ACCESS NET before any reductions.

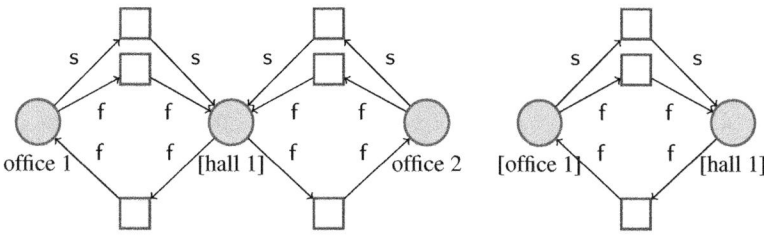

(b) After the unlocked doors reduction.

(c) After equivalent rooms and redundant transitions reductions.

Fig. 4. Applying reductions to a simplified ACCESS NET for an office building

Redundant Transitions Reduction. If two transitions represent identical access rules and move tokens from the same sources to the same destinations, then one of the two transitions can be deleted. This reduction does not follow the pattern of defining an equivalence relation on places for the sake of merging places. Instead if two transitions are equivalent according to the following definition, then one of the transitions can be arbitrarily deleted.

Definition 7 (Equivalent up to Redundant Transitions). *Two transitions t_1 and t_2 are equivalent up to redundant transitions, written $\overset{tr}{\sim}$, iff:*

1. *$H(t_1) = H(t_2)$, that is, the transitions are enabled at exactly the same times.*
2. *There exists a bijective mapping $\mu : \text{in}(t_1) \rightarrow \text{in}(t_2)$ such that for every place p_1 where $(p_1, t_1) \in \text{in}(t_1)$, then whenever $(p_2, t_2) = \mu(p_1, t_1)$, we have:*

$$p_1 = p_2 \quad \textit{and} \quad W((p_1, t_1), s) = W((p_2, t_2), s) \textit{ for every } s \in S \, .$$

3. *There exists a bijective mapping $\nu : \text{out}(t_1) \rightarrow \text{out}(t_2)$ such that for every place p_1 where $(t_1, p_1) \in \text{out}(t_1)$, then whenever $(t_2, p_2) = \nu(t_1, p_1)$, we have:*

$$p_1 = p_2 \quad \textit{and} \quad W((t_1, p_1), s) = W((t_2, p_2), s) \textit{ for every } s \in S \, .$$

This definition says that two transitions are equivalent if they are enabled at exactly the same times and if their incoming and outgoing edges can be put into a bijective correspondence of equivalent edges. It is straightforward to show that $\overset{tr}{\sim}$ is an equivalence relation. For each equivalence class of transitions, all of the transitions in that class can be deleted except for one arbitrary representative.

Equivalent Rooms Reduction. If two rooms are equivalent in the sense that they are only reachable from the same rooms according to the same access control rules, then the two rooms can be merged into a single room.

Definition 8 (Equivalent Rooms). *First, we define two transitions as being* equivalent up to $q_1 = q_2$, *written* $\overset{q_1=q_2}{\sim}$ *in the same way as* $\overset{tr}{\sim}$ *from the redundant transitions reduction with one change. Instead of requiring of μ and ν that $p_1 = p_2$, we require only that*

$$p_1 = p_2 \qquad or \qquad p_1 = q_1 \ and \ p_2 = q_2 \qquad or \qquad p_1 = q_2 \ and \ p_2 = q_1$$

That is, the transitions are redundant under an assumption that $q_1 = q_2$. Then two rooms q_1 and q_2 are equivalent rooms, *denoted $q_1 \overset{pl}{\sim} q_2$ if and only if*

1. *There exists a bijective mapping $\mu : \mathsf{pred}(q_1) \rightarrow \mathsf{pred}(q_2)$ such that for every transition $t \in \mathsf{pred}(q_1)$, we have $t \overset{q_1=q_2}{\sim} \mu(t)$.*
2. *There exists a bijective mapping $\nu : \mathsf{succ}(q_1) \rightarrow \mathsf{succ}(q_2)$ such that for every transition $t \in \mathsf{succ}(q_1)$, we have $t \overset{q_1=q_2}{\sim} \nu(t)$.*

It is straightforward to show that $\overset{pl}{\sim}$ is an equivalence relation. Figure 4(c) shows the result of applying the equivalent rooms and redundant doors reductions to Fig. 4(b). We see that office 1 and office 2 have been merged into a single place [office 1]. These reductions correspond naturally to our intuition, as from the perspective of token reachability, all of the offices and all of the halls look the same as long as they are connected to each other though "unlocked areas."

All three reductions, unlocked doors, redundant transitions, and equivalent rooms, are sound with respect to token reachability. Furthermore, unlocked doors and redundant transitions are complete with respect to token reachability (though equivalent rooms is not). Proofs of these facts are given in our companion technical report [10]. At a high-level, the reductions merge "equivalent" places that satisfy the same set of properties, in order to construct an abstraction. This abstraction is similar in ways to canonical abstraction in the TVLA program analysis framework [22].

Untiming. Regarding tick transitions, the definition for state transitions allows arbitrary time steps and describes an infinite state space. However, only the the initial time and the boundaries of time intervals referenced by time-dependent transitions need to be considered during verification. To this end, we apply a standard untiming construction as described in Alur and Dill [1]. The untiming construction is especially simplified in the case of ACCESS NETS since the model has a single timer.

5   Case Study: Office Security

To validate the feasibility of our approach, we modeled a part of the Engineering Center Office Tower (ECOT) at the University of Colorado, Boulder and a set of synthetic access control rules. Furthermore, we have completely modeled an actual, large office building with multiple floors, occupied by many businesses using a real access control

Table 1. Dependence of explicit-state model checking using Spin on the size of the building for verifying a valid property. In each test case run, we show the size of the ACCESS NET (number of rooms, transitions, and persons) along with the number states observed by Spin, the total memory used by Spin, and the total time for the model checking to run.

Model	Rooms	Transitions	Persons	States	Memory (MB)	Time (s)
ECOT 8	17	38	3	1603	13.9	0.1
ECOT 7,8	50	120	3	20429	22.7	2.7
ECOT 6,7,8	92	222	3	93578	103.6	22.8

policy. With these models, we applied explicit-state model checking using Spin [15] and bounded model checking [4] using our implementation based on the Yices SMT solver [8] (other verification techniques could apply). With this study, we are interested in how the building and access control policy is encoded as an ACCESS NET model and how feasible is model checking. We also look at how much the state space can be reduced using the techniques from Sect. 4.

To create our ACCESS NET model of ECOT, we examined CAD drawings of the sixth, seventh, and eighth floors of the building (which is where the Computer Science Department is located). The access control policy involved three access types, student, faculty, and maintenance and consisted of the following rules:

1. Any faculty can enter any office. Anybody in an office can exit it.
2. Any maintenance can enter a mechanical room or janitorial room. Anybody in one of these rooms can exit it.
3. Any student can only enter a conference room accompanied by a faculty and only between 9:00 a.m. and 5:00 p.m. Conference rooms can be exited freely.

As perhaps expected, the state space grows quickly even for our relatively small models by either increasing the number of places and transitions or the number of tokens. Fortunately, the topology and access policies that we work with are amenable to reduction, which apply regardless of model checking technique. We first consider verification of a valid property using Spin on unreduced models and look at the growth in verification resources as a function of model size. Then, we look at the cost of discovering property violations. We consider not only explicit-state model checking but also bounded model checking, which is insensitive to number of tokens. Finally, we look at the effectiveness of reduction.

Verifying Valid Properties. Table 1 shows the relationship between the resources required for explicit-state model checking and number of rooms and transitions in an ACCESS NET, while Table 2 considers the dependence on number of persons. All of our tests were executed on a Linux server with 32 GB memory and sixteen 2.93GHz Intel Xeon X7350 CPUs. In the test runs in these two tables, we checked that "a student can never be in a particular office (826) and a faculty member can never be in a specific mechanical room (805A)," which is valid in these models. There were no uses of time in any of these models (i.e., we did not use rule 3 regarding the conference rooms here).

In Table 1, we see that Spin works with reasonable memory and time constraints, but the state space blows up quite quickly as we add additional rooms (by successively

Table 2. Dependence of explicit-state model checking using Spin on the number of persons in the model for verifying a valid property. We started with one person of each type and then successively added one faculty at a time.

Model	Rooms	Transitions	Persons	States	Memory (MB)	Time (s)
ECOT 8	17	38	3	1603	13.9	0.1
ECOT 8	17	38	4	12523	15.8	0.7
ECOT 8	17	38	5	70763	26.1	4.3
ECOT 8	17	38	6	318283	89.1	22.4
ECOT 8	17	38	7	1209355	405.3	97.9

adding the rooms on the 7th and 6th floors). In these tests, we started one token of each type in a public room on the 8th floor.

For increasing number of persons, we see the number of states considered by Spin also grows rapidly, as does the increase in memory and time consumption, as shown in Table 2. In these tests, we started with one token of each type and then successively added one token of type faculty at a time. We chose the faculty type, as it leads to the largest state space.

Discovering Property Violations. Both of the previous examples checked properties that could not be violated (and thus required an exhaustive exploration of the state space). Here, we consider violated properties. First, we consider the same set of ACCESS NET models from Table 1 that do not use timed transitions. The violated property was "a faculty member cannot be in a particular office on the 8th floor (826)." The test runs are shown in the top half of Table 3.

We then looked at a set of timed models that adds the conference room rule (rule 3), that is, that a student can only enter a conference room with a faculty member between 9:00 a.m. and 5:00 p.m. In this case, the initial state was a student and a faculty on the 7th floor at 9:00 a.m. The violated property was "a student cannot be in the conference room (831) at 6:00 p.m." This property can be violated by the faculty letting the student into the conference room between 9:00 a.m. and 5:00 p.m. and then the student remaining in the room after 5:00 p.m. until 6:00 p.m.

Table 2 shows rapid explosion in the number of states considered by Spin as we increase the number of tokens. A potential advantage of bounded model checking is its insensitivity to number of tokens, and thus, we applied it to the property violation cases of Table 3. Table 4 presents these results. We confirm that the Yices-based bounded model checker finds the same witnesses as Spin in a reasonable amount of time and space. Note that our BMC implementation is currently a prototype.

Reductions. The redundant structure of ECOT is particularly well-suited to the reductions described in Sect. 4. Even after adding in the 5th floor, ECOT reduces to just four rooms! In the reduced model, there is one public room, one representative office, one representative maintenance room, and one representative conference room. Table 5 shows the results from the reductions; the memory and time measurements show the cost of computing the reduced model. In all cases, after applying all reductions, the models are so small that the model checking times are negligible (and thus not shown in the table). The rows labeled 'some reductions' show the effect of performing only

Table 3. Discovering a property violation using Spin in breadth-first search mode. We consider the set of ACCESS NET models without timed transitions from Table 1 and a new set with timed transitions.

Model	Rooms	Transitions	Persons	States	Memory (MB)	Depth	Time (s)
Without Timed Transitions							
ECOT 8	17	38	3	556	4.8	2	0.0
ECOT 7,8	50	120	3	2961	10.5	5	0.3
ECOT 6,7,8	92	222	3	10730	46.0	6	2.4
With Timed Transitions							
ECOT 8	17	42	3	6897	7.1	6	0.1
ECOT 7,8	50	124	3	64323	68.5	9	6.0

Table 4. Discovering a property violation using the Yices-based BMC (untimed models). Note that BMC does not require a bound on the number of persons.

Model	Memory (MB)	Time (s)	Depth
ECOT 8	6.4	0.2	2
ECOT 7,8	38.4	5.7	5
ECOT 6,7,8	104.9	21.7	6

the unlocked doors and redundant transitions reductions (Definitions 6 and 7). The rows labeled 'all reductions' add the equivalent rooms reduction (Definition 8), which is all reductions described in Sect. 4. In our model, all faculty can access all offices, but in a slight variant, we may have a unique access policy for each office. In this case, the equivalent rooms reduction would have no effect giving reduced models analogous to the cases with 'some reductions.'

Real-World Example. We also obtained the complete access control specification for an actual four-story, multi-tenant office building. The building houses roughly 200 employees during working hours. Our model of the building had about 200 rooms and 230 doors. The operators of the building can assign up to 24 different access types. Due to the exponential dependence of our model on the number of people in the model, we could not simulate all access types at once. We selected two access types that were more interesting and ran a simple slicing reduction (not described in Sect. 4) that removes transitions for the excluded access types.

Without reductions, this model is too large for the explicit-state model checker, but the reductions are very effective (see Table 6). After reductions, we can prove safety properties very efficiently. Note that the restrictions in the number of persons does not apply to BMC that was run for an unbounded number of persons. This makes the BMC approach especially appealing because the number of people in the model does not directly affect the encoding size. The BMC implementation ran for an hour on the full model without reduction, searching up to depth 7, but was unable to find a violation. The running time on the reduced model was significantly smaller (30s) for a depth 30.

Table 5. Size of reduced models and resource requirements to calculate the reduction. The marking ($<$) indicates something below the granularity of our measurements, while (*) indicates a case where we fail to run Spin possibly because of the model size.

Model	Rooms	Transitions	Persons	States	Model Reduction Memory (MB)	Time (s)
ECOT 8						
no reductions	17	38	3	1603	N/A	N/A
some reductions	6	16	3	37	$<$	$<$
all reductions	4	6	3	20	$<$	$<$
ECOT 7, 8						
no reductions	50	120	3	20429	N/A	N/A
some reductions	23	62	3	167	$<$	0.1
all reductions	4	6	3	20	4.1	0.6
ECOT 6, 7, 8						
no reductions	92	222	3	93578	N/A	N/A
some reductions	47	124	3	423	5.1	0.2
all reductions	4	6	3	20	5.1	4.5
ECOT 5, 6, 7, 8						
no reductions	138	336	3	*	N/A	N/A
some reductions	74	194	3	859	5.1	0.4
all reductions	4	6	3	20	5.1	18.1

Table 6. Results of explicit-state model checking for real office building

Model	Rooms	Transitions	Persons	States	Memory (MB)	Time (s)
before reductions	207	460	2	N/A	N/A	N/A
after reductions	10	15	2	25	13.9	1.7

6   Related Work

Sampemane et al. present a specification formalism for role-based access control to physical spaces that allow novel uses of physical spaces, while ensuring that resources in these spaces are not misused [23]. Similarly, Bauer et al. present a framework for modeling and reasoning about personnel credentials and their delegation for physical as well as cyber access control using theorem proving [3]. The previously cited works present formalizations that support the addition, deletion, and modification of access control policies. Our work is complementary: we focus on modeling the physical topology of the building and reasoning about its interplay with access control mechanisms.

Dynamical models of buildings have been investigated both at the *macroscopic levels*, wherein, pedestrian flows are often modeled as continuous, without distinguishing the behavior of each individual pedestrian [14] and at *microscopic levels* with an agent-based model of individual actions. Applications of these simulations have included techniques to predict the time to evacuate large and complex buildings [18,13,24,21]. These models inevitably use a graph-based representation to capture the building topology. Our work offers a systematic model that also takes into account the different access levels and the complex software-controlled access policies that are virtually standard in modern buildings.

Model checking has also been applied in the past to check access control policy for computer network systems. The model proposed here is similar to the role-based access control (RBAC) model used for mediating access to electronic resources in an organization [9]. The verification of access control policies for organizational systems has been considered in the past. For instance, Jha et al. [17] present a formalization of various RBAC models and characterize the computational complexity of some analysis problems. Guelev et al. present a model-checking approach for verifying both the permissivity as well as the security of access control policies [12].

Our work on physical spaces bears many similarities to role-based access control policies. For instance, our model assumes that permissions are provided based on certain well-defined organizational roles, which can be finitely many and well-known *a priori*. However, the verification problem is inherently different. Unlike network topologies, buildings have a non-trivial spatial layout, whose modeling at the appropriate level of detail is critical. Furthermore, buildings tend to be larger with more rooms, doors, passageways with a rich variety of access enforcement mechanisms. Building access control rules vary with time unlike network access control rules. Finally, the need for mandatory transitions is also quite unique. Nevertheless, as witnessed by the success of our abstraction-based approaches, buildings also present large amount of regularity that can be exploited through simple reduction schemes to significantly reduce the complexity of property verification.

Our work makes use of a translation to existing model checking tools including Spin for explicit state model checking [5,15], as well as a bounded model checker [4] implemented using the SAT-modulo theory solver Yices [20,8]. Other fast SMT solvers include solvers such as Z3 [7,2].

7   Conclusion

Although we have focused on reachability properties, we can consider ACCESS NETS that model and verify other aspects of physical spaces. For example, other potential applications include checking for *detectability* of violations (e.g., by adding observability to the semantics) or modeling *evacuation* plans for buildings. In summary, we have presented a formal model, ACCESS NETS, for analyzing access control policies for physical spaces. The model can express many aspects that are relevant such as physical topology, role-based access policies, and time-dependent access rules. Formal verification techniques can be used on these models, thereby making computer-aided validation of access control policies possible. Furthermore, we have demonstrated that although the state-space does explode, domain-specific state-space reduction techniques are quite effective in reducing the complexity of the verification problem.

Acknowledgments. We thank the anonymous reviewers for their helpful comments.

References

1. Alur, R., Dill, D.L.: A theory of timed automata. Theor. Comput. Sci. 126(2) (1994)
2. Barrett, C., Deters, M., Oliveras, A., Stump, A.: Design and results of the third annual satis-fiability modulo theories competition (SMT-Comp 2007). International Journal on Artificial Intelligence Tools 17(4) (2008)
3. Bauer, L., Garriss, S., Reiter, M.K.: Efficient proving for practical distributed access-control systems. In: Biskup, J., López, J. (eds.) ESORICS 2007. LNCS, vol. 4734, pp. 19–37. Springer, Heidelberg (2007)
4. Biere, A., Cimatti, A., Clarke, E., Zhu, Y.: Symbolic model checking without BDDs. In: Cleaveland, W.R. (ed.) TACAS 1999. LNCS, vol. 1579, p. 193. Springer, Heidelberg (1999)
5. Clarke, E., Grumberg, O., Peled, D.: Model Checking (1999)
6. Clarke, E.M., Grumberg, O., Long, D.E.: Model checking and abstraction. ACM Trans. Pro-gram. Lang. Syst. 16(5) (1994)
7. de Moura, L., Bjørner, N.S.: Z3: An efficient SMT solver. In: Ramakrishnan, C.R., Rehof, J. (eds.) TACAS 2008. LNCS, vol. 4963, pp. 337–340. Springer, Heidelberg (2008)
8. Dutertre, B., de Moura, L.: The YICES SMT solver,
   http://yices.csl.sri.com/tool-paper.pdf
9. Ferraiolo, D.F., Kuhn, D.R., Chandramouli, R.: Role-based Access Control (2003)
10. Frohardt, R., Chang, B.-Y.E., Sankaranarayanan, S.: Access Nets: Modeling access to phys-ical spaces (extended version). Technical Report CU-CS-1076-10, Department of Computer Science, University of Colorado, Boulder (2010)
11. Genrich, H.J., Lautenbach, K.: System modelling with high-level Petri nets. Theor. Comput. Sci. 13(1) (1981)
12. Guelev, D.P., Ryan, M.D., Schobbens, P.-Y.: Model-checking access control policies. In: Zhang, K., Zheng, Y. (eds.) ISC 2004. LNCS, vol. 3225, pp. 219–230. Springer, Heidelberg (2004)
13. Helbing, D., Farkas, I., Vicsek, T.: Simulating dynamical features of escape panic. Nature 407(6803) (2000)
14. Henderson, L.: The statistics of crowd fluids. Nature 229 (1971)
15. Holzmann, G.: The SPIN Model Checker (2003)
16. Jensen, K.: Coloured Petri nets and the invariant-method. Theor. Comput. Sci. 14(3) (1981)
17. Jha, S., Li, N., Tripunitara, M.V., Wang, Q., Winsborough, W.H.: Towards formal verifi-cation of role-based access control policies. IEEE Transactions on Dependable and Secure Computing (TDSC) 5(4) (2008)
18. Lovas, G.: Modeling and simulation of pedestrian traffic flow. Transportation Research B 28(6) (1994)
19. Murata, T.: Petri nets: Properties, analysis and applications. Proc. IEEE 77(4) (1989)
20. Nieuwenhuis, R., Oliveras, A., Tinelli, C.: Solving SAT and SAT modulo theories: From an abstract DPLL procedure to DPLL(T). J. ACM 53(6) (2006)
21. Pelechano, N., Malkawi, A.: Evacuation simulation models: Challenges in modeling high rise building evacuation with cellular automata approaches. Automation in Construction 17(4) (2008)
22. Sagiv, M., Reps, T., Wilhelm, R.: Parametric shape analysis via 3-valued logic. ACM Trans. Program. Lang. Syst. 24(3) (2002)
23. Sampemane, G., Naldurg, P., Campbell, R.H.: Access control for active spaces. In: Computer Security Applications, ACSAC (2002)
24. Shen, T.: ESM: A building evacuation simulation model. Building and Environment 40(5) (2005)

Join-Lock-Sensitive Forward Reachability Analysis for Concurrent Programs with Dynamic Process Creation[*]

Thomas Martin Gawlitza[1], Peter Lammich[2], Markus Müller-Olm[2], Helmut Seidl[3], and Alexander Wenner[2]

[1] CNRS/VERIMAG, France
Thomas.Gawlitza@imag.fr
[2] Institut für Informatik, Westfälische Wilhelms-Universität Münster, Germany
{peter.lammich,markus.mueller-olm,alexander.wenner}@wwu.de
[3] Technische Universität München, Germany
seidl@in.tum.de

Abstract. Dynamic Pushdown Networks (DPNs) are a model for parallel programs with (recursive) procedures and dynamic process creation. *Constraints* on the sequences of spawned processes allow to extend the basic model with joining of created processes [2]. Orthogonally DPNs can be extended with nested locking [9]. Reachability of a regular set R of configurations in presence of stable constraints as well as reachability without constraints but with nested locking are based on computing the set of predecessors $\mathrm{pre}^*(R)$. In the present paper, we present a *forward*-propagating algorithm for deciding reachability for DPNs. We represent sets of executions by sets of *execution trees* and show that the set of all execution trees resulting in configurations from R which either allow a lock-sensitive execution or a join-sensitive execution, is *regular*. Here, we rely on basic results about *macro tree transducers*. As a second contribution, we show that reachability is decidable also for DPNs with both nested locking and joins.

1 Introduction

Bouajjani et al. [2] introduced (Constrained) Dynamic Pushdown Networks ((C)DPNs) for modeling parallel programs with (potentially recursive) procedures and dynamic process creation. They propose an algorithm inspired by the pre*-algorithm for Pushdown Systems that, under the mild assumption that all constraints are *stable*, computes the set of all predecessors of a given regular set of configurations. Stable constraints are, for instance, capable of modeling *fork-join* parallelism as considered by Esparza and Podelski [4], Müller-Olm and Seidl [10], Seidl and Steffen [11].

Only weak forms of synchronization can be expressed in CDPNs. In order to deal with *nested* locking, Lammich et al. [9] introduced another mechanism for restricting executions. For unconstrained DPNs, they introduce *action trees*[1] to represent sets of related executions. Generalizing the acquisition history techniques of Kahlon et al. [6, 7], they construct a finite tree automaton to check whether an action tree represents

---

[*] This work was partially funded by the DFG project OpIAT (MU 1508/1-1 and SE 551/13-1) and the ANR project ASOPT.
[1] Action trees are called execution trees in Lammich et al. [9].

a *lock-sensitive* execution. This allows them to perform a lock-sensitive backward reachability analysis for unconstrained DPNs with nested locking.

The techniques of Lammich et al. [9] cannot directly be adapted to perform a lock-sensitive *forward* reachability analysis, since the set of all possible executions cannot always be represented by a regular set of action trees. In this paper, we therefore propose an augmented version of action trees, which we call *execution trees* throughout the present paper. Our construction should be seen in analogy to contextfree grammars where the linear derivation process can be represented in treelike form by representing subderivations referring to distinct sections of sentential forms in distinct subtrees. We show that the set of executions can be represented by a *regular* set of execution trees. This enables us to use tree automata techniques for forward reachability analysis. Moreover, by applying known results for *macro tree transducers*, we show that every tree regular property of action trees can be translated into a tree regular property of execution trees. This allows us to re-use the results of Lammich et al. [9] to perform a *forward* reachability analysis for DPNs with joins as well as a lock-sensitive forward reachability analysis for DPNs with nested locking. The algorithms we obtain in this way are both natural and not less efficient than the corresponding algorithms for backward reachability analysis of Bouajjani et al. [2] and Lammich et al. [9], respectively. These algorithms for *forward* reachability are our first contribution.

In programming languages which support multithreaded programming such as JAVA and C with POSIX threads, joins and locks may occur simultaneously in programs. Therefore, as our second contribution, we provide an algorithm for performing a *forward* reachability analysis that is simultaneously join- and lock-sensitive. Following the approach of Lammich et al. [9], we construct a finite tree automaton which accepts all action trees for which a schedule exists that is simultaneously lock-sensitive and join-sensitive. This tree automaton can be used with both, the forward analysis techniques of this paper, and the backward analysis techniques of Lammich et al. [9]. Note that such an automaton cannot be constructed by simply intersecting a tree automaton for lock-sensitive action trees with a tree automaton for join-sensitive action trees, since action trees may represent multiple executions. Hence, an action tree may represent a lock-sensitive execution and a different join-sensitive execution, but no execution that is simultaneously join- and lock-sensitive.

Before we proceed with the technical constructions, we consider an introductory example written in a real-world programming language:

Example 1. We consider the following C program that uses POSIX threads:

```
pthread_mutex_t m = PTHREAD_MUTEX_INITIALIZER;
void* f(void* x) {
  pthread_mutex_lock(&m); printf("A"); printf("B\n");
  pthread_mutex_unlock(&m); }
int main() { pthread_t t[10]; int i;
  for (i = 0; i < 10; i++) pthread_create(&t[i],NULL,f,NULL);
  for (i = 0; i < 10; i++) pthread_join(t[i],NULL);
  printf("End!\n"); return 0; }
```

Here, a main process creates 10 child-processes, waits until all these processes terminate, prints *End!*, and terminates. Each child-process prints *AB*. The lock m guarantees that the critical section of f is not used by two different processes at the same time. The main process does not need to acquire the lock m, since it only may access the printer when no child-process is alive. A lock-sensitive reachability analysis which does not take joining into account, may flag a spurious warning that exclusive access to the printer might be violated. Likewise, a join-sensitive reachability analysis which ignores the locking cannot exclude potential violations. In order to exclude such false alarms, a reachability analysis is required which is simultaneously join- and lock-sensitive.   □

2   Dynamic Pushdown Networks

Let us first introduce some notation: The Boolean lattice $\{\bot, \top\}$ is denoted by $\mathbb{B}$. The natural numbers are denoted by $\mathbb{N}$. We assume $0 \in \mathbb{N}$ and set $\mathbb{N}_+ := \mathbb{N} \setminus \{0\}$. The domain of a partial function $f : A \rightsquigarrow B$ is denoted by $\mathrm{dom}(f)$. $\oplus$ denotes the update operator for partial functions, i.e., for $f, g : A \rightsquigarrow B$ and $x \in A$, $(f \oplus g)(x)$ equals $g(x)$ if $x \in \mathrm{dom}(g)$ and $f(x)$ otherwise. We write $\{x_1 \mapsto y_1, \ldots, x_n \mapsto y_n\}$ for the partial function that maps x_i to y_i for all $i \in \{1, \ldots, n\}$ and is undefined otherwise.

Let Act be a non-empty set of *actions*. The specific action sp $\notin$ Act represents the spawning of a new process. We set $\overline{\mathsf{Act}} := \mathsf{Act} \cup \{\mathsf{sp}\}$. A *Dynamic Pushdown Network* (DPN) M is a tuple $(\mathsf{Act}, P, \Gamma, \Delta)$ where P is a finite set of *control states*, Γ is a finite set of *stack symbols*, and Δ is a finite set of *transition rules* of the following forms:

$$\text{(Base) } p\gamma \xrightarrow{a} p'\gamma' \qquad\qquad \text{(Push) } p\gamma \xrightarrow{a} p'\gamma_1\gamma_2$$
$$\text{(Pop) } p\gamma \xrightarrow{a} p' \qquad\qquad \text{(Spawn) } p\gamma \xrightarrow{\mathsf{sp}} p'\gamma' \triangleright p_s\gamma_s$$

Here, $p, p', p_s \in P$, $a \in \mathsf{Act}$, and $\gamma, \gamma', \gamma_1, \gamma_2 \in \Gamma$. Intuitively, DPNs extend pushdown systems by (Spawn)-rules, that create a new process as a side effect.

A *configuration* of a DPN $M = (\mathsf{Act}, P, \Gamma, \Delta)$ is an *unranked* tree where each node in the tree is labeled with an element from $P\Gamma^*$. Intuitively, each node of the tree denotes a process and is labeled with the current configuration of the process. The children of a process are the processes that were spawned by the parent process. Formally, we represent nodes in trees by sequences of natural numbers: A set $T \subseteq \mathbb{N}_+^*$ is called a *tree domain* iff (1) T is finite, and (2) prefix-closed, i.e., $l \in T$ implies $l' \in T$ for all prefixes l' of l, and (3) if $li \in T$ with $i > 1$ then also $l(i-1) \in T$. The set of all tree domains is denoted by $\mathcal{T}^{\mathbb{N}_+}$. Accordingly, a configuration c is a partial mapping $c : \mathbb{N}_+^* \rightsquigarrow P\Gamma^*$ where the domain $\mathrm{dom}(c)$ is a tree domain. Let $\mathcal{C}$ denote the set of all configurations of M. Within a configuration c, processes are organized hierarchically. Each element $l \in \mathrm{dom}(c)$ denotes a process. The set $\{li \in \mathrm{dom}(c) \mid i \in \mathbb{N}_+\}$ contains all child-processes of l within the configuration c. For $c(l) = pw$ with $p \in P, w \in \Gamma^*$, p is the control-state and w the stack of the process l within the configuration c. We call a configuration c_0 an *initial configuration* iff $c_0 = \{\epsilon \mapsto p\gamma\}$ for some $p \in P$ and some $\gamma \in \Gamma$, i.e. it contains a single process with a single symbol on its stack.

A single execution step of a DPN on a configuration applies a local rewrite step to the control-state and stack of one of the processes of the configuration. For all transition rules $r \in \Delta$ and all processes $l \in \mathbb{N}_+^*$, we define the partial function $\mapsto_r^l : \mathcal{C} \rightsquigarrow \mathcal{C}$ that applies r to the process l as follows:

$$\mapsto^l_{p\gamma \overset{a}{\hookrightarrow} p'w'}(c) := c \oplus \{l \mapsto p'w'w\} \qquad \qquad \text{if } c(l) = p\gamma w$$

$$\mapsto^l_{p\gamma \overset{sp}{\hookrightarrow} p'\gamma' \triangleright p_s\gamma_s}(c) := c \oplus \{l \mapsto p'\gamma'w, \mathrm{nc}(l, \mathrm{dom}(c)) \mapsto p_s\gamma_s\} \quad \text{if } c(l) = p\gamma w$$

Here, $\mathrm{nc}(l, T) := l \cdot \min\{i \in \mathbb{N}_+ \mid l \cdot i \notin T\}$ is the sequence of natural numbers denoting the next child of process l which can be added to the tree domain T preserving the tree domain property.

Constraint Structures. In this paragraph we define *constraint structures* that allow us to restrict sequences of execution steps of DPNs. The idea is to disable undesired execution steps depending on a global state, that is computed in parallel to the actual configuration of the DPN. Constraint structures will later be used to define join-lock sensitive executions. Formally a constraint structure is a tuple $\mathbb{C} = (\mathbb{S}, \mathbb{T}, s_0)$ where $\mathbb{S}$ is a non-empty set of *global states*, $s_0 \in \mathbb{S}$ is an *initial state*, and $\mathbb{T} : \mathbb{N}_+^* \times \overline{\mathsf{Act}} \to \mathbb{S} \rightsquigarrow \mathbb{S}$ is a *global state transformer*. For $l \in \mathbb{N}_+^*$, $a \in \overline{\mathsf{Act}}$, and $s \in \mathbb{S}$, $\mathbb{T}(l, a)(s)$ denotes the global state resulting from applying action a to process l in global state s, or is undefined. If $\mathbb{T}(l, a)(s)$ is undefined, we consider the constraint to be violated. In this case, the corresponding action cannot be performed, i.e. the corresponding transition rule is not applicable. In order to capture this, we define the partial function by

$$^{\mathbb{C}}\!\mapsto^l_r((s, c)) := (\mathbb{T}(l, \overline{\mathsf{Act}}(r))(s), \mapsto^l_r(c)) \quad \text{if } \mathbb{T}(l, \overline{\mathsf{Act}}(r))(s) \text{ and } \mapsto^l_r(c) \text{ are defined}$$

Here, $\overline{\mathsf{Act}}(r)$ denotes the action of the transition rule r. The transition rule r is applied to the process l as before and the global state is transformed according to the transformer of the constraint structure. Thus, the function is only defined if the transformation of the global state is defined. Whenever the next global state is undefined, the constraint structure $\mathbb{C}$ prevents the application of r to l.

The set of configurations reachable from an initial configuration c_0 under a constraint structure $\mathbb{C}$ is defined as $\mathrm{post}^*_{\mathbb{C},M}(c_0) = \{c_0\} \cup \{c \mid \exists k \in \mathbb{N}_+, l_1, \dots, l_k \in \mathbb{N}_+^*, r_1, \dots, r_k \in \Delta, s \in \mathbb{S}. (s, c) = {}^{\mathbb{C}}\!\mapsto^{l_k}_{r_k}(\cdots{}^{\mathbb{C}}\!\mapsto^{l_1}_{r_1}(s_0, c_0)\cdots)\}$. One goal of this paper is to present an algorithm to check whether a set R of configurations is reachable from an initial configuration c_0, given one of the constraint structures $\mathbb{C} \in \{\mathbb{C}^u, \mathbb{C}^j, \mathbb{C}^l, \mathbb{C}^{jl}\}$ defined in the following. Formally, this is equivalent to checking whether

$$\mathrm{post}^*_{\mathbb{C},M}(c_0) \cap R \neq \emptyset.$$

Join/Lock-Constraints. In the present paper we consider joins together with nested locking. For that, let $L = \{1, \dots, n\}$ be a fixed, finite set of locks. We assume a fixed set of actions $\mathsf{Act} = \{\mathsf{jo}, \$, \epsilon\} \cup \{\mathsf{acq}(i), \mathsf{rel}(i) \mid i \in L\}$. The action jo blocks the current process until all child-processes of the current process are stopped. The action $\$$ stops a process. The action ϵ represents actions unrelated to joining and locking. $\mathsf{acq}(i)$ acquires and $\mathsf{rel}(i)$ releases the lock i.

Unconstrained. For dealing with *unconstrained* DPNs, we define the constraint structure $\mathbb{C}^u := (\{\top\}, \mathbb{T}^u, \top)$ by $\mathbb{T}^u(l, a)(\top) := \top$ for all $l \in \mathbb{N}_+^*, a \in \overline{\mathsf{Act}}$. This constraint structure never disables any execution steps.

Joins. For dealing with joins we define a constraint structure that keeps track of whether existing processes have stopped or not. Processes can only make steps if they have not stopped and jo-steps can only be performed if all child processes have stopped. Hence we define $\mathbb{C}^j := (\mathbb{S}^j, \mathbb{T}^j, s_0^j)$ by $\mathbb{S}^j := \mathbb{N}_+^* \rightsquigarrow \mathbb{B}$, $s_0^j(\epsilon) = \bot$, $s_0^j(l)$ is undefined for all $l \in \mathbb{N}_+^* \setminus \{\epsilon\}$, and

$$
\mathbb{T}^j(l,a)(s) := \begin{cases} s & \text{if } s(l) = \bot, a = \mathsf{jo}, \\ & \quad \forall i \in \mathbb{N}_+.\, li \in dom(s) \Rightarrow s(li) = \top \\ s \oplus \{l \mapsto \top\} & \text{if } s(l) = \bot, a = \$ \\ s \oplus \{\mathsf{nc}(l, dom(s)) \mapsto \bot\} & \text{if } s(l) = \bot, a = \mathsf{sp} \\ s & \text{if } s(l) = \bot, a \notin \{\mathsf{jo}, \$, \mathsf{sp}\} \end{cases}
$$

for all $s \in \mathbb{S}^j$, all $l \in dom(s)$, and all $a \in \overline{\mathsf{Act}}$. For all $s \in \mathbb{S}^j$ and all $l \in \mathbb{N}_+^*$, $s(l) = \top$ iff the process l exists and it is stopped.

Locks. For dealing with locks we define a constraint structure that keeps track of the set of locks held by each existing process. acq-steps can only be performed if the corresponding lock is held by no process and rel-steps require the corresponding lock to be held by the process. Formally, we define $\mathbb{C}^l := (\mathbb{S}^l, \mathbb{T}^l, s_0^l)$ by $\mathbb{S}^l := \mathbb{N}_+^* \rightsquigarrow 2^L$, $s_0^l(\epsilon) = \emptyset$, $s_0^l(l)$ is undefined for all $l \in \mathbb{N}_+^* \setminus \{\epsilon\}$, and

$$
\mathbb{T}^l(l,a)(s) := \begin{cases} s \oplus \{l \mapsto (s(l) \cup \{i\})\} & \text{if } a = \mathsf{acq}(i), i \notin \bigcup_{l' \in dom(s)} s(l') \\ s \oplus \{l \mapsto (s(l) \setminus \{i\})\} & \text{if } a = \mathsf{rel}(i), i \in s(l) \\ s \oplus \{\mathsf{nc}(l, dom(s)) \mapsto \emptyset\} & \text{if } a = \mathsf{sp} \\ s & \text{if } a \notin \{\mathsf{acq}(i), \mathsf{rel}(i), \mathsf{sp} \mid i \in L\} \end{cases}
$$

for all $s \in \mathbb{S}^l$, all $l \in dom(s)$, and all $a \in \overline{\mathsf{Act}}$. For all $s \in \mathbb{S}^l$ and all $l \in \mathbb{N}_+^*$, $s(l)$ is the set of locks that are acquired by the process l, provided that the process l exists. Here, we only consider non-reentrant locks, i.e., a process that already owns a lock i is not allowed to acquire i again. However, under certain conditions, DPNs with reentrant locks can be simulated by DPNs with non-reentrant locks at a cost that is exponential in the maximal nesting depth of locks (see Kidd et al. [8], Lammich et al. [9]).

Products of Constraint Structures. For all constraint structures $\mathbb{C}_1 = (\mathbb{S}_1, \mathbb{T}_1, s_0^{(1)})$ and $\mathbb{C}_2 = (\mathbb{S}_2, \mathbb{T}_2, s_0^{(2)})$, we define the *product* $\mathbb{C}_1 \times \mathbb{C}_2$ of $\mathbb{C}_1$ and $\mathbb{C}_2$ by

$$
\mathbb{C}_1 \times \mathbb{C}_2 := (\mathbb{S}_1 \times \mathbb{S}_2, \mathbb{T}_1 \times \mathbb{T}_2, (s_0^{(1)}, s_0^{(2)})),
$$

where $(\mathbb{T}_1 \times \mathbb{T}_2)(l,a)((s_1, s_2)) := (\mathbb{T}_1(l,a)(s_1), \mathbb{T}_2(l,a)(s_2))$ for all $l \in \mathbb{N}_+^*$, all $a \in \overline{\mathsf{Act}}$, and all $(s_1, s_2) \in \mathbb{S}_1 \times \mathbb{S}_2$ iff $\mathbb{T}_1(l,a)(s_1)$ and $\mathbb{T}_2(l,a)(s_2)$ are defined.

Joins and Locks. For dealing with joins and locks simultaneously, we define the constraint structure $\mathbb{C}^{jl} := \mathbb{C}^j \times \mathbb{C}^l$. A DPN together with the constraint structure $\mathbb{C}^{jl}$ is called a *join-lock-DPN* for short.

Example 2. The behavior of the C program of Example 1 can be safely over-approximated by the join-lock-DPN with the following transition rules:

$$
p_m m \xrightarrow{\mathsf{sp}} p_m m \triangleright p_f f \quad p_m m \xrightarrow{\mathsf{jo}} \$_m m \quad p_f f \xrightarrow{\mathsf{acq}(1)} q_f f \quad q_f f \xrightarrow{\mathsf{rel}(1)} r_f f \quad r_f f \xrightarrow{\$} \$_f f
$$

The main process $p_m m$ may create arbitrary many child-processes $p_f f$ and may terminate (go into the state $\$_m$) as soon as all child-processes are stopped. Each child-process acquires the lock 1, releases the lock 1 and then stops. Because of the semantics of locks, two different child-processes may never be in state q_f simultaneously. Moreover, because of the semantics of joins, all child-processes must be in state $\$_f$, before the main-process can reach state $\$_m$. □

3   Forward Reachability

In this section we present our approach for checking forward reachability using only operations on regular sets of trees.

Configurations. In order to explicitly describe sets of configurations of a DPN $M = (\text{Act}, P, \Gamma, \Delta)$ using regular tree languages, i.e. tree automata, we represent the unranked trees c from the set $\mathcal{C}$ by *ranked* trees. For that, we use *lists* constructed with cons and nil. As a shorthand we later write lists $\text{cons}(a_1, \ldots, \text{cons}(a_k, \text{nil}) \ldots)$ as $[a_1; \ldots; a_k]$. The set C of ranked trees which we will use is specified by the tree grammar:

$$LG ::= \text{nil} \mid \text{cons}(\Gamma, LG) \qquad LC ::= \text{nil} \mid \text{cons}(C, LC) \qquad C ::= P(LG, LC)$$

Hence a configuration is a ranked tree where the root node is labeled with the control state of the initial process. The root node has two branches. One is the list of stack symbols of the initial process. The other is the list of processes spawned by the initial process, where the last process spawned is the first in the list. For each spawned process the list contains a configuration with the process as initial process. The function $f : \mathcal{C} \to C$ captures the relation between the unranked and ranked model of configurations. It is defined by $f(c) := f(c, \epsilon)$ for all $c \in \mathcal{C}$, where, for all $c \in \mathcal{C}$ and all $l \in \text{dom}(c)$, $f(c, l) := p([a_1; \ldots; a_m], [c'_k; \cdots; c'_1])$ if $c(l) = p a_1 \ldots a_m, p \in P, a_1, \ldots, a_m \in \Gamma$, $\{i \in \mathbb{N}_+ \mid l \cdot i \in \text{dom}(c)\} = \{1, \ldots, k\}$, and $c'_1 = f(c, l\, 1), \ldots, c'_k = f(c, l\, k)$. Recall that $l\, 1$ is the first and $l\, k$ the last process spawned by process l within configuration c. Since f is a bijection, all functions and concepts defined in Section 2 can be transferred to the new representation and in the following we redefine the set $\mathcal{C}$ to be the set C of ranked trees. Hence a configuration $c \in \mathcal{C}$ is now a ranked tree and an initial configuration is represented by a term of the form $p([\gamma], \text{nil})$ with $p \in P$ and $\gamma \in \Gamma$.

Known Results. For all pushdown systems M, $\text{pre}^*(R)$ and $\text{post}^*(R)$ are regular, whenever $R \subseteq \mathcal{C}$ is a regular set of configurations. Bouajjani et al. [1] provide a construction which, starting from a finite automaton for R, successively adds transitions until an automaton for $\text{pre}^*(R)$ is obtained. Bouajjani et al. [2] applied a generalization of this construction to implement pre^*-operators for DPNs with *stable* constraints. The post^*-operator for DPNs, however, does *not* preserve regularity as shown in Bouajjani et al. [2] for a word model of configurations. This also holds for the tree model of this paper:

Example 3 (A Non-Regular post^*-Image). We consider the DPN $M = (\text{Act}, P, \Gamma, \Delta)$ that is defined by $P = \{p, q, p', q', r, r', \$\}$, $\Gamma = \{a\}$, and

$$\Delta = \{pa \overset{\text{sp}}{\hookrightarrow} qa \triangleright ra, \ ra \overset{\$}{\hookrightarrow} \$, \ qa \overset{\epsilon}{\hookrightarrow} paa, \ pa \overset{\text{jo}}{\hookrightarrow} p', \ p'a \overset{\text{sp}}{\hookrightarrow} q'a \triangleright r'a, \ q'a \overset{\epsilon}{\hookrightarrow} p'\}.$$

Here, $\mathrm{post}^*_{\mathbb{C}^u,M}(p([a], \mathsf{nil}))$ is not regular, since the process can spawn at most k processes of type $r'a$ after spawning k processes of type ra.   □

Execution Trees. We avoid the problem of non-regularity by introducing *execution trees*. Execution trees can be regarded as configuration trees with a history of rule applications that lead from an initial configuration to the reached configuration. Inner nodes of execution trees are annotated with rules of the DPN and leaf nodes contain information about the current control state and, if existent, the current top-most stack symbol.

Starting from the root node, the leftmost branch of an execution tree contains the rules applied to the initial process in the order of application. Whenever a new process was spawned, the corresponding sp-rule has a separate branch containing the rules applied to the new process. Additionally, if a stack symbol is pushed that is later popped, the push-node has two branches: The left one describes the execution up to popping the stack symbol and the right one describes the rest of the execution.

To this end, we consider the set Δ of all transition rules of the DPN M as a ranked alphabet where *Push*-rules have rank 1 or 2, *Spawn*-rules have rank 2, *Base*-rules have rank 1, and *Pop*-rules have ranks 0. Additionally, for $p \in P$ and $\gamma \in \Gamma$, we introduce symbols $\langle p, \gamma \rangle$ of rank 0. The set X of execution trees is then described by the following regular tree grammar:

$$\mathrm{XT} ::= \langle\mathsf{Base}\rangle(\mathrm{XT}) \mid \langle\mathsf{Push}\rangle(\mathrm{XT}, \mathrm{XT}) \mid \langle\mathsf{Pop}\rangle \mid \langle\mathsf{Spawn}\rangle(\mathrm{XT}, \mathrm{X})$$
$$\mathrm{XN} ::= \langle\mathsf{Base}\rangle(\mathrm{XN}) \mid \langle\mathsf{Push}\rangle(\mathrm{XN}) \mid \langle\mathsf{Push}\rangle(\mathrm{XT}, \mathrm{XN}) \mid \langle\mathsf{Spawn}\rangle(\mathrm{XN}, \mathrm{X}) \mid \langle P \times \Gamma \rangle$$
$$\mathrm{X} ::= \mathrm{XT} \mid \mathrm{XN}$$

Here, Base is the set of Base-rules, Push is the set of Push-rules, Pop is the set of Pop-rules, and Spawn is the set of Spawn-rules. The elements of the set X are the execution trees, where XT (*terminated execution trees*) contains the execution trees that end with popping the stack-symbol of the current stacklevel, and XN (*not yet terminated execution trees*) contains the execution trees that do not pop the stack-symbol of the current stacklevel.

An execution tree t reaches a configuration $\mathsf{c}(t)$. We can extract this configuration by $\mathsf{c}(t) := \mathsf{c}(t, \mathsf{nil}, \mathsf{nil})$ with:

$$\mathsf{c}(\langle p, \gamma \rangle, w, \bar{c}) := p(\mathsf{cons}(\gamma, w), \bar{c})$$
$$\mathsf{c}(\langle p\gamma \overset{a}{\hookrightarrow} p'\gamma' \rangle(t), w, \bar{c}) := \mathsf{c}(t, w, \bar{c})$$
$$\mathsf{c}(\langle p\gamma \overset{a}{\hookrightarrow} p'\gamma_1\gamma_2 \rangle(t), w, \bar{c}) := \mathsf{c}(t, \mathsf{cons}(\gamma_2, w), \bar{c})$$
$$\mathsf{c}(\langle p\gamma \overset{a}{\hookrightarrow} p'\gamma_1\gamma_2 \rangle(t_1, t_2), w, \bar{c}) := \mathsf{c}(t_2, w, \mathsf{ch}(t_1, \bar{c}))$$
$$\mathsf{c}(\langle p\gamma \overset{a}{\hookrightarrow} p' \rangle, w, \bar{c}) := p'(w, \bar{c})$$
$$\mathsf{c}(\langle p\gamma \overset{\mathsf{sp}}{\hookrightarrow} p\gamma \triangleright p_s\gamma_s \rangle(t, t_s), w, \bar{c}) := \mathsf{c}(t, w, \mathsf{cons}(\mathsf{c}(t_s), \bar{c}))$$
$$\mathsf{ch}(\langle p, \gamma \rangle, \bar{c}) := \bar{c}$$
$$\mathsf{ch}(\langle p\gamma \overset{a}{\hookrightarrow} p'\gamma' \rangle(t), \bar{c}) := \mathsf{ch}(t, \bar{c})$$
$$\mathsf{ch}(\langle p\gamma \overset{a}{\hookrightarrow} p'\gamma_1\gamma_2 \rangle(t), \bar{c}) := \mathsf{ch}(t, \bar{c})$$
$$\mathsf{ch}(\langle p\gamma \overset{a}{\hookrightarrow} p'\gamma_1\gamma_2 \rangle(t_1, t_2), \bar{c}) := \mathsf{ch}(t_2, \mathsf{ch}(t_1, \bar{c}))$$
$$\mathsf{ch}(\langle p\gamma \overset{a}{\hookrightarrow} p' \rangle, \bar{c}) := \bar{c}$$
$$\mathsf{ch}(\langle p\gamma \overset{\mathsf{sp}}{\hookrightarrow} p\gamma \triangleright p_s\gamma_s \rangle(t, t_s), \bar{c}) := \mathsf{ch}(t, \mathsf{cons}(\mathsf{c}(t_s), \bar{c}))$$

Here ch is an auxiliary function that extracts the list of configurations of all spawned processes in an execution tree. The function is used to collect the configurations of processes which were spawned in left branches of push-nodes. Note that initial configurations $p([\gamma], \text{nil})$ are represented by execution trees consisting of a single node $\langle p, \gamma \rangle$.

The mappings c and ch for extracting the configuration can be interpreted as total deterministic *macro tree transducers* (see, e.g., Engelfriet and Vogler [3] for definitions and fundamental results), which use each of their input and output parameters exactly once. The pre-image of a regular set of trees w.r.t. the translation of any macro tree transducer is again regular [3]. By carefully inspecting the macro tree transducers realizing the mappings c and ch, we obtain:

Lemma 1. *For every regular set C of configurations, $c^{-1}(C)$ is a regular set of execution trees. If C is given by a nondeterministic finite tree automaton with n states and m transitions, a finite tree automaton for $c^{-1}(C)$ can be constructed in time $\mathcal{O}(m^2 + |\Delta| \cdot n^4 + |\Delta| \cdot m \cdot n^2 + |P| \cdot |\Gamma| \cdot n)$.*

Due to lack of space, the proof of this and some other lemmas is deferred to the extended version of this paper [5].

We now define a semantics $^{C}\!\!\mapsto^l_r$ on execution trees that is compatible with the semantics $^{C}\!\!\mapsto^l_r$ on configurations. For that, for all $r \in \Delta$, we define the partial function $\mapsto_r : X \rightsquigarrow X$ that applies r to the root process of an execution tree as follows:

$$\mapsto_{p\gamma \xrightarrow{a} p'\gamma'} (\langle p, \gamma \rangle) := \langle p\gamma \xrightarrow{a} p'\gamma' \rangle (\langle p', \gamma' \rangle)$$

$$\mapsto_{p\gamma \xrightarrow{a} p'\gamma_1\gamma_2} (\langle p, \gamma \rangle) := \langle p\gamma \xrightarrow{a} p'\gamma_1\gamma_2 \rangle (\langle p', \gamma_1 \rangle)$$

$$\mapsto_{p\gamma \xrightarrow{a} p'} (\langle p, \gamma \rangle) := \langle p\gamma \xrightarrow{a} p' \rangle$$

$$\mapsto_{p\gamma \xrightarrow{sp} p'\gamma' \triangleright p_s\gamma_s} (\langle p, \gamma \rangle) := \langle p\gamma \xrightarrow{sp} p'\gamma' \triangleright p_s\gamma_s \rangle (\langle p', \gamma' \rangle, \langle p_s, \gamma_s \rangle)$$

$$\mapsto_r (\langle p\gamma \xrightarrow{a} p'\gamma' \rangle(t)) := \langle p\gamma \xrightarrow{a} p'\gamma' \rangle(\mapsto_r(t))$$

$$\mapsto_r (\langle p\gamma \xrightarrow{a} p'\gamma_1\gamma_2 \rangle(t)) := \begin{cases} \langle p\gamma \xrightarrow{a} p'\gamma_1\gamma_2 \rangle(t') & \text{if } t' \in \text{XN} \\ \langle p\gamma \xrightarrow{a} p'\gamma_1\gamma_2 \rangle(t', \langle s(c(t')), \gamma_2 \rangle) & \text{if } t' \in \text{XT} \\ \text{where } t' = \mapsto_r(t) \end{cases}$$

$$\mapsto_r (\langle p\gamma \xrightarrow{a} p'\gamma_1\gamma_2 \rangle(t, t')) := \langle p\gamma \xrightarrow{a} p'\gamma_1\gamma_2 \rangle(t, \mapsto_r(t'))$$

$$\mapsto_r (\langle p\gamma \xrightarrow{sp} p'\gamma' \triangleright p_s\gamma_s \rangle(t, t_s)) := \langle p\gamma \xrightarrow{sp} p'\gamma' \triangleright p_s\gamma_s \rangle(\mapsto_r(t), t_s)$$

Here, $s(p(w, \bar{c})) := p$ for all $p(w, \bar{c}) \in C$ extracts the control-state of the root process of an execution tree. It is used to extract the control state at the end of a left branch of a push-node. This control-state is the initial control-state for the continued execution on the right branch.

We define $\mapsto^l_r(t)$ to be the application of $\mapsto_r$ to the subtree of the execution tree which has the process identified by $l \in \mathbb{N}^*_+$ as root process. One can find the specific subtree by counting the number of sp-rules along the leftmost branch starting from the root node. If the correct sp-rule was found, we descend into the right branch and continue. If we arrive at the end of a left branch of a push-node, we continue at the right branch of that node. Analogously to Section 2 we define $^{C}\!\!\mapsto^l_r$ and the set $\text{tpost}^*_{C,M}(\langle p, \gamma \rangle) = \{\langle p, \gamma \rangle\} \cup \{t \mid \exists k \in \mathbb{N}_+, l_1, \ldots, l_k \in \mathbb{N}^*_+, r_1, \ldots, r_k \in \Delta, s \in$

$\mathbb{S}$. $(s,t) = {}^{\mathcal{C}}\!\!\mapsto_{r_k}^{l_k}(\cdots {}^{\mathcal{C}}\!\!\mapsto_{r_1}^{l_1}(s_0, \langle p, \gamma\rangle)\cdots)\}$ of successors of an execution tree representing an initial configuration for execution trees. An execution tree is called *consistent* iff there exists some $p \in P$ and some $\gamma \in \Gamma$ such that $t \in \text{tpost}^*_{\mathcal{C}^u, M}(\langle p, \gamma\rangle)$, i.e. $\text{tpost}^*_{\mathcal{C}^u, M}(\langle p, \gamma\rangle)$ is the set of consistent execution trees starting in $p\gamma$. We then have:

Lemma 2. $c({}^{\mathcal{C}}\!\!\mapsto_r^l(t)) = {}^{\mathcal{C}}\!\!\mapsto_r^l(c(t))$ *holds for all execution trees* $t \in X$, *all transition rules* $r \in \Delta$, *all positions* $l \in \mathbb{N}_+^*$ *and constraint structures* $\mathcal{C}$.

Thus, to check reachability we can check $c(\text{tpost}^*_{\mathcal{C}, M}(\langle p, \gamma\rangle)) \cap R \neq \emptyset$ or equivalently

$$\text{tpost}^*_{\mathcal{C}, M}(\langle p, \gamma\rangle) \cap c^{-1}(R) \neq \emptyset.$$

We have already mentionend, that $c^{-1}(R)$ is regular if R is regular. In order to obtain an algorithm which allows to check reachability solely based on operations on regular sets of trees, it remains to show that $\text{tpost}^*_{\mathcal{C}, M}(\langle p, \gamma\rangle)$ is regular as well. We first show this for unconstrained DPNs, i.e. for $\mathcal{C} = \mathcal{C}^u$.

Regular characterization of $\text{tpost}^*_{\mathcal{C}, M}(\langle p, \gamma\rangle)$. Let $p \in P$ and $\gamma \in \Gamma$. Our goal is to compute the set $\text{tpost}^*_{\mathcal{C}^u, M}(\langle p, \gamma\rangle)$ of all execution trees that can be reached starting from the execution tree $\langle p, \gamma\rangle$ without any restrictions due to the constraint structure. For that we construct a finite tree automaton which recognizes $\text{tpost}^*_{\mathcal{C}^u, M}(\langle p, \gamma\rangle)$.

For all control states $p, p' \in P$ and all stack symbols $\gamma \in \Sigma$, we inductively define the set $\mathcal{T}^{p, \gamma, p'}$ (resp. $\mathcal{N}^{p, \gamma}$) of *terminated* (resp. *not yet terminated*) execution trees with initial control state p and top-most stack symbol γ and terminating with control state p' (resp. not terminating) as follows:

Open Leaf: For all $p \in P$, and all $\gamma \in \Gamma$: $\langle p, \gamma\rangle \in \mathcal{N}^{p, \gamma}$
Pop: For all $r = p\gamma \xrightarrow{a} p' \in \Delta$: $\langle r\rangle \in \mathcal{T}^{p, \gamma, p'}$
Base: For all $r = p\gamma \xrightarrow{a} p'\gamma' \in \Delta$, and all $p'' \in P$:
    If $t \in \mathcal{T}^{p', \gamma', p''}$, then $\langle r\rangle(t) \in \mathcal{T}^{p, \gamma, p''}$.
    If $t \in \mathcal{N}^{p', \gamma'}$, then $\langle r\rangle(t) \in \mathcal{N}^{p, \gamma}$.
Push: For all $r = p\gamma \xrightarrow{a} p'\gamma_1\gamma_2 \in \Delta$, and all $p'', p''' \in P$:
    If $t_1 \in \mathcal{T}^{p', \gamma_1, p''}$ and $t_2 \in \mathcal{T}^{p'', \gamma_2, p'''}$, then $\langle r\rangle(t_1, t_2) \in \mathcal{T}^{p, \gamma, p'''}$.
    If $t_1 \in \mathcal{T}^{p', \gamma_1, p''}$ and $t_2 \in \mathcal{N}^{p'', \gamma_2}$, then $\langle r\rangle(t_1, t_2) \in \mathcal{N}^{p, \gamma}$.
    If $t_1 \in \mathcal{N}^{p', \gamma_1}$, then $\langle r\rangle(t_1) \in \mathcal{N}^{p, \gamma}$.
Spawn: For all $r = p\gamma \xrightarrow{sp} p'\gamma' \triangleright p_s\gamma_s \in \Delta$, and all $p'', p_s' \in P$:
    If $t \in \mathcal{T}^{p', \gamma', p''}$ and $t_s \in \mathcal{T}^{p_s, \gamma_s, p_s'} \cup \mathcal{N}^{p_s, \gamma_s}$, then $\langle r\rangle(t, t_s) \in \mathcal{T}^{p, \gamma, p''}$.
    If $t \in \mathcal{N}^{p', \gamma'}$ and $t_s \in \mathcal{T}^{p_s, \gamma_s, p_s'} \cup \mathcal{N}^{p_s, \gamma_s}$, then $\langle r\rangle(t, t_s) \in \mathcal{N}^{p, \gamma}$.

Thus, we get:

Theorem 1. *1.* $\text{tpost}^*_{\mathcal{C}^u, M}(\langle p, \gamma\rangle) = \bigcup_{p' \in P} \mathcal{T}^{p, \gamma, p'} \cup \mathcal{N}^{p, \gamma}$.
2. The sets $\mathcal{T}^{p, \gamma, p'}$, $\mathcal{N}^{p, \gamma}$, *and finally* $\text{tpost}^*_{\mathcal{C}^u, M}(\langle p, \gamma\rangle)$ *can be recognized by a finite tree automaton that can be constructed in time* $\mathcal{O}(|P|^2 \cdot (|\Gamma| + |\Delta|))$.

Proof (Sketch). Statement 1 can be shown by straight-forward induction. We focus on Statement 2: The states of the finite tree automaton correspond to the sets $\mathcal{T}^{p, \gamma, p'}$ and $\mathcal{N}^{p, \gamma}$. Hence, we have $|P|^2 \cdot |\Gamma|$ states. Moreover, there are $\mathcal{O}(|P| \cdot |\Gamma| + |P|^2 \cdot |\Delta|)$ transition rules. This gives us the desired complexity estimation. □

Hence, we can effectively check reachability for unconstrained DPNs using only operations on regular tree languages, i.e. finite tree automata. To close the gap to DPNs with a constraint structure, we observe, that the order in which rules are applied to processes running in parallel in an unconstrained DPN is irrelevant for the finally reached execution tree. However, this is not the case for DPNs with a constraint structure, since the order of rule applications determines how the global state of the constraint structure is transformed. Consequently, there may be orders which are not feasible, since a necessary transformation is undefined. To capture this, we define a *schedule* $(l_1, a_1), \ldots, (l_k, a_k)$ of an execution tree t as a sequence of process-labels and actions, such that there exists $p \in P$, $\gamma \in \Gamma$ and rules $r_1, \ldots, r_k \in \Delta$, with $\overline{\mathrm{Act}}(r_i) = a_i$, such that $t = \mapsto_{r_k}^{l_k} (\cdots \mapsto_{r_1}^{l_1} (\langle p, \gamma \rangle) \cdots)$. Each consistent execution tree has at least one schedule. A schedule is call *executable* under a constraint structure iff additionally $\mathbb{T}(l_k, a_k)(\cdots \mathbb{T}(l_1, a_1)(s_0) \cdots)$ is defined. Then, $\mathrm{tpost}^*_{\mathbb{C}, M}(\langle p, \gamma \rangle)$ is exactly the set of consistent execution trees starting in $p\gamma$ that have an executable schedule under $\mathbb{C}$. As a consequence we can write $\mathrm{tpost}^*_{\mathbb{C}, M}(\langle p, \gamma \rangle) = \mathrm{tpost}^*_{\mathbb{C}^u, M}(\langle p, \gamma \rangle) \cap H_\mathbb{C}$, where $H_\mathbb{C}$ is a set of execution trees that contains all consistent execution trees that have an executable schedule and no consistent execution tree that has no executable schedule. Then our reachability problem boils down to checking

$$\mathrm{tpost}^*_{\mathbb{C}^u, M}(\langle p, \gamma \rangle) \cap H_\mathbb{C} \cap \mathrm{c}^{-1}(R) \neq \emptyset.$$

In the remainder of this paper, we construct regular sets $H_\mathbb{C}$ for all constraint structures $\mathbb{C} \in \{\mathbb{C}^j, \mathbb{C}^l, \mathbb{C}^{jl}\}$. Thus, checking reachability reduces to checking emptiness of intersections of regular sets of trees.

4   Action Trees

At the end of the last section we have observed that, in order to check reachability under a constraint structure, we need to specify a regular set of execution trees that contains all consistent execution trees with an executable schedule and no consistent execution tree without an executable schedule. We have also observed that executability of a schedule depends only on the actions of the rules and identities of the processes taking part in the execution. Consequently, we do not need the full power of the execution tree model to capture executability. Indeed, it is simpler to characterize executability if the left branches of push-nodes are inlined as in the trees used by Lammich et al. [9]. Therefore, in this section, we introduce *action trees* as an abstraction of execution trees that does this inlining and omits information about control states and stack contents.

Formally, the set of action trees $\mathcal{T}^{\mathrm{Act}}$ is defined by the tree grammar $\mathcal{T}^{\mathrm{Act}} ::= \epsilon \mid \langle \mathrm{Act} \rangle (\mathcal{T}^{\mathrm{Act}}) \mid \langle \mathrm{sp} \rangle (\mathcal{T}^{\mathrm{Act}}, \mathcal{T}^{\mathrm{Act}})$. The root node and each right child of an sp-node within an action tree represents a process that performs the actions of the left-most path starting from this node and ending in a leaf.

Schedules. For all $l \in \mathbb{N}^*_+$, $a \in \overline{\mathrm{Act}}$, we define the partial function $\longmapsto^l_a : \mathcal{T}^{\mathrm{Act}} \rightsquigarrow \mathcal{T}^{\mathrm{Act}}$, that constructs action trees by

$$\begin{aligned}
\rightarrowtail_a^l(\epsilon) &:= \langle a\rangle(\epsilon) & &\text{if } l = \epsilon, a \in \mathsf{Act}\\
\rightarrowtail_{\mathsf{sp}}^l(\epsilon) &:= \langle\mathsf{sp}\rangle(\epsilon,\epsilon) & &\text{if } l = \epsilon\\
\rightarrowtail_a^l(\langle a'\rangle(t)) &:= \langle a'\rangle(\rightarrowtail_a^l(t)) & &\text{if } a' \in \mathsf{Act}\\
\rightarrowtail_a^l(\langle\mathsf{sp}\rangle(t,t_s)) &:= \langle\mathsf{sp}\rangle(\rightarrowtail_a^l(t),t_s) & &\text{if } l = \epsilon\\
\rightarrowtail_a^l(\langle\mathsf{sp}\rangle(t,t_s)) &:= \langle\mathsf{sp}\rangle(t,\rightarrowtail_a^{l'}(t_s)) & &\text{if } l = 1\cdot l'\\
\rightarrowtail_a^l(\langle\mathsf{sp}\rangle(t,t_s)) &:= \langle\mathsf{sp}\rangle(\rightarrowtail_a^{(i-1)\cdot l'}(t),t_s) & &\text{if } l = i\cdot l', i > 1
\end{aligned}$$

$\rightarrowtail_a^l(t)$ appends the action a to the process l of the action tree. Identification of processes is similar as in the case of execution trees.

A schedule of an action tree t is a finite sequence $(l_1,a_1),\ldots,(l_k,a_k)$, where $l_i \in \mathbb{N}_+^*$ and $a_i \in \overline{\mathsf{Act}}$ for all $i \in \{1,\ldots,k\}$, with $t = \rightarrowtail_{a_k}^{l_k}(\cdots\rightarrowtail_{a_1}^{l_1}(\epsilon)\cdots)$. Action trees always have at least one schedule in contrast to execution trees, where only consistent execution trees have a schedule. Recall that a schedule is called executable under a constraint structure $\mathbb{C}$ iff $\mathbb{T}(l_k,a_k)(\cdots\mathbb{T}(l_1,a_1)(s_0)\cdots)$ is defined.

Execution Trees and Action Trees. Each execution tree t can be abstracted to an action tree $\mathsf{a}(t)$ by cutting away unnecessary information. We define $\mathsf{a}(t) := \mathsf{a}(t,\epsilon)$, where:

$$\begin{aligned}
\mathsf{a}(\langle p,\gamma\rangle,x) &:= x\\
\mathsf{a}(\langle p\gamma \xrightarrow{a} p'\gamma'\rangle(t),x) &:= \langle a\rangle(\mathsf{a}(t,x))\\
\mathsf{a}(\langle p\gamma \xrightarrow{a} p'\gamma_1\gamma_2\rangle(t),x) &:= \langle a\rangle(\mathsf{a}(t,x))\\
\mathsf{a}(\langle p\gamma \xrightarrow{a} p'\gamma_1\gamma_2\rangle(t_1,t_2),x) &:= \langle a\rangle(\mathsf{a}(t_1,\mathsf{a}(t_2,x)))\\
\mathsf{a}(\langle p\gamma \xrightarrow{a} p'\rangle,x) &:= \langle a\rangle(x)\\
\mathsf{a}(\langle p\gamma \xrightarrow{\mathsf{sp}} p\gamma \triangleright p_s\gamma_s\rangle(t,t_s),x) &:= \langle\mathsf{sp}\rangle(\mathsf{a}(t,x),\mathsf{a}(t_s))
\end{aligned}$$

The mapping a for extracting action trees can again be interpreted as a total deterministic macro tree transducer. We get:

Lemma 3. *For every regular set T of action trees, $\mathsf{a}^{-1}(T)$ is a regular set of execution trees. If T is given by a nondeterministic finite tree automaton with n states and m transitions, a finite tree automaton for $\mathsf{a}^{-1}(T)$ can be constructed in time $\mathcal{O}(|P|\cdot|\Gamma|\cdot n + |\Delta|\cdot m\cdot n^2)$.*

Moreover, scheduling of action trees is compatible with that of execution trees:

Lemma 4. *A consistent execution tree t has an executable schedule under a constraint structure $\mathbb{C}$ iff $\mathsf{a}(t)$ has an executable schedule.*

Consequently, for the set $T_{\mathbb{C}}$ of all action trees that have an executable schedule under the constraint structure $\mathbb{C}$, each consistent execution tree $t \in \mathsf{a}^{-1}(T_{\mathbb{C}})$ has an executable schedule. Vice versa, each consistent execution tree $t \notin \mathsf{a}^{-1}(T_{\mathbb{C}})$ has no executable schedule. Thus, we define $H_{\mathbb{C}} := \mathsf{a}^{-1}(T_{\mathbb{C}})$. Since a^{-1} preservers regularity, $H_{\mathbb{C}}$ is regular if $T_{\mathbb{C}}$ is regular.

Lammich et al. [9] showed how to construct a tree automaton check[l] that accepts the set $T_{\mathbb{C}^l}$ of all action trees that can be scheduled lock-sensitively, i.e. have an executable schedule under $\mathbb{C}^l$. A tree automaton check[j] that accepts the set $T_{\mathbb{C}^j}$ of all action trees that can be scheduled join-sensitively, i.e. have an executable schedule under $\mathbb{C}^j$, can be

– rather straightforwardly – constructed in polynomial time as well. The tree automaton check^j checks that all child-processes that are spawned before a jo-action are stopped using the action \$ and the action \$ is only performed at the end of branches.

The language $T_{\mathbb{C}^{jl}}$, however, need not to be the intersection of the languages $T_{\mathbb{C}^j}$ and $T_{\mathbb{C}^l}$.The reason is that the set of join-sensitive schedules and the set of lock-sensitive schedules of t might be disjoint.

5   Join-Lock-Sensitive Schedules of Action Trees

In this section we construct a deterministic bottom-up tree automaton check^{jl} which recognizes the set of all action trees that can be scheduled join-lock-sensitively. We restrict ourselves to action trees where each single process in isolation uses locks in a well-nested fashion, releases all locks before stopping, and does not try to perform actions after the stop action. We call such action trees join-lock-well-formed, a notion defined more formally in the next paragraph.

Well-Formedness. A sequence of actions $a_1 \cdots a_k$ is called *well-nested* iff its lock operations are a prefix of a sequence from the context-free language $U ::= \epsilon \mid U \cdot U \mid$ acq$(1) \cdot U \cdot$rel$(1) \mid \cdots \mid$ acq$(n) \cdot U \cdot$rel(n). It is called *non-reentrant* iff each acquired lock is released before it is acquired again, i.e., for each $a_i = $ acq(j), $a_{i'} = $ acq(j), $i < i'$, there is an i'' with $i < i'' < i'$ and $a_{i''} = $ rel(j), and, symmetrically, each released lock is re-acquired before it is released again, i.e., for each $a_i = $ rel(j), $a_{i'} = $ rel(j), $i < i'$ there is an i'' with $i < i'' < i'$ and $a_{i''} = $ acq(j). A sequence of actions is called *well-formed* iff it is both well-nested and non-reentrant. It is called *join-lock-well-formed* iff (1) it is well-formed, (2) there is no action after the action \$, and (3) if the sequence ends with the action \$, then its sequence of lock operations is from U, i.e., all acquired locks are released before terminating with the action \$.

An action tree is called *join-lock-well-formed* iff the actions of each process form a join-lock-well-formed sequence. A join-lock-DPN M is called *join-lock-well-formed* iff all action trees that correspond to consistent execution trees of M are join-lock-well-formed. Note that the set of join-lock-well-formed action trees is regular. Thus, we can use the techniques presented above to check whether a DPN is join-lock-well-formed.

Acquisition-Structures. For defining the tree automaton check^{jl}, we use a modified version of *acquisition structures* as introduced by Lammich et al. [9].

An acquisition of a lock i without a matching release is called a *final acquisition* of i. A matching release means, that the same process releases the lock, i.e., that there is a release of i on the leftmost path starting at the acquisition node. Symmetrically, a release of i without a matching acquisition is called an *initial release*. Acquisitions and releases that are not final acquisitions or initial releases are called *usages*.

Let t be a join-lock-well-formed action tree. We first check the following properties, that are obviously necessary for the existence of a join-lock-sensitive schedule: (1) Every lock is finally acquired at most once. (2) For every process, the last action of all child-processes that are spawned before some join is \$. We write ok(t) iff t fulfills the requirements (1) and (2). The evaluation of the predicate ok can easily be implemented by a deterministic bottom-up tree automaton where the complexity of the construction is exponential in the number of locks.

To each subtree of a join-lock-well-formed action tree, we assign an acquisition structure that can be used for constructing a join-lock-sensitive schedule. In this paper we define an acquisition structure either to be $\bot$ or a tuple $(A, R, R_{jo}, U, \rightarrow_A, J)$ where:

- A is the set of acquired locks (final acquisitions and usages).
- R is the set of initially released locks. Note that, due to well-nestedness, only the root process of the subtree may contain initial releases.
- R_{jo} is the set of locks that are initially released after the next join. If the root process contains no join operation, we have $R_{jo} = \emptyset$. Moreover, we have $R_{jo} \subseteq R$.
- U is the set of locks whose usages are required for termination of the root process, including locks whose usages are required for termination of spawned processes the root process joins with.
- $\rightarrow_A \subseteq L^2$ is the *acquisition graph*. We have $i \rightarrow_A j$ iff there is an acquisition of j after a final acquisition of i.
- $J \in \mathbb{B}$ is $\top$ iff the root process performs at least one jo.

The acquisition structure $as(t)$ of an action tree t is defined by the following rules, if the subtrees of t have non-bottom acquisition structures and the side conditions of the rules are fulfilled. In any other case, we set $as(t) := \bot$.

$$
\begin{aligned}
as(\epsilon) := as(\langle \$\rangle(\epsilon)) &:= (\emptyset, \emptyset, \emptyset, \emptyset, \emptyset, \bot) \\
as(\langle \epsilon \rangle(t)) &:= as(t) \\
as(\langle acq(i)\rangle(t)) &:= (A \cup \{i\}, R \setminus \{i\}, R_{jo} \setminus \{i\}, U \cup \{i\}, \rightarrow_A, J), && \text{if } i \in R \\
as(\langle acq(i)\rangle(t)) &:= (A \cup \{i\}, R, R_{jo}, U, \rightarrow_A \cup \{i\} \times A, J), && \text{if } i \notin R \\
as(\langle rel(i)\rangle(t)) &:= (A, R \cup \{i\}, R_{jo}, U, \rightarrow_A, J) \\
as(\langle jo\rangle(t)) &:= (A, R, R, U, \rightarrow_A, \top) \\
as(\langle sp\rangle(t, t')) &:= (A \cup A', R, R_{jo}, U, \rightarrow_A \cup \rightarrow_{A'}, \bot), && \text{if } J = \bot \\
as(\langle sp\rangle(t, t')) &:= (A \cup A', R, R_{jo}, U \cup U', \rightarrow_A \cup \rightarrow_{A'}, \top), \\
&&& \text{if } J = \top \text{ and } R_{jo} \cap U' = \emptyset
\end{aligned}
$$

where $as(t) = (A, R, R_{jo}, U, \rightarrow_A, J)$ and $as(t') = (A', R', R'_{jo}, U', \rightarrow_{A'}, J')$. We prove that a join-lock-well-formed action tree t can be scheduled join-lock-sensitively iff $ok(t)$ and $as(t) = (A, R, R_{jo}, U, \rightarrow_A, J)$ with acyclic $\rightarrow_A$. Since the number of acquisition structures is finite, a deterministic bottom-up tree automaton check[jl] can be constructed that accepts the action trees that satisfy the above property:

Theorem 2. *There is a deterministic bottom-up tree automaton* check[jl] *which accepts a join-lock-well-formed action tree t iff t can be scheduled join-lock-sensitively;* check[jl] *can be constructed in time at most exponential in the number of locks.*

Proof (Sketch). Due to lack of space only a sketch is presented here. The complete proof can be found in the extended version of this paper [5].

The complexity estimate for check[jl] follows from the fact that the number of acquisition structures is exponentially bounded in the number of locks.

Assume that check^{jl} does not accept t. Hence, not ok(t) or as$(t) = \bot$ or as$(t) = (A, R, R_{\mathrm{jo}}, U, \to_A, J)$ with cyclic $\to_A$. First of all, it is easy to see that there is no join-lock sensitive schedule if ok(t) does not hold. If as$(t) = \bot$, this results from a failed $R_{\mathrm{jo}} \cap U' = \emptyset$ check in the second sp-rule of m. This means that there is a process that spawns another process and then joins, while it holds a lock that is required by the spawned process for termination. Hence, no lock-sensitive schedule is possible. The edges in $\to_A$ capture ordering constraints on final acquisitions of locks: $i \to_A j$ means, that there is a final acquisition of i that must be scheduled before the final acquisition of j, if any. If $\to_A$ is cyclic, these constraints obviously cannot be fulfilled.

If check^{jl} accepts t, then ok(t) holds and as$(t) = (A, R, R_{\mathrm{jo}}, U, \to_A, J)$ with an acyclic $\to_A$. We first choose a total ordering $<$ on the locks with $\to_A \subseteq <$. Then, we construct inductively a schedule $s(t')$ for each subtree t' of t with the following properties: (1) The actions in $s(t')$ form a suffix of a join-lock-well-formed action sequence. (2) $s(t')$ is join-sensitive, i.e. steps of spawned processes are scheduled before the respective join operations. (3) Acquisitions in $s(t')$ respect the ordering $<$ in the sense that only locks $i > j$ are acquired after an unmatched acquisition of j. (4) Only required locks are used before termination, i.e. before termination of the root process, all acquired locks are released and are from U' (where as$(t') = (A', R', R'_{\mathrm{jo}}, U', \to_A', J')$).

The construction of this schedule is straightforward except for subtrees of the form $t' = \langle \mathrm{sp} \rangle (t_1, t_2)$. In this case, $s(t')$ is constructed as a specific shuffling of $s(t_1)$ and $s(t_2)$. Then, by (1) and (2), the schedule $s(t)$ constructed for the entire tree t is join-lock sensitive. $\square$

We are now prepared to put all parts together:

Theorem 3. *Let $M = (\mathrm{Act}, P, \Gamma, \Delta)$ be a join-lock-well-formed join-lock-DPN, $p \in P, \gamma \in \Gamma$, and R a regular set of configurations. It can be decided whether a configuration from R can be reached by M, starting from the configuration $p(\lceil \gamma \rceil, \mathrm{nil})$ through an execution that respects joins and locks simultaneously, i.e., whether or not*

$$\mathrm{post}^*_{\mathbb{C}^{\mathrm{jl}}, M}(p(\lceil \gamma \rceil, \mathrm{nil})) \cap R \neq \emptyset$$

holds, by checking the following intersection of regular sets:

$$\mathrm{tpost}^*_{\mathbb{C}^{\mathrm{u}}, M}(\langle p, \gamma \rangle) \cap a^{-1}(T) \cap \mathrm{c}^{-1}(R) \neq \emptyset$$

where T is the language of check^{jl}. The complexity is polynomial in the size of M and in that of a tree automaton recognizing R and exponential only in the number of locks.

6   Conclusion

We have developed a *forward* propagating algorithm for analyzing reachability in Dynamic Pushdown Networks. The key idea was to represent all possible executions by means of a regular set of execution trees. We then showed how to restrict the set of all possible executions to executions that respect joins and locks simultaneously. By that, we obtained an algorithm for analyzing reachability w.r.t. join-lock-sensitive executions. Our algorithms are polynomial in the size of the DPN as well as in the size of the finite tree automaton describing the set of configurations to be reached and exponential only in the number of locks used by the DPN.

It would be interesting to explore to what extent nested locking can be combined with concepts that are more general than joins, e.g. *stable* constraints as considered by Bouajjani et al. [2]. It might also be challenging to see which other properties can be decided for the different classes of DPNs beyond reachability. Finally, it is left to future work to practically evaluate the provided techniques on real world examples.

References

[1] Bouajjani, A., Esparza, J., Maler, O.: Reachability analysis of pushdown automata: Application to model-checking. In: Mazurkiewicz, A., Winkowski, J. (eds.) CONCUR 1997. LNCS, vol. 1243, pp. 135–150. Springer, Heidelberg (1997)

[2] Bouajjani, A., Müller-Olm, M., Touili, T.: Regular symbolic analysis of dynamic networks of pushdown systems. In: Jayaraman, K., de Alfaro, L. (eds.) CONCUR 2005. LNCS, vol. 3653, pp. 473–487. Springer, Heidelberg (2005)

[3] Engelfriet, J., Vogler, H.: Macro tree transducers. J. Comput. Syst. Sci. 31(1), 71–146 (1985)

[4] Esparza, J., Podelski, A.: Efficient algorithms for pre* and post* on interprocedural parallel flow graphs. In: POPL, pp. 1–11 (2000)

[5] Gawlitza, T.M., Lammich, P., Müller-Olm, M., Seidl, H., Wenner, A.: Join-locksensitive forward reachability analysis for concurrent programs with dynamic process creation, http://cs.uni-muenster.de/sev/publications/ (extended version)

[6] Kahlon, V., Gupta, A.: An automata-theoretic approach for model checking threads for LTL properties. In: Proc. of LICS 2006, pp. 101–110. IEEE Computer Society, Los Alamitos (2006)

[7] Kahlon, V., Ivančić, F., Gupta, A.: Reasoning about threads communicating via locks. In: Etessami, K., Rajamani, S.K. (eds.) CAV 2005. LNCS, vol. 3576, pp. 505–518. Springer, Heidelberg (2005)

[8] Kidd, N., Lal, A., Reps, T.W.: Language strength reduction. In: Alpuente, M., Vidal, G. (eds.) SAS 2008. LNCS, vol. 5079, pp. 283–298. Springer, Heidelberg (2008)

[9] Lammich, P., Müller-Olm, M., Wenner, A.: Predecessor sets of dynamic pushdown networks with tree-regular constraints. In: Bouajjani, A., Maler, O. (eds.) CAV 2009. LNCS, vol. 5643, pp. 525–539. Springer, Heidelberg (2009)

[10] Müller-Olm, M., Seidl, H.: On optimal slicing of parallel programs. In: STOC, pp. 647–656 (2001)

[11] Seidl, H., Steffen, B.: Constraint-based inter-procedural analysis of parallel programs. Nord. J. Comput. 7(4), 375 (2000)

Verifying Deadlock-Freedom of Communication Fabrics

Alexander Gotmanov[1], Satrajit Chatterjee[2], and Michael Kishinevsky[2]

[1] Intel Corporation, Moscow, Russia
alexander.gotmanov@intel.com
[2] Intel Corporation, Hillsboro, Oregon, USA
{satrajit.chatterjee,michael.kishinevsky}@intel.com

Abstract. Avoiding message dependent deadlocks in communication fabrics is critical for modern microarchitectures. If discovered late in the design cycle, deadlocks lead to missed project deadlines and suboptimal design decisions. One approach to avoid this problem is to get high level of confidence on an early microarchitectural model. However, formal proofs of liveness even on abstract models are hard due to large number of queues and distributed control. In this work we address liveness verification of communication fabrics described in the form of high-level microarchitectural models which use a small set of well-defined primitives. We prove that under certain realistic restrictions, deadlock freedom can be reduced to unsatisfiability of a system of Boolean equations. Using this approach, we have automatically verified liveness of several non-trivial models (derived from industrial microarchitectures), where state-of-the-art model checkers failed and pen and paper proofs were either tedious or unknown.

Keywords: liveness, deadlocks, communication fabrics, networks-on-chip, microarchitecture, high-level models, formal verification.

1 Introduction

Consider a simple system consisting of two agents and a trivial communication fabric. Each agent generates requests for the other and processes incoming requests to produce responses. Requests and responses share the same physical channel but use different virtual channels to avoid deadlock. Even on an abstract microarchitectural model of this system, automatically verifying liveness is intractable using existing model checkers. (For the curious, the precise model we consider here is shown in Figure 3 using the XMAS notation which will be explained in Section 3.) Now suppose k is the number of credits allocated to each virtual channel in the system. If we use ABC [3] to verify liveness on the abstract microarchitectural model, we find that for $k = 1$ and $k = 2$, ABC is able to verify liveness in less than a second. However, for $k = 3$ (which is not even enough to saturate the link) ABC cannot prove liveness in 18 hours. ABC checks liveness by converting it into a safety problem [4] which it then proves using

R. Jhala and D. Schmidt (Eds.): VMCAI 2011, LNCS 6538, pp. 214–231, 2011.

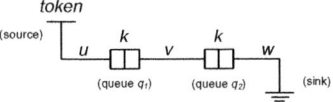

Fig. 1. A simple xMAS model with a source that generates tokens, two queues that can store k elements each and a sink. The components are connected by channels u, v and w.

interpolation. It is important to note that we add critical safety invariants [5, §5] which enable interpolation to converge. Classical LTL model checking as implemented in NuSMV [1] does worse on this example: it takes 11 hours to prove the $k = 1$ case.

The above example is probably the simplest example that is interesting from a liveness perspective. Most of our real examples involve much more complicated agents and fabrics with several different types of messages, multiple virtual channels with ordering constraints between them, deep pipelining and dozens of messages simultaneously in-flight.

In this paper we present a lightweight, *automatic* approach that allows us to prove liveness on a large class of real examples drawn from the domain of communication fabrics. Our microarchitectural models are described by instantiating and connecting components from a library of primitives. We refer to these models as xMAS networks (xMAS stands for eXecutable MicroArchitectural Specification). The properties to be verified are specified on these networks. The semantics of xMAS networks are specified using synchronous equations for each primitive. Thus every xMAS network has an associated synchronous system which we call the *synchronous model*.[1] The modeling methodology is described in more detail in [6] and its use in safety verification is described in [5]. Our definition of deadlock in xMAS models (see Section 4) is *local* i.e. it permits part of the model to be forever blocked while the rest continues processing packets. Such local deadlocks are also called livelocks.

The main idea behind our method is to exploit the high-level structure of the model in order to reason about liveness. We show that all non-live behaviors of xMAS network, or *structural deadlocks*, can be characterized by pure structural reasoning. Unreachable structural deadlocks are ruled out using safety invariants which are also obtained through automatic analysis of the model.

Our method is best explained on a simple example. Consider the system shown in Figure 1 which has a source that non-deterministically creates packets and a sink that non-deterministically consumes packets. The source and sink are connected by two queues in series. It is obvious that the system is live (i.e. activity on channels never ceases) as long as the sink is fair i.e. it always eventually consumes packets, and the source is fair i.e. it always eventually sends packets.

---

[1] If there is a combinational cycle in the synchronous model, the corresponding xMAS network is *ill-formed*. We do not consider such networks in the paper.

Consider a fair execution S of model M in Figure 1 and assume that in this execution channel v eventually becomes inactive (we say "stuck inactive" and express it in the paper using LTL[2] as $\mathbb{F}\,\mathbb{G}(inactive)$). If v stops transferring then q_1 must be out of tokens and unable to send or q_2 must have become filled to its maximum capacity and unable to receive. To formalize the argument, we describe "eventual stuck-at" states of channel v and queues q_1, q_2 by Boolean variables

$$\mathbf{Inactive}(v) \equiv \text{"}v \text{ eventually stuck inactive"},$$
$$\mathbf{Empty}(q) \equiv \text{"}q \text{ eventually stuck empty"},$$
$$\mathbf{Full}(q) \equiv \text{"}q \text{ eventually stuck full"}.$$

Note: to visually differentiate between the propositional statements capturing the instantaneous state of the system (e.g. a queue is empty now) and the temporal statements such as the eventual stuck-at properties, throughout the paper we use bold font for the temporal statements and their functions.

Then for every execution S of model M, it is true that

$$\mathbf{Inactive}(v) \Rightarrow \mathbf{Empty}(q_1) + \mathbf{Full}(q_2).$$

Queue q_1 can become empty, only if its input channel u stops sending tokens (let us denote that as $\mathbf{Idle}(u)$). Similarly, if queue q_2 is full then its output channel w must forever block, i.e. stop receiving tokens ($\mathbf{Block}(w)$). Therefore,

$$\mathbf{Empty}(q_1) \Rightarrow \mathbf{Idle}(u),$$
$$\mathbf{Full}(q_2) \Rightarrow \mathbf{Block}(w),$$
$$\mathbf{Inactive}(v) \Rightarrow \mathbf{Idle}(u) + \mathbf{Block}(w).$$

The consequent of last implication is obviously in contradiction with our fairness assumptions. Indeed, in fair execution source is required to periodically produce tokens and sink is required to periodically consume tokens, which is captured by

$$\mathbf{Fair} = \neg\,\mathbf{Idle}(u) \cdot \neg\,\mathbf{Block}(w).$$

Finally, we conclude that

$$\mathbf{Fair} \Rightarrow \neg\,\mathbf{Inactive}(v).$$

Also note that it is possible to perform all deductions completely automatically by forming a set of all equations and assumptions and checking it for combinational satisfiability.

The overall flow of our deadlock analysis is as follows:

– We first construct the characteristic function of all structural deadlocks in the XMAS system. This characteristic function is expressed entirely as a function of "eventually stuck at" variables similar to $\mathbf{Idle}$ and $\mathbf{Block}$ discussed above.

---

[2] Linear Temporal Logic. We use $\mathbb{G}$, $\mathbb{F}$, and $\mathbb{X}$ to represent "globally", "eventually", and "next" operators in LTL .

- We then derive local and global invariants of the xMAS model using an efficient automatic technique [5]. The invariants are formulated in terms of instantaneous variables (such as the current occupancies of various queues). Hence to use these invariants to prune out unreachable deadlocks we need to link stuck-at variables with instantaneous variables.
- Finally, we check the combined system of equations (structural deadlocks and model invariants) for satisfiability using an off-the-shelf SAT solver. If the problem is unsatisfiable then the xMAS system has no deadlocks. If there is a solution, one can examine it to construct a deadlock state which may be unreachable. Unreachable deadlocks may require additional invariants to rule out.

We start with a review of related work in Section 2. Next, Section 3 introduces xMAS primitives and Section 4 defines a few useful properties of xMAS models. Section 5 presents the basic structural deadlock analysis which is extended to rule out unreachable deadlocks using safety invariants in Section 6. Finally, we present experimental results for xMAS models of real microarchitectures in Section 7 and conclude with Section 8.

2   Related Work

Since the literature on detecting deadlocks in interconnect networks is large, we review only the most relevant work here. Most techniques for proving deadlock-freedom of interconnect structures are based on search and elimination of cycles in channel dependency graphs. Simple textbook static analysis techniques such as proving absence of structural cycles [7, §14.1] do not apply in our examples since there are cycles due to message and resource dependencies. Duato extends this analysis to structurally cyclic dependency graphs in which cycles can be broken by a particular choice of an adaptive routing function [8]. Recently, Taktak et al. [15] extended Duato's method to handle message dependencies in agents (e.g. responses generated as a result of requests) and Verbeek and Schmaltz formalized some of these arguments in ACL2 [16]. However, this general line of deadlock analysis critically depends on assuming a very structured network with specific assumptions on how routers and agents behave (e.g. see [15, §2.2] for a list of assumptions). Therefore these techniques cannot be directly used to analyze arbitrary xMAS models, and indeed in practice it is non-trivial to check that the assumptions used in the deadlock analysis hold on the microarchitecture. The method presented in this paper does not require any such assumptions. Finally, note that the router and agent models considered in these approaches can be captured in xMAS and the techniques in our paper can be used to argue liveness on the resultant models.

Also, closely related to the above is a rich body of *prescriptive* techniques to avoid deadlocks in various specific network-on-chip proposals ([12] is a good entry point). Clearly, these cannot be of use to reason about deadlock freedom in general microarchitectures.

There is a large body of work on analysis of systems of finite state machines connected by unbounded FIFO queues (as opposed to small FIFO queues which are the norm in hardware). In general, reachability in these systems is undecidable and most of the work seeks to identify decidable subclasses. Ghafari et al.[10] is a good entry point though note that one of the conditions for decidability there is that the communication graph must be acyclic which limits its application in our domain.

The first step of our method – generation of structural deadlocks – is somewhat reminiscent of structural deadlock analysis in Petri nets [2]. However, rather than modeling the communication fabric with colored Petri nets, which leads to a significant overhead of using explicit back-pressure arcs, colors, and complexity in modeling the data-path, and then applying a graph theoretic analysis, we derive deadlock equations directly from more compact and natural xMAS specifications by characterizing xMAS primitives using LTL statements.

An alternative approach is to create executable models of the hardware and use model checking or theorem proving techniques to argue deadlock-freedom. Although model checking is useful to find bugs, as we saw above, it cannot converge on proofs even for the simplest examples. Theorem proving techniques (e.g. [14,13,9]) require expertise in formal methods and significant human effort to find suitable decompositions for proofs or suitable refinement relationships. With this work, we are aiming to exploit the high-level structure of our models to obtain the scalability of theorem proving with the automation of model checking.

Finally, there has been interesting work recently in using termination analysis based on synthesizing ranking functions to reason about some liveness properties of multi-threaded programs [11]. However, it remains to be seen if these techniques can be usefully applied to hardware. Also note that the approach presented in this paper is fundamentally different from synthesizing ranking functions and presents an alternative way to reason about liveness based on creating simple abstractions of components for liveness analysis.

3   xMAS **Primitives**

xMAS model is a network of primitives connected via typed data *channels*. In this paper we assume that all types are inhabited by only finitely many values and treat types as sets of values. In the synchronous model, a channel x with type α has two Boolean signals $x.irdy$ (for "initiator ready") and $x.trdy$ (for "target ready") for control handshake between communicating components and one signal $x.data$ that has type α for the data.

A channel is connected to exactly two components: one component called the *initiator* that "writes" to the channel via its *output* port and another component called the *target* that "reads" from the channel via its *input* port.[3] In the synchronous model, the initiator drives irdy and data signals (and reads trdy) whereas the target drives trdy (and reads irdy and data). Intuitively, a data element (or a packet) is transferred across a channel in those cycles when both irdy and trdy are true. We call such cycles *transfer* cycles. Note that a channel

---

[3] All input and output ports of a component should be connected to channels.

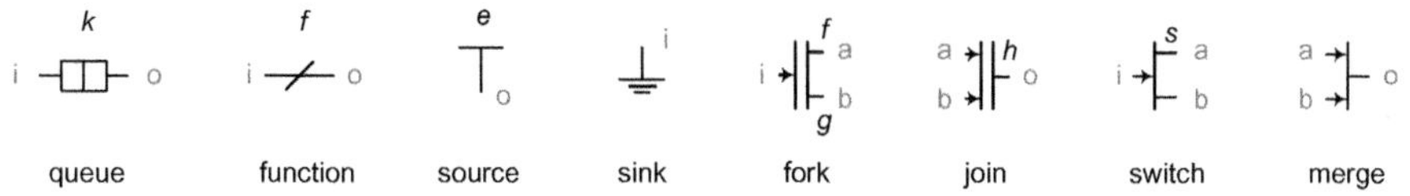

Fig. 2. A key showing the symbols for the various primitives used to model micro architectural blocks. The italicized letters (k, f, e, g, h and s) indicate parameters. Whenever we use these primitives in a diagram we need to specify values for these parameters. Often, to avoid clutter we do not show these values explicitly trusting that they are clear from the context. The gray letters (i, o, a, and b) indicate port names.

stores no state. It is represented in diagrams by a line. For example, in Figure 1, there are three channels u, v and w. For channel u, the initiator is the source and the target is the first queue.

Figure 2 shows the library of primitives. Each primitive is formally specified by its synchronous equations. For brevity we do not present these equations here but they can be found in previous papers [5,6]. Also note that even though the set of primitives is small, many other useful microarchitectural blocks such as credit logic, virtual channels, routers, out-of-order queues, scoreboards, etc. can be constructed as macro-blocks out of these primitives [6].

A *function* primitive is used to model transformations on the data. It is parameterized by a combinational function which is applied to an incoming packet to produce the outgoing packet. Note that using functions one can easily convert types of messages (e.g., from requests to responses) and hence model message dependencies both inside the fabric and in the model of the environment.

A *fork* is a primitive with one input and two outputs. Intuitively, a fork takes an input packet and creates a packet at each output. It coordinates the input and outputs so that a transfer only takes place when the input is ready to send and both the outputs are ready to receive.

A *join* is the dual of a fork. It has two inputs and one output and is parameterized by a two-input combinational function that specifies how the output packet is to be constructed from the two input packets. Like a fork, it ensures that a transfer only takes place when the inputs are ready to send and the output is ready to receive.

A *switch* is a primitive to route packets in the network. It has one input port and two output ports and is parameterized by a switching function that specifies how an incoming packet is to be routed (i.e. to which output).

Arbitration is modeled by a *merge* primitive that selects one packet among two competing packets. A merge has two input ports and one output port. Requests for a shared resource are modeled by sending packets to a merge, and a grant is modeled by the selected packet. It is guaranteed that the requests are served fairly, i.e. that each of them will eventually be served.

A *queue* primitive is used to store packets. It is parameterized by a positive integer k that indicates its capacity. In our set of primitives, the queue is the only delay element: even if the queue is empty, an input packet is visible at the output only after 1 cycle.

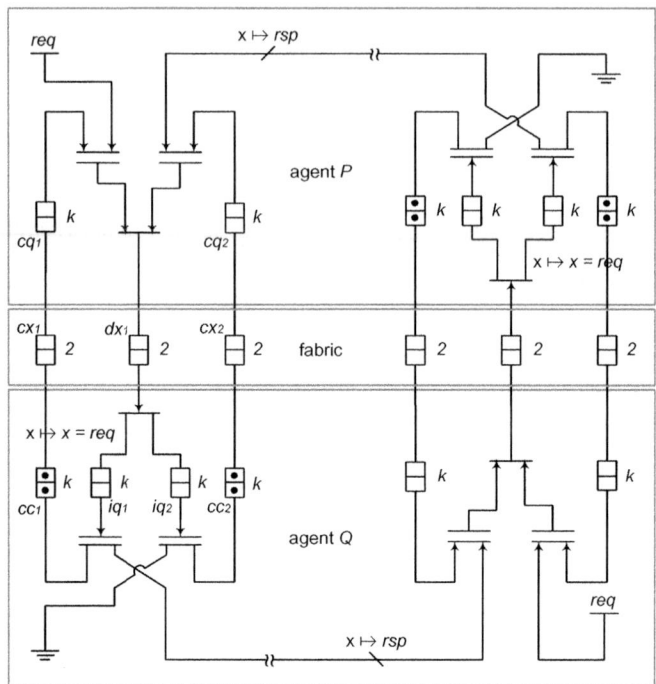

Fig. 3. Example showing a pair of agents communicating over a simple fabric (see text for details). Since each symbol has a precise formal semantics (see Section 3) this figure is a precise executable description.

Finally, *source* and *sink* primitives are used to create and consume packets non-deterministically.

Example. Figure 3 shows two agents P and Q communicating over a trivial fabric composed of six queues. Packets are modeled by an enumerated type that has two values: *req* (request) and *rsp* (response). Each agent creates new requests for the other agent. When an agent receives a request, it produces a response (by changing the packet type using a function) after a non-deterministic delay. The packet type conversion introduces a message dependence between requests and responses inside the agents. The response is sent back to the original agent where it is sunk when the sink is ready to receive it. Implementation of the non-deterministic delay macro block using XMAS primitives is shown in Figure 4(a). Thus each agent behaves like a master that produces requests and responses and a target that consumes responses and requests.

Communication between agents is done through the virtual channels. Consider agent P as example. It sends requests and responses to agent Q through the shared channel and the data transfer queue, dx_1, and then to two ingress queues iq_1 and iq_2, one per message type. An arbiter modeled by the merge primitive

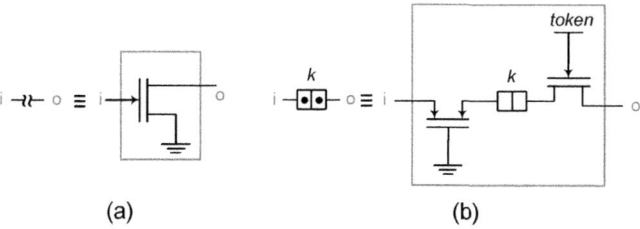

Fig. 4. Two macro-blocks used in Figure 3 and their implementation using xMAS primitives: a non-deterministic delay (a) and a credit counter (b). The functions of the forks in the two figures are identity.

selects fairly between *req* and *rsp* messages that are exposed to arbitration only if they have credit tokens inside the corresponding credit queues, cq_1 and cq_2. Credits are initialized inside the credit counters cc_1 and cc_2 to the values equal to the sizes of the ingress queues iq_1 and iq_2, i.e. to k. Implementation of the credit counter (using a queue) is shown in Figure 4 (b). Credits are returned through fabric credit queues, cx_1 and cx_2.

Due to correct sizing of credit counters, this system is free from deadlock. However if credit counters are sized incorrectly to provide more credits (say k + 1) than the capacity k of the ingress queues, the system deadlocks: responses can get blocked behind requests in the fabric data queues dx_1 and dx_2, while in turn requests blocking these queues cannot make forward progress to their ingress queues that are full due to over-provisioning of credits.

4   Channel Properties

Formally we define an execution of an xMAS network as an execution of the corresponding synchronous model, i.e., an infinite sequence of its consecutive states as computed by the next state functions that are composed from the equations for individual xMAS primitives. Note that synchronous models of xMAS networks are usually non-deterministic due to sources and sinks. To reason about xMAS model behavior, we use statements of LTL. For example, the LTL statement $\mathbb{G}\mathbb{F}(u.irdy)$ is true for an execution S if $u.irdy$ is true infinitely often in S. We denote this by:

$$S \models \mathbb{G}\mathbb{F}(u.irdy).$$

If some LTL formula ϕ is true for *all* executions of model M, we write $M \models \phi$ (or simply ϕ when there are no doubts about the model).

4.1   Persistency

Persistency is a desirable property of channel control signals. It significantly limits possible deadlocks and allows for simpler definitions of channel liveness.

It can be formulated as two LTL properties, one for *irdy* and the other for *trdy*. The former (*forward* persistency) guarantees that the initiator will keep sending the data until transfer occurs. The latter (*backward* persistency) states that the target will keep its input channel unblocked until transfer occurs.

$$\text{FwdPersistency}(u) \equiv \mathbb{G}((u.irdy \cdot \neg u.trdy) \Rightarrow \mathbb{X} u.irdy),$$
$$\text{BwdPersistency}(u) \equiv \mathbb{G}((u.trdy \cdot \neg u.irdy) \Rightarrow \mathbb{X} u.trdy).$$

Theorem 1. *Every channel u of any* XMAS *model M is persistent:*

$$M \models \text{FwdPersistency}(u), \qquad M \models \text{BwdPersistency}(u).$$

4.2 Life and Death of Channels

In Section 1, we illustrated a possible channel deadlock by the absence of transfers:

$$\textbf{Inactive}(v) \equiv \mathbb{F}\,\mathbb{G}(\neg(v.irdy \cdot v.trdy)).$$

This definition is too strict for real applications. Communication fabrics are typically engineered to operate correctly even when some sources never inject packets into the network. Therefore channel liveness is defined as a "leads-to" property so that an idle channel that never wants to transfer a message is considered live:

$$\textbf{Live}(u) \equiv \mathbb{G}(u.irdy \Rightarrow \mathbb{F}\,u.trdy). \tag{1}$$

Respectively, its negation defines channel's deadlock:

$$\textbf{Dead}(u) \equiv \neg\,\textbf{Live}(u) = \mathbb{F}(u.irdy \cdot \mathbb{G}\,\neg u.trdy). \tag{2}$$

Note that a channel can be live in one execution S_1, but may enter deadlock in another execution S_2. We say that there is a deadlock on channel u, if $\exists S.S \models$ **Dead**(u).

For a persistent channel, a simpler liveness condition can be used.

Theorem 2. *If channel u is persistent then*

$$\textbf{Live}(u) = \mathbb{F}\,\mathbb{G}(\neg u.irdy) + \mathbb{G}\,\mathbb{F}(u.trdy), \tag{3}$$
$$\textbf{Dead}(u) = \mathbb{G}\,\mathbb{F}(u.irdy) \cdot \mathbb{F}\,\mathbb{G}(\neg u.trdy). \tag{4}$$

Since all channels of XMAS model are persistent (Theorem 1), the above theorem can be used for checking liveness of all channels.

4.3 Fairness of Sinks and Sources

If sinks of the system do not periodically consume messages the system gets into a trivial deadlock. It is therefore necessary to assume that some of system sinks are *fair*. Fairness of a sink with input channel v is defined as follows:

$$\textbf{FairReceive}(v) \equiv \mathbb{G}\,\mathbb{F}(v.trdy). \tag{5}$$

Similarly some of the sources (such as a source initializating the credit logic in Figure 4 (b)) must be fair to avoid deadlocks. A source with output channel v is fair if:

$$\mathbf{FairSend}(v) \equiv \mathbb{G}\,\mathbb{F}(v.irdy). \tag{6}$$

A conjunction of fairness statements for *all* fair sources and sinks gives a compound fairness assumption for the model M denoted as $\mathbf{Fair}_M$.

5   Characterizing Structural Deadlocks

In this section we derive a system of Boolean equations characterizing structural deadlocks in xMAS model.

5.1   Variables

Let us first precisely define two inactive "stuck-at" states of a channel:

$$\mathbf{Idle}(u) \equiv \mathbb{F}\,\mathbb{G}(\neg u.irdy) \qquad\qquad \mathbf{Block}(u) \equiv \mathbb{F}\,\mathbb{G}(\neg u.trdy).$$

The characterization of the channel deadlock from Theorem 2 can be expressed in a slightly different form,

$$\mathbf{Dead}(u) = \neg\,\mathbb{F}\,\mathbb{G}(\neg u.irdy) \cdot \mathbb{F}\,\mathbb{G}(\neg u.trdy) = \neg\,\mathbf{Idle}(u) \cdot \mathbf{Block}(u). \tag{7}$$

Observe that **Idle** and **Block** have complete information to characterize channel deadlock. Moreover they can be propagated through xMAS primitives. Consider, for example, a fork (Figure 2) and assume that $S \models \mathbf{Block}(a)$ holds for fork's output a. Then $S \models \mathbf{Block}(i)$ also holds for the fork's input i. In fact, the following equality holds:

$$\mathbf{Block}(i) = \mathbf{Block}(a) + \mathbf{Block}(b). \tag{8}$$

Our immediate goal is to characterize all xMAS primitives with equations similar to (8). When conjuncted together for a given model M, these equations will describe all structural deadlocks in M. Before that we need to define a few more variables to capture data values on channels and internal state of queues and merges. All these variables correspond to "eventually stuck at" LTL expressions. While some of them are defined for separate data values which may appear exhaustive, recall that xMAS models are abstract microarchitectural models and therefore only few values relevant for control decisions are modeled.

Given channel $u : \alpha$ and a value x, $x \in \alpha$, we define

$$\mathbf{Idle}^x(u) \equiv \mathbb{F}\,\mathbb{G}(\neg u.irdy + (u.data \neq x)), \tag{9}$$
$$\mathbf{Block}(u) \equiv \mathbb{F}\,\mathbb{G}(\neg u.trdy). \tag{10}$$

Note that $\mathbf{Idle}^x(u)$ is a refinement of $\mathbf{Idle}(u)$. $S \models \mathbf{Idle}^x(u)$ holds during execution S if and only if the initiator of channel u eventually stops sending packets with value x. It is straightforward to see that $\mathbf{Idle}(u) = \prod_{x \in \alpha} \mathbf{Idle}^x(u)$ for channel $u : \alpha$. We will also use a generalized notation:

$$\mathbf{Idle}^{p(x)}(u) \equiv \prod_{x \in \alpha\,:\,p(x)} \mathbf{Idle}^x(u),$$

where $u : \alpha$ and $p(x)$ is arbitrary predicate on α.

Now, given a merge m, define

$$\mathbf{Select}_0(m) \equiv \mathbb{F}\,\mathbb{G}(m.u = 0), \tag{11}$$
$$\mathbf{Select}_1(m) \equiv \mathbb{F}\,\mathbb{G}(m.u = 1). \tag{12}$$

Merge variables $\mathbf{Select}_0(m)$ and $\mathbf{Select}_1(m)$ capture possible "stuck at" behavior of the internal state of the merge primitive. $S \models \mathbf{Select}_i(m)$ holds in execution S if the "priority" variable $m.u$ selecting input of merge m eventually gets stuck at value i (see merge definition in [5]).

Given a queue q of size k with output channel $o : \alpha$ and a value x, $x \in \alpha$, define

$$\mathbf{Full}(q) \equiv \mathbb{F}\,\mathbb{G}(q.num = k), \tag{13}$$
$$\mathbf{Empty}(q) \equiv \mathbb{F}\,\mathbb{G}(q.num = 0), \tag{14}$$
$$\mathbf{Idle}^x(q) \equiv \mathbb{F}\,\mathbb{G}((q.num = 0) + (q.front \neq x)), \tag{15}$$

where $q.num$ is a number of packets in the queue and $q.front$ is a data value of the first packet (see the queue definition in [5]). Queue variables $\mathbf{Full}(q)$, $\mathbf{Empty}(q)$, $\mathbf{Idle}^x(q)$ are not necessary[4] but handy for dealing with queue invariants (Section 6). $\mathbf{Idle}(q)$ and $\mathbf{Idle}^{p(x)}(q)$ are defined in complete analogy with channel variables.

5.2   Deadlock Equations

Following is a list of equations characterizing all xMAS primitives. The proof is a straightforward exercise in LTL and is based on the definition of xMAS primitives. It can be automatically carried out in NuSMV. We assume that input and output channels of all primitives are persistent and named as in Figure 2.

Function. Let α be type of channel i, and β be the type of channel o. For each value $y \in \beta$,

$$\mathbf{Block}(i) = \mathbf{Block}(o),$$
$$\mathbf{Idle}^y(o) = \prod_{x \in \alpha\,:\,f(x)=y} \mathbf{Idle}^x(i).$$

---

[4] They can be expressed through "stuck-at" variables at input and output channels of the queue.

Fork. Fork is parameterized by two functions f and g. However, it can be equivalently decomposed to a fork with identity functions followed by two function primitives. We assume this simpler fork in the equations below.

Let α be a type of channel i. For each value $x \in \alpha$,

$$\mathbf{Block}(i) = \mathbf{Block}(a) + \mathbf{Block}(b),$$
$$\mathbf{Idle}^x(a) = \mathbf{Idle}^x(i) + \mathbf{Block}(b),$$
$$\mathbf{Idle}^x(b) = \mathbf{Idle}^x(i) + \mathbf{Block}(a).$$

Join. Writing deadlock equations for a join is tricky since the output of a join in general could be functionally dependent on both inputs. However, in our examples drawn from the domain of communication fabrics, joins are only used to control access to resources. Therefore, the join function depends only on at most one input of the join (called the *functional* input) i.e. it is of the form $h : \alpha \rightarrow \gamma$ (instead of $h : \alpha \times \beta \rightarrow \gamma$). In such cases the other input carries tokens (i.e. values having the unit type). Given such a join with the restricted function $h : \alpha \rightarrow \gamma$, for simplifying deadlock equations we can further assume that h is an identity function and represent a more general restricted join by composing with a function primitive.

Let α be a type of channel a. For each value $x \in \alpha$,

$$\mathbf{Block}(a) = \mathbf{Block}(o) + \mathbf{Idle}(b), \qquad \mathbf{Block}(b) = \mathbf{Block}(o) + \mathbf{Idle}(a),$$
$$\mathbf{Idle}^x(o) = \mathbf{Idle}^x(a) + \mathbf{Idle}(b).$$

Switch. Let α be the type of switch channels i, a, and b, and $s : \alpha \rightarrow \mathrm{Bool}$ be the switching function. For all values $x \in \alpha$,

$$\mathbf{Block}(i) = \mathbf{Idle}(i) + \mathbf{Block}(a) \cdot \mathbf{Idle}^{\neg s(x)}(i) + \mathbf{Block}(b) \cdot \mathbf{Idle}^{s(x)}(i),$$
$$\mathbf{Idle}^x(a) = \neg s(x) + \mathbf{Idle}^x(i),$$
$$\mathbf{Idle}^x(b) = s(x) + \mathbf{Idle}^x(i).$$

Merge. Let α be the type of merge channels a, b, and o. For each value $x \in \alpha$,

$$\mathbf{Block}(a) = \mathbf{Idle}(a) + \mathbf{Select}_1(m) \cdot \mathbf{Block}(o) + \mathbf{Select}_0(m),$$
$$\mathbf{Block}(b) = \mathbf{Idle}(b) + \mathbf{Select}_0(m) \cdot \mathbf{Block}(o) + \mathbf{Select}_1(m),$$
$$\mathbf{Idle}^x(o) = \mathbf{Idle}^x(a) \cdot \mathbf{Idle}^x(b) + \mathbf{Idle}^x(a) \cdot \mathbf{Select}_1(m) + \mathbf{Idle}^x(b) \cdot \mathbf{Select}_0(m).$$

Note that the above equations leave $\mathbf{Select}_0(m)$ and $\mathbf{Select}_1(m)$ variables unbound. Therefore they can generate a lot of "false" solutions. For example, solutions with $\mathbf{Select}_0(m) = \mathbf{Select}_1(m) = 1$ are not prohibited, however they obviously cannot be satisfied in any execution. We need additional equations to capture mutual exclusivity of $\mathbf{Select}_0(m)$ and $\mathbf{Select}_1(m)$ and other constraints characterizing the internal state of the merge primitive.

$$\textbf{Select}_1(m) \Rightarrow \neg \textbf{Select}_0(m),$$
$$\textbf{Select}_1(m) \Rightarrow \textbf{Idle}(b) + \textbf{Block}(o),$$
$$\textbf{Select}_0(m) \Rightarrow \textbf{Idle}(a) + \textbf{Block}(o),$$
$$\textbf{Block}(o) \Rightarrow \textbf{Select}_0(m) + \textbf{Select}_1(m).$$

Queue. Let α be type of channel o. For each value $x \in \alpha$,

$$\textbf{Block}(i) = \textbf{Full}(q),$$
$$\textbf{Idle}^x(o) = \textbf{Idle}^x(q).$$

As in the case of merge, we need to provide additional constraints for the internal state of a queue to exclude false deadlocks. For each value $x \in \alpha$,

$$\textbf{Empty}(q) \Rightarrow \neg \textbf{Full}(q),$$
$$\textbf{Full}(q) \Rightarrow \textbf{Block}(o),$$
$$\textbf{Empty}(q) = \textbf{Idle}(q),$$
$$\textbf{Block}(o) \Rightarrow \textbf{Idle}(i) + \textbf{Full}(q),$$
$$\neg \textbf{Block}(o) \Rightarrow (\textbf{Idle}^x(i) = \textbf{Idle}^x(q)).$$

Finally, the equation that states that a blocked queue can only have one value stuck at its head. This equation is formulated for every pair of values. For every $x, y \in \alpha$, $x \neq y$,

$$\textbf{Block}(o) \Rightarrow \textbf{Idle}^x(q) + \textbf{Idle}^y(q).$$

5.3   Sources and Sinks

There are no deadlock equations for sources and sinks, however some of them may have associated fairness assumptions as explained in Section 4.2. It is easy to see that fairness assumption for a source with output channel u can be rewritten as $\neg \textbf{Idle}(u)$, while fairness of a sink with input v is equivalent to $\neg \textbf{Block}(v)$. Hence a compound fairness assumption $\textbf{Fair}_M$ can be formulated using only **Idle** and **Block** variables.

5.4   Checking Structural Deadlocks

Given XMAS model M with restricted joins let us denote a conjunction of the deadlock equations for all primitives of M as $\textbf{StructDead}_M$. The main result of this section states that deadlock equations hold for all executions of M:

Theorem 3. *For every* XMAS *model* M *with restricted joins*

$$M \models \textbf{StructDead}_M.$$

Assume now that we want to prove absence of deadlock on channel u of model M under certain fairness assumptions $\mathbf{Fair}_M$. To do so it is sufficient to prove unsatisfiability of $\mathbf{StructDead}_M \cdot \mathbf{Fair}_M \cdot \mathbf{Dead}(u)$, where $\mathbf{Dead}(u)$ is defined by (7). If this formula is unsatisfiable then model M has no execution, which simultaneously satisfies $\mathbf{Fair}_M$ and $\mathbf{Dead}(u)$. Hence channel u is live in every fair execution of M regardless of the initial state of the system. The example of Figure 1 can be proven deadlock-free in this way.

6   Adding Reachability Constraints

To rule out unreachable solutions and enable liveness proofs for practical examples, $\mathbf{Fair}_M$, $\mathbf{StructDead}_M$ and $\mathbf{Dead}(u)$ should be augmented with the additional model invariants, i.e. equations which hold for all *reachable* states of M, and do not hold for some of the unreachable states. We will refer to conjunction of all additional invariants as $\mathbf{Inv}_M$. For fully automatic proofs, $\mathbf{Inv}_M$ can be generated using local invariants and global *flow invariants* from [5]. A flow invariant is a linear equation relating occupancies of different queues in xMAS network. It holds in every reachable state. For example, an xMAS model in Figure 5 has the following flow invariant

$$q_1.num + q_2.num = q_3.num. \tag{16}$$

Although this xMAS model has no reachable deadlocks, $\mathbf{Fair}_M \cdot \mathbf{StructDead}_M \cdot \mathbf{Dead}(i)$ has 2 satisfying solutions: $\mathbf{Empty}(q_1) = \mathbf{Empty}(q_2) = \mathbf{Full}(q_3) = 1$ and $\mathbf{Full}(q_1) = \mathbf{Full}(q_2) = \mathbf{Empty}(q_3) = 1$. Hence Theorem 3 is not sufficient to prove deadlock-freedom. On the other hand, it is easy to see that (16) is in contradiction with both of the above assignments. Indeed, as follows from (16) in any reachable eventual stuck-at state it is impossible to have both q_1 and q_2 empty and the q_3 full, as well as it is impossible to have both top queues full and the bottom queue empty. Note that in the above reasoning we used the instantaneous $q.num$ variables to reason about LTL "stuck-at" variables $\mathbf{Full}$ and $\mathbf{Empty}$. The translation is straightforward for this particular example, but let us illustrate the general approach.

For every queue q of size k let us introduce an auxiliary integer variable $\mathbf{N}(q)$ that characterizes possible occupancies of queue q that occur infinitely often in a given execution S,

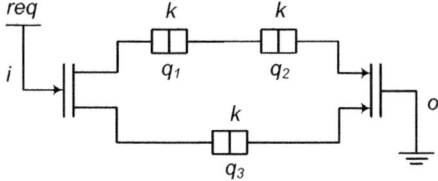

Fig. 5. Example of xMAS model requiring flow invariant $q_1.num + q_2.num = q_3.num$ to prove liveness. All channels are of unit type with single *req* value.

$$\mathbf{N}(q) \in \{n \colon \; \mathbb{G}\mathbb{F}(q.num = n)\}. \tag{17}$$

Conceptually, $\mathbf{N}(q)$ is similar to "stuck-at" variables (9-15) with only difference that constraint (17) allows for $\mathbf{N}(q)$ to non-deterministically assume any value from its execution-dependent domain. Following equations relate $\mathbf{N}(q)$ to $\mathbf{Empty}(q)$, $\mathbf{Full}(q)$ and $\mathbf{Block}(o)$ variables, where o is an output channel of q

$$0 \leq \mathbf{N}(q) \leq k, \tag{18}$$
$$\mathbf{Empty}(q) \Rightarrow \mathbf{N}(q) = 0, \tag{19}$$
$$\mathbf{Full}(q) \Rightarrow \mathbf{N}(q) = k, \tag{20}$$
$$\mathbf{Block}(o) \cdot \neg\,\mathbf{Empty}(q) \Rightarrow \mathbf{N}(q) > 0, \tag{21}$$
$$\mathbf{Block}(o) \cdot \neg\,\mathbf{Full}(q) \;\Rightarrow \mathbf{N}(q) < k. \tag{22}$$

On one hand constraints (18-22) relate "stuck-at" variables with $\mathbf{N}(q)$, while on the other hand, $\mathbf{N}(q)$ variables can be used to reformulate any flow invariant.

Theorem 4. *Given an* XMAS *model M, consider a predicate ψ on the queue occupancies. If*

$$M \models \mathbb{G}\left(\psi(q_1.num, \ldots, q_r.num)\right) \tag{23}$$

then for every execution S of M, $\exists\,\mathbf{N}(q_1), \ldots, \mathbf{N}(q_r)$ satisfying (17) such that

$$S \models \psi(\mathbf{N}(q_1), \ldots, \mathbf{N}(q_r)). \tag{24}$$

Using Theorem 4, we can now construct $\mathbf{Inv}_M$ from equations (18-22) and (24) capturing reachability constraints provided by original invariant (23). Note that predicate ψ in (23) can be arbitrarily complex. In particular, ψ can be defined as conjunction of all invariants we want to capture.

For the network in Figure 5, equations (18-22) provide:

$$\mathbf{Empty}(q_i) \Rightarrow \mathbf{N}(q_i) = 0, \qquad\qquad i = 1, 2, 3, \tag{25}$$
$$\mathbf{Full}(q_i) \Rightarrow \mathbf{N}(q_i) = k, \qquad\qquad i = 1, 2, 3. \tag{26}$$

Applying Theorem 4 with the predicate $\psi(q_1.num, q_2.num, q_3.num) = (q_1.num + q_2.num = q_3.num)$ gives

$$\mathbf{N}(q_1) + \mathbf{N}(q_2) = \mathbf{N}(q_3). \tag{27}$$

Now it is easy to see that $\mathbf{Empty}(q_1) = \mathbf{Empty}(q_2) = \mathbf{Full}(q_3) = 1$ and (25-27) lead to $0 + 0 = k$, while $\mathbf{Full}(q_1) = \mathbf{Full}(q_2) = \mathbf{Empty}(q_3) = 1$ and (25-27) lead to $k + k = 0$. Both statements are false for any positive value of k. Therefore, $\mathbf{Fair}_M$, $\mathbf{StructDead}_M$, $\mathbf{Inv}_M$ and $\mathbf{Dead}(i)$ cannot be simultaneously satisfied by any execution. Hence channel i is live in every fair execution, which also satisfies flow invariant (16).

Approach we described can be generalized to handle wider class of flow invariants from [5], which count tokens satisfying some properties. Consider for example an invariant such as

$$q_1.num^{p_1} + q_2.num^{p_2} = q_3.num^{p_3},$$

where $q.num^p$ is number of tokens in queue q satisfying predicate $p(x)$. It can be translated to

$$\mathbf{N}(q_1)^{p_1} + \mathbf{N}(q_2)^{p_2} = \mathbf{N}(q_3)^{p_3},$$

where $\mathbf{N}(q)^p$ is an integer variable with LTL constraint similar to (17) i.e.

$$\mathbf{N}(q)^p \in \{n \colon \mathbb{G}\mathbb{F}(q.num^p = n)\}.$$

Variables $\mathbf{N}(q)^p$ can be characterized by equations similar to (18-22), and generalization of Theorem 4 is straightforward.

7   Results

We have applied techniques described in this paper to prove deadlock-freedom of a number of xMAS models, including those derived from industrial microarchitectures. Drawn from the domain of communication fabrics, they are characterized by deeply pipelined logic for multi-phase transactions, presence of ordering logic and several virtual channels, and peer-to-peer traffic.

We compared our approach for liveness verification with state-of-the-art model checkers ABC version 91206p (using conversion to safety [4]) and NuSMV version 2.4. We only show comparisons with ABC since ABC outperformed NuSMV on all examples that we looked at. Note that we add safety invariants corresponding to global flow invariants [5, §5] which ABC retains after the liveness to safety transformation as additional safety properties on the transformed model. In our experience this dramatically improves the convergence of interpolation on the transformed model.

Table 1. Experimental results using ABC

Example	i	r	n	depth	time
Fig. 3 ($k = 1$)	6	28	60	(11, 10)	1.06
Fig. 3 ($k = 2$)	6	37	128	(12, 13)	2.63
Fig. 3 ($k = 3$)	6	38	211	BMC 34	-
SMF1	4	83	455	BMC 31	-
SMF2	4	137	1200	BMC 17	-

Table 1 shows the results of running ABC on 5 benchmarks. The first 3 are derived from Figure 3 with different values of the parameter k. The next two examples SMF1 and SMF2 are industrial examples of messaging fabrics where the microarchitects wanted to ensure that no deadlocks are introduced by allowing an agent to send packets to itself using the messaging fabric. SMF1 allows complete reordering of messages whereas SMF2 imposes some ordering restrictions on packets to guarantee producer-consumer ordering. SMF1 and SMF2 are parameteric models and we set the parameter values to obtain minimal configurations for comparing with ABC.

230 A. Gotmanov, S. Chatterjee, and M. Kishinevsky

Table 2. Experimental results using the proposed method. All instances are proved UNSAT in less than 1 second.

Example	c	q	v	e	f
Figure 3	54	12	176	241	4
SMF1	57	20	182	257	4
SMF2	71	24	232	322	6

Column i in the table is the number of primary inputs (oracles); r and n are number of registers and AIG nodes (after lightweight synthesis but before liveness to safety conversion). A depth of (m, n) means interpolation converged in n iterations when starting from a BMC of depth $1 + m$. The time is in seconds (on a 3GHz Intel Xeon CPU) with a timeout of 12 hours indicated by a dash (and we show the final BMC depth in the previous column). Note that we are able to obtain proofs only for the first two benchmarks using ABC.

Table 2 shows the results of applying the method proposed in this paper to the 5 examples. Columns c and q refer to the number of channels and queues in the model. Columns v and e refer to the number of variables and equations constructed for the satisfiability problem. Finally column f indicates the number of flow invariants added to rule out unreachable deadlocks. These flow invariants are generated automatically according to the algorithm in [5, §5] (which takes negligible run-time). Note that Table 2 has only 1 row for Figure 3. This is because the formulation of the structural deadlock problem and the flow invariants do not depend on the size of the queues and hence is independent of k. Finally, we note that in all cases, the resulting satisfiability problem was solved by Minisat in less than 1 second.

8 Conclusion

The method presented in this paper allows us to obtain proofs of deadlock freedom on real examples which were previously intractable. Although the comparisons with ABC have been done on minimal configurations, our method is far more scalable than brute-force model checking. For instance, our method has no trouble accommodating much larger configurations.

Finally, although our method is sound, it is not complete since false deadlocks may be found. Although in all our practical examples so far, flow invariants have sufficed to rule out all false deadlocks, it is possible that in some cases they may not be adequate. However, if liveness proof fails, our method always provides a concrete deadlock scenario: By looking at the positive literals of a satisfying solution, one can re-construct the deadlock state. This counter-example can be analyzed manually or be presented as *safety* problem for a model checker to rule out.

Acknowledgment. We thank Sayak Ray for implementing the liveness to safety conversion in ABC and for careful reading of an earlier draft.

References

1. NuSMV home page, http://nusmv.irst.itc.it/
2. Barkaoui, K., Dutheillet, C., Haddad, S.: An efficient algorithm for finding structural deadlocks in colored Petri nets. In: Ajmone Marsan, M. (ed.) ICATPN 1993. LNCS, vol. 691, pp. 69–88. Springer, Heidelberg (1993)
3. Berkeley Logic Synthesis and Verification Group: ABC: A system for sequential synthesis and verification, http://www.eecs.berkeley.edu/~alanmi/abc/
4. Biere, A., Artho, C., Schuppan, V.: Liveness checking as safety checking. Electronic Notes in Theoretical Computer Science 66(2), 160–177 (2002)
5. Chatterjee, S., Kishinevsky, M.: Automatic generation of inductive invariants from high-level microarchitectural models of communication fabrics. In: Touili, T., Cook, B., Jackson, P. (eds.) CAV 2010. LNCS, vol. 6174, pp. 321–338. Springer, Heidelberg (2010)
6. Chatterjee, S., Kishinevsky, M., Ogras, U.Y.: Quick formal modeling of communication fabrics to enable verification. In: Proc. IEEE High Level Design Validation and Test Workshop (HLDVT), pp. 42–49 (2010)
7. Dally, W., Towles, B.: Principles and Practices of Interconnection Networks. Morgan Kaufmann, San Francisco (2004)
8. Duato, J.: A necessary and sufficient condition for deadlock-free adaptive routing in wormhole networks. IEEE Trans. Paral. Distrib. Syst. 6(10), 1055–1067 (1995)
9. Gebremichael, B., Vaandrager, F.W., Zhang, M., Goossens, K.G.W., Rijpkema, E., Rădulescu, A.: Deadlock prevention in the æthereal protocol. In: Borrione, D., Paul, W. (eds.) CHARME 2005. LNCS, vol. 3725, pp. 345–348. Springer, Heidelberg (2005)
10. Ghafari, N., Gurfinkel, A., Klarlund, N., Trefler, R.J.: Algorithmic analysis of piecewise fifo systems. In: FMCAD, pp. 45–52 (2007)
11. Gotsman, A., Cook, B., Parkinson, M., Vafeiadis, V.: Proving that non-blocking algorithms don't block. In: POPL 2009: Proc. of Symp. on Principles of Prog. Lang., pp. 16–28. ACM, New York (2009)
12. Hansson, A., Goossens, K., Rădulescu, A.: Avoiding message-dependent deadlock in network-based systems on chip. VLSI Design 2007 (May 2007)
13. Manolios, P., Srinivasan, S.K.: Automatic verification of safety and liveness for pipelined machines using web refinement. ACM Trans. Des. Autom. Electron. Syst. 13(3), 1–19 (2008)
14. McMillan, K.L.: Circular compositional reasoning about liveness. In: Pierre, L., Kropf, T. (eds.) CHARME 1999. LNCS, vol. 1703, pp. 342–345. Springer, Heidelberg (1999)
15. Taktak, S., Desbarbieux, J.L., Encrenaz, E.: A tool for automatic detection of deadlock in wormhole networks on chip. ACM Trans. Design Autom. Electr. Syst. 13(1) (1995)
16. Verbeek, F., Schmaltz, J.: Formal specification of networks-on-chips: deadlock and evacuation. In: DATE 2010, pp. 1701–1706 (2010)

Static Analysis of Finite Precision Computations

Eric Goubault and Sylvie Putot

CEA LIST, Laboratory for the Modelling and Analysis of Interacting Systems,
Point courrier 94, Gif-sur-Yvette, F-91191 France
Firstname.Lastname@cea.fr

Abstract. We define several abstract semantics for the static analysis
of finite precision computations, that bound not only the ranges of values
taken by numerical variables of a program, but also the difference with
the result of the same sequence of operations in an idealized real number semantics. These domains point out with more or less detail (control
point, block, function for instance) sources of numerical errors in the program and the way they were propagated by further computations, thus
allowing to evaluate not only the rounding error, but also sensitivity to
inputs or parameters of the program. We describe two classes of abstractions, a non relational one based on intervals, and a weakly relational
one based on parametrized zonotopic abstract domains called affine sets,
especially well suited for sensitivity analysis and test generation. These
abstract domains are implemented in the Fluctuat static analyzer, and
we finally present some experiments.

1 Introduction

In this article, we discuss several abstract domains for proving properties about
the potential loss of accuracy in numerical programs using finite-precision arithmetics, such as IEEE 754 floating-point numbers, fixed point semantics, and
even integers with finite range. The goal of such abstractions is not to find runtime errors, but rather to automatically prove the the computation made by a
program (using finite-precision arithmetics) conforms to what was expected by
the programmer (using real-number semantics). These properties are of utmost
importance in the field of embedded systems (see the Patriot bug for instance
[27]) and in computer architecture and numerical simulation (see for instance
[24]). Take as explanatory example the following simple C program:

```
1   float x=[0,1];  float y=(x−1)*(x−1)*(x−1)*(x−1);
2   float z=x*x;
3   float z=z*z−4*x*z+6*z−4*x+1;  float t=z−y;
```

Using our analysis, we will find automatically (in our fully-fledged analyzer
Fluctuat, in less than 0.01 seconds) that y is in the real number semantics
within 0 and 1 with a negligible error in the floating-point number semantics in
$[-4.2.10^{-7}, 4.2.10^{-7}]$ whereas z is in $[-1.70, 2.25]$ (real number semantics) with
an error in the floating-point number semantics of $[-2.1.10^{-6}, 2.1.10^{-6}]$ mostly

R. Jhala and D. Schmidt (Eds.): VMCAI 2011, LNCS 6538, pp. 232–247, 2011.

due to line 3. We will actually see in Section 5 that using other mechanisms, implemented in Fluctuat [5], we can improve a lot these bounds and even prove that t is almost 0, showing that z is the same calculation in real numbers as y. On other examples, we will also demonstrate the use of Fluctuat to hint at less well behaved rounding error.

This paper is bridging the gaps between the initial proposal [11] and the actual implementation in the Fluctuat tool as demonstrated in [17,3,5]. It describes in particular the relational abstraction of the imprecision errors, never published before.

Related Work. This article is linked with earlier work by the authors, in particular concerning the relational abstractions of real numbers using zonotopes [15,16] and is improving on [11,14].

Other proposals have been made to analyze imprecision errors, most notably [1], in which floating-point variables are represented as a triplet: its floating-point value, its value computed using the real-number semantics, and its intended value that the programmer ultimately wanted to compute. The first two components correspond to our semantic model, although the error is not decomposed along the history of computation in [1]. The last component allows for computing the "model error" and not only the "implementation error", but this is also feasible with our relational abstraction described in Sections 4.1 and 4.2, see for instance Example 3. Finally, our approach uses abstract interpretation and thus is fully automatic, whereas the approach of [1] is based on Hoare proofs and thus is interactive.

More generally, the subject of analyzing the floating-point number semantics has gained importance in the early 2000s in fully-fledged static analyzers. A common approach to go from a real number abstraction to a floating-number abstract semantics is to use linearization, see [20,21], as implemented in APRON [25]. This approach allows for correctly abstracting the floating-point semantics, but does not decompose it into its real number and error decomposition. Also, the approach we are taking in Section 4.2 allows for finer results, even though the computation of the decomposition of errors along the computation history makes results less precise when we ask for finer information of the location of these errors. For instance, we only find with these techniques, using linearizations of polyhedra (APRON/Polka): y in $[0, 1]$ in real numbers, in $[-5.96.10^{-7}, 1.00000059604653]$ in the floating-point semantics, but no relation between the two abstract semantic values, and z in $[-7, 6.75]$ in real numbers, and in $[-3.000002384, 5.7500668]$ in floating-point numbers and no relation between real and floating-point values. So we are even unable to prove with linearizations of polyhedra that the imprecision error, notwithstanding its origin, is small. Even the concretization of y obtained by our technique is better (in $[-4.17.10^{-7}, 1.000000417]$) and much better for z indeed.

Contents. We begin by describing briefly the concrete semantics of finite-precision computations, focusing mostly on floating-point numbers, in Section 2. This semantics is non-standard in that it attributes to each variable x a triplet (f^x, r^x, e^x) where f^x (resp. r^x, e^x) is its floating-point (resp. real number, error) value. In Section 3, we detail the first natural abstraction, by intervals, of the values and the decomposition of error terms. We then describe in Section 4 a more accurate zonotopic abstraction, using affine sets, of the values and errors.

We will see that different choices of abstraction lead to a different way to see the triplet (f^x, r^x, e^x). With intervals, f^x will be first computed, then we will deduce e^x. Finally, r^x can be deduced by $e^x + f^x$, or computed directly. Whereas relational abstractions naturally apply to real numbers, but not to their finite-precision approximations: we will first compute r^x, then deduce e^x and f^x. We discuss in Section 5 the implementation of these abstractions, and show detailed examples and benchmarks.

2   Modelling Finite Precision Computations

We insist here more specifically on the modelling of more standard floating-point numbers; however the domains presented hereafter are perfectly well suited to the handling of fixed-point numbers. Indeed, an abstract domain for the analysis of programs in fixed-point numbers is implemented in our static analyzer Fluctuat.

2.1   Finite Precision Computations

Floating-point arithmetic. We recall here very briefly some basic properties of floating-point arithmetic, and refer the reader to [10,22] for instance for more details. The IEEE 754 standard [7] specifies the way most processors handle finite-precision approximation of real numbers known as floating-point numbers. It specifies four rounding modes. When the rounding mode is fixed, it then uniquely specifies the result of rounding of a real number to a floating-point number. Let $\uparrow \colon \mathbb{R} \to \mathbb{F}$ be the function that returns the rounded value of a real number r. Whatever the rounding mode and the precision of the floating-point analyzed are, there exist two positive constants δ_r and δ_a (which value depend on the format of the floating-point numbers), such that the error $r^x - \uparrow r^x$ when rounding a real number r^x to its floating-point representation $\uparrow r^x$ can be bounded by

$$|r^x - \uparrow r^x| \leq max(\delta_r | \uparrow r^x|, \delta_a). \tag{1}$$

For any arithmetic operator on real numbers $\diamond \in \{+, -, \times, /\}$, we note $\diamond_{\mathbb{F}}$ the corresponding operator on floating-point numbers, with rounding mode the one of the execution of the analyzed program. IEEE-754 standardises these four operations, as well as the square root: the result of the floating-point operation is the same as if the operation were performed on the real numbers with the given inputs, then rounded.

We are not interested in run-time errors or exceptions: when an overflow or undefined behaviour is encountered, our analysis simply reports $\top$ as a result.

Integers. Machine integers have finite range: we consider modular arithmetic, where adding one to the maximum value representable in a given data type gives the minimum value of this data type. The difference with natural integers is an error term in our model (the "real" value being the natural integer).

Fixed-point arithmetic. Fixed-point numbers are a finite approximation of real numbers with a fixed number of digits before and after the radix. They are essentially integer numbers scaled by a specific factor determined by the type. The main differences with floating-point arithmetic are that the range of values is very limited, and that the absolute rounding error is bounded and not the relative error. As the only properties we will use in our abstractions, are a function giving the rounded value $\uparrow r^x$ of a real number r^x, and a range for the rounding error $r^x - \uparrow r^x$ (no abstraction of the relative error is used), all the work below naturally applies to the analysis of fixed-point arithmetic.

2.2 Concrete Model

The underlying idea of the concrete model, first sketched in [11], then further described in more details in [18], and meanwhile implemented in a first version of the Fluctuat static analyzer [12], is to describe the difference of behaviour between the execution of a program in real numbers and in floating-point numbers. For that, the concrete value of a program variable is a triplet (f^x, r^x, e^x), where $f^x \in \mathbb{F}$ is the value of the variable if the program is executed with a finite-precision semantics, r^x is the value of the same variable if the program is executed with a real numbers semantics, and e^x is the rounding error, that is $e^x = r^x - f^x$. A variation of the same idea is used in the context of formal proof in [1], where the concrete model of a floating-point variable relies on its floating-point and idealized real values.

Another idea of [11,18,12], also developed here, is that it could be of interest for a static analysis to decompose the error term e^x along its provenance in the source code of the analyzed program, in order to point out the main sources of numerical discrepancy. For that, depending on the level of detail required, control points, blocks, or functions of a program can be annotated by a label ℓ, which will be used to identify the errors introduced during a computation. We note $\mathcal{L}$ the set of labels of the program, and $\mathcal{L}^+$ the set of words over these labels, then we express the error term as a sum

$$e^x = \bigoplus_{u \in \mathcal{L}^+} e_u, \tag{2}$$

where $e_u \in \mathbb{R}$ is the contribution to the global error of operations involved in word u. A word of length n thus identifies an order n error, which originates from several points in the program, and as for labels, we can choose different levels of abstraction of multiple sources of errors. We refer to [18] for details about this.

Our concrete model also models integers. The semantics of machine integers does not introduce rounding errors, but there are two sources of error terms. First, the effect of rounding errors on a floating-point variable that is cast in an integer i, is considered as an error term e^i. Second, the effect of the finite representation of integers by modular arithmetic is also expressed as an error term, as compared to a computation with infinite integers.

We will now describe two different abstractions of this concrete model.

3   A Non Relational Abstraction

3.1   Interval Abstraction of Values and Error Decomposition

The first natural idea to get an efficient abstract domain of our concrete model, is to abstract the values and errors with intervals, and to agglomerate all errors of order greater than one in a remaining interval term. This is what was first implemented in the Fluctuat static analyzer, and partially described in [12]. Correctness of the transfer functions is based on the separate Galois connection abstraction on each of the component of the triplet (f^x, r^x, e^x) of the collecting semantics based on the concrete semantics of Section 2.2.

Interval arithmetic. We denote intervals by bold letters. For two intervals with real bounds $\boldsymbol{x} = [\underline{x}, \overline{x}]$ and $\boldsymbol{y} = [\underline{y}, \overline{y}]$, we define:

$$\boldsymbol{x} + \boldsymbol{y} = [\underline{x} + \underline{y}, \overline{x} + \overline{y}]; \quad \boldsymbol{x} - \boldsymbol{y} = [\underline{x} - \overline{y}, \overline{x} - \underline{y}]$$
$$\boldsymbol{x} \times \boldsymbol{y} = [\min(\underline{xy}, \underline{x}\overline{y}, \overline{x}\underline{y}, \overline{xy}), \max(\underline{xy}, \underline{x}\overline{y}, \overline{x}\underline{y}, \overline{xy})]$$

The same operators can also be defined over finite precision approximations of the real numbers (typically floating-point numbers), for the current rounding mode. Finally, for the implementation, we need to define an abstraction of interval arithmetic over real numbers: we thus need the same operators defined over the set of floating-point of arbitrary precision p, noted $\mathbb{F}_p$, with outward rounding:

$$\boldsymbol{x} +_{\mathbb{F}_p} \boldsymbol{y} = [\underline{x} +_{\mathbb{F}_p}^{-\infty} \underline{y}, \overline{x} +_{\mathbb{F}_p}^{\infty} \overline{y}], \tag{3}$$

where $+_{\mathbb{F}_p}^{-\infty}$ (resp. $+_{\mathbb{F}_p}^{\infty}$) denotes the plus operator on floating-point numbers with an arbitrary precision p and rounding towards minus infinity (resp. rounding towards plus infinity).

Abstract model. An abstract element x is a triplet

$$x = \left(f^x, \ r^x, \ \bigoplus_{l \in \mathcal{L}} e_l^x \oplus e_{ho}^x \right) \tag{4}$$

where $\boldsymbol{f}^x = [\underline{f^x}, \overline{f^x}]$ bounds the finite precision value, with $(\underline{f^x}, \overline{f^x}) \in \mathbb{F} \times \mathbb{F}$, $\boldsymbol{r}^x = [\underline{r^x}, \overline{r^x}]$ bounds the real value, with $(\underline{r^x}, \overline{r^x}) \in \mathbb{R} \times \mathbb{R}$, $\boldsymbol{e}_l^x = [\underline{e_l^x}, \overline{e_l^x}]$ bounds the first-order contribution of control point l on the error between the real and the computed value of variable x, and $\boldsymbol{e}_{ho}^x = [\underline{e_{ho}^x}, \overline{e_{ho}^x}]$ the sum of all higher-order contributions (most of the time negligible), with $(\underline{e_l^x}, \overline{e_l^x}) \in \mathbb{R} \times \mathbb{R}$, for all l in $\mathcal{L} \cup ho$. The first-order errors are the propagated elementary rounding errors that can be associated to a specific control point. Higher-order errors appear in non affine arithmetic operations, and are non longer associated to a specific control point: they occur for instance when multiplying two error terms. The sum of the error intervals over-approximates the global error e^x due to finite precision computation or to initial errors on inputs.

3.2   Transfer Functions for Arithmetic Operations

Constants and inputs. For an interval $\boldsymbol{r}^x = [\underline{r^x}, \overline{r^x}]$, we note $\uparrow \boldsymbol{r}^x = [\uparrow \underline{r^x}, \uparrow \overline{r^x}]$. Using bound (1), we can over-approximate the rounding error of a real value given in interval $\boldsymbol{r}^x$ to its finite precision representation, by the interval

$$e(\boldsymbol{r}^x) = [-u^x, u^x] \cap (\boldsymbol{r}^x - \uparrow \boldsymbol{r}^x), \tag{5}$$

where $u^x = \max(\delta_r \max(|\uparrow \underline{r^x}|, |\uparrow \overline{r^x}|), \delta_a)$. This expresses the fact that we can compute the error as the intersection of the abstraction of bound given by (1), and the actual difference between the real and the finite precision values. The right-hand side or the left-hand side will be more accurate in different cases, depending for instance on the width of the range of values abstracted.

Arithmetic operations. Then, using this abstraction of the rounding error with the fact that the arithmetic operations on floating-point operations are correctly rounded (Section 2.1), we define the transfer function for expression $z = x \diamond^n y$ at label n. When $\diamond$ is the plus or minus operator, we have:

$$z = (\boldsymbol{f}^x \diamond_{\mathbb{F}} \boldsymbol{f}^y, \; \boldsymbol{r}^x \diamond \boldsymbol{r}^y, \; \bigoplus_{l \in \mathcal{L} \cup ho} (e_l^x \diamond e_l^y) \oplus e(\boldsymbol{f}^x \diamond \boldsymbol{f}^y)),$$

where the new error term $e(\boldsymbol{f}^x \diamond \boldsymbol{f}^y)$ is associated to label n. Indeed, the error on the result of an arithmetic operation combines the propagation of existing errors on the operands, plus a new round-off error term.
For the multiplication, we define:

$$z = (\boldsymbol{f}^x \times_{\mathbb{F}} \boldsymbol{f}^y, \; \boldsymbol{r}^x \times \boldsymbol{r}^y, \; \bigoplus_{l \in \mathcal{L} \cup ho} (\boldsymbol{f}^x \times e_l^y + \boldsymbol{f}^y \times e_l^x) \oplus \sum_{(l,k) \in (\mathcal{L} \cup ho)^2} e_l^x e_k^y \oplus e(\boldsymbol{f}^x \times \boldsymbol{f}^y)).$$

The semantics for the division x/y is defined using a first-order Taylor expansion to compute the inverse of $\boldsymbol{f}^y \bigoplus_{l \in \mathcal{L} \cup ho} e_l^y$: the approximation error is bounded and seen as an additional error. This expansion is all the more accurate as the errors are small compared to the value.

Integer computations. The cast of a floating-point (or fixed-point) number to an integer, as long as it does not result in an overflow of the integer result, is not seen as an additional error, so that the real value $\boldsymbol{r}^x$ is also cast in an integer. Let us note $(int)(\boldsymbol{r}^x)$ the result of casting a real variable to an integer, and $(int)(\boldsymbol{a})$ its extension to an interval $\boldsymbol{a}$, then we define $i = (int)x$ by:

$$i = \left((int)(\boldsymbol{f}^x), \; (int)(\boldsymbol{r}^x), \; \left(\sum_{l \in \mathcal{L} \cup ho} e_l^x + [-1, 1] \right) \cap ((int)(\boldsymbol{r}^x) - (int)(\boldsymbol{f}^x)) \right),$$

where the error is fully assigned to the label of the rounding operation: the sources of errors in previous computations are thus lost, we only keep track of the fact that rounding errors on floating-point computation can have an impact on an integer variable.

The addition, subtraction and multiplication on integer variables can be directly extended from their floating-point version (same propagation of existing errors, no additional rounding error, but an additional error of MAX_INT-MIN_INT if an overflow occurs). The integer division can be interpreted by a division over reals (error propagation with no additional error) followed by a cast to an integer.

3.3   Order-Theoretic Operations

Join. The most natural join operation between two abstract values is to define it by component-wise join on the intervals:

$$x \cup y = \left(\boldsymbol{f}^x \cup \boldsymbol{f}^y, \ \boldsymbol{r}^x \cup r^y, \ \bigoplus_{l \in \mathcal{L}} (e_l^x \cup e_l^y) \oplus (e_{ho}^x \cup e_{ho}^x) \right),$$

where the join of two intervals a and b is $a \cup b = [\min(\underline{a}, \underline{b}), \max(\overline{a}, \overline{b})]$. This join operation presents an inconvenience: when joining abstract values coming from different control flows, the joined abstract value will contain the elementary errors coming from these different control flows, so that the sum of the elementary errors of this joined value can be larger than when first computing the sums of errors then joining the result. In practice, in order to overcome this problem, we keep in the abstract domain an interval representing the global error, that is obtained by interval join of the global error, and which is thus more accurate than the decomposed sum.

Test interpretation. Our analysis relies on the assumption that the control flow of the program is the same for the finite precision and real values of the program. If this is found not to be the case when evaluating a boolean condition in real and in floats, an unstable test is indicated. The finite precision control flow is followed: this can give unsound error bounds, but the user is indicated which test to look at. A solution to avoid this assumption is to follow the two control flows and at the next join, merge the abstract values, by adding to the abstract value of the finite precision control-flow, the difference with the value of the real value control-flow as a rounding error. However, this can become quite costly and will not be expanded further in this paper.

Now, with the assumption that the finite precision and real values take the same control-flow, we define the meet operation by $x \cap y = (\boldsymbol{f}^x \cap \boldsymbol{f}^y, \ \boldsymbol{r}^x \cap r^y, \ e^x)$, where the meet of two intervals a and b is $a \cap b = [\max(\underline{a}, \underline{b}), \min(\overline{a}, \overline{b})]$. (by convention, the interval which lower bound is greater than the upper bound is the empty interval) The hypothesis that the finite precision and real control flow are the same also allows to reduce the error terms.

3.4   Fixpoint Iteration

In order to ensure termination of the fixpoint computation, we define the following natural widening operator on abstract values, by applying the component-wise classical interval widening on each elementary terms:

$$x \nabla y = \left(\boldsymbol{f}^x \nabla \boldsymbol{f}^y, \ \boldsymbol{r}^x \nabla r^y, \ \bigoplus_{l \in \mathcal{L}} (e_l^x \nabla e_l^y) \oplus (e_{ho}^x \nabla e_{ho}^x) \right),$$

where the widening on intervals is for instance the classical one proposed of [4]. Note that it is most of the time necessary to operate a semantic loop unrolling to ensure a good convergence of fixpoint computations [16].

4   A Zonotopic Abstraction

The abstraction of Section 3 naturally suffers from the over-estimation of interval analysis. We will now present an abstraction of the triplet (f^x, r^x, e^x) relying on a zonotopic weakly-relational abstract domain for the analysis of real value variables, based on ideas from affine arithmetic [2]: these domains that we developed over the last few years use a parametrization of zonotopes we call affine sets, that allow an accurate and computationally efficient functional abstraction of input-output relations on the values of real variables [14,15,8,9].

As the good algebraic properties of real numbers do not hold on floating-point (or fixed-point) number, the relational domains do not apply directly on finite precision values. We will present here how we can use them to bound the real value r^x and the error e^x of the triplet (f^x, r^x, e^x). From this, the finite precision value of variables can be bounded by the reduced product of $r^x - e^x$ with the intersection of a direct interval computation of f^x. Hints on previous work on the subject were given in [26,13,14], but never actually described a relational abstraction of the error terms.

After a quick introduction in Section 4.1 to affine sets for real value estimation, we focus in section 4.2 on their use to abstract the full value (f^x, r^x, e^x).

4.1   Zonotopic Abstract Domain for Real Values

Affine arithmetic [2] is a more accurate extension of interval arithmetic, that takes into account linear correlation between variables. An affine form $\hat{x}$ is a formal sum over a set of noise symbols ε_i: $\hat{x} = \alpha_0^x + \sum_{i=1}^{n} \alpha_i^x \varepsilon_i$, where $\alpha_i^x \in \mathbb{R}$ and the noise symbols ε_i are independent symbolic variables with unknown value in $[-1, 1]$. The coefficients $\alpha_i^x \in \mathbb{R}$ are the partial deviations to the center $\alpha_0^x \in \mathbb{R}$ of the affine form. These deviations can express uncertainties on the values of variables, for instance when inputs or parameters are given in a range of values, but also uncertainty coming from computation. The sharing of the same noise symbols between variables expresses implicit dependency. The values that a variable x defined by an affine form $\hat{x}$ can take is in the range

$$\gamma(\hat{x}) = \left[\alpha_0^x - \sum_{i=1}^{n} |\alpha_i^x|, \alpha_0^x + \sum_{i=1}^{n} |\alpha_i^x| \right]. \tag{6}$$

Assignment. The assignment of a variable x whose value is given in a range $[a, b]$, is defined as a centerd form using a fresh noise symbol $\varepsilon_{n+1} \in [-1, 1]$, which indicates unknown dependency to other variables: $\hat{x} = \frac{(a+b)}{2} + \frac{(b-a)}{2} \varepsilon_{n+1}$.

Affine operations. The result of linear operations on affine forms is an affine form. For two affine forms $\hat{x}$ and $\hat{y}$, and a real number λ, we get

$$\lambda \hat{x} + \hat{y} = (\lambda \alpha_0^x + \alpha_0^y) + \sum_{i=1}^{n} (\lambda \alpha_i^x + \alpha_i^y) \varepsilon_i$$

Multiplication. For non affine operations, we select an approximate linear resulting form, and bounds for the error committed using this approximate form are computed, that create a new noise term added to the linear form:

$$\hat{x}\hat{y} = \alpha_0^x \alpha_0^y + \sum_{i=1}^{n} (\alpha_i^x \alpha_0^y + \alpha_i^y \alpha_0^x) \varepsilon_i + \left(\sum_{i=1}^{n} |\alpha_i^x \alpha_i^y| + \sum_{i<j}^{n} |\alpha_i^x \alpha_j^y + \alpha_j^x \alpha_i^y| \right) \varepsilon_{n+1}.$$

The joint concretization of these affine forms is a center-symmetric polytope, that is a zonotope. We defined in [15,8,9] abstract domains based on extensions of these affine forms, with an order relation, and corresponding join and meet operators. In particular, we defined in [9] a meet operation using a logical product of our affine sets with an abstract domain over the noise symbols: the constraints generated by the tests are interpreted over the noise symbols of the affine forms. We do not detail these operations here, we will refer in the rest of the paper to $\hat{x} \cup \hat{y}$ and $\hat{x} \cap \hat{y}$ for respectively the join and meet over two affine forms $\hat{x}$ and $\hat{y}$. The order relation on abstract values ensures the geometric ordering for the zonotope including the current variables and the inputs of the program, that is we have a functional abstraction of the behaviour of the program.

4.2   Abstract Domain for Finite Precision Computations

The triplet (f^x, r^x, e^x) is now abstracted using two sets of noise symbols: the ε_i^r that model the uncertainty on the real value, and the ε_i^e that model the uncertainty on the error. An abstract value consists of an interval and two affine forms: $x = (\boldsymbol{f}^x, \hat{r}^x, \hat{e}^x)$. The uncertainty on the real value also introduces an uncertainty on the error, which is partially modelled:

$$\hat{r}^x = r_0^x + \sum_i r_i^x \varepsilon_i^r$$

$$\hat{e}^x = e_0^x + \sum_i e_i^x \varepsilon_i^r + \sum_l e_l^x \varepsilon_l^e$$

In the error expression $\hat{e}^x$, $e_l^x \varepsilon_l^e$ expresses the uncertainty on the rounding error committed at point l of the program (its center being in e_0^x), and its propagation through further computations, while $e_i^x \varepsilon_i^r$ expresses the propagation of the uncertainty on value at point i, on the error term; it allows to model dependency between errors and values.

Transfer functions. We now define the transfer function for expression $z = x \diamond^n y$ at label n. When $\diamond$ is the plus or minus operator, we define:

$$\hat{r}^z = \hat{r}^x \diamond \hat{r}^y,$$
$$\hat{e}^z = \hat{e}^x \diamond \hat{e}^y + new_{\varepsilon^e}(e(\gamma(\hat{r}^z - \hat{e}^x \diamond \hat{e}^y))),$$
$$\boldsymbol{f}^z = (\boldsymbol{f}^x \diamond \boldsymbol{f}^y) \cap (\hat{r}^z - \hat{e}^z)$$

where γ is the interval concretization on affine forms defined by (6), interval function e is the interval abstraction of the rounding error defined in (5), and function new_{ε^e} creates a new error noise symbol: for an interval I, we define $new_{\varepsilon^e}(I) = mid(I) + dev(I)\varepsilon^e_{n+1}$, where ε^e_{n+1} is a fresh error noise symbol, $mid(\iota) = \frac{\underline{I}+\overline{I}}{2}$ denotes the center of the interval, and $dev(I) = \frac{\overline{I}-\underline{I}}{2}$ the deviation to its center. The affine form for the real value is obtained by the operation on affine forms $\hat{r}^x \diamond \hat{r}^y$ as defined in Section 4.1. Then the error is obtained by the sum of the propagation of the existing error $\hat{e}^x \diamond \hat{e}^y$ still by affine arithmetic, and of the new error of rounding the result in real numbers of $\hat{r}^z - \hat{e}^x \diamond \hat{e}^y$ to the floating-point result f^z.

For the multiplication, we define:

$$\hat{r}^z = \hat{r}^x \hat{r}^y,$$
$$\hat{e}^z = \hat{r}^y \hat{e}^x + \hat{r}^x \hat{e}^y - \hat{e}^x \hat{e}^y + new_{\varepsilon^e}(e(\gamma(\hat{r}^z - (\hat{r}^y \hat{e}^x + \hat{r}^x \hat{e}^y - \hat{e}^x \hat{e}^y)))),$$
$$\boldsymbol{f}^z = (\boldsymbol{f}^x \boldsymbol{f}^y) \cap (\hat{r}^z - \hat{e}^z).$$

The real value is obtained by the multiplication on affine forms $\hat{r}^x \hat{r}^y$ as defined in Section 4.1. The propagation of the existing errors, obtained by expressing $\hat{r}^x \hat{r}^y - (\hat{r}^x - \hat{e}^x)(\hat{r}^y - \hat{e}^y)$, is computed by $\hat{r}^y \hat{e}^x + \hat{r}^x \hat{e}^y - \hat{e}^x \hat{e}^y$. The operations occurring in this expression are those over affine forms, with partially shared noise symbols between the real and error affine forms. When the propagation error is computed, we can finally deduce the new rounding error due to the multiplication by $new_{\varepsilon^e}(e(\gamma(\hat{r}^z - (\hat{r}^y \hat{e}^x + \hat{r}^x \hat{e}^y - \hat{e}^x \hat{e}^y))))$.

Note that we chose not to separate the higher-order from the first-order term as in the non-relational semantics. Indeed, this decomposition would be more costly for no gain of accuracy. But most of all, we noticed that the higher-order terms tend to converge much more slowly in fixpoint iterations than if agglomerated as proposed here.

Using more refined properties of floating-point numbers. Some specific properties of floating-point numbers can be used to refine the estimation of the new error in some cases. For instance, the well-known Sterbenz Theorem [28] that says that is x and y are two floating-point numbers such that $\frac{y}{2} \leq x \leq 2y$, then the result of $x - y$ is a floating-point number, so that no new rounding error is added in this case. This allows to refine the subtraction by writing $\hat{e}^z = \hat{e}^x - \hat{e}^x$ when the floating-point values of x and y satisfy the hypotheses of Sterbenz Theorem. Note that it is more accurate to verify the satisfaction of this condition on the affine forms $\hat{r}^x - \hat{e}^x$ and $\hat{r}^y - \hat{e}^y$ than on the intervals $\boldsymbol{f}^x$ and $\boldsymbol{f}^y$.

Example 1. Let x, y, and z be double precision floating-point numbers, and x initially given in range $[0, 2]$ for the following sequence of instructions:

```
1  x := [0,2];
2  y = 0.75*x;
3  z = x-y;
```

With the interval analysis, we get $\boldsymbol{f}^z = [-1.5, 2]$ and $\boldsymbol{e}^z = [-1.11e^{-16}, 1.11e^{-16}]_2 + [-2.22e^{-16}, 2.22e^{-16}]_3$. Indeed, as no relation is kept between x and y, the value of z is computed inaccurately, and so is the error, as it does not realize that Sterbenz theorem applies. Whereas with the relational analysis, $\hat{r}^x = 1 + \varepsilon_1^r$, $\hat{r}^y = 0.75 + 0.75\varepsilon_1^r$, $\hat{e}^y = 1.11e^{-16}\varepsilon_2^e$, and finally $\hat{r}^z = 0.25 + 0.25\varepsilon_1^r \in [0, 0.5]$ and $\hat{e}^z = -1.11e^{-16}\varepsilon_2^e \in [-1.11e^{-16}, 1.11e^{-16}]$ as Sterbenz theorem applies.

Casts from floating-point value to integers. For lack of place, we only detail a very simple version of the cast. As already stated, the truncation due to the cast is not seen in itself as an error. So, the affine form for the real value is also cast to an integer, which results in a partial loss of relation, of amplitude bounded by 1. If the error on x was not zero, a loss of relation also applies. For the floating-point value, the cast directly applied to the interval value will be more accurate than $r^i - e^i$. The cast $i = (int)x$ then writes

$$\hat{r}^i = \hat{r}^x + new_{\varepsilon^r}([-1,1])$$

$$\hat{e}^i = \begin{cases} 0 & \text{if } e^x = 0 \\ new_{\varepsilon^e}([-1,1]) & \text{if } \gamma(e^x) \in [-1,1] \\ e^x + new_{\varepsilon^e}([-1,1]) & \text{otherwise} \end{cases}$$

$$\boldsymbol{f}^i = (int)\boldsymbol{f}^x$$

Order-theoretic operations. The join operation is computed component-wise, using the join over intervals and affine forms $x \cup y = (\boldsymbol{f}^x \cup \boldsymbol{f}^y, \hat{r}^x \cup \hat{r}^y, \hat{e}^x \cup \hat{e}^y)$. Note that we do not have here the over-estimation problem over errors that we had with the non-relational join. Indeed, the join we define over affine forms keeps only the greatest common relation (see [15,8,9]). It will thus lose the sources of errors that are not common to all execution paths of the programs, but will assign them to the label of the corresponding join operator.

As in the non relational abstraction, we make the assumption for the analysis that the control flow of the program is the same for the floating-point and real executions (see Section 3.3 for the discussion of this assumption), so that we interpret the tests over the real and floating-point values. For the meet operation, we thus interpret $\hat{r}^x \cap \hat{r}^y$ and $\hat{r}^x - \hat{e}^x \cap \hat{r}^y - \hat{e}^y$. Remember (it was briefly stated in Section 4.1, see [9] for more details) that the interpretation of tests yields constraints on the noise symbols. By lack of place, we will not detail this formally here.

Fixpoint computation, widening. We described in [15,8,9] fixpoint iterations and widening operators for affine sets, along with some convergence results on fixpoint computations. They can be applied here component-wise to our abstract values.

Remark: computing the finite precision value only. Simpler variations of this abstract domain can be used to compute the finite precision value only, basically using only one affine form. Each operation creates a new noise symbol that is used either to over-approximate a non-affine operation, either to add a rounding error, or both. The results for the finite precision value would be comparable to those we obtain through our more decomposed abstract domain, though some slight differences would be due to a different interpretation of tests and to the different decomposition (the results for the direct computation of the values would be slightly more accurate in general).

5   Implementation and Results

These abstract domains are among those implemented in the Fluctuat analyzer, some of the case studies realized with the zonotopic abstract domain on real industrial programs, are reported in [17,3,5]. We discuss here the implementation in finite precision, and present benchmarks and some results on simple examples.

We now have at our disposal for the analysis, floating-point numbers with an arbitrary precision p, instead of real numbers (using the MPFR [6] library). For the non relational abstract domain, where operations on real numbers occur on interval bounds, the abstraction by operations with numbers in $\mathbb{F}_p$ is kept correct by using all such operations in interval arithmetic with outward rounding, as in (3) for the addition. The affine forms of the relational domain can also be computed using finite precision coefficients: the computation is made sound by over-approximating the rounding error committed on these coefficients and agglomerating the resulting error in new noise terms. Keeping track of these particular noise terms is interesting as they quantify the overestimation in the analysis specifically due to the use of finite precision for the analysis.

Finally, before eventually using a widening to ensure termination of the analysis, it proved interesting to use a convergence acceleration operator for the computation of fixpoint, obtained by the progressive reduction of the precision p of the floating-point used for the analysis (see [17], Section 2.4 for more details).

We now present some experiments made using Fluctuat, using both the non-relational and the relational abstract semantics; part of the programs (the academic ones) can be found at http://www.lix.polytechnique.fr/~goubault/ NAME[.c][.apron]. Times are given on an Intel Core 2 Duo 2GHz, 4Gb of RAM, running under MacOS Snow Leopard, and include all the mechanisms used in Fluctuat, including for instance alias analysis.

Let us first come back to the introductory example of Section 1: with the relational domain using 1000 subdivisions, in 78 seconds we get for the real value of t, $r^t \in [-2.10^{-6}, 2.10^{-6}]$ instead of $[-1.95, 1.94]$ without subdivision, and $[-8, 8]$ with the non-relational domain. We already saw that the rounding errors where negligible, we now also have that the two computations for y and z are functionally very close in real numbers.

Example 2. Take the following simple program that implements 100 iterations of a scheme proposed by Muller [23] and analyzed by Kahan, to demonstrate the effect of finite precision on computation.

```
1    x0 = 11/2.0;
2    x1 = 61/11.0;
3    for (i=1 ; i<=100 ; i++) {
4      x2 = 111 - (1130 - 3000/x0) / x1;
5      x0 = x1;   x1 = x2; }
```

Computed with exact numbers, this sequence should converge to 6. However, this fixed point is repulsive, while the fixed point 100 is attractive. This means that any perturbation from the exact sequence converging to this repulsive fixed point will eventually lead to the attractive one. Thus, when computed in finite precision, whatever the precision used, this sequence will eventually converge to 100. Fluctuat, with the interval abstract domain, and using floating-point numbers with 500 bits of precision, indeed finds in less than 0.15 second that $x2$ after the loop has a float value equal to 100, a real value equal to 5.999..., and a global error equal to $-94.000...$, due to lines 2 and 4, and to higher order errors. As a matter of fact, it is in particular because $x1$ is not represented exactly that the dynamical system converges towards the attractive fixpoint (in floating-point numbers). The fixed point for an arbitrary number of iterations will be $\top$ for the real value and error. Using APRON with Polka (polyhedra) and linearization, we find $x1$ equal to 5.999... in real-numbers and $x1$ equal to top (since the eighth iterate) in floating-point numbers, even though we unravelled all 100 iterations and infinite precision computation is made by the analyzer - this is due to the linearization scheme.

Example 3. The function below computes (Householder method) the inverse of the square root of the input I. The loop stops when the difference between two successive iterates is below a criterion that depends on a value eps.

```
1    xn = 1.0/I; i = 0; residu = 2.0*eps;
2    while (fabs(residu) > eps) {
3      xnp1 = xn*(1.875+I*xn*xn*(-1.25+0.375*I*xn*xn));
4      residu = 2.0*(xnp1-xn)/(xn+xnp1);
5      xn = xnp1; i++; }
6    O = 1.0/xnp1;   sbz = O- sqrt(I);
```

This algorithm is known to quickly converge when in real numbers, whatever the value of eps is. However, in finite precision, the stopping criterion must be defined with caution: for instance, executed in simple precision, with eps=10^{-8}, the program never terminates for some inputs, for instance $I = 16.000005$. Analyzed with Fluctuat for an input in $[16, 16.1]$, we obtain that the number of iterations i of the algorithm is potentially unbounded. We also obtain that $residu$ has a real value bounded in $[-3.66e^{-9}, 3.67e^{-9}]$ and a floating-point value is bounded in $[-2.79e^{-7}, 2.79e^{-7}]$ (50 subdivisions), so that the real value satisfies the stopping criterion but not the floating-point value, which is also signalled by an unstable test on the loop condition. Now, analyzing the same program but now for double precision variables, Fluctuat is able to prove in 3 seconds that the number of iterations is always 6 (both the real value and the floating-point value satisfy the stopping criterion). Also, bounding the variable sbz, Fluctuat is also able to bound the method error, so that we prove that the program indeed computes something that is close to the square root: the real and float value of sbz are found in $[-1.03e^{-8}, -1.03e^{-8}]$, with an error due to the use of finite precision in $[-1.05e^{-14}, 1.05e^{-14}]$. The non-relational analysis does not manage to bound the values of variables nor the number of iterations.

Example 4. Consider the following set of second-order linear recursive filters:

```
1    xn = 1.0/I;  i = 0;  residu = 2.0*eps;
2    while (fabs(residu) > eps) {
3      xnp1 = xn*(1.875+I*xn*xn*(-1.25+0.375*I*xn*xn));
4      residu = 2.0*(xnp1-xn)/(xn+xnp1);
5      xn = xnp1;  i++; }
6    O = 1.0/xnp1;   sbz = O- sqrt(I);
```

We find in 90 seconds, with the relational abstraction (the non-relational abstraction does not converge): S in $[-15.08, 16.58]$ with error in $[-7.9.10^{-14}, 7.9.10^{-14}]$ (coming mostly from line 5). When unrolling the first 200 iterations, we find the better estimate (convergence is actually very fast): S in $[-5.63, 7.13]$, with error in $[-2.93.10^{-14}, 2.93.10^{-14}]$. Our abstraction allows for test case generation, both in values (see for instance [5]) and for errors: indeed, similarly as in [5], one can easily maximize or minimize the form $\hat{e}^x = e_0^x + \sum_i e_i^x \varepsilon_i^r + \sum_l e_l^x \varepsilon_l^e$ by choosing the right inputs, i.e. the values for ε_i^r (see Section 4.2). Here we find input values that allow for S to reach -0.92 and 5.36 (in real-numbers) and using the subdivision mechanism of Fluctuat [5], we find even better: [-4.81,6.33]. For errors, we find inputs reaching $-2.49.10^{-14}$ and $2.6.10^{-14}$ very close to the static analysis result.

Example 5. We finally consider a conjugate gradient algorithm applied to a class of matrices close to a Lagrangian in one dimension, discretized in a 4×4 matrix. Fluctuat shows that the error is coming from mostly evalA, the evaluation of the perturbed Lagrangian (error in $[-9.22.10^{-6}, 9.22.10^{-6}]$), the scalar product function (error in $[-6.61.10^{-6}, 6.61.10^{-6}]$), and the multiply add routine for matrices ($[-5.46.10^{-6}, 5.46.10^{-6}]$) for $xi[1]$. The influence of the perturbation of the Lagrangian matrix is negligible (of the order of $2.56.10^{-11}$), as well as the influence of the perturbation of the initial condition (of the order of $1.98.10^{-10}$): this is a well-known phenomenon for well-behaved problems such as this one, called orthogonality defects, see [19].

In terms of performance (time and memory), the relational abstract domain is of the same order of complexity as the zonotopic domain for the analysis of real values (though of course a little more costly, as there will be the error noise symbols on top of the value noise symbols). For this abstract domain for the analysis of real values, benchmarks and comparisons with other classical abstract domains (APRON implementation) were presented in [8,9].

Finally, here is a table of some experiments made using Fluctuat on real codes coming from industry, which involve some intricate numerical computations:

246 E. Goubault and S. Putot

Program	#LOC	Analysis	Time(s)	Memory(Mo)
subset of navigation code	~10000	fixpoint	33	20
physical process monitoring	~800	fixpoint	188	94
subset of navigation code	~1000	unfolding 20000 it	520	16

6 Conclusion and Future Work

We presented in this paper non-relational and relational abstractions of finite-precision computations allowing for determining precisely not only the bounds of variables in real-number and finite precision (in particular, floating-point number) semantics, but also the discrepancy between these two semantics, and their causes. The amount of information delivered is more important than in a classical floating-point analysis, however we can obtain better results, in a very economical manner, both in time and memory. This extra information also allows us to generate interesting outcomes such as worst-case inputs.

As a last word, let us notice that the rounding error of (normalized) floating-point computations is classically bounded in relative error. In a relational analysis, we would thus like to express the new rounding error of a real number defined by an affine form over noise symbols, as a function of these noise symbols. However, this is no longer expressible purely as an affine form, hence we simply use a noise symbol to abstract the whole range of error. A future direction could be to enhance the abstract domain with the relative error, when particularizing our technique to floating-point arithmetic.

References

1. Boldo, S., Filliâtre, J.-C.: Formal Verification of Floating-Point Programs. In: 18th IEEE International Symposium on Computer Arithmetic (June 2007)
2. Comba, J.L.D., Stolfi, J.: Affine arithmetic and its applications to computer graphics. In: SEBGRAPI 1993 (1993)
3. Conquet, E., Cousot, P., Cousot, R., Goubault, E., Ghorbal, K., Lesens, D., Putot, S., Turin, M.: Space software validation using abstract interpretation. In: Proceedings of DASIA (2009)
4. Cousot, P., Cousot, R.: Static determination of dynamic properties of programs. In: Proceedings of the Second International Symposium on Programming, Dunod, Paris, France, pp. 106–130 (1976)
5. Delmas, D., Goubault, E., Putot, S., Souyris, J., Tekkal, K., Védrine, F.: Towards an industrial use of FLUCTUAT on safety-critical avionics software. In: Alpuente, M., Cook, B., Joubert, C. (eds.) FMICS 2009. LNCS, vol. 5825, pp. 53–69. Springer, Heidelberg (2009)
6. Zimmerman, P., et al.: The MPFR library, http://www.mpfr.org/
7. IEEE 754 Standard for Binary Floating-Point Arithmetic, revision (2008), http://ieeexplore.ieee.org/servlet/opac?punumber=4610933
8. Ghorbal, K., Goubault, E., Putot, S.: The zonotope abstract domain taylor1+. In: Bouajjani, A., Maler, O. (eds.) CAV 2009. LNCS, vol. 5643, pp. 627–633. Springer, Heidelberg (2009)

9. Ghorbal, K., Goubault, E., Putot, S.: A logical product approach to zonotope intersection. In: Touili, T., Cook, B., Jackson, P. (eds.) CAV 2010. LNCS, vol. 6174, pp. 212–226. Springer, Heidelberg (2010)
10. Goldberg, D.: What every computer scientist should know about floating-point arithmetic. ACM Comput. Surv. 23(1), 5–48 (1991)
11. Goubault, É.: Static analyses of the precision of floating-point operations. In: Cousot, P. (ed.) SAS 2001. LNCS, vol. 2126, pp. 234–259. Springer, Heidelberg (2001)
12. Goubault, É., Martel, M., Putot, S.: Asserting the precision of floating-point computations: A simple abstract interpreter. In: Le Métayer, D. (ed.) ESOP 2002. LNCS, vol. 2305, pp. 209–212. Springer, Heidelberg (2002)
13. Goubault, É., Putot, S.: Weakly relational domains for the analysis of floating-point computations. Presented at NSAD (2005)
14. Goubault, É., Putot, S.: Static analysis of numerical algorithms. In: Yi, K. (ed.) SAS 2006. LNCS, vol. 4134, pp. 18–34. Springer, Heidelberg (2006)
15. Goubault, E., Putot, S.: Perturbed affine arithmetic for invariant computation in numerical program analysis. CoRR, abs/0807.2961 (2008)
16. Goubault, E., Putot, S.: A zonotopic framework for functional abstractions. CoRR, abs/0910.1763 (2009), http://arxiv.org/abs/0910.1763
17. Goubault, É., Putot, S., Baufreton, P., Gassino, J.: Static analysis of the accuracy in control systems: Principles and experiments. In: Leue, S., Merino, P. (eds.) FMICS 2007. LNCS, vol. 4916, pp. 3–20. Springer, Heidelberg (2008)
18. Martel, M.: Propagation of roundoff errors in finite precision computations: A semantics approach. In: Le Métayer, D. (ed.) ESOP 2002. LNCS, vol. 2305, pp. 194–208. Springer, Heidelberg (2002)
19. Meurant, G.: The Lanczos and Conjugate Gradient Algorithm; from theory to finite precision computation. SIAM, Philadelphia (2006)
20. Miné, A.: Relational abstract domains for the detection of floating-point run-time errors. In: Schmidt, D. (ed.) ESOP 2004. LNCS, vol. 2986, pp. 3–17. Springer, Heidelberg (2004)
21. Miné, A.: Symbolic methods to enhance the precision of numerical abstract domains. In: Emerson, E.A., Namjoshi, K.S. (eds.) VMCAI 2006. LNCS, vol. 3855, pp. 348–363. Springer, Heidelberg (2005)
22. Monniaux, D.: The pitfalls of verifying floating-point computations. ACM Trans. Program. Lang. Syst. 30(3), 1–41 (2008)
23. Muller, J.-M.: Arithmétique des Ordinateurs. Masson (1989)
24. Muller, J.-M., Brisebarre, N., de Dinechin, F., Jeannerod, C.-P., Lefèvre, V., Melquiond, G., Revol, N., Stehlé, D., Torres, S.: Handbook of Floating-Point Arithmetic. Birkhäuser, Boston (2010)
25. APRON Project. Numerical abstract domain library (2007), http://apron.cri.ensmp.fr
26. Putot, S., Goubault, É., Martel, M.: Static analysis-based validation of floating-point computations. In: Alt, R., Frommer, A., Kearfott, R.B., Luther, W. (eds.) Dagstuhl Seminar 2003. LNCS, vol. 2991, pp. 306–313. Springer, Heidelberg (2004)
27. Skeel, R.: Roundoff error and the patriot missile. SIAM News (1992)
28. Sterbenz, P.H.: Floating point computation. Prentice-Hall, Englewood Cliffs (1974)

An Evaluation of Automata Algorithms for String Analysis

Pieter Hooimeijer[1,*] and Margus Veanes[2]

[1] University of Virginia
pieter@cs.virginia.edu
[2] Microsoft Research
margus@microsoft.com

Abstract. There has been significant recent interest in automated reasoning techniques, in particular constraint solvers, for string variables. These techniques support a wide variety of clients, ranging from static analysis to automated testing. The majority of string constraint solvers rely on finite automata to support regular expression constraints. For these approaches, performance depends critically on fast automata operations such as intersection, complementation, and determinization. Existing work in this area has not yet provided conclusive results as to which core algorithms and data structures work best in practice.

In this paper, we study a comprehensive set of algorithms and data structures for performing fast automata operations. Our goal is to provide an apples-to-apples comparison between techniques that are used in current tools. To achieve this, we re-implemented a number of existing techniques. We use an established set of regular expressions benchmarks as an indicative workload. We also include several techniques that, to the best of our knowledge, have not yet been used for string constraint solving. Our results show that there is a substantial performance difference across techniques, which has implications for future tool design.

1 Introduction

There has been significant recent interest in decision procedures for string constraints. Traditionally, many analyses and automated testing approaches relied on their own built-in models to reason about string values [5,8,9,21,23,28]. Recent work on string analysis has focused on providing external decision procedures that reason about strings [2,11,12,15,24,26,27]. The separation of string decision procedures from their client analyses is desirable because it allows for the independent development of more scalable algorithms.

Existing string decision procedures vary significantly in terms of feature sets. Although most tools support regular expression constraints in one form or another, there is no strong consensus on which features are necessary. Many programming languages provide a variety of string manipulating functions. For example, the user manual for PHP lists 111 distinct string manipulation functions [20], and the System.Text namespace in the .NET class library contains

---

* This work was done during an internship at Microsoft Research.

R. Jhala and D. Schmidt (Eds.): VMCAI 2011, LNCS 6538, pp. 248–262, 2011.

more than a dozen classes that deal with Unicode encodings [19]. Constraint solving tools must strike a balance between expressive utility and other concerns like scalability and generality.

In this paper, we focus on a subclass of string decision procedures that support regular expression constraints and use finite automata as their underlying representation. This includes the DPRLE [11], JSA [5], and Rex [26,27] tools, as well as a prototype from our recent work [12]. These tools are implemented in different languages, they parse different subsets of common regular expression idioms, they differ in how they use automata internally, and the automata data structures themselves are different. However, each approach relies crucially on the efficiency of basic automaton operations like intersection and determinization/complementation. Existing work provides reasonable information on the relative performance of the tools as a whole, but does not give any insight into the relative efficiency of the individual data structures.

Our goal is to provide an apples-to-apples comparison between the core algorithms that underlie these solvers. To achieve this, we have performed a faithful re-implementation in C# of several often-used automaton data structures. We also include several data structures that, to the best of our knowledge, have not yet featured in existing work on string decision procedures. We conduct performance experiments on an established set of string constraint benchmarks. We use both ASCII and UTF-16 encodings where possible, to investigate the impact of alphabet size on the various approaches. Our testing harness includes a relatively full-featured regular expression parser that is based on the .NET framework's built-in parser. By fixing factors like the implementation language and the front-end parser, and by including a relatively large set of regular expression features, we aim to provide practical insight into which data structures are advisable for future string decision procedure work.

This paper makes the following contributions:

- To the best of our knowledge, we provide the first performance comparison of automata data structures (and associated algorithms) designed for string decision procedures. We pay special attention to isolating the core operations of interest.
- We present several approaches that have not yet been used for string decision procedures. We demonstrate that these approaches frequently out-perform existing approaches.

The rest of this paper is structured as follows. Section 2 gives formal definitions of the automata constructs of interest. Section 3 presents the design and implementation of the data structures under consideration. In Sectino 4, we provide experimental results using those data structures. We discuss closely related work in Section 5, and we conclude in Section 6.

2   Preliminaries

We assume familiarity with classical automata theory [13]. We work with a representation of automata where several transitions from a source state to a target state may be combined into a single *symbolic move*. Symbolic moves have labels that denote *sets of characters* rather than individual characters. This representation naturally separates the structure of automata graph from the representation used for the character sets that annotate the edges. In this context, classical finite automata can be viewed as a special case in which each label is a singleton set. The following definition builds directly on the standard definition of finite automata.

Definition 1. *A Symbolic Finite Automaton or SFA A is a tuple* $(Q, \Sigma, \Delta, q^0, F)$, *where Q is a finite set of states, Σ is the input alphabet, $q^0 \in Q$ is the initial state, $F \subseteq Q$ is the set of final states and $\Delta : Q \times 2^\Sigma \times Q$ is the move relation.*

We indicate a component of an SFA A by using A as a subscript. The word *symbolic* stems from the intension that a move (q, ℓ, p) denotes the *set* of transitions $[\![(q, \ell, p)]\!] \stackrel{\text{def}}{=} \{(q, a, p) \mid a \in \ell\}$. We let $[\![\Delta]\!] \stackrel{\text{def}}{=} \cup\{[\![\rho]\!] \mid \rho \in \Delta\}$. An SFA A denotes the finite automaton $[\![A]\!] \stackrel{\text{def}}{=} (Q_A, \Sigma_A, [\![\Delta_A]\!], q_A^0, F_A)$. The *language* $L(A)$ *accepted by* A is the language $L([\![A]\!])$ accepted by $[\![A]\!]$.

An ϵSFA A may in addition have moves where the label is ϵ, denoting the corresponding epsilon move in $[\![A]\!]$. For $\rho = (p, \ell, q)$, let $Src(\rho) \stackrel{\text{def}}{=} p$, $Tgt(\rho) \stackrel{\text{def}}{=} q$, $Lbl(\rho) \stackrel{\text{def}}{=} \ell$. We use the following notation for the set of moves starting from a given state q in A: $\Delta_A(q) \stackrel{\text{def}}{=} \{\rho \mid \rho \in \Delta_A, Src(\rho) = q\}$ and furthermore will allow lifting functions to sets. For example, $\Delta_A(Q) \stackrel{\text{def}}{=} \cup\{\Delta_A(q) \mid q \in Q\}$. We write Δ_A^ϵ for the set of all epsilon moves in Δ_A and Δ_A^{ℓ} for $\Delta_A \setminus \Delta_A^\epsilon$. An ϵSFA A is *clean* if for all $\rho \in \Delta_A^{\ell}$, $Lbl(\rho) \neq \emptyset$; A is *normalized* if for all $q \in Q_A$, if $\rho_1, \rho_2 \in \Delta_A^{\ell}(q)$ and $Tgt(\rho_1) = Tgt(\rho_2)$ then $\rho_1 = \rho_2$; A is *total* if for all states $q \in Q_A$, $\Sigma_A = \bigcup_{\rho \in \Delta_A(q)} Lbl(\rho)$. Let $\complement$ denote the complement operation over character sets. For making an SFA A total, do the following: for all $q \in Q_A$ such that $\ell = \complement(\bigcup_{\rho \in \Delta_A(q)} Lbl(\rho)) \neq \emptyset$, add $(q, \ell, sink)$ to Δ_A, and add the state $sink$ to Q_A and the move $(sink, \Sigma, sink)$ to Δ_A. Epsilon elimination from an ϵSFA is straightforward and makes use of union [27]. Also, any SFA can easily be made clean and normalized. When we say SFA we assume that epsilon moves are not present.

We assume a translation from regex (extended regular expression) patterns to ϵSFAs that follows closely the standard algorithm, see e.g., [13, Section 2.5]. A sample regex and corresponding ϵSFA are illustrated in Figure 1.

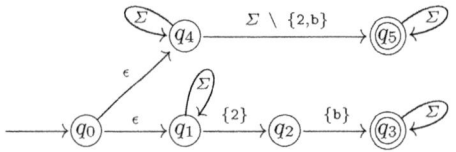

Fig. 1. ϵSFA generated from regex 2b| [^2b]

3   Automata Data Structures and Algorithms

In this section, we describe the automaton data structures and algorithms of interest. We assume a graph-based data structure for the automata; each transition edge is annotated with a data structure that represents the label of that transition. Section 3.1 describes the data structures we use for those annotations. In Section 3.2, we discuss lazy and eager algorithms for two key operations on automata: language intersection (using the cross product construction) and language difference (using the subset construction). Later, in Section 4, we will evaluate experimentally how well each data structure/algorithm combination performs.

3.1   Representing Character Sets

We start by defining an interface for character set operations. This interface represents all the operations that the higher-level automata algorithms use to perform intersection and complementation. We then discuss several representations that can be used to implement this interface. A given representation affects both the performance of the algorithms discussed below; it also affects how effectively the algorithms can be combined with existing solvers.

Definition 2. Let I denote an ordered set of indices. A *minterm* of a finite nonempty sequence $(\ell_i)_{i \in I}$ of nonempty subsets of Σ is a sequence $(\ell'_i)_{i \in I}$ where each ℓ'_i is equal to either ℓ_i or $\complement(\ell_i)$, and $\bigcap_{i \in I} \ell'_i \neq \emptyset$, where $\bigcap_{i \in I} \ell'_i$ is the set *represented* by the minterm.

Intuitively, a minterm (ℓ'_1, ℓ'_2) of a sequence (ℓ_1, ℓ_2) of two nonempty subsets $\ell_1, \ell_2 \subseteq \Sigma$ represents a minimal nonempty region $\ell'_1 \cap \ell'_2$ of a Venn diagram for ℓ_1 and ℓ_2, see Figure 2. Note that the *collection of all minterms* of a given sequence

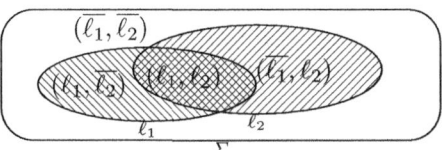

Fig. 2. Intuition behind minterms of (ℓ_1, ℓ_2)

of nonempty sets over Σ represents a *partition* of Σ.[1]

Character set solver interface:

Boolean operations: union ($\cup$), intersection ($\cap$), and complement ($\complement$).

Nonemptiness check: decide if a given set is nonempty.

Minterm generation: compute all minterms for a given sequence of character sets.

For any character set representation, we can use an algorithm similar to that of Figure 3 to perform the minterm computation in terms of repeated complementation and intersections. This algorithm is similar in spirit to the standard *Quine-McCluskey algorithm* for minimizing Boolean functions. We compute intersections combinatorially in rank order; once a given combination reaches the

---

[1] A *partition of* Σ is a collection of nonempty subsets of Σ such that every element of Σ is in exactly one of these subsets.

Input: Finite nonempty sequence of nonempty sets $(\ell_i)_{i \in I}$.
Rank propagation: Iterate over *ranks* $r \leq |I|$ and construct S_r:

$$S_0 = \{\emptyset\}$$
$$S_{r+1} = \{J \cup \{i\} \mid J \in S_r, i \in I \setminus J, \ell_i \cap \bigcap_{j \in J} \ell_j \neq \emptyset\}$$

Output: Set of all $J \in \bigcup_r S_r$ such that $(\bigcap_{i \in J} \ell_i) \cap (\bigcap_{i \in I \setminus J} \mathsf{C}(\ell_i)) \neq \emptyset$.

Fig. 3. Minterm generation algorithm

empty set at rank i, we know that derived combinations of rank $i' > i$ are necessarily empty (and thus uninteresting). In practice, we use this algorithm for every character set representation.

For each character-set representation we discuss how the above operations are supported, and indicate how the minterm generation is implemented.

Character sets as BDDs. In the general case, regexes, and string operations involving regexes, assume Unicode UTF-16 character encoding. This means that characters correspond to 16-bit bit-vectors. For the special case of ASCII range (resp. extended ASCII range) the number of bits is 7 (resp. 8). Independent of the number of bits, the general idea behind the BDD encoding is that each bit of a character corresponds to a variable of the BDD. The crucial point is to determine a good variable order for the BDD encoding. In order to do so, we considered typical uses of regexes, and in a separate evaluation determined an order which yielded BDDs of small size.

Based on the evaluation, a good choice of order turned out to be one where the highest bit has the lowest ordinal, in particular, for 16 bits, the MSB has ordinal 0 and the LSB has ordinal 15. This decision was, in part, based on the observation that typical regexes make extensive use of predefined character patterns called *character classes* where several bits are clustered and yield compact BDDs, such as \w (matches any word character), \W (matches any non-word character), \d (matches any decimal digit), p{Lu} (matches any single character in the Unicode general category Lu of uppercase letters), etc. There are a total of 30 general Unicode categories and the character class \w is a union of 7 of those categories (namely categories 0 (Lu), 1 (Ll), 2 (Lt), 3 (Lm), 4 (Lo), 8 (Nd) and 18 (Pc)). In total, the class \w *alone* denotes a set of characters consisting of 323 nonoverlapping ranges, totaling 47057 characters. Let β_p denote the BDD of a character pattern p. The BDD $\beta_{\backslash w}$ has 1656 nodes. Note that Boolean operations with the above set interpretation correspond directly to Boolean operations over BDDs.

As an example, consider the pattern [\w-[\da-d]], which denotes the set of all word characters that are neither decimal digits nor characters a through d, i.e., $\beta_{[\backslash w - [\backslash da - d]]} = \beta_{\backslash w} \cap \mathsf{C}(\beta_{\backslash d} \cup \beta_{a-d})$. We write $\llbracket \beta \rrbracket$ for the set of characters represented by β, thus for example $\llbracket \beta_1 \cap \beta_2 \rrbracket = \llbracket \beta_1 \rrbracket \cap \llbracket \beta_2 \rrbracket$. It is easy to write infeasible character patterns. For example, [\W-[\D]] denotes an empty set since $\llbracket \beta_{\backslash d} \rrbracket \subset \llbracket \beta_{\backslash w} \rrbracket$ and

$$\llbracket \beta_{\backslash w} \cap \mathsf{C}(\beta_{\backslash D}) \rrbracket = \llbracket \mathsf{C}(\beta_{\backslash w}) \cap \mathsf{C}(\mathsf{C}(\beta_{\backslash d})) \rrbracket = \mathsf{C}(\llbracket \beta_{\backslash w} \rrbracket) \cap \llbracket \beta_{\backslash d} \rrbracket.$$

Performing nonemptiness checking for BDDs is trivial because the empty BDD $\beta^\perp$ is unique. Similarly, the BDD of all characters $\beta^\top$ is unique. Except for $\beta^\perp$ and $\beta^\top$, two BDDs are not guaranteed to be identical by construction even though they are isomorphic when representing the same sets. However, checking isomorphism (equivalence) of BDDs is linear. Equivalence checking is used prior to calling the minterm algorithm in order to eliminate duplicate sets from the input sequence.

Character sets as bitvector predicates. A common alternative representation for character sets is to use interval arithmetic over bitvectors or integers. Here we assume that we are working in the context of a constraint solver that provides built-in support for bit vectors. We write BV^n for the sort of characters used by the solver, which is assumed to be a sort of n-bit vectors for a given fixed $n \in \{7, 8, 16\}$. Standard logic operations as well as standard arithmetic operations over BV^n, such as '$\leq$', are assumed to be built-in and can be used to form predicates for expressing character ranges. Let $\varphi_\mathrm{p}(\chi)$ denote a predicate (with a single *fixed* free variable $\chi{:}\mathrm{BV}^n$) corresponding to the regex character pattern p and let $[\![\varphi_\mathrm{p}]\!]$ denote the set of all characters a for which $\varphi_\mathrm{p}(a)$ is true modulo the built-in theories. For example, consider BV^7 and the character pattern \w, the predicate $\varphi_{\backslash\mathrm{w}}$ is as follows where each disjunct corresponds to a Unicode category (the Unicode categories 2 , 3 and 4 are empty for the ASCII character range):

$$(\text{'A'} \leq \chi \wedge \chi \leq \text{'Z'}) \vee (\text{'a'} \leq \chi \wedge \chi \leq \text{'z'}) \vee (\text{'0'} \leq \chi \wedge \chi \leq \text{'9'}) \vee \chi = \text{'\_'}$$

where '$..$' is the bitvector representation of a character. The Boolean operations are directly supported by the corresponding built-in logical operators. For example $[\![\varphi_{[\backslash\mathrm{w}-[\backslash\mathrm{d}a-d]]}]\!] = [\![\varphi_{\backslash\mathrm{w}} \wedge \neg(\varphi_{\backslash\mathrm{d}} \vee \varphi_{\mathrm{a}-\mathrm{d}})]\!] = [\![\varphi_{\backslash\mathrm{w}}]\!] \cap \complement([\![\varphi_{\backslash\mathrm{d}}]\!] \cup [\![\varphi_{\mathrm{a}-\mathrm{d}}]\!])$

For the ASCII range (or extended ASCII range), the direct range representation has several advantages by being succinct and taking advantage of the built-in optimizations of the underlying solver. Based on our experiments, however, for full Unicode the representation produces predicates that do not scale. Instead, we use *if-then-else* (*Ite*) terms, supported in all state-of-the-art constraint solvers, to encode *Shannon expansions*, thus mimicking BDDs. An *Ite*-term is a term $Ite(\psi, t_1, t_2)$ that equals t_1, if ψ is true; equals t_2, otherwise. We explain the main idea. Given a BDD β the corresponding predicate $Ite[\beta]$ is constructed as follows where all shared subterms are constructed only once (and cached) and are thus maximally shared in the resulting term of the solver. Given a BDD β (other than $\beta^\perp$ or $\beta^\top$) we write $BitIs0(\beta)$ for the predicate over $\chi{:}\mathrm{BV}^n$, that is true if and only if the i'th bit of χ is 0, where $i = n - ordinal(\beta) - 1$ (recall that $ordinal(\beta)$ is the reverse bit position).

$$Ite[\beta] \stackrel{\text{def}}{=} \begin{cases} true, & \text{if } \beta = \beta^\top; \\ false, & \text{if } \beta = \beta^\perp; \\ Ite(BitIs0(\beta), Ite[Left(\beta)], Ite[Right(\beta)]), & \text{otherwise.} \end{cases}$$

It follows from the definition that $[\![\beta]\!] = [\![Ite[\beta]]\!]$.

A nonemptiness check of $[\![\varphi]\!]$ for a character predicate φ is conducted by checking whether the formula φ is *satisfiable* by using the constraint solver. For minterm generation we use an incremental constraint solving technique that is sometimes called *cube-formula* solving [26]. The core idea behind the technique is as follows:

Given a finite sequence of character formulas $\varphi = (\varphi_i)_{i<m}$ and distinct Boolean variables $\boldsymbol{b} = (b_i)_{i<m}$ define $Cube(\varphi, \boldsymbol{b}) \overset{\text{def}}{=} \bigwedge_{i<m} \varphi_i \Leftrightarrow b_i$. A *solution* of $Cube(\varphi, \boldsymbol{b})$ is an assignment M of truth values to $\boldsymbol{b}$ such that $M \models Cube(\varphi, \boldsymbol{b})$. Given a solution M of $Cube(\varphi, \boldsymbol{b})$, let $\varphi_M \overset{\text{def}}{=} \bigwedge_{i<m, M\models b_i} b_i \wedge \bigwedge_{i<m, M\models \neg b_i} \neg b_i$.

We use the following iterative model generation procedure to generate the set S of all solutions of $Cube(\varphi, \boldsymbol{b})$. Although the procedure is exponential in (n in) the *worst case* due to the inherent complexity of the problem, it seems to work well in practice [26]. The algorithm assumes that the solver is capable of model generation, rather than just checking existence of a model, which is the case for most state-of-the-art constraint solvers and in particular SMT solvers.

Minterm generation with cubes: Input is a nonempty sequence of satisfiable character predicates φ. Output is the set $\mathbf{M}$ of solutions of $Cube(\varphi, \boldsymbol{b})$.
   Initialize: Let $\mathbf{M}_0 = \emptyset$ and $\psi_0 = Cube(\varphi, \boldsymbol{b})$.
   Iterate: If ψ_i has a model M let $\mathbf{M}_{i+1} = \mathbf{M}_i \cup \{M\}$ and $\psi_{i+1} = \psi_i \wedge \neg \varphi_M$, otherwise let $\mathbf{M} = \mathbf{M}_i$ and stop.

3.2   Primitive Automata Algorithms

The algorithms on automata that we are most interested in, and that we will focus on here, are *product* $A \times B$ and *difference* $A - B$, where difference provides a way of checking *subset* constraints between regular expressions as well as doing *complementation* $\bar{B}$ such that $L(\bar{B}) = \Sigma^* \setminus L(B)$ and *determinization* of B, $Det(B)$, as special cases. The algorithms assume a representation of SFAs where move labels are symbolic and use a *character set solver* that provides the functionality discussed in Section 3.1. Both algorithms also have *lazy* versions that do not construct the full automaton: lazy difference is *subset checking* $L(A) \subseteq L(B)$ (with witness in $L(A) \setminus L(B)$ if $L(A) \subsetneq L(B)$), and lazy product is *disjointness checking* $L(A) \cap L(B) = \emptyset$ (with witness in $L(A) \cap L(B)$ if $L(A) \cap L(B) \neq \emptyset$). We do not describe the lazy versions explicitly, since, apart from not constructing the resulting automaton, they are similar to the eager versions.

The product algorithm is shown in Figure 4. Note that the character set solver is used for performing intersection and nonemptiness check on labels. The difference algorithm, shown in Figure 5, makes, in addition, essential use of minterm generation during an implicit determinization of the subtracted automaton B in $A - B$. Intuitively, the algorithm is a combined product and complementation algorithm. The main advantage of the combination is *early pruning of search stack S* by keeping the resulting automaton *clean*. In our implementation, the difference algorithm uses a standard set implementation to represent state sets, denoted by $State\{\dots\}$ in Figure 5, to represent subsets of automata states. The difference algorithm uses three different kinds of set data structures, each with

Input: ϵSFAs A and B over Σ.
Initialize: Eliminate epsilons from A and B.
    Let S be a stack, initially $S = (\langle q_A^0, q_B^0 \rangle)$.
    Let V be a hashtable, initially $V = \{\langle q_A^0, q_B^0 \rangle\}$.
    Let Δ be a hashtable, initially $\Delta = \emptyset$.
Search: While S is nonempty, repeat the following.
    Pop $\langle q_1, q_2 \rangle$ from S.
      For each $\rho_1 \in \Delta_A(q_1)$ and $\rho_2 \in \Delta_B(q_2)$, let $\ell = Lbl(\rho_1) \cap Lbl(\rho_2)$, if $\ell \neq \emptyset$:
        Let $p_1 = Tgt(\rho_1)$, $p_2 = Tgt(\rho_2)$ and add $(\langle q_1, q_2 \rangle, \ell, \langle p_1, p_2 \rangle)$ to Δ.
        If $\langle p_1, p_2 \rangle \notin V$ then add $\langle p_1, p_2 \rangle$ to V and push $\langle p_1, p_2 \rangle$ to S.
Output: $A \times B = (\langle q_A^0, q_B^0 \rangle, \Sigma, V, \{q \in V \mid q \in F_A \times F_B\}, \Delta)$.

Fig. 4. Product algorithm for symbolic automata. Constructs $A \times B$ such that $L(A \times B) = L(A) \cap L(B)$.

Input: ϵSFAs A and B over Σ.
Initialize: Eliminate epsilons from A and B and make B *total*.
    Let $q^0 = \langle q_A^0, State\{q_B^0\} \rangle$.
    Let S be a stack, initially $S = (q^0)$.
    Let V, F, and Δ be hashtables. Initially $V = \{q^0\}$ and $\Delta = \emptyset$.
    Initially $F = \{q^0\}$, if $q_A^0 \in F_A$ and $q_B^0 \notin F_B$; $F = \emptyset$, otherwise.
Search: While S is nonempty repeat the following.
    Pop $\langle p, Q \rangle$ from S. Let $\Delta_B(Q) = \{\rho_i\}_{i \in I}$ and let $\ell_i = Lbl(\rho_i)$ for $i \in I$.
    Compute minterms: Compute **M** as the set of all minterms of the sequence $(\ell_i)_{i \in I}$. Here
    minterms are given as subsets of I. For $J \in$ **M** let $\ell_J = \bigcap_{i \in J} \ell_i \cap \bigcap_{i \in I \setminus J} \complement(\ell_i)$.
    For each minterm $J \in$ **M:**
      For each A move $\rho \in \Delta_A(p)$ such that $Lbl(\rho) \cap \ell_J \neq \emptyset$:
        Let $P = State\{Tgt(\rho_i) \mid i \in J\}$.
        Let $q = \langle Tgt(\rho), P \rangle$.
        Add $(\langle p, Q \rangle, Lbl(\rho) \cap \ell_J, q)$ to Δ.
        If $q \notin V$ then add q to V and push q to S.
        If $Tgt(\rho) \in F_A$ and $P \cap F_B = \emptyset$ then add q to F.
Output: $A - B = (q^0, \Sigma, V, F, \Delta)$.

Fig. 5. Difference algorithm. Constructs $A - B$ such that $L(A - B) = L(A) \setminus L(B)$.

different strengths: character sets, state sets, and hashtables for algorithm variables, where the character set representation depends on the character set solver.

Note that the difference algorithm reduces to complementation of B when $L(A) = \Sigma^*$, e.g., when $A = (q_A^0, \Sigma, \{q_A^0\}, \{q_A^0\}, \{(q_A^0, \Sigma, q_A^0)\})$. Then the condition $Lbl(\rho) \cap \ell_J \neq \emptyset$ above is trivially true, since $Lbl(\rho) \cap \ell_J = \ell_J$, for $\rho \in \Delta_A$. Consequently, there is no pruning of the search stack S then with respect to A, and the full complement $\bar{B}$ is constructed. Moreover, $\bar{B}$ is *deterministic*, since for any two distinct moves $(\langle p, Q \rangle, \ell_J, q)$ and $(\langle p, Q \rangle, \ell_{J'}, q')$ that are added to Δ above, $\ell_J \cap \ell_{J'} = \emptyset$ by definition of minterms. It follows that the difference algorithm also provides a *determinization* algorithm for B: construct $\bar{B}$ as above and let $Det(B) = (q_{\bar{B}}^0, \Sigma_{\bar{B}}, Q_{\bar{B}}, Q_{\bar{B}} \setminus F_{\bar{B}}, \Delta_{\bar{B}})$.

4   Experiments

In this section we first compare the performance of the product and difference algorithms with respect to different character set representations and eager vs. lazy versions of the algorithms. For the predicate representation of character

	A_0	A_1	A_2	A_3	A_4	A_5	A_6	A_7	A_8	A_9
$|Q|$:	36	30	31	17	11	18	4573	104	2228	42
$|\Delta^\epsilon|$:	25	15	10	11	4	14	8852	99	3570	32
$|\Delta^f|$:	36	24	28	15	11	13	148	96	524	40

Fig. 6. Sizes of ϵSFAs A_{i-1} constructed for regexes #i for $1 \le i \le 10$ in [27, Table I], where each regex is assumed to have an implicit start-anchor ˆ and end-anchor $.

sets we use Z3 as the constraint solver. Integration with Z3 uses the .NET API that is publicly available [31]. All experiments were conducted on a laptop with an Intel dual core T7500 2.2GHz processor. We then compare the performance of our implementation with the dk.brics.automaton library that underlies the Java String Analyzer (JSA) [5].

Our experiment uses a set of ten benchmark regexes that have previously been used to evaluate string constraint solving tools [12,27]. The regexes are representative for various practical usages and originate from a case study [18]. The sizes of the automata constructed from the regexes are shown in Figure 6.

For each pair $(A_i, A_j)_{i,j<10}$ we conducted the following experiments to compare different character set representations, algorithmic choices, and the effect of the size of the alphabet. For product we ignored the order of the arguments due to commutativity, thus there are 55 pairs in total, and for difference there are 100 pairs in total. Figure 7 shows the evaluation results for the difference algorithm and the product algorithm, respectively. The times exclude the construction time of ϵSFAs from the regexes but *include* the epsilon elimination time to convert ϵSFAs to SFAs that is a preprocessing step in the algorithms. The total time to construct the ϵSFAs for the 10 regexes (including parsing) was 0.33 seconds (for both UTF16 as well as ASCII). For parsing the regexes we use the built-in regex parser in .NET.

The top columns correspond to the eager vs. lazy versions of the algorithms and the secondary columns correspond to whether the result is an empty automaton or a nonempty automaton. The rows correspond to the different algorithmic choices: *BDD-X* denotes the use of the BDD based solver where X is ASCII or UTF16; *Pred-ASCII* denotes the use of predicate encoding of character sets using Z3 predicates over BV^7; *Pred-UTF16* denotes the use of predicate encoding of character sets using Z3 *Ite*-term encodings of BDDs over BV^{16}; *Range-ASCII* denotes the use of standard range representation for ASCII character sets as *hashsets of character pairs*; *Hash-ASCII* denotes the use of *hashsets of individual characters* as character sets.

We excluded the evaluation results for most of the *Range-UTF16* and *Hash-UTF16* cases, since too many instances either timed out or caused an out-of-memory exception. The only case that completed for the same number of instances was lazy difference with *Range-UTF16* character set representation, but is approximately 70 times slower in total experiment time compared to *BDD-UTF16*. In the difference experiment, 5 instances either timed out or caused an out-of-memory exception, involving the automata A_6 and A_8 in all cases. One of the hardest instances that terminated was checking $L(A_8) \subseteq L(A_9)$ that took

	Eager		Lazy	
Difference	**Empty**	**Nonempty**	**Empty**	**Nonempty**
BDD-ASCII	(8).33/.007	(78)36/.008	(8).33/.006	(87)41/.001
BDD-UTF16	(8).56/.02	(78)38/.02	(8).52/.012	(87)41/.01
Pred-ASCII	(8)1.6/.06	(78)72/.08	(8)1.6/.06	(87)58/.02
Pred-UTF16	(8)5.5/.12	(78)179/.24	(8)5.3/.12	(87)66/.11
Range-ASCII	(8).9/.03	(78)67/.03	(8)1/.03	(87)44/.003
Hash-ASCII	(8).9/.03	(78)67/.03	(8)1/.03	(87)45/.003
brics-ASCII	(9)32/.015	(72)273/.016		
brics-UTF16	(9)39/.11	(72)341/.44		

	Eager		Lazy	
Product	**Empty**	**Nonempty**	**Empty**	**Nonempty**
BDD-ASCII	(29)9.7/.001	(26)90/.002	(29)9.7/.001	(26)19/.001
BDD-UTF16	(29)9.7/.001	(26)92/.003	(29)9.7/.001	(26)19/.001
Pred-ASCII	(29)10/.003	(26)142/.003	(29)10/.004	(26)25/.007
Pred-UTF16	(29)10/.01	(26)150/.05	(29)10/.01	(26)25/.03
Range-ASCII	(29)10/.002	(23)16/.005	(29)10/.002	(26)69/.001
Hash-ASCII	(29)10/.002	(23)16/.005	(29)10/.002	(26)70/.001
brics-ASCII	(25)66/.015	(19)65/.016		
brics-UTF16	(25)66/.03	(19)70/.09		

Fig. 7. Experimental evaluation of the SFA algorithms. Each entry in the tables has the form $(n)t/m$ where n is the *number of combinations solved*, t is the *total time* it took to solve the n instances, m is the *median*. Time is in seconds. For product, the eager experiment constructs $A_i \times A_j$ for $0 \le i \le j < 10$; the lazy experiment tests emptiness of $L(A_i) \cap L(A_j)$ for $0 \le i \le j < 10$. For difference, the eager experiment constructs $A_i - A_j$ for $0 \le i, j < 10$; the lazy experiment tests if $L(A_i) \subseteq L(A_j)$ $(L(A_i - A_j) = \emptyset)$ for $0 \le i, j < 10$. Timeout for each instance (i, j) was 20 min.

14 minutes with *Range-UTF16* and 1.3 seconds with *BDD-UTF16*, where the minterm generation algorithm is used heavily.

With the BDD representation, the size of the alphabet turns out not to play a major role in the algorithms, although the BDD sizes are typically considerably larger for UTF16 (hundreds or even thousands of nodes) compared to ASCII (tens of nodes). This is a useful indication that BDDs work surprisingly well as character sets and may even work for UTF32 encoding (which we have not tried). In several non-BDD cases, many individual experiments timed out. The BDD character set based algorithms are an *order of magnitude faster in the median for UTF16*. As expected, all the lazy versions of the algorithms are faster in the nonempty case. The eager constructions are however needed when converting the resulting SFAs to *symbolic language acceptors* for combination with other theories [27]. Symbolic language acceptors for SFAs are made use of for example in the parameterized unit testing framework Pex [23], where regexes are handled in branch conditions of .NET programs using SFAs with Pred-UTF16 representation of character sets, integration of the algorithms in this paper into Pex is currently ongoing work.[2]

[2] http://www.rise4fun.com/

Comparison with `brics`. For this comparison we first serialized the automata A_i, $i < 10$, in textual format. This is for two reasons: 1) to provide a fair comparison *at the level of automata algorithms*, i.e., to exclude differences in the automata constructed from the regexes; 2) to avoid semantic differences regarding the meaning of the notations used in the regexes. In the measurements we bootstrapped the automata by excluding the time to deserialize and to reconstruct the automata in *brics*, but included the time to add epsilon transitions (that add extra character interval transitions), as this is effectively equivalent to epsilon elimination using the *brics* library.

The Java code responsible for the lazy difference experiment is

```
... construct Ai, Aj, epsAi, epsAj ...
long t = System.currentTimeMillis();
boolean empty = (Ai.addEpsilons(epsAi)).subsetOf(Aj.addEpsilons(epsAj));
t = System.currentTimeMillis() - t;
```

using the `brics.Automaton` method `subsetOf`. The eager experiment used the `brics.Automaton` method `minus`. The code for the product experiment is similar (using `intersection`). For running each instance we assigned 1.5GB to the java runtime (which was the maximum possible). For all cases involving A_6, the product and difference experiments timed out or caused an out-of-memory exception. For the product experiment all cases involving A_8 also timed out. The instance $L(A_8) \subseteq L(A_8)$ did not time out using brics, while caused an out-of-memory exception using our tool during minterm generation.

	Product		Difference	
	Empty	Nonempty	Empty	Nonempty
BDD-ASCII	.022/.001	.024/.001	.32/.005	.33/.001
BDD-UTF16	.022/.001	.024/.001	.54/.015	.78/.002
Pred-ASCII	.07/.003	.07/.004	1.6/.06	2/.01
Pred-UTF16	.2/.01	.2/.01	5.2/.12	8.2/.05
brics-ASCII	.14/.001	.2/.015	.1/.016	.8/.016
brics-UTF16	.6/.03	1.4/.05	3.6/.05	24.8/.08

Fig. 8. Lazy difference and product experiment times with A_6 and A_8 excluded. Each entry is *total/median* in seconds. For product, 21 instances are empty and 15 instances are nonempty. For difference, 8 instances are empty and 56 instances are nonempty.

For a better comparison of the easy cases we conducted a separate experiment where both A_6 and A_8 are excluded from the experiments and considered the lazy versions only. Thus, there are total of 36 product instances and 64 difference instances. The outcome of this experiment is shown in Figure 8. Let t_X^{op} denote the total time for experiment row X and operation op in Figure 8. Then:

$$t^{\text{prod}}_{\text{brics}-\text{ASCII}}/t^{\text{prod}}_{\text{BDD}-\text{ASCII}} \approx 7, \quad t^{\text{prod}}_{\text{brics}-\text{UTF16}}/t^{\text{prod}}_{\text{BDD}-\text{UTF16}} \approx 43,$$
$$t^{\text{diff}}_{\text{brics}-\text{ASCII}}/t^{\text{diff}}_{\text{BDD}-\text{ASCII}} \approx 1.4, \quad t^{\text{diff}}_{\text{brics}-\text{UTF16}}/t^{\text{diff}}_{\text{BDD}-\text{UTF16}} \approx 21.$$

5   Related Work

In this section we discuss related work, focusing on automated reasoning techniques; Figure 9 provides a brief overview. DPRLE [11] has two associated implementations: a fully verified core algorithm written in Gallina [6], and the OCaml implementation used for the experiments. The Gallina specification is designed primarily to help discharge proof obligations (using Coq's built-in inversion lemmas for cons lists, for example). This specification is of limited interest, since it is not actually designed to be executed. The OCaml implementation relies heavily on OCaml's built-in hashtable data structure. The transition function is modeled using two separate mappings: one for character-consuming transitions (state -> state -> character set) and one for ϵ–transitions (state -> state set). This representation reflects the fact that the main DPRLE algorithms rely heavily on tracking states across automaton operations [11].

The Rex tool provides a SFA representation that is similar to the formal definition given in Section 2. The core idea, based on work by van Noord and Gerdeman [22], is to represent automaton transitions using logical predicates. Rex works in the context of *symbolic language acceptors*, which are first-order encodings of symbolic automata into the theory of algebraic datatypes. The Rex implementation uses the Z3 satisfiability modulo theories(SMT) solver [7] to solve the produced constraints. The encoding process and solving process are completely disjoint. This means that many operations, like automaton intersection, can be offloaded to the underlying solver. For example, to find a string w that matches two regular expressions, r_1 and r_2, Rex can simply assert the existence of w, generate symbolic automaton encodings for r_1 and r_2, and assert that s is accepted by both those automata. We refer to this as a *Boolean encoding* of the string constraints.

The initial Rex work [27] explores various optimizations, such as minimizing the symbolic automata prior to encoding them. These optimizations make use of the underlying SMT solver to find combinations of edges that have internally-consistent move conditions. Subsequent work [26] explored the trade-off between the Boolean encoding and the use of automata-specific algorithms for language intersection and language difference. In this case, the automata-specific algorithms make repeated calls to Z3 to solve *cube formulae* to enumerate edges

Technique Name	Data structure	Corresponds to
Christensen, Moller, et al. (JSA) [5]	Char. ranges (Java, Unicode)	Eager Range
Hooimeijer and Weimer (DPRLE) [11]	Single-char. hashset (OCaml; ASCII)	Eager Hashset
Hooimeijer and Weimer [12]	Char. ranges (C++; ASCII)	Lazy Range
Minamide [21,28]	Single-char. functional set (OCaml; ASCII)	Eager Hashset
Veanes, Halleux, and Tillmann [27]	Unary pred. (C# and Z3[31]; Unicode)	Lazy predicate
Henriksen, Jensen, et al. [10,29]	BDDs C	Eager BDD

Fig. 9. Existing automata-based string analyses and, the data structures they use, and the closest-matching experimental prototype tested in this paper

with co-satisfiable constraints. In practice, this approach is not consistently faster than the Boolean encoding.

The Java String Analyzer (JSA) by Christensen *et al.* [5] uses finite automata internally to represent strings. The underlying dk.brics.automaton library is not presented as a constraint solving tool, but it is used in that way. The library represents automata using a pointer-based graph representation of node and edge objects; edges represent contiguous character ranges. The library, which is written in Java, includes a deterministic automaton representation that is specialized for matching given strings efficiently. This is not a common use case for constraint solving, since the goal there is to efficiently *find* string assignments rather than verify them. Several other approaches include a built-in model of string operations; Minamide [21] and Wassermann and Su [28] rely on an ad-hoc OCaml implementation that uses that language's built-in applicative data structures.

In previous work, we present a lazy backtracking search algorithm for solving regular inclusion constraints [12]. The underlying automaton representation, written in C++, is based on the Boost Graph Library [25], which allows for a variety of adjacency list representations. We annotate transitions with integer ranges, similar to JSA. The implementation pays special attention to memory management, using fast pool allocation for small objects such as the abstract syntax tree for regular expressions. This implementation uses lazy algorithms intersection and determinization algorithms, allowing for significant performance benefits relative to DPRLE [11] and the original Rex [27] implementation.

Other Approaches. Bjørner *et al.* describe a set of string constraints based on common string library functions [2]. The approach is based on a direct encoding to a combination of theories provided by the Z3 SMT solver [7]. Supported operations include substring extraction (and, in general, the combination of integer constraints with string constraints), but the work does not provide an encoding for regular sets.

The Hampi tool [15] uses an eager bitvector encoding from regular expressions to bitvector logic. The encoding does not use quantification, and requires the enumeration of all positional shifts for every subexpression. The Kaluza tool extends this approach to systems of constraints with multiple variables and concatenation [24].

The MONA implementation [10] provides decision procedures for several varieties of monadic second–order logic (M2L). MONA relies on a highly-optimized BDD-based representation for automata. The implementation has seen extensive engineering effort; many of the optimizations are described in a separate paper [16]. We are not aware of any work that investigates the use of multiterminal BDDs for nondeterministic finite automata directly. In this paper, we restrict our attention to a class of graph-based automata representations.

There is a wide range of application domains that, at some level, rely on implicit or explicit automata representations. Fang *et al.* [30] use an automaton-based method to model string constraints and length bounds for abstract interpretation. There is significant work on using automata for arithmetic constraint solving; Boigelot and Wolper provide an overview [4]. A subset of work on explicit state space model checking (e.g., [3]) has focused on general algorithms to perform fast state space reduction. Similarly, there is theoretical work on word equations that involves automata [1,17], as well as algorithms work on the efficient construction of automata from regular expressions (e.g., [14]).

6   Conclusions

In this paper we presented a study of automata representations for efficient intersection and difference constructions. We conducted this study to evaluate which combination of data structures and algorithms is most effective in the context of string constraint solving. Existing work in this area has consistently included performance comparisons at the tool level, but has been largely inconclusive regarding which automata representations work best in general. To answer this question, we re-implemented a number of data structures in the same language (C#) using a front-end parser that correctly handles a large subset of .NET's regular expression language, and using a UTF-16 alphabet. Our experiments showed that, over the sample inputs under consideration, the BDD-based representation provides the best performance when paired with the lazy versions of the intersection and difference algorithms. This suggests that future string decision procedure work can achieve significant direct benefits by using this combination of data structure (BDD) and algorithm (lazy) as a starting point. To the best of our knowledge, no existing tools currently use this combination.

Acknowledgment. We thank Nikolaj Bjørner for discussions that lead to the BDD character set representation idea and for continuous support with Z3.

References

1. Bala, S.: Regular language matching and other decidable cases of the satisfiability problem for constraints between regular open terms. In: Diekert, V., Habib, M. (eds.) STACS 2004. LNCS, vol. 2996, pp. 596–607. Springer, Heidelberg (2004)
2. Bjørner, N., Tillmann, N., Voronkov, A.: Path feasibility analysis for string-manipulating programs. In: Kowalewski, S., Philippou, A. (eds.) TACAS 2009. LNCS, vol. 5505, pp. 307–321. Springer, Heidelberg (2009)
3. Blom, S., Orzan, S.: Distributed state space minimization. J. Software Tools for Technology Transfer 7(3), 280–291 (2005)
4. Boigelot, B., Wolper, P.: Representing arithmetic constraints with finite automata: An overview. In: Stuckey, P.J. (ed.) ICLP 2002. LNCS, vol. 2401, pp. 1–19. Springer, Heidelberg (2002)
5. Christensen, A.S., Møller, A., Schwartzbach, M.I.: Precise Analysis of String Expressions. In: Cousot, R. (ed.) SAS 2003. LNCS, vol. 2694, pp. 1–18. Springer, Heidelberg (2003)
6. Coquand, T., Huet, G.P.: The calculus of constructions. Information and Computation 76(2/3), 95–120 (1988)
7. de Moura, L., Bjørner, N.S.: Z3: An Efficient SMT Solver. In: Ramakrishnan, C.R., Rehof, J. (eds.) TACAS 2008. LNCS, vol. 4963, pp. 337–340. Springer, Heidelberg (2008)

8. Godefroid, P., Kieżun, A., Levin, M.Y.: Grammar-based whitebox fuzzing. In: PLDI 2008, Tucson, AZ, USA, June 9-11 (2008)
9. Godefroid, P., Klarlund, N., Sen, K.: DART: directed automated random testing. In: PLDI 2005, pp. 213–223 (2005)
10. Henriksen, J.G., Jensen, J., Jørgensen, M., Klarlund, N., Paige, B., Rauhe, T., Sandholm, A.: Mona: Monadic second-order logic in practice. In: Brinksma, E., Steffen, B., Cleaveland, W.R., Larsen, K.G., Margaria, T. (eds.) TACAS 1995. LNCS, vol. 1019. Springer, Heidelberg (1995)
11. Hooimeijer, P., Weimer, W.: A decision procedure for subset constraints over regular languages. In: PLDI, pp. 188–198 (2009)
12. Hooimeijer, P., Weimer, W.: Solving string constraints lazily. In: ASE 2010 (2010)
13. Hopcroft, J.E., Ullman, J.D.: Introduction to Automata Theory, Languages, and Computation. Addison-Wesley, Reading (1979)
14. Ilie, L., Yu, S.: Follow automata. Information and Computation 186(1), 140–162 (2003)
15. Kieżun, A., Ganesh, V., Guo, P.J., Hooimeijer, P., Ernst, M.D.: HAMPI: a solver for string constraints. In: ISSTA 2009, pp. 105–116. ACM, New York (2009)
16. Klarlund, N., Møller, A., Schwartzbach, M.I.: MONA implementation secrets. International Journal of Foundations of Computer Science 13(4), 571–586 (2002)
17. Kunc, M.: What do we know about language equations? In: Harju, T., Karhumäki, J., Lepistö, A. (eds.) DLT 2007. LNCS, vol. 4588, pp. 23–27. Springer, Heidelberg (2007)
18. Li, N., Xie, T., Tillmann, N., de Halleux, P., Schulte, W.: Reggae: Automated test generation for programs using complex regular expressions. In: ASE 2009 (2009)
19. MSDN Library. System.text namespace, http://msdn.microsoft.com/en-us/library/system.text.aspx
20. PHP Manual. Pcre; posix regex; strings, http://php.net/manual/en/book.strings.php
21. Minamide, Y.: Static approximation of dynamically generated web pages. In: WWW 2005, pp. 432–441 (2005)
22. Van Noord, G., Gerdemann, D.: Finite state transducers with predicates and identities. Grammars 4 (2001)
23. Pex, http://research.microsoft.com/projects/pex
24. Saxena, P., Akhawe, D., Hanna, S., Mao, F., McCamant, S., Song, D.: A symbolic execution framework for javascript. In: SP 2010. IEEE Computer Society, Los Alamitos (2010)
25. Siek, J.G., Lee, L.-Q., Lumsdaine, A.: The Boost Graph Library: User Guide and Reference Manual. Addison-Wesley Professional, Reading (2001)
26. Veanes, M., Bjørner, N., de Moura, L.: Symbolic automata constraint solving. In: Fermüller, C.G., Voronkov, A. (eds.) LPAR-17. LNCS, vol. 6397, pp. 640–654. Springer, Heidelberg (2010)
27. Veanes, M., de Halleux, P., Tillmann, N.: Rex: Symbolic Regular Expression Explorer. In: ICST 2010. IEEE, Los Alamitos (2010)
28. Wassermann, G., Su, Z.: Sound and precise analysis of web applications for injection vulnerabilities. In: PLDI 2007, pp. 32–41. ACM, New York (2007)
29. Yu, F., Alkhalaf, M., Bultan, T.: An automata-based string analysis tool for PHP. In: Esparza, J., Majumdar, R. (eds.) TACAS 2010. LNCS, vol. 6015, pp. 154–157. Springer, Heidelberg (2010)
30. Yu, F., Bultan, T., Ibarra, O.H.: Symbolic string verification: Combining string analysis and size analysis. In: Kowalewski, S., Philippou, A. (eds.) TACAS 2009. LNCS, vol. 5505, pp. 322–336. Springer, Heidelberg (2009)
31. Z3, http://research.microsoft.com/projects/z3

Automata Learning with Automated Alphabet Abstraction Refinement[*]

Falk Howar, Bernhard Steffen, and Maik Merten

University of Dortmund, Chair of Programming Systems,
Otto-Hahn-Str. 14, 44227 Dortmund, Germany
Tel.: ++49-231-755-7759; Fax: ++49-231-755-5802
{falk.howar,steffen,maik.merten}@cs.tu-dortmund.de

Abstract. Abstraction is the key when learning behavioral models of
realistic systems, but also the cause of a major problem: the introduction
of non-determinism. In this paper, we introduce a method for refining a
given abstraction to automatically regain a deterministic behavior on-
the-fly during the learning process. Thus the control over abstraction
becomes part of the learning process, with the effect that detected non-
determinism does not lead to failure, but to a dynamic alphabet abstraction refinement. Like automata learning itself, this method in general
is neither sound nor complete, but it also enjoys similar convergence
properties even for infinite systems as long as the concrete system itself
behaves deterministically, as illustrated along a concrete example.

1 Introduction

Most systems in use today lack adequate specifications or make use of underspecified components. In fact, the much propagated component-based software
design style naturally leads to under specified systems, as most libraries only provide very partial specifications of their components. We observed this dilemma
in the telecommunication area: specifications of telecommunication protocols are
usually provided as natural language text documents with no formal link to the
actual implementation. This hampers the application of any kind of formal validation techniques like model based testing [8] or model checking [11], and it
makes it hard to keep them up to date. Automata learning techniques [16] have
been proposed to overcome this situation, by allowing to construct and later
update behavioral models automatically. This has been illustrated in a number of case studies like e.g. the above mentioned concrete setting of Computer
Telephony Integrated (CTI) systems [17,16], for Web Services [22], protocol specifications [23] or communication protocol entities [7].

All these scenarios had one thing in common: the learned systems were 'wrapped'
in a kind of test harness, which in addition to providing access to the system to

---

[*] This work was partially supported by the European Union FET Project CON-
NECT: Emergent Connectors for Eternal Software Intensive Networked Systems
(http://connect-forever.eu/).

R. Jhala and D. Schmidt (Eds.): VMCAI 2011, LNCS 6538, pp. 263–277, 2011.
© Springer-Verlag Berlin Heidelberg 2011

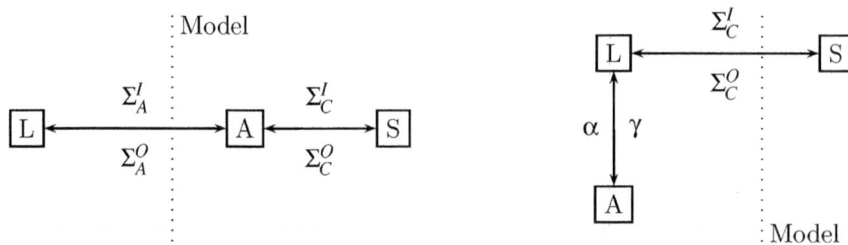

Fig. 1. Traditional use of abstraction (left) and abstraction as part of the learning process (right)

be learned also took care of the abstraction inherent in the definition of the considered behavioral perspective, like hiding certain parameters, abstracting time to causality, or treating certain resources (e.g., phones) symbolically. This meant that the learning algorithm was not confronted with the real system, but only with its wrapper-based abstraction (see left half of Fig. 1), whose adequacy therefore was critical to the success of the whole learning enterprise. In the figure, Σ^I denotes an input alphabet and Σ^O an output alphabet. By *Sigma$_C$* we denote an alphabet at the concrete level, while Σ_A refers to an abstract (symbolic) alphabet. As the employed active learning techniques assume a deterministic behavior, this meant in particular that this abstraction (from Σ_C to Σ_A) had to impose a deterministic behavior on the concrete system. This is a very strong requirement when dealing with black box systems, which led to many manual modifications of the wrapper in the course of a single learning experiment; each one requiring a complete restart of the learning process, using the refined alphabet.

In this paper we propose a method to automatically refine a given abstraction until a level is reached where this abstraction imposes a deterministic behavior on the concrete system. Like automata learning itself, this method is in general neither sound nor complete, but it also enjoys similar convergence properties even for infinite systems (in fact, both the alphabet and the state set of the concrete systems may by infinite) as long as the concrete system itself behaves deterministically. Key to this method is the switch from the learning scenario shown in the left of Fig. 1 to the one in the right, which allows the learning algorithm (L) to control the abstraction. Technically this is achieved by a change of perspective: Rather than working at the abstract level, the learner is sitting now at the concrete level in order to observe the concrete system behavior for a set of representatives of the equivalence classes imposed by the abstraction. Thus abstraction is no longer a 'filter' between the concrete system and the learning algorithm, but rather a teacher, helping the learner to choose adequate representative tests. This learner is able to automatically resolve *controllable* non-determinism, i.e. non-determinism which is due to the imposed abstraction. Thus the control over abstraction becomes part of the learning process, with the effect that detected non-determinism does not lead to failure, but to a dynamic refinement of the abstraction.

Related Work: We are not aware of any learning framework exploiting alphabet abstraction refinement for treating the problem of undesired non-determinism. Closest is the work reported in [14], where the learning alphabet is automatically refined (i.e. extended) to capture previously missing aspects of system interaction during learning-based assume guarantee reasoning [12]. In contrast, our notion refinement concerns the granularity of an abstraction. This notion is reminiscent of predicate abstraction as presented in [10,18] for model checking, and specifically used as a preprocess for learning in [2].

However, in contrast to these approaches, which are white box in the sense that a concrete system description is available, our approach is black box, and therefore requires a 'behavioral' description of the equivalence classes of the refined abstractions in terms of witnesses (cf. Section 3). We expect that this approach will be particularly fruitful when dealing with parameterized resp. abstract alphabets (cf. [5,6,15,26]).

Outline: In Section 2 we introduce the theoretical framework we use for alphabet abstraction refinement and show the existence of a coarsest deterministic alphabet abstraction. Section 3 presents the integration of the proposed abstraction refinement into existing active learning algorithms, while Section 4 discusses an illustrating example scenario, before we conclude in the final section.

2   Alphabet Abstraction Refinement

Mealy automata have turned out to be a very good automata model for learning in practice, and, indeed, also in this paper we will use them in the later parts. However for the ease of exposition, we will introduce our new method for *alphabet abstraction refinement* (AAR) first for the structurally simpler setting of deterministic automata. Please note that we do not require the finiteness of the alphabet or the set of states. They are not necessary for the correctness of the method, but only for the convergence of the corresponding algorithm. The subsequent generalization to the setting of (countable) Mealy automata is then straightforward.

In order to emphasize that the systems we are aiming at do not need to be finite state themselves, we directly introduce the following notion of countable automata. Of course, automata which we produce will continue to be finite state: they are finite state views/approximations of potentially infinite state systems. This is why we prefer to call this learning process regular extrapolation (see also RERS challenge [9]).

Definition 1. *A deterministic countable automaton (DCA) is a tuple $Sys = \langle Q, q_0, \Sigma, \delta, F \rangle$ where*

- *Q is a countable nonempty set of states,*
- *$q_0 \in Q$ is the initial state,*
- *Σ is a countable alphabet,*

- $\delta : Q \times \Sigma \rightarrow Q$ is the transition function, and
- $F \subseteq Q$ is the set of accepting states.

Intuitively, a DCA evolves through states $q \in Q$, and whenever one applies an input symbol (or action) $a \in \Sigma$, the machine moves to a new state according to $\delta(q,a)$. A word $w \in \Sigma^*$ is accepted by the DCA if and only if the DCA reaches an accepting state $q_i \in F$ after processing the word starting from its initial state. We write $q \xrightarrow{a} q'$ to denote that on input symbol a the DCA moves from state q to state q'. The transition function $\delta : Q \times \Sigma \rightarrow Q$ can be extended to $\delta' : Q \times \Sigma^* \rightarrow Q$ such that for all states $q, q' \in Q$ letters $a \in \Sigma$ and words $w \in \Sigma^*$ the following holds: $\delta'(q,\varepsilon) = q$, and $\delta'(q,aw) = \delta'(\delta(q,a),w)$.

2.1   A Sketch of Classical Automata Learning

Automata learning tries to construct a deterministic automaton representation that matches the behavior of a given target automaton on the basis of observations of the target automaton and optionally some further information on its internal structure. *Active* learning algorithms [3,4] learn finite state acceptors or Mealy machines by *actively* posing *membership* queries and *equivalence* queries to the target automaton in order to extract behavioral information, and by refining successively an hypothesis-automaton based on the answers. A membership query collects the output that a string (a potential run) will produce on the automaton, and an equivalence query compares the hypothesis automaton with the target automaton for equivalence, in order to determine whether the learning procedure was successfully completed. In this case experimentation can stop.

In principle, learning starts with a one state hypothesis automaton that treats all words over the considered alphabet (of elementary observations) alike and refines this automaton on the basis of query results iterating two steps. Here, the dual way of how states are characterized is central:

- by words reaching them. A prefix-closed set S of words reaching each state of an automaton exactly once defines a spanning tree of the automaton. The algorithm will construct such a set S. Extending the spanning tree to also contain all the one-letter continuations of the words in S (referred to as $SA(= S \times \Sigma)$) will result in a tree covering also all the transitions of the automaton.
- by their future behavior wrt. a dynamically increasing vector of strings from Σ^*. Let this vector be denoted by D. This characterization is too coarse throughout the learning process and will be refined continuously following the pattern of the well-known Nerode congruence [21].

During the learning process, membership queries are used to refine the current hypothesis. Every time a stable hypothesis (closed under the transition function) exists, an equivalence query is performed. In case the hypothesis is not equivalent to the target system, a counterexample highlighting some difference is returned and exploited to further refine the hypothesis.

The following section introduces the notion of *determinism preserving abstraction* (DPA) and states that any abstraction has a unique greatest DPA. Our learning algorithm, subsequently presented in Section 3, resolves detected non-determinism of a given abstraction by (optimal) refinement. Rather than failing in response to non-determinism, the algorithm automatically also 'learns' the corresponding greatest DPA.

2.2 Determinism Preserving Abstraction

Assume an unknown DCA *Sys* together with a finite abstraction given in terms of a pair of adjoint functions (α, γ), i.e., $\alpha : \Sigma_C \to \Sigma_A$, where sets annotated with C denote sets of (potentially infinite) concrete alphabet symbols and sets annotated with A denote sets of finite abstract input symbols. The set of abstract input symbols Σ_A will evolve throughout the learning process according to the refinement in response to detected non-determinism. The concretization function $\gamma : \Sigma_A \to \Sigma_C$ is required to satisfy that $\gamma \circ \alpha$ is the identity: i.e., each $\gamma(a)$ has to be an element of $\alpha^{-1}(a)$.

Like for verification, when learning behavioral models of real systems, finding the right level of abstraction is essential. It is necessary to make the learning problem tractable, and it allows one to automatically arrive at tailored views focusing on the parts of interest. Let us therefore assume that Σ_A is a finite abstraction of the concrete alphabet Σ_C, identifying what we would like to distinguish of the behavior of *Sys*, and $\alpha : \Sigma_C \to \Sigma_A$ is the corresponding (abstraction) function. By α-equivalence we denote the equivalence relation $\equiv_\alpha$ over Σ_C^* induced by α, i.e.:

$$\forall v, w \in \Sigma^* \, . \, v =_\alpha w \iff |v| - |w| \wedge \forall 1 \leq i \leq |v|. \, \alpha(v_i) = \alpha(w_i)$$

Typical prerequisite of active learning techniques is that there exists a deterministic acceptor (the *membership oracle*) for individual behaviors (words). Unfortunately, even if *Sys* itself would be such a deterministic acceptor[1], its abstraction to observations in Σ_A^* is in general not deterministic, i.e., there exist words $w_1, w_2 \in \Sigma_C^*$ with

- *Sys* accepts w_1 but rejects w_2 and
- w_1 and w_2 are α-equivalent.

This has the fatal effect that typical active learning solutions would simply fail in their attempt to learn the behavior at this level of abstraction. For the rest of this section we will show that there exists a 'best' or coarsest intermediate abstraction $\alpha_{c,o} : \Sigma_C \to \Sigma_{c,o}$ which refines α in a deterministic fashion, i.e.:

$$\forall w_1, w_2 \in \Sigma^* \, . \, w_1 \equiv_\alpha w_2 \implies (w_1 \in L(Sys) = w_2 \in L(Sys))$$

Abstractions like this are said to *preserve determinism*.

---

[1] Indeed, in practice one tests the real system to check for membership, and in most scenarios, the concrete system is supposed to have deterministic behavior.

The following corollary to our main theorem (Theorem 1) formulates concisely the backbone of our enhanced learning algorithm, which on demand refines the considered abstraction in an 'optimal' fashion, while in particular avoiding any problems due to non-determinism introduced by the abstraction (see Section 3). The corollary could also be proved as an independent theorem using lattice theoretic arguments. On the other hand, it is a direct consequence of the more constructive argument underlying the correctness proof for our enhanced partition refinement algorithm.

Corollary 1 (DCA: Alphabet Abstraction Refinement)
Let $Sys = \langle Q, q, \Sigma_C, \delta, F \rangle$ be a DCA and $\alpha : \Sigma_C \rightarrow \Sigma_A$ a (finite abstraction) function. Then there exists an (abstraction) function $\alpha_{c,o} : \Sigma_C \rightarrow \Sigma_{c,o}$ refining α in a deterministic fashion with

- *$\exists \alpha_o . \ \alpha = \alpha_o \circ \alpha_{c,o}$ and*
- *for all abstractions $\alpha_d : \Sigma_C \rightarrow \Sigma_d$ imposing a deterministic behavior on Sys, we have: $\exists \alpha_r : \Sigma_d \rightarrow \Sigma_A . \ \alpha = \alpha_r \circ \alpha_d \implies \exists \alpha_{r'} : \Sigma_d \rightarrow \Sigma_{c,o}. \ \alpha_{c,o} = \alpha_{r'} \circ \alpha_d$.*

The following section generalizes this theorem to fit the further development of this paper. The resulting theorem, which works for countable Mealy machines (see below), is then proved in parallel with the presentation of the partition refinement algorithm for constructing the greatest determinism preserving abstraction in Section 3.

In order to show that such 'optimal' abstractions also exist in the slightly more complicated setting of Mealy automata, let us first pinpoint the essence of the difference. Rather than accepting words, Mealy automata produce an output after processing an (input) word. As in the case of DCA, we generalized the notion to allow countable sets of alphabets and states.

Definition 2. *A countable Mealy machine (CMM) is defined as a tuple $Sys = \langle Q, q_0, \Sigma, \Omega, \delta, \lambda \rangle$ where*

- *Q is a countable nonempty set of states,*
- *$q_0 \in Q$ is the initial state,*
- *Σ is a countable input alphabet,*
- *Ω is a finite output alphabet,*
- *$\delta : Q \times \Sigma \rightarrow Q$ is the transition function, and*
- *$\lambda : Q \times \Sigma \rightarrow \Omega$ is the output function.*

Intuitively, a countable Mealy machine evolves through states $q \in Q$, and whenever one applies an input symbol (or action) $a \in \Sigma$, the machine moves to a new state according to $\delta(q,a)$ and produces an output according to $\lambda(q,a)$.

One can regard DCAs as CMMs whose output alphabet has just two symbols, one for acceptance and one for rejection. With this intuition in mind it is not surprising that the corresponding corollary looks almost identical.

Corollary 2 (CMM: Alphabet Abstraction Refinement)
Let $Sys = \langle Q, q_0, \Sigma_C, \Omega, \delta, \gamma \rangle$ be an deterministic CMM and $\alpha : \Sigma_C \to \Sigma_A$ an arbitrary (abstraction) function. Then there exists an (abstraction) function $\alpha_{c,o} : \Sigma_C \to \Sigma_{C,o}$ refining α in an deterministic fashion with

- $\exists \alpha_o \, . \, \alpha = \alpha_o \circ \alpha_{c,o}$ *and*
- *for all abstractions $\alpha_d : \Sigma_C \to \Sigma_d$ imposing a deterministic behavior on Sys, we have: $\exists \alpha_r : \Sigma_d \to \Sigma_A \, . \, \alpha = \alpha_r \circ \alpha_d \implies \exists \alpha_{r'} : \Sigma_d \to \Sigma_{C,o}. \; \alpha_{c,o} = \alpha_{r'} \circ \alpha_d$*

We will provide a partition refinement algorithm for the construction of the desired deterministic abstraction function via abstraction refinement.

3   Automated Alphabet Abstraction Refinement

In this section, we develop our partition refinement-based algorithm for alphabet abstraction refinement in the setting of Mealy machines, the system model we consider most adequate for practical applications. In this setting, we fix the output alphabet Ω (in the DCA case just 'accept' and 'reject'), and, given some initial abstraction Σ_A of the input alphabet Σ_C, we learn the coarsest abstraction that refines Σ_A and preserves determinism.

Our learning algorithm works directly on a representation system R for α-equivalence, i.e., initially, for each symbol of Σ_A we have a unique symbol of Σ_C, its concretization, which is used to query the concrete system *Sys*, whenever its abstraction appears in a membership query. This way, membership queries will never encounter non-determinism. This problem only arises when handling counterexamples. They can contain arbitrary alphabet symbols of Σ_C. Non-determinism can then be detected, when the counterexample transformed to an α-equivalent word consisting only of symbols in R produces a different output, as shown in Fig. 2. Here, the topmost line depicts the concrete input sequence defining the counterexample and the second line its transformation into the corresponding α-equivalent input sequence in R^*.

This is the point where classical learning would simply fail, and where our partition refinement-based technique shows its power. Key to our technique is the *'semantic'* way of maintaining a representation system during the refinement-based evolution of the input alphabet in terms of *witnesses*:

Definition 3 (Witness). *Let Sys be a Mealy machine, $p, d \in \Sigma_C^*$, $c, c' \in \Sigma_C$. We call $(p, c | c', d) \in \Sigma^* \times \Sigma^2 \times \Sigma^*$ a witness (of the inequivalence of c and c'), iff*

$$\lambda'(p \cdot c \cdot d) \neq \lambda'(p \cdot c' \cdot d),$$

where $\lambda'(w)$ denotes $\lambda(\delta'(q_0, w))$ defined by $\delta'(q, aw) = \delta'(\delta(q, a), w)$.

Witnesses form a *middle-congruence*. This middle-congruence can be used to refine the alphabet in the same fashion as the (Nerode) right-congruence is used to refine the set of states. We have:

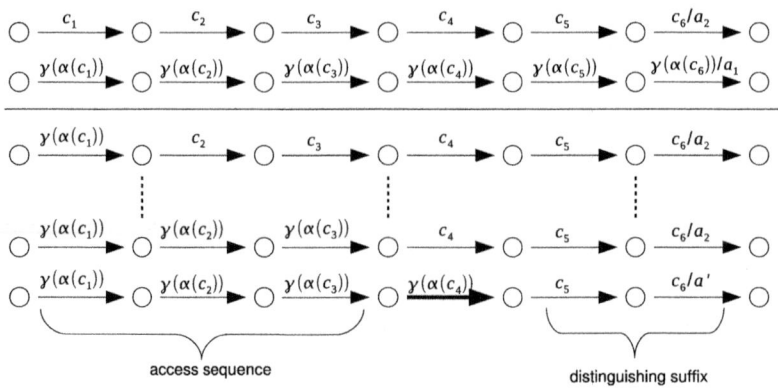

Fig. 2. Processing of counterexamples

Lemma 1. *Every counterexample exposing non-determinism can be decomposed into a prefix p, a concrete symbol $\bar{c}$ and a suffix d, such that*

$$(\gamma(\alpha(p)),\ \bar{c}|\gamma(\alpha(\bar{c})),\ d)$$

is a witness.

Sketch of Proof: Let us now assume a counterexample exposing non-determinism, i.e., of the kind as indicated by the first two lines of Fig. 2, where the symbols in each column are assumed to be α-equivalent. Then we proceed as indicated by the lower part of Fig. 2 by successively replacing the input symbols from left to right according to the following pattern:

$$\lambda'(\gamma(\alpha(p)) \cdot \bar{c} \cdot d)\ =\ \lambda'(\gamma(\alpha(p)) \cdot \gamma(\alpha(\bar{c})) \cdot d)$$

until the test fails, which is guaranteed to happen, because the fully transformed counterexample has a different output symbol. In Fig. 2, e.g., the replacement of the third counterexample input by its α-equivalent standard representative still works, but replacing the fourth input leads to an observable change of the output (a_2 becomes a'): There exists an index i, such that $(\gamma(\alpha(c_1 \ldots c_{i-1})),\ c_i|\gamma(\alpha(c_i)),\ c_{i+1} \ldots c_m)$ is a witness.   □

The witnesses found by counterexamples will become the key to the semantic refinement of α and γ:

$$\alpha_{new}(c) = \begin{cases} \alpha_{old}(c) & \text{if } c \notin \alpha_{old}(\bar{c}) \\ \alpha_{new}(\bar{c}) & \text{if } \lambda'(\gamma(\alpha(p)) \cdot \bar{c} \cdot d) \\ & = \lambda'(\gamma(\alpha(p)) \cdot c \cdot d) \\ \alpha_{new}(\gamma_{old}(\alpha_{old}(\bar{c}))) & \text{if } c \in \alpha_{old}(\bar{c}) \setminus \alpha_{new}(\bar{c}) \end{cases}$$

$$\gamma_{new}(a) = \begin{cases} \gamma_{old}(a) & \text{if } a \neq \alpha_{old}(\bar{c}) \\ \bar{c} & \text{if } a = \alpha_{new}(\bar{c}) \\ \gamma_{old}(\alpha_{old}(a)) & \text{if } a = \alpha_{old}(\bar{c}) \wedge a \neq \alpha_{new}(\bar{c}) \end{cases}$$

As indicated by the term partition refinement, the semantic refinement of α only splits the equivalence class $\alpha_{old}(\bar{c})$, and abstracts all other concrete symbols as before (first line in the definition of $\alpha_{new}(c)$). The class $\alpha_{old}(\bar{c})$ itself splits into

- one subclass for all concrete symbols that behave like $\bar{c}$ on the witness (second line in the definition of $\alpha_{new}(c)$), and
- a second subclass for all the remaining elements of $\alpha_{old}(\bar{c})$ (third line in the definition of $\alpha_{new}(c)$).

The definition of γ_{new} arises then straightforwardly as shown in the definition of $\gamma_{new}(c)$. After each such refinement step, which adds an abstract symbol whose equivalence class is concretely represented by $\bar{c}$, the learning procedure continues by establishing closedness and consistency.

Thinking in terms of partitions and partition refinement is the key for proving the optimality of our alphabet abstraction algorithm. Let therefore

- $Part(\Sigma_C)$ and $Part(\Sigma_C^*)$ be the set of all partitions over Σ_C and Σ_C^*, respectively, and,
- for any $p,d \in \Sigma_C^*$, $c,c' \in \Sigma_C$ let $Ref_{(p,c|c',d)} : Part(\Sigma^*) \rightarrow Part(\Sigma^*)$ be the function that refines any partition over Σ_C^* according to a witness $(p,c|c',d)$ as described above. Furthermore, let
- $\alpha : \Sigma_C \rightarrow Part(\Sigma_A)$ be an arbitrary abstraction function, and
- $Part_d$ be the set of all partitions over Σ_C that refine the partition induced by $\equiv_\alpha$ and at the same time preserve determinism.

Then we have:

Lemma 2. *Let Sys be a system and $(p,c|c',d)$ be a witness. Then being an upper bound for $Part_d \subseteq Part(\Sigma_C)$ is invariant under the application of $Ref_{(p,c|c',d)}$.*

Proof: Let P be an upper bound for $Part_d$ and Q be an arbitrary element of $Part_d$. Then we can prove the required $Q \subseteq Ref_{(p,c|c',d)}(P)$ by contraposition as follows: $(z_1,z_2) \notin Ref_{(p,c|c',d)}(P)$ implies $(z_1,z_2) \notin Q$.
Let therefore $z_1,z_2 \in \Sigma_C$ with $(z_1,z_2) \notin Ref_{(p,c|c',d)}(P)$ and w.l.o.g. with $(z_1,z_2) \in P$. This means that z_1 and z_2 must have been split by $Ref_{(p,c|c',d)}$ and therefore that w.l.o.g. $\lambda'(p \cdot z_1 \cdot d) = \lambda'(p \cdot c' \cdot d)$ and $\lambda'(p \cdot z_2 \cdot d) \neq \lambda'(p \cdot c' \cdot d)$. Thus $\lambda'(p \cdot z_1 \cdot d) \neq \lambda'(p \cdot z_2 \cdot d)$. Thus, together with $Q \in Part_d$ we obtain as desired $(z_1,z_2) \notin Q$.   □

This theorem obviously implies that every abstraction constructed during our alphabet abstraction refinement procedure induces an upper bound for $Part_d$.

If we now assume that we have a perfect equivalence oracle (which is standard for classical automata learning), we can combine this result with the correctness result for classical learning in order to obtain:

Theorem 1 (Optimality relative to perfect Equivalence Oracles). *Let Sys be a deterministic system and α an abstraction on the input alphabet of Sys. Moreover, let us assume that we have a perfect equivalence oracle. Then we have upon termination of our refinement enhanced learning procedure:*

- *The last alphabet refinement ended at the coarsest refinement of α that preserves determinism.*
- *The learned automaton is behaviorally indistinguishable from Sys under the computed refined abstraction of the alphabet. In particular it can be used to reliably predict the Sys output for any (abstract) input word.*

This result shows that our elaboration of automata learning is very much in line with the also partition refinement-based approach of L^*. Like there, the correctness depends on a reliable equivalence oracle or counterexample finder. In addition, all the intermediately constructed hypotheses are optimal in the sense that they concisely reflect all the considered observations: they are the state minimal automata (here Mealy machines) labeled with elements of a coarsest alphabet abstraction which are consistent will all the currently available observations. The formal proof of this statement follows a straightforward pattern for partition refinement algorithms. For many practical applications, like e.g., test generation, regression testing, or (behavioral) specification mining, this optimality result is both very valuable, and the best one could expect.

Similar to classical learning, where the complexity is always considered relative to the number of states of the final system Q, we also considered the complexity relative to the final size of the abstract alphabet Σ_A^f. As every round introduced by handling a counterexample either introduces a new state or a refinement of the alphabet, one can easily conclude that the algorithm terminates after at most $|Q| + |\Sigma_A^f|$ rounds, which is at the same time the maximum number of required equivalence queries.

Membership queries are required to complete the observation table and to treat counterexamples. The treatment of counterexamples will cause at most one membership query for every of its steps. Thus, the number of membership queries for treating counterexamples can be estimated by $m \cdot (|Q| + |\Sigma_A^f|)$, where m is the maximal length of a counterexample. The size of the final observation table can be estimated by $O(|\Sigma_A^f| \cdot |Q|^2)$, cf. [24,25]. Accordingly, the total number of required membership queries is at most $|\Sigma_A^f| \cdot |Q|^2 + m \cdot (|Q| + |\Sigma_A^f|)$. In summary we obtain:

Theorem 2 (Complexity). *Assuming that equivalence and membership queries both have some constant cost, our new learning algorithm has an overall complexity of: $O(|\Sigma_A| \cdot |Q|^2 + m \cdot (|Q| + |\Sigma_A|))$.*

Under the very reasonable assumption that the maximum length of the counterexamples m does not grow faster than the number of states $|Q|$, our complexity result reduces to $O(|\Sigma_A| \cdot |Q|^2)$, exactly the result known for classical automata learning. It should be noted, however, that this result, besides suppressing constant factors as usual in classical complexity theory, is also based on the assumption of constant time membership and equivalence oracles. Having in mind

```
enum {msg,recv} event;                         // events to occur
pdu p, ack;                                     // pdus
packet buffer = 0;                              // incoming data
seq_nr expect = 0;                              // next expected seq. nr
while (true) {
    wait_for_event(&event);                     // wait for event
    switch (event) {
    msg:
        from_lower_layer(&p);                   // read new message
        if (buffer==0 &&                        // if buf empty and
                (p.seq % 2 == expect % 2)) {    // and seq matches
            buffer = p.data;
            expect++;                           // increment exp. seq. nr
            indicate_to_upper_layer();          // indicate new data
        }
        break;
    recv:
        if (buffer==0) break;                   // skip if buffer emtpy
        data_to_upper_layer(&buffer);           // forward data
        ack.seq = (expect-1) % 2;               // ack. delivery
        to_lower_layer(&ack);
        break;
    }
}
```

Fig. 3. Pseudocode of protocol entity

that equivalence oracles may not be realizable at all in practice, this might look quite unrealistic. Experiences made in the context of the ZULU challenge [13] though suggest that often equivalence oracles may be substitutable by fast counterexample finders. In fact, we were able to reduce the effort for realizing such a counterexample finder to very few membership queries [19]. This shows the potential of practical approaches and heuristics and it was one of the motivating observations that led us to founding the RERS initiative for experimental automata learning [9].

It should also be noted that the termination of our algorithm does not necessarily require Σ_C to be finite or *Sys* to be regular: It is sufficient that there exists a regular deterministic abstraction of *Sys*, as is illustrated in the next section.

4   An Example Run of the Algorithm

In this section, we will apply the method for abstraction refinement to a basic example to illustrate the integration with classical automata learning for Mealy machines (cf. [20,25]). The pseudo code for our example is given in Fig. 3. It specifies a protocol entity that to the next upper layer provides primitives to receive and indicate messages and to the next lower layer exposes primitives

-	msg(0,d)	recv
ε	ind	–
msg(0,d)	–	ack(0)
msg(0,d) recv	–	–
recv	ind	–
msg(0,d) msg(0,d)	–	ack(0)
msg(0,d) recv msg(0,d)	–	–
msg(0,d) recv recv	–	–

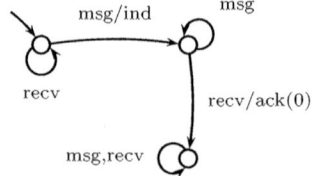

Fig. 4. Observation Table and hypothesis at the end of the first learning phase

to receive messages and to send acknowledgements. The component internally uses an continually increasing Integer variable to keep track of sequence numbers assigned to messages. Due to the counter, this system has infinitely many states even if we abstract from the content of the messages. We will show, how our algorithm refines the input alphabet just enough to reveal its Alternating Bit Protocol like stop-and-go behavior, which is regular.

Initially we assume an abstraction that has two concrete representative elements $msg(0,d)$ and $recv$, where msg and $recv$ denote two different primitives, and d some concrete instantiation of data. The abstraction refinement algorithm then is assumed to be able to partition the set of all possible inputs to the system according to this abstraction.

The learning algorithm will use an Observation Table and initialize the set of distinguishing suffixes D as $\{msg(0,d), recv\}$, the set of access sequences S as $\{\varepsilon\}$ and the set of continuations SA accordingly. During the first round of learning the algorithm will find two additional access sequences $msg(0,d)$ and $msg(0,d)recv$. Fig. 4 shows the resulting observation table and the resulting abstract hypothesis. Now, let the three-lettered word $msg(72,d')\ recv\ msg(73,d'')$ be the counterexample that is provided by the equivalence oracle. We first apply the current abstraction component-wisely to the counterexample. This results in the abstract word $msg\ recv\ msg$, which will be concretized to $msg(0,d)\ recv\ msg(0,d)$. The original counterexample and its representative will, when run on the system, lead to different outputs:

$$msg(72,d')\ \ recv\ \ msg(73,d'')\ \ :\ \ ind\ ack(0)\ ind$$
$$msg(0,d)\ \ \ \ recv\ \ msg(0,d)\ \ \ \ :\ \ ind\ ack(0)\ \ \ -$$

At this point classic automata learning and a static abstraction would fail. The too coarse abstraction produces a conflict in observations that would be interpreted as result of inherent non-deterministic behavior or without interpretation simply as a failure of the experimental setup. Here, the proposed abstraction refinement method comes into play. The corresponding detailed analysis of the counterexample is shown in Fig. 5. The prefixes of the counterexample will component-wisely (one symbol at time) replaced by their according representative elements. The resulting word is then executed on the system. At one point the system's behavior will switch from producing the same output as for the original counterexample to producing different output. In this case replacing

candidate	reaction	processing
msg(72,d') recv msg(73,d")	ind ack(0) ind	-
msg(0,d) recv msg(73,d")	ind ack(0) ind	replace $msg(72,d')$ by $\gamma(\alpha(msg(72,d')))$
msg(0,d) recv msg(73,d")	ind ack(0) ind	replace $recv$ by $\gamma(\alpha(recv))$
msg(0,d) recv msg(0,d)	ind ack(0) -	replace $msg(73,d")$ by $\gamma(\alpha(msg(73,d")))$

Fig. 5. Treatment of a counterexample

-	msg(0,d)	recv
ε	ind	-
msg(0,d)	-	ack(0)
msg(0,d) recv	-	-
msg(0,d) recv msg(73,d")	-	ack(1)
recv	ind	-
msg(73,d")	ind	-
msg(0,d) msg(0,d)	-	ack(0)
msg(0,d) msg(73,d")	-	ack(0)
msg(0,d) recv msg(0,d)	-	-
msg(0,d) recv recv	-	-
msg(0,d) recv msg(73,d") msg(0,d)	-	ack(1)
msg(0,d) recv msg(73,d") recv	ind	-
msg(0,d) recv msg(73,d") msg(73,d")	-	ack(1)

(hypothesis automaton labels: recv msg1, msg0/ind, msg0 msg1; recv/ack(1), recv/ack(0); msg0, msg1/ind, msg0 recv)

Fig. 6. Observation Table and hypothesis after termination

$msg(73,d'')$ will result in a different (conflicting) observation. We thus use the transformed prefix and the original element at the current position of the counterexample to refine the abstraction on the alphabet. The abstract symbol msg will be split into the abstract symbols $msg0$ and $msg1$. The witness revealing the difference is $(msg(0,d) \ recv, \ msg(0,d)|msg(73,d''), \ \varepsilon)$.

After processing the counterexample is completed, the newly found representative element is passed to the learning algorithm as a new alphabet symbol. Assuming the learning algorithm will use this symbol only to extend the set of continuations SA and not in the set D as well (which is sufficient), the learning algorithm will after a second round terminate with a hypothesis that is equivalent to the behavior of the actual system. The resulting observation table and hypothesis are shown in Fig. 6.

5   Conclusion

We have presented an on-the-fly method for refining a given abstraction to automatically regain a deterministic behavior, a must for active learning. With this method detected non-determinism does no longer lead to failure, but to a dynamic abstraction refinement. Like automata learning itself, this method is in general neither sound nor complete, but it also enjoys similar convergence properties as long as the concrete (not necessarily finite) system itself behaves deterministically. From a practical perspective, our method allows users to 'experimentally' try abstractions and to let the algorithm care for the determinism requirement.

Our experience with a prototypical implementation of the enhanced learning algorithm is quite promising. We applied it, e.g., to the case study discussed in [1]. While Aarts et al. used a priori knowledge and hand tailored an abstraction in their case study in several iterations, we could simply provide a far too coarse initial abstraction, which was then automatically refined by our algorithm to terminate with the same result.

References

1. Aarts, F., Schmaltz, J., Vaandrager, F.: Inference and abstraction of the biometric passport. In: Margaria, T., Steffen, B. (eds.) ISoLA 2010. LNCS, vol. 6415, pp. 673–686. Springer, Heidelberg (2010)
2. Alur, R., Cerný, P., Madhusudan, P., Nam, W.: Synthesis of interface specifications for java classes. In: Palsberg, J., Abadi, M. (eds.) POPL, pp. 98–109. ACM, New York (2005)
3. Angluin, D.: Learning regular sets from queries and counterexamples. Information and Computation 2(75), 87–106 (1987)
4. Balcázar, J.L., Díaz, J., Gavaldà, R.: Algorithms for learning finite automata from queries: A unified view. In: Advances in Algorithms, Languages, and Complexity, pp. 53–72 (1997)
5. Berg, T., Jonsson, B., Raffelt, H.: Regular inference for state machines with parameters. In: Baresi, L., Heckel, R. (eds.) FASE 2006. LNCS, vol. 3922, pp. 107–121. Springer, Heidelberg (2006)
6. Berg, T., Jonsson, B., Raffelt, H.: Regular inference for state machines using domains with equality tests. In: Fiadeiro, J.L., Inverardi, P. (eds.) FASE 2008. LNCS, vol. 4961, pp. 317–331. Springer, Heidelberg (2008)
7. Bohlin, T., Jonsson, B.: Regular inference for communication protocol entities. Technical report, Department of Information Technology, Uppsala University, Schweden (2009)
8. Broy, M., Jonsson, B., Katoen, J.-P., Leucker, M., Pretschner, A.: Model-Based Testing of Reactive Systems. In: Broy, M., Jonsson, B., Katoen, J.-P., Leucker, M., Pretschner, A. (eds.) Model-Based Testing of Reactive Systems. LNCS, vol. 3472, pp. 607–609. Springer, Heidelberg (2005)
9. TU Dortmund Chair of Programming Systems, Department of Computer Science. RERS - A Challenge In Active Learning, http://leo.cs.tu-dortmund.de:8100/ (version from 20.06.2010)
10. Clarke, E., Grumberg, O., Jha, S., Lu, Y., Veith, H.: Counterexample-guided abstraction refinement for symbolic model checking. J. ACM 50(5), 752–794 (2003)
11. Clarke, E.M., Grumberg, O., Peled, D.A.: Model checking. Springer, Heidelberg (1999)
12. Cobleigh, J.M., Giannakopoulou, D., Păsăreanu, C.S.: Learning assumptions for compositional verification. In: Garavel, H., Hatcliff, J. (eds.) TACAS 2003. LNCS, vol. 2619, pp. 331–346. Springer, Heidelberg (2003)
13. Combe, D., de la Higuera, C., Janodet, J.-C., Ponge, M.: Zulu - Active learning from queries competition, http://labh-curien.univ-st-etienne.fr/zulu/index.php (version from 01.08.2010)
14. Gheorghiu Bobaru, M., Păsăreanu, C.S., Giannakopoulou, D.: Automated assume-guarantee reasoning by abstraction refinement. In: Gupta, A., Malik, S. (eds.) CAV 2008. LNCS, vol. 5123, pp. 135–148. Springer, Heidelberg (2008)

15. Grinchtein, O., Jonsson, B., Pettersson, P.: Inference of event-recording automata using timed decision trees. In: Baier, C., Hermanns, H. (eds.) CONCUR 2006. LNCS, vol. 4137, pp. 435–449. Springer, Heidelberg (2006)
16. Hagerer, A., Hungar, H.: Model generation by moderated regular extrapolation. In: Kutsche, R.-D., Weber, H. (eds.) FASE 2002. LNCS, vol. 2306, pp. 80–95. Springer, Heidelberg (2002)
17. Hagerer, A., Margaria, T., Niese, O., Steffen, B., Brune, G., Ide, H.D.: Efficient regression testing of CTI-systems: Testing a complex call-center solution. Annual review of communication, Int. Engineering Consortium (IEC) 55, 1033–1040 (2001)
18. Henzinger, T.A., Jhala, R., Majumdar, R., Sutre, G.: Lazy abstraction. In: POPL 2002: Proceedings of the 29th ACM SIGPLAN-SIGACT Symposium on Principles of Programming Languages, pp. 58–70. ACM, New York (2002)
19. Howar, F., Steffen, B., Merten, M.: From zulu to rers: Lessons learned in the zulu challenge. In: Margaria, T., Steffen, B. (eds.) ISoLA 2010. LNCS, vol. 6415, pp. 687–704. Springer, Heidelberg (2010)
20. Margaria, T., Niese, O., Raffelt, H., Steffen, B.: Efficient test-based model generation for legacy reactive systems. In: HLDVT 2004: Proceedings of the High-Level Design Validation and Test Workshop, Ninth IEEE International. IEEE Computer Society, Los Alamitos (2004)
21. Nerode, A.: Linear Automaton Transformations. Proceedings of the American Mathematical Society 9(4), 541–544 (1958)
22. Raffelt, H., Margaria, T., Steffen, B., Merten, M.: Hybrid test of web applications with webtest. In: Proc. of the 2008 Workshop on Testing, Analysis, and Verification of Web Services and Applications (TAV-WEB 2008), pp. 1–7. ACM, New York (2008)
23. Raffelt, H., Steffen, B., Berg, T., Margaria, T.: Learnlib: a framework for extrapolating behavioral models. International Journal on Software Tools for Technology Transfer (STTT) 11(5), 393–407 (2009)
24. Rivest, R.L., Schapire, R.E.: Inference of finite automata using homing sequences. Inf. Comput. 103(2), 299–347 (1993)
25. Shahbaz, M., Groz, R.: Inferring mealy machines. In: Cavalcanti, A., Dams, D.R. (eds.) FM 2009. LNCS, vol. 5850, pp. 207–222. Springer, Heidelberg (2009)
26. Shahbaz, M., Li, K., Groz, R.: Learning parameterized state machine model for integration testing. In: COMPSAC 2007: Proceedings of the 31st Annual International Computer Software and Applications Conference, Washington, DC, USA, vol. 2, pp. 755–760. IEEE Computer Society, Los Alamitos (2007)

Towards Complete Reasoning
about Axiomatic Specifications

Swen Jacobs and Viktor Kuncak

École Polytechnique Fédérale de Lausanne (EPFL), Switzerland
`firstname.lastname@epfl.ch`

Abstract. To support verification of expressive properties of functional programs, we consider algebraic style specifications that may relate multiple user-defined functions, and compare multiple invocations of a function for different arguments. We present decision procedures for reasoning about such universally quantified properties of functional programs, using local theory extension methodology. We establish new classes of universally quantified formulas whose satisfiability can be checked in a complete way by finite quantifier instantiation. These classes include single-invocation axioms that generalize standard function contracts, but also certain many-invocation axioms, specifying that functions satisfy congruence, injectivity, or monotonicity with respect to abstraction functions, as well as conjunctions of some of these properties. These many-invocation axioms can specify correctness of abstract data type implementations as well as certain information-flow properties. We also present a decidability-preserving construction that enables the same function to be specified using different classes of decidable specifications on different partitions of its domain.

1 Introduction

A promising approach to precision and scalability in software verification is to let developers write the specifications of procedures, then use modern satisfiability-modulo theory solvers to automatically prove verification conditions that use such specifications. Recent results in modular verification have been obtained using e.g. tools VCC [2] and Jahob [12]. In this paper, we follow the idea of the high-level analysis of Hob [10] tool, and focus particularly on checking that specified functions are correctly used to implement the desired higher-level functionality. We simplify the problem by considering purely functional instead of imperative code. However, we consider more complex program properties than those checked by most previous automated verification approaches. Most of the existing approaches for specifying a function f use contracts that establish a relationship between a given input, x, and the output of the function, $f(x)$. Such contracts can be expressed as universally quantified statements $\forall x. \Phi(x, f(x))$, where Φ is a formula expressing the desired property of the function. Contracts are therefore a very special case among the classes of function specifications.

Algebraic specifications. In this paper, we consider a broader class of specifications that follow algebraic specification style. Our specifications may relate

R. Jhala and D. Schmidt (Eds.): VMCAI 2011, LNCS 6538, pp. 278–293, 2011.

multiple different functions, using, for example, abstraction functions to specify the behavior of an abstract data type implementation. Moreover, our properties may include *multiple universal quantifiers*, which allows us to express congruence, monotonicity, injectivity, and non-interference properties of functions. Such properties cannot be directly expressed using standard pre/post condition specifications, which refer to an arbitrary, but *only one* function invocation.

Sound, complete and terminating approach. We study the verification problem for such properties from the theorem proving point of view. In analogy with modular verification of contracts, our verification conditions (VCs) contain as assumptions certain universally quantified formulas (specifying the behavior of basic functions). As the goal, the VCs contain further universally quantified formulas that express the behavior of functions composed from basic ones. The key challenge in proving such VCs is the presence of quantifiers in their assumptions. Current SMT provers typically have incomplete support for quantifiers. Therefore, they typically cannot establish that a quantified formula is satisfiable. This limits their ability to provide meaningful counterexamples to the developer.

In this paper, we overcome the incompleteness of quantifier reasoning for a number of properties of interest. We use the methodology of local theory extensions [13] to obtain complete quantifier-instantiation strategies. We therefore arrive at decision procedures for quantified formulas about functions in the presence of decidable theories of primitive operations (such as linear arithmetic and algebraic data types). The procedure can prove the validity of universally quantified properties of functions, where functions themselves are specified using universally quantified axioms. Our algorithms are counterexample generating decision procedures. They terminate for all specifications in the identified classes. Given a formula, they either prove its validity, or generate a counterexample. The completeness for counterexamples is a significant aspect of usability, because it helps users identify concrete inputs that cause errors. At the same time, the completeness for generating proofs provides a higher degree of confidence compared to bounded-exhaustive test-case generation [4].

Single-invocation and many-invocation axioms. As our first class of properties that specify a function f we consider *single-invocation* axioms of the form $\forall \bar{x}.\Phi(\bar{x}, f(\bar{x}))$ for a formula Φ in a decidable theory. We show that it suffices to instantiate the universal quantifier over $\bar{x}$ only with $\bar{a}$ such that $f(\bar{a})$ occurs in the property being proved. Such completeness of instantiation has not been stated before, and is not to be taken for granted: we show that such instantiation is *incomplete* for general *two-invocation* axioms of the form $\forall \bar{x}, \bar{y}.\Phi(\bar{x}, \bar{y}, f(\bar{x}), f(\bar{y}))$. Despite this limitation, we identify a number of useful subclasses of two-invocation axioms that also remain local and decidable. These include properties of functions such as monotonicity, injectivity, congruence, and non-interference, all under a given abstraction function.

Locality of sufficiently surjective recursive abstractions. The results on both single-invocation and many-invocation axioms are particularly useful in the presence of recursively defined functions. Recent results [15, 17] show the decidability of theories of algebraic data types with recursive abstraction functions which includes e.g. functions to compute set or multiset content, size, or height of algebraic data type (ADT) values. We verify that, like [15], the results of [17] can be naturally explained using Ψ-locality. We present a more abstract algorithm than the description in [17], possibly leading to more efficient future implementations.

Combination results. Given several classes of axioms for which reasoning is complete, a question arises whether they can be combined. We consider combinations of axioms that are separately local, and show several positive and negative results for the locality of their combinations. Finally, we give a positive result on *piecewise* combinations of local axioms. This is of significant practical value, because it enables functions to be specified using different local axiomatizations on different regions of their input domain, and generates a local axiomatization as a result.

In summary, we show a number of new decidability results for theories that support quantifiers, by showing that these quantifiers can be finitely instantiated in a complete way. Thus, we extend the predictability and efficiency of quantifier-free reasoning to an interesting class of axiomatically specified functions. Proofs have been omitted due to lack of space. They can be found in the technical report [8].

2   Example

Fig. 1 shows an illustrative functional program in the notation of the Scala programming language. We specify functions using global assertions written in Scala extended with a $\forall$ operator for universal quantification.

Many interesting properties of functional programs can be expressed using contracts. Contracts assign a pre- and a postcondition to every function, where the postcondition may depend on the value of function parameters. The specification of function merge in Fig. 1 illustrates how we can encode contracts using universally quantified axioms. The result of the function is a list containing the elements of both input lists. We express this requirement using an abstraction function content, mapping a list to the set of elements it contains. We show locality for such specifications in sections 4 and 5.

However, many other interesting properties of functions are *not* expressible through contracts, because they compare the values of different invocations of the function. Consider a user-defined equality on data structures, defined by the abstraction function content: $x \sim y \iff \text{content}(x) = \text{content}(y)$. By definition, $\sim$ is an equivalence relation, but it may or may not satisfy the *congruence* axiom: $x \sim y \rightarrow f(x) \sim f(y)$. Congruence states that the equivalence is preserved under application of data structure operations, and is generally a desirable property. For example, the function even in Figure 1 takes a list and returns the sublist containing the (integer) elements that are even numbers. The second assertion after even definition shows how to specify the congruence of even with respect to equivalence determined by content.

```
def merge(l1: List, l2: List): List = { ... }
assert(∀l1 : List ⇒ ∀l2 : List ⇒ content(merge(l1,l2)) = content(l1) ∪ content(l2))

def even(l : List): List = { ... }
assert(∀l: List ⇒ content(even(l)) ⊆ content(l))
assert(∀l1 : List ⇒ ∀ l2 : List ⇒
          content(l1) = content(l2)  →  content(even(l1)) = content(even(l2)))

def insert(c : Int, l: List): List = { ... }
assert(∀c: Int ⇒ ∀l1 : List ⇒ ∀l2 : List⇒
          content(l1) ⊆ content(l2)  →  content(insert(c,l1)) ⊆ content(insert(c,l2)))

def fill(l: List): List = { ... }
assert(∀l: List ⇒ if (content(l).size < 3) content(fill(l)).size=3
                    else content(fill(l)) = content(l) )

def main(c: Int, l1: List, l2: List): List = merge(even(l1), fill(insert(c,l2)))

case class Employee(name : String, age : Int, bankAccountNo : Int)
def samePublic1(e1 : Employee, e2 : Employee) : Boolean =
  { e1.name = e2.name && e1.age = e2.age }
def samePublic(el1 : List[Employee], el2 : List[Employee]) : Boolean =
    zip(el1,el2).forAll(samePublic1) && length(el1)=length(el2)
assert(equivalence(samePublic))

def averageAge(emp : List[Employee]) : Int = { ... }
// information flow property: averageAge does not depend on private data
assert(∀l1: List[Employee] ⇒ ∀l2: List[Employee] →
  samePublic(l1,l2)  →  averageAge(l1) = averageAge(l2)
```

Fig. 1. Example of Functional Program Specified Using Axioms

For other functions, such as insert in Fig. 1, we may require stronger properties, such as monotonicity with respect to the pre-order. The pre-order can be induced by an abstraction function that maps into an ordered structure. In case of the content abstraction, the starting point is the subset ordering, and we define $x \preceq y \iff$ content$(x) \subseteq$ content(y). Then, we expect a function that inserts a given element into the data structure to satisfy $x \preceq y \rightarrow$ insert$(c, x) \preceq$ insert(c, y).

It can also be useful to specify the data that a function is allowed to access. For example, averageAge in Fig. 1 is a function that should not access the private information about employees. We specify this by first defining an equivalence relation samePublic1 on employees, abstracting from the private data bankAccountNo, then an equivalence relation on lists of employees (which are equivalent if they have the same length and elements at the same position in a list are in relation samePublic1), and finally assert that whenever two lists are equivalent wrt. samePublic, then averageAge will give the same result for both lists. The results in Section 6 ensure complete reasoning about specifications that take the form of congruence, monotonicity, or injectivity.

We may also wish to combine specifications using conjunctions or if-then-else. As an example of combination using conjunction, the function even in Fig. 1 should satisfy the congruence, and, in addition, it should return a subset of the original list. As an example of combination by if-then-else, the fill function should insert additional elements into lists with less than 3 elements (so that the result has 3 distinct elements), and otherwise should not change the list content. Sections 7 and 8 establish results on preserving the decidability of reasoning when combining specifications.

As with the usual contracts, our overall goal is to verify partial correctness of programs in a modular way. We wish to check the properties of functions such as main in Figure 1, assuming the assertions of the functions it calls. The properties we check can be universally quantified and can include contracts, as well as e.g. congruence or monotonicity. When the function verified (e.g. main) is not recursive, proving such contracts reduces to deciding quantifier-free formulas in the theory given by the specifications of the functions called. The approach that we introduce allows us to decide such questions. Moreover, if a property does not hold, we obtain a counterexample that points us to the weakness in our specification or code, which we can use to make the appropriate correction.

3   Background

The notion of *local theory extensions* is key to our decidability results. We give a short introduction to the concept, which was developed by Sofronie-Stokkermans [13]. For more details, we refer to [5,7,13].

Theories and models. Consider a signature $\Pi = (\Sigma, \mathsf{Pred})$, where Σ is a set of function symbols and Pred a set of predicate symbols (both with given arities). A Π-*structure* $\mathcal{M}$ consists of a non-empty set of elements M, a total function $f^{\mathcal{M}} : M^n \to M$ for every n-ary function symbol $f \in \Sigma$, as well as a set $P^{\mathcal{M}} \subseteq M^n$ for every n-ary predicate symbol $P \in \mathsf{Pred}$. We regard *theories* as sets of formulas closed under consequences, defined by a set of *axioms*. A given (Π-)structure $\mathcal{M}$ is a *model* of a theory $\mathcal{T}$ iff every axiom of $\mathcal{T}$ is satisfied by $\mathcal{M}$. If a formula F is satisfied by a structure $\mathcal{M}$, we write $\mathcal{M} \models F$. If F is true in all models of $\mathcal{T}$, we write $\models_{\mathcal{T}} F$. If no model of $\mathcal{T}$ satisfies F, we write $F \models_{\mathcal{T}} \square$, where $\square$ represents the empty clause.

Local theory extensions. *Theory extensions* extend a given theory with new function symbols, defined by a set of axioms. *Locality* of the extension ensures that reasoning about these symbols can be reduced to reasoning in the base theory by finite instantiation of the axioms. The new symbols are called *extension symbols*, terms starting with extension symbols are *extension terms*.

Consider a background theory $\mathcal{T}$ with signature $\Pi_0 = (\Sigma_0, \mathsf{Pred})$, and an extension $\Pi = (\Sigma_0 \cup \Sigma_1, \mathsf{Pred})$ of this signature with extension symbols in Σ_1. An *augmented Π-clause* is a Π-formula $\forall \overline{x}.\ \Phi(\overline{x}) \vee C(\overline{x})$, where $\Phi(\overline{x})$ is an arbitrary

Π_0-formula and $C(\overline{x})$ is a disjunction of Π-literals. We say that it is Σ_1-*ground* if $C(\overline{x})$ is ground. A *theory extension* of a theory $\mathcal{T}$ with signature Π_0 is given by a set $\mathcal{K}$ of augmented Π-clauses, representing axioms for the extension symbols.

A substitution σ is a function mapping variables to terms. By $F\sigma$ we denote the result of simultaneously replacing each free variable x in F with $\sigma(x)$. For a set of formulas $\mathcal{K}$, define $\mathsf{st}(\mathcal{K})$ as the set of ground subterms appearing in $\mathcal{K}$. For a set of Π-formulas $\mathcal{K}$ and a Π-formula G, let

$$\mathcal{K}[G] = \{\ F\sigma\ |\ F \in \mathcal{K} \text{ and } \sigma \text{ is such that}$$
$$f(\overline{t})\sigma \in \mathsf{st}(\mathcal{K} \cup G) \text{ for each extension subterm } f(\overline{t}) \text{ of } F,$$
$$\text{and } \sigma(x) = x \text{ if } x \text{ does not appear in an extension term }\},$$

i.e. $\mathcal{K}[G]$ is the result of matching extension terms in $\mathcal{K}$ to ground terms in $\mathcal{K} \cup G$. We consider theory extensions with the following locality property (defined in [13]):

(ELoc)   For every set G of Σ_1-ground augmented Π-clauses, we have
$$\mathcal{K} \cup G \models_{\mathcal{T}} \square \iff \mathcal{K}[G] \cup G \models_{\mathcal{T}} \square$$

Decidability and model generation. Assuming (ELoc), satisfiability of G modulo $\mathcal{T} \cup \mathcal{K}$ is decidable whenever $\mathcal{K}[G] \cup G$ is finite and belongs to a decidable fragment of $\mathcal{T}$ (plus free functions). In particular, if G is ground, and all variables in $\mathcal{K}$ appear in extension terms, then $\mathcal{K}[G] \cup G$ is ground, and decidability of the ground fragment of $\mathcal{T}$ is sufficient. As mentioned in [5], model-generating decision procedures for $\mathcal{T}$ can be used to produce models for $\mathcal{T} \cup \mathcal{K}$.

Identifying local theory extensions. To formulate a sufficient condition for theory extensions satisfying (ELoc), we need some additional definitions.

A *partial Π-structure* is the same as a Π-structure, except that function symbols may be assigned partial functions. In a partial structure $\mathcal{M}$, terms are evaluated wrt. a variable assignment β as in total structures, except that the evaluation of $\beta(f(t_1,\ldots,t_n))$ is undefined if either $(\beta(t_1),\ldots,\beta(t_n))$ is not in the domain of $f^{\mathcal{M}}$, or at least one of the $\beta(t_i)$ is undefined. A partial Π-structure $\mathcal{M}$ and a variable assignment β *weakly satisfy* a literal L if either all terms in L are defined and the usual notion of satisfaction applies, or if at least one of the terms in L is undefined. Based on weak satisfaction of literals, weak satisfaction of formulas is defined recursively in the usual way. If $\mathcal{M}$ satisfies F for all variable assignments β, $\mathcal{M}$ is a *weak partial model* of F.

For $\Pi = (\Sigma, \mathsf{Pred})$, a total Π-structure $\mathcal{M}$ is a *completion* of a partial Π-structure $\mathcal{M}'$ if (1) $M = M'$, (2) for every $f \in \Sigma$: $f^{\mathcal{M}}(\overline{x}) = f^{\mathcal{M}'}(\overline{x})$ whenever $f^{\mathcal{M}'}(\overline{x})$ is defined, and (3) for every $P \in \mathsf{Pred}$: $P^{\mathcal{M}} = P^{\mathcal{M}'}$.

For extensions of a theory $\mathcal{T}$ with signature $\Pi_0 = (\Sigma_0, \mathsf{Pred})$ with a set of axioms $\mathcal{K}$ with signature $\Pi = (\Sigma_0 \cup \Sigma_1, \mathsf{Pred})$, define the completability property

(Comp$_\mathsf{w}$)   For every weak partial Π-model $\mathcal{M}$ of $\mathcal{T} \cup \mathcal{K}$ where Σ_0-functions are total, there exists a completion which is a model of $\mathcal{T} \cup \mathcal{K}$

A formula F is Σ_1-*flat* if it does not contain occurrences of function symbols below a Σ_1-symbol. A Σ_1-flat formula F is Σ_1-*linear* if all extension terms in F

which contain the same variable are syntactically equal, and no extension term in F contains two or more occurrences of the same variable.

Theorem 1 (Completability implies extended locality [13]). *If $\mathcal{K}$ consists of Σ_1-linear augmented clauses and the extension of $\mathcal{T}$ with $\mathcal{K}$ satisfies* (Comp$_w$), *then it also satisfies* (ELoc).

Combinations and chains of extensions. For combining several local theory extensions with different extension functions, two approaches have been considered in the literature. If we have two extensions of $\mathcal{T}$ with $\mathcal{K}_1$ and $\mathcal{K}_2$, respectively, that introduce disjoint sets of function symbols and individually satisfy (Comp$_w$), then the extension of $\mathcal{T}$ with $\mathcal{K}_1 \cup \mathcal{K}_2$ also satisfies (Comp$_w$) [14]. On the other hand, an extended theory can be extended again, so we can extend $\mathcal{T}$ with $\mathcal{K}_1$, then $\mathcal{T} \cup \mathcal{K}_1$ with $\mathcal{K}_2$, and so on, if every extension satisfies (Comp$_w$).

These combination results allow us to efficiently reason about programs containing multiple user-specified functions: if two functions are defined separately (i.e. they don't appear in the definition of each other), then the combination of both axioms is also a local extension, and if one is defined in terms of the other, we can use a chain of extensions. There are currently no combination results for mutually recursive functions.

In sections 5 to 8, we introduce several classes of axioms and prove that they satisfy (Comp$_w$), and thus the locality property (ELoc).

4   Reasoning about ADTs with Abstractions

In this section, we introduce a logic that allows us to reason about axiomatic specifications of functional programs. We consider the theory of ADTs with recursive abstraction functions introduced in [17] as our base theory, and use the framework of local theory extensions [13] to reason about axiomatic specifications of additional functions that manipulate these data structures. The syntax of our logic, parametrized by element and collection theory, can be found in Fig. 2. In the rest of the paper, we will prove decidability of this logic.

Several decidability results for recursive functions over algebraic data types are presented in [15, 17]. Whereas [15] uses local theory extensions, [17] uses a criterion of sufficient surjectivity, related to the notion of counting constraints of [19]. In the following, we give a decision procedure that follows [17] but uses local theory extensions. It decides satisfiability of ground formulas in our logic (see Fig. 2; we ignore additional function symbols $f \notin \Sigma_T$ for now, but they could easily be added as free function symbols).

We present our decision procedure for the specific ADT of binary trees, but it generalizes to data types with other constructors. Our decision procedure is parametrized by an *element theory* $\mathcal{T}_E$, a *collection theory* $\mathcal{T}_C$ and an *abstraction function* α, which is recursively defined on the tree structure by $\mathcal{K}_\alpha = \{\alpha(\mathsf{Leaf}) = \mathsf{empty}, \ \forall t_1, e, t_2.\ \alpha(\mathsf{Node}(t_1, e, t_2) = \mathsf{combine}(\alpha(t_1), e, \alpha(t_2))\}$, where empty is a ground term in $\mathcal{T}_C$ and combine is a function which maps two

Element terms:	E	$::= e \mid T_E$
Tree terms:	T	$::= t \mid \mathsf{Leaf} \mid \mathsf{Node}(T, E, T) \mid \mathsf{Left}(T) \mid \mathsf{Right}(T) \mid f(T)$ for $f \notin \Sigma_T$
Collection terms:	C	$::= c \mid \alpha(T) \mid T_C$
Element literals:	L_E	$::= \mathcal{L}_E$ (given by $\mathcal{T}_E$)
Tree literals:	L_T	$::= T = T$
Collection literals:	L_C	$::= C = C \mid C \leq C \mid \mathcal{L}_C$ (given by $\mathcal{T}_C$)
Ground Formulas:	φ	$::= L_E \mid L_T \mid L_C \mid \varphi \wedge \varphi \mid \varphi \vee \varphi \mid \neg\varphi$
Axioms:	ϕ	$::= \forall x.\Phi(x, f(x))^\star \mid (\mathsf{Con}) \mid (\mathsf{Mon}) \mid (\mathsf{Inj})$
Conjunctive comb.:	$\phi^\wedge$	$::= \phi \mid (\mathsf{Con}) \wedge (\mathsf{Mon}) \mid (\mathsf{Con}) \wedge (\mathsf{Inj}) \mid \forall x.\Phi(x, f(x)) \wedge (\mathsf{Con})^\star$
		$\mid \forall x.\Phi(x, f(x)) \wedge (\mathsf{Inj})^\star \mid \forall x.\Phi(x, f(x)) \wedge (\mathsf{Con}) \wedge (\mathsf{Inj})^\star$
Piecewise comb.:	$\phi^\vee$	$::= \bigwedge_j \left((\bigwedge_i \varphi_j(x_i)) \rightarrow \phi_j^\wedge \right)^\star$
Formulas:	ϕ^+	$::= \phi^\vee \wedge \varphi$

Cases marked with $\star$ require additional side conditions, see Sect. 5 to 8.

Fig. 2. Syntax of our logic

arguments of collection sort and one argument of element sort to a value of collection sort.[1] We assume that α is *sufficiently surjective* as defined in [17].

Key steps of the decision procedure. We give a decision procedure for conjunctions of literals. It can be lifted to arbitrary ground formulas by using the well-known $DPLL(\mathcal{T})$ approach.

Purification and flattening. We purify the formula s.t. every literal only contains symbols from one of the theories $\mathcal{T}_E, \mathcal{T}_C$ or $\mathcal{T}_T$ (the theory of trees). Then we flatten tree terms s.t. constructors and selectors are only applied to tree variables (and arbitrary element terms), and tree disequalities do not contain non-variable terms. Both can be done by introduction of fresh variables.

Elimination of selectors. We rewrite equations $t = \mathsf{Left}(t_1)$ to $t_1 = \mathsf{Node}(t_L, e, t_R) \wedge t = t_L$, and $t = \mathsf{Right}(t_1)$ to $t_1 = \mathsf{Node}(t_L, e, t_R) \wedge t = t_R$, where t_L, t_R and e are always fresh variables.

Unification of tree literals. We apply unification on the positive tree literals (see [17] for details). If unification fails, we have shown unsatisfiability. Otherwise, we obtain a solution σ that can be seen as a substitution for tree and element variables. We apply this substitution to the formula and call the result G. Tree variables t with $\sigma(t) = t$ will in the following be called *parameter variables*. If for any disequality $x \neq y$ between tree or element variables we have $\sigma(x) = \sigma(y)$, then we also have shown unsatisfiability. Otherwise, we continue.

Adding additional constraint P. To ensure equisatisfiability to the original problem, we have to add an additional constraint P that depends on the abstraction function α, as well as on the variables and terms of tree sort in the given formula. Generation of P for content and other abstraction functions is given in [17].

---

[1] Typically, we consider theories of sets or multisets as collection theory, but integers or even booleans can also be considered as "collections".

Partial evaluation of α. We partially evaluate α in $G \wedge P$ by adding, for every term $\alpha(\mathsf{Node}(T_1, e, T_2))$, the recursive definition $\alpha(\mathsf{Node}(T_1, e, T_2)) = \mathsf{combine}(\alpha(T_1), e, \alpha(T_2))$, and recursively for the subterms T_1 and T_2. The set of all these recursive definitions, including $\alpha(\mathsf{Leaf}) = \mathsf{empty}$, will be called $\mathcal{K}_\alpha[G]$ (note that all terms in P which appear below α are also in G, so the set of needed definitions does not depend on P). G may still contain equalities of the form $\alpha(T_j) = c_j$, where T_j may be either a parameter variable or a term containing parameter variables. In the latter case, $\mathcal{K}_\alpha[G]$ contains all recursive definitions to uniquely determine $\alpha(T_j)$, given the values $\alpha(t_i)$ for all parameter variables t_i and values of element variables e_i appearing in T_j.

Solving the resulting problem. The resulting formula, when considering α as a free function symbol, is equisatisfiable to the original one. We can check its satisfiability with a combined decision procedure for $\mathcal{T}_T \cup \mathcal{T}_C \cup \mathcal{T}_E$.

Correctness of the decision procedure. It is clear that the preprocessing steps are satisfiability-preserving. Therefore, we only state that the constraint G (in the theory $\mathcal{T}_T \cup \mathcal{T}_c \cup \mathcal{T}_E \cup \mathcal{K}_\alpha$, where $\mathcal{K}_\alpha$ are the universal recursive definitions of α) is equisatisfiable to the resulting formula $G \wedge P \wedge \mathcal{K}_\alpha[G]$ in $\mathcal{T}_T \cup \mathcal{T}_c \cup \mathcal{T}_E$.

Theorem 2 (Correctness of Decision Procedure for Abstraction Functions). *Let G be a conjunction of literals which has been preprocessed as mentioned above, let P be as defined in [17] (based on G and α), and $\mathcal{K}_\alpha$ and $\mathcal{K}_\alpha[G]$ as defined above. Then* $G \models_{\mathcal{T}_T \cup \mathcal{T}_c \cup \mathcal{T}_E \cup \mathcal{K}_\alpha} \Box \iff G \cup P \cup \mathcal{K}_\alpha[G] \models_{\mathcal{T}_T \cup \mathcal{T}_c \cup \mathcal{T}_E} \Box.$

Compared to [17], we improved efficiency of the decision procedure by removing the case split on (dis)equalities of variables, which are now partially determined by unification, and then negotiated by a combined decision procedure for the base theory. Also, we do not need to convert formula P to DNF, since our correctness argument works for arbitrary boolean structure of P.

5   Complete Reasoning about Single-Invocation Axioms

Suppose we are given a function f, and we wish to prove $P(f(\bar{t}_1), \ldots, f(\bar{t}_n))$ for all values of free variables in P. In condition P, function f is applied to arbitrary terms $\bar{t}_1, \ldots, \bar{t}_n$ from some decidable theory, such as the theory of linear arithmetic, lists, sets, or trees. We wish to prove P valid using only a contract-like specification of f as an assumption. Consider a contract for f with a quantifier-free precondition $\mathsf{Pre}(\bar{x})$ and a quantifier-free postcondition $\mathsf{Post}(\bar{x}, r)$, with r denoting the resulting value. We model such a contract as the formula $\forall \bar{x}.\Phi(\bar{x}, f(\bar{x}))$, where $\Phi(\bar{x}, r)$ is $\mathsf{Pre}(\bar{x}) \to \mathsf{Post}(\bar{x}, r)$. Our goal is to show that the contract implies the desired property, that is, that the following formula is valid: $(\forall \bar{x}.\Phi(\bar{x}, f(\bar{x}))) \to P(f(\bar{t}_1), \ldots, f(\bar{t}_n))$. Equivalently, we aim to show that $(\forall \bar{x}.\Phi(\bar{x}, f(\bar{x}))) \wedge \neg P(f(\bar{t}_1), \ldots, f(\bar{t}_n))$ is an unsatisfiable formula.

In this section we show that we can reduce such satisfiability problems to the simpler *quantifier-free* satisfiability problem $\left(\bigwedge_{i=1}^n \Phi(\bar{t}_i, f(\bar{t}_i)) \right) \wedge \neg P(f(\bar{t}_1), \ldots, f(\bar{t}_n))$, in which the universal quantifier is instantiated only with the terms t_i. Note that the above instantiation confirms two important special cases. First, when $\Phi(\overline{x}, r)$ specifies the behavior of f completely, that is, r is unique for a given $\overline{x}$, then the axiom is simply a form of one-point rule applied to f as a variable. Second, if we view P as a program that invokes f, then the instantiation principle above reflects modular reasoning by inlining contracts. While it is known that such reasoning is sound, this is usually shown using operational semantics. In our formulation, the approach is sound thanks to quantifier instantiation. Moreover, the following theorem shows that this approach is also complete, as a consequence of a locality result.

Theorem 3 (Locality for Single-Invocation Axioms). *Let T be a theory with signature $\Pi_0 = (\Sigma_0, \mathsf{Pred})$, f a fresh function symbol and $\Phi(\overline{x}, f(\overline{x}))$ a $(\Sigma_0 \cup \{f\}, \mathsf{Pred})$-formula with $\overline{x}$ as the vector of all free variables and $f(\overline{x})$ the only non-ground term containing f. Then $(\mathsf{Comp_w})$ holds for the extension of T with $\forall \overline{x}.\ \Phi(\overline{x}, f(\overline{x}))$ if and only if $\models_T \forall \overline{x} \exists y.\ \Phi(\overline{x}, y)$.*

By Thm. 1, $(\mathsf{Comp_w})$ implies (ELoc), which ensures that we can decide satisfiability of formulas with respect to such axioms by simply adding one instance of the axiom for every occurrence of the function symbol in a given formula.[2]

The side condition $\models_T \forall \overline{x} \exists y.\ \Phi(\overline{x}, y)$ guarantees that the specification is consistent. It holds whenever there exists a function f with $\forall \overline{x}.\ \Phi(\overline{x}, f(\overline{x}))$. Consequently, if we have proved that some function satisfies its contract, we can use finite instantiation to reason about the contract in a complete way.

Let us also remark that Thm. 3 subsumes the decidability result from field constraint analysis [18] in a more systematic form, by expressing it as a locality result. We have shown that this result applies also to contracts of functional programs. Moreover, in addition to better understanding, locality gives us efficient implementations in the form of incremental instance generation [6].

Loss of locality for general many-invocation axioms. In general, the straightforward modification of Thm. 3 for axioms with multiple function invocations does not hold. Consider the background theory of integers $T_{\mathbb{Z}}$ and its extension with strict monotonicity

$$\forall x_1, x_2.\ x_1 < x_2 \rightarrow f(x_1) < f(x_2). \qquad (\mathsf{SMon})$$

Although the axiom is consistent, the extension of $T_{\mathbb{Z}}$ with (SMon) is not local (and thus cannot satisfy $(\mathsf{Comp_w})$). Indeed, take $G = \{f(0) = 0, f(2) = 1\}$. Then $(\mathsf{SMon})[G] \cup G$ is $T_{\mathbb{Z}}$-satisfiable, but $(\mathsf{SMon}) \cup G$ is unsatisfiable, because a strictly monotonic function on integers cannot have $f(0) = 0$ and $f(2) = 1$. Despite this negative result, in the next sections we show that in a number of cases of interest we can also obtain locality results for many-invocation axioms.

---

[2] Note that in this case, we do not need the restriction to augmented clauses, since for any G the local instantiation of $\Phi(\overline{x}, f(\overline{x}))$ can easily be shown to be equivalent to the instantiation of its augmented CNF (where Π_0-formulas are treated as literals).

6   Complete Reasoning about Many-Invocation Axioms

In this section, we push decidability of reasoning over axiomatic specifications beyond function contracts to more expressive axiom classes.

Congruence. We want to consider axiomatic specifications which go beyond contracts, in that they allow multiple function invocations. We start with congruence properties, as defined for function even in Fig. 1.

We consider equivalence relations $\sim$ on data types given by abstraction functions like content, i.e. $x \sim y \iff \mathrm{content}(x) = \mathrm{content}(y)$.

The following result allows us to reason about specifications ensuring congruence of a function wrt. an equivalence relation $\sim$. In the following Theorem, the equivalence relation $\dot\sim$ may be defined by $\overline{x}\dot\sim\overline{y} \iff \bigwedge_{i=1}^{n} x_i \sim y_i$, but it can also be any other equivalence relation on the domain of f.

Theorem 4 (Locality of Congruence). *If T is a theory with equivalence relations $\sim$ and $\dot\sim$, then* (Comp$_w$) *holds for the extension of T with a function f satisfying*

$$\forall \overline{x}, \overline{y}. \ \ \overline{x}\dot\sim\overline{y} \ \rightarrow \ f(\overline{x}) \sim f(\overline{y}). \tag{Con}$$

This theorem allows us to decide satisfiability problems with user-defined functions that are specified to be congruent with respect to a given abstraction, such as the averageAge function in the Fig. 1 example.

Monotonicity. Another important requirement for many functions is monotonicity wrt. a given abstraction, as specified for function insert in Fig. 1.

By ordering data structures wrt. the given abstraction, we define a new order with $x \preceq y \iff \mathrm{content}(x) \subseteq \mathrm{content}(y)$.

Because it is defined by a function, such a user-defined order satisfies the defining properties of the original order, except antisymmetry (unless the abstraction function is injective). That is, if the original order is a total order then the user-defined order will be a total preorder, if it is a lattice the user-defined order will be a prelattice, etc.

The following theorem extends known results on local extensions with monotone functions [16, 7] to the case of preorders and bounded (semi-)prelattices:

Theorem 5 (Locality of Monotonicity). *Let T be a theory with a binary relation $\preceq$ such that either (i) $\preceq$ is a total order, or (ii) $\preceq$ defines a bounded semi-lattice. Let $R(x, y)$ be a binary predicate which is transitive in T. Then*
(i) (Jacobs, Sofronie-Stokkermans [7])
   (Comp$_w$) *holds for the extension of T with a function f satisfying*

$$\forall \overline{x}, \overline{y}. \ \ R(\overline{x}, \overline{y}) \ \rightarrow \ f(\overline{x}) \preceq f(\overline{y}). \tag{Mon}$$

(ii) (Comp$_w$) *is already satisfied if $\preceq$ is a total preorder, or defines a bounded semi-prelattice.*

For the abstraction of data structures to their set of elements, $\preceq$ is a bounded prelattice, and for abstractions to their length or size, it is a total preorder.

Injectivity. Another important property of functions manipulating data structures is injectivity. The following result allows us to decide specifications that require injectivity of a function wrt. a given abstraction, and is a generalization of known locality results wrt. equality [5]:

Theorem 6 (Locality of Injectivity). *If $\mathcal{T}$ is a theory with equivalence relations $\sim$ and $\dot\sim$ such that (in every model of $\mathcal{T}$)[3] there are infinitely many equivalence classes wrt. $\sim$, then $(\mathsf{Comp_{w,f}})$[4] holds for the extension of $\mathcal{T}$ with a function f satisfying*

$$\forall \overline{x}, \overline{y}.\ \neg(\overline{x}\dot\sim\overline{y}) \ \rightarrow\ \neg(f(\overline{x}) \sim f(\overline{y})). \tag{Inj}$$

7   Complete Reasoning about Conjunctive Combinations

In this Section, we consider the problem of reasoning about specifications which impose several axioms from the classes introduced in Sect. 5 and 6 on the same function, as for function even from Fig. 1.

Theorem 7 (Locality of Conjunctive Combinations 1). *Let $\mathcal{T}$ be a theory with equivalence relations $\sim$ and $\dot\sim$.*

(i) *Let $\Phi(x, f(x))$ be as in Thm. 3. Then $(\mathsf{Comp_w})$ holds for the extension of $\mathcal{T}$ with a function f satisfying $(\mathsf{Con}) \cup \forall \overline{x}.\ \Phi(\overline{x}, f(\overline{x}))$ if and only if*
  $\models_{\mathcal{T}} \forall \overline{x_1}, \overline{x_2}, y_1.\ (\overline{x_1}\dot\sim\overline{x_2} \wedge \Phi(\overline{x_1}, y_1)) \rightarrow \exists y_2.\ y_1 \sim y_2 \wedge \Phi(\overline{x_2}, y_2))$.

(ii) *Let $\preceq$ and $R(x, y)$ be as in Thm. 5, and furthermore such that*
  $\models_{\mathcal{T}} x \preceq y \wedge y \preceq x \iff x \sim y$. *Then $(\mathsf{Comp_w})$ holds for the extension of $\mathcal{T}$ with a function f satisfying $(\mathsf{Con}) \cup (\mathsf{Mon})$.*

(iii) *$(\mathsf{Comp_w})$ holds for the extension of $\mathcal{T}$ with a function f satisfying $(\mathsf{Con}) \cup (\mathsf{Inj})$ if and only if $|dom(f)/\dot\sim| \leq |codom(f)/\sim|$.*

In contrast to these positive results, an extension with $(\mathsf{Mon}) \cup (\mathsf{Inj})$ or $(\mathsf{Con}) \cup (\mathsf{Mon}) \cup (\mathsf{Inj})$ will in general not be local. This essentially corresponds to strict monotonicity, mentioned as a counterexample to locality at the end of Sect. 5. We can however obtain some more positive results:

Theorem 8 (Locality of Conjunctive Combinations 2). *Let $\mathcal{T}$ be a theory with equivalence relations $\sim$ and $\dot\sim$, and $\Phi(\overline{x}, f(\overline{x}))$ as in Thm. 3. Then*

---

[3] In fact, it would be sufficient to have a notion similar to *stable infiniteness* wrt. the equivalence classes, i.e. whenever a formula is satisfiable, it is also satisfiable in a model with infinitely many equivalence classes.

[4] $(\mathsf{Comp_{w,f}})$ is a weaker form of $(\mathsf{Comp_w})$ that only considers embeddability of models where partial functions have a finite domain. It implies the slightly weakened locality condition $(\mathsf{ELoc_f})$, which requires G to be finite.

(i) (Comp$_w$) *holds for the extension of* T *with a function* f *satisfying*
(Inj) $\cup \forall \bar{x}.\ \Phi(\bar{x}, f(\bar{x}))$ *if*
$\models_T \forall \bar{x_1}, \bar{x_2}, y_1.\ (\neg(\bar{x_1} \sim \bar{x_2}) \wedge \Phi(\bar{x_1}, y_1) \rightarrow \exists^\infty y_2.\ y_1 \not\sim y_2 \wedge \Phi(\bar{x_2}, y_2)).$

(ii) (Comp$_w$) *holds for the extension of* T *with a function* f *satisfying* (Con) $\cup$
(Inj) $\cup \forall x.\ \Phi(x, f(x))$ *if and only if*
$\models_T \quad \forall \bar{x_1}, \bar{x_2}, y_1.\ (\bar{x_1} \sim \bar{x_2} \wedge \Phi(\bar{x_1}, y_1) \rightarrow \exists y_2.\ y_1 \sim y_2 \wedge \Phi(\bar{x_2}, y_2))$ *and*
$|dom(f)/\sim| \leq |codom(f)/\sim|.$

Above, $\exists^\infty y_2$ means that there exist infinitely many values y_2 in different equivalence classes wrt. $\sim$. Combination of contracts with (Mon) is in general not local, not even with the restriction to contracts which allow monotone functions.

8   Complete Reasoning about Piecewise Combinations

In some cases, it is desirable to use specifications with a case distinction over different partitions of the function domain, as for function fill in Fig. 1.

While single-invocation axioms allow case distinctions intrinsically, this is not the case for the other axiom classes we introduced, or local theory extensions in general. In the following, we consider sets of axioms $\mathcal{K}(f(\bar{x}_1), \ldots, f(\bar{x}_n))$, where in each axiom there may be up to n invocations of f. We first show that we can have different local axiomatizations in disjoint subsets of the domain, and the resulting "piecewise" axiomatization will again be local. Furthermore, we show that a piecewise local axiomatization can also be obtained for non-disjoint subsets of the domain, as long as the overlaps are finite.

In the following, we use restrictions of formulas $\mathcal{K}(f(\bar{x}_1), \ldots, f(\bar{x}_n))$ to a subset of the domain of f, specified by a formula $\Phi(\bar{x})$. We denote by $\bigwedge_{i=1}^n \Phi(\bar{x}_i) \rightarrow \mathcal{K}(f(\bar{x}_1), \ldots, f(\bar{x}_n))$ the set of augmented Π-clauses $\{\forall \bar{x}_1, \ldots, \bar{x}_n.\ \bigwedge_{i=1}^n \Phi(\bar{x}_i) \rightarrow F \vee C \mid F \vee C \in \mathcal{K}(f(\bar{x}_1), \ldots, f(\bar{x}_n))\}$. We state that such restrictions do not destroy locality properties:

Lemma 1. *Let* T *be a* Π_0*-theory and* $\mathcal{K}(f(\bar{x}_1), \ldots, f(\bar{x}_n))$ *a set of augmented* Π*-clauses such that* $T \subseteq T \cup \mathcal{K}(f(\bar{x}_1), \ldots, f(\bar{x}_n))$ *satisfies* (Comp$_w$). *For any* Π_0*-formula* $\Phi(\bar{x})$, *the extension* $T \subseteq T \cup (\Phi(\bar{x}) \rightarrow \mathcal{K}(f(\bar{x}_1), \ldots, f(\bar{x}_n)))$ *also satisfies* (Comp$_w$).

Lem. 1 and the next theorem allow piecewise combinations satisfying (Comp$_w$):

Theorem 9 (Locality of Disjoint Piecewise Combinations). *Let* T *be a* Π_0*-theory and consider* Π_0*-formulas* $\Phi_1(\bar{x}), \Phi_2(\bar{x})$ *such that* $\models_T \neg(\Phi_1(\bar{x}) \wedge \Phi_2(\bar{x}))$. *If* $\mathcal{K}_1(f(\bar{x}_1), \ldots, f(\bar{x}_n))$ *and* $\mathcal{K}_2(f(\bar{x}_1), \ldots, f(\bar{x}_m))$ *are* Π*-formulas such that* (Comp$_w$) *holds for both* $T \subseteq T \cup (\bigwedge_{i=1}^n \Phi_1(\bar{x}_i) \rightarrow \mathcal{K}_1(f(\bar{x}_1), \ldots, f(\bar{x}_n))$ *and* $T \subseteq T \cup (\bigwedge_{i=1}^m \Phi_2(\bar{x}_i) \rightarrow \mathcal{K}_2(f(\bar{x}_1), \ldots, f(\bar{x}_m))$, *then* (Comp$_w$) *also holds for* $T \subseteq T \cup \mathcal{K}$, *with*

$$\begin{aligned}
\mathcal{K} = \quad & (\textstyle\bigwedge_{i=1}^n \Phi_1(\bar{x}_i)) \rightarrow \mathcal{K}_1(f(\bar{x}_1), \ldots, f(\bar{x}_n)) \\
\cup \ & (\textstyle\bigwedge_{i=1}^m \Phi_2(\bar{x}_i)) \rightarrow \mathcal{K}_2(f(\bar{x}_1), \ldots, f(\bar{x}_m)).
\end{aligned}$$

Repeated application of Thm. 9 directly gives a locality result for arbitrarily many case distinctions.

Non-disjoint subsets with a finite intersection. If the overlap between cases is finite, we can preserve completeness by instantiating the axioms additionally for all elements in the overlap. To this end, consider a closure operator Ψ on ground terms and the more general notion of Ψ-completability [5]

(Comp$_w^\Psi$)   For every weak partial Π-model $\mathcal{M}$ of $\mathcal{T} \cup \mathcal{K}$ where Σ_0-functions are total and the definition domain of Σ_1-functions is closed under Ψ, there exists a completion which is a model of $\mathcal{T} \cup \mathcal{K}$,

which implies the Ψ-locality condition

(ELoc$^\Psi$)   For every set G of Σ_1-ground augmented Π-clauses, we have
$$\mathcal{K} \cup G \models_{\mathcal{T}} \square \iff \mathcal{K}^\Psi[G] \cup G \models_{\mathcal{T}} \square$$

with $\mathcal{K}^\Psi[G]$ defined like $\mathcal{K}[G]$, except extension terms may be in $\Psi(\mathrm{st}(\mathcal{K} \cup G))$.

Then, with a suitable Ψ we can prove Ψ-locality for piecewise combinations with finite overlaps:

Theorem 10 (Locality of Piecewise Combinations with Finite Intersection). *Let $\mathcal{T}$ be a theory with signature $\Pi_0 = (\Sigma_0, \mathsf{Pred})$ and consider Π_0-formulas $\Phi_1(\overline{x}), \Phi_2(\overline{x})$ such that in every $\mathcal{T}$-model $\mathcal{M}$, the set $O = \{\overline{x} \in M | \Phi_1(\overline{x}) \wedge \Phi_2(\overline{x})\}$ is finite. Let furthermore T_0 be a set of Σ_0-terms such that in every such model $\mathcal{M}$, $O \subseteq \{t^{\mathcal{M}} \mid t \in T_0\}$.*

If $\mathcal{K}_1(f(\overline{x}_1), \ldots, f(\overline{x}_n))$ and $\mathcal{K}_2(f(\overline{x}_1), \ldots, f(\overline{x}_m))$ are sets of augmented Π-clauses such that (Comp$_w$) holds for both the extensions of $\mathcal{T}$ with $(\bigwedge_{i=1}^{n} \Phi_1(\overline{x}_i) \rightarrow \mathcal{K}_1(f(\overline{x}_1), \ldots, f(\overline{x}_n))$ and $(\bigwedge_{i=1}^{m} \Phi_2(\overline{x}_i) \rightarrow \mathcal{K}_2(f(\overline{x}_1), \ldots, f(\overline{x}_m))$, then (Comp$_w^\Psi$) holds for the extension of for $\mathcal{T}$ with $\mathcal{K}$, where $\Psi(T) = T \cup \{f(t)|t \in T_0\}$ and

$$\begin{aligned}
\mathcal{K} = \ &(\textstyle\bigwedge_{i=1}^{n} \Phi_1(\overline{x}_i)) \rightarrow \mathcal{K}_1(f(\overline{x}_1), \ldots, f(\overline{x}_n)) \\
&\cup (\textstyle\bigwedge_{i=1}^{m} \Phi_2(\overline{x}_i)) \rightarrow \mathcal{K}_2(f(\overline{x}_1), \ldots, f(\overline{x}_m)).
\end{aligned}$$

Thm. 10 can easily be extended to a combination of arbitrarily many pieces, where $O = \{\overline{x} \in M | \Phi_i(\overline{x}) \wedge \Phi_j(\overline{x})$, for some $i \neq j\}$.

9   Related Work

Local theory extensions are one of the few approaches that allow us to obtain decision procedures for quantified satisfiability problems modulo a background theory. They have proved useful in the verification of parametrized systems [9] and properties of data structures [5,15], and in reasoning about certain properties of numerical functions [14] and functions in ordered domains [16]. Algebraic data types with size functions are shown to be decidable in [19]. Further results on handling quantified formulas in a complete way include decidable fragments of the theory of arrays [1] and of pointer data structures [11, 18], as well as certain classes of formulas that can be decided with an appropriate instantiation strategy [3]. An overview of results on local theory extensions can be found in [7].

Note that each locality result needs to be proved separately for each class of axioms of interest. A contribution of our paper is to identify new classes of local theories, and to show that they are useful in verification of new classes of properties of functional programs.

Acknowledgements. We thank Viorica Sofronie-Stokkermans for detailed comments on drafts of this paper, as well as the original suggestion to generalize the monotonicity axiom from [16] to the version in [7]. We thank Philippe Suter for discussions related to Section 4.

References

1. Bradley, A.R., Manna, Z., Sipma, H.B.: What's decidable about arrays? In: Emerson, E.A., Namjoshi, K.S. (eds.) VMCAI 2006. LNCS, vol. 3855, pp. 427–442. Springer, Heidelberg (2005)
2. Cohen, E., Dahlweid, M., Hillebrand, M., Leinenbach, D., Moskal, M., Santen, T., Schulte, W., Tobies, S.: VCC: A practical system for verifying concurrent C. In: Berghofer, S., Nipkow, T., Urban, C., Wenzel, M. (eds.) TPHOLs 2009. LNCS, vol. 5674, pp. 23–42. Springer, Heidelberg (2009)
3. Ge, Y., de Moura, L.: Complete instantiation for quantified SMT formulas. In: Bouajjani, A., Maler, O. (eds.) CAV 2009. LNCS, vol. 5643, pp. 306–320. Springer, Heidelberg (2009)
4. Gligoric, M., Gvero, T., Jagannath, V., Khurshid, S., Kuncak, V., Marinov, D.: Test generation through programming in UDITA. In: International Conference on Software Engineering, ICSE (2010)
5. Ihlemann, C., Jacobs, S., Sofronie-Stokkermans, V.: On local reasoning in verification. In: Ramakrishnan, C.R., Rehof, J. (eds.) TACAS 2008. LNCS, vol. 4963, pp. 265–281. Springer, Heidelberg (2008)
6. Jacobs, S.: Incremental instance generation in local reasoning. In: Bouajjani, A., Maler, O. (eds.) CAV 2009. LNCS, vol. 5643, pp. 368–382. Springer, Heidelberg (2009)
7. Jacobs, S.: Hierarchic Decision Procedures for Verification. PhD thesis, Saarland University, Germany (2010)
8. Jacobs, S., Kuncak, V.: On complete reasoning about axiomatic specifications. Technical Report EPFL-REPORT-151486, EPFL (2010)
9. Jacobs, S., Sofronie-Stokkermans, V.: Applications of hierarchical reasoning in the verification of complex systems. Electronic Notes in Theoretical Computer Science 174(8), 39–54 (2007)
10. Lam, P., Kuncak, V., Rinard, M.: Generalized typestate checking for data structure consistency. In: Cousot, R. (ed.) VMCAI 2005. LNCS, vol. 3385, pp. 430–447. Springer, Heidelberg (2005)
11. McPeak, S., Necula, G.C.: Data structure specifications via local equality axioms. In: Etessami, K., Rajamani, S.K. (eds.) CAV 2005. LNCS, vol. 3576, pp. 476–490. Springer, Heidelberg (2005)
12. Podelski, A., Wies, T.: Counterexample-guided focus. In: 37th ACM SIGACT-SIGPLAN Symposium on Principles of Programming Languages (2010)

13. Sofronie-Stokkermans, V.: Hierarchic reasoning in local theory extensions. In: Nieuwenhuis, R. (ed.) CADE 2005. LNCS (LNAI), vol. 3632, pp. 219–234. Springer, Heidelberg (2005)
14. Sofronie-Stokkermans, V.: Efficient hierarchical reasoning about functions over numerical domains. In: Dengel, A.R., Berns, K., Breuel, T.M., Bomarius, F., Roth-Berghofer, T.R. (eds.) KI 2008. LNCS (LNAI), vol. 5243, pp. 135–143. Springer, Heidelberg (2008)
15. Sofronie-Stokkermans, V.: Locality results for certain extensions of theories with bridging functions. In: Schmidt, R.A. (ed.) CADE-22. LNCS, vol. 5663, pp. 67–83. Springer, Heidelberg (2009)
16. Sofronie-Stokkermans, V., Ihlemann, C.: Automated reasoning in some local extensions of ordered structures. Journal of Multiple-Valued Logic and Soft Computing 13(4-6), 397–414 (2007)
17. Suter, P., Dotta, M., Kuncak, V.: Decision procedures for algebraic data types with abstractions. In: 37th ACM SIGACT-SIGPLAN Symposium on Principles of Programming Languages (2010)
18. Wies, T., Kuncak, V., Lam, P., Podelski, A., Rinard, M.: Field constraint analysis. In: Emerson, E.A., Namjoshi, K.S. (eds.) VMCAI 2006. LNCS, vol. 3855, pp. 157–173. Springer, Heidelberg (2005)
19. Zhang, T., Sipma, H.B., Manna, Z.: Decision procedures for recursive data structures with integer constraints. In: Basin, D., Rusinowitch, M. (eds.) IJCAR 2004. LNCS (LNAI), vol. 3097, pp. 152–167. Springer, Heidelberg (2004)

String Analysis as an Abstract Interpretation

Se-Won Kim and Kwang-Moo Choe

Korea Advanced Institute of Science and Technology

Abstract. We formalize a string analysis within abstract interpretation framework. The abstraction of strings is given as a conjunction of predicates that describes the common configuration changes on the reference pushdown automaton while processing the strings. We also present a family of pushdown automata called ϵ bounded pushdown automata. This family covers all context-free languages, and by using this family of pushdown automata, we can prevent abstract values from becoming infinite conjunctions and guarantee that the operations required in the analyzer are computable.

1 Introduction

The baseline of the correctness of a document-generating program is that all documents generated by the program should be syntactically correct. The syntax is usually defined by a context-free grammar or equivalently a pushdown automaton, which we call the *reference* of the syntax.

The current verification techniques for this property use resolution of constraints, which over-approximate the output of the program. This approach was first introduced in [5], and was adopted in [9,21,15] and other semantic analyses based on them. Though this approach has been quite useful in many applications, it has some drawbacks.

- It is hard to recover the precision lost during the constraint generation. In [9], the ignored branch conditions become the main cause of false alarms.
- Integration with other analysis is not easy because they use constraints as the target of verification.
- The constraints usually trace the flow of strings only for the shallow variables like the local and global variables[4]. If the program heavily involves heap or structured data, they often fail to capture the precise flow within the constraints.
- It may require manually provided *hot-spots*. Each hot-spot is composed of one program point and a variable whose possible string values should be verified.
- It rejects the constraints that generate valid substrings of the reference, and implicitly enforces whole and complete program for the verification.

We alleviate these problems by designing a string analysis within abstract interpretation framework[6,7,8], and let it benefit from various abstract interpretation techniques. The contributions of this paper are:

R. Jhala and D. Schmidt (Eds.): VMCAI 2011, LNCS 6538, pp. 294–308, 2011.

- We suggest a novel abstraction of strings. These abstract values express the key characteristics of strings that compose the output documents.
- Our string analysis can be used for all context-free references.
- Practically, our abstract domain and abstract operations can be plugged into a conventional analysis framework. This makes it easy to compose string analysis with other analysis and to benefit from the various techniques devoloped for abstract interpretation.

We outline the remainder of this paper. We first define notations and terminologies and see one motivating example that cannot be verified by the previous constraint generation approach. After that, we thoroughly study the meaning of one string from the view of the reference automaton and apply this knowledge to the design of a new abstract domain for strings. We compare our work with previous approaches and conclude.

2 Preliminary

We assume the reference is given as a pushdown automaton (henceforth PDA).

Definition 1 (PDA). *A PDA* **A** *is a tuple defined as* $\mathbf{A} = (Q, \Sigma, \Gamma, \Delta, q_0, Z_0, Q_F)$

- Q *is the finite set of states.*
- Σ *is the finite set of input symbols.*
- Γ *is the finite set of stack symbols.*
- $\Delta \subseteq Q \times \Gamma^* \times (\Sigma \cup \{\epsilon\}) \times Q \times \Gamma^*$ *is the finite set of actions. An action* $(q_1, \gamma_1, a, q_2, \gamma_2) \in \Delta$ *is written as* $q_1\gamma_1 \overset{a}{\mapsto} q_2\gamma_2$.
- $q_0 \in Q$ *is the initial state.*
- $Z_0 \in \Gamma$ *is the initial stack content.*
- $Q_F \subseteq Q$ *is the set of final states.*

A configuration of PDA consists of a state and stack content. If the current state is q and the stack content is $Z_1, Z_2 \ldots, Z_n$ from the top, we denote it as $qZ_1Z_2 \cdots Z_n$. Reading a from the input, the PDA configuration changes from $q_1\gamma_1\gamma$ to $q_2\gamma_2\gamma$ if $q_1\gamma_1 \overset{a}{\mapsto} q_2\gamma_2 \in \Delta$. This PDA transition is written as $q_1\gamma_1\gamma \overset{a}{\mapsto} q_2\gamma_2\gamma$. If the PDA configuration changes from $q_1\gamma_1$ to $q_2\gamma_2$ while reading $w \in \Sigma^*$, we denote it as $q_1\gamma_1 \overset{w}{\mapsto} q_2\gamma_2$. If PDA configuration can be changed from $q_1\gamma_1$ to $q_2\gamma_2$, we denote it as $q_1\gamma_1 \overset{*}{\mapsto} q_2\gamma_2$. The language that the automaton **A** accepts is defined as

$$L(\mathbf{A}) = \{w \in \Sigma^* \mid q_0Z_0 \overset{w}{\mapsto} q_F, \ q_F \in Q_F\}.$$

We denote state by p and q, stack symbol by X, Y, and Z, input by w. Note that we can transform this stateful PDA to a stateless PDA if we remove the set Q from the tuple and let the set of stack symbol be the disjoint union of Q and Γ, and ensure the state is always at the stack top. In this vein, we use η, γ, δ and κ to represent a PDA configuration or a part of it, which may contain state symbol at the first position. For a configuration $q\gamma$, if $q\gamma = \gamma_1\gamma_2$, we say γ_1 (resp. γ_2) is a *prefix* (resp. *suffix*) of configuration $q\gamma$. We resort to the stateful PDA definitions for three reasons.

- The stateful PDAs are practically more convenient for describing PDAs.
- The distinguished first symbols of configurations help us identify the start of a configuration in a graph structure representing set of configurations. This graph structure is introduced in Section 4.
- The state can be an extra space for integration of other facilities. For example, input preprocessors based on finite state transducers can be integrated into a stateless parser as additional state actions.

3   Motivating Example

In this section, we demonstrate the weakness of constraint generation approach by one simple scenario. Let us assume that we are developing a program that should generate document described by the PDA in Fig. 1a. In the middle of the development, we have the program[1] in Fig. 1b, which constructs valid substring of the document.

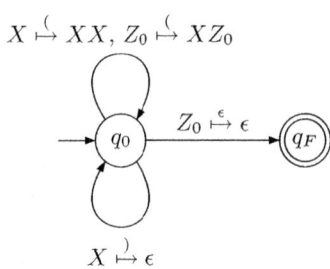

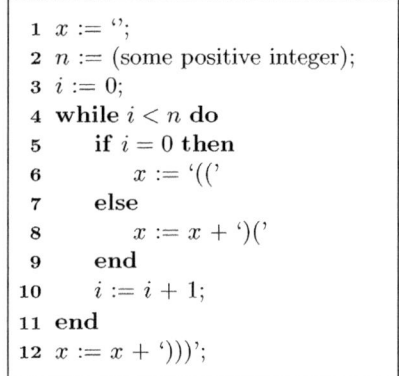

```
1  x := '';
2  n := (some positive integer);
3  i := 0;
4  while i < n do
5      if i = 0 then
6          x := '(('
7      else
8          x := x + ')('
9      end
10     i := i + 1;
11 end
12 x := x + ')))';
```

(a) A PDA for matching parentheses. State transition is represented by the start and end node of the edge, and stack behavior and input symbol is shown on edges. q_F is the final state.

(b) A program in the middle of development. It generates a valid substring of matching parentheses.

Fig. 1. A reference PDA and an incomplete target program

When we apply constraint generation approach in [5] to verify this program, we get the following constraints that track the flow of string values.

$$X_1 \to \epsilon \qquad\qquad X_4 \to X_1 \mid X_9 \qquad X_6 \to ((\qquad\qquad X_8 \to X_4)($$
$$X_9 \to X_6 \mid X_8 \qquad X_{11} \to X_1 \mid X_9 \qquad X_{12} \to X_{11}))) $$

Each X_i represents the possible set of strings that the variable x can have after executing the ith line. Since the program constructs only part of its output

---

[1] The loop sturucture of this snippet is from a web application written in PHP, SchoolMate v1.5.4.

document, the resolution based on the language inclusion within the reference simply fails. However, we assume that the programmer supplies the left and right context of X_{12} by manually adding the rule $S \rightarrow (X_{12}$ to the constraints and uses S as the hot-spot for the verification.

Nevertheless, the constraints suggest that the program might generate '()))' by the derivation $S \Rightarrow (X_{12} \Rightarrow (X_{11}))) \Rightarrow (X_1))) \Rightarrow ())$), which leads to a false alarm. This false alarm is caused by ignoring the value of n and the control flow that depends on it. There can be two ways to remove this false alarm:

- Run the sign and flow analysis before constraint generator and use the analysis result to transform the program before the constraint generation, or let the constraint generator take into account the analysis result during the constraint generation.
- Run the string analysis simultaneously with sign and flow analysis in one framework.

In this paper, we develop the theoretical facilities for the second approach. The second approach is conceptually simpler in that it requires only abstract domain and abstract operations for strings, and has strictly more opportunity to correctly verify programs. It can also support modular string analysis: we can verify incomplete programs and help find bugs early during the development.

4 PDA Configuration Changes Caused by One String

In this section, we study configuration changes caused on the reference PDA while reading a string. We devise an algorithm which builds a finite representation of all possible PDA configuration changes caused by the given string. We also study a condition for PDAs which is closely related to the complexity of the representation. Throughout this section, we assume the reference PDA is given as $\mathbf{A} = (Q, \Sigma, \Gamma, \Delta, q_0, Z_0, Q_F)$.

4.1 The Need

If the output document is to be correctly processed by the reference PDA, each fragment, which we assume is one of the string literals in the program, successively transforms the PDA configuration from the initial configuration to the accepting. The first fragment transforms the initial configuration to another, and the second fragment transforms the ending configuration of the first fragment to another. This process continues to the last fragment, which must transform the configuration to the accepting at the end. This observation leads us to consider the PDA configuration changes caused by string literals in the program. The same idea was used in [17] for deterministic $LR(k)$ languages. They regard parse actions as *black box* mappings from one parse stack to another. On the other hand, we look into the detailed inner workings of configuration transitions on a string in more general non-deterministic PDAs.

4.2   Configuration Change

For each string literal, we only need to know all pairs of the initial configuration before processing the string and the last configuration after processing it.

Definition 2 (configuration change). *If for a string $w \in \Sigma^*$, $q_0 Z_0 \overset{*}{\mapsto} \delta\eta \overset{w}{\mapsto} \delta'\eta$ and the suffix η is intact (never popped nor read) while processing w, we say w has a configuration change $\delta \leadsto \delta'$.*

We deliberately omitted the suffix η for the configuration change. It is natural since the bottom η is not relevant as a change caused by the given string. Note that the most conservative choice for η is ϵ. If the bottom η is chosen aggressively to be maximal, we say the resulting configuration change is *minimal*.

4.3   Algorithm for Computing Minimal Configuration Changes

We present the algorithm for finding all minimal configuration changes. This is enough since each configuration change can be obtained by appending valid fragment η to one of the minimal configuration changes. We assume that the input string is $w = a_1 a_2 \cdots a_n$, and n denotes the length of the input.

The algorithm has two phases:

1. It computes all reachable configurations before processing w. The configurations are represented as a finite graph(actually, a relaion '$\succ$' on a finite set $\mathcal{I}$), which we refer as *the initial closure*. The closure represents reachable configurations after processing possible left context of w.
2. Based on the initial closure, it extends the graph while reading the actual input. A valid path in the graph extension corresponds to δ' of a minimal configuration change $\delta \leadsto \delta'$ of w. It also simultaneously constructs a grammar whose sentence corresponds to δ of $\delta \leadsto \delta'$.

Our algorithm is based on the algorithm of [18], which applies tabular parsing to pushdown transducers. This technique also has been applied to parsing sentence with wild cards[19], parsing sentence of ambiguous grammar[3] and linear-time suffix parsing of deterministic pushdown languages[23]. Our algorithm constructs the relation '$\succ$' and a context-free grammar. The relation represents a set of reachable configurations, which is similar to [18,23,19,3]. The difference is on the constructed grammar. The constructed grammar in [18,23,19,3] represents the output of pushdown transducers, that is, all the possible parse of the given string. On the other hand, the constructed grammar of our algorithm represents the prefixes of configurations which had been read from the initial closure while processing the input.

The Relation '$\succ$'. The binary relation '$\succ$' is on the finite set of *items*,

$$\mathcal{I} = \{[q\gamma]_* \mid q\gamma \text{ is a prefix of } q_0 Z_0 \dashv\}$$
$$\cup \{[q\gamma]_i \mid i = * \vee (i \in \mathbb{Z} \wedge 0 \leq i \leq n), \exists \gamma_1 \overset{a}{\mapsto} \gamma_2 \in \Delta. \; q\gamma \text{ is a prefix of } \gamma_2\},$$

Initial relation: $[q_0]_* \succ [q_0 Z_0]_* \succ [q_0 Z_0 \dashv]_*$.

If

$$pX_1 \cdots X_m \overset{a}{\mapsto} qY_1 \cdots Y_l \in \Delta$$
$$[p]_* \succ [\gamma_1 X_1]_* \succ \cdots \succ [\gamma_m X_m]_* \succ [\gamma]_*$$

then

$$[q]_* \succ [qY_1]_* \succ \cdots \succ [qY_1 \cdots Y_l]_* \succ [\gamma]_*$$

Fig. 2. The condition for the initial closure

where the fresh stack symbol '$\dashv$' denotes the end of configurations. Intuitively, each $[q\gamma X]_i$ (resp. $[q]_i$) represents one stack symbol X(resp. a state symbol q) and the relation '$\succ$' represents 'is on top of' relation between symbols. Let us call $[\gamma_1]_{i_1} \succ [\gamma_2]_{i_2}$ an *edge*. The relation as a whole represents a set of configurations. The non-negative integer index i of an item represents the length of the input read when the relation is extended. If the edge is constructed as the initial closure, where the arbitrary input is used, we use '$*$' for the index.

For convenience, we abbreviate $[\gamma_1]_{i_1} \succ [\gamma_2]_{i_2}, [\gamma_2]_{i_2} \succ [\gamma_3]_{i_3}, \ldots, [\gamma_{k-1}]_{i_{k-1}} \succ [\gamma_k]_{i_k}$ as one chain: $[\gamma_1]_{i_1} \succ [\gamma_2]_{i_2} \succ \cdots \succ [\gamma_k]_{i_k}$.

The Initial Closure. The *initial closure* is the minimal relation that satisfies the condition in Fig. 2. Its construction starts with the relation that represents the initial configuration, and extends the relation by simulating the PDA actions on the relation. Note that PDA actions on the relation are *additive*: they do not destruct edges for popping symbols.

The initial closure describes all possible PDA configurations after reading some input.

Theorem 1. $\exists \gamma_1, \ldots, \gamma_m.\ [p]_* \succ [\gamma_1 Z_1]_* \succ \cdots \succ [\gamma_m Z_m]_* \succ [q_0 Z_0 \dashv]_*$, *if and only if* $q_0 Z_0 \overset{*}{\mapsto} p Z_1 \cdots Z_m$.

The initial closure can also be used for checking the validity of a prefix.

Corollary 1. $\exists \gamma_1, \ldots, \gamma_m, \gamma, Z.\ [p]_* \succ [\gamma_1 Z_1]_* \succ \cdots \succ [\gamma_m Z_m]_* \succ [\gamma Z]_*$, *if and only if* $\exists \eta.\ q_0 Z_0 \overset{*}{\mapsto} p Z_1 \cdots Z_m \eta$.

All the proof of the propositions in this paper can be found in [14].

Processing the Actual Input. The minimal configuration changes of the given input w can be obtained from the smallest extension of the initial closure and the smallest set of production rules that satisfy the rule in Fig. 3. Their construction starts with the initial closure and empty set of production rules, and repeats the rule in Fig. 3 until there can be no additional edges and production rules.

If
$$pX_1 \cdots X_m \overset{a}{\mapsto} qY_1 \cdots Y_l \in \Delta$$
$$[p]_{i_0} \succ [\gamma_1 X_1]_{i_1} \succ \cdots \succ [\gamma_m X_m]_{i_m} \succ [\gamma]_{i_{m+1}}$$

and if

1. $i_0 = * \wedge a \in \{\epsilon, a_1\}$, then $k = |a|$ and
   - Let $\Upsilon = ([qY_1 \cdots Y_l]_k \succ [\gamma]_{i_{m+1}})$
   - Add $\Upsilon \to pX_1 \cdots X_m$
2. $i_j \in \mathbb{Z} \wedge i_{j+1} = * \wedge a \in \{\epsilon, a_{i_0+1}\}$, then $k = i_0 + |a|$ and
   - Let $\Upsilon = ([qY_1 \cdots Y_l]_k \succ [\gamma]_{i_{m+1}})$
   - Two cases:
     - If $j = m$, then add $\Upsilon \to ([\gamma_m X_m]_{i_m} \succ [\gamma]_{i_{m+1}})$
     - If $j < m$, then add $\Upsilon \to ([\gamma_j X_j]_{i_j} \succ [\gamma_{j+1} X_{j+1}]_{i_{j+1}}) X_{j+1} \cdots X_m$
3. $i_{m+1} \in \mathbb{Z} \wedge a \in \{\epsilon, a_{i_0+1}\}$, then $k = i_0 + |a|$.

If one of the above three conditions is satisfied,

$$[q]_k \succ [qY_1]_k \succ \cdots \succ [qY_1 \cdots Y_l]_k \succ [\gamma]_{i_{m+1}}$$

Fig. 3. Processing the actual input $w = a_1 a_2 \cdots a_n$. The construction starts with the initial closure.

Essentially, the rule in Fig. 3 simulates PDA actions on the relation as the rule in Fig. 2. The increased complexity comes from its additional workload:

- It reads input symbols from left to right and uses the variable k to denote the length of the input read. It uses k for the index of the items that represent the symbols pushed by the current action.
- It transcribes the *deficiency* of configuration into a production rule. The deficiency occurs when we directly or indirectly use the edges in the initial closure for popping symbols.

Before the details of Fig. 3, we show some properties first, which will help us understand the algorithm.

Lemma 1. *If* $[\gamma_1]_{i_1} \succ [\gamma_2]_{i_2}$ *then,* $(i_1, i_2 \in \mathbb{Z} \wedge i_1 \geq i_2)$ *or* $(i_1 \in \mathbb{Z} \wedge i_2 = *)$ *or* $(i_1 = i_2 = *)$.

The constructed context-free grammar uses $Q \cup \Gamma$ as the set of terminal, and $([\gamma_1]_{i_1} \succ [\gamma_2]_{i_2})$'s for non-terminals, whose language represents the symbols read from the initial closure to construct the edge. From the algorithm, we can verify that the referred non-terminals have more restricted form.

Lemma 2. *If* $([\gamma_1]_{i_1} \succ [\gamma_2]_{i_2})$ *appears in a production rule added by the rule in Fig. 3, then* $i_1 \in \mathbb{Z}$ *and* $i_2 = *$.

In other words, only the edges that cross the boundary of the initial closure are required for the grammar.

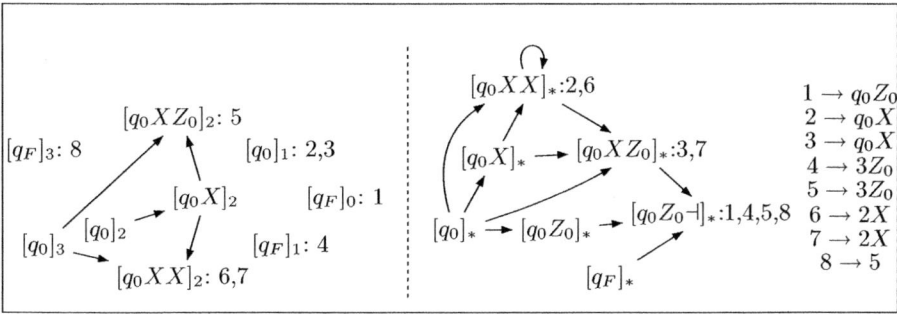

Fig. 4. The result of computing minimal configuration changes on the input ')()' with the PDA in Fig. 1a

Understanding the Rule in Fig. 3. When the algorithm discovers an action,

- whose pop symbols match a sequence of items in '$\succ$',
- and whose input symbol a is at the current position of the input,

it adds the sequence of edges for the push. The indexes of the pushed items are the length of the input read so far. The reasoning behind the production rule construction for each cases are:

1. Case $i_0 = *$: By Lemma 1, $i_0 = i_1 = \cdots = i_{m+1} = *$. In this case, all pop symbols are from the initial closure. We transcribe the deficient fragment $pX_1 \cdots X_m$ from the sequence of the popped items, and remember this fragment as a possible deficiency required for constructing the edge $[qY_1 \cdots Y_l]_k \succ [\gamma]_*$.
2. Case $i_j \in \mathbb{Z} \wedge i_{j+1} = *$: By Lemma 1, $i_0, \ldots, i_j \in \mathbb{Z} \wedge i_{j+1} = \cdots = i_{m+1} = *$.
   - Case $j = m$: No pop symbols are directly from the initial closure. However, the last edge is crossing the boundary of the initial closure, and we are using this edge for popping X_m. In this case, we have only the indirect deficiency for using the last edge, and need to refer it as a possible deficiency required for constructing the edge $[qY_1 \cdots Y_l]_k \succ [\gamma]_*$.
   - Case $j < m$: In this case, we have both kinds of deficiency. We need to append the indirect deficiency, which is referred by the non-terminal, and the direct deficiency transcribed from the items of the initial closure.
3. Case $i_{m+1} \in \mathbb{Z}$: By Lemma 1, $i_0, \ldots, i_{m+1} \in \mathbb{Z}$. Since there is neither direct nor indirect deficiency, it simply add no production rule.

In Fig. 4, we show the result for the input ')()' using the PDA in Fig. 1a as the reference. The relation '$\succ$' is represented as arrows. The initial closure lies on the right of the dotted line, and the edges from processing the actual input lies on the left of the dotted line. For conciseness, those edges that should have crossed the dotted line are represented as the additional number labels on items. For example, the label 1 on $[q_F]_0$ and $[q_0 Z_0 \dashv]_*$ represents the edge from $[q_F]_0$ to $[q_0 Z_0 \dashv]_*$. These number labels are also used in the constucted grammar, which is on the right of the initial closure.

Interpretation of the Result

Theorem 2. *For the input w, there exists $[q]_{i_0} \succ [\gamma_1 Z_1]_{i_1} \succ \cdots \succ [\gamma_m Z_m]_{i_m} \succ [\gamma Z]_*$ where $i_0 = |w| \wedge i_m \in \mathbb{Z}$ and $\eta \in L([\gamma_m Z_m]_{i_m} \succ [\gamma Z]_*)^2$, if and only if w has the minimal configuration change $\eta \leadsto q Z_1 \cdots Z_m$.*

By Theorem 2, the minimal configuration changes from Fig. 4 are $q_0 X Z_0 \leadsto q_0 Z_0$, $q_0 X X \leadsto q_0 X$, and $q_0 X Z_0 \leadsto q_F$.

When the input is ϵ, there is one additional minimal configuration change $\epsilon \leadsto \epsilon$ besides the configuration changes computed from Fig. 3. This trivial configuration change can not be computed by the algorithm because the algorithm finds configuration changes that involve at least one PDA action.

4.4   The Finiteness Condition: ϵ Boundedness

We suggest a condition for PDAs that makes the number of minimal configuration changes finite for any input string.

Definition 3 (ϵ bounded). *A PDA $\mathbf{A}$ is ϵ bounded if there exists a positive constant k s.t. $q_0 Z_0 \overset{*}{\mapsto} \gamma_1 \overset{\epsilon}{\mapsto} \gamma_2 \overset{\epsilon}{\mapsto} \cdots \overset{\epsilon}{\mapsto} \gamma_m$ implies $-k \leq |\gamma_1| - |\gamma_m| \leq k$.*

Theorem 3. *The followings are equivalent for the PDA $\mathbf{A}$.*

- *The PDA is ϵ bounded.*
- *For any input, the size of the minimal configuration change is linearly bounded.*
- *For any input, the number of minimal configuration changes is finite.*

The family of ϵ bounded PDAs contains many practical PDAs. This family includes any no delay or finite delay PDAs. It contains simple machines[10] and super-deterministic PDAs[12]. This family also includes any deterministic pushdown parser whose transition involves only finite number of consecutive ϵ actions. We can directly use these PDAs for the analysis.

It turns out that the ϵ bounded PDAs can express any context-free languages. In [13], it is shown that any context-free language has an equivalent no delay PDA, which is ϵ bounded. The construction of such PDA is essentially based on a non-deterministic topdown parser for the grammar in Greibach normal form. Therefore, if the given reference PDA is not ϵ bounded, we can use another PDA which is ϵ bounded and describes the same language.

5   Formalizing String Analysis

In this section, we design a string analysis for the given reference PDA $\mathbf{A}$. We first define the abstract domain $(\mathcal{C}_{\mathbf{A}}, \sqsubseteq)$, correctness relation as a Galois connection between $(2^{\Sigma^*}, \subseteq)$ and $(\mathcal{C}_{\mathbf{A}}, \sqsubseteq)$. We show the abstract concatenation operation and simple widening operation. We also revisit the previous motivating example equipped with the domain.

---

[2] This is the set of sentences derived from the non-terminal $[\gamma_m Z_m]_{i_m} \succ [\gamma Z]_*$.

5.1 The Predicate Domain

The main idea of our abstraction is that we can regard a configuration change of the reference PDA $\mathbf{A}$ as a predicate for string:

$$\delta \rightsquigarrow \delta'(w) = \exists \eta. \ (q_0 Z_0 \overset{*}{\mapsto} \delta \eta) \wedge (\eta \text{ is intact while } \delta \eta \overset{w}{\mapsto} \delta' \eta).$$

If at least one string has the configuration change $\delta \rightsquigarrow \delta'$, we say $\delta \rightsquigarrow \delta'$ is *inhabited*.

Lemma 3. *For inhabited predicates $\delta \rightsquigarrow \delta'$ and $\delta \eta \rightsquigarrow \delta' \eta$, $\delta \rightsquigarrow \delta'$ implies $\delta \eta \rightsquigarrow \delta' \eta$.*

Let us represent the above syntactic implication between inhabited predicates as $\delta \rightsquigarrow \delta' \Rightarrow \delta \eta \rightsquigarrow \delta' \eta$. The inhabited predicates along with $\lambda w. \ true$ and $\lambda w. \ false$ form a well-founded complete lattice using '$\Rightarrow$' as the order, where the supremum is $\lambda w. \ true$ and the infimum is $\lambda w. \ false$.

5.2 The Domain $(\mathcal{C}_{\mathbf{A}}, \sqsubseteq)$

Since the domain of predicates does not have the best abstraction property in general, we define the analysis domain $(\mathcal{C}_{\mathbf{A}}, \sqsubseteq)$ which is basically the conjunction completion[6, Example 6.6] of the predicate domain.

The set $\mathcal{C}'_{\mathbf{A}}$ is a collection of conjunctions of inhabited predicates. We will use $C = \bigwedge_{i \in I} \eta_i \rightsquigarrow \kappa_i$ to denote a conjunction, and c to denote one inhabited predicate. We allow set operation on the conjunctions regarding them as sets of predicates. We demand two additional conditions for each conjunction $C \in \mathcal{C}'_{\mathbf{A}}$:

- Each predicate of C is not related to other predicates in C by '$\Rightarrow$'.
- The conjunction C is inhabited. i.e. $\exists w \in \Sigma^*. \ \forall i \in I. \ \eta_i \rightsquigarrow \kappa_i(w)$.

The first condition is necessary for the order $\sqsubseteq$, which is defined below, to be antisymmetric. This condition can be enforced for any set of inhabited predicates P by the *norm* function: $norm(P) = \bigwedge \{c \in P \mid \forall c' \in P. \ (c' \Rightarrow c) \Rightarrow (c = c')\}$. The second condition prevents many different elements from having the same concrete meaning of empty set of strings. Now, the set $\mathcal{C}_{\mathbf{A}}$ is defined as $\mathcal{C}_{\mathbf{A}} = \mathcal{C}'_{\mathbf{A}} \cup \{\perp\}$.

Definition 4 ($\sqsubseteq$). *For $C_1, C_2 \in \mathcal{C}'_{\mathbf{A}}$, $C_1 \sqsubseteq C_2$ if and only if $\forall c_2 \in C_2. \ \exists c_1 \in C_1. \ c_1 \Rightarrow c_2$. The $\perp$ is the infimum of $(\mathcal{C}_{\mathbf{A}}, \sqsubseteq)$.*

The $\perp$ is the identity of $\bigsqcup$, and we define $\bigsqcup \emptyset = \perp$. The *least upper bound* of non-empty $S \subseteq \mathcal{C}'_{\mathbf{A}}$ is

$$\bigsqcup S = \bigwedge \{c \in \bigcup S \mid \forall C' \in S. \ \exists c' \in C'. \ c' \Rightarrow c\}.$$

Theorem 4. *The domain $(\mathcal{C}_{\mathbf{A}}, \sqsubseteq)$ is a complete lattice.*

5.3   The Galois Connection

The concretization of a conjunction $C \in \mathcal{C}'_\mathbf{A}$ is the common inhabitants of all the predicates in C,

$$\gamma(C) = \{w \in \Sigma^* \mid \forall c \in C.\ c(w)\}.$$

We define $\gamma(\bot) = \emptyset$. The abstraction of non-empty set of strings $S \subseteq \Sigma^*$ is the normalized conjunction of common predicates of all the string in S,

$$\alpha(S) = norm(\{c \mid \forall w \in S.\ c(w)\}).$$

For the empty set, we define $\alpha(\emptyset) = \bot$.

Fact 1. *If the reference PDA A is ϵ bounded, the abstraction of a string is finite and computable: the abstraction is the same as the normalized conjunction of all minimal configuration changes of the string.*

Theorem 5. *The Galois connection, $(2^{\Sigma^*}, \subseteq) \xleftrightarrow[\alpha]{\gamma} (\mathcal{C}_\mathbf{A}, \sqsubseteq)$ holds.*

5.4   Abstract String Concatenation Operation

Now we define the abstract string concatenation operation $\odot$ for conjunctions. Generaly, the *best* abstract transfer functions on Galois connection between complete lattices can be induced by the functions α, γ and the concrete semantics after removing redundancy in the abstract domain[8]. However, we could not find the redundancy elimination as a computable function. Hence, we manually define a *correct* abstract concatenation operation.

We first consider operation $\odot_1$ on predicates:

$$\eta_1 \rightsquigarrow \kappa_1 \odot_1 \eta_2 \rightsquigarrow \kappa_2 = \begin{cases} \eta_1 \rightsquigarrow \kappa_2 \delta & \text{if } \kappa_1 = \eta_2 \delta, \\ \eta_1 \delta \rightsquigarrow \kappa_2 & \text{if } \kappa_1 \delta = \eta_2 \text{ and } \eta_1 \delta \text{ is a valid prefix,} \\ \lambda w.\ true & \text{otherwise.} \end{cases}$$

Basically, the $\odot_1$ operation is simple composition of two configuration changes. It recovers and fixes the implicit configuration as much as it is needed to compose with the other predicate. If they can not be concatenated, the result is $\lambda w.\ true$. The operation $\odot$ on the conjunction is defined as

$$C_1 \odot C_2 = norm(\{c \mid c = c_1 \odot_1 c_2 \neq \lambda w.\ true, c_1 \in C_1, c_2 \in C_2\}).$$

The $\bot$ is zero of $\odot$ operation, i.e. $\bot \odot C = C \odot \bot = \bot \odot \bot = \bot$.

Theorem 6. *The operator $\odot$ is associative, and a correct upper approximation of concatenation operation.*

5.5   The Widening Operator

Although we can design a computable analysis for ϵ bounded reference PDAs thanks to Fact. 1 and $\odot$ operation, the analysis can be non-terminating. Let's consider the program on the right and the reference automaton in Fig. 1a. After the nth visit of line 3, the abstract value of the variable x at the

```
1  x := '';
2  while e do
3      x := ')' + x + '(';
4  end
```

head of the loop is $q_0 X^{n+1} \rightsquigarrow q_0 X^{n+1} \wedge q_0 X^n Z_0 \rightsquigarrow q_0 X^n Z_0$.

To guarantee the termination, we use the set intersection as the widening operator on conjunctions. We can use this widening at a loop after bounded number of iterations. When the reference PDA has a decision procedure for inclusion(e.g. [12,1,16,22]), it is possible to avoid using the widening operator. Instead, we can use the result from the literature and effectively find the maximum size of predicates. However, finding the maximum size is not recommendable since it requires investigation of the global structure[3] of the program and finding a feasible left context string for each abstract value. This approach is impossible for modular analysis. Usually, the heuristic constant bound of the size or the widening operator described earlier are sufficient for verification.

5.6   Example Revisited

We will analyze the program in Fig. 1b with a sign domain for integers, and $(\mathcal{C}_{\mathbf{A}}, \sqsubseteq)$ for strings, simultaneously. The sign domain is $\{\lambda n.\ false,\ \lambda n.\ n = 0,\ \lambda n.\ n > 0,\ \lambda n.\ n < 0,\ \lambda n.\ true\}$. One peculiar aspect of this program is that the conditional on line 5 takes $true$ branch only at the first iteration and this fact is crucial to the verification. Thus, we use the trace partitioning[20] technique and achieve the effect of loop unrolling by using token set $\{*, 1, 2+\}$. Here, the token $*$ means the control is not in the loop, and the token 1 means it is in the loop and doing the first iteration, and the token 2+ means it is in the loop and after the first iteration. We use the tuple of control location, token and abstract memory state for analysis. The label l_i is for labeling the location after the statement on line i, and the abstract memory state is the set of pairs of a variable name and its abstract value. Then, the stabilized abstract value on l_{11} is $(l_{11}, *, \{i : \lambda n.\ n > 0,\ n : \lambda n.\ n > 0,\ x : q_0 X \rightsquigarrow q_0 XXX \wedge q_0 Z_0 \rightsquigarrow q_0 XX Z_0\})$ which takes into account the abstract values escaped from all iterations. Finally, the abstract value after line 12 is $(l_{12}, *, \{i : \lambda n.\ n > 0,\ n : \lambda n.\ n > 0,\ x : q_0 X \rightsquigarrow q_0 \wedge q_0 X Z_0 \rightsquigarrow q_F\})$ since the abstraction of ')))' is $q_0 XXX \rightsquigarrow q_0 \wedge q_0 XXX Z_0 \rightsquigarrow q_F$.

From the result, we have verified that the string in x after line 12 is correct subsentence of the reference PDA. More specifically, it has the effect of popping one symbol X, and also can make up a whole sentence when it is appended to a string that has the abstract value $q_0 Z_0 \rightsquigarrow q_0 X Z_0$. Note that we don't need any string analysis specific preprocessing for the program before the analysis.

---

[3] For the simpler cases where a context-free grammar can be regarded as the program, we refer you to [16,22].

6   Related Work

In [17], the authors used the idea that a string can be represented by a function in $P \to P$ that maps a parse stack to resulting parse stack after processing the string. They subsequently approximate set of strings as the mapping between abstract parse stacks. Roughly speaking, our abstraction directly uses a mapping in $P \to P$ and its functional domain restriction as an abstraction for set of strings. While [17] supports $LR(k)$ languages, ours can support all context-free languages and modular analysis. In [4], the authors devised a string analyzer in an abstract interpretation framework. Their analyzer can verify the output of program at the level of regular languages.

In [26], the author presented a type system for document-generating program. The type-checking is based on constraint generation and verifying the constraints by an extended Earley parser. This technique can be used for any context-free grammar. Since the type for string is one of the non-terminals, the supported abstraction for string is inherently finite.

Abstract parsing[9] can provide abstraction for strings as a finite mapping from one stack top to a set of stack fragment that can be pushed on the stack top after reading the strings. This technique is very fast and precise for HTML generating programs. One weak point of this technique is that, it does not provide abstraction for strings which pop the initial stack top. For example, they do not directly provide the abstraction for ')' in matched parentheses parser. This makes their abstraction not enough for designing abstract interpretation. However, they allow this kind of string to appear in the middle of data flow equations when some stack symbols already have been pushed onto the initial stack top by the preceding vocabulary string of the equation.

The analysis in [15] uses the verification and grammar transformation for parenthesis languages described in [16] to check the XML validity of the output. The characteristic function $c(x)$ and $d(x)$ in [16] for string x is closely related to our abstraction. For a string x, the values of $d(x)$ and $c(x) + d(x)$ correspond respectively to the size of η and κ, where $\eta \rightsquigarrow \kappa$ is a minimal configuration change for x. The technique in [22] uses the verification and grammar transformation for balanced languages. The ρ function in [22, Section 2] maps a string to the sequence of unmatched close tags and open tags. These close tags and open tags match respectively η and the reverse of κ. The techniques in [15,22] can check the XML validity after grammar transformation. In our approach, we can check the XML validity without requiring a seperate phase by using an ϵ bounded PDA which also encodes the XML validity condition.

Substring parsing can provide useful information about document fragments. We used the parsing algorithm in [18] with different grammar construction. Their algorithm can handle arbitrary context-free language and gives all the possible parse for the input in a form of context-free grammar. The parser in [25] also handles arbitrary context-free grammar. However, this parser does not find all possible parses. The $LR(k)$ substring recognizer in [2,11] decides whether the string is a substring of the language in linear time without constructing the parse.

7   Discussion and Ongoing Work

The algorithm in Section 4 takes $O(n^3)$ if we decompose the PDA actions to smaller ones, and listing all the minimal configuration changes can take exponential time in the worst case. However, in practical languages, the number of minimal configuration changes does not show the exponential behavior. The main reason is that as the string gets longer the number of possible context for the string usually decreases.

We have implemented our string analysis on Soot framework[24] as a proof of concept. We have tested the analyzer on small reference PDAs and programs. We are planning to analyze more realistic programs for practical reference languages.

The $LR(k)$ parsers are not ϵ bounded in general, and the abstraction of abstract parsing [9] is based on collecting possible parse stacks. We are currently working on formalizing abstract parsing using configuration changes and abstract interpretation framework[6] to support modular abstract parsing.

Acknowledgments. This work was supported by the Engineering Research Center of Excellence Program of Korea Ministry of Education, Science and Technology(MEST) / National Research Foundation of Korea(NRF) (Grant 2010-0001714).

References

1. Alur, R., Madhusudan, P.: Visibly pushdown languages. In: STOC 2004: Proceedings of the Thirty-Sixth Annual ACM Symposium on Theory of Computing, pp. 202–211. ACM, New York (2004)
2. Bates, J., Lavie, A.: Recognizing substrings of LR(k) languages in linear time. ACM Trans. Program. Lang. Syst. 16(3), 1051–1077 (1994)
3. Billot, S., Lang, B.: The structure of shared forests in ambiguous parsing. In: Proceedings of the 27th Annual Meeting on Association for Computational Linguistics, pp. 143–151. Association for Computational Linguistics, Morristown (1989)
4. Choi, T.-H., Lee, O., Kim, H., Doh, K.-G.: A practical string analyzer by the widening approach. In: APLAS, pp. 374–388 (2006)
5. Christensen, A.S., Møller, A., Schwartzbach, M.I.: Precise analysis of string expressions. In: Cousot, R. (ed.) SAS 2003. LNCS, vol. 2694, pp. 1–18. Springer, Heidelberg (2003), http://www.brics.dk/JSA/
6. Cousot, P., Cousot, R.: Abstract interpretation frameworks. Journal of Logic and Computation 2(4), 511–547 (1992)
7. Cousot, P., Cousot, R.: Abstract interpretation: a unified lattice model for static analysis of programs by construction or approximation of fixpoints. In: POPL 1977: Proceedings of the 4th ACM SIGACT-SIGPLAN Symposium on Principles of Programming Languages, pp. 238–252. ACM, New York (1977)
8. Cousot, P., Cousot, R.: Systematic design of program analysis frameworks. In: POPL 1979: Proceedings of the 6th ACM SIGACT-SIGPLAN Symposium on Principles of Programming Languages, pp. 269–282. ACM, New York (1979)
9. Doh, K.-G., Kim, H., Schmidt, D.A.: Abstract parsing: Static analysis of dynamically generated string output using LR-parsing technology. In: Palsberg, J., Su, Z. (eds.) SAS 2009. LNCS, vol. 5673, pp. 256–272. Springer, Heidelberg (2009)

10. Friedman, E.P.: The inclusion problem for simple languages. Theor. Comput. Sci. 1(4), 297–316 (1976)
11. Goeman, H.: On parsing and condensing substrings of LR languages in linear time. Theor. Comput. Sci. 267(1-2), 61–82 (2001)
12. Greibach, S.A., Friedman, E.P.: Superdeterministic pdas: A subcase with a decidable inclusion problem. J. ACM 27(4), 675–700 (1980)
13. Greibach, S.A.: A new normal-form theorem for context-free phrase structure grammars. J. ACM 12(1), 42–52 (1965)
14. Kim, S.-W.: Proofs for formalizing string analysis within abstract interpretation framework. Technical report, KAIST (2010),
    http://pllab.kaist.ac.kr/~sewon.kim/papers/pf-saai-tr.pdf
15. Kirkegaard, C., Møller, A.: Static analysis for java servlets and JSP. In: Yi, K. (ed.) SAS 2006. LNCS, vol. 4134, pp. 336–352. Springer, Heidelberg (2006)
16. Knuth, D.E.: A characterization of parenthesis languages. Information and Control 11(3), 269–289 (1967)
17. Kong, S., Choi, W., Yi, K.: Abstract parsing for two-staged languages with concatenation. In: GPCE 2009: Proceedings of the Eighth International Conference on Generative Programming and Component Engineering, pp. 109–116. ACM, New York (2009)
18. Lang, B.: Deterministic techniques for efficient non-deterministic parsers. In: Loeckx, J. (ed.) ICALP 1974. LNCS, vol. 14, pp. 255–269. Springer, Heidelberg (1974)
19. Lang, B.: Parsing incomplete sentences. In: Proceedings of the 12th conference on Computational linguistics, pp. 365–371. ACL, Morristown (1988)
20. Mauborgne, L., Rival, X.: Trace partitioning in abstract interpretation based static analyzers. In: Sagiv, M. (ed.) ESOP 2005. LNCS, vol. 3444, pp. 5–20. Springer, Heidelberg (2005)
21. Minamide, Y.: Static approximation of dynamically generated web pages. In: WWW 2005: Proceedings of the 14th International Conference on World Wide Web, pp. 432–441. ACM, New York (2005)
22. Minamide, Y., Tozawa, A.: Xml validation for context-free grammars. In: APLAS, pp. 357–373 (2006)
23. Nederhof, M.-J., Bertsch, E.: Linear-time suffix parsing for deterministic languages. J. ACM 43(3), 524–554 (1996)
24. Vallée-Rai, R., Hendren, L., Sundaresan, V., Lam, P., Gagnon, E., Co, P.: Soot - a java optimization framework. In: Proceedings of CASCON 1999, pp. 125–135 (1999)
25. Rekers, J., Koorn, W.: Substring parsing for arbitrary context-free grammars. SIGPLAN Not. 26(5), 59–66 (1991)
26. Thiemann, P.: Grammar-based analysis of string expressions. In: TLDI 2005: Proceedings of the 2005 ACM SIGPLAN International Workshop on Types in Languages Design and Implementation, pp. 59–70. ACM, New York (2005)

ExplainHoudini: Making Houdini Inference Transparent

Shuvendu K. Lahiri[1] and Julien Vanegue[2]

[1] Microsoft Research
shuvendu@microsoft.com
[2] Microsoft Corporation
jvanegue@microsoft.com

Abstract. Houdini is a simple yet scalable technique for annotation inference for modular contract checking. The input to Houdini is a set of candidate annotations, and the output is a consistent subset of these candidates. Since this technique is most useful as an annotation assistant for user-guided refinement of annotations, understanding the reason for the removal of annotations is crucial for a user to refine the set of annotations, and classify false errors easily. This is especially true for applying Houdini to large legacy modules with thousands of procedures and deep call chains. In this work we present a method *ExplainHoudini* that explains the reason why a given candidate was removed, purely in terms of the existing candidates. We have implemented this algorithm and provide preliminary experience of applying it on large modules.

1 Introduction

Static analysis aims to check a property on a program with high coverage without executing the code. However, automatic static analysis of most non-trivial properties on real programs is undecidable. This fact either manifests in spurious warnings (false alarms) or non-termination of static analysis tools. For example, tools based on abstract interpretation [5] may generate false alarms when the intermediate invariants cannot be captured in the underlying abstract domains (which are mostly fixed); on the other hand, extensible tools based on predicate abstraction [10] or interpolants [15] may diverge while performing automated refinement of abstractions.

User-specified intermediate contracts or annotations (preconditions, postconditions etc.) are helpful in minimizing the false alarms for static analysis. In recent years, a number of contract-checking tools for real programs have been developed including ESC/Java [9] (for Java), Spec# [3] (for C#), HAVOC [4], and VCC [6](for C). These tools can be used to check a range of properties, starting from the absence of runtime defects (such as absence of null dereferences), to simple object type-state properties (such as a lock is acquired before a release) to more complex functional correctness properties. The research problems for these tools vary depending on the type of properties being checked. For example, the main challenges in tools proving functional correctness (mainly in the

R. Jhala and D. Schmidt (Eds.): VMCAI 2011, LNCS 6538, pp. 309–323, 2011.
© Springer-Verlag Berlin Heidelberg 2011

hands of verification experts) are in devising efficiently-checkable logics for expressing data invariants, and exploiting data encapsulation for reasoning about composition of multiple modules [3,6]. On the other hand, the main hurdle for (extended static) checking simple user-defined properties lies in the annotation overhead required for a (non-expert) user to check a property with high coverage and low false alarm [9,1]. This work concerns the latter.

In the extended static checking [9,1] scenario for large code bases, the user drives the verification process. The user first adds the property to be checked using procedure contracts and instrumented assertions. The next steps alternate between adding a few core annotations and directing an annotation inference assistant to generate a set of simple intermediate annotations. A desirable property of the inference assistant is to be *configurable* by an average user, be *scalable* to large codebases, and provide *transparency* in providing feedback about the inference.

HOUDINI [8] is a simple yet scalable annotation inference technique that meets most of these requirements. The input to Houdini is a set of candidate annotations (or "guesses"), and the output is a consistent subset of these candidates. It is a greatest fixed point algorithm that removes candidates that cannot be proved by modular checking. It is *configurable* by allowing the user to specify a set of guesses using a set of simple patterns. For example, a user may add a candidate precondition for any procedure that all pointer arguments are non-null [8], or that the lock parameters are released [1], or even guess exceptions to module invariants [13]. The underlying analysis uses a theorem prover and does not require defining new abstract semantics. It is *scalable* as the inference converges linearly in the number of candidates; and often much earlier if only a small number of candidates are removed[1]. It also uses procedure modular checking that does not involve inspecting long interprocedural counterexamples. It is *transparent* to a great extent as the user can inspect the set of annotations that were inferred.

However, when applying HOUDINI on large modules, we have spent most of the effort in understanding the reason a candidate annotation is removed [13,1]. There are several reasons a candidate could be removed: (i) it does not hold, (ii) the existing annotations are not strong enough, or (iii) prover incompleteness. Understanding the reason is crucial for classifying false alarms from true bugs, and refining the set of annotations. In fact, the authors of the original article of HOUDINI rightly mention [8]:

> *Surprisingly, our experience indicates that presenting the refuted annotations and the causes thereof is the most important aspect of the user interface.*

To address this partially, the tool displayed the call-site where a candidate precondition was removed, and possibly an intraprocedural path that lead to the

---

[1] In contrast to a least fixed point based forward predicate abstraction approach that can solve the same problem [10].

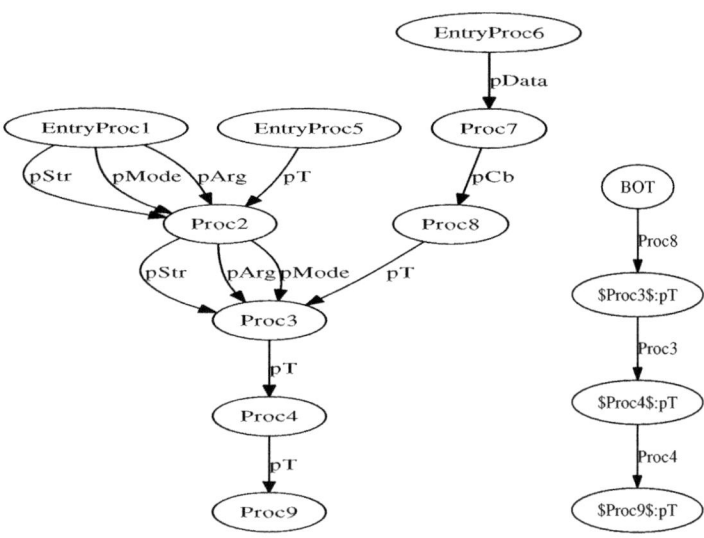

Fig. 1. (a) Dependency of candidates removed for `Proc9`. (b) Output of EXPLAINHOU-
DINI for the candidates removed for `Proc9`.

removal. Although this is useful, it provides very little interprocedural information to understand the cause of the removal.

Let us illustrate the problem with the graph in Figure 1 (a). The graph on
the left represents a subset of candidates removed when applying the HOUDINI
implementation in `HAVOC` for annotation inference on a large Windows module
measuring more than 250KLOC, containing more than 3000 procedures. The
candidates correspond to preconditions that pointer parameters are *trusted*; that
is, the pointer was either allocated inside the kernel, or had undergone a sanitization by calling one of the designated procedures [1]. The graph represents
a small slice of the overall graph of candidates removed — the slice contains
candidates removed from the procedure `Proc9` and its callers[2]. Each node in
the graph corresponds to a procedure, and an edge (p, c, q) represents that the
candidate c of procedure q was removed while checking the body of p. Instead
of showing the entire annotation on the edges (which can be verbose), we just
show the parameter contained in the candidate.

Although the graph shows the local cause such as the call-site where a precondition was removed, it provides little interprocedural information. For instance,
it is not clear if the candidate for `pT` parameter of the method `Proc9` was removed because there is a pointer flowing from one of the roots (say one of the
parameters `pMode` of `EntryProc1`) in this graph without sanitization (true bug),

---

[2] The names of the procedures and the parameters have been obfuscated due to security reasons.

or whether there is a missing precondition or postcondition along the path that would have ensured that the candidate was provable (false alarm). Initial attempt at tracing the call chains from a removed candidate back to the roots of the graph manually was extremely time consuming. Matters get worse when candidate postconditions are involved; one not only has to look at all the transitive callers of a given procedure, but all the callees of these transitive callers as well, resulting in huge graphs. For a module of this size, one can end up spending a few minutes to sometimes several hours trying to understand the root cause of an annotation removal to certify true bugs.

In this work, we provide a step towards making HOUDINI more transparent by providing a more meaningful interprocedural reason of the annotation removal in addition to the above graph. Our goal is much less modest compared to the work on automatic *refinement* (e.g. [11]) to suggest new annotations, or even suggest which procedures to refine. For a run of HOUDINI, we provide a notion of *cause* for the removal of a candidate in terms of another removed candidate whenever possible (or $\perp$ otherwise). These causes can be composed to provide an interprocedural path from $\perp$ to a candidate that was removed; the path captures a sequence of candidate removal ultimately leading to the removal of a candidate. It is an interprocedural explanation of the removal *purely in terms of the candidates removed*. We provide an algorithm EXPLAINHOUDINI, which computes the cause for each removed annotation by adding a simple "replay" mechanism to any HOUDINI implementation. The algorithm is extremely simple (does not require any more functionality from the theorem prover than what HOUDINI requires), modular (does not require analyzing large interprocedural traces that may be infeasible for large modules), and does not require changing the search heuristics in HOUDINI.

Figure 1 (b) displays the output of EXPLAINHOUDINI on the removed candidate for Proc9. Here, each node represents a candidate (prefixed with procedure name) and the edge denotes the procedure whose checking removed the annotation. The node BOT marks the $\perp$ node. An edge from c' to c denotes that the cause of c is c'. The interprocedural dependency graph suggests that the candidate precondition on the pT parameter of Proc9 cannot be removed until the candidate on pT parameter of Proc3 was removed. However, the removal of this candidate on pT parameter from Proc3 cannot be explained in terms of the existing candidates. The information narrows down the choice of places to inspect to understand the false alarm. The information strongly suggests that the pointer from the root does not flow into Proc9, and the false alarm can most likely be found out by looking at the procedures in the path of the explanation. We encourage the reader to revisit the graph after gaining familiarity with the notion of causality captured by these graphs in Section 3.

In the rest of the paper, we provide some background on HOUDINI (Section 2), formalize cause and describe EXPLAINHOUDINI (Section 3), and provide preliminary experience on applying it on a couple of large modules (Section 4).

2   Background

In this section, we formalize the concepts in this paper, and present the HOUDINI algorithm [8].

2.1   Source and Assertion Languages

We assume that the source language supports standard features of most imperative programming languages such as variable assignment ($x := e$) statements, conditional statements (if (e) s else t), sequential composition ($s; t$), and procedure calls. Accesses to the heap (dereferencing pointers ($*x$) or object fields ($x.f$)) is modeled as reads and writes to global map variables that model the entire heap or individual fields in the heap [9,4,3]. To enable a uniform formalism, we assume that loops are modeled as tail-recursive procedures.

In addition to assertions present in the program (using **assert** ϕ statements), each procedure can be decorated with preconditions and postconditions. A precondition on a procedure p is specified as **requires** ϕ to denote that the condition ϕ is true whenever the procedure p is invoked. A postcondition on a procedure p is specified as **ensures** ϕ to denote that the condition ϕ is true whenever the procedure p returns. The language of ϕ constitutes the *assertion language* for the program. These assertions are well-scoped Boolean expressions over program variables (parameters, globals, return variables), including accesses to fields in objects (e.g. **requires** $x.f < 5$). The latter is desugared as read over the global map modeling the heap. The assertion language also permits the use of ghost variables and fields to write these specifications. The preconditions and postconditions together constitute the *contract* for a procedure[3]. A program $P = \{p_1, \ldots, p_k\}$ constitutes a set of procedures, where some are marked as *entry* procedures (no callers), and some are marked as *external* procedures (without a body).

2.2   Modular Contract Checking and Contract Inference

A modular contract checker verifies that each procedure in a program P can verify its contracts with respect to the contracts of its callees. To perform a modular verification of a procedure p, a procedure call $h(e)$ is replaced by the following sequence of statements: (i) assert the preconditions of h, (ii) scramble all the globals (including the heap map) that could be modified by h and (iii) assume the postconditions of h. For the resultant call-free procedure, a logical formula called the *verification condition* (VC) is generated that encodes the correctness of the procedure p with respect to its contracts. If the formula is valid, then p satisfies its contracts. A failure indicates that some postcondition of p or a precondition of one of the callees of p could not be proved.

---

[3] For simplicity, we have ignored the issue of modifies clauses in the formalism. For the purpose of this paper, they can be regarded as additional postconditions involving the global heap map that express the facts that remain unchanged.

Let $\mathcal{A}$ denote a set of annotations where $\mathcal{A}_p \subseteq \mathcal{A}$ denotes the annotations for a procedure $p \in P$, i.e., $\mathcal{A} = \bigcup_{p \in P} \mathcal{A}_p$. For a procedure $p \in P$ and two sets of annotations $\mathcal{A}$ and $\mathcal{A}'$, we define CHECKVC$(p, \mathcal{A}, \mathcal{A}')$ to be a method that checks the procedure p against the contracts in $\mathcal{A}$, *assuming* the contracts in $\mathcal{A}'$. In other words, the contracts in $\mathcal{A}'$ are "free", i.e. they are not checked. For example, a postcondition $a \in \mathcal{A}'$ for a procedure $p \in P$ can be assumed at a call-site of p but is not checked when the body of p is analyzed. The generalization to allow unchecked assumptions will be useful when we describe the HOUDINI algorithm later in this section.

Definition 1 (Contract checking). *For a set of procedures $P = \{p_1, \ldots, p_k\}$ and a set of annotations $\mathcal{A} = \bigcup_{p \in P} \mathcal{A}_p$, is* CHECKVC$(p, \mathcal{A}, \{\})$ = VERIFIED *for every $p \in P$?*

Definition 2 (Contract inference). *For a set of procedures $P = \{p_1, \ldots, p_k\}$ and a set of annotations $\mathcal{A} = \bigcup_{p \in P} \mathcal{A}_p$, does there exist (infer) a set of annotations $\mathcal{A}' = \bigcup_{p \in P} \mathcal{A}'_p$, such that* CHECKVC$(p, \mathcal{A} \cup \mathcal{A}', \{\})$ = VERIFIED *for every $p \in P$?*

A restricted form of the contract inference is the *monomial predicate abstraction* problem [10]:

Definition 3 (Monomial predicate abstraction). *For a set of procedures $P = \{p_1, \ldots, p_k\}$, a set of annotations $\mathcal{A} = \bigcup_{p \in P} \mathcal{A}_p$, and a set of candidate annotations $\mathcal{C} = \bigcup_{p \in P} \mathcal{C}_p$, does there exist (infer) a set of annotations $\mathcal{A}' = \bigcup_{p \in P} \mathcal{A}'_p$, such that (i) $\mathcal{A}'_p \subseteq \mathcal{C}_p$ for each $p \in P$ and (ii)* CHECKVC$(p, \mathcal{A} \cup \mathcal{A}', \{\})$ = VERIFIED *for every $p \in P$?*

Care has to be taken to not allow candidate preconditions on entry procedures and candidate postconditions on external procedures that do not have a body. One can trivially satisfy the requirement for contract inference with a candidate precondition of **requires** false for each entry procedure of a program. Similarly, a candidate postcondition **ensures** false for a external procedure can lead to unsoundness. In both these cases, these annotations are always going to be assumed and never checked.

2.3   Houdini Algorithm

HOUDINI [8] is an algorithm for solving the monomial predicate abstraction problem described earlier. Given a program P annotated with a set of contracts $\mathcal{A}$ and a set of candidate contracts $\mathcal{C}$, the algorithm employs a greatest fixed-point algorithm over the set of candidates: it starts with the entire set of candidates in $\mathcal{C}$ and successively removes a candidate $c \in \mathcal{C}$ if it is unable to prove c using the CHECKVC() procedure. It converges when no candidates can be removed. Let $\mathcal{A}' \subseteq \mathcal{C}$ be the set of annotations that were not removed during the fixed-point algorithm — the algorithm guarantees that CHECKVC$(p, \mathcal{A}', \mathcal{A})$ = VERIFIED for every $p \in P$. Further, if CHECKVC$(p, \mathcal{A}' \cup \mathcal{A}, \{\})$ = VERIFIED for every

---

Algorithm 1. HOUDINI

Require: A program $P = \{p_1, p_2, \ldots, p_k\}$
Require: A set of contracts $\mathcal{A} = \bigcup_{p \in P} \mathcal{A}_p$
Require: A set of candidate contracts $\mathcal{C} = \bigcup_{p \in P} \mathcal{C}_p$
Ensure: A set of inferred contracts $\mathcal{A}' = \bigcup_{p \in P} \mathcal{A}'_p$, such that $\mathcal{A}'_p \subseteq \mathcal{C}_p$ for each $p \in P$

1: $WL \leftarrow P$ // Add all procedures to the worklist
2: **for** $p \in P$ **do**
3:   $\mathcal{R}_p \leftarrow \{\}$
4: **end for**
5: **while** $\neg$ISEMPTY(WL) **do**
6:   $p \leftarrow$ DEQUEUE(WL)
7:   **if** CHECKVC($p, \mathcal{C}, \mathcal{A}$) $\neq$ VERIFIED **then**
8:     Let c be the candidate contract that was not proved
9:     $q \leftarrow$ PROC(c)
10:    CAUSE(c) $\leftarrow$ EXPLAINHOUDINI($p, c, \mathcal{A}, \mathcal{C}, \mathcal{R}$)
11:    $\mathcal{C}_q \leftarrow \mathcal{C}_q \setminus \{c\}$
12:    $\mathcal{R}_q \leftarrow \mathcal{R}_q \cup \{c\}$
13:    **if** c is a precondition **then**
14:        $WL \leftarrow WL \cup \{q\}$
15:    **else**
16:        $WL \leftarrow WL \cup \{q\} \cup$ CALLERS(q) //q is the same as p in this case
17:    **end if**
18:   **end if**
19: **end while**
20: **return** $\bigcup_{p \in P} \mathcal{C}_p$

$p \in P$, then the algorithm returns "yes" to the monomial predicate abstraction decision problem.

Algorithm 1 describes the algorithm in detail. The   highlighted   line can be ignored now. The algorithm maintains a worklist WL of procedures that are pending to be analyzed. This is initialized with all the procedures in P (line 5). The variable $\mathcal{R}_p$ tracks the set of candidates removed from $\mathcal{C}_p$ at any instant, and is initialized to $\{\}$ (line 3). At every iteration, the algorithm extracts a procedure p from the worklist (line 6) and checks the procedure p with respect to $\mathcal{A} \cup \mathcal{C}$. Notice that the algorithm uses CHECKVC($p, \mathcal{C}, \mathcal{A}$) (in line 7) to ensure that none of the assertions in $\mathcal{A}$ are checked (although they may be assumed) during the contract inference stage.

If the check fails for a candidate assertion $c \in \mathcal{C}$, then it extracts the procedure q containing this assertion (using the procedure PROC() in line 9), removes it from $\mathcal{C}_q$ and adds it to $\mathcal{R}_q$. Finally, it updates WL with q and all the callers of q (only when c is a postcondition of q). It returns the set of candidate assertions that have not been removed as the inferred set of annotations. The algorithm also guarantees that the maximum set of candidates are retained irrespective of the removal order [8,12].

```
typedef struct _B{
   int g;
   int h;
}B, *PB;

PB gb; //global

ensures probed(p)
void Probe(PVOID p);
```

```
cand_requires probed(q)
cand_ensures probed(q)
void Inner6(PB q)
{
   assert probed(q);
   q->h = 25;
}
```

```
requires probed(gb)
void Inner5()
{
   PB b = gb;
   Inner6(b);
}
```

```
cand_requires probed(q)
cand_ensures probed(q)
void Inner4(PB q)
{
   assert probed(q);
   q->h = 10;
}
```

```
cand_requires probed(q)
cand_ensures probed(q)
void Inner3(PB q)
{
   assert probed(q);
   q->g = 5; // TRUE BUG
}
```

```
cand_requires probed(q)
cand_ensures probed(q)
ensures q ⟹ probed(q)
void Inner2(PB q)
{
   if (q)
       Probe(q);
}
```

```
cand_requires probed(q)
cand_ensures probed(q)
void Inner1(PB q)
{
   Inner2(q);
   Inner3(q);
   if (q)
       Inner4(q);
}
```

```
cand_ensures probed(p)
void Entry(PB p)
{
   Inner1(p);
   Probe(gb);
   Inner5();
}
```

Fig. 2. Running example. The additional annotations are underlined. The highlighted annotations are the inferred candidates after adding the additional annotations.

An alternate implementation may use CHECKVC$(p, \mathcal{A} \cup \mathcal{C}, \{\})$ in line 7 and terminate when an annotation $a \in \mathcal{A}$ cannot be proved. The above algorithm tries to find a subset of the candidates in $\mathcal{C}$ that are provable *assuming* the annotations in $\mathcal{A}$. This is often desirable in practice when $\mathcal{A}$ contains multiple annotations; the inferred annotations can serve as additional annotations that can remove some of the false alarms, even though all the annotations in $\mathcal{A}$ may not be provable (and may indeed be bugs).

2.4   Example

Consider the C example in Figure 2 — we will use this example to illustrate concepts in this paper. The example consists of seven procedures with Entry as the entry procedure and a set of internal procedures Innerx. We check the *probe-before-use* property on this example — every input pointer (pointers reachable from the globals and inputs to the entry procedures) needs to be sanitized with a call to a procedure Probe before being used (dereferenced) [1]. This is modeled by a ghost field inside each pointer that tracks whether it has been probed — the formula *probed*(q) denotes that the pointer q is probed. The procedure Probe has a postcondition to ensure that a pointer is probed in the post-state. The property is instrumented by adding an assertion before every dereference of a pointer (in procedures Inner3, Inner4 and Inner6). For this example, only the procedure Inner3 has a violation of the property.

The annotations in **requires** , **ensures** and **assert** denote the set $\mathcal{A}$. The annotations in **cand_requires** denote the set of candidate annotations $\mathcal{C}$ — let us ignore them initially. Let us also pretend that the underlined <u>annotations</u> are not present initially. An attempt at modular contract checking of this example produces three counterexamples, one for each of the **assert** statements.

At this point, a user would add the set of guesses using the following instrumentation (say in HAVOC [1]) — for any pointer argument p of a procedure, add **cand_requires** *probed*(p) (except for entry procedures) and **cand_ensures** *probed*(p) (except for external procedures with no bodies). This results in the set of candidate annotations present in the program. Running HOUDINI on this example unfortunately removes all the candidates, and infers an empty set of annotations that does not reduce the set of warnings for the example.

Let us assume that the user now adds the annotations that are <u>underlined</u>. Performing modular checking still yields the same three assertion failures. Running HOUDINI(with the candidates) in the presence of the additional annotations in $\mathcal{A}$ yields new inferred annotations (highlighted). With these inferred annotations, a modular checking only produces one assertion failure (in Inner3) corresponding to a true bug.

3   ExplainHoudini

Recall that a candidate annotation $c \in \mathcal{C}$ is removed by HOUDINI when it is unable to prove c while checking the annotations of a procedure modularly. There can be several reasons for the removal of a candidate annotation: (1) it does not hold, (2) the set of annotations of the procedure and its callees are not strong enough to prove c, or (3) the theorem prover may be incomplete in proving c. Ideally, the notion of cause should provide feedback for distinguishing between these cases and perhaps suggest additional annotations in the case of (2) to refine the current annotation set. However, our goal is less ambitious we simply want to show the user the *interprocedural* reason why HOUDINI failed to prove an annotation, purely in terms of the candidate annotations. It is left to the user to use this information to refine the candidate set, identify true errors, or fix prover incompleteness.

In this section, we first define a notion of local *cause* for the removal of a candidate purely in terms of other candidates, and then describe an algorithm EXPLAINHOUDINI that computes the cause for candidates that are removed. Finally, we illustrate the working of this algorithm on the running example.

3.1   Cause

For a run of the HOUDINI algorithm (Algorithm 1), consider a candidate $c \in \mathcal{C}$ that was removed. Let $\mathcal{R}_c \subseteq \mathcal{C}$ contain the set of candidates that were removed prior to the removal of c. Further, let p_c be the procedure whose checking removed c. For such a c, we define a set CAUSESET(c) $\subseteq \mathcal{R}_c$ as follows: a $c' \in$ CAUSESET(c) iff the following conditions hold:

1. $c' \in \mathcal{R}_c$, and
2. there exists a $\mathcal{R}_1 \subseteq \mathcal{R}_c$ such that:

(a) $\textsc{CheckVC}(p_c, \{c\}, \mathcal{A} \cup (\mathcal{C} \setminus \mathcal{R}_1)) = \text{VERIFIED}$, and
(b) $\textsc{CheckVC}(p_c, \{c\}, \mathcal{A} \cup ((\mathcal{C} \setminus \mathcal{R}_1)) \setminus \{c'\}) \neq \text{VERIFIED}$.

Intuitively, a c' belongs to $\textsc{CauseSet}(c)$ if there is a subset $\mathcal{R}_1$ of $\mathcal{R}_c$ such that (a) the removal of $\mathcal{R}_1$ from $\mathcal{C}$ does not affect the provability of c, and (b) the removal of $\mathcal{R}_1 \cup \{c'\}$ makes c unprovable. Note that the two conditions imply that $c' \notin \mathcal{R}_1$. Moreover, since $c' \in \mathcal{R}_c$, c' has to be different from c.

In other words, $\textsc{CauseSet}(c)$ contains a set of candidates removed before the removal of c, such that there exists an order of removing candidates where c would not be removed unless c' was removed. The intuition is as follows: if the presence of *all* the candidates in $\mathcal{C}$ is not strong enough to prove c, then $\textsc{CauseSet}(c)$ will be empty; otherwise, the set of candidates in $\mathcal{C}$ is not strong enough to prove some $c' \in \textsc{CauseSet}(c)$. Since there is a removal order in which c cannot be removed until c' is removed, we label c' as a likely cause for the removal of c.

Although $\textsc{CauseSet}(c)$ may contain multiple potential causes for each c, considering all possible causes may be overwhelming and may be expensive to compute. In the rest of paper, we will describe a method that concisely describes a *single candidate removal sequence* for each candidate contract c. Let $\mathcal{R}$ be the set of candidates that are removed when the HOUDINI algorithm terminates. For each $c \in \mathcal{R}$, we define $\textsc{Cause}(c) \in \mathcal{R} \cup \{\bot\}$, such that:

1. $\textsc{Cause}(c) \in \textsc{CauseSet}(c)$, when $\textsc{CauseSet}(c) \neq \{\}$, and
2. $\textsc{Cause}(c) = \bot$, otherwise

For a candidate c that was removed, one can also record the intraprocedural trace that removed c as part of $\textsc{Cause}(c)$ in addition to the candidate c' that forms the cause. These causes can be composed to provide an interprocedural path from $\bot$ to a candidate c that was removed, denoting a candidate removal sequence that terminates in the removal of the particular candidate c.

3.2   Example Revisited

Figure 3 shows a graph (for the running example in Figure 2) where a node represents a candidate annotation $c \in \mathcal{R}$ that was removed, and there is an edge (c', p, c) to represent $\textsc{Cause}(c) = c'$, where $c' \in \{\bot\} \cup \mathcal{R}$ and c was removed during $\textsc{CheckVC}(p, \ldots)$. Each annotation node has a prefix pk: to indicate the procedure p that the annotation belongs to and the position of the annotation k in the list of annotations for p (to account for duplicate candidates).

It is useful to understand the candidate removal for the procedures that have false alarms (Inner4 and Inner6). Observe that the edge $(\bot,$ Inner5, $Inner6$0) indicates that the reason for the removal of this precondition cannot be explained in terms of the existing candidates. This is indeed true, as we need the additional annotation **requires** *probed*(gb) for Inner5 (that is not captured by the set of candidates) to retain this candidate precondition. On the other hand, the graph indicates that HOUDINI cannot remove the precondition of Inner4 until the postcondition of Inner3 is present. Similarly, the

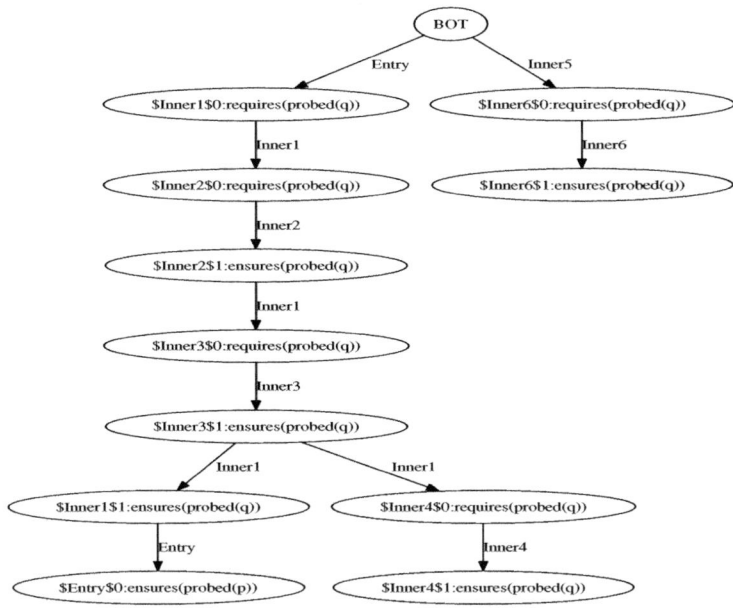

Fig. 3. The output of ExplainHoudini on the running example (in the absence of any of the <u>additional</u> annotations)

postcondition of `Inner3` can be removed only after the precondition of `Inner3` has been removed, which in turn requires the postcondition of `Inner2` to be removed. This process continues all the way where the precondition of `Inner1` is removed inside `Entry`. Although the graph shows the interprocedural causality why HOUDINI removed the precondition of `Inner4`, it is not clever enough to identify the procedure that has to be refined (`Inner2`) and the additional annotation (**ensures** q $\implies$ *probed*(q)) that can remove the spurious warning. This is consistent with the vision of a transparent inference that performs a scalable analysis to perform simple tasks and leaves the difficult task to the user. While walking the path of causes backwards, it is easy to spot the place that has to be refined and the candidate for a user.

3.3 Algorithm

We now describe the EXPLAINHOUDINI algorithm (Algorithm 2) that computes the CAUSE() for each of the removed candidates. This procedure is invoked during the HOUDINI algorithm (Algorithm 1) just before a candidate c is removed from $\mathcal{C}$ and added to $\mathcal{R}$ — this is indicated by the highlighted line in the algorithm. In addition to c, this procedure is invoked with (i) the procedure p whose checking removes c, (ii) the set of annotations $\mathcal{A}$, (iii) the present set of candidate annotations $\mathcal{C}$, and (iv) the set $\mathcal{R}$ that contain the candidates removed so far. The algorithm returns the cause of the annotation c.

Algorithm 2. EXPLAINHOUDINI(p, c, $\mathcal{A}$, $\mathcal{C}$, $\mathcal{R}$)

Require: A procedure $p \in P$
Require: A candidate contract $c \in \mathcal{C}_q$, where $q \in \{p\} \cup \text{CALLEES}(p)$
Require: A set of contracts $\mathcal{A} = \bigcup_{r \in P} \mathcal{A}_r$
Require: The current set of candidate contracts $\mathcal{C} = \bigcup_{r \in P} \mathcal{C}_r$
Require: A set of candidate contracts already removed $\mathcal{R} = \bigcup_{r \in P} \mathcal{R}_r$
Ensure: $c' \in \{\bot\} \cup \mathcal{R}_r$, where $r \in \{p\} \cup \text{CALLEES}(p)$
 1: $\mathcal{Q} \leftarrow (\mathcal{R}_p \cap \{c' \mid c' \text{is a candidate precondition}\})$
 2: **for all** $q \in \text{CALLEES}(p)$ **do**
 3:    $\mathcal{Q} \leftarrow \mathcal{Q} \cup (\mathcal{R}_q \cap \{c' \mid c' \text{is a candidate postcondition}\})$
 4: **end for**
 5: $c' \leftarrow \bot$
 6: **while** CHECKVC(p, $\{c\}$, $\mathcal{A} \cup \mathcal{C} \cup \mathcal{Q}$) = VERIFIED **do**
 7:    $c' \leftarrow$ DEQUEUE($\mathcal{Q}$)
 8: **end while**
 9: **return** c'

Since c was removed while checking p, c has to be either (i) a postcondition of p, or (ii) a precondition to one of the callees of p (including p if p calls itself). The set $\mathcal{Q}$ collects the removed candidates that are present as assumptions while checking p — this includes the candidate preconditions of p (line 1) and the candidate postconditions of all the callees of p (line 3).

The loop (line 6) is iterated while CHECKVC(p, $\{c\}$, $\mathcal{A} \cup \mathcal{C} \cup \mathcal{Q}$) is successful. If this check is not successful, then we return the value in c'. If the body of the loop is never executed, then the returned value is $\bot$. This case indicates that c was not provable with the entire set of candidates in $\mathcal{C}$; therefore CAUSESET(c) = $\{\}$, and consequently CAUSE(c) = $\bot$. Otherwise, each loop iteration removes one candidate c' non-deterministically from $\mathcal{Q}$, using the procedure DEQUEUE($\mathcal{Q}$) that extracts a candidate c' from $\mathcal{Q}$. When the returned value in c' is not $\bot$, it is easy to see that $c' \in$ CAUSESET(c). Since $c' \in \mathcal{Q} \subseteq \mathcal{R}$, and c was provable until c' was not removed, c' satisfies the definition of the CAUSESET(c). The only thing to observe is that the while loop (line 6) terminates. If $\mathcal{Q}$ ever becomes empty, we are guaranteed that the check CHECKVC(p, $\{c\}$, $\mathcal{A} \cup \mathcal{C}$) will fail, because this check is the same as performed in the HOUDINI algorithm before invoking EXPLAINHOUDINI. However, in many cases, the loop will terminate much earlier than $\mathcal{Q}$ becoming empty. Finally, although the soundness of the algorithm does not depend on the choice of implementation of the DEQUEUE($\mathcal{Q}$) procedure, our implementation maintains a priority queue sorted by latest removal time of the candidates in $\mathcal{Q}$.

3.4 Optimizations

The above presentation of the algorithm only requires CHECKVC(p, $\mathcal{C}$, $\mathcal{A}$) to check a procedure p with respect to a set of annotations A and return either VERIFIED or an annotation c that was violated. This makes it easy to integrate with any off-the-shelf implementation of HOUDINI. However, the algorithm can benefit from richer functionalities of $\textsc{CheckVC}(p, \mathcal{C}, \mathcal{A})$. We discuss a couple of such optimizations that are likely to signficantly reduce the number of times the loop in line 6 has to be executed:

– If $\textsc{CheckVC}(p, \mathcal{C}, \mathcal{A})$ (in $\textsc{Houdini}$ algorithm) can return an intraprocedural control-flow path starting from the entry of p to the annotation that was violated, the set of $\textsc{Callees}(p)$ in line 2 can be restricted to only the ones along the intraprocedural path. This utility can be easily integrated into the verification condition generation algorithm [14], and is available in several existing tools such as ESC/Java and Boogie [2].

– Let the $\textsc{CheckVC}(p, \{c\}, \mathcal{A} \cup \mathcal{C} \cup \mathcal{Q})$ (in $\textsc{ExplainHoudini}$) also return a minimal unsatisfiable core of annotations $\mathcal{A}' \subseteq \mathcal{A} \cup \mathcal{C} \cup \mathcal{Q}$ when the check succeeds. Intuitively, $\mathcal{A}'$ represents the annotations that were responsible for proving the candidate c. If such functionality is present, then one can choose c' in line 7 from the annotations in $\mathcal{A}' \cap \mathcal{Q}$. This will have the advantage of choosing those annotations for c' that are more likely to be the cause of c.

4   Evaluation

We have integrated $\textsc{ExplainHoudini}$ with the implementation of $\textsc{Houdini}$ in the HAVOC property checker for C. The $\textsc{Houdini}$ implementation uses the Boogie [2] verification condition generator and the Z3 [7] SMT solver to implement the $\textsc{CheckVC}()$ procedure. Our current implementation does not contain the optimizations mentioned in Section 3.4 yet.

We report preliminary experience on using $\textsc{ExplainHoudini}$ on two large modules in Windows (we have concealed the names of the components for security reasons). The property being checked is the *probe-before-use* described earlier in Section 2.4 and the set of candidates are similar to the ones in the running example. Instead of inspecting the reason for every candidate removed by $\textsc{Houdini}$, a user typically looks at the candidates for the procedures that reported the alarms.

Figure 4 presents a summary of the results for two examples named A and B. For each example, we report the number of candidates and the number of annotations retained. We compare the overhead of $\textsc{ExplainHoudini}$ by reporting the number of calls to $\textsc{CheckVC}()$ and the overall runtime with and without using $\textsc{ExplainHoudini}$ (indicated by "w" and "w/o" respectively). The absolute runtimes are not very representative of an optimized implementation of $\textsc{Houdini}$ — the current implementation has huge overhead due to parsing files for input to Boogie and can be improved by at least an order of magnitude. In terms of the number of calls to $\textsc{CheckVC}()$, the overhead of $\textsc{ExplainHoudini}$ is around 51% for A and 33% for B. In terms of the overall runtime, the overhead of $\textsc{ExplainHoudini}$ is around 36% for A and 29% for B. Given that it can help reduce manual post-processing effort, this is fairly acceptable. We believe that the optimizations in Section 3.4 will further reduce this overhead.

More interestingly, we measured the size of the causality graphs ("Explain size") generated with and without $\textsc{ExplainHoudini}$ per removed candidates.

Ex	LOC	# Pr	# Cand	# Infrd	w/o ExplainHoudini					w ExplainHoudini				
							Explain size					Explain size		
					# Chk	Time	Avg	Min	Max	# Chk	Time	Avg	Min	Max
A	260K	3108	3026	1415	4972	312m	2.46	1	19	7514	426m	1.45	1	7
B	88K	680	550	269	1097	48m	2.27	1	14	1456	62m	1.22	1	3

Fig. 4. Overhead and quality of EXPLAINHOUDINI on two modules. "#" is used to denote the number of various entities. "LOC" denotes the lines of code. "Pr" denotes procedures, "Cand" denotes candidates, "Infrd" denotes inferred, "Chk" is a call to CHECKVC(). "Time" denotes the total time for inference in minutes. "Explain size" denotes the size (number of edges) of the graph per removed candidate.

The graph without EXPLAINHOUDINI contains all the annotations on the (transitive) callers that were removed before a procedures candidate was removed (similar to the graph in Figure 1 (a)). We report the average, maximum and minimum sizes (denoted as "Explain Size") of these graphs for each module. With EXPLAINHOUDINI, the average size of the graphs is reduced by more than 40% for both the examples and the maximum size has considerably reduced. The average graph size is small for these benchmarks because more than 50% of the graphs have a size of 1. However, for the example A, there are 119 graphs with more than 5 nodes without EXPLAINHOUDINI, but only 2 graphs with more than 5 nodes with EXPLAINHOUDINI. Similarly, for the example B, there are 40 graphs with more than 3 nodes without EXPLAINHOUDINI, but 0 graphs with more than 3 nodes with EXPLAINHOUDINI. The results suggest that EXPLAINHOUDINI can often provide simpler explanations for annotation removal.

To understand the reason for the shallow explanation graphs, we sampled a few of the removed candidates. In most cases, a candidate *probed*(p) for a parameter p was removed because the caller passed the value of a field q->f to p, where q is a parameter of the caller. Since we only track *probed*(q) at the caller, HOUDINI was unable to prove *probed*(q->f) at the call site. In other cases, caller passed a global or the return value of another procedure to p for which there are no candidates at present.

5   Conclusion

For large software modules, understanding the cause of (candidate) contract violations is often most the time-consuming step in refining annotations and classifying errors. We have augmented the HOUDINI algorithm with EXPLAIN-HOUDINI to provide concise explanation for the removal of a candidate contract. We are exploring the optimizations in Section 3.4 to reduce the overhead of EXPLAINHOUDINI and providing the user with likely annotations to refine the existing set of annotations.

Acknowledgements. We thank the anonymous reviewers for useful suggestions on improving the paper.

References

1. Ball, T., Hackett, B., Lahiri, S.K., Qadeer, S., Vanegue, J.: Towards scalable modular checking of user-defined properties. In: Leavens, G.T., O'Hearn, P., Rajamani, S.K. (eds.) VSTTE 2010. LNCS, vol. 6217, pp. 1–24. Springer, Heidelberg (2010)
2. Barnett, M., Chang, B.E., DeLine, R., Jacobs, B., Leino, K.R.M.: Boogie: A modular reusable verifier for object-oriented programs. In: de Boer, F.S., Bonsangue, M.M., Graf, S., de Roever, W.-P. (eds.) FMCO 2005. LNCS, vol. 4111, pp. 364–387. Springer, Heidelberg (2006)
3. Barnett, M., Leino, K.R.M., Schulte, W.: The spec# programming system: An overview. In: Barthe, G., Burdy, L., Huisman, M., Lanet, J.-L., Muntean, T. (eds.) CASSIS 2004. LNCS, vol. 3362, pp. 49–69. Springer, Heidelberg (2005)
4. Condit, J., Hackett, B., Lahiri, S.K., Qadeer, S.: Unifying type checking and property checking for low-level code. In: Principles of Programming Languages (POPL 2009), pp. 302–314 (2009)
5. Cousot, P., Cousot, R.: Abstract interpretation: A Unified Lattice Model for the Static Analysis of Programs by Construction or Approximation of Fixpoints. In: Principles of Programming Languages (POPL 1977), pp. 238–252 (1977)
6. Dahlweid, M., Moskal, M., Santen, T., Tobies, S., Schulte, W.: Vcc: Contract-based modular verification of concurrent c. In: International Conference on Software Engineering (ICSE 2009), Companion Volume, pp. 429–430 (2009)
7. de Moura, L.M., Bjørner, N.: Z3: An efficient smt solver. In: Ramakrishnan, C.R., Rehof, J. (eds.) TACAS 2008. LNCS, vol. 4963, pp. 337–340. Springer, Heidelberg (2008)
8. Flanagan, C., Leino, K.R.M.: Houdini, an annotation assistant for ESC/Java. In: Oliveira, J.N., Zave, P. (eds.) FME 2001. LNCS, vol. 2021, pp. 500–517. Springer, Heidelberg (2001)
9. Flanagan, C., Leino, K.R.M., Lillibridge, M., Nelson, G., Saxe, J.B., Stata, R.: Extended static checking for Java. In: Programming Language Design and Implementation (PLDI 2002), pp. 234–245 (2002)
10. Graf, S., Saïdi, H.: Construction of abstract state graphs with PVS. In: Grumberg, O. (ed.) CAV 1997. LNCS, vol. 1254, pp. 72–83. Springer, Heidelberg (1997)
11. Henzinger, T.A., Jhala, R., Majumdar, R., McMillan, K.L.: Abstractions from proofs. In: Symposium on Principles of Programming Languages (POPL), pp. 232–244. ACM, New York (2004)
12. Lahiri, S.K., Qadeer, S.: Complexity and algorithms for monomial and clausal predicate abstraction. In: Schmidt, R.A. (ed.) CADE 2009. LNCS, vol. 5663, pp. 214–229. Springer, Heidelberg (2009)
13. Lahiri, S.K., Qadeer, S., Galeotti, J.P., Voung, J.W., Wies, T.: Intra-module inference. In: Bouajjani, A., Maler, O. (eds.) CAV 2009. LNCS, vol. 5643, pp. 493–508. Springer, Heidelberg (2009)
14. Leino, K.R.M., Millstein, T., Saxe, J.B.: Generating error traces from verification-condition counterexamples. Sci. Comput. Program. 55(1-3) (2005)
15. McMillan, K.L.: Interpolation and sat-based model checking. In: Hunt Jr., W.A., Somenzi, F. (eds.) CAV 2003. LNCS, vol. 2725, pp. 1–13. Springer, Heidelberg (2003)

Abstract Probabilistic Automata*

Benoît Delahaye[1], Joost-Pieter Katoen[2], Kim G. Larsen[3], Axel Legay[1],
Mikkel L. Pedersen[3], Falak Sher[2], and Andrzej Wąsowski[4]

[1] INRIA/IRISA, Rennes, France
[2] RWTH Aachen University, Software Modeling and Verification Group, Germany
[3] Aalborg University, Denmark
[4] IT University of Copenhagen, Denmark

Abstract. Probabilistic Automata (PAs) are a widely-recognized mathematical framework for the specification and analysis of systems with non-deterministic and stochastic behaviors. This paper proposes Abstract Probabilistic Automata (APAs), that is a novel abstraction model for PAs. In APAs uncertainty of the non-deterministic choices is modeled by may/must modalities on transitions while uncertainty of the stochastic behaviour is expressed by (underspecified) stochastic constraints. We have developed a complete abstraction theory for PAs, and also propose the first specification theory for them. Our theory supports both satisfaction and refinement operators, together with classical stepwise design operators. In addition, we study the link between specification theories and abstraction in avoiding the state-space explosion problem.

1 Introduction

Probabilistic Automata (PAs) constitute a mathematical framework for the specification and analysis of non-deterministic probabilistic systems. They have been developed by Segala [23] to model and analyze asynchronous, concurrent systems with discrete probabilistic choice in a formal and precise way. PAs are akin to Markov decision processes (MDPs). A detailed comparison with models such as MDPs, as well as generative and reactive probabilistic transition systems is given in [22]. PAs are recognized as an adequate formalism for randomized distributed algorithms and fault tolerant systems. They are used as semantic model for formalisms such as probabilistic process algebra [20] and a probabilistic variant of Harel's statecharts [12]. An input-output version of PAs is the basis of PIOA and variants thereof [7,5]. PAs have been enriched with notions such as weak and strong (bi)simulations [23], decision algorithms for these notions [6] and a statistical testing theory [8]. This paper brings two new contributions to the field of probabilistic automata: the theories of *abstraction* and of *specification*.

Abstraction is pivotal to combating the state explosion problem in the modeling and verification of realistic systems such as randomized distributed algorithms. It aims at model reduction by collapsing sets of concrete states to

---

* Work partially funded by VKR Centre of Excellence — MT-LAB. Part of the work was performed during Wąsowski's stay at INRIA/Rennes.

R. Jhala and D. Schmidt (Eds.): VMCAI 2011, LNCS 6538, pp. 324–339, 2011.
© Springer-Verlag Berlin Heidelberg 2011

abstract states, e.g., by partitioning the concrete state space. This paper presents a three-valued abstraction of PAs. The main design principle of our model, named *Abstract Probabilistic Automata* (APAs), is to abstract sets of distributions by constraint functions. This generalizes earlier work on interval-based abstraction of probabilistic systems [14,11,15]. To abstract from action transitions, we introduce *may* and *must* modalities in the spirit of modal transition systems [18]. If all states in a partition p have a must-transition on action a to some state in partition p', the abstraction yields a must-transition between p and p'. If some of the p-states have no such transition while others do, it gives rise to a may-transition between p and p'. Our model shall be viewed as a combination of both Modal Automata [19] and Constraint Markov Chains (CMC) [3] that are abstractions for transition systems and Markov Chains, respectively.

We also propose the first specification theory for PAs, equipped with all essential ingredients of a compositional design methodology: a satisfaction relation (to decide whether a PA is an implementation of an APA), a consistency check (to decide whether the specification admits an implementation), a refinement (to compare specifications in terms of inclusion of sets of implementations), logical composition (to compute the intersection of sets of implementations), and structural composition (to combine specifications). Our framework also supports incremental design [9]. To the best of our knowledge, the theory of APAs is the first specification theory for PAs in where both logical and structural compositions can be computed within the same framework.

Our notions of refinement and satisfaction are, as usual, characterized in terms of inclusion of sets of implementations. One of our main theorems shows that for the class of deterministic APAs, refinement coincides with inclusion of sets of implementations. This latter result is obtained by a reduction from APAs to CMCs, for which a similar result holds. Hence, APAs can also be viewed as a specification theory for Markov Chains (MCs). The model is as expressive as CMCs, and hence more expressive than other theories for stochastic systems such as Interval Markov Chains [13,2,11].

Our last contribution is to propose an *abstraction-based* methodology that allows to simplify the behavior of APAs with respect to the refinement relation – such an operation is crucial to avoid state-space explosion. We show that our abstraction preserves weak refinement, and that weak refinement is a precongruence with respect to parallel composition. These results provide the key ingredients to allow *compositional* abstraction of PAs.

Organisation of the paper. In Section 2, we introduce the concepts of APAs and a satisfaction relation with respect to PAs. We also propose a methodology to decide whether an APA is consistent. Refinement relations and abstraction of APAs are discussed in Section 3. Other compositional reasoning operators such as conjunction and composition as well as their relation with abstraction are presented in Section 4. Section 5 discusses the relation between CMCs and APAs and proposes a class of deterministic APAs for which strong and weak refinements coincide with inclusion of sets of implementations. Finally, Section 6 concludes the paper and proposes directions for future research. Due to space limitation, proofs and larger examples are given in a long version of this paper [10].

2 Specifications and Implementations

We now introduce the main models of the paper: first *Probabilistic Automata*, and then the new abstraction—*Abstract Probabilistic Automata*.

Implementations. A PA [23] resembles a non-deterministic automaton, but its transitions target probability distributions over states instead of single states. Hence, PAs can be seen as a combination of Markov Chains and non-deterministic automata or as Markov Decision Processes allowing non-determinism.

Definition 1 (Probabilistic automata). *A probabilistic automaton is a tuple* (S, A, L, AP, V, s_0), *where:*

- S *is a finite set of states with initial state* $s_0 \in S$,
- A *is a finite set of actions,*
- $L: S \times A \times Dist(S) \to \mathbb{B}_2$ *is a two-valued transition function,*
- AP *is a finite set of valuations, and*
- $V: S \to 2^{AP}$ *is a state-labeling function.*

Here $\mathbb{B}_2 = \{\bot, \top\}$, with $\bot < \top$. $L(s, a, \mu)$ identifies the *transition* of the automaton: $\top$ indicates its presence and $\bot$ indicates its absence. We write $s \xrightarrow{a} \mu$ meaning $L(s, a, \mu) = \top$. In the rest of the paper, we assume that PAs are *finitely branching*, i.e., for any state s, the number of pairs (a, μ) such that $s \xrightarrow{a} \mu$ is finite. The *labeling function* V indicates the propositions (or properties) that are valid in a state. A *Markov Chain* (MC) is a PA, where, for each $s \in S$, there exists exactly one triple (s, a, μ) such that $L(s, a, \mu) = \top$.

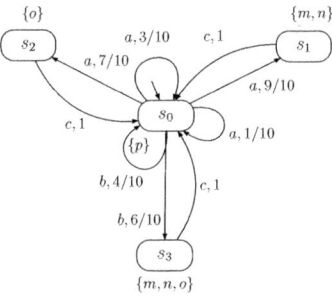

Fig. 1. An example PA

Example 1. Figure 1 presents a PA with $L(s_0, a, \mu) = \top$, where $\mu(s_0) = 3/10$ and $\mu(s_2) = 7/10$. We adopt a notational convention that represents $L(s_0, a, \mu) = \top$ by a set of arrows with tails located close to each other on the boundary of s_0, and heads targeting the states in the support of μ.

In state s_0, a non-deterministic choice takes places on action a between the distributions μ and μ' with $\mu'(s_0) = 1/10$ and $\mu'(s_1) = 9/10$.

Specifications. A Constraint Markov Chain (CMC) [3] is a MC equipped with a constraint on the next-state probabilities from any state. Roughly speaking, an implementation for a CMC is thus a MC, whose next-state probability distribution satisfies the constraint associated with each state. Let $Sat(\varphi)$ denote the set of distributions that satisfy constraint function φ, and $C(S)$ the set of constraint functions defined on state space S.

A *Modal Automaton* [17,18] is an automaton whose transitions are typed with *may* and *must* modalities. Informally, a must transition is available in every model of the specification, while a may transition needs not be.

An *Abstract Probabilistic Automaton* (APA) is an abstraction that represents a possibly infinite set of PAs. APAs combine Modal Automata and CMCs – the abstractions for labelled transition systems and Markov Chains, respectively.

Definition 2. *An* abstract PA *is a tuple* (S, A, L, AP, V, s_0) *such that:*

- S, A, AP *and* s_0 *are defined as before*
- $L : S \times A \times C(S) \longrightarrow \mathbb{B}_3$ *is a three-valued state-constraint function, and*
- $V : S \longrightarrow 2^{2^{AP}}$ *maps a state onto a set of admissible valuations.*

Here, $\mathbb{B}_3 = \{\bot, ?, \top\}$ denotes a *complete lattice* with the following ordering $\bot < ? < \top$ and meet ($\sqcap$) and join ($\sqcup$) operators. A CMC is thus an APA, where for each $s \in S$, there exists exactly one triple (s, a, φ) such that $L(s, a, \mu) = \top$, while an *Interval Markov Chain* (IMC) [13] is a CMC whose constraints are disjunctions of intervals. The labeling $L(s, a, \varphi)$ identifies the "type" of the constraint function $\varphi \in C(S)$: $\top$, $?$ and $\bot$ indicate a *must*, a *may* and the absence of a constraint function, respectively. We could have limited ourselves to constraints denoting unions of intervals of probability values. However, as we shall soon see, polynomial constraints are needed to support *both* conjunction *and* parallel composition. Like for CMCs, states of an APA are labeled with a set of subsets of atomic propositions. A single set of propositions represents properties that should be satisfied by an implementation state. A powerset models a disjunctive choice of properties. Later, we shall see that any APA whose states are labelled with a set of subsets of atomic propositions can be turned into an equivalent (in the sense of implementations set) APA whose states are labeled with a set that contains only a single subset of AP.

Finally, observe that a PA is an APA in which every transition (s, a, μ) is represented by a *must*-transition (s, a, φ) with $Sat(\varphi) = \{\mu\}$, and each state-label consists of a single set of propositions.

Example 2. Consider the APA N given in Figure 2. State s_0 has three outgoing transitions: a *must* a-transition (s_0, a, φ_x), a *may* a-transition (s_0, a, φ_y), and a *may* b-transition (s_0, b, φ_z). Due to the constraint, each of these transitions can cover several transitions in a concrete implementation PA. As an example, the a-transition $(s_0, a, (1/10, 9/10, 0, 0))$ of the PA given in Figure 1 is satisfying the *must* a-transition (s_0, a, φ_x).

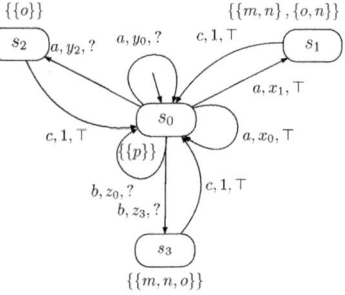

$$\varphi_x \equiv x_1 \geq 0.9 \wedge x_0 + x_1 = 1$$
$$\varphi_y \equiv y_2 \leq 0.8 \wedge y_0 + y_2 = 1$$
$$\varphi_z \equiv z_3 \geq 0.5 \wedge z_0 + z_3 = 1$$

Fig. 2. An example APA

In the rest of the paper we distinguish deterministic APAs. The distinction will be of particular importance when comparing APAs in Section 3.1. In APAs, the non-determinism can arise due to sets of valuations in states, or due to actions that label transitions:

Definition 3 (Deterministic APA). *An APA $N = (S, A, L, AP, V, s_0)$ is*

- *action-deterministic, if $\forall s \in S.\forall a \in A.\ |\{\varphi \in C(S) \mid L(s, a, \varphi) \neq \bot\}| \leq 1$.*
- *valuation-deterministic, if $\forall s \in S.\forall a \in A.\forall \varphi \in C(S)$ with $L(s, a, \varphi) \neq \bot$:*

$$\forall \mu', \mu'' \in Sat(\varphi), s', s'' \in S, (\mu'(s') > 0 \wedge \mu''(s'') > 0 \Rightarrow V(s') \cap V(s'') = \emptyset).$$

N is deterministic iff it is both action-deterministic and valuation-deterministic.

Satisfaction. We relate APA specifications to PAs implementing them, by extending the definitions of satisfaction introduced in [13]. We start with the following definition that relates distributions between set of states. We use $Dist(S)$ to denote a set of *probability distributions* on the finite set S in the usual way.

Definition 4. ($\Subset_R^\delta$). *Let S and S' be non-empty sets of states. Given $\mu \in Dist(S)$, $\mu' \in Dist(S')$, a function $\delta : S \rightarrow (S' \rightarrow [0,1])$, and a binary relation $R \subseteq S \times S'$, μ is simulated by μ' with respect to R and δ, denoted as $\mu \Subset_R^\delta \mu'$, iff*

1. *for all $s \in S$, if $\mu(s) > 0$, then $\delta(s)$ is a distribution on S',*
2. *for all $s' \in S'$, $\sum_{s \in S} \mu(s) \cdot \delta(s)(s') = \mu'(s')$, and*
3. *if $\delta(s)(s') > 0$, then $(s, s') \in R$.*

In the rest of the paper, we write $\mu \Subset_R \mu'$ iff there exists a function δ such that $\mu \Subset_R^\delta \mu'$. Such δ is called a correspondence function.

We are now ready to define the satisfaction relation between PAs and APAs.

Definition 5 (Satisfaction relation). *Let $P = (S, A, L, AP, V, s_0)$ be a PA and $N = (S', A, L', AP, V', s_0')$ be an APA. $R \subseteq S \times S'$ is a satisfaction relation iff, for any $(s, s') \in R$, the following conditions hold:*

1. *$\forall a \in A, \forall \varphi' \in C(S') : L'(s', a, \varphi') = \top \implies \exists \mu \in Dist(S) : L(s, a, \mu) = \top$ and $\exists \mu' \in Sat(\varphi')$ such that $\mu \Subset_R \mu'$,*
2. *$\forall a \in A, \forall \mu \in Dist(S) : L(s, a, \mu) = \top \implies \exists \varphi' \in C(S') : L'(s', a, \varphi') \neq \bot$ and $\exists \mu' \in Sat(\varphi')$ such that $\mu \Subset_R \mu'$, and*
3. *$V(s) \in V'(s')$.*

We say that P satisfies N, denoted $P \models N$, iff there exists a satisfaction relation relating s_0 and s_0'. If $P \models N$, P is called an implementation *of N.*

Thus, a PA P is an implementation of an APA N iff any must-transition of N is matched by a must-transition of P that agrees on the probability distributions specified by the constraint, and reversely, P does not contain must-transitions that do not have a corresponding (may- or must-) transition in N. The set of all implementations of N is given by $[\![N]\!] = \{P \mid P \models N\}$.

Example 3. The relation $R = \{(s_0, s_0), (s_1, s_1), (s_2, s_2), (s_3, s_3)\}$ is a satisfaction relation between the PA P given in Figure 1 and the APA N of Figure 2.

Consistency. An APA N is *consistent* iff it admits at least one implementation. We say that a state s is *consistent* if $V(s) \neq \emptyset$ and $L(s, a, \varphi) = \top \implies Sat(\varphi) \neq \emptyset$. An APA is *locally consistent* if all its states are consistent. It is easy to see that a locally consistent APA is also consistent, i.e. has at least one implementation. However, inconsistency of a state does not imply inconsistency of the specification. In order to decide whether a specification is consistent, we proceed as usual and propagate inconsistent states with the help of a *pruning operator β* that filters out distributions leading to inconsistent states. This operator is applied until a fixed point is reached, i.e., until the specification does not contain inconsistent states (it is locally consistent). See [10] for details.

Theorem 1. *For any APA N, it holds:* $[\![N]\!] = [\![\beta(N)]\!]$.

As the set of states of N is finite, the fixed point computation will always terminate. By the above theorem, we have that $[\![N]\!] = [\![\beta^*(N)]\!]$.

3   Abstraction and Refinement

In this section we introduce *Refinement* that allows to compare APAs. We also propose an *abstraction-based* methodology that permits to simplify the behavior of APAs with respect to the refinement relation.

3.1   Refinement

A refinement compares APAs with respect to their sets of implementations. More precisely, if APA N refines APA N', then the set of implementations of N should be included in the one of N'. The ultimate refinement relation that can be defined between APAs is thus *Thorough Refinement* that exactly corresponds to inclusion of sets of implementations.

Definition 6 (Thorough refinement). *Let $N = (S, A, L, AP, V, s_0)$ and $N' = (S', A, L', AP, V', s_0')$ be APAs. We say that N thoroughly refines N', denoted $N \preceq_T N'$, iff $[\![N]\!] \subseteq [\![N']\!]$.*

For most specification theories, it is known that deciding thorough refinement is computationally intensive (see for example [1]). For many models such as Modal automata or CMCs, one can partially avoid the problem by working with a syntactical notion of refinement. This definition, which is typically strictly stronger than thorough refinement, is easier to check. The difference between syntactic and semantic refinements resembles the difference between simulations and trace inclusion for transition systems.

We consider two syntactical refinements. These relations extend two well known refinement relations for CMCs and IMCs by combining them with the refinement defined on modal automata. We start with the strong refinement.

Definition 7 (Strong refinement). *Let* $N = (S, A, L, AP, V, s_0)$ *and* $N' = (S', A, L', AP, V', s'_0)$ *be APAs.* $R \subseteq S \times S'$ *is a strong refinement relation iff, for all* $(s, s') \in R$, *the following conditions hold:*

1. *$\forall a \in A. \forall \varphi' \in C(S'). L'(s', a, \varphi') = \top \implies \exists \varphi \in C(S). L(s, a, \varphi) = \top$ and there exists a correspondence function $\delta : S \to (S' \to [0, 1])$ such that $\forall \mu \in Sat(\varphi). \exists \mu' \in Sat(\varphi')$ with $\mu \Subset_R^\delta \mu'$,*
2. *$\forall a \in A. \forall \varphi \in C(S). L(s, a, \varphi) \neq \bot \implies \exists \varphi' \in C(S'). L'(s', a, \varphi') \neq \bot$ and there exists a correspondence function $\delta : S \to (S' \to [0, 1])$ such that $\forall \mu \in Sat(\varphi). \exists \mu' \in Sat(\varphi')$ with $\mu \Subset_R^\delta \mu'$, and*
3. *$V(s) \subseteq V'(s')$.*

We say that N strongly refines N', denoted $N \preceq_S N'$, iff there exists a strong refinement relation relating s_0 and s'_0.

Observe that strong refinement imposes a "fixed-in-advance" δ in the simulation relation between distributions. This assumption is lifted with the definition of *weak refinement*:

Definition 8 (Weak refinement). *Let* $N = (S, A, L, AP, V, s_0)$ *and* $N' = (S', A, L', AP, V', s'_0)$ *be APAs.* $R \subseteq S \times S'$ *is a weak refinement relation iff, for all* $(s, s') \in R$, *the following conditions hold:*

1. *$\forall a \in A. \forall \varphi' \in C(S'). L'(s', a, \varphi') = \top \implies \exists \varphi \in C(S). L(s, a, \varphi) = \top$ and $\forall \mu \in Sat(\varphi). \exists \mu' \in Sat(\varphi')$ with $\mu \Subset_R \mu'$,*
2. *$\forall a \in A. \forall \varphi \in C(S). L(s, a, \varphi) \neq \bot \implies \exists \varphi' \in C(S'). L'(s', a, \varphi') \neq \bot$ and $\forall \mu \in Sat(\varphi). \exists \mu' \in Sat(\varphi')$ with $\mu \Subset_R \mu'$, and*
3. *$V(s) \subseteq V'(s')$.*

We say that N weakly refines N', denoted $N \preceq N'$, iff there exists a weak refinement relation relating s_0 and s'_0.

It is easy to see that the above definitions are combinations of the definitions of strong and weak refinement of CMCs with the *modal refinement* of Modal Automata. Hence algorithms for checking weak and strong refinements for APAs can be obtained by combining existing fixed-point algorithms for CMCs [4] and Modal Automata [19]. For the class of polynomial-constraint APAs, the upper bound for deciding weak/strong refinement is thus exponential in the number of states and doubly-exponential in the size of the constraints [4]. Both strong and weak refinement imply inclusion of sets of implementations. However, the converse is not true. The following theorem classifies the refinement relations.

Theorem 2. *Thorough refinement is strictly finer than weak refinement, and weak refinement is strictly finer than strong refinement.*

Proof. We present a sketch of the proof and refer to [10] for details. By definition, we have that $\preceq_S$ implies $\preceq$. By observing the definition of satisfaction relation, one can easily deduce that $\preceq_S$ and $\preceq$ imply $\preceq_T$. Consider now the APAs N_1

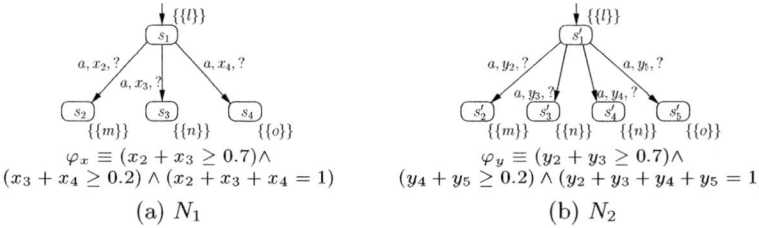

Fig. 3. APAs N_1 and N_2 such that $N_1 \preceq N_2$, but not $N_1 \preceq_S N_2$

and N_2 given in Figure 3. It is easy to see that $N_1 \preceq N_2$. However, we have that $N_1 \npreceq_S N_2$. Informally, one can see that State s_3' and State s_4' of N_2 both correspond to State s_3 of N_1. Thus, the probability mass x_3 of going to state s_3 in N_1 has to be distributed on s_3' and s_4' in order to match probabilities y_3 and y_4. The latter shall be achieved with the correspondence function δ that defines the refinement relation. The crucial point is that this correspondence function will depend on the exact value of x_3, thus δ cannot be precomputed and we have that $\preceq$, but not $\preceq_S$ holds.

Similarly, $\preceq$ does not imply $\preceq_T$. Consider the APAs N_3 and N_4 given in Figure 4. It is easy to see that $\preceq_T$ holds between N_3 and N_4. However, State s_2 of N_3 cannot refine State s_2' or s_3'. Indeed, State s_2 has more implementations than s_2' and s_3' taken separately.   □

We have just seen that thorough refinement is strictly finer than strong and weak refinement. In Section 5, we will propose a class of deterministic APAs on which the three relations coincide.

3.2   Abstraction

This section covers the abstraction of APA. The rationale is to partition the state space, i.e., group (disjoint) sets of states by a single abstract state. Let N and M be APA with state space S and S', respectively. An *abstraction* function $\alpha : S \to S'$ is a surjection. The inverse of abstraction function α is the *concretization* function $\gamma : S' \to 2^S$. The state $\alpha(s)$ denotes

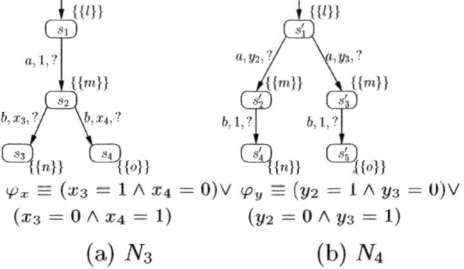

Fig. 4. APAs N_3 and N_4

the abstract counterpart of state s while $\gamma(s')$ represents the set of all (concrete) states that are represented by the abstract state s'. Abstraction is lifted to distributions as follows. The abstraction of $\mu \in Dist(S)$, denoted $\alpha(\mu) \in Dist(S')$, is uniquely defined by $\alpha(\mu)(s') = \mu(\gamma(s'))$ for all $s' \in S'$.

Abstraction is lifted to sets of states, or sets of distributions in a pointwise manner. It follows that $\varphi' = \alpha(\varphi)$ iff $Sat(\varphi') = \alpha(Sat(\varphi))$. The abstraction of

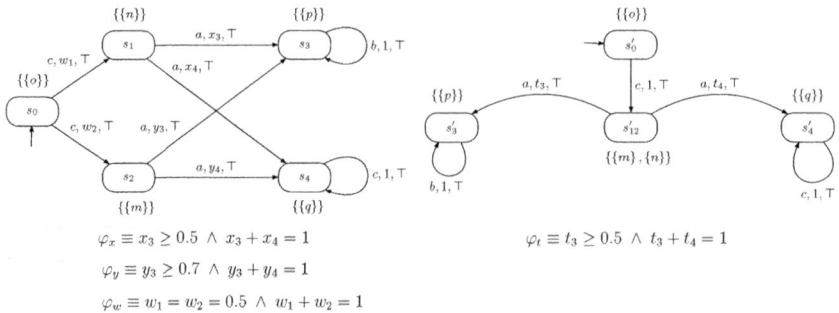

Fig. 5. The APA N (left) is abstracted by the APA N' (right), i.e. $N' = \alpha(N)$

the product of constraint functions φ and φ' is given as $\alpha(\varphi \cdot \varphi') = \alpha(\varphi) \cdot \alpha(\varphi')$. These ingredients provide the basis to define the abstraction of an APA.

Definition 9 (Abstraction). *Given APA* $N = (S, A, L, AP, V, s_0)$, *the abstraction function* $\alpha : S \to S'$ *induces the APA* $\alpha(N) = (S', A, L', AP, V', \alpha(s_0))$, *where for all* $a \in A$, $s' \in S'$ *and* $\varphi' \in C(S')$:

$$
L'(s', a, \varphi') = \begin{cases}
\top & \begin{array}{l} \text{if } \forall s \in \gamma(s') : \exists \varphi \in C(S) : L(s, a, \varphi) = \top, \text{and} \\ Sat(\varphi') = \alpha(\bigcup_{(s,\varphi) \in \gamma(s') \times C(S) : L(s,a,\varphi) = \top} Sat(\varphi)) \end{array} & (a) \\[2em]
? & \begin{array}{l} \text{if } \exists s \in \gamma(s') : \exists \varphi \in C(S) : L(s, a, \varphi) \neq \bot, \text{and} \\ Sat(\varphi') = \alpha(\bigcup_{(s,\varphi) \in \gamma(s') \times C(S) : L(s,a,\varphi) \neq \bot} Sat(\varphi)) \end{array} & (b) \\[2em]
\bot & \text{otherwise} & (c)
\end{cases}
$$

and $V'(s') = \bigcup_{\forall s \in \gamma(s')} V(s)$

Item (a) asserts that if there are must transitions (s, a, φ) from all states $s \in \gamma(s')$, then the must transition (s', a, φ') represents the total behavior. Item (b) asserts that a may a-transition emanating from s' represents the total behaviour of all transitions (s, a, φ) for $s \in \gamma(s')$, if not all states in $\gamma(s')$ have a must a-transition, and there is a a-transition on modality different from $\bot$. Item (c) asserts that if no state in $\gamma(s')$ has an a-transition, then s' also does not have an a-transition.

The result of abstracting APA N is the APA $\alpha(N)$ that is able to mimic all behaviours of N, but possibly exhibits more behaviour.

Lemma 1. *For any APA* N, $\alpha(N)$ *is an APA.*

Example 4. Consider the APA $N = (S, A, L, AP, V, s_0)$ and $N' = (S', A, L', AP, V', s_0')$ depicted in Fig. 5. Let the abstraction function $\alpha : S \to S'$ be given by $\alpha(s_0) = s_0'$, $\alpha(s_1) = s_{12}' = \alpha(s_2)$, $\alpha(s_3) = s_3'$ and $\alpha(s_4) = s_4'$. Both states s_1

and s_2 in N have a must a-transition. These are abstracted in N' by a single must a-transition satisfied by distributions in the union of satisfaction sets of φ_x and φ_y.

Observe that the abstract version of an APA is always weaker in term of refinement than the original APA.

Theorem 3. *For any APA N and abstraction function α, $N \preceq \alpha(N)$.*

4   Compositional Reasoning

APAs can serve as a specification theory for systems with both non-deterministic and stochastic behaviors. Any good specification theory shall be equiped with a *conjunction operation* that allows to combine multiple requirements into a single specification, and a *composition operation* that allows specifications to be combined structurally. Studying these two operations for APAs is the subject of this section.

4.1   Conjunction

Conjunction, also called *logical composition*, allows combining two specifications into a single specification, that has the conjunctive behavior of the two operands. More precisely, conjunction allows to compute the intersection of sets of implementations. In this paper, conjunction will be defined for action-deterministic APAs with the same action alphabet. The generalization to non-deterministic APAs with dissimilar alphabets, which is already known to be complex for the case of Modal Automata [21], is postponed for future work. The conjunction operation is a mix between the corresponding operation for modal automata and CMCs.

Definition 10 (Conjunction). *Let $N = (S, A, L, AP, V, s_0)$ and $N' = (S', A, L', AP, V', s'_0)$ be action-deterministic APAs sharing actions sets and atomic propositions sets. The conjunction of N and N' is the APA $N \wedge N' = (S \times S', A, \tilde{L}, AP, \tilde{V}, (s_0, s'_0))$ such that*

- $\tilde{L}$ *is defined as follows. For all $a \in A$ and $(s, s') \in S \times S'$,*
  - *If there exists $\varphi \in C(S)$ such that $L(s, a, \varphi) = \top$ and for all $\varphi' \in C(S')$, we have $L'(s', a, \varphi') = \bot$, or if there exists $\varphi' \in C(S')$ such that $L'(s', a, \varphi') = \top$ and for all $\varphi \in C(S)$, we have $L(s, a, \varphi) = \bot$, then $\tilde{L}((s, s'), a, false) = \top$.*
  - *Else, if either for all $\varphi \in C(S)$, we have $L(s, a, \varphi) = \bot$ or for all $\varphi' \in C(S')$, we have $L'(s', a, \varphi') = \bot$, then for all $\tilde{\varphi} \in C(S \times S')$, $\tilde{L}((s, s'), a, \tilde{\varphi}) = \bot$.*
  - *Otherwise, for all $\varphi \in C(S)$ and $\varphi' \in C(S')$ such that $L(s, a, \varphi) \neq \bot$ and $L'(s', a, \varphi') \neq \bot$, define $\tilde{L}((s, s'), a, \tilde{\varphi}) = L(s, a, \varphi) \sqcup L'(s', a, \varphi')$ with $\tilde{\varphi}$ the new constraint in $C(S \times S')$ such that $\tilde{\mu} \in Sat(\tilde{\varphi})$ iff*

∗ the distribution $\mu : t \to \sum_{t' \in S'} \tilde{\mu}((t, t'))$ is in $Sat(\varphi)$, and
∗ the distribution $\mu' : t' \to \sum_{t \in S} \tilde{\mu}((t, t'))$ is in $Sat(\varphi')$.
  • Finally, for all other $\tilde{\varphi}' \in C(S \times S')$, let $\tilde{L}((s, s'), a, \tilde{\varphi}') = \bot$.
 − $\tilde{V}((s, s')) = V(s) \cap V'(s')$.

Observe that the conjunction of two action-deterministic APAs is an action-deterministic APA. The conjunction operation may introduce inconsistent states. Hence, any conjunction operation has to be followed by a pruning operation. Finally, observe that the conjunction of two APAs with interval constraints is not necessarily an APA with interval constraints, but could be an APA whose constraints are systems of linear inequalities (see [10] for an example).

The following theorem states that the pruned conjunction of two action-deterministic APAs matches their greatest lower bound with respect to refinement.

Theorem 4. *Let N, N', and N'' be action-deterministic consistent APAs. It holds that $\beta^*(N \wedge N') \preceq N$ and, if $N'' \preceq N$ and $N'' \preceq N'$, then $N'' \preceq \beta^*(N \wedge N')$.*

4.2   Parallel Composition

We now propose a composition operation that allows to combine two APAs. We then show how composition and abstraction can collaborate to avoid state-space explosion.

In our theory, the composition operation is parametrized with a set of synchronization actions. This set allows to specify on which actions the two specifications should collaborate and on which actions they can behave individually. The composition of two must transitions is a must transition, but composing a must with a may leads to a may transition.

Definition 11 (Parallel composition of APAs). *Let $N = (S, A, L, AP, V, s_0)$ and $N' = (S', A', L', AP', V', s'_0)$ be APAs and assume $AP \cap AP' = \emptyset$. The parallel composition of N and N' w.r.t. synchronization set $\bar{A} \subseteq A \cap A'$, written as $N \|_{\bar{A}} N'$, is given as $N \|_{\bar{A}} N' = (S \times S', A \cup A', \tilde{L}, AP \cup AP', \tilde{V}, (s_0, s'_0))$ where*

 − $\tilde{L}$ *is defined as follows:*
   • *For all $(s, s') \in S \times S'$, $a \in \bar{A}$, if there exists $\varphi \in C(S)$ and $\varphi' \in C(S')$, such that $L(s, a, \varphi) \neq \bot$ and $L'(s', a, \varphi') \neq \bot$, define $\tilde{L}((s, s'), a, \tilde{\varphi}) = L(s, a, \varphi) \sqcap L'(s', a, \varphi')$ with $\tilde{\varphi}$ the new constraint in $C(S \times S')$ such that $\tilde{\mu} \in Sat(\tilde{\varphi})$ iff there exists $\mu \in Sat(\varphi)$ and $\mu' \in Sat(\varphi')$ such that $\tilde{\mu}(u, v) = \mu(u) \cdot \mu'(v)$ for all $u \in S$ and $v \in S'$.
   If either for all $\varphi \in C(S)$, we have $L(s, a, \varphi) = \bot$, or $\forall \varphi' \in C(S')$, we have $L'(s', a, \varphi') = \bot$ then for all $\tilde{\varphi} \in C(S \times S')$, $\tilde{L}((s, s'), a, \tilde{\varphi}) = \bot$.*
   • *For all $(s, s') \in S \times S'$, $a \in A \setminus \bar{A}$, and for all $\varphi \in C(S)$, define $\tilde{L}((s, s'), a, \tilde{\varphi}) = L(s, a, \varphi)$ with $\tilde{\varphi}$ the new constraint in $C(S \times S')$ such that $\tilde{\mu} \in Sat(\tilde{\varphi})$ iff for all $u \in S$ and $v \neq s', \tilde{\mu}(u, v) = 0$ and the distribution $\mu : t \mapsto \tilde{\mu}(t, s')$ is in $Sat(\varphi)$.*

- *For all $(s, s') \in S \times S'$, $a \in A' \setminus \bar{A}$, and for all $\varphi' \in C(S')$, define $\tilde{L}((s, s'), a, \tilde{\varphi}') = L'(s', a, \varphi')$ with $\tilde{\varphi}'$ the new constraint in $C(S \times S')$ such that $\mu' \in Sat(\tilde{\varphi}')$ iff for all $u \neq s$ and $v \in S', \mu'(u, v) = 0$ and the distribution $\mu' : t' \mapsto \mu'(s, t')$ is in $Sat(\varphi')$.*
  - *$\tilde{V}$ is defined as follows: for all $(s, s') \in S \times S'$, $\tilde{V}((s, s')) = \{\tilde{B} = B \cup B' \mid B \in V(s) \text{ and } B' \in V'(s')\}$.*

Contrary to the conjunction operation, Composition is defined for both dissimilar alphabets and non-deterministic APAs. Since PAs are a restriction of APAs, their compositions is defined in the same way. By inspecting Definition 11, one can see that the composition of two APAs whose constraints are systems of linear inequalities (or polynomial constraints) may lead to an APA whose constraints are polynomial. One can also see that the conjunction of two APAs with polynomial constraints is an APA with polynomial constraints. The class of polynomial constraints APAs is closed under all compositional design operations.

The following theorem characterizes the relation between parallel composition and weak refinement.

Theorem 5. *Given a synchronization set $\bar{A}$, the parallel composition operator $\|_{\bar{A}}$ defined above is a precongruence with respect to weak refinement.*

The fact that abstraction preserves weak refinement (cf. Theorem 3), and that weak refinement is a pre-congruence w.r.t. parallel composition, enables us to apply abstraction in a component-wise manner. That is to say, rather than first generating (the typically large PA) $M\|_{\bar{A}}N$, and then applying abstraction, it allows for first applying abstraction, yielding $\alpha_1(M)$ and $\alpha_2(N)$, respectively, and then constructing $\alpha_1(M)\|_{\bar{A}}\alpha_2(N)$. Possibly a further abstraction of $\alpha_1(M)\|_{\bar{A}}\alpha_2(N)$ can be employed. The next theorem shows that component wise abstraction is as powerful as applying the combination of the "local" abstractions to the entire model.

Theorem 6. *Let M and N be APA, $\bar{A}$ a synchronization set, and α_1, α_2 be abstraction functions, then:*

$$\alpha_1(M) \|_{\bar{A}} \alpha_2(N) = (\alpha_1 \times \alpha_2)(M \|_{\bar{A}} N) \qquad \text{up to isomorphism}$$

The above theorem helps avoiding state-space explosion when combining systems by allowing for abstraction as soon as possible.

5   Completeness and Relation with CMCs

In this section, we propose a class of APAs on which thorough and strong refinements coincide. For doing so, we will compare the expressiveness power of APAs and CMCs, showing that APAs can also act as a specification theory for MCs. We now introduce an important definition that will be used through the rest of the section.

Definition 12. *We say that an APA* $N = (S, A, L, AP, V, s_0)$ *is in a single valuation normal form iff all its admissible valuations sets are singletons, i.e. for all* $s \in S$, *we have* $|V(s)| = 1$.

It is worth mentioning that any APA with a single valuation in the initial state can be turned into an APA in single valuation normal form that accepts the same set of implementations (see [10] for such a transformation that preserves determinism).

Some results on CMCs. We recap the definitions of MCs and CMCs. Informally, a MC is a PA with a single probability distribution per state.

Definition 13 (Markov Chain). $P = \langle Q, q_0, \pi, A, V \rangle$ *is a Markov Chain if* Q *is a set of states containing the initial state* q_0, A *is a set of atomic propositions,* $V : Q \to 2^A$ *is a state valuation, and* $\pi : Q \to (Q \to [0, 1])$ *is a probability transition function:* $\sum_{q' \in Q} \pi(q)(q') = 1$ *for all* $q \in Q$.

We now formally introduce CMC, our abstraction theory for MCs.

Definition 14 (Constraint Markov Chain). *A Constraint Markov Chain is a tuple* $C = \langle Q, q_0, \psi, AP, V \rangle$ *where* Q *is a finite set of states,* $q_0 \in Q$ *is the initial state,* $\psi : Q \to (Dist(Q) \to \{0, 1\})$ *is a constraint function, AP is a set of atomic propositions and* $V : Q \to 2^{2^{AP}}$ *is a state labeling function.*
   For each state $q \in Q$, *the constraint function* ψ *is such that, for all distribution* π *on* Q, $\psi(q)(\pi) = 1$ *iff the distribution* π *is allowed in state* q.

We say that a CMC C is deterministic iff for all states $q, q', q'' \in Q$, if there exists $\pi' \in Dist(Q)$ such that $(\psi(q)(\pi') \wedge (\pi'(q') \neq 0))$ and $\pi'' \in Dist(Q)$ such that $(\psi(q)(\pi'') \wedge (\pi''(q'') \neq 0))$, then we have that $V(q') \cap V(q'') = \emptyset$. Single valuation normal form of CMCs is defined similarly as for APAs. The satisfaction relation between MCs and CMCs as well as the notions of weak and strong refinements are also defined similarly as for APAs. We will use the following result.

Theorem 7 ([3]). *For deterministic CMCs in single valuation normal form, strong refinement coincides with thorough and weak refinement.*

On the relation between CMCs and APAs. We now show that APAs can act as a specification theory for MCs. For doing so, we propose a satisfaction relation between MCs and APAs. Our definition is in two steps. First we show how to use PAs as a specification theory for MCs. Then, we use the existing relation between PAs and APAs to conclude.

Definition 15. *Let* $P = (S, A, L, AP, V, s_0)$ *be a PA with* $A \cap AP = \emptyset$. *Let* $M = \langle Q, q_0, \pi, A_M, V_M \rangle$ *be a bipartite Markov chain such that (1)* $Q = Q_N \cup Q_D$, *with* $Q_N \cap Q_D = \emptyset$, *for all* $q, q' \in Q_N, \pi(q, q') = 0$ *and for all* $q, q' \in Q_D$, $\pi(q)(q') = 0$, *(2)* $q_0 \in Q_D$, *and (3)* $A_M = A \cup AP$. *Let* $\mathcal{R} \subseteq Q_D \times S$. $\mathcal{R}$ *is a satisfaction relation iff whenever* $q \mathcal{R} s$, *we have*

1. $V_M(q) = V(s)$.
2. *For all action $a \in A$ and distribution μ over S such that $L(s, a, \mu) = \top$, there exists $q' \in Q_N$ such that $V(q') = V(s) \cup \{a\}$, $\pi(q)(q') > 0$, and $\pi(q') \Subset_{\mathcal{R}} \mu$.*
3. *For all state $q' \in Q_N$ such that $\pi(q, q') > 0$, there exists an action $a \in A$ and a distribution μ over S such that $V(q') = V(s) \cup \{a\}$, $L(s, a, \mu) = \top$, and $\pi(q') \Subset_{\mathcal{R}} \mu$.*

We say that M satisfies P iff there exists a satisfaction relation $\mathcal{R}$ such that $q_0 \, \mathcal{R} \, s_0$.

The satisfaction relation between MCs and APAs follows directly. We say that a MC M satisfies an APA N, which we write $M \models_{MC} N$, iff there exists a PA P such that M satisfies P and P satisfies N.

Expressivity Completeness.   In the previous section, we have proposed a satisfaction relation for MCs with respect to APAs. We now propose the following theorem that relates the expressive power of CMCs and APAs.

Theorem 8. *Let $N = (S, A, L, AP, V, s_0)$ be a deterministic APA in single valuation normal form and such that $AP \cap A = \emptyset$. There exists a deterministic CMC $\widehat{N}$ in single valuation normal form such that for all MC M, $M \models_{MC} N \iff M \models \widehat{N}$.*

We have just shown that for all APA N, there exists a CMC $\widehat{N}$ such that $\llbracket N \rrbracket_{MC} = \llbracket \widehat{N} \rrbracket$. The reverse of the theorem also holds up to a syntactical transformation that preserves sets of implementations (see [10] for details). This result together with Theorem 7 leads to the following important result.

Theorem 9. *For deterministic APAs with single valuations in the initial state, strong refinement coincides with thorough and weak refinement.*

6   Conclusion

This paper presents a novel abstraction for PAs and proposes the first specification theory for them. In addition, the paper also studies the relation between abstraction and compositional design in combating the state-space explosion problem.

There are various directions for future research. The first of them being to implement and evaluate our results. This would require to design efficient algorithms for the compositional design operators. Also, it would be of interest to embed our abstraction procedure in a CEGAR model checking algorithm. Another interesting direction would be to design an algorithm to decide thorough refinement and characterize the complexity of this operation. Finally, one should also consider a continuous-timed extension of our model inspired by [16].

References

1. Beneš, N., Křetínský, J., Larsen, K.G., Srba, J.: Checking thorough refinement on modal transition systems is EXPTIME-complete. In: Leucker, M., Morgan, C. (eds.) ICTAC 2009. LNCS, vol. 5684, pp. 112–126. Springer, Heidelberg (2009)
2. Caillaud, B., Delahaye, B., Larsen, K.G., Legay, A., Pedersen, M.L., Wąsowski, A.: Decision Problems for Interval Markov Chains (2010), http://www.cs.aau.dk/~mikkelp/doc/IMCpaper.pdf (Research report)
3. Caillaud, B., Delahaye, B., Larsen, K.G., Legay, A., Pedersen, M.L., Wąsowski, A.: Compositional design methodology with constraint Markov chains. In: QEST. IEEE, Los Alamitos (2010)
4. Caillaud, B., Delahaye, B., Larsen, K.G., Legay, A., Pedersen, M.L., Wąsowski, A.: Compositional design methodology with constraint Markov chains. Submitted to TCS. Elsevier, Amsterdam (2010)
5. Canetti, R., Cheung, L., Kaynar, D.K., Liskov, M., Lynch, N.A., Pereira, O., Segala, R.: Analyzing security protocols using time-bounded task-pioas. Discrete Event Dynamic Systems 18(1), 111–159 (2008)
6. Cattani, S., Segala, R.: Decision algorithms for probabilistic bisimulation. In: Brim, L., Jančar, P., Křetínský, M., Kučera, A. (eds.) CONCUR 2002. LNCS, vol. 2421, pp. 371–385. Springer, Heidelberg (2002)
7. Cheung, L., Lynch, N.A., Segala, R., Vaandrager, F.W.: Switched pioa: Parallel composition via distributed scheduling. TCS 365(1-2), 83–108 (2006)
8. Cheung, L., Stoelinga, M., Vaandrager, F.W.: A testing scenario for probabilistic processes. J. ACM 54(6) (2007)
9. de Alfaro, L., Henzinger, T.A.: Interface-based design. In: Engineering Theories of Software-intensive Systems. NATO Science Series: Mathematics, Physics, and Chemistry, vol. 195, pp. 83–104. Springer, Heidelberg (2005)
10. Delahaye, B., Katoen, J.-P., Larsen, K.G., Legay, A., Pedersen, M.L., Sher, F., Wąsowski, A.: Abstract probabilistic automata (2010), http://perso.bretagne.ens-cachan.fr/~delahaye/VMCAI11-long.pdf
11. Fecher, H., Leucker, M., Wolf, V.: Don't know in probabilistic systems. In: Valmari, A. (ed.) SPIN 2006. LNCS, vol. 3925, pp. 71–88. Springer, Heidelberg (2006)
12. Jansen, D.N., Hermanns, H., Katoen, J.-P.: A probabilistic extension of uml statecharts. In: Damm, W., Olderog, E.-R. (eds.) FTRTFT 2002. LNCS, vol. 2469, pp. 355–374. Springer, Heidelberg (2002)
13. Jonsson, B., Larsen, K.G.: Specification and refinement of probabilistic processes. In: LICS, pp. 266–277. IEEE, Los Alamitos (1991)
14. Jonsson, B., Larsen, K.G.: Specification and refinement of probabilistic processes. In: LICS, pp. 266–277. IEEE, Los Alamitos (1991)
15. Katoen, J.-P., Klink, D., Leucker, M., Wolf, V.: Three-valued abstraction for continuous-time markov chains. In: Damm, W., Hermanns, H. (eds.) CAV 2007. LNCS, vol. 4590, pp. 316–329. Springer, Heidelberg (2007)
16. Katoen, J.-P., Klink, D., Neuhäußer, M.R.: Compositional abstraction for stochastic systems. In: Ouaknine, J., Vaandrager, F.W. (eds.) FORMATS 2009. LNCS, vol. 5813, pp. 195–211. Springer, Heidelberg (2009)
17. Larsen, K.G., Nyman, U., Wąsowski, A.: Modal I/O automata for interface and product line theories. In: De Nicola, R. (ed.) ESOP 2007. LNCS, vol. 4421, pp. 64–79. Springer, Heidelberg (2007)

18. Larsen, K.G., Thomsen, B.: A modal process logic. In: LICS, pp. 203–210. IEEE, Los Alamitos (1988)
19. Larsen, K.G.: Modal specifications. In: AVMFSS, pp. 232–246. Springer, Heidelberg (1989)
20. Parma, A., Segala, R.: Axiomatization of trace semantics for stochastic nondeterministic processes. In: QEST, pp. 294–303. IEEE, Los Alamitos (2004)
21. Raclet, J.-B., Badouel, E., Benveniste, A., Caillaud, B., Legay, A., Passerone, R.: Modal interfaces: unifying interface automata and modal specifications. In: EM-SOFT, pp. 87–96. ACM, New York (2009)
22. Segala, R.: Probability and nondeterminism in operational models of concurrency. In: Baier, C., Hermanns, H. (eds.) CONCUR 2006. LNCS, vol. 4137, pp. 64–78. Springer, Heidelberg (2006)
23. Segala, R., Lynch, N.A.: Probabilistic simulations for probabilistic processes. NJC 2, 250–273 (1995)

Distributed and Predictable Software Model Checking

Nuno P. Lopes[1] and Andrey Rybalchenko[2]

[1] INESC-ID / IST, TU Lisbon
[2] Technische Universität München

Abstract. We present a predicate abstraction and refinement-based algorithm for software verification that is designed for the distributed execution on compute nodes that communicate via message passing, as found in today's compute clusters. A successful adaptation of predicate abstraction and refinement from sequential to distributed setting needs to address challenges imposed by the inherent non-determinism present in distributed computing environments. In fact, our experiments show that up to an order of magnitude variation of the running time is common when a naive distribution scheme is applied, often resulting in significantly worse running time than the non-distributed version. We present an algorithm that overcomes this pitfall by making deterministic the counterexample selection in spite of the distribution, and still efficiently exploits distributed computational resources. We demonstrate that our distributed software verification algorithm is practical by an experimental evaluation on a set of difficult benchmark problems from the transportation domain.

1 Introduction

There has been a recent rapid growth of the amount of computing resources clustered in data centers together with their increasing availability for wide access. Compute clusters can be found in academic institutions, and today it is even possible to rent computers from major providers. A typical cluster offers a large number of compute nodes interconnected via a high throughput and low latency network. The number of available CPUs can be up to one hundred and more, however usually they do not share any memory, i.e., the communication between compute nodes is via message passing over the network.

Such clusters open unprecedented opportunities for amplifying the scalability of software model checking tools. Software model checking [12] can be abstractly viewed as a tree construction, where nodes correspond to sets of program states and edges are labeled by program statements. The goal is to compute a set of nodes that contains all states that the program can reach, and then check if error states were included. Computation of child nodes is an expensive task that requires invocation of a decision procedure. This tree construction procedure has a promising potential for distribution. However, to the best of our knowledge, such computing infrastructure has not yet been utilized for software model checking.

R. Jhala and D. Schmidt (Eds.): VMCAI 2011, LNCS 6538, pp. 340–355, 2011.

In this paper we present a distributed version of a software model checking algorithm that is designed for the distributed execution on compute nodes that communicate via message passing. Our algorithm implements a prominent approach to software verification that is based on predicate abstraction and its counterexample-guided refinement [2,3,6,8]. Based on preliminary experiments, we decided to use a centralized approach with a single master node and a set of worker nodes. The master node keeps the reachability tree and a queue of nodes whose successors need to be computed by the workers. In addition, each worker node maintains a partial reachability tree that is used to locally check if a computed set of program states has been already reached. Although theoretically the master node is a bottleneck of our approach, our preliminary experiments indicated that in practice neither CPU nor network usage reach their limits.

A successful adaptation of a predicate abstraction-based model checking algorithm from sequential to distributed setting needs to address challenges imposed by the inherent non-determinism present in distributed computing environments. Since the success of predicate abstraction-based verifiers crucially depends on the choice of counterexamples used to discover predicates, any deviation from an intended program exploration strategy, and hence a counterexample selection strategy, e.g., BFS, can significantly impact the verifier running time.

Message queues, different link latencies and CPU speeds make counterexample selection non-deterministic, i.e., different verification runs can discover different series of counterexamples. Such lack of predictability can have a two-fold negative impact. First, the verification time can increase due to a suboptimal exploration strategy. In fact, our experiments with a naive distribution scheme summarized by the table in Fig. 1 show that up to an order of magnitude variation of the running time can occur[1]. Due to the random counterexample choice, the running time of the naive distributed algorithm can be up to two times slower than the sequential algorithm. Second, the outcome of the verification is practically impossible to reproduce. (Note however that computed proofs can still be checked, since the proof validity is independent of how it was computed.)

In this paper we present an algorithm that addresses the predictability requirement. Our algorithm overcomes this efficiency pitfall by making deterministic the counterexample selection in spite of the distribution. While achieving the desired deterministic behavior at the level of abstraction refinement, the algorithm does not impose any synchronization during the reachability computation, which is necessary to achieve the full utilization of available resources.

We implemented our distributed algorithm as an extension of the model checker ARMC [17] by using the DAHL distribution framework [14]. We demonstrate that our distributed software verification algorithm is practical by an experimental evaluation on a set of difficult benchmark problems from the transportation domain. For the evaluation we used a compute cluster with 40 CPUs on commodity workstations. In the experiments we observed a linear scalability in the number of CPUs with the factor 0.4–0.5, that is, with 40 CPUs our

---

[1] The naive approach distributes the computation of reachable states among workers without any attempt to control the counterexample discovery.

Test	Slowdown			
	5 nodes	10 nodes	20 nodes	40 nodes
larger_scale1_lb	1.03	1.79	2.63	3.29
larger_scale1_ub	–	–	–	–
scale1_lb	1.16	1.36	1.22	1.80
scale1_ub	1.63	33.21	13.90	1.04
timing	1.13	1.04	1.00	1.01
gasburner	1.92	2.08	1.71	2.18
rtall_tcs	1.48	1.37	1.29	2.94

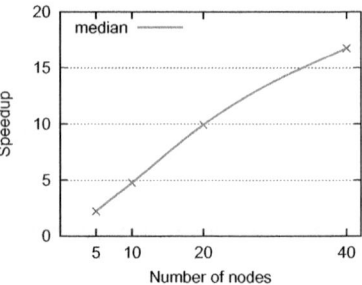

Fig. 1. On the left, we show the slowdown – the ratio between the best and the worst running time – of a naive distributed algorithm computed for three runs for each example. In larger_scale1_ub, the naive distribution did not succeed due to reaching the memory limit of 2 GB caused by a very large number of predicates collected in several days of running time. On the right, the summary of our experimental evaluation is presented. The graph presents the correlation of speedup – ratio between the running time in the sequential and distributed settings – and the number of compute nodes.

implementation is up to 20 times faster (the median value over all benchmarks) than the sequential one, see Figure 1 and Section 5 for more details. We also observed that our algorithm reduces the variation of running time across different model checker runs to negligible 1–3% (in contrast to 150–3300% as witnessed by the table of Figure 1 for the naive distribution).

In summary, this paper makes the following contributions:

- To the best of our knowledge, the first distributed model checking algorithm based on predicate abstraction and its counterexample guided refinement that offers predictable execution behavior and linear scalability;
- A practical implementation of the proposed algorithm;
- An experimental evaluation of the algorithm on a network of workstations demonstrating the effectiveness of the approach.

Related work. Previous efforts for utilizing distributed computation environments were focused on symbolic and explicit model checking algorithms, [5, 9, 13, 20]. Overcoming memory limitations of a single workstation was their primary objective, yet some implementations also delivered increase of performance. For example, the parallel Murϕ verifier [20] achieves near-linear speedups with up to 60 machines. The algorithm distributes the state space across the machines using a (static) hash function. The algorithm of [5] also shows near-linear speedups with up to ten machines. None of these algorithms needed to address the determinacy issues arising due to iterative abstraction refinement.

Jha [11] proposes d-IRA, a parallel version of refinement based model checking for hybrid systems, and shows near-linear speedups when executed on four CPUs (on the same machine). Our algorithm is similar to d-IRA in its usage of a master-slave architecture and counterexample generation entirely performed by the master. The crucial difference lies in the granularity of distribution. d-IRA lets each worker compute a relaxation of the full system for a single counterexample, while our algorithm distributes each abstract reachability computation.

Holzmann et al. [10] exploit the availability of multiple CPUs in the Swarm tool that runs several instances of a model checker in parallel with different state space exploration strategies. Each instance runs reachability computation sequentially, while our algorithm targets its distribution.

Venet and Brat [21] propose an algorithm for distributed pointer analysis that was shown to scale up to four CPUs. Similarly to our algorithm, the proposed algorithm uses a master node to distribute the global state and assign the work pieces. The main difference lies in the distribution scheme, since it uses work pieces that are individual C source files, while our algorithm distributes at the level of individual statements.

Monniaux [16] presents an algorithm for distributed abstract interpretation with widening, and its evaluation on five CPUs. The algorithm uses a master node to distribute the work pieces that are created at branch or dispatch points in the source code. The algorithm of [16] makes distributed abstract interpretation deterministic by requiring the associativity and commutativity of the join operator. In contrast, our algorithm achieves determinism through a deterministic counterexample selection scheme.

Prabhu et al. [18] present a 0CFA specific algorithm that exploits the parallelism and computation power of GPUs, achieving speedups up to 72x.

2   Example

We illustrate our distributed algorithm on a simple example program. First, we show how the choice of counterexamples for the predicate discovery affects the overall execution of the reachability computation. Then, we demonstrate what our algorithm does to make the counterexample selection process deterministic.

Consider the program in Figure 2 for which we want to check the validity of the assertion in the last line. On the right we present the corresponding control-flow graph, in which $\ell_{\mathcal{I}}$ is the initial location and $\ell_{\mathcal{E}}$ is the error location. The edges are annotated with transition relations, i.e., logical formulas over the program variables and their primed versions that represent the effect of executing the program statement. Our goal is to prove that the error location $\ell_{\mathcal{E}}$ is not reachable. Intuitively, the assertion validity can be proved by keeping track of the following two observations, so-called predicates, about the program: $x \geq 1$ and $y \geq 1$.

Now we consider how this program is verified by a distributed verification algorithm. The algorithms keeps track of a fixed set of predicates over variables and traces how the predicate validity changes when the program state is modified by executing program statements. For the sake of illustration we omit the details of how the reachability trees are constructed and focus on counterexamples, which are paths through a reachability tree that lead to the error locations, and their use for predicate discovery.

```
if (x > 0) {
    y = x;
} else if (x == 0) {
    y = 2;
} else {
    y = 1;
    y = y + 1;
}
assert(y >= 1);
```

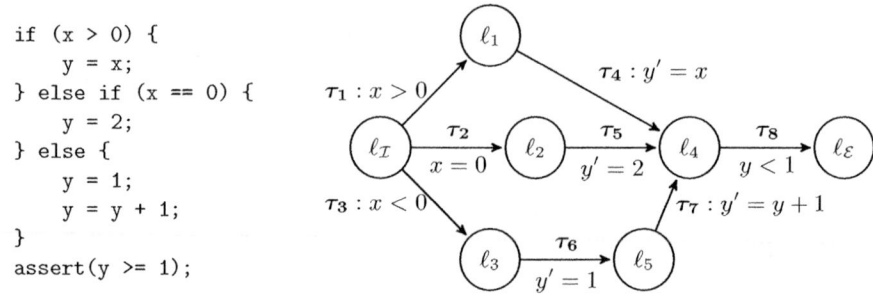

Fig. 2. An example C program and its control-flow graph. To simplify the figure, we omit update expressions $x' = x$ and $y' = y$ in the transition relations.

Naive distribution. In the case of naive distribution we do not impose any constraints on the counterexample selection. First, we attempt to prove the program correct without keeping track of any predicates. In this case we could discover any of the three counterexamples $\pi_1 = \tau_1\tau_4\tau_8$, $\pi_2 = \tau_2\tau_5\tau_8$, and $\pi_3 = \tau_3\tau_6\tau_7\tau_8$, since any path through the program that leads to the assertion appears to be feasible when we omit any reasoning about the values of program variables. By applying a predicate discovery procedure on these counterexamples, e.g., the one based on interpolation [7, 19], we obtain the following set of predicates, respectively: $\mathcal{P}_1 = \{x \geq 1, y \geq 1\}$, $\mathcal{P}_2 = \{y \geq 2\}$, and $\mathcal{P}_3 = \{y \geq 1, y \geq 2\}$.

Now we continue by considering each possible counterexample, i.e., we simulate how the verification proceeds if π_1, π_2, or π_3 was discovered and provided predicates. For each of the scenarios we now assume that the algorithm keeps track of the discovered set of predicates $\mathcal{P}_1$, $\mathcal{P}_2$, or $\mathcal{P}_3$ respectively.

In the first case, no further counterexample is found, which means that the program is proved correct using $\mathcal{P}_1$. For the cases 2 and 3, the algorithm can discover either $\pi_{2.1} = \tau_1\tau_4\tau_8$ or $\pi_{2.2} = \tau_3\tau_6\tau_7\tau_8$, and $\pi_{3.1} = \tau_1\tau_4\tau_8$, respectively. For these paths the predicate discovery yields the following sets of predicates, respectively: $\mathcal{P}_{2.1} = \{y \geq 2, x \geq 1, y \geq 1\}$, $\mathcal{P}_{2.2} = \{y \geq 2, y \geq 1\}$, and $\mathcal{P}_{3.1} = \{y \geq 1, y \geq 2, x \geq 1\}$.

Taking the sets of predicates $\mathcal{P}_{2.1}$ or $\mathcal{P}_{3.1}$ into consideration leads to the completion of the correctness proof in the respective cases. For the scenario that discovered the predicates $\mathcal{P}_{2.2}$, another refinement iteration is needed, which discovers and analyzes the counterexample $\pi_{2.2.1} = \tau_1\tau_4\tau_8$ producing the predicates $\mathcal{P}_{2.2.1} = \{y \geq 2, y \geq 1, x \geq 1\}$.

In summary, we have the following four scenarios of executing the naive distribution, which are determined by the discovered sequences of counterexamples: π_1, $(\pi_2, \pi_{2.1})$, $(\pi_2, \pi_{2.2}, \pi_{2.2.1})$, and $(\pi_3, \pi_{3.1})$.

Our simple example indicates that depending on the choice of counterexamples to perform refinement, which is non-deterministic in a naive distribution, the verification algorithm can take one, two, or three iterations, which results in a significant variation of the execution time. For complex, large program, the difference in behavior can be significantly bigger.

Predictable distribution. Now we demonstrate how our deterministic coun-terexample selection can be enforced. First, we define a total ordering $\prec$ on counterexample paths, which can be the lexicographic ordering where individ-ual transitions are compared by considering their names. Assume that we define $\tau_1 \prec \cdots \prec \tau_8$, which yields for example that $\tau_1 \tau_4 \tau_8 \prec \tau_2 \tau_3 \tau_8$.

Now we can use the ordering to select the shortest minimal discovered coun-terexample. However, when committing to the selection of a candidate coun-terexample we need to take into consideration the possibility that a smaller counterexample – currently under construction in the distributed environment – can be discovered later on. This means that we need to wait until the reachability tree construction reaches the depth of the candidate.

For example, assume that the counterexamples π_2 and π_3 are already discov-ered and π_2 is the candidate for selection, since π_2 is shorter than π_3. We still need to wait until the reachability tree construction reaches the depth 3, which is the length of π_2. Finally, π_1 will be discovered and since $\pi_1 \prec \pi_2$, it will be selected for the predicate discovery.

Thus, the deterministic selection approach leads to the predictable execution of the verification algorithm while leaving unconstrained the order on which the reachability tree is explored. The induced cost of waiting for the completion of the tree construction up to the depth determined by the candidate counterexample does not lead to a significant overhead in practice, as our experiments indicate.

In the remaining sections we provide a detailed description of our distributed verification algorithm, which is based on the idea illustrated in this section.

3 Preliminaries

In this section we define programs and computations, and provide a brief descrip-tion of predicate abstraction-based approach to program verification together with a counterexample-guided abstraction refinement procedure.

Programs and computations. We assume an abstract representation of pro-grams by transition systems [15]. A *program* $P = (\Sigma, s_\mathcal{I}, \mathcal{T}, s_\mathcal{E})$ is given by a set of program *states* Σ, an *initial* state $s_\mathcal{I} \in \Sigma$, a set of *transitions* $\mathcal{T}$, and an *error* state $s_\mathcal{E} \in \Sigma$. Each transition $\tau \in \mathcal{T}$ has a corresponding *transition relation* $\rho_\tau \subseteq \Sigma \times \Sigma$. The error state $s_\mathcal{E}$ is used to represent assertion statements commonly present in programming languages. Each failed assertion leads to $s_\mathcal{E}$.

A *computation* of P is a sequence of states $s_1, s_2, \ldots$ such that s_1 is the initial state, i.e., $s_1 = s_\mathcal{I}$, and there is a transition $\tau \in \mathcal{T}$ between each pair of consecutive states s and s', i.e., $(s, s') \in \rho_\tau$. A state s is *reachable* if it appears in some computation. The program is *safe* if the error state is *not* reachable.

A *path* is a sequence of transitions. Let $\circ$ be the *relational composition* function for binary relation over states, i.e., for $X, Y \subseteq \Sigma \times \Sigma$ we have $X \circ Y = \{(s, s') \mid \exists s'' \in \Sigma : (s, s'') \in X \wedge (s'', s') \in Y\}$. Then, a path relation ρ_π is a relational composition of transition relations along the path, i.e., for $\pi = \tau_1 \ldots \tau_n$ we have $\rho_\pi = \rho_{\tau_1} \circ \cdots \circ \rho_{\tau_n}$. A path is *feasible* if its path relation is not empty.

Predicate abstraction. Our goal is to verify if a given program is safe. To achieve this, we need to consider all reachable states and check if the error state appears among them. The set of all reachable states can be computed iteratively using the function $post : (\mathcal{T} \times 2^{\Sigma}) \to 2^{\Sigma}$ such that $post(\tau, S) = \{s' \mid \exists s \in S : (s, s') \in \rho_\tau\}$. Its least fixed point above $\{s_\mathcal{I}\}$ is the set of reachable states, i.e.,

$$s \text{ is reachable if and only if } s \in lfp(\lambda S. \bigcup_{\tau \in \mathcal{T}} post(\tau, S), \{s_\mathcal{I}\}) .$$

The exact computation of the set of reachable states is a undecidable problem, however for the verification purposes a sufficiently close *abstraction* is enough. The framework of abstract interpretation [4] provides a formal foundation for the approximate, yet sound abstraction of reachable states, where abstraction is defined as an *over-approximation*. Given an abstraction function $\alpha : 2^{\Sigma} \to 2^{\Sigma}$ such that $\forall S \subseteq \Sigma : S \subseteq \alpha(S)$, we construct an *abstraction* $post^{\#}$ of $post$ as follows: $post^{\#}(\tau, S) = \alpha(post(\tau, S))$. Our abstraction puts together and operates on sets of program states. We call such sets *abstract states* and let $\Sigma^{\#} = 2^{\Sigma}$ be the set of all abstract states. The least fixed point of $post^{\#}$ above the abstraction of the initial state is an over-approximation of the reachable states, i.e.,

$$lfp(\lambda S. \bigcup_{\tau \in \mathcal{T}} post^{\#}(\tau, S), \alpha(\{s_\mathcal{I}\})) \supseteq lfp(\lambda S. \bigcup_{\tau \in \mathcal{T}} post(\tau, S), \{s_\mathcal{I}\}) .$$

If the error state is not included in the over-approximation then the program is safe, that is, we obtain a sound method for verifying program safety.

The abstraction function α can be constructed automatically from a given set of basic building blocks, called *predicates*, where a predicate represents a set of program states. Given a set of predicates $\mathcal{P} = \{P_1, \ldots, P_n\}$, where $P_i \subseteq \Sigma$, and a *theorem prover* that can decide validity of subset inclusion between sets of states represented in a logical language, we obtain an implementation of an abstraction function $\alpha^{\mathcal{P}} : 2^{\Sigma} \to 2^{\Sigma}$ as follows: $\alpha^{\mathcal{P}}(S) = \cap\{P \in \mathcal{P} \mid S \subseteq P\}$.

Abstraction refinement. In order to verify program safety using predicate abstraction, we need to supply a set of predicates. Predicates can be derived in a goal-oriented way by using the counterexample-guided abstraction refinement approach [3]. The crux of this approach to predicate discovery lies in leveraging *spurious counterexamples*, which are program paths that expose the coarseness of the abstraction function determined by the currently used set of predicates.

A path $\pi = \tau_1 \ldots \tau_n$ is a spurious counterexample if the abstract reachability computation along the path leads to the error states, i.e.,

$$s_{\mathcal{E}} \in post^{\#}(\tau_n, post^{\#}(\tau_{n-1}, \ldots post^{\#}(\tau_1, \alpha^{\mathcal{P}}(\{s_\mathcal{I}\})))) ,$$

but the actual, not abstracted path does not lead to the error state, i.e., $(s_\mathcal{I}, s_{\mathcal{E}}) \notin \rho_\pi$. By analyzing a spurious counterexample using automated reasoning techniques, e.g., proofs [8] and interpolation [7], we extract a set of new predicates that *excludes* the spurious counterexample. Let REFINE : $\mathcal{T}^{+} \to 2^{\Sigma}$

be a refinement function that extracts predicates from spurious counterexamples. Then, after adding the extracted set of predicates to the abstraction function and obtaining $\alpha^{\mathcal{P} \cup \text{REFINE}(\pi)}$, the error state is no longer reachable via abstract reachability computation along π.

4   Predictable Distributed Verification Algorithm

This section presents our distributed algorithm for the predicate abstraction-based verification of program safety together with counterexample guided abstraction refinement. Our algorithm is parametrized. Its first parameter is the function REFINE, which takes a spurious counterexample and returns a set of predicates that, when used by the abstraction function, leads to the elimination of the counterexample during the abstract reachability computation. The second parameter is a total ordering on program paths $\prec$, which can be defined by the lexicographic extension of a total order on program transitions' names.

We designed our algorithm for the execution in a centralized environment that consists of a master node and a set of worker nodes, where there is a bidirectional communication link between the master and each of the workers. We assume that messages are received in the same order they were sent with respect to a single sender. This assumption greatly simplifies the algorithm and does not impose any practical restriction, since it can be established by using the TCP transport protocol which is ubiquitously available.

Our algorithm consists of four building blocks given by the procedures MAIN-MASTER, MAINWORKER, ADDNODE, and the function SELECTCOUNTEREX-AMPLE. The master node executes the procedure MAINMASTER as the main event processing loop, which in turn can invoke ADDNODE and SELECTCOUN-TEREXAMPLE. Each worker executes MAINWORKER, which in turn can execute ADDNODE. The procedure ADDNODE takes as the first input parameter a flag indicating whether ADDNODE is executed on the master or on a worker.

We describe each building block of our algorithm in details, while referring to the program in Figure 2 as a running example.

Procedure MainMaster. Figure 3 shows the implementation of MAINMAS-TER. This procedure maintains the central reachability tree by keeping the nodes whose successors need to be computed in an outgoing queue, which is processed by workers, and putting the computed successors to the tree.

The master starts by adding the abstraction of the initial program state to the queue (line 4), and then waits (while idling at line 7) for workers to join the system and ask for work.

The master handles three kinds of events. "EventJoin w" indicates that a worker node w wants to join the system, "EventAskForNode w" is sent by a worker w if it asks for work, and "EventReachedNode n" delivers a computed successor to the master.

When a worker w wants to join the system, it sends a EventJoin w event to the known address of the master node. Upon reception, the master registers the worker (line 9) and sends the current set of predicates to the worker (line 10).

procedure MAINMASTER
input
    $P = (\Sigma, s_{\mathcal{I}}, \mathcal{T}, s_{\mathcal{E}})$ - program
vars
    $\mathcal{P} \subseteq 2^{\Sigma}$ - finite set of predicates over states
    $Reach \subseteq \Sigma^{\#}$ - reachable abstract states
    $Parent \subseteq \Sigma^{\#} \times \mathcal{T} \times \Sigma^{\#}$ - parent relation between abstract states
    $Depth : \Sigma^{\#} \to \mathbb{N}$ - depth of abstract states
    $DepthBound \in \mathbb{N} \cup \{\infty\}$ - minimal depth of reachable error abstract state
    $Queue \in (\Sigma^{\#})^{*}$ - queue of abstract states
    $Workers, IdleWorkers$ - worker nodes and their idle subset
begin
1    $Reach := \{\alpha^{\mathcal{P}}(\{s_{\mathcal{I}}\})\}$
2    $Depth := \lambda x.0$
3    $DepthBound := \infty$
4    $Queue := \alpha^{\mathcal{P}}(\{s_{\mathcal{I}}\})$
5    $\mathcal{P} := Parent := Workers := IdleWorkers := \emptyset$
6   **repeat**
7   **match** INPUTEVENT() **with**
8 | EventJoin w ->
9          $Workers := \{w\} \cup Workers$
10   **send** $(w, \text{EventPreds } \mathcal{P})$
11 | EventAskForNode w ->
12   **if** $Queue$ is not empty **then**
13          $n := $ take from $Queue$
14   **send** $(w, \text{EventDoNode } (n, Depth(n)))$
15   **else**
16          $IdleWorkers := \{w\} \cup IdleWorkers$
17   **if** $IdleWorkers = Workers$ **then**
18   **if** $DepthBound = \infty$ **then**
19   **return** "program P is safe"
20   **else**
21              $\pi := $ SELECTCOUNTEREXAMPLE()
22   **if** $\rho_{\pi} = \emptyset$ **then**
23                $\mathcal{P} := $ REFINE$(\pi) \cup \mathcal{P}$
24   **for each** $w' \in Workers$ **do**
25   **send** $(w', \text{EventPreds } \mathcal{P})$
26   **send** $(w, \text{EventDoNode } (\alpha^{\mathcal{P}}(\{s_{\mathcal{I}}\}), 0))$
27                $Reach := \{\alpha^{\mathcal{P}}(\{s_{\mathcal{I}}\})\}$
28                $Depth := \lambda x.0$
29                $DepthBound := \infty$
30                $Parent := Queue := \emptyset$
31   **else**
32   **return** "counterexample π"
33 | EventReachedNode(n, d, m, τ) ->
34   ADDNODE("master", n, d, m, τ)
35   **if** $n \in s_{\mathcal{E}} \wedge Depth(n) < DepthBound$ **then**
36          $DepthBound := Depth(n)$
end.

Fig. 3. Procedure MAINMASTER

The master handles workers requests for work according to two scenarios depending on the work availability, either (lines 12–14) or (lines 15–32). If there is work available, then the master sends a piece of work to the worker. Otherwise, the worker is queued in the list of idle workers (line 16). If all the registered workers become idle, then it means the reachability computation has terminated, either by exploring the full tree or reaching the depth bound. The program is correct if no counterexamples have been found upon termination (lines 18–19). Otherwise, the master selects a counterexample by calling the function SELECT-COUNTEREXAMPLE and checks its feasibility (lines 21–22). If the counterexample is not feasible, then it is analyzed by applying REFINE and the discovered predicates are broadcasted to all workers (lines 23–25). Finally, we restart the reachability computation by initializing the relevant data structures.

When a new abstract state is computed by a worker and the worker determines that the state might have not been reached before, the state is sent to the master, where the final decision if the state should be added to the tree is made (line 34). If the added abstract state contains the error state of the program and its depth is less than the current depth bound, then the algorithm adjusts the counterexample depth bound (lines 35–36).

Procedure MainWorker. We present the implementation of MAINWORKER in Figure 4.

When a worker is started, first it joins the system by sending a join message to the master (line 3), and then asks for a piece of work (line 4). Afterwards, the worker processes the events received from the master (lines 5–15).

Workers handle two kinds of events. "EventPreds $\mathcal{P}$" is received before the abstract reachability computation begins. This event is used to update the set of predicates, as well as to reset the relevant data structures (lines 7–10). The other event kind processed by workers is "EventDoNode n", which comes from the master and contains an abstract state whose immediate successors should be computed by the worker. Upon receiving such an event, the worker applies the one-step abstract reachability operator on the received abstract state, adds the result to its local reachability tree (lines 12–14), and, if a computed abstract state appears to have not been discovered previously, sends it to the master. Finally, the worker asks for a new piece of work.

Procedure AddNode. See Figure 5 for the implementation of the procedure ADDNODE. This procedure is used to add an abstract state to the abstract reachability tree and is responsible for discarding those abstract states that represent program states already appearing in the tree.

ADDNODE starts by pruning nodes that are subsumed by the abstract state that we are trying to add (line 1). The checks for the depth are part of the implementation to enforce deterministic execution. So, we only allow a node to prune other if its depth is smaller. As an optimization, if the abstract state that we are trying to add is already present in the tree at the same depth, then we only update the parent relation, as the recomputation of the node is unnecessary (lines 2–3). Finally, if the abstract state is not subsumed by any other one present

```
       procedure MainWorker
       input
           P = (Σ, s_I, T, s_E) - program
           self - this node
           master - master node
       vars
           P ⊆ 2^Σ - finite set of predicates over states
           Reach ⊆ Σ^# - reachable abstract states
           Parent ⊆ Σ^# × T × Σ^# - parent relation between abstract states
           Depth : Σ^# → IN - depth of abstract states
       begin
1          Depth := λx.0
2          P := Parent := Reach := ∅
3          send (master, EventJoin self)
4          send (master, EventAskForNode self)
5          repeat
6              match InputEvent() with
7              | EventPreds P' ->
8                  P := P'
9                  Depth := λx.0
10                 Parent := Reach := ∅
11             | EventDoNode (m, d) ->
12                 for each τ ∈ T do
13                     n := α^P(post(τ, m))
14                     AddNode("worker", n, d + 1, m, τ)
15                 send (master, EventAskForNode self)
       end
```

Fig. 4. Procedure MainWorker

in the tree (again, with a lower depth), then it is added to the tree (lines 4–7). The last step of AddNode involves putting the recently added node to the work queue. As the work queue is maintained by the master, the worker has to send the abstract state to the master for further processing (line 15), while the master directly adds it to its queue (line 10–14). If there is an idle worker, the master immediately sends the state to such a worker for processing (lines 10–12).

Function SelectCounterexample. Figure 6 presents the implementation of the function SelectCounterexample. This function deterministically selects one counterexample from the reachability tree.

SelectCounterexample generates all the counterexample paths, and then selects the minimal path according to total order ≺. It works in a breadth-first way and traverses the reachability tree backwards from the reachable error states.

First, SelectCounterexample initializes the paths list with the reachable error states (line 1) and then expands these paths iteratively by following the parent relation (lines 4–7). Then, when all shortest counterexample paths are found (i.e., when the start state is first reached), the loop terminates (lines 8–9).

---

procedure ADDNODE
input
    $mode \in \{$"master", "worker"$\}$ - execution mode
    $n \in \Sigma^{\#}$ - node to add
    $d \in \mathbb{N}$ - depth of node n
    $m \in Reach$ - parent of node n
    $\tau \in \mathcal{T}$ - transition from m to n
begin

1    $Reach := Reach \setminus \{n' \in Reach \mid n' = n \wedge Depth(n') > d \vee$
                                        $n' \subset n \wedge Depth(n') \geq d\}$
2   **if** $n \in Reach \wedge Depth(n) = d$ **then**
3       $Parent := \{(m, \tau, n)\} \cup Parent$
4   **else if** $\forall n' \in Reach : \neg(n \subseteq n' \wedge d \geq Depth(n'))$ **then**
5       $Reach := \{n\} \cup Reach$
6       $Parent := \{(m, \tau, n)\} \cup Parent$
7       $Depth := Depth[n \mapsto d]$
8   **match** $mode$ **with**
9 | "master" ->
10   **if** $IdleWorkers \neq \emptyset$ **then**
11           $w :=$ pick and remove one from $IdleWorkers$
12   **send** $(w, \texttt{EventDoNode } (n, d))$
13   **else**
14           $Queue :=$ add n to $Queue$
15 | "worker" -> **send** $(master, \texttt{EventReachedNode } (n, d, m, \tau))$
end

Fig. 5. Procedure ADDNODE

The set of paths in *ErrorPaths* is then guaranteed to include counterexample paths of equal, shortest length. Finally, the minimal counterexample wrt. $\prec$ is selected from the list and returned to the caller.

Correctness. In order to state the correctness of our algorithm, we present the following statements.

Invariant 1. *A node n with depth d cannot be subsumed by a larger node n' with depth d' if $d < d'$.*

Lemma 1. SELECTCOUNTEREXAMPLE *is deterministic.*

Proof. (Sketch) As the algorithm uses a total ordering function and it works only with data that is independent of the execution (transition identifiers), the algorithm is deterministic.

Lemma 2. *Workers are deterministic.*

Proof. (Sketch) First, assuming no messages are lost, every worker updates its set of predicates when an iteration begins. Second, the computation done by a

```
     function SELECTCOUNTEREXAMPLE
     vars
         PathsSofar, ErrorPaths ⊆ Σ# × T* - partial counterexamples with start state
     begin
1        PathsSofar  :=  {(n, ϵ) | n ∈ Reach ∧ sε ∈ n}
2        ErrorPaths  :=  ∅
3        do
4            for each (n, π) ∈ PathsSofar do
5                PathsSofar  :=  PathsSofar \ {(n, π)}
6                    for each (m, τ, n) ∈ Parent such that m ∈ Reach do
7                        PathsSofar  :=  {(m, τ · π)} ∪ PathsSofar
8            ErrorPaths  :=  {(n, π) ∈ PathsSofar | sI ∈ n}
9        while ErrorPaths = ∅
10       return min(≺, ErrorPaths)
     end
```

Fig. 6. Function SELECTCOUNTEREXAMPLE

worker is itself deterministic, which depends only on the input state and the predicates set.

Theorem 1. *Every execution of the* MAINMASTER *algorithm on a given program computes the same fixpoint in the same number of iterations.*

Proof. (Sketch) First, the ADDNODE procedure ensures that every subsumed node in the tree gets pruned and every non-subsumed node gets added (w.r.t. Invariant 1), disregarding the order that the input is given. Second, MAINMASTER ensures that all non-subsumed nodes up to the lowest height are computed. Therefore all shortest counterexamples are found in an iteration. Finally, by Lemmas 1 and 2 and the previous observations, we have that the algorithm picks counterexamples deterministically.

5   Experiments

In this section we describe our experiments with an implementation of our distributed algorithm as an extension of the model checker ARMC [17].

Benchmarks. For the experimental evaluation we used a set of benchmarks from the transportation domain [1] and a standard hybrid system example, gasburner. Our benchmarks are automata-theoretic models compiled from complex specifications that describe communication, timing and data manipulation aspects and are represented using a combination of CSP, Duration Calculus, and Object-Z. Table 1 provides some details about the size of the benchmarks.

As a baseline for our evaluation we used the results obtained by executing the sequential model checker ARMC. As Table 2 demonstrates, our benchmarks are difficult (for the sequential algorithm) and require verification time in order of hours.

Table 1. Size of benchmark programs and details their verification in sequential setting

Test	Program size		# Predicates	Max. length of	Refinement
	# Variables	# Transitions		counterexamples	iterations
larger_scale1_lb	16	6127	154	15	32
larger_scale1_ub	16	6127	217	25	46
scale1_lb	15	3337	98	15	20
scale1_ub	15	3337	182	25	37
timing	47	99093	17	17	14
gasburner	19	3124	209	41	64
rtall_tcs	20	18757	50	15	30

Table 2. Running time, in hours, for the sequential (BFS) and distributed cases for 10, 20, and 40 nodes, together with the speedup

Test	Running time, hours				Speedup		
	Sequential	Distributed			10 nodes	20 nodes	40 nodes
		10 nodes	20 nodes	40 nodes			
larger_scale1_lb	1.8	2.9	1.4	0.7	0.62	1.33	2.66
larger_scale1_ub	50.9	9.8	4.6	2.3	5.18	11.06	22.13
scale1_lb	0.3	0.2	0.1	0.1	1.15	2.37	4.24
scale1_ub	5.9	2.7	1.3	0.6	2.17	4.67	9.24
timing	0.7	0.1	0.1	0.04	5.64	10.95	16.73
gasburner	5.5	1.1	0.6	0.3	4.75	9.90	18.35
rtall_tcs	1.0	0.1	0.1	0.04	9.44	19.13	28.76
Median					4.75	9.90	16.73

Setup. The tests were run on a cluster of AMD Opteron 252 (2.6 Ghz) machines, with 3 GB of RAM, 64 KB of L1 caches, and 1 MB of L2 cache each, running Linux kernel version 2.6.24. The computers were connected through a gigabit LAN with an average round-trip time (RTT) of 0.14 ms.

Our implementation of the distributed model checker was compiled using the SICStus Prolog compiler 4.0.5 and the DAHL distribution framework [14].

We verified our benchmarks in five configurations using 5, 10, 20, and 40 compute nodes. Each of the experiments was executed three times to investigate the predictability of our distributed algorithm.

Results. Our experiments show encouraging results, see Table 2. We observe a reduction in order of magnitude of the running time, which decreased hours to minutes. The speedup – ratio between the running times in the sequential and distributed setting – is on par with the number of utilized compute nodes and grows linearly with the number of worker nodes.

Besides the overall positive outcome of the running time evaluation, the experiments also show that our implementation can still be improved. We observe that the efficiency of our algorithm – the ratio between the speedup and the number of compute nodes – is between 40 and 50%, which leaves significant space for improvement. We also observed that the difference between running times of the same example across multiple runs is below 1–3%, which indicates the predictability of our algorithm.

References

1. Automatic Verification and Analysis of Complex Systems (AVACS), http://www.avacs.org
2. Ball, T., Majumdar, R., Millstein, T.D., Rajamani, S.K.: Automatic Predicate Abstraction of C Programs. In: PLDI (2001)
3. Clarke, E., Grumberg, O., Jha, S., Lu, Y., Veith, H.: Counterexample-Guided Abstraction Refinement. In: Emerson, E.A., Sistla, A.P. (eds.) CAV 2000. LNCS, vol. 1855. Springer, Heidelberg (2000)
4. Cousot, P., Cousot, R.: Abstract Interpretation: a Unified Lattice Model for Static Analysis of Programs by Construction or Approximation of Fixpoints. In: POPL (1977)
5. Garavel, H., Mateescu, R., Smarandache, I.: Parallel State Space Construction for Model-Checking. In: Dwyer, M.B. (ed.) SPIN 2001. LNCS, vol. 2057, p. 217. Springer, Heidelberg (2001)
6. Graf, S., Saïdi, H.: Construction of Abstract State Graphs with PVS. In: Grumberg, O. (ed.) CAV 1997. LNCS, vol. 1254, Springer, Heidelberg (1997)
7. Henzinger, T.A., Jhala, R., Majumdar, R., McMillan, K.L.: Abstractions from Proofs. In: POPL (2004)
8. Henzinger, T.A., Jhala, R., Majumdar, R., Sutre, G.: Lazy Abstraction. In: POPL (2002)
9. Heyman, T., Geist, D., Grumberg, O., Schuster, A.: Achieving Scalability in Parallel Reachability Analysis of Very Large Circuits. In: Emerson, E.A., Sistla, A.P. (eds.) CAV 2000. LNCS, vol. 1855. Springer, Heidelberg (2000)
10. Holzmann, G.J., Joshi, R., Groce, A.: Tackling Large Verification Problems with the Swarm Tool. In: Havelund, K., Majumdar, R. (eds.) SPIN 2008. LNCS, vol. 5156, pp. 134–143. Springer, Heidelberg (2008)
11. Jha, S.K.: d-IRA: A Distributed Reachability Algorithm for Analysis of Linear Hybrid Automata. In: Egerstedt, M., Mishra, B. (eds.) HSCC 2008. LNCS, vol. 4981, pp. 618–621. Springer, Heidelberg (2008)
12. Jhala, R., Majumdar, R.: Software Model Checking. ACM Computing Surveys 41(4) (2009)
13. Lerda, F., Sisto, R.: Distributed-Memory Model Checking with SPIN. In: Dams, D.R., Gerth, R., Leue, S., Massink, M. (eds.) SPIN 1999. LNCS, vol. 1680, p. 22. Springer, Heidelberg (1999)
14. Lopes, N.P., Navarro, J.A., Rybalchenko, A., Singh, A.: Applying Prolog to Develop Distributed Systems. Theory and Practice of Logic Programming 10(4-6), 691–707 (2010)
15. Manna, Z., Pnueli, A.: Temporal Verification of Reactive Systems: Safety. Springer, Heidelberg (1995)
16. Monniaux, D.: The Parallel Implementation of the Astrée Static Analyzer. In: APLAS (2005)

17. Podelski, A., Rybalchenko, A.: ARMC: The Logical Choice for Software Model Checking with Abstraction Refinement. In: PADL (2007)
18. Prabhu, T., Ramalingam, S., Might, M., Hall, M.: EigenCFA: Accelerating flow analysis with GPUs. In: POPL (2011)
19. Rybalchenko, A., Sofronie-Stokkermans, V.: Constraint Solving for Interpolation. In: Cook, B., Podelski, A. (eds.) VMCAI 2007. LNCS, vol. 4349, pp. 346–362. Springer, Heidelberg (2007)
20. Stern, U., Dill, D.L.: Parallelizing the Murφ Verifier. Formal Methods in System Design 18(2), 117–129 (2001)
21. Venet, A., Brat, G.: Precise and Efficient Static Array Bound Checking for Large Embedded C Programs. In: PLDI (2004)

Access Analysis-Based Tight Localization of Abstract Memories

Hakjoo Oh[1], Lucas Brutschy[2], and Kwangkeun Yi[1]

[1] Seoul National University
[2] RWTH Aachen University

Abstract. On-the-fly localization of abstract memory states is vital for economical abstract interpretation of imperative programs. Such localization is sometimes called "abstract garbage collection" or "framing". In this article we present a new memory localization technique that is more effective than the conventional reachability-based approach. Our technique is based on a key observation that collecting the reachable memory parts is too conservative and the accessed parts are usually tiny subsets of the reachable. Our technique first estimates, by an efficient pre-analysis, the set of locations that will be accessed during the analysis of each code block. Then the main analysis uses the access-set results to trim the memory entries before analyzing code blocks. In experiments with an industrial-strength global C static analyzer, the technique is applied right before analyzing each procedure's body and reduces the average analysis time and memory by 92.1% and 71.2%, respectively, without sacrificing the analysis precision. Localizing more frequently such as at loop bodies and basic blocks as well as procedure bodies, the generalized localization additionally reduces analysis time by an average of 31.8%.

1 Introduction

In global abstract interpretation of imperative programs, memory localization (sometimes called "abstract garbage collection" or "framing") is vital for reducing analysis cost [5, 8, 14, 16, 24]. Not to mention the immediate benefit of the reduced memory footprint, memory localization has other important impact on cost reduction. In flow-sensitive, semantically dense global abstract interpretation, code blocks such as procedure bodies are repeatedly analyzed (often needlessly) with different input memory states. Localization makes input memory states smaller, which results in more general summaries for the blocks. More general summaries reduce re-computations of blocks by increasing the chance of reusing the previously computed analysis results. For example, consider a code x=0;f();x=1;f(); and assume that x is not used inside f. Without localization, f is analyzed twice because the input state to f is changed at the second call. If x is removed from the input state (localization), the analysis result of f for the first call can be reused for the second call without re-analyzing the procedure.

The conventional localization scheme is reachability-based [5, 23, 24, 8, 21, 20, 14, 16]. When applied to procedure bodies, reachability-based approaches allow a procedure to be analyzed with only a memory portion that is reachable from

R. Jhala and D. Schmidt (Eds.): VMCAI 2011, LNCS 6538, pp. 356–370, 2011.

Table 1. Reachability-based approach is too conservative. The table shows a comparison of accessed and reachable (abstract) memory portions during abstract interpretations of 5 open-source programs. For each a/b (r%), a is the average number of memory entries accessed in the called procedures, b is the average size of the reachable input state, and r is their ratio.

Program	LOC	accessed memory / reachable memory
spell-1.0	2,213	5 / 453 (1.1%)
gzip-1.2.4a	7,327	22 / 1,002 (2.2%)
jwhois-3.0.1	9,344	28 / 830 (3.4%)
bc-1.06	13,093	24 / 824 (2.9%)
less-290	18,449	86 / 1,546 (5.6%)

actual parameters or global variables. Because the reachable portion is often smaller than the entire memory state, analysis cost is reduced, both in time and memory. The method is popular in various kinds of program analysis: for example, in shape analysis [23, 8, 21, 14, 6] and higher-order flow analysis [16, 5].

However, the reachability-based approach has inefficient aspects especially in analyzing real C programs. This is mainly because large parts of the reachable portion of input states are not actually accessed, i.e. the values are neither read nor written during the analysis. For example, Table 1 shows, given a reachability-based localized input state to a procedure, how much is actually accessed inside the (directly or transitively) called procedures. The results show that only few reachable memory entries were actually accessed: procedures accessed only 1.1%–5.6% of reachable memory states. Nonetheless, the reachability-based approach propagates all the reachable parts to procedures. It is therefore possible for a procedure body to be needlessly recomputed for input memory states whose only differences lie in the reachable-but-non-accessed portions. This means that the reachability-based approach can be too conservative for real C programs and hence is inefficient in both time and memory cost. This observation was made while investigating the reasons for the inefficiency of an industrial-strength static analyzer [11–13, 18, 19] that uses the reachability-based localization.

In this paper, we present a localization technique that is more aggressive than reachability-based approach. In addition to excluding unreachable memory entries from the localized state, we also exclude memory entries that are reachable but possibly not accessed. The main problem is to find the memory parts that will be accessed during the analysis of a block *before* actually analyzing the block. We solve the problem by staging: (1) the set of abstract locations that will be used during the analysis of a code block is conservatively estimated by a pre-analysis; (2) then, the actual analysis uses the information and filters out memory parts that will not be accessed within the block. The pre-analysis applies a conservative abstraction to the abstract semantics of the original analysis and quickly finds an over-approximation of resources that the actual analysis requires. This over-approximate nature of our pre-analysis ensures the correctness of our approach (Section 3.2).

The time savings by our new localization method are significant: when applied to each procedure's body, our access-based localization reduces the analysis time by on average 92.1% over reachability-based localization. We implemented our approach inside an industrial-strength interval-domain-based abstract interpreter [11–13, 18, 19]. In experiments, the technique reduces analysis time by 78.5%–98.5%, on average 92.1%, and peak memory consumption by 33.0–81.2%, on average 71.2%, over the reachability-based approach for a variety of open-source C benchmarks (2K–100KLOC). Moreover, our technique enables the largest four programs of our benchmarks to be analyzed, which could not be analyzed with the reachability-based approach because of the analysis running out of memory.

We generalize the idea of localization at procedure entries to localization of arbitrary code blocks. When applying localization to such smaller code blocks, we have to carefully select localization targets because localizing operations introduce performance overhead. We present a block selection strategy that is flexible to balance actual cost reduction against the overhead. The generalized localization reduces the analysis time by 8.5–53.7%, on average 31.8%, on top of the procedure-level localization.

This paper makes the following contributions.

- We present a new localization technique, access-based localization. We employ a pre-analysis that is a conservative abstraction of the abstract semantics of the actual analysis. As far as we know published program analyzers do not perform access-based localization: previous analyses use reachability-based techniques (e.g., [16, 8, 20]) or their variants (e.g., [5, 15]).
- We present a generalized localization algorithm that applies to arbitrary code blocks as well as procedure bodies. As far as we know, other published program analyzers apply localization only to procedures.
- We prove the effectiveness of our technique by experiments with industrial-strength C static analyzer [11–13, 18, 19].

Example 1. Consider the C code in Fig. 1 and an interval analysis of the code. The analysis begins with an empty memory state ($\lambda x.\bot$). The abstract memory state right before calling f at line 7 (after parameter bound) is represented by Fig. 1(a). Here, s denotes a structure with fields $\{a, b\}$ allocated at line 5. The abstract locations of each field are represented by $\langle l_5, a \rangle$ and $\langle l_5, b \rangle$, which initially have bottom values. p is a parameter of f and g is a global variable.

Reachability-based localization collects all reachable memory entries: global variable g, parameter p, and structure fields $\langle l_5, a \rangle$ and $\langle l_5, b \rangle$ that are reachable by dereferencing p. Fig. 1(b) shows the resulting localized memory.

Our approach additionally filters the memory entries for $\langle l_5, b \rangle$ and g. Our pre-analysis infers that only the abstract locations $\{p, \langle l_5, a \rangle\}$ could be accessed during actual analysis of f. The actual analysis uses the results and trims memory entries, resulting in the memory state shown in Fig. 1(c). Note that, because the localized memory (Fig. 1(c)) does not contain $\langle l_5, b \rangle$, the update to location $\langle l_5, b \rangle$ at line 8 does not cause f to be re-analyzed at the subsequent call to f (line 8). On the other hand, with reachability-based localization, f will be analyzed again at the second call.

```
1: struct S { int a; int b; }
2: int g = 0;
3: void f (S* p) { p->a = 1; }
4: void main() {
5:      S *s = (S*)malloc(sizeof S);
6:      s->a = 0;
7:      s->b = 0; f(s);        // first call to f
8:      s->b = 1; f(s); }      // second call to f
```

$$s \mapsto \langle l_5, \{a,b\} \rangle \qquad p \mapsto \langle l_5, \{a,b\} \rangle \qquad p \mapsto \langle l_5, \{a,b\} \rangle$$
$$p \mapsto \langle l_5, \{a,b\} \rangle \qquad \langle l_5, a \rangle \mapsto [0,0] \qquad \langle l_5, a \rangle \mapsto [0,0]$$
$$\langle l_5, a \rangle \mapsto [0,0] \qquad \langle l_5, b \rangle \mapsto [0,0]$$
$$\langle l_5, b \rangle \mapsto [0,0] \qquad g \mapsto [0,0]$$
$$g \mapsto [0,0]$$

(a) Non-localized memory (b) Reachability-based localization (c) Access-based localization

Fig. 1. Example code and abstract memories right before calling procedure f at line 7

Outline. Section 2 presents our analysis framework. Section 3 develops our approach on top of our analysis framework. Section 4 shows experimental results. Section 5 presents related work and discussion.

2   Setting: Baseline Analyzer

We describe our localization technique on top of a flow-sensitive and context-insensitive abstract interpreter of C programs, based on the interval abstract domain. We present the representation of programs (Section 2), abstract domain, and abstract semantics (Section 2).

Our abstract domain and semantics are rather conventional, similar to ones used in other abstract interpretations for C or binary programs (e.g., [2]). Our abstract semantics estimate numeric and pointer values within a monolithic abstract interpretation.

Program Representation. We assume that a program is represented by a supergraph. A supergraph consists of control flow graphs of all procedures with interprocedural edges connecting each call-site to its callee and callees to return-sites. Each command in a node $n \in Node$ in the graph has one of the following types:

$$\mathtt{set}(lv, e) \mid \mathtt{alloc}(lv, a) \mid \mathtt{call}(f_x, e)$$

where expression e, l-value expression lv, and allocation expression a are defined as follows:

$$\text{expression } e \rightarrow n \mid e + e \mid lv \mid \&lv$$
$$\text{l-value } \quad lv \rightarrow x \mid *e \mid e[e] \mid e.x$$
$$\text{allocation } a \rightarrow [e]_l \mid \{x\}_l$$

An expression may be a constant integer (n), a binary operation $(e + e)$, an l-value expression (lv), or an address-of expression $(\&lv)$. An l-value may be a variable (x), a pointer dereference $(*e)$, an array access $(e\,[e])$, or a field access $(e\,.x)$. Expressions and l-value expressions have no side-effects. All program variables, including formal parameters, have unique names. The command $\mathtt{set}\,(lv\,,e)$ assigns the value of e into the location of lv. The command $\mathtt{alloc}\,(lv\,,a)$ allocates an array $[e]_l$ or a structure $\{x\}_l$, where e is the size of the array, x is the field name, and the subscript l is the label of the allocation site. For simplicity, we only consider structures with one field in this explanation.

A call-site in a program is represented by a call node and its corresponding return node. A call node $\mathtt{call}\,(f_x,e)$ indicates that it invokes a procedure f, its formal parameter is x, and actual parameter is e. For simplicity, we assume that there are no function pointers and only consider procedures with one parameter. Edges are assembled by two functions $\mathsf{predof} \in \mathit{Node} \to 2^{\mathit{Node}}$ and $\mathsf{succof} \in \mathit{Node} \to 2^{\mathit{Node}}$, which map each node to its predecessors and successors, respectively.

Static Analysis. In our analysis, the set of (possibly infinite) concrete memory states are represented by an abstract memory state $\hat{\mathit{Mem}} = \hat{\mathit{Addr}} \xrightarrow{\text{fin}} \hat{\mathit{Val}}$, denoting a finite map from abstract locations $(\hat{\mathit{Addr}})$ to the abstract values $(\hat{\mathit{Val}})$.

$$\hat{\mathit{Addr}} = \mathit{Var} + \mathit{AllocSite} + \mathit{AllocSite} \times \mathit{FieldName}$$
$$\hat{\mathit{Val}} = \hat{\mathbb{Z}} \times 2^{\hat{\mathit{Addr}}} \times 2^{\mathit{AllocSite} \times \hat{\mathbb{Z}} \times \hat{\mathbb{Z}}} \times 2^{\mathit{AllocSite} \times 2^{\mathit{FieldName}}}$$
$$\hat{\mathbb{Z}} = \{\bot\} \cup \{[l,u] \mid l \in \mathbb{Z} \cup \{-\infty\} \wedge u \in \mathbb{Z} \cup \{+\infty\} \wedge l \le u\}$$

An abstract location may be a program variable (Var), an allocation site $(\mathit{AllocSite})$, or a structure field $(\mathit{AllocSite} \times \mathit{FieldName})$. All elements of an array allocated at l are abstracted by l. The abstract location for field x of a structure allocated at l is represented by $\langle l, x \rangle$ (the analysis is field-sensitive). An abstract value is a quadruple. Numeric values are tracked by the interval values $(\hat{\mathbb{Z}})$. Points-to information is kept by the second component $(2^{\hat{\mathit{Addr}}})$: it indicates pointer targets an abstract locations may point to. Allocated arrays of memory locations are represented by array blocks $(2^{\mathit{AllocSite} \times \hat{\mathbb{Z}} \times \hat{\mathbb{Z}}})$: an array block $\langle l, o, s \rangle$ consists of abstract base address (l), offset (o), and size (s). A structure block $\langle l, \{x\} \rangle \in 2^{\mathit{AllocSite} \times 2^{\mathit{FieldName}}}$ abstracts structure values that are allocated at l and have a set of fields $\{x\}$.

We first define two functions $\hat{\mathcal{V}}$ and $\hat{\mathcal{L}}$ that compute abstract values and locations, respectively. Given an expression e and an abstract memory state $\hat{m}$, $\hat{\mathcal{V}}(\in e \to \hat{\mathit{Mem}} \to \hat{\mathit{Val}})$ evaluates the abstract value of e under $\hat{m}$. Similarly, $\hat{\mathcal{L}}(\in lv \to \hat{\mathit{Mem}} \to 2^{\hat{\mathit{Addr}}})$ evaluates the set of abstract locations of lv under $\hat{m}$.

$$
\begin{aligned}
\hat{\mathcal{V}}(n)(\hat{m}) &= \langle [n,n], \bot, \bot, \bot \rangle & \hat{\mathcal{L}}(x)(\hat{m}) &= \{x\} \\
\hat{\mathcal{V}}(e_1 + e_2)(\hat{m}) &= \hat{\mathcal{V}}(e_1)(\hat{m}) \hat{+} \hat{\mathcal{V}}(e_2)(\hat{m}) & \hat{\mathcal{L}}(*e)(\hat{m}) &= \hat{\mathcal{V}}(e)(\hat{m}).2 \cup \{l \mid \langle l,o,s \rangle \in \hat{\mathcal{V}}(e)(\hat{m}).3\} \\
\hat{\mathcal{V}}(lv)(\hat{m}) &= \bigsqcup \{\hat{m}(\hat{\mathit{Addr}}) \mid & &\cup \{\langle l,x \rangle \mid \langle l, \{x\} \rangle \in \hat{\mathcal{V}}(e)(\hat{m}).4\} \\
&\quad \hat{\mathit{Addr}} \in \hat{\mathcal{L}}(lv)(\hat{m})\} & \hat{\mathcal{L}}(e_1\,[e_2])(\hat{m}) &= \{l \mid \langle l,o,s \rangle \in \hat{\mathcal{V}}(e_1)(\hat{m}).3\} \\
\hat{\mathcal{V}}(\&lv)(\hat{m}) &= \langle \bot, \hat{\mathcal{L}}(lv)(\hat{m}), \bot, \bot \rangle & \hat{\mathcal{L}}(e.x)(\hat{m}) &= \{\langle l,x \rangle \mid \langle l, \{x\} \rangle \in \hat{\mathcal{V}}(e)(\hat{m}).4\}
\end{aligned}
$$

where, $\hat{\mathcal{V}}(e)(\hat{m}).n$ indicates the n-th element of the tuple that $\hat{\mathcal{V}}(e)(\hat{m})$ evaluates. We skip the conventional definition of the abstract binary $(\hat{+})$ and join $(\sqcup)$ operations. In our analysis, all of the array elements are smashed into a single element, and hence, the definition of $\hat{\mathcal{L}}(e_1[e_2])$ does not involve e_2.

For each node n, we define a transfer function $\hat{f} : Node \rightarrow \hat{Mem} \rightarrow \hat{Mem}$ that, given an input memory state, computes the effect of the command in node n on the input state :

$$\hat{f}\ n\ \hat{m} = \begin{cases} \hat{m}\{\hat{\mathcal{V}}(e)(\hat{m}) /\!\!/ \hat{\mathcal{L}}(lv)(\hat{m})\} & \text{if } n = \texttt{set}(lv,e) \\ \hat{m}\{\langle \bot, \bot, \{\langle l, [0,0], \hat{\mathcal{V}}(e)(\hat{m}).1\rangle\}, \bot\rangle /\!\!/ \hat{\mathcal{L}}(lv)(\hat{m})\} & \text{if } n = \texttt{alloc}(lv,[e]_l) \\ \hat{m}\{\langle \bot, \bot, \bot, \{\langle l, \{x\}\rangle\}\rangle /\!\!/ \hat{\mathcal{L}}(lv)(\hat{m})\} & \text{if } n = \texttt{alloc}(lv,\{x\}_l) \\ \hat{m}\{\hat{\mathcal{V}}(e)(\hat{m}) /\!\!/ \hat{\mathcal{L}}(x)(\hat{m})\} & \text{if } n = \texttt{call}(f_x,e) \end{cases}$$

where, $\hat{m}\{v /\!\!/ \{l_1,\ldots,l_k\}\}$ means $\hat{m}\{l_1 \mapsto (\hat{m}(l_1) \sqcup v)\} \cdots \{l_k \mapsto (\hat{m}(l_k) \sqcup v)\}$. The effect of node $\texttt{set}(lv,e)$ is to (weakly) assign the abstract value of e into the locations in $\hat{\mathcal{L}}(lv)(\hat{m})$[1]. The array allocation command $\texttt{alloc}(lv,[e]_l)$ creates a new array block with offset 0 and size e. The structure block command $\texttt{alloc}(lv,\{x\}_l)$ creates a new structure block. In both cases, we use the allocation site l as a base address, which means that many, possibly infinite, concrete locations are summarized by finite abstract locations. The call node command $\texttt{call}(f_x,e)$ binds the formal parameter x to the value of actual parameter e. Please note that the output of the call node is the memory state that flows into the body of the called procedure, not the memory state returned from the call.

Airac computes a fixpoint table $\mathcal{T} \in Node \rightarrow \hat{Mem}$ that maps each node in the program to its output abstract memory state. The abstract memory state at each program point approximates all the concrete memory states occurring at the node in the concrete executions. The map is defined by the least fixpoint of the following function:

$$\hat{\mathcal{F}} : (Node \rightarrow \hat{Mem}) \rightarrow (Node \rightarrow \hat{Mem})$$

$$\hat{\mathcal{F}}(T) = \lambda n.\hat{f}\ n\ (\textstyle\bigsqcup_{p \in \mathsf{predof}(n)} T(p))$$

Fig. 2(a) (without the shaded line) shows the worklist-based fixpoint algorithm. In addition, we use widening and narrowing [7], the worklist order is weak topological ordering [4].

3   Memory Localization by Access Analysis

This section describes our localization technique. We first describe localization for procedure bodies: Section 3.1 develops the reachability-based localization on top of our analysis framework (Section 2) and Section 3.2 extends it to our access-based approach for procedures. We then generalize the procedure-level localization for arbitrary code blocks in Section 3.3.

---

[1] For brevity, we consider only weak updates. Applying strong update is orthogonal to our technique we present in this paper.

3.1   Conventional Reachability-Based Localization for Procedures

We first formalize the reachability-based approach on top of our baseline analyzer Airac. We call our analyzer based on this approach $\mathsf{Airac}_{\mathsf{Reach}}$.

When calling a procedure, $\mathsf{Airac}_{\mathsf{Reach}}$ passes the memory parts that are reachable from global variables or parameters. Formally, given a call node $\texttt{call}(f_x, e)$ and its input memory state $\hat{m}$ (parameter-bound), $\mathsf{Airac}_{\mathsf{Reach}}$ computes the following set of abstract locations (let Globals be the set of global variables in the program):

$$\mathcal{R}(f_x, \hat{m}) = \mathsf{Reach}(\mathsf{Globals}, \hat{m}) \cup \mathsf{Reach}(\{x\}, \hat{m})$$

We use $\mathsf{Reach}(X, \hat{m})$ to denote the set of abstract locations in $\hat{m}$ that are (directly or transitively) reachable from a location set X.

$$\mathsf{Reach}(X, \hat{m}) = \mathsf{lfp}(\lambda Y. X \cup \mathsf{OneHop}(Y, \hat{m}))$$

$\mathsf{OneHop}(X, \hat{m})$ is the set of locations that are directly reachable from X:

$$\mathsf{OneHop}(X, \hat{m}) = \bigcup_{x \in X} \hat{m}(x).2 \cup \{l \mid \langle l, o, s \rangle \in \hat{m}(x).3\} \cup \{\langle l, f \rangle \mid \langle l, \{f\} \rangle \in \hat{m}(x).4\}$$

Given an input memory $\hat{m}$ to a call node $\texttt{call}(f_x, e)$, the definition of the transfer function $\hat{f}$ is changed as follows:

$$\hat{f} \; \texttt{call}(f_x, e) \; \hat{m} \;\; = \;\; \hat{m}'|_{\mathcal{R}(f_x, \hat{m}')} \text{ where } \hat{m}' = \hat{m}\{\hat{\mathcal{V}}(e)(\hat{m})/\!\!/\{x\}\}$$

We also have to consider procedure returns. When a procedure returns to a return node, in order to recover the local information from the corresponding call node, we combine the returned memory with the memory parts that were not propagated to called procedures from the call node. Note that the issue of cutpoints [20] is not involved in our analysis because our semantics is store-based and every object is represented by a fixed location.

3.2   Access-Based Localization for Procedures

For performing the localization more aggressively, we separate the entire analysis into two phases: (1) the set of abstract locations that are accessed by a procedure during actual analysis is conservatively estimated by a pre-analysis; (2) then, the actual analysis uses the access-information and filters out memory entries that will definitely not be accessed by called procedures. The pre-analysis is derived from the abstract semantics of the original analysis by applying conservative abstractions. We call our analyzer based on the new technique $\mathsf{Airac}_{\mathsf{ProcAcc}}$.

Pre-analysis. For ensuring the correctness of the actual analysis, the pre-analysis should be an over-approximation of the actual analysis. The pre-analysis should not only find locations that are accessed in real executions, but find a set of abstract locations that contains all locations required by the actual analysis. For example, consider an expression $*p$. Suppose p points to a variable a during real execution. Suppose further, during actual analysis, p points to variables a and b, where b is a by-product of abstraction. In this case, our pre-analysis results should contain both a and b because both locations will be accessed in actual analysis. Hence we derive the pre-analysis from actual analysis of interest rather than using a separate pre-analysis such as an existing pointer analysis.

Our pre-analysis computes a map access $\in ProcId \rightarrow 2^{A\hat{d}dr}$ that maps each procedure to a set of abstract locations that are possibly accessed (directly or transitively) during the actual analysis of the procedure body. In order to compute such a map, we first instrument the analysis (Section 2) so that accessed locations are collected during the course of the analysis. Then the abstract semantics of the analysis is conservatively abstracted to a less precise but more efficient analysis, the pre-analysis.

Fig. 2(a) shows how we collect abstract locations during the original analysis. Without the shaded line, the algorithm is a normal fixpoint algorithm. With the shaded line, the algorithm performs an analysis recording accessed locations. After the effect of a node n is computed (using $\hat{f}$), the abstract locations that are accessed during the evaluation of n are collected by collect. Throughout the analysis, the accessed locations for n are accumulated in $\mathcal{A}(n)$. When the analysis terminates, all the abstract locations that have been accessed during the analyses of n are collected by $\mathcal{A}(n)$.

In order to define function collect, we define two functions $\hat{\mathcal{A}\mathcal{V}} \in e \rightarrow \hat{Mem} \rightarrow 2^{A\hat{d}dr}$ and $\hat{\mathcal{A}\mathcal{L}} \in lv \rightarrow \hat{Mem} \rightarrow 2^{A\hat{d}dr}$. Given an expression e (resp., lv) and a memory state $\hat{m}$, $\hat{\mathcal{A}\mathcal{V}}(e)(\hat{m})$ (resp., $\hat{\mathcal{A}\mathcal{L}}(lv)(\hat{m})$) collects abstract locations that are accessed during the evaluation of $\hat{\mathcal{V}}(e)(\hat{m})$ (resp., $\hat{\mathcal{L}}(lv)(\hat{m})$). $\hat{\mathcal{A}\mathcal{V}}$ and $\hat{\mathcal{A}\mathcal{L}}$ are naturally derived by examining the definition of $\hat{\mathcal{V}}$ and $\hat{\mathcal{L}}$.

$$
\begin{aligned}
\hat{\mathcal{A}\mathcal{V}}(n)(\hat{m}) &= \emptyset & \hat{\mathcal{A}\mathcal{L}}(x)(\hat{m}) &= \emptyset \\
\hat{\mathcal{A}\mathcal{V}}(e_1 + e_2)(\hat{m}) &= \hat{\mathcal{A}\mathcal{V}}(e_1)(\hat{m}) \sqcup \hat{\mathcal{A}\mathcal{V}}(e_2)(\hat{m}) & \hat{\mathcal{A}\mathcal{L}}(*e)(\hat{m}) &= \hat{\mathcal{A}\mathcal{V}}(e)(\hat{m}) \\
\hat{\mathcal{A}\mathcal{V}}(lv)(\hat{m}) &= \hat{\mathcal{A}\mathcal{L}}(lv)(\hat{m}) \sqcup \hat{\mathcal{L}}(lv)(\hat{m}) & \hat{\mathcal{A}\mathcal{L}}(e_1[e_2])(\hat{m}) &= \hat{\mathcal{A}\mathcal{V}}(c_1)(\hat{m}) \\
\hat{\mathcal{A}\mathcal{V}}(\&lv)(\hat{m}) &= \hat{\mathcal{A}\mathcal{L}}(lv)(\hat{m}) & \hat{\mathcal{A}\mathcal{L}}(e.x)(\hat{m}) &= \hat{\mathcal{A}\mathcal{V}}(e)(\hat{m})
\end{aligned}
$$

Consider $\hat{\mathcal{A}\mathcal{V}}$ (defined in the left column) first. When $e = n$, we see that the definition of $\hat{\mathcal{V}}$ does not read (nor write to) any location, and hence there are no accessed locations ($\emptyset$). When $e = e_1 + e_2$, accessed locations are just collected recursively. When an l-value lv is used as an r-value (the third case), from the definition of $\hat{\mathcal{V}}(lv)(\hat{m})$, we see that abstract locations of lv and abstract locations that are accessed during the evaluation of $\hat{\mathcal{L}}(lv)(\hat{m})$ are accessed, which are collected by $\hat{\mathcal{L}}(lv)(\hat{m})$ and $\hat{\mathcal{A}\mathcal{L}}(lv)(\hat{m})$, respectively. When an l-value lv is used as an address-of expression (the last case), from the definition of $\hat{\mathcal{V}}(\&lv)(\hat{m})$, we see that abstract locations that lv denotes ($\hat{\mathcal{L}}(lv)(\hat{m})$) are not accessed during the evaluation of $\hat{\mathcal{V}}(\&lv)(\hat{m})$ and hence the fourth case only includes $\hat{\mathcal{A}\mathcal{L}}(lv)(\hat{m})$.

Similarly, the definition of $\hat{\mathcal{A}\mathcal{L}}$ (defined in the right column) is derived from the definition of $\hat{\mathcal{L}}$. For example, $\hat{\mathcal{A}\mathcal{L}}(x)(\hat{m})$ is $\emptyset$ because $\hat{\mathcal{L}}(x)(\hat{m})$ just produces a location x but does not read (resp., write) any value from (resp., to) x. Note that, when $lv = e_1[e_2]$ (the third case), we do not collect the locations accessed during the evaluation of e_1 because the definition of $\hat{\mathcal{L}}$ for this case does not involve e_2 (array elements are smashed into a single element in the analysis).

$\mathcal{W} \in Worklist = 2^{Node}$
$\mathcal{T} \in \text{Table} = Node \to \hat{Mem}$
$\hat{f} \in Node \to \hat{Mem} \to \hat{Mem}$
$\mathcal{A} \in Node \to 2^{\hat{Addr}}$

$old, new \in \hat{Mem}$
$\hat{f}' \in Node \to \hat{Mem} \to \hat{Mem}$
$\mathcal{A} \in Node \to 2^{\hat{Addr}}$

$FixpointIterate\ (\mathcal{W}, \mathcal{T}) =$
$\mathcal{W} := Node$
$\mathcal{T} := \lambda n.\bot_{\hat{Mem}}$
repeat
    $n := \mathsf{choose}(\mathcal{W})$
    $m := \hat{f}\ n\ (\bigsqcup_{p \in \mathsf{predof}(n)} \mathcal{T}(p))$
    $\boxed{\mathcal{A}(n) := \mathcal{A}(n) \cup \mathsf{collect}(n, \bigsqcup_{p \in \mathsf{predof}(n)} \mathcal{T}(p))}$
    if $m \not\sqsubseteq \mathcal{T}(n)$
        $\mathcal{W} := \mathcal{W} \cup \mathsf{succof}(n)$
        $\mathcal{T}(n) := \mathcal{T}(n) \sqcup m$
until $\mathcal{W} = \emptyset$
return $\mathcal{T}$

(a) The (worklist-based) analysis algorithm

$Preliminary\ (old, new) =$
$new := \bot_{\hat{Mem}}$
repeat
    $old := new$
    for all $n \in Node$ **do**
        $new := \hat{f}'\ n\ new$
        $\mathcal{A}(n) := \mathcal{A}(n) \cup \mathsf{collect}(n, new)$
until $new \sqsubseteq old$
return new

(b) The pre-analysis algorithm

Fig. 2. (a) Collecting accessed abstract locations during a (worklist-based) fixpoint computation. Without the shaded line, it shows a normal worklist algorithm. The shaded line collects abstract locations that are accessed by node n currently being analyzed. (b) The pre-analysis performs flow-insensitive fixpoint computation.

Using $\hat{\mathcal{AV}}$ and $\hat{\mathcal{AL}}$, function collect collects abstract locations that are accessed during the analysis of each command. collect is derived from the definition of the transfer function $\hat{f}$, which is similar to the derivation of $\hat{\mathcal{AV}}$ and $\hat{\mathcal{AL}}$.

$$\mathsf{collect}(n, \hat{m}) = \begin{cases} \hat{\mathcal{AL}}(lv)(\hat{m}) \cup \hat{\mathcal{AV}}(e)(\hat{m}) \cup \hat{\mathcal{L}}(lv)(\hat{m}) & \text{if } n = \mathtt{set}(lv, e) \\ \hat{\mathcal{AL}}(lv)(\hat{m}) \cup \hat{\mathcal{AV}}(e)(\hat{m}) \cup \hat{\mathcal{L}}(lv)(\hat{m}) & \text{if } n = \mathtt{alloc}(lv, [e]_l) \\ \hat{\mathcal{AL}}(lv)(\hat{m}) \cup \hat{\mathcal{L}}(lv)(\hat{m}) & \text{if } n = \mathtt{alloc}(lv, \{x\}_l) \\ \hat{\mathcal{AV}}(e)(\hat{m}) \cup \hat{\mathcal{L}}(x)(\hat{m}) & \text{if } n = \mathtt{call}(f_x, e) \end{cases}$$

The problem now is to collect accessed locations in an efficient way. If we used the algorithm of Fig. 2(a) as our pre-analysis, the pre-analysis would take more time than the actual analysis. In order to get a more efficient pre-analysis, we apply the following two abstractions to the analysis of Fig. 2(a): (1) we ignore the orders of program statements, that is, we perform a flow-insensitive analysis; (2) We ignore parts of the semantics that are not directly related to computing abstract locations. In the abstract value $\hat{Val}$, for example, the interval values ($\hat{\mathbb{Z}}$) have nothing to do with abstract locations. The flow function ($\hat{f}$) and abstract evaluation $\hat{\mathcal{V}}$ are changed so that interval values are not computed any more. We call the changed functions $\hat{f}'$ and $\hat{\mathcal{V}}'$, respectively.

In general, the pre-analysis can be derived using any conservative abstraction of the original analysis. However, we chose the above two abstractions because it is efficient enough in practice and it is precise enough to track reachability

along the dynamically allocated locations and structure fields. We believe that
filtering out not only unused variables but also unused allocated locations and
fields is vital for the performance of our localization technique.

Fig. 2(b) shows our pre-analysis algorithm. It uses a flow-insensitive fixpoint
computation. The analysis starts with a bottom memory state ($\perp_{\widehat{Mem}}$). The
state is iteratively updated by flow functions for all nodes in the program until
the resulting state is subsumed by the state of the previous iteration. After the
effect of a node n is computed (using $\hat{f}'$), the abstract locations that are accessed
during the evaluation of n are collected using function collect.

The set access(f) of abstract locations that are (directly or transitively) accessed by procedure f is defined as follows:

$$\mathsf{access}(f) = \bigcup_{g \in \mathsf{callees}(f)} \left(\bigcup_{n \in \mathsf{nodesof}(g)} \mathcal{A}(n) \right)$$

where, callees(f) denotes the set of procedures, including f, that are reachable
from f via the call-graph and nodesof(f) the set of nodes in procedure f.

Actual Analysis. The actual analysis is the same as $\mathsf{Airac_{Reach}}$ except that
$\mathsf{Airac_{ProcAcc}}$ uses access information (access) and additionally excludes
non-accessed memory parts. Given an input memory state $\hat{m}$ to a call node
$\mathtt{call}(f_x, e)$, reachable locations $\mathcal{R}(f_x, \hat{m})$, and accessed locations access(f), the
transfer function $\hat{f}$ for the call statement $\mathtt{call}(f_x, e)$ is changed as follows:

$$\hat{f} \; \mathtt{call}(f_x, e) \; \hat{m} \;\; = \;\; (\hat{m}'|_{\mathcal{R}(f_x, \hat{m}')})|_{\mathsf{access}(f)} \text{ where } \hat{m}' = \hat{m}\{\hat{\mathcal{V}}(e)(\hat{m})/\!\!/\{x\}\}$$

After parameter binding ($\hat{m}'$) the memory is first restricted to the reachable
locations ($\mathcal{R}(f_x, \hat{m}')$) and then the resulting memory is restricted to access(f).
The reason why we restrict the memory to $\mathcal{R}(f_x, \hat{m}') \cap \mathsf{access}(f)$ is that access(f)
may have locations that are unreachable, i.e., not contained in $\mathcal{R}(f_x, \hat{m}')$, because
our pre-analysis is less precise than the actual analysis. Hence, the memory states
localized by our approach are always smaller than or equal to those localized by
the reachability-based approach. Procedure returns are handled as in $\mathsf{Airac_{Reach}}$.

3.3   Access-Based Localization for Arbitrary Code Blocks

We generalize the access-based, procedural localization ($\mathsf{Airac_{ProcAcc}}$) for code
blocks smaller than procedures. Given a code block, it is straightforward to
collect accessed locations for the block because our pre-analysis provides access
information ($\mathcal{A}$ in Fig. 2) for each node in the control flow graph. We localize
the input memories to the block according to the access information for the
block, and analyze the block with the localized memory state, which avoids re-
computations and speeds up memory operations. We select localization target
blocks before starting the actual analysis.

For effectiveness, we have to carefully select blocks to apply localization. Localization improves the analysis performance, but at the same time, introduces a
performance overhead. At the entry of a selected block, additional set-operations
to localize the input memory state have to be performed and at the exit of the

block, non-localized memory portions of the input memory have to be merged with the output of the block. In order to balance against the localization overhead, we select code blocks $\langle entry, exit, B \rangle$ that consists of one $entry$ node, one $exit$ node, and a selected block B that satisfy the following properties:

- the $entry$ (respectively, the $exit$) node strictly dominates (respectively, post-dominates) all nodes in B, and B contains all nodes that are strictly dominated and post-dominated by the $entry$ and $exit$, respectively
- code block size $|B| \geq k$ for parameter k

Using the parameter k, we are able to find a balance between actual reduction and overhead introduced by localizing operations. The above selection strategy is applied recursively: a block satisfying the requirements can be selected inside another selected block.

4   Experiments

We check the performance of our new localization technique by experiments with Airac, a global abstract interpretation engine in an industrialized bug-finding analyzer [11–13, 18, 19]. Because we focus on comparing the performance between different localization schemes, we disabled some improvement techniques for Airac. Specifically, we did not use context pruning, narrowing, and return-site sensitivity [18, 19]. These techniques improve analysis' precision and speed but make it hard to only measure the net effect of respective localization schemes.

From our baseline analyzer Airac, which does not use localization, we have made three analyzers Airac$_{Reach}$, Airac$_{ProcAcc}$, and Airac$_{GenAcc}$ that respectively use procedure-level reachability-based, procedure-level access-based, and generalized access-based localization and differ from Airac only in their respective localization schemes. Hence, performance differences, if any, are solely attributed to the different localization methods. We set the minimum block size k to 6 for Airac$_{GenAcc}$, which was shown to be most efficient in our setting. The analyzers are written in OCaml.

We have analyzed 15 software packages. Fig. 3 shows our benchmark programs. All experiments were done on a Linux 2.6 system running on a Pentium4 3.2 GHz box with 4 GB of main memory.

We use three performance measures: (1) *#iters* is the total number of iterations during the worklist algorithm (the number of iterations of the outside loop in Fig. 2(a); (2) *time* is the CPU time spent; (3) *MB* is the peak memory consumption.

Airac vs. Airac$_{Reach}$: The results show that the reachability-based localization reduces the analysis time and memory for most programs. Airac$_{Reach}$ consistently reduces *#iters* of Airac by 54.9% on average and reduces the analysis time by 36.7% on average. The effectiveness is clear from the fact that Airac$_{Reach}$ reduces analysis time of Airac more than 50% for programs httptunnel, gzip, jwhois, parser and bc. However, for some programs (spell and make), Airac$_{Reach}$ took

Program	LOC	Proc	BB	Airac (w.o. localization)			Airac$_{Reach}$			
				#iters	time(sec)	MB	#iters	time(sec)	MB	Save$_1$
spell-1.0	2,213	31	782	37,085	46.1	29	23,249	53.0	23	-15.0%
barcode-0.96	4,460	57	2,634	38,742	105.7	291	17,997	92.6	125	12.4%
httptunnel-3.3	6,174	110	2,757	444,354	2808.9	284	201,046	1383.2	154	50.8%
gzip-1.2.4a	7,327	135	6,271	1,327,464	12,756.2	886	393,338	2,866.6	333	77.5%
jwhois-3.0.1	9,344	73	5,147	428,584	3,424.5	633	198,249	1,185.4	254	65.4%
parser	10,900	325	9,298	5,707,185	196,318.8	2,917	2,327,303	60,577.8	1,048	69.1%
bc-1.06	13,093	134	4,924	5,677,277	87,988.5	767	800,474	13,879.2	335	84.2%
twolf	19,700	222	14,610	∞	∞	∞	2,375,894	27,230.3	1,199	N/A
tar-1.13	20,258	222	10,800	6,244,121	157,545.0	2,916	3,819,726	113,061.4	1,797	28.2%
less-382	23,822	382	10,056	7,654,188	148,015.7	2,445	2,998,969	137,827.3	1,480	6.9%
make-3.76.1	27,304	191	11,061	6,162,145	126,908.8	2,757	4,013,647	142,325.6	1,954	-12.1%
wget-1.9	35,018	434	16,544	∞	∞	∞	∞	∞	∞	N/A
screen-4.0.2	44,734	589	31,792	∞	∞	∞	∞	∞	∞	N/A
bison-2.4	56,361	1,203	20,781	∞	∞	∞	∞	∞	∞	N/A
bash-2.05a	105,174	959	28,675	∞	∞	∞	∞	∞	∞	N/A

(a) Properties of the benchmarks and analysis results for Airac and Airac$_{Reach}$

Program	Airac$_{ProcAcc}$				Airac$_{GenAcc}$($k=6$)			
	#iters	time:total(pre)	MB	Save$_2$	#iters	time:total(pre)	MB	Save$_3$
spell-1.0	5,512	2.4 (0.2)	5	95.4%	4,857	2.1 (0.3)	5	13.5%
barcode-0.96	9,433	9.4 (0.6)	25	89.8%	7,213	5.5 (1.4)	21	41.6%
httptunnel-3.3	17,072	31.4 (1.3)	36	97.7%	14,824	21.6 (2.4)	24	31.0%
gzip-1.2.4a	78,471	94.8 (1.3)	73	96.7%	47,454	54.5 (8.0)	67	42.5%
jwhois-3.0.1	99,815	254.8 (1.2)	170	78.5%	73,000	188.1 (18.5)	148	26.2%
parser	206,173	890.0 (3.8)	224	98.5%	173,285	617.0 (9.2)	245	30.7%
bc-1.06	146,407	730.9 (4.1)	106	94.7%	123,398	542.7 (8.5)	116	25.8%
twolf	520,561	1,037.7 (7.5)	332	96.2%	337,837	480.4 (20.0)	260	53.7%
tar-1.13	360,009	2,524.0 (6.0)	338	97.8%	219,109	1,638.3 (15.9)	351	35.1%
less-382	1,223,535	26,817.6 (40.7)	466	80.5%	833,643	18,766.7 (95.0)	528	30.0%
make-3.76.1	1,149,151	19,015.2 (39.4)	580	86.6%	894,843	17,405.7 (75.9)	740	8.5%
wget-1.9	526,975	6,735.8 (20.8)	609	N/A	366,051	3,823.3 (48.5)	623	43.2%
screen-4.0.2	6,402,974	340,849.0 (281.5)	2,458	N/A	4,699,777	274,280.3 (667.1)	2,958	19.5%
bison-2.4	305,988	2,487.3 (13.1)	301	N/A	234,751	1,696.6 (37.7)	302	31.8%
bash-2.05a	370,429	2,011.3 (20.2)	439	N/A	251,175	1,142.7 (59.5)	416	43.2%

(b) Analysis results for Airac$_{ProcAcc}$ and Airac$_{GenAcc}$

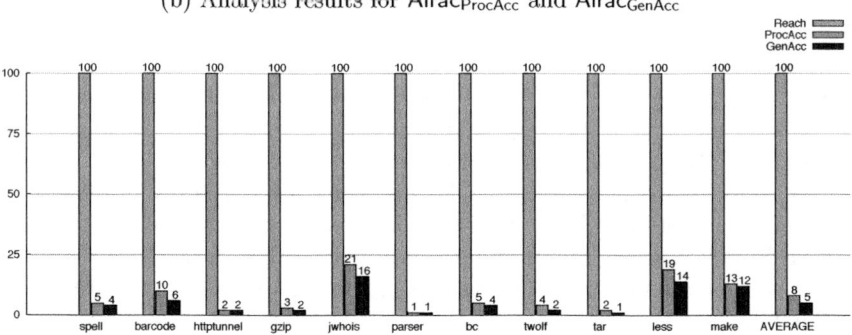

(c) Comparison of analysis time among Airac$_{Reach}$, Airac$_{ProcAcc}$ and Airac$_{GenAcc}$.

Fig. 3. Lines of code (**LOC**) are given before preprocessing. The number of procedures (**Proc**), basic blocks in the supergraph (**BB**) in programs are given after preprocessing. *time* for Airac$_{ProcAcc}$ and Airac$_{GenAcc}$ is the total time that includes pre-analysis time. The pre-analysis time is shown inside parentheses. *Save$_1$* shows time savings of Airac$_{Reach}$ against Airac. *Save$_2$* shows time savings of Airac$_{ProcAcc}$ against Airac$_{Reach}$. *Save$_3$* shows time savings of Airac$_{GenAcc}$ against Airac$_{ProcAcc}$. Entries with ∞ mean missing data because of the analysis running out of memory.

more time than Airac. This is mainly because of the overhead of localizing operations at procedure calls.

Airac$_{Reach}$ vs. Airac$_{ProcAcc}$: Overall, Airac$_{ProcAcc}$ saved 78.5%–98.5%, on average 92.1%, of the analysis time of Airac$_{Reach}$. The analysis time of Airac$_{ProcAcc}$ includes pre-analysis time. The significant time savings are caused by the synergy between reduction (on average 74.3%) in the number of iterations (#*iters*) and improved speed (on average 4.0x) of memory operations. Iterations are reduced because Airac$_{ProcAcc}$'s more general summaries more effectively avoid re-computation of procedures at different call-sites. Speed is improved because each procedure is analyzed with smaller memory states.

Moreover, our technique noticeably saves peak memory consumption by on average 71.2%. The reduction enabled Airac$_{ProcAcc}$ to analyze the largest four programs (wget, screen, bison, bash) that cannot be analyzed by Airac$_{Reach}$.

Airac$_{ProcAcc}$ is at least as precise as Airac$_{Reach}$. In principle, more aggressive localization improves precision of our analysis because unnecessary memory entries are not passed to procedures and needless widenings are avoided. In the experiments (similar to one performed in [18]), Airac$_{ProcAcc}$'s precision was the same with Airac$_{Reach}$ or slightly improved.

Airac$_{ProcAcc}$ vs. Airac$_{GenAcc}$: Airac$_{GenAcc}$ additionally saved, on average 31.8%, of the analysis time of Airac$_{ProcAcc}$. Memory costs between them is nearly the same (1.9% is reduced). Memory costs for Airac$_{GenAcc}$ sometimes increase (e.g., parser), because we cache access sets for each localization block.

5   Related Work and Discussion

In static program analysis, localization is a well-known idea for reducing analysis cost, however, research has been mainly focused on reachability-based approach. For example, in shape analysis, reachability-based localization has been used to improve the scalability of interprocedural analysis [6, 20, 21, 14, 8, 24, 23]. Rinetzky et al. [20, 21] define a shape analysis in which called procedures are only passed with reachable parts of the heap. Marron et al. [14] reformulate the idea of [20] for graph-based heap models. In separation-logic-based program verification (both by-hand and automatic checking [3]), one typically reasons about a command with respect to its footprint (memory cells that the command accesses) in isolation. However, (even) in separation-logic-based program analysis, the framing, which is expressed in accessibility in logic, is conventionally implemented based on reachability [8, 24, 23]: Gotsman et al. [8] and Yang et al. [24, 23] split states based on reachability. Similar reachability-based techniques are also popular in higher-order flow analyses [9, 10, 16]. Jagannathan et al. [10] use "an abstract form of garbage collection" that removes unreachable bindings. Might et al. [16] formalize the abstract-garbage-collecting control-flow analysis and show that removing unreachable cells significantly improves the analysis performance.In this paper, we present a new approach to localization that is access-based.

Chen et al. [5] use a mixture of reachability- and access-based localization, but, their approach is more restricted than ours. During reachability-based localization, they try to infer accessed locations by evaluating expressions two times. However, because input states are not at a fixpoint during the course of the analysis, the accessed locations cannot be completely determined. By contrast our approach makes access-based localization always possible.

Might et al. [15] observes that reachability is overly conservative, and presents a refined localization technique that is orthogonal to our method. From the reachability-based localized state, they additionally exclude some resources that are governed by unsatisfiable conditions. The resulting localized state may contain non-accessed resources that are not governed by such conditions, which could be filtered by our technique. And, since our technique does not consider unsatisfiable conditions, their technique can improve ours.

We do not argue that our access-based localization is cost-effective in general. Our abstract domain (numeric intervals) is non-relational and, consequently, partitioning of the memory states is relatively simple. But, the partitioning operation will become costly when analysis' abstract semantics involves relational information such as in analysis with relational domain [17] or storeless semantics [20]. In these cases, not only the resources that are directly accessed by a code block but also resources that are indirectly required to keep relational information should be considered. Hence, localizing operation gets more complicated. We have a plan to investigate our technique for relational analysis.

It is also a well-known idea to scale an analysis by using an efficient pre-analysis. For example, flow-insensitive pre-analysis has been used in dataflow analysis [1], pointer analysis [22]. Our work is an instance of these lines of research: we use a pre-analysis to localize memory states in actual analysis.

Lastly, one noteworthy point is that designing a correct pre-analysis with a right balance of accuracy and cost was relatively easy in our case because the underlying analysis was designed as an abstract interpretation. Our pre-analysis was simply a further abstraction of the underlying (actual) abstract interpreter.

Acknowledgements. This work was supported by the Engineering Research Center of Excellence Program of Korea Ministry of Education, Science and Technology(MEST) / National Research Foundation of Korea(NRF) (Grant 2010-0001718) and the Brain Korea 21 Project, School of Electrical Engineering and Computer Science, Seoul National University in 2010.

References

1. Adams, S., Ball, T., Das, M., Lerner, S., Rajamani, S.K., Seigle, M., Weimer, W.: Speeding up dataflow analysis using flow-insensitive pointer analysis. In: Hermenegildo, M.V., Puebla, G. (eds.) SAS 2002. LNCS, vol. 2477, pp. 230–246. Springer, Heidelberg (2002)
2. Allamigeon, X., Godard, W., Hymans, C.: Static analysis of string manipulations in critical embedded C programs. In: Yi, K. (ed.) SAS 2006. LNCS, vol. 4134, pp. 35–51. Springer, Heidelberg (2006)
3. Berdine, J., Calcagno, C., O'Hearn, P.W.: Symbolic execution with separation logic. In: APLAS, pp. 52–68 (2005)
4. Bourdoncle, F.: Efficient chaotic iteration strategies with widenings. In: Int. Conf. on Formal Methods in Prog. and their Appl, pp. 128–141 (1993)

5. Chen, L., Harrison III, W.L.: An efficient approach to computing fixpoints for complex program analysis. In: Int. Conf. on Supercomp., pp. 98–106 (1994)
6. Chong, S., Rugina, R.: Static analysis of accessed regions in recursive data structures. In: Cousot, R. (ed.) SAS 2003. LNCS, vol. 2694, pp. 463–482. Springer, Heidelberg (2003)
7. Cousot, P., Cousot, R.: Comparing the Galois connection and widening/narrowing approaches to abstract interpretation. In: Bruynooghe, M., Wirsing, M. (eds.) PLILP 1992. LNCS, vol. 631, pp. 269–295. Springer, Heidelberg (1992)
8. Gotsman, A., Berdine, J., Cook, B.: Interprocedural shape analysis with separated heap abstractions. In: Yi, K. (ed.) SAS 2006. LNCS, vol. 4134, pp. 240–260. Springer, Heidelberg (2006)
9. Harrison III, W.L.: The Interprocedural Analysis and Automatic Parallelization of Scheme Programs. PhD thesis, Center for Supercomputing Research and Development, University of Illinois at Urabana-Champaign (February 1989)
10. Jagannathan, S., Thiemann, P., Weeks, S., Wright, A.: Single and loving it: must-alias analysis for higher-order languages. In: POPL, pp. 329–341 (1998)
11. Jhee, Y., Jin, M., Jung, Y., Kim, D., Kong, S., Lee, H., Oh, H., Park, D., Yi, K.: Abstract interpretation + impure catalysts: Our Sparrow experience. Presentation at the Workshop of the 30 Years of Abstract Interpretation, San Francisco (January 2008), http://ropas.snu.ac.kr/ kwang/paper/30yai-08.pdf
12. Jung, Y., Kim, J., Shin, J., Yi, K.: Taming false alarms from a domain-unaware C analyzer by a bayesian statistical post analysis. In: Hankin, C., Siveroni, I. (eds.) SAS 2005. LNCS, vol. 3672, pp. 203–217. Springer, Heidelberg (2005)
13. Jung, Y., Yi, K.: Practical memory leak detector based on parameterized procedural summaries. In: ISMM, pp. 131–140 (2008)
14. Marron, M., Hermenegildo, M., Kapur, D., Stefanovic, D.: Efficient context-sensitive shape analysis with graph based heap models. In: Hendren, L. (ed.) CC 2008. LNCS, vol. 4959, pp. 245–259. Springer, Heidelberg (2008)
15. Might, M., Chambers, B., Shivers, O.: Model checking via ΓCFA. In: Cook, B., Podelski, A. (eds.) VMCAI 2007. LNCS, vol. 4349, pp. 59–73. Springer, Heidelberg (2007)
16. Might, M., Shivers, O.: Improving flow analyses via ΓCFA: Abstract garbage collection and counting. In: ICFP, pp. 13–25 (2006)
17. Miné, A.: The octagon abstract domain. Higher-Order and Symbolic Computation 19(1), 31–100 (2006)
18. Oh, H.: Large spurious cycle in global static analyses and its algorithmic mitigation. In: APLAS (2009)
19. Oh, H., Yi, K.: An algorithmic mitigation of large spurious interprocedural cycles in static analysis. In: Software: Practice and Experience (2010)
20. Rinetzky, N., Bauer, J., Reps, T., Sagiv, M., Wilhelm, R.: A semantics for procedure local heaps and its abstractions. In: POPL, pp. 296–309 (2005)
21. Rinetzky, N., Sagiv, M., Yahav, E.: Interprocedural shape analysis for cutpoint-free programs. In: Hankin, C., Siveroni, I. (eds.) SAS 2005. LNCS, vol. 3672, pp. 284–302. Springer, Heidelberg (2005)
22. Xu, G., Rountev, A., Sridharan, M.: Scaling CFL-reachability-based points-to analysis using context-sensitive must-not-alias analysis. In: Drossopoulou, S. (ed.) ECOOP 2009. LNCS, vol. 5653, pp. 98–122. Springer, Heidelberg (2009)
23. Yang, H., Lee, O., Berdine, J., Calcagno, C., Cook, B., Distefano, D., O'Hearn, P.: Scalable shape analysis for systems code. In: Gupta, A., Malik, S. (eds.) CAV 2008. LNCS, vol. 5123, pp. 385–398. Springer, Heidelberg (2008)
24. Yang, H., Lee, O., Calcagno, C., Distefano, D., O'Hearn, P.: On scalable shape analysis. Technical Memorandum RR-07-10, Queen Mary University of London, Department of Computer Science (November 2007)

Decision Procedures for Automating Termination Proofs

Ruzica Piskac[1] and Thomas Wies[2]

[1] École Polytechnique Fédérale de Lausanne (EPFL), Switzerland
[2] Institute of Science and Technology (IST), Austria

Abstract. Automated termination provers often use the following schema to prove that a program terminates: construct a relational abstraction of the program's transition relation and then show that the relational abstraction is well-founded. The focus of current tools has been on developing sophisticated techniques for constructing the abstractions while relying on known decidable logics (such as linear arithmetic) to express them. We believe we can significantly increase the class of programs that are amenable to automated termination proofs by identifying more expressive decidable logics for reasoning about well-founded relations. We therefore present a new decision procedure for reasoning about multiset orderings, which are among the most powerful orderings used to prove termination. We show that, using our decision procedure, one can automatically prove termination of natural abstractions of programs.

1 Introduction

The standard technique for proving program termination is to construct a *ranking function* [11]. A ranking function maps the states of the program into some well-founded domain, i.e., a set equipped with a well-founded ordering. The mapping is such that, with each transition taken by the program, the value of the ranking function decreases in the ordering. The canonical well-founded ordering for constructing ranking functions is the strict order on the natural numbers. However, constructing *global* ranking functions for this ordering (i.e., functions that decrease with every transition of the program) requires a lot of ingenuity.

Despite the general result of undecidability of the halting problem, recent advances in program analysis have brought forth tools that can automatically prove termination of real-world programs [3, 6, 5]. The success of these tools is due to the development of new proof techniques for termination [15, 23]. These techniques avoid the construction of a global termination argument and, instead, decompose the program into simpler ones. Each of these simpler programs is then proved terminating independently, by constructing a simpler ranking function. The automation of these proof techniques relies on decision procedures for reasoning about constraints on well-founded domains. The existing tools use known decidable logics such as linear arithmetic to express these constraints [22, 4], which effectively restricts the range of ranking functions that can be constructed automatically. We believe that by providing decision procedures for more sophisticated well-founded domains, one can significantly increase the class of programs that are amenable to automated termination proofs.

R. Jhala and D. Schmidt (Eds.): VMCAI 2011, LNCS 6538, pp. 371–386, 2011.
© Springer-Verlag Berlin Heidelberg 2011

Among the most powerful well-founded domains for proving program termination are multiset orderings [9]. In this paper, we present a decision procedure for automated reasoning about such orderings. A multiset is an unordered collection of elements from a base set, where each element may occur multiple times. For instance, $\{1, 2, 2, 3\}$ is a multiset of natural numbers. This multiset is equal to the multiset $\{1, 3, 2, 2\}$ but different from the multiset $\{1, 2, 3\}$. A (strict) ordering $\prec$ on the base set S can be lifted to an ordering $\prec_m$ on (finite) multisets over S as follows. For two multisets X and Y, $X \prec_m Y$ holds iff X and Y are different and for every element $x \in S$ which occurs more times in X than in Y, there exists an element $y \in S$ which occurs more times in Y than in X and $x \prec y$. For instance, $\{1, 1, 1, 2, 2\} <_m \{1, 3\}$ since $1 < 3$ and $2 < 3$. Multiset orderings are interesting because they inherit important properties of the ordering on the base set. In particular, the multiset ordering $\prec_m$ is well-founded iff the ordering $\prec$ on the base set is well-founded [9]. Multiset orderings have been traditionally used for manual termination proofs in program verification [9, 7], term rewriting systems [8, 1], and theorem proving [16, 2]. The question whether reasoning about multiset orderings can be effectively automated was open.

Contributions. In this paper, we present a new logic called POSSUM for expressing ordering constraints on finite multisets. The logic is parameterized by the theory of the base set, which can be an arbitrary theory equipped with a preorder (not necessarily well-founded). We show that if the base theory is decidable then so is its extension to a multiset ordering. What is more, we show that if the base theory is decidable in NP then the satisfiability problem for its POSSUM extension is NP-complete. Our decision procedure can be easily implemented using off-the-shelf SMT solvers. We demonstrate the usefulness of our decision procedure for proving termination of interesting programs. We therefore believe that it can be a useful component of future automated termination provers.

2   Examples

We motivate the usefulness of our decision procedure for proving termination through two examples.

Example 1: counting leaves in a tree. Our first example is a program taken from [9] and shown in Figure 1. The termination behavior of this program is representative for many programs that traverse algebraic data types.

The program COUNTLEAVES counts the number of leaves in a binary tree. For this purpose it maintains a stack S that contains all subtrees of the input tree *root* that still need to be traversed. In each iteration the first element y is removed from S. If y is a leaf then the count is increased. Otherwise the subtrees of y are pushed on the stack. Then the computation continues with the updated stack.

In order to prove termination of program COUNTLEAVES we need to find a well-founded ordering on the states of the program that decreases with every iteration of the loop. This well-founded ordering needs to capture the fact that in each loop iteration either some tree is removed from the stack, or some tree on the stack is replaced by finitely many smaller trees. This can be naturally expressed in terms of a multiset ordering. We therefore abstract the program COUNTLEAVES by a program over multisets.

```
prog CountLeaves(root : Tree) : int =
    var S : Stack[Tree] = root
    var c : int = 0
    do
        y := head(S)
        if leaf(y) then
            S := tail(S)
            c := c + 1
        else S := left(y) · right(y) · tail(S)
    until S = ε
    return c
```

Fig. 1. Program COUNTLEAVES: counting the leaves in a binary tree

```
prog AbsCountLeaves(root : Tree) =
    var X_S : multiset[Tree] = {root}
    do
        y := choose(X_S)
        if leaf(y) then X_S := X_S \ {y}
        else X_S := (X_S \ {y}) ⊎ {left(y)} ⊎ {right(y)}
    until X_S = ∅
```

Fig. 2. Multiset abstraction of program COUNTLEAVES

The result of this abstraction is shown in Figure 2. The program ABSCOUNTLEAVES is obtained from program COUNTLEAVES by mapping the stack S to a multiset X_S, i.e., in program ABSCOUNTLEAVES we abstract from the order of the elements in S. In program ABSCOUNTLEAVES the stack operations are replaced by operations on multisets. For instance, the operation $head(S)$ is abstracted by the operation $choose(X_S)$ that non-deterministically chooses an element from the multiset X_S. The computation of such multiset abstractions of programs could be automated by combining techniques developed in [27] and [24, 5]. In this paper we focus on automating the termination proofs for the resulting multiset program.

We prove termination of program ABSCOUNTLEAVES by proving that for every iteration of the loop, the variable X_S decreases in the ordering $\prec_m$. The ordering $\prec_m$ is the multiset extension of the subtree ordering $\prec$ on the trees stored in the multiset. The subtree ordering is well-founded; consequently, so is its multiset extension. Termination of program ABSCOUNTLEAVES is therefore implied by the validity of the *termination condition* given in Figure 3. The decision procedure presented in this paper decides the validity of such termination conditions (respectively, unsatisfiability of their negation). In Section 3 we show how the decision procedure works on a formula similar to the one shown in Figure 3.

Example 2: computing negation normal form. Our second example is a rewrite system that computes the negation normal form of a propositional formula. It consists of the three rewrite rules shown in Figure 4. The three rules are applied non-deterministically to any matching subformula.

$$X_S \neq \emptyset \wedge X_S(y) > 0 \wedge$$
$$(X_S' = X_S \setminus \{y\} \vee X_S' = (X_S \setminus \{y\}) \uplus \{left(y)\} \uplus \{right(y)\}) \; \rightarrow \; X_S' \prec_m X_S$$

Fig. 3. Termination condition for program ABSCOUNTLEAVES

$$\neg\neg F \rightsquigarrow F$$
$$\neg(F \wedge G) \rightsquigarrow \neg F \vee \neg G$$
$$\neg(F \vee G) \rightsquigarrow \neg G \wedge \neg G$$

Fig. 4. Rewrite system for computing negation normal form

In order to prove termination of this rewrite system, Dershowitz [8] suggested the following mapping from a propositional formula F to a multiset of natural numbers X_F. Let $[G]$ denote the number of operators other than $\neg$ that occur in G, then define

$$X_F = \{ [G] \mid \neg G \text{ is a subformula of } F \}$$

We can then prove that, for each rewrite rule applied to a formula F, X_F decreases in the multiset extension $<_m$ of the ordering $<$ on natural numbers. This amounts to checking validity of the following two implications:

$$X_F = X_F' \uplus \{x, x\} \rightarrow X_F' <_m X_F$$
$$X_F = Y \uplus \{x\} \wedge x > 0 \wedge X_F' = Y \uplus \{x - 1, x - 1\} \rightarrow X_F' <_m X_F$$

Again, these checks can be automated using our decision procedure.

3   Decision Procedure Through an Example

We now explain our decision procedure through an example. The decision procedure is parameterized by the theory of the base elements comprising the multisets. For instance, in the first example given in Section 2, the base theory is the theory of trees with the subtree ordering. This theory is decidable in NP [28]. In general, the base theory can be any decidable theory equipped with a preorder. Our decision procedure reduces the formula with ordering constraints over multisets to a formula containing ordering constraints on the base elements. Satisfiability of the reduced formula is then checked using the decision procedure of the base theory.

To demonstrate how our decision procedure works, we apply it to the following formula, which is a slightly generalized version of the negated termination condition given in Figure 3:

$$Y \subseteq X \wedge X' = (X \setminus Y) \uplus Z \wedge Z \prec_m Y \wedge \neg(X' \prec_m X) \tag{1}$$

This formula is unsatisfiable in the theory of preordered multisets (where the base theory is the theory of all preordered sets). The reduction of the formula works as follows. First we purify and flatten the input formula by introducing fresh variables for multisets and base elements to separate the multiset constraints from constraints in the base theory. In our example there are no base theory constraints. So, purification and flattening of formula (1) results in the formula:

$$Y \subseteq X \wedge X' = X_1 \uplus Z \wedge X_1 = X \setminus Y \wedge Z \prec_m Y \wedge \neg(X' \prec_m X)$$

The next step is to replace all multiset atoms by their point-wise definitions on the base elements. This gives the following formula:

$$
\begin{aligned}
&(\forall x. \, Y(x) \leq X(x)) \wedge \\
&(\forall x. \, X'(x) = X_1(x) + Z(x)) \wedge \\
&(\forall x. \, X_1(x) = \max\{X(x) - Y(x), 0\}) \wedge \\
&(\exists y. Z(y) \neq Y(y)) \wedge (\forall z. \, Y(z) < Z(z) \rightarrow \exists y. \, Z(y) < Y(y) \wedge z \prec y) \wedge \\
&((\forall x. X'(x) = X(x)) \vee \exists x'. \, X(x') < X'(x') \wedge \forall x. \, X'(x) < X'(x) \rightarrow \neg(x' \prec x)))
\end{aligned}
$$

Next, we skolemize all existentially quantified variables. In our example this introduces two Skolem constants e_1, e_2 and one Skolem function w. The resulting formula is:

$$
\begin{aligned}
&(\forall x. \, Y(x) \leq X(x)) \wedge \\
&(\forall x. \, X'(x) = X_1(x) + Z(x)) \wedge \\
&(\forall x. \, X_1(x) = \max\{X(x) - Y(x), 0\}) \wedge \\
&Z(e_1) \neq Y(e_1) \wedge (\forall y'. \, Y(y') < Z(y') \rightarrow Z(w(y')) < Y(w(y')) \wedge y' \prec w(y'))) \wedge \\
&((\forall x. X'(x) = X(x)) \vee X(e_2) < X'(e_2) \wedge \forall x. \, X'(x) < X(x) \rightarrow \neg(e_2 \prec x))
\end{aligned}
$$

The idea is now to replace each remaining universal quantifier with a finite conjunction by instantiating each quantifier with finitely many ground terms generated from the constants appearing in the formula and the introduced Skolem functions. The problem is that finite instantiation is in general incomplete because the Skolem functions coming from the ordering constraints generate an infinite Herbrand universe. Before instantiation we therefore first conjoin the skolemized formula with additional axioms that further constrain the Skolem functions. In our example, we add the two axioms:

$$\forall x \, y. \, Y(x) < Z(x) \wedge w(x) \prec y \rightarrow Y(y) \leq Z(y), \quad \forall x. \, Z(x) = Y(x) \rightarrow w(x) = x$$

We will show in Section 6 that this step is sound and ensures that instantiation of the strengthened formula with the terms $e_1, e_2, w(e_1)$ and $w(e_2)$ is sufficient for proving unsatisfiability of the original constraint. The instantiated formula is a quantifier-free formula over symbols of the base theory (such as the preorder $\prec$), the theory of linear arithmetic, and the theory of free function symbols (the multisets and the Skolem functions). The satisfiability of such formulas can be decided using a Nelson-Oppen combination of the decision procedures for the corresponding component theories. In our example, the instantiated formula implies the following disjunction:

$$
\begin{aligned}
&Z(e_1) \neq Y(e_1) \wedge X'(e_1) = X(e_1) - Y(e_1) + Z(e_1) \wedge X'(e_1) = X(e_1) \vee \\
&X'(e_2) = X(e_2) - Y(e_2) + Z(e_2) \wedge X(e_2) < X'(e_2) \wedge Y(e_2) \geq Z(e_2) \vee \\
&X'(w(e_2)) = X(w(e_2)) - Y(w(e_2)) + Z(w(e_2)) \wedge \\
&\quad\quad Z(w(e_2)) < Y(w(e_2)) \wedge X'(w(e_2)) \geq X(w(e_2)) \vee \\
&e_2 \prec w(e_2) \wedge \neg(e_2 \prec w(e_2))
\end{aligned}
$$

Observe that each of the disjuncts is unsatisfiable and, hence, so is the original formula (1).

4 Preliminaries

Before we describe the logic and decision procedure for multiset orderings, we briefly fix our formal framework.

Sorted logic. A *signature* Σ is a tuple (S, Ω), where S is a countable set of sorts and Ω is a countable set of function symbols f. Every $f \in \Omega$ is associated with an arity $n \geq 0$ and a sort $s_1 \times \cdots \times s_n \to s_0$ with $s_i \in S$ for all $i \leq n$. Function symbols of arity 0 are called *constant symbols*. For the description of our problem we will consider three sorts: $S = \{\text{int}, \text{bool}, \text{elem}\}$. We treat predicates of sort $s_1 \times \cdots \times s_n$ as function symbols of sort $s_1 \times \ldots \times s_n \to \text{bool}$. We say that a signature Σ_1 extends a signature Σ_2 if Σ_1 contains at least the sorts and function symbols of Σ_2. Let V be a countably infinite set of sorted variables, disjoint from Ω. Terms are built as usual from the function symbols in Ω and variables taken from V. We denote by $t : s$ that term t has sort s. A term t is *ground*, if no variable appears in t. We denote by $\text{Terms}(\Sigma)$ the set of all ground Σ-terms. An *atom* is either constructed from the equality symbol $t_1 = t_2$ applied to terms t_1 and t_2 of the same sort, or by applying a predicate symbol to terms of the respective sorts. Formulas are built from atoms as usual, using boolean connectives and quantifiers. A formula F is called *closed* or a *sentence* if no variable appears free in F.

Structures. Given a signature $\Sigma = (S, \Omega)$, a Σ-*structure* α is a function that maps each sort $s \in S$ to a non-empty set $\alpha(s)$ and each function symbol $f \in \Omega$ of sort $s_1 \times \cdots \times s_n \to s_0$ to a function $\alpha(f) : \alpha(s_1) \times \cdots \times \alpha(s_n) \to \alpha(s_0)$. Set $\alpha(s)$ is also called α-domain of the sort s. We assume that all structures interpret the sort bool by the set of Booleans $\{\text{true}, \text{false}\}$, and the sort int by the set of all integers $\mathbb{Z}$. The sort elem will serve as our base set for defining multisets. We speak of $\alpha(\text{elem})$ simply as the *domain* of α and often identify the two.

For a Σ-structure α and a *variable assignment* $\beta : V \to \alpha(S)$, the evaluation of a term (respectively a formula) in α, β is defined as usual. In particular, we use the standard interpretations for the equality symbol and propositional connectives. A quantified variable of sort s ranges over all elements of $\alpha(s)$. For ground terms t we skip the variable assignment and simply write $\alpha(t)$ for its evaluation in α. The notions of satisfiability, validity, and entailment of formulas are also defined as usual. We write $\alpha, \beta \models F$ if α satisfies F under β. Similarly, we write $\alpha \models F$ if α satisfies F for all variable assignments β. In this case we also call α a *model* of F.

Theories. A Σ-*theory* $\mathcal{T}$ for a signature Σ is simply a set of Σ-structures. Sometimes we identify a theory by a set of Σ-sentences $\mathcal{K}$, meaning the set of all Σ-models of $\mathcal{K}$. We then call $\mathcal{K}$ the *axioms* of the theory. The satisfiability problem for a Σ-theory $\mathcal{T}$ and a set of Σ-formulas $\mathcal{F}$ is to decide whether a given $F \in \mathcal{F}$ is satisfiable in some structure of $\mathcal{T}$. If the set of formulas $\mathcal{F}$ is clear from the context, we simply speak of the satisfiability problem of the theory $\mathcal{T}$. A Σ_2-theory $\mathcal{T}_2$ is an *extension* of a Σ_1-theory $\mathcal{T}_1$ if Σ_2 is an extension of Σ_1 and for every $\alpha \in \mathcal{T}_2$, the restriction $\alpha|_{\Sigma_1}$ of α to the sorts and symbols of Σ_1 is a structure in $\mathcal{T}_1$. A Σ-theory $\mathcal{T}$ is called *stably infinite* with respect to a set of formulas $\mathcal{F}$, if for every formula $F \in \mathcal{F}$ which is satisfiable in $\mathcal{T}$, there exists a model α of F in $\mathcal{T}$, such that the domain of α has infinite cardinality.

5 POSSUM: **Multiset Constraints over Preordered Sets**

In this section we formally define the constraints whose satisfiability we study in this paper. Before we define the syntax and semantics of these constraints, we first define the theories of preordered sets and their extensions to finite preordered multisets.

5.1 Finite Multisets over Preordered Sets

We assume that Σ_{elem} is a signature containing at least the binary predicate symbol $\preceq$ over sort elem. Let $\mathcal{F}_{\text{elem}}$ be the set of all quantifier-free ground formulas over signature Σ_{elem}. We will use the formula $t_1 \prec t_2$ as syntactic sugar for the formula $t_1 \neq t_2 \wedge t_1 \preceq t_2$. A binary relation R defined on a set E, such that R is reflexive and transitive is called a *preorder* and set (E, R) is called a preordered set. A theory of preordered sets $\mathcal{T}_{\text{elem}}$ is a Σ_{elem}-theory such that for all structures $\alpha \in \mathcal{T}_{\text{elem}}$, $(\alpha(\text{elem}), \alpha(\preceq))$ is a preordered set, i.e., every structure $\alpha \in \mathcal{T}_{\text{elem}}$ satisfies the following two axioms:

$$\forall x : \text{elem. } x \preceq x \quad (\text{refl}) \qquad \forall x, y, z : \text{elem. } x \preceq y \wedge y \preceq z \rightarrow x \preceq z \quad (\text{trans})$$

For the rest of this paper, we fix such a theory $\mathcal{T}_{\text{elem}}$. We require that the satisfiability problem for $\mathcal{F}_{\text{elem}}$ and $\mathcal{T}_{\text{elem}}$ is decidable. We further require that $\mathcal{T}_{\text{elem}}$ is stably-infinite with respect to the formulas $\mathcal{F}_{\text{elem}}$. We call $\mathcal{T}_{\text{elem}}$ the *base theory*.

Let Ω_{la} be the function and constant symbols of linear integer arithmetic

$$\Omega_{\text{la}} = \{+, -, \max, \min, \ldots, -2, -1, 0, 1, 2, \ldots, -2\cdot, -1\cdot, 0\cdot, 1\cdot, 2\cdot\}$$

with their appropriate sorts (the function symbol $C\cdot$ denotes multiplication with integer constant C). We assume that these symbols are disjoint from the symbols in Σ_{elem}. We represent multisets as function symbols of sort elem $\rightarrow$ int. Let $\mathcal{M}$ be a countably infinite set of function symbols of this sort, disjoint from the symbols in Σ_{elem} and Ω_{la}. Further, let Σ_{mset} be the signature Σ_{elem} extended with the symbols $\mathcal{M}$ and Ω_{la}. We then define the theory $\mathcal{T}_{\text{mset}}$ of finite preordered multisets over $\mathcal{T}_{\text{elem}}$ as follows. The theory $\mathcal{T}_{\text{mset}}$ is the set of all structures α such that α is an extension of a structure in $\mathcal{T}_{\text{elem}}$ to a Σ_{mset}-structure and α satisfies the following conditions:

- α gives the standard interpretation to the arithmetic symbols, and
- α interprets each $X \in \mathcal{M}$ as a finite multiset, i.e., (1) for all $e \in \alpha(\text{elem})$, $\alpha(X)(e) \geq 0$ and (2) there are only finitely many $e \in \alpha(\text{elem})$ such that $\alpha(X)(e) > 0$.

5.2 Syntax and Semantics of POSSUM **Formulas**

Syntax. Figure 5 defines the POSSUM formulas. A POSSUM formula is an arbitrary propositional combination of atomic formulas. The atomic formulas are relations between multiset expressions, relations between arithmetic expressions, atoms over the base signature Σ_{elem}, and restricted quantified formulas $\mathsf{F}^{\forall}$. An example of a base signature atom is the formula $e_1 \preceq e_2$, where e_1 and e_2 are two constants of sort elem. The

top-level formulas:
$$F ::= A \mid F \wedge F \mid \neg F$$
$$A ::= M = M \mid M \subseteq M \mid K = K \mid K \leq K \mid M \preceq_m M \mid A_{\mathsf{elem}} \mid F^\forall$$
$$M ::= X \mid \emptyset \mid \{t^K\} \mid M \cap M \mid M \cup M \mid M \uplus M \mid M \setminus M \mid \mathsf{setOf}(M)$$
$$K ::= k \mid C \mid K + K \mid C \cdot K$$

restricted quantified formulas:
$$F^\forall ::= \forall x : \mathsf{elem}.F^\forall \mid \forall x : \mathsf{elem}.F^{\mathsf{in}}$$
$$F^{\mathsf{in}} ::= A^{\mathsf{in}} \mid F^{\mathsf{in}} \wedge F^{\mathsf{in}} \mid \neg F^{\mathsf{in}}$$
$$A^{\mathsf{in}} ::= t^{\mathsf{in}} \leq t^{\mathsf{in}} \mid t^{\mathsf{in}} = t^{\mathsf{in}} \mid E^{\mathsf{in}} \preceq E^{\mathsf{in}} \mid E^{\mathsf{in}} = E^{\mathsf{in}}$$
$$t^{\mathsf{in}} ::= X(E^{\mathsf{in}}) \mid C \mid t^{\mathsf{in}} + t^{\mathsf{in}} \mid C \cdot t^{\mathsf{in}}$$
$$E^{\mathsf{in}} ::= x \mid t$$

terminals:
A_{elem} - ground Σ_{elem}-atom ; X - multiset ; k - integer variable; C - integer constant
t - ground Σ_{elem}-term of sort elem; x - variable of sort elem

Fig. 5. Syntax for Multiset Constraints over Preordered Sets (POSSUM)

formulas $F^\forall$ express universal quantification over formulas of sort elem. The formulas below the quantifiers can express arithmetic relations between multiplicities $X(x)$ of the quantified variables or ordering constraints between these variables. Using these quantified formulas we can, for instance, express that some constant e is maximal in a multiset X: $\forall x. X(x) > 0 \rightarrow x \preceq e$. The important restriction for the formulas below the universal quantifiers is that the quantified variables x are not allowed to appear below function symbols of the base signature Σ_{elem}. This is enforced by allowing only ground Σ_{elem}-terms t below the quantifiers. Note also that there are no POSSUM formulas with $F^\forall$ atoms that have an alternating quantifier prefix. We call a subset $\mathcal{F}$ of POSSUM formulas *quantifier-bounded* if the number of quantified variables appearing in $F^\forall$ subformulas of formulas in $\mathcal{F}$ is bounded.

Semantics. POSSUM formulas are interpreted in the structures of the theory $\mathcal{T}_{\mathsf{mset}}$. The semantics of POSSUM formulas extends the semantics of first-order formulas defined in Section 4. Note that with the exception of atomic formulas that express relations on multisets, all atomic formulas are first-order formulas. Thus, we only need to define the semantics of formulas of the form $M_1 = M_2$, $M_1 \subseteq M_2$, and $M_1 \preceq_m M_2$. Let α be a structure in $\mathcal{T}_{\mathsf{mset}}$. First, we extend the interpretation $\alpha(X)$ of multisets $X \in \mathcal{M}$ in α to multiset expressions. The interpretation is defined point-wise for all $e \in \alpha$ and recursively on the structure of the expression:

$$\alpha(\emptyset)(e) = 0$$
$$\alpha(\{t^K\})(e) = \text{if } \alpha(t) = e \text{ then } \alpha(K) \text{ else } 0$$
$$\alpha(M_1 \cup M_2)(e) = \max\{\alpha(M_1)(e), \alpha(M_2)(e)\}$$
$$\alpha(M_1 \cap M_2)(e) = \min\{\alpha(M_1)(e), \alpha(M_2)(e)\}$$
$$\alpha(M_1 \uplus M_2)(e) = \alpha(M_1)(e) + \alpha(M_2)(e)$$

$$\alpha(M_1 \setminus M_2)(e) = \max\{\alpha(M_1)(e) - \alpha(M_2)(e), 0\}$$
$$\alpha(\mathsf{setOf}(M))(e) = \min\{\alpha(M)(e), 1\}$$

For defining the interpretations of the predicate symbols $=$, $\subseteq$, and $\preceq_m$ on multisets we define corresponding relations $=_m$, $\subseteq_m$, and $\preceq_m$ on the meta level. Let m_1, m_2 be functions $\alpha(\mathsf{elem}) \to \mathbb{N}$. The relations $=_m$ and $\subseteq_m$ are defined point-wise as expected:

$$m_1 =_m m_2 \quad \Leftrightarrow \quad \forall e \in \alpha(\mathsf{elem}).m_1(e) = m_2(e)$$
$$m_1 \subseteq_m m_2 \quad \Leftrightarrow \quad \forall e \in \alpha(\mathsf{elem}).m_1(e) \leq m_2(e)$$

For defining the multiset ordering we identify $\prec$ with the irreflexive reduct of the relation $\alpha(\preceq)$. The relation $\preceq_m$ is then defined as follows:

$$m_1 \preceq_m m_2 \quad \Leftrightarrow \quad \forall e_1 \in \alpha.\, m_1(e_1) > m_2(e_1) \Rightarrow$$
$$\exists e_2 \in \alpha.m_2(e_2) > m_1(e_2) \wedge e_1 \prec e_2 \tag{2}$$

Note that this is not the standard definition of the multiset ordering that was originally used in [9]. However, in order to reduce the number of multiset variables we use the simpler definition (2). For finite multisets, definition (2) is equivalent to the standard one (for proof see [1, Lemma 2.5.6, p.24]).

6   Decision Procedure

We now describe the decision procedure for POSSUM. The idea of the decision procedure is to reduce satisfiability of a POSSUM formula to satisfiability of a formula in a particular first-order theory, namely, the disjoint combination of the base theory $\mathcal{T}_{\mathsf{elem}}$, the theory of linear integer arithmetic, and the theory of uninterpreted function symbols.

Reduction to a first-order theory. In the following, we show how to decide conjunctions of POSSUM literals. The extension of the decision procedure to arbitrary Boolean combinations of literals is straightforward. Thus, let F be a fixed POSSUM conjunction. The first step of our decision procedure is to rewrite F into a quantified first-order formula by expanding all multiset constraints to their point-wise definitions.

For two multiset variables X and Y we denote by $L_{X,Y}$ the multiset $X \setminus Y$ and by $U_{X,Y}$ the multiset $Y \setminus X$. Similarly, for a given element x we use $L_{X,Y}(x)$ as a shorthand for the expression $X(x) - Y(x)$ and $U_{X,Y}(x)$ for $Y(x) - X(x)$. The algorithm for rewriting F is then as follows:

1. Purify and flatten all multiset constraints in F:
   $C[M] \rightsquigarrow X_f = M \wedge C[X_f]$
   where $X_f \in \mathcal{M}$ is a fresh multiset and M is
   (a) either of the form $M_1 \cup M_2$, $M_1 \cap M_2$, $M_1 \uplus M_2$, $M_1 \setminus M_2$, and at least one M_i is not a multiset $X \in \mathcal{M}$
   (b) or of the form $\emptyset$, $\{t^k\}$, $\mathsf{setOf}(M_1)$, and they are not in a conjunct of the form $X = M$ or $M = X$ for some multiset $X \in \mathcal{M}$.

2. Replace all multiset atoms by their point-wise definitions

$$
\begin{aligned}
C[X = \emptyset] &\rightsquigarrow C[\forall x.\, X(x) = 0] \\
C[X = \{e^k\}] &\rightsquigarrow C[X(e) = k \wedge \forall x.\, x \neq e \rightarrow X(e) = 0] \\
C[X = Y \cup Z] &\rightsquigarrow C[\forall x.\, X(x) = \max\{Y(x), Z(x)\}] \\
C[X = Y \cap Z] &\rightsquigarrow C[\forall x.\, X(x) = \min\{Y(x), Z(x)\}] \\
C[X = Y \uplus Z] &\rightsquigarrow C[\forall x.\, X(x) = Y(x) + Z(x)] \\
C[X = Y \setminus Z] &\rightsquigarrow C[\forall x.\, X(x) = \max\{Y(x) - Z(x), 0\}] \\
C[X = Y] &\rightsquigarrow C[\forall x.\, X(x) = Y(x)] \\
C[X \preceq_m Y] &\rightsquigarrow C[\forall x.\, L_{X,Y}(x) > 0 \rightarrow \exists y.\, U_{X,Y}(y) > 0 \wedge x \prec y]
\end{aligned}
$$

3. Compute negation normal form, i.e., push all negations down to the atoms
4. Skolemize all existentially quantified variables
5. For every multiset X occurring in the formula add the formula $\forall x.\, X(x) \geq 0$ as an additional conjunct

After rewriting, the resulting formula is of the form $\mathcal{K} \wedge G$ where G is a ground formula and $\mathcal{K}$ is a conjunction of universally quantified formulas. Clearly, each step of the rewriting transforms the input formula into an equisatisfiable formula.

Lemma 1. *The formulas F and $\mathcal{K} \wedge G$ are equisatisfiable in the theory of preordered multisets.*

Quantifier instantiation. We will now show that there exists a finite and computable set of ground terms $T_{\mathcal{K},G}$ of sort elem such that $\mathcal{K} \wedge G$ is equisatisfiable to the formula $\mathcal{K}[T_{\mathcal{K},G}] \wedge G$, where $\mathcal{K}[T_{\mathcal{K},G}]$ is a ground formula obtained by instantiating all quantified variables appearing in $\mathcal{K}$ with the terms in T.

Throughout the rest of this section we denote by E the set of all ground terms of sort elem appearing in $\mathcal{K} \wedge G$. The set E contains the ground terms appearing in the initial formula F and Skolem constants that have been introduced for top-level existentially quantified variables in Step 4 of the rewrite algorithm. Zarba showed in [29] that for formulas F without ordering constraints on multisets and formulas $\mathsf{F}^\forall$, the theory $\mathcal{K}$ is (what is now known as) a *stably local theory extension* [25]. This means that if F does not contain ordering constraints then F is equisatisfiable to the formula $\mathcal{K}[E] \wedge G$. The reason for locality of $\mathcal{K}$ in this case is simply that instantiation of the quantifiers in $\mathcal{K}$ with terms of sort elem will not create new terms of the same sort. Unfortunately, in the presence of ordering constraints this is no longer true, i.e., instantiation of $\mathcal{K}$ with the terms in E alone is not sufficient.

For illustration of this behavior, reconsider the defining formula (2) for the ordering constraint $X \preceq_m Y$. This formula contains $\forall \exists$ quantification over variables of sort elem. Skolemization of this formula thus gives

$$
\forall x.\, L_{X,Y}(x) > 0 \rightarrow U_{X,Y}(w_{X,Y}(x)) > 0 \wedge x \prec w_{X,Y}(x) \tag{3}
$$

where $w_{X,Y}$ is a fresh Skolem function. We call these Skolem functions $\preceq_m$-*witness functions* and terms constructed from these functions $\preceq_m$-*witnesses*. Instantiation of formula (3) with a term $e \in E$ generates a new $\preceq_m$-witness $w_{X,Y}(e)$ of sort elem, which is not already contained in E. For completeness we have to instantiate $\mathcal{K}$ recursively with these $\prec_m$-witnesses.

We now show that we can put additional constraints on the $\prec_m$-witness functions such that we only need to consider finitely many $\prec_m$-witnesses for the instantiation of $\mathcal{K}$. These additional constraints are as follows. First, we enforce that the $\prec_m$-witness function $w_{X,Y}$ only chooses maximal elements in the multiset $U_{X,Y}$ and, second, we require that each element outside $L_{X,Y}$ is mapped to itself. Formally, these constraints are expressed by the following two axioms:

$$\forall x\, y.\, L_{X,Y}(x) > 0 \wedge w_{X,Y}(x) \prec y \;\rightarrow\; U_{X,Y}(y) = 0 \tag{4}$$
$$\forall x.\, L_{X,Y}(x) = 0 \;\rightarrow\; w_{X,Y}(x) = x \tag{5}$$

The existence of such constrained witness functions is guaranteed by the fact that we restrict ourselves to finite multisets. In particular, given a $\prec_m$-witness function $w_{X,Y}$ satisfying axiom (3), we can define a new witness function that maps every e in $L_{X,Y}$ to the maximal element of some ascending chain starting from $w_{X,Y}(e)$ in $U_{X,Y}$. Finiteness of the multiset $U_{X,Y}$ guarantees the existence of such a maximal element.

For the rest of this section let W be the set of all $\prec_m$-witness functions occurring in $\mathcal{K}$ and let $\mathcal{K}_W$ be the conjunction of axioms (4) and (5) for all $w_{X,Y} \in W$.

Lemma 2. *The formulas $\mathcal{K} \wedge G$ and $\mathcal{K} \wedge \mathcal{K}_W \wedge G$ are equisatisfiable in the theory of preordered multisets.*

Let $T_{W,E}$ be the smallest set of ground terms that satisfies the following two conditions: (i) $E \subseteq T_{W,E}$ and (ii) if $t \in T_{W,E}$ and $w_{X,Y} \in W$ then $w_{X,Y}(t) \in T_{W,E}$. For a term $t \in T_{W,E}$ of the form $t = w_n \ldots w_1(e)$ where $e \in S$, we define $t_0 = e$ and denote by t_i, for $1 \leq i \leq n$, the subterm $w_i \ldots w_1(e)$ of t. We call $t \in T_{W,E}$ a strict chain in a structure α iff α satisfies $t_i \prec t_{i+1}$ for all i with $0 \leq i < n$. We say that a strict chain $t \in T_{W,E}$ in a structure α is *maximal* if t is not a proper subterm of any other strict chain $t' \in T_{W,E}$ in α. For a structure α and a set of ground terms T, we denote by $\alpha(T)$ the set $\alpha(T) = \{\alpha(t) \mid t \in T\}$.

Now, define $T_{\mathcal{K},G}$ as the set of all terms $t \in T_{W,E}$ such that each function $w_{X,Y}$ occurs at most once in t. Clearly, the set $T_{\mathcal{K},G}$ is finite, since W is finite. We can now show that in models of $\mathcal{K} \wedge \mathcal{K}_W$, the terms $T_{W,E}$ are partitioned into finitely many equivalence classes, each of which is represented by some term in $T_{\mathcal{K},G}$.

Lemma 3. *For all models α of $\mathcal{K} \wedge \mathcal{K}_W$, $\alpha(T_{W,E}) = \alpha(T_{\mathcal{K},G})$.*

Proof. Let α be a model of $\mathcal{K} \wedge \mathcal{K}_W$. Note that from strictness of $\prec$, and axioms (3) and (5) follows that for all terms t of sort elem and $w_{X,Y} \in W$, either $\alpha \models w_{X,Y}(t) = t$ or $\alpha \models t \prec w_{X,Y}(t)$ holds.

The proof goes by contradiction. Thus, assume there exists $t \in T_{W,E}$ such that $\alpha(t) \notin \alpha(T_{\mathcal{K},G})$. Then remove all function applications w_i from t for which $\alpha \models w_i(t_{i-1}) = t_{i-1}$, obtaining a term $t' \in T_{W,E}$. Then t' is a strict chain and $\alpha \models t = t'$. From this we conclude that $\alpha(t') \notin \alpha(T_{\mathcal{K},G})$ and therefore $t' \notin T_{\mathcal{K},G}$. Hence, there exists i, j with $1 \leq i < j < k$ and multiset variables X, Y such that $w'_i = w'_j = w_{X,Y} \in W$. We then have $\alpha \models t'_{i-1} \prec w_{X,Y}(t'_{i-1})$. Based on strictness of $\prec$, axiom

(5) and axiom $\forall x.L_{X,Y}(x) \geq 0$ we conclude $\alpha \models L_{X,Y}(t'_{i-1}) > 0$. Similarly, we conclude $\alpha \models L_{X,Y}(t'_{j-1}) > 0$. By transitivity of $\prec$ and construction of t', we further have that α satisfies $w_{X,Y}(t'_{i-1}) \prec w_{X,Y}(t'_{j-1})$. From axiom (4) we then conclude $\alpha \models U_{X,Y}(w_{X,Y}(t'_{j-1})) = 0$. However, from axiom (3) follows $\alpha \models U_{X,Y}(w_{X,Y}(t'_{j-1})) > 0$, which gives us a contradiction.   □

From Lemma 3 follows that we only need to instantiate the axioms $\mathcal{K} \wedge \mathcal{K}_W$ with the terms in $T_{\mathcal{K},G}$.

Lemma 4. *The formulas $\mathcal{K} \wedge \mathcal{K}_W \wedge G$ and $\mathcal{K}[T_{\mathcal{K},G}] \wedge \mathcal{K}_W[T_{\mathcal{K},G}] \wedge G$ are equisatisfiable in the theory of preordered multisets.*

The formula $\mathcal{K}[T_{\mathcal{K},G}] \wedge \mathcal{K}_W[T_{\mathcal{K},G}] \wedge G$ can now be purified obtaining an equisatisfiable formula $G_{elem} \wedge G_{la} \wedge G_{euf}$ such that the three conjuncts G_{elem}, G_{la}, and G_{euf} only share constant symbols and:

- G_{elem} is a constraint over symbols in the theory $\mathcal{T}_{elem}$
- G_{la} is a linear integer arithmetic constraint, and
- G_{euf} is a constraint built from uninterpreted function symbols and equality

We can thus check satisfiability of F by checking satisfiability of $G_{elem} \wedge G_{la} \wedge G_{euf}$ in the disjoint combination of the theory $\mathcal{T}_{elem}$, the theory of linear integer arithmetic, and the theory of uninterpreted function symbols with equality. By our assumptions on the theory $\mathcal{T}_{elem}$, this combined theory can be decided using standard Nelson-Oppen combination techniques [18].

Theorem 1. *The satisfiability problem for POSSUM formulas is decidable.*

Complexity. We will now establish that the satisfiability problem for the quantifier-bounded fragments of POSSUM is in NP, provided the base theory $\mathcal{T}_{elem}$ is also decidable in NP. Since POSSUM formulas subsume propositional logic this bound is tight.

We have seen in the previous section that we can reduce a POSSUM conjunction F to a ground formula $\mathcal{K}[T_{\mathcal{K},G}] \wedge \mathcal{K}_W[T_{\mathcal{K},G}] \wedge G$ whose satisfiability can be decided using the decision procedure of the base theory. However, the size of the resulting formula can be exponential in the size of the input formula F because the size of the set $T_{\mathcal{K},G}$ used for the instantiation is exponential in the number of $\prec_m$-witness functions W. The following lemma implies that this exponential blowup can be avoided.

Lemma 5. *If the formula $\mathcal{K} \wedge \mathcal{K}_W \wedge G$ is satisfiable then it has a model α such that $|\alpha(T_{\mathcal{K},G})| \in \mathcal{O}(|W|^2 \cdot |E|)$.*

Proof. Assume $\mathcal{K} \wedge \mathcal{K}_W \wedge G$ is satisfiable and let α_0 be one of its models. Further, let $n = |W|$ and $m = |E|$. From α_0 we construct a model α with $|\alpha(T_{\mathcal{K},G})| \in \mathcal{O}(n^2 m)$ by collapsing redundant strict chains in α_0. For this purpose, we choose a set T of strict chains in α_0 such that for every term $e \in E$ and witness function $w_{X,Y} \in W$, there is at most one chain $t \in T$ that starts in $L_{X,Y}$, i.e., t contains $w_{X,Y}(e)$ as a subterm. Formally, let $E_=$ be the quotient of E with respect to the interpretation of the equality predicate $=$ in α_0 and denote by $[e] \in E_=$ the equivalence class of $e \in E$. Let T be a maximal subset T of $T_{K,G}$ such that (i) each $t \in T$ is a maximal strict chain in α_0, and (ii) for each $w \in W$, if there is some $t \in T$ which contains w and starts in $e \in E$ then there is no other $t' \in T$ which contains $w(e')$ as a subterm, for any $e' \in [e]$. Clearly such a set T exists. Let T^* be the set of all subterms $t_0, \ldots, t_k$ of the chains $t \in T$, where k is the length of chain t.

We now construct α from α_0 by collapsing all strict chains in α_0 to the chains in T. First, we let α agree with α_0 on the interpretation of all sorts and all symbols that are not witness functions. For each witness function $w \in W$ and $v \in \alpha(\mathsf{elem})$, we then define $\alpha(w)(v)$ as follows: if $v = \alpha_0(e)$ for some $e \in E$, $\alpha_0(w(e)) \neq \alpha_0(e)$, and there is some term $t \in T^*$ with $t = w(t')$ for some t' containing $e' \in [e]$, choose one such term t and define $\alpha(w)(v) = \alpha_0(t)$. In all other cases define $\alpha(w)(v) = \alpha_0(w)(v)$. Note that from the definition of T and α follows that for all $t \in T^*$, $\alpha(t) = \alpha_0(t)$. Thus all terms in T^* are still strict chains in α.

We first prove that α is still a model of $K \wedge K_W \wedge G$. Since α_0 is a model of $K \wedge K_W \wedge G$ and α agrees with α_0 on all symbols that are not witness functions, we immediately conclude that α is also a model of G and all axioms of K that do not mention the witness functions. The fact that α still satisfies the remaining axioms (3)-(5) for all $w \in W$ also easily follows from the definition of α. In particular, if for some w and v, $\alpha(w)(v) \neq \alpha_0(w)(v)$ then, by definition, $v = \alpha(e)$ for some $e \in E$ and $\alpha(w)(v) = \alpha(t)$ for some term $t \in T^*$ such that t contains $e' \in [e]$. From the fact that t is a strict chain in α starting in e' and the transitivity of $\prec$ follows $\alpha \models e' \prec t$. Since $e' \in [e]$ we further have $\alpha \models e = e'$ and hence $\alpha \models e \prec w(e)$. Thus α still satisfies axiom (3). The proofs for the other two axioms are similar.

For proving that $|\alpha(T_{K,G})| \in \mathcal{O}(n^2 m)$ first note that by construction of α we have $\alpha(T^*) = \alpha(T_{K,G})$. We thus need to count the number of elements in T^*. For this purpose, fix $e \in E$ and let k be the maximal length of the chains t in T that start from some $e' \in [e]$. From strictness of the chains and Lemma 3 follows $k \leq n$. We then have by condition (ii) of the definition of T that there are at most $n - k + 1$ chains t in T that start from some $e' \in [e]$. Each of these chains has at most length k by assumption and thus at most $k + 1$ subterms. It follows that T^* contains at most $(n - k + 1)(k + 1)$ terms with some $e' \in [e]$ as a subterm. From $\max_{1 \leq k \leq n} \{(n - k + 1)(k + 1)\} \in \mathcal{O}(n^2)$ we then conclude $|T^*| \in \mathcal{O}(n^2 m)$. □

From Lemma 5 follows that we can guess a polynomial subset T of the terms $T_{K,G}$ and then use this subset to instantiate the axioms in $K \wedge K_W$. The size of the resulting formula $K[T] \wedge K_W[T] \wedge G$ is then polynomial in the size of the input formula, provided we bound the number of quantified variables in $\mathsf{F}^\forall$ subformulas of the input.

Theorem 2. *If the base theory $\mathcal{T}_{\mathsf{elem}}$ is decidable in NP then for the quantifier-bounded fragments of its* POSSUM *extension, the satisfiability problem is NP-complete.*

Practical Considerations. Our decision procedure is amenable to practical implementations using off-the-shelf SMT-solvers. In particular, using techniques developed for local theory extensions [13], we can postpone the exponential decomposition phase of guessing the terms used for instantiation, by generating these terms lazily from models produced by the SMT solver. Also note that in practical applications such as checking validity of constraints generated from termination proofs, all multiset ordering constraints $X \prec_m Y$ will typically have negative polarity. Since only positive occurrences of such constraints generate $\prec_m$-witness functions, the set of terms $T_{K,G}$ will, in most practical cases, already be polynomial in the size of the input constraint.

7 Further Related Work

The logic POSSUM extends the logic of multisets with integers, which was shown to be NP-complete by Zarba [29]. This extension is non-trivial. In particular, Zarba only considers a disjoint combination of a base theory with the theory of multisets and does not support ordering constraints on multisets. Such constraints generate axioms with $\forall \exists$ quantification, which require a more intricate argument to establish completeness of local instantiation. The logic of multisets with cardinality constraints [20] also subsumes Zarba's logic and was shown to be NP-complete [21]. It is incomparable to our logic because it also does not support ordering constraints. On the other hand, POSSUM can only express very restricted cardinality constraints. In [14] the theory of sets with cardinality constraints over totally ordered base sets was shown to be decidable in NP. This result can be generalized to multisets. Decidability of multisets over partially ordered base sets and with general cardinality constraints is open.

Local theory extensions [25] formalize the general category of theories for which local quantifier instantiation techniques are complete. Some local theory extension of orders have been studied in [26]. Our extension of preorders to multiset orderings is an instance of the so called Ψ-local theory extensions, which have been introduced in [12].

Simplification orderings are a common tool to prove termination of term rewrite systems [8, 1]. Among the most widely used simplification orderings are recursive path orderings [8] (which have originally been defined in terms of multiset orderings), lexicographic path orderings [1], and Knuth-Bendix orderings [10]. Constraint solving has been shown to be decidable in NP for each of these orderings [17, 30, 19]. Unlike simplification orderings, we do not require that the underlying order is total. Thus, one can use our decision procedure to prove termination even in cases where there are no natural total orderings, such as Example 1 in Section 2.

8 Conclusion

We presented POSSUM, a new logic and decision procedure for reasoning about multiset orderings. POSSUM can express constraints over complex well-founded orderings, which makes it a useful tool for proving termination. The logic subsumes linear integer arithmetic which has been traditionally used to express ranking functions in automated termination proofs. We established that the satisfiability problem for POSSUM is NP-complete, provided the base theory is in NP. Thus it has the same complexity as quantifier-free linear integer arithmetic. Furthermore, our decision procedure is susceptible to a practical implementation. We thus believe that POSSUM provides a valuable tool for extending the scope of existing termination provers. Our next step is to implement the decision procedure and make it available as a component for SMT solvers.

Acknowledgments. We thank Viktor Kuncak for inspiring discussions and his valuable comments on an earlier draft of this paper.

References

1. Baader, F., Nipkow, T.: Term Rewriting and All That. Cambridge University Press, Cambridge (1998)
2. Bachmair, L., Ganzinger, H.: Resolution theorem proving. In: Handbook of Automated Reasoning, pp. 19–99. MIT Press, Cambridge (2001)
3. Berdine, J., Cook, B., Distefano, D., O'Hearn, P.W.: Automatic termination proofs for programs with shape-shifting heaps. In: Ball, T., Jones, R.B. (eds.) CAV 2006. LNCS, vol. 4144, pp. 386–400. Springer, Heidelberg (2006)
4. Colón, M.A., Sipma, H.B.: Synthesis of linear ranking functions. In: Margaria, T., Yi, W. (eds.) TACAS 2001. LNCS, vol. 2031, pp. 67–81. Springer, Heidelberg (2001)
5. Cook, B., Podelski, A., Rybalchenko, A.: Abstraction refinement for termination. In: Hankin, C., Siveroni, I. (eds.) SAS 2005. LNCS, vol. 3672, pp. 87–101. Springer, Heidelberg (2005)
6. Cook, B., Podelski, A., Rybalchenko, A.: TERMINATOR: Beyond safety. In: Ball, T., Jones, R.B. (eds.) CAV 2006. LNCS, vol. 4144, pp. 415–418. Springer, Heidelberg (2006)
7. Deng, Y., Sangiorgi, D.: Ensuring termination by typability. Inf. Comput. 204(7), 1045–1082 (2006)
8. Dershowitz, N.: Orderings for term-rewriting systems. In: Symposium on Foundations of Computer Science (SFCS), pp. 123–131 (1979)
9. Dershowitz, N., Manna, Z.: Proving termination with multiset orderings. Commun. ACM 22(8), 465–476 (1979)
10. Dick, J., Kalmus, J., Martin, U.: Automating the Knuth Bendix Ordering. Acta Inf. 28(2), 95–119 (1990)
11. Floyd, R.W.: Assigning meanings to programs. In: Proc. Amer. Math. Soc. Symposia in Applied Mathematics, vol. 19, pp. 19–31 (1967)
12. Ihlemann, C., Jacobs, S., Sofronie-Stokkermans, V.: On local reasoning in verification. In: Ramakrishnan, C.R., Rehof, J. (eds.) TACAS 2008. LNCS, vol. 4963, pp. 265–281. Springer, Heidelberg (2008)
13. Jacobs, S.: Incremental instance generation in local reasoning. In: Bouajjani, A., Maler, O. (eds.) CAV 2009. LNCS, vol. 5643, pp. 368–382. Springer, Heidelberg (2009)
14. Kuncak, V., Piskac, R., Suter, P.: Ordered sets in the calculus of data structures. In: Dawar, A., Veith, H. (eds.) CSL 2010. LNCS, vol. 6247, pp. 34–48. Springer, Heidelberg (2010)
15. Lee, C.S., Jones, N.D., Ben-Amram, A.M.: The size-change principle for program termination. In: POPL, pp. 81–92 (2001)
16. Martín-Mateos, F.-J., Ruiz-Reina, J.-L., Alonso, J.-A., Hidalgo, M.J.: Proof pearl: A formal proof of higman's lemma in ACL2. In: Hurd, J., Melham, T. (eds.) TPHOLs 2005. LNCS, vol. 3603, pp. 358–372. Springer, Heidelberg (2005)
17. Narendran, P., Rusinowitch, M., Verma, R.M.: RPO Constraint Solving Is in NP. In: Gottlob, G., Grandjean, E., Seyr, K. (eds.) CSL 1998. LNCS, vol. 1584, pp. 385–398. Springer, Heidelberg (1999)
18. Nelson, G., Oppen, D.C.: Simplification by cooperating decision procedures. ACM TOPLAS 1(2), 245–257 (1979)
19. Nieuwenhuis, R.: Simple LPO constraint solving methods. Inf. Process. Lett. 47(2), 65–69 (1993)
20. Piskac, R., Kuncak, V.: Decision procedures for multisets with cardinality constraints. In: Logozzo, F., Peled, D.A., Zuck, L.D. (eds.) VMCAI 2008. LNCS, vol. 4905, pp. 218–232. Springer, Heidelberg (2008)

21. Piskac, R., Kuncak, V.: Linear arithmetic with stars. In: Gupta, A., Malik, S. (eds.) CAV 2008. LNCS, vol. 5123, pp. 268–280. Springer, Heidelberg (2008)
22. Podelski, A., Rybalchenko, A.: A complete method for the synthesis of linear ranking functions. In: Steffen, B., Levi, G. (eds.) VMCAI 2004. LNCS, vol. 2937, pp. 239–251. Springer, Heidelberg (2004)
23. Podelski, A., Rybalchenko, A.: Transition invariants. In: LICS 2004 (2004)
24. Podelski, A., Rybalchenko, A.: Transition predicate abstraction and fair termination. ACM TOPLAS 29(3), 15 (2007)
25. Sofronie-Stokkermans, V.: Hierarchic reasoning in local theory extensions. In: Nieuwenhuis, R. (ed.) CADE 2005. LNCS (LNAI), vol. 3632, pp. 219–234. Springer, Heidelberg (2005)
26. Sofronie-Stokkermans, V., Ihlemann, C.: Automated reasoning in some local extensions of ordered structures. In: ISMVL (2007)
27. Suter, P., Dotta, M., Kuncak, V.: Decision procedures for algebraic data types with abstractions. In: 37th ACM SIGACT-SIGPLAN Symposium on Principles of Programming Languages, POPL (2010)
28. Venkataraman, K.N.: Decidability of the purely existential fragment of the theory of term algebras. Journal of the ACM (JACM) 34(2), 492–510 (1987)
29. Zarba, C.G.: Combining multisets with integers. In: Voronkov, A. (ed.) CADE 2002. LNCS (LNAI), vol. 2392, p. 363. Springer, Heidelberg (2002)
30. Zhang, T., Sipma, H.B., Manna, Z.: The Decidability of the First-Order Theory of Knuth-Bendix Order. In: Nieuwenhuis, R. (ed.) CADE 2005. LNCS (LNAI), vol. 3632, pp. 131–148. Springer, Heidelberg (2005)

Collective Assertions

Stephen F. Siegel and Timothy K. Zirkel*

Verified Software Laboratory, Department of Computer and Information Sciences
University of Delaware, Newark, DE 19716, USA
{siegel,zirkeltk}@udel.edu
http://vsl.cis.udel.edu

Abstract. We introduce the notion of *collective assertions* for message-passing-based parallel programs with distributed memory, such as those written using the Message Passing Interface. A single collective assertion comprises a set of locations in each process and an expression on the global state. The semantics are defined as follows: whenever control in a process reaches one of the locations, a "snapshot" of the local state of that process is sent to a coordinator; once a snapshot has been received from each process, the expression is evaluated on the global state formed by uniting the snapshots. We have extended the Toolkit for Accurate Scientific Software (TASS), a verifier based on symbolic execution and explicit state enumeration, to check that collective assertions hold on all possible executions of a C/MPI program. We give several examples of such programs, show that many properties of them are naturally expressed as collective assertions, and use TASS to verify or refute these.

1   Introduction

Assertions are an important tool for developing reliable sequential programs. They are used to specify correct behavior, reveal faults, and isolate defects. They can be checked at runtime, or verified statically using a number of different techniques. Most importantly, they are easy to use, since they do not require a developer to learn much beyond the expression syntax of the programming language.

In this paper, we focus on distributed memory, message-passing, multiprocess programs, such as those expressed using the Message Passing Interface (MPI, [10]). This includes most programs used in high-performance scientific computing. In this domain, the success of assertions is less clear. This is not surprising: the most difficult and subtle defects in such programs involve the interaction of multiple processes, yet the programming languages and libraries used by developers support only assertions local to a single process.

There has been research to develop *global assertions* in distributed programs, i.e., assertions that may refer to the global state. While these might prove useful in certain cases, it is our view that they are not appropriate for expressing many of the properties that arise naturally in the domain of interest. We now give an example illustrating the problem.

---

* Supported by the U.S. National Science Foundation grants CCF-0733035 and CCF-0953210, and the University of Delaware Research Foundation.

R. Jhala and D. Schmidt (Eds.): VMCAI 2011, LNCS 6538, pp. 387–402, 2011.

```
int first = PID*NX/NPROCS;
int nxl = (PID+1)*NX/NPROCS - first;
int left = (PID+NPROCS-1)%NPROCS;
int right = (PID+1)%NPROCS;
int time = 0;
float u[nxl+2];

/* ... initialize u ... */
for (time=1; time<=nsteps; time++) {
  send(u[1],     left);
  recv(u[nxl+1], right);
  send(u[nxl],   right);
  recv(u[0],     left);
  assert PROC[right].u[0] == u[nxl] &&
   PROC[left].u[PROC[left].nxl+1] == u[1];
  /* ... local update of u ... */
}
```

	Proc 0	Proc 1	Proc 2
1.		send left	
2.			send left
3.		recv right	
4.	send left		
5.			recv right
6.			send right
7.		send right	
8.			recv left
9.			**assert**

Fig. 1. Left: block-distributed 1d diffusion solver with global assertion. Right: an execution fragment in which the assertion, if interpreted literally, fails.

The numerical solution of the "diffusion equation" is a standard example used in many parallel programming texts. In one dimension, the standard solution manipulates a one-dimensional array u of length NX of real values. The algorithm iterates through discrete time steps. At each time step, the value of each cell in u is updated using a formula that is a function of the current value of that cell and those of its left and right neighbors. Assume a cyclic domain, so there is no need for special handling at the boundary. A typical (distributed-memory) parallel version of the algorithm is outlined in C-like pseudocode in Fig. 1 (left). Each of the NPROCS processes executes a copy of this code. The processes may still exhibit different behaviors because each has a unique ID number (PID) between 0 and NPROCS − 1, inclusive.

The original array is block-distributed so that each process "owns" a contiguous slice of length nxl of the original array. Assume NX ≥ NPROCS, so that nxl ≥ 1 on each process. To update the cell on the left boundary of its slice, a process needs the value of the right-most cell of its left neighbor; a similar issue holds at the right boundary. This problem is managed by having each process maintain a left and right *ghost cell*: the left ghost cell to mirror the value of the left neighbor's right-most (ordinary) cell, and a similar cell for the right neighbor. To incorporate the ghost cells, u is given length nxl + 2, with the ghost cells in positions 0 and nxl + 1. At each time step, the processes update their ghost cells using the communication operations shown. To simplify the discussion, assume asynchronous communication with unbounded channels, i.e., a message sent by a send operation can always be buffered, so the routine shown will not deadlock. After the exchange completes, a process updates its cells in the usual way, and proceeds to the next time step.

Suppose we wish to assert the correctness of the ghost cell exchange. From the point of view of one process, this might be stated informally as "after the ghost cell exchange, the value of my right neighbor's left ghost cell agrees with the value of my right-most non-ghost cell," with a similar statement for the left neighbor. To express this requires some notation to refer to variables in other processes. We write PROC[i].x to denote a variable x in the process with PID i, where i is an integer-valued expression. Using this notation, the desired assertion appears in the pseudocode. As with other statements, one assertion appears in each process, though the asserted expressions differ because each process has its own PID.

Let us assume these assertions are given the obvious semantics: that when control reaches an assertion, the expression is evaluated in the current global state, and the assertion is violated if it evaluates to *false*. (Leave aside for now the question of how this could be implemented.) It is not hard to see the assertion can fail on many executions, such as the one in Fig. 1 (right). In that execution fragment, process 2 reaches the assertion before its right neighbor, process 0, has received any message. When the assertion is evaluated, the value of u[0] on process 0 will not necessarily agree with that of u[nxl] on process 2. But there is nothing wrong with this execution—it is the assertion that is broken.

How can we fix the problem? We might alter the semantics by restricting the set of executions on which the assertion should be evaluated. For example, we could declare that the assertion imposes a barrier, and is not evaluated until all processes reach it. There are two problems with this approach. First, it does not capture the intuitive property that the developer has in mind, which applies to all executions, not just the subset which synchronize at the assertion. Hence it leaves a large number of legal executions untested, and as we shall see in Sec. 4 (in the *wildcard_gather* example) there are natural assertions that hold for all executions in which the assertion is treated as a barrier, but fail on other executions. Second, if the assertions are to be used for runtime checks, as they usually are, the additional forced synchronization would be unacceptable from a performance view. Surely one desirable quality of any assertion system should be that the assertions not change the set of possible behaviors of the program. Similar comments apply to other possible restrictions, such as forcing the communication to be synchronous, or forcing all processes to move in lockstep.

A more precise informal statement of the desired property might be "for all $i \geq 1$, the value of my right-most non-ghost cell at time step i after the exchange agrees with the value of my right neighbor's left ghost cell whenever it is in time step i just after the exchange." But it is not clear how this could be made precise using standard assertions, at least without performing complex modifications to the program (e.g., by adding and maintaining history variables).

The solution proposed in this paper is the *collective assertion*. Like a global assertion, a collective assertion may refer to the state of several processes, but unlike a global assertion, the process states may have existed at (very) different times in the execution. A collective assertion is specified by placing an assertion statement in each process. When control in that process reaches the assertion, a snapshot of the process state is taken. Once every process has reached its assertion, these snapshots are composed into a single global state (ignoring the buffered messages), in which all the asserted expressions are evaluated. Only at this point—just after the last process reaches the assertion—is the assertion determined to have passed or failed. With this semantics, the ghost cell assertion in our example will hold on every execution—and never for vacuous reasons.

A collective assertion is analogous to the *collective operations* of MPI [10, Chap. 5]. These are communication primitives which involve a set of processes, and include barrier, broadcast, gather, reduction, and other operations. Like our collective assertion, an MPI collective operation requires a statement in each process; each process contributes something to the operation upon executing that statement; and the operation as a whole does not complete until every process has made its contribution. Unlike MPI's collectives, however, our assertions never impose any additional synchronization, since we want the program to exhibit the same set of behaviors whether the assertions are turned on or off.

In this paper, we present formal definitions of *collective assertions* and their semantics. We have realized these notions in our Toolkit for Accurate Scientific Software [11]. TASS uses symbolic execution and explicit state enumeration techniques [7,6] to verify that safety properties of C/MPI programs hold for all possible executions within user-specified bounds. We discuss how we have implemented collective assertion verification in TASS, report on experiments designed to gauge the cost of verifying the assertions, give several additional examples of properties that are naturally expressed using them, and report on our success using TASS on those examples. These include examples where TASS is used to verify the equivalence of two programs. We conclude with a discussion of related work, and various ways the techniques may be extended in the future.

2   Model

For a formal description, we need a model. The model we use is based on [1, Def. 2.31]. For sets X and Y, let $\mathsf{Func}(X, Y)$ denote the set of all functions from X to Y. For $f \in \mathsf{Func}(X, Y)$, $x \in X$, $y \in Y$, $f[x := y]$ denotes the function which is the same as f, except possibly at x, where it returns y. Let X^* denote the set of finite sequences of elements of X and $\mathsf{len}(\sigma)$ the length of a sequence σ.

Let $n \geq 1$ and $\mathsf{Var}_1, \ldots, \mathsf{Var}_n$ be n mutually disjoint sets of *variables*. Let Val be a set of *values*. Let Chan be a set of *channels*, each with a *capacity* $\mathsf{cap}(c) \in \{1, 2, \ldots\}$. Let $V \subseteq \mathsf{Var} \overset{\text{def}}{=} \bigcup_i \mathsf{Var}_i$, and $\mathsf{Eval}(V) \overset{\text{def}}{=} \mathsf{Func}(V, \mathsf{Val})$. The set of *communication actions* is $\mathsf{Comm} \overset{\text{def}}{=} \{c!e, c?x \mid c \in \mathsf{Chan}, x \in \mathsf{Var}, e \in \mathsf{Expr}\}$, where Expr denotes the set of expressions over Var. The exact syntax of expressions is not important, but we assume all expressions are side-effect free.

Definition 1. *A* **program graph** *over* (V, Chan) *is a tuple*

$$\mathsf{PG} = (\mathsf{Loc}, \mathsf{Act}, \mathsf{Effect}, \hookrightarrow, \mathsf{Loc}_0, g_0), \tag{1}$$

where $\mathsf{Cond}(V)$ *denotes the set of boolean-valued expressions over* V *and*

1. Loc *is a set of* locations *and* Act *is a set of* actions,
2. Effect: $\mathsf{Act} \times \mathsf{Eval}(V) \to \mathsf{Eval}(V)$ *is the* effect function,
3. $\hookrightarrow \subseteq \mathsf{Loc} \times \mathsf{Cond}(V) \times (\mathsf{Act} \cup \mathsf{Comm}) \times \mathsf{Loc}$ *is the* conditional transition relation,
4. $\mathsf{Loc}_0 \subseteq \mathsf{Loc}$ *is a set of* initial locations, $g_0 \in \mathsf{Cond}(V)$ *is the* initial condition.

We write $l \overset{g:\alpha}{\hookrightarrow} l'$ *to denote that* $\langle l, g, \alpha, l' \rangle \in \hookrightarrow$.

Definition 2. *A* **channel system** CS *over* $(\mathsf{Var}, \mathsf{Chan})$ *is a tuple* $[\mathsf{PG}_1 | \cdots | \mathsf{PG}_n]$, *where for each* i, $\mathsf{PG}_i = (\mathsf{Loc}_i, \mathsf{Act}_i, \mathsf{Effect}_i, \hookrightarrow_i, \mathsf{Loc}_{i,0}, g_{i,0})$ *is a program graph over* $(\mathsf{Var}_i, \mathsf{Chan})$.

Semantics. We assume an expression semantics is given; this specifies how to extend any $\eta \in \mathsf{Eval}(\mathsf{Var})$ to some $\tilde{\eta} \in \mathsf{Eval}(\mathsf{Expr})$. The elements of $\mathsf{Eval}(\mathsf{Chan}) \overset{\text{def}}{=} \mathsf{Func}(\mathsf{Chan}, \mathsf{Val}^*)$ are *channel evaluations*. Let ξ_0 denote the channel evaluation that maps every channel to the empty sequence. The sets of *(global) states* and *initial states* are defined by

$$\mathsf{State} = \mathsf{Loc}_1 \times \cdots \times \mathsf{Loc}_n \times \mathsf{Eval}(\mathsf{Var}) \times \mathsf{Eval}(\mathsf{Chan})$$
$$I = \{\langle l_1, \ldots, l_n, \eta, \xi_0 \rangle \in \mathsf{State} \mid \forall 0 < i \leq n. (l_i \in \mathsf{Loc}_{0,i} \wedge \eta \models g_{0,i})\}.$$

A *transition* is a triple $\langle s, \alpha, s' \rangle$, where $s = \langle l_1, \ldots, l_i, \ldots, l_n, \eta, \xi \rangle$, $s' \in \mathsf{State}$, $\alpha \in \mathsf{Act} \overset{\text{def}}{=} \bigcup_i \mathsf{Act}_i \cup \{\tau\}$, and one of the following holds:

1. for some i, $\alpha \in \mathsf{Act}_i$, $l_i \overset{g:\alpha}{\hookrightarrow} l_i'$, $\eta \models g$, and $s' = \langle l_1, \ldots, l_i', \ldots, l_n, \mathsf{Effect}(\alpha, \eta), \xi \rangle$,
2. $\alpha = \tau$ and for some i, $l_i \overset{g:c?x}{\hookrightarrow} l_i'$, $\mathsf{len}(\xi(c)) = k > 0$, $\xi(c) = v_1 \cdots v_k$, $\eta \models g$, and $s' = \langle l_1, \ldots, l_i', \ldots, l_n, \eta[x := v_1], \xi[c := v_2 \cdots v_k] \rangle$, or
3. $\alpha = \tau$ and for some i, $l_i \overset{g:c!e}{\hookrightarrow} l_i'$, $\mathsf{len}(\xi(c)) = k < \mathsf{cap}(c)$, $\xi(c) = v_1 \cdots v_k$, $\eta \models g$, and $s' = \langle l_1, \ldots, l_i', \ldots, l_n, \eta, \xi[c := v_1 v_2 \cdots v_k \tilde{\eta}(e)] \rangle$.

We write $s \overset{\alpha}{\to} s'$ to denote that $\langle s, \alpha, s' \rangle$ is a transition. We say s is *terminal* if there is no transition departing from s, i.e., none of the form $s \overset{\alpha}{\to} s'$.

An *execution fragment* is a (finite or infinite) sequence $\rho = s_0 \overset{\alpha_0}{\to} s_1 \overset{\alpha_1}{\to} \cdots$. We say ρ is *initial* if $s_0 \in I$. The *length* of ρ is the number of transitions.

3 Collective Assertions

Definition 3. *Let* CS *be a channel system and* $\mathsf{Loc} \overset{\text{def}}{=} \bigcup_{1 \leq i \leq n} \mathsf{Loc}_i$. *A* collective assertion σ *is a function from a subset* $\mathsf{dom}(\sigma)$ *of* Loc *to* $\mathsf{Cond}(\mathsf{Var})$.

Hence σ involves some set of locations, and to each such location it associates a global expression. Note the locations may be in several processes, and there may be several locations in the same process. Although it is not required by the definition, we will see that if σ is to have any chance of holding, $\mathsf{dom}(\sigma)$ must have at least one location in each process.

Let Σ be a set of collective assertions such that, for any location l, $l \in \mathsf{dom}(\sigma)$ for at most one $\sigma \in \Sigma$. Let $\mathsf{ALoc} = \{l \in \mathsf{Loc} \mid \exists \sigma \in \Sigma. l \in \mathsf{dom}(\sigma)\}$. The elements of ALoc are the *assertion locations*. Given $l \in$ ALoc, let assert(l) denote the unique $\sigma \in \Sigma$ such that $l \in \text{dom}(\sigma)$.

Let $\rho = s_0 \xrightarrow{\alpha_0} s_1 \xrightarrow{\alpha_1} \cdots \xrightarrow{\alpha_{m-1}} s_m$ be a finite execution fragment. We now define what it means for Σ to hold on ρ. The definition requires that every process encounter the same assertions in the same order. (This is also the case with MPI's collective operations.) Write $s_j = \langle l_{j,1}, \ldots, l_{j,n}, \eta_j, \xi_j \rangle$ ($0 \leq j \leq m$).

We define a sequence $\Lambda_i^j \in (\text{Eval}(\text{Var}_i) \times \text{Loc}_i)^*$ for each $1 \leq i \leq n$ and $1 \leq j \leq m$. This sequence contains the accumulated snapshots from process i after reaching state s_j in ρ. The definition is by induction on j. For $j = 0$,

$$\Lambda_i^0(s) = \begin{cases} \langle \eta_0|_{\text{Var}_i}, l_{0,i} \rangle & \text{if } l_{0,i} \in \text{ALoc} \\ \text{the empty sequence} & \text{otherwise} \end{cases} \qquad (1 \leq i \leq n). \qquad (2)$$

Hence $\Lambda_i^0(s)$ is a sequence of length 1 or 0, depending on whether $l_{0,i}$ is an assertion location. Note $\eta_0|_{\text{Var}_i}$ denotes the restriction of η_0 to Var_i, and captures the values of the local variables for PG_i.

Now assume $1 \leq j \leq m$ and we have defined Λ_i^{j-1} for all i. The transition α_{j-1} lies in some process PG_i. If $l_{j,i} \in \text{ALoc}$ then $\Lambda_i^j = \Lambda_i^{j-1}.\langle \eta_j|_{\text{Var}_i}, l_{j,i} \rangle$. Otherwise, $\Lambda_i^j = \Lambda_i^{j-1}$.

Let $\Lambda_i = \Lambda_i^m$; this is the final sequence of snapshots at the end of ρ.

Note that given $\chi_i \in \text{Eval}(\text{Var}_i)$ for each $1 \leq i \leq n$, we can form their union $\chi = \bigcup_i \chi_i \in \text{Eval}(\text{Var})$: for any $v \in \text{Var}$, $\chi(v) = \chi_i(v)$, where $v \in \text{Var}_i$. This is the "composite" global state formed from the local snapshots.

Let $k \geq 1$. If $\text{len}(\Lambda_i) \geq k$, write $\Lambda_i[k] = \langle \eta_i^k, l_i^k \rangle$ for the kth element of Λ_i. We say that Σ *holds at the kth occurrence in ρ* if

1. $\forall 1 \leq i, j \leq n.((\text{len}(\Lambda_i) \geq k \wedge \text{len}(\Lambda_j) \geq k) \Rightarrow \text{assert}(l_i^k) = \text{assert}(l_j^k))$, and
2. $(\forall 1 \leq i \leq n.\text{len}(\Lambda_i) \geq k) \Rightarrow \bigcup_{1 \leq i \leq n} \eta_i^k \models \bigwedge_{i=1}^n \sigma(l_i^k)$.

The first constraint says all processes which have reached their k^{th} assertion location agree on the kth assertion to be checked. The second says that if all processes have reached the kth assertion, the asserted expressions hold at the composite state.

Definition 4. *Let Σ, ρ, and the Λ_i be defined as above. The collective assertion set Σ holds on ρ if (i) for all $k \geq 1$, Σ holds at the kth occurrence in ρ, and (ii) if s_m is a terminal state then all Λ_i have the same length. We say CS satisfies Σ if Σ holds on every finite initial execution fragment of CS.*

Note there are three ways in which Σ can fail to hold for ρ: (1) the collective assertions are encountered in different orders by two processes, (2) the final state is terminal, yet there remain assertions entered by some processes but not by others, or (3) all processes have entered an assertion but the asserted expression fails to hold in the composite state.

```
 1  procedure  check(⟨s, Λ₁, ..., Λₙ⟩ ∈ AState \ {s_V}): AState is
 2  │  if ∀j.len(Λⱼ) = 0 then return ⟨s, Λ₁, ..., Λₙ⟩;
 3  │  choose j such that len(Λⱼ) > 0 and let σ = assert(peek(Λⱼ));
 4  │  if ∃i.(len(Λᵢ) > 0 ∧ assert(peek(Λᵢ)) ≠ σ) then return s_V;  /*out of order*/
 5  │  if ∃j.len(Λⱼ) = 0 then return ⟨s, Λ₁, ..., Λₙ⟩;
 6  │  foreach j ∈ {1. ..., n} do Λ'ⱼ, ⟨ηⱼ, lⱼ⟩ ← dequeue(Λⱼ);
 7  │  if ⋃_{1≤j≤n} ηⱼ ⊭ ⋀_{j=1}^{n} σ(lⱼ) then return s_V;  /* assertion failure */
 8  │  return ⟨s, Λ'₁, ..., Λ'ₙ⟩;

 9  procedure  next(⟨s, Λ₁, ..., Λₙ⟩ ∈ AState \ {s_V}, s →ᵅ s'): AState is
10  │  let i be the index of the process to which α belongs;
11  │  let ⟨l₁, ..., lₙ, η, ξ⟩ = s;
12  │  if lᵢ ∈ ALoc then return check⟨s', Λ₁, ..., enqueue(Λᵢ, ⟨η|_{Var_i}, lᵢ⟩), ..., Λₙ⟩;
13  │  return ⟨s', Λ₁, ..., Λₙ⟩;
```

Fig. 2. Next state function for ATS. Function **dequeue** returns both the left-most element and the sequence obtained by removing that element; **peek** just returns the leftmost element; **enqueue** returns the sequence obtained by appending the given element on the right. Also, assert(⟨η, l⟩) = assert(l).

3.1 The Extended Transition System

We now define an extended transition system ATS which can be used to determine whether a channel system satisfies a collective assertion set Σ. The approach mirrors the definition above, with one adjustment. Instead of waiting until termination to check the assertions, an assertion is checked as soon as there is at least one snapshot queued from each process. From a practical point of view, this allows a violation to be reported earlier—as soon as the last process reaches the assertion. Also, as soon as an assertion is checked, the snapshots can be dequeued, reducing the memory required to store the snapshots.

The states in ATS model the snapshot queues and include a terminal *violation state* s_V:

$$\mathsf{AState} \stackrel{\text{def}}{=} (\mathsf{State} \times (\mathsf{Eval}(\mathsf{Var}_1) \times \mathsf{Loc}_1)^* \times \cdots \times (\mathsf{Eval}(\mathsf{Var}_n) \times \mathsf{Loc}_n)^*) \cup \{s_V\}.$$

The initial states are all states of the form check⟨$s, \Lambda_1^0(s), \ldots, \Lambda_n^0(s)$⟩, where $s \in I$ and $\Lambda_i^0(s)$ is as in (2). The function check, defined in Fig. 2, first checks that no out-of-order violation has occurred. Then, if there is at least one entry in each queue, it dequeues one snapshot from each and checks the assertion at the resulting composite state. It returns the violation state if any check fails.

Given any $\tilde{s} = \langle s, \ldots \rangle \in \mathsf{AState}$ and any transition $s \stackrel{\alpha}{\to} s'$, there is a transition $\tilde{s} \stackrel{\alpha}{\to} \mathsf{next}(\tilde{s}, s \stackrel{\alpha}{\to} s')$ in ATS, where the function next is defined in Fig. 2.

Define a predicate Φ on AState as follows: for $\tilde{s} \in \mathsf{AState}$,

$$\Phi(\tilde{s}) \Leftrightarrow (\tilde{s} \text{ is terminal} \Rightarrow (\tilde{s} \neq s_V \land \forall i.\mathsf{len}(\Lambda_i) = 0)), \tag{3}$$

where $\tilde{s} = \langle s, \Lambda_1, \ldots, \Lambda_n \rangle$ if $\tilde{s} \in \mathsf{AState} \setminus \{s_V\}$. We claim

Theorem 1. CS *satisfies* Σ *if and only if* Φ *holds at every state reachable from an initial state in* ATS.

Proof. Let A be the set of all finite execution fragments ρ of CS such that Σ does not hold on ρ but Σ does hold on any proper prefix of ρ. Let B be the set of all finite execution fragments in ATS that terminate in a state at which Φ does not hold. We claim there is a surjective map from A to B. This will complete the proof, since it implies $A = \emptyset \Leftrightarrow B = \emptyset$.

Given $\rho = s_0 \xrightarrow{\alpha_0} \cdots \xrightarrow{\alpha_{m-1}} s_m \in A$, let $\tilde{\rho}$ be the execution fragment in ATS $\tilde{s}_0 \xrightarrow{\alpha_0} \cdots \xrightarrow{\alpha_{m-1}} \tilde{s}_m$, where $\tilde{s}_0$ is the initial state corresponding to s_0 and $\tilde{s}_{j+1} = \mathsf{next}(\tilde{s}_j, s_j \xrightarrow{\alpha_j} s_{j+1})$ for $0 \leq j \leq m - 1$. There are two possibilities: either (i) there exists k such that Σ does not hold at the kth occurrence in ρ, or (ii) Σ holds at the kth occurrence in ρ for all k, but s_m is a terminal state and $\exists 1 \leq i, j \leq n.\mathsf{len}(\Lambda_i) > \mathsf{len}(\Lambda_j)$. In the first case, $\tilde{s}_m = s_V$, so $\tilde{\rho} \in B$. In the second case, $\tilde{s}_m = \langle s_m, \Lambda'_1, \ldots, \Lambda'_n \rangle$ is terminal and $\Lambda'_i > 0$, since, whenever elements are removed from the queues (line 6 of Fig. 2), one element is removed from each queue. Hence $\tilde{\rho} \in B$ in this case as well. Conversely, given any $\tilde{\rho} \in B$, $\tilde{\rho}$ ends at either s_V or a terminal state with a non-empty snapshot queue. In the first case it must arise in the above way from a $\rho \in A$ satisfying (i); in the second from a ρ satisfying (ii). $\square$

Hence the validity of a set of collective assertions is an invariant property for the extended transition system. It can therefore be verified using standard techniques, such as depth-first search of the reachable states.

4   Implementation and Experiments

In this section we discuss how we have implemented collective assertion verification in TASS, describe the results of some preliminary experiments carried out with that implementation, and give several more examples of properties that are naturally expressed using collective assertions.

4.1   Overview of TASS

TASS takes as input a C/MPI program and an integer $n \geq 1$, and verifies a number of safety properties of an n-process instance of the program. Absence of deadlock, buffer overflows, memory leaks, and (ordinary) assertion violations are some of the properties checked. Currently only standard-mode blocking MPI functions are supported, but this is being expanded to a much larger subset of MPI. Not every C language feature is supported at this time, but many of the most commonly-used features are, including multi-dimensional arrays, structs, pointers and pointer arithmetic, and dynamically allocated data.

TASS uses symbolic execution to reason about all possible inputs to the program. The program inputs are represented as symbolic constants; operations result in symbolic expressions in those symbolic constants. An additional boolean-valued path condition variable is used to keep track of the guards that had to evaluate to *true* in order for the current path to have been executed. Automated theorem proving techniques are used to determine if the path condition becomes unsatisfiable, whether an array index is out of bounds, and so on. TASS has its own internal support for simplifying symbolic expressions, placing them into a canonical formal, and dispatching some of the proof obligations; for those it cannot dispatch itself, it uses CVC3 [2].

TASS allows the user to specify an arbitrary initial condition. In practice this is used to place bounds on certain inputs (array sizes, loop iterations) in order to make the number of states tractable. Without such bounds it is possible that TASS will never return because the state space is infinite. In general, TASS is applied to configurations that are smaller than those the program would typically encounter in use, but within the specified bounds it performs an exhaustive exploration of all possible program behaviors and inputs.

Partial order reduction [5] is a family of techniques for reducing the number of states that need to be explored in order to verify a class of properties. TASS uses the MPI-specific POR technique, the *urgent algorithm* [12]. Given a state s, the urgent algorithm can conclude that it is safe to explore only those transitions enabled in a single process, rather than all enabled transitions. We say such a process is "urgent" at s. If more than one process is urgent, a heuristic is used to select one of them. (By default, TASS chooses the first urgent process it finds.) Any such heuristic is sound, i.e., if a violation exists within the specified bounds, one will be found. But the number of states explored can differ greatly with the heuristic, in ways that are usually difficult to predict.

TASS can also use *comparative symbolic execution* [13] to verify that two programs are functionally equivalent (i.e., "input-output" equivalent). The basic idea is to construct a model in which the two programs run sequentially—one after the other—and at the end the outputs are compared. The state space of this model is then exhaustively explored. This technique is particularly useful in computational science, for comparing a complex parallel version of a program (the "implementation") to a simple, trusted sequential version ("specification").

4.2   Collective Assertion Specification and Verification in TASS

The assertions are specified as pragmas inserted into the code at the desired locations. Fig. 3 gives examples of the pragmas used in the 1d-diffusion code. We have already discussed the 'PROC' notation for referring to a variable in another process. We have also added support for existential and universal quantifiers.

An identifier (GHOSTS or COMPARE) gives a name to the collective assertion of which the pragma is a part. One collective assertion $\sigma = \sigma(\text{id})$ is created for each identifier id, and σ consists of all location-expression pairs specified by a pragma with identifier id. The location is the point in the source code immediately following the pragma.

Collective assertions can also be used when comparing two programs, particularly to specify the expected correspondence between variables at various control points. The semantics are easily defined: if one program has n processes, and

```
for (time = 1; time <= nsteps; time++) {
  exchange_ghost_cells();
#pragma TASS collective assert GHOSTS u[nxl] == PROC[right].u[0] \
    && u[1] == PROC[left].u[PROC[left].nxl+1];
  update();
#pragma TASS joint assert COMPARE forall {int i | 1<=i && i<=nxl} \
    u[i]==spec.u[first+i-1];
}
```
(a) main loop in parallel version (implementation)

```
for (time = 1; time <= nsteps; time++) {
  update();
#pragma TASS joint assert COMPARE true;
}
```
(b) main loop in sequential version (specification)

Fig. 3. TASS collective assertion pragmas in 1d-diffusion code

the other m, we can consider the two programs together to be a single program with $n + m$ processes running concurrently. All of the definitions of Sections 2 and 3 apply; the urgent POR scheme will automatically avoid exploring the unnecessary interleavings resulting from this combination. An advantage of this approach over the standard comparative method is that if a discrepancy is detected, it can be reported immediately, rather than waiting until both programs have terminated. It is also helpful in isolating the source of a fault.

The keyword `joint` can be used in place of `collective` to indicate a collective assertion that is to be used when comparing two programs. These pragmas will be ignored when verifying either program individually. Typically, the asserted expression in the specification will be vacuous ("`true`") so the pragma in the specification is used only to label a location. A reasonable policy is to forbid references to implementations within the specification, while implementations can and should refer to the specification.

A joint assertion is used in Fig. 3. It asserts the values of the non-ghost cells held by this process agree with the corresponding values in the specification. This is checked at the end of each time step, rather than only at termination.

TASS verifies collective assertions by performing a depth-first search of the transition system ATS defined in Section 3. To implement this, we added local state queues to the state, and a special handler is executed whenever a process reaches a collective location. One implementation detail concerns the way the local state snapshots are stored in each state. In TASS, these process states are immutable objects which are created using the Flyweight design pattern. Hence the queues contain only references to the process states, each of which was created at an earlier point in the execution. If the entire process state data were instead duplicated in each state, the memory required to store the states would be prohibitively large.

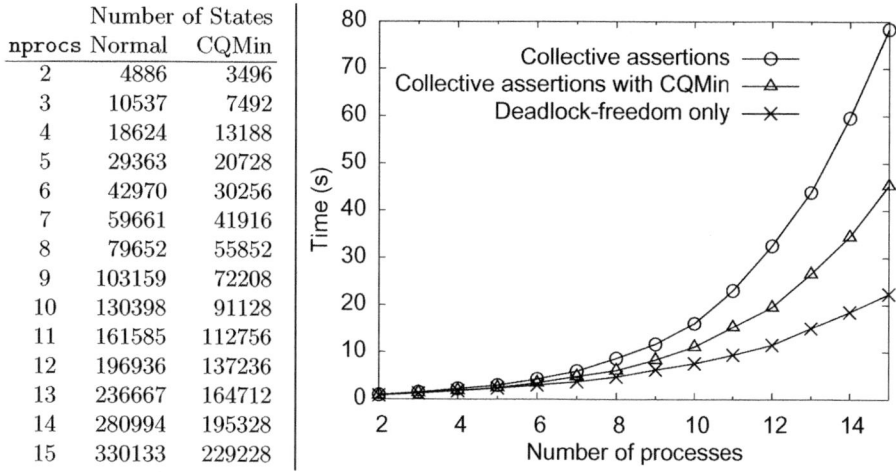

	Number of States	
nprocs	Normal	CQMin
2	4886	3496
3	10537	7492
4	18624	13188
5	29363	20728
6	42970	30256
7	59661	41916
8	79652	55852
9	103159	72208
10	130398	91128
11	161585	112756
12	196936	137236
13	236667	164712
14	280994	195328
15	330133	229228

Fig. 4. Verification of diffusion1d, comparing parallel and sequential versions. NX is bounded by 3*nprocs, NSTEPS by 2. For each value of nprocs, three experiments were run: (a) verifying only absence of potential deadlock, (b) verifying that and the collective assertions, and (c) same as (b) but using the queue-minimizing heuristic (CQMin).

4.3   Scaling Experiment

After successfully verifying the two collective assertions in small configurations of the 1d-diffusion code, we decided to scale this example to gauge the cost of verifying the assertions. We scaled the number of processes n from 2 to 15 and for each n conducted three experiments. All three involve using TASS to compare the sequential and parallel versions, as well as verify absence of deadlocks.

In the first experiment, used as a baseline, we turned the assertion checking off (so only the deadlock property was checked). In the second experiment, we checked the collective assertion and the deadlock property using the default heuristic for the urgent POR scheme. In the third experiment, we checked the assertion and the deadlock property, but used a novel *collective queue minimization* heuristic. This heuristic selects, among all "urgent" processes, a process with the shortest local state queue. The idea is to try to keep the processes as "close together" as possible. In some cases, such as this diffusion example, this heuristic essentially imposes a barrier at the collective assertion point. In other cases, it will not impose such a barrier, and it would not be safe to do so (see example *wildcard_gather* below). As described in Section 4.1, in all cases the heuristic is safe, i.e., a violation will be found if one exists.

In each case, we recorded the verification time and the number of states explored. All were run on a 2.8GHz quad-core Intel i7 iMac with 16GB RAM.

The results are shown in Fig. 4. Note that there is a substantial cost to collective assertion checking in terms of time: up to 4× at the worst case. Nevertheless, even the maximum time of 80 seconds is not unreasonable. There is no difference in the number of states between the baseline and the first collective assertion experiment because (1) both use the same POR algorithm and (2) in this example, the state space is a tree, so there is never a case where the introduction of the snapshots can cause a pair of states that matched in the first case to fail to match in the second. The queue minimization heuristic led to a reduction in the number of states and cut the runtime almost in half.

4.4   Further Examples

We examined the examples distributed with TASS for other opportunities where collective assertions could express useful properties. We have found such opportunities in virtually every case and report on a representative sample here. We then used TASS to verify these assertions.

```
for (i=0; i<N; i++) {              for (i=1; i<=N; i++) {
    x = x + a[i];                      x = ((i-1)*x + a[i-1])/i;
    #pragma TASS joint assert C true;  #pragma TASS joint assert C x*i==spec.x;
}                                  }
m = x/N;                           m = x;
#pragma TASS joint assert M true;  #pragma TASS joint assert M m == spec.m;
```

Fig. 5. Two ways to compute the mean of an array of floating-point numbers

Mean. This is an example where the assertion is more complicated that just "$x = y$". Fig. 5 shows two different ways to compute the mean of an array of N floating-point numbers. The first corresponds exactly to the standard definition: it sums the elements and divides the result by N. The second computes a "running mean": after the ith iteration the value of x should be the mean of the first i numbers. The assertion relating these is x*i==spec.x, which is checked at the end of each loop iteration. A joint assertion at the end claims the final results should agree, which indeed holds. (This relies on the fact that TASS interprets arithmetic to take place over the mathematical reals instead of floating-point numbers.) When verified with N bounded above by 10, TASS explored 132 states and took 0.3 seconds.

Wildcard_gather. This example demonstrates that it is not always safe to verify a collective assertion by imposing a barrier at the assertion. The program of Fig. 6 is composed of a root process (rank 0) and $n-1$ worker processes. Each worker sends one number to the root, which in this case happens to be the worker's PID. The root receives these in whatever order they arrive (using a wildcard receive) and inserts the number into an array at the position which is the rank of the sending process. The routine is called twice in a row.

   The collective assertion is invoked once by each process in each call. It asserts that the value stored in the root's array agrees with the value sent. The code is incorrect: a race condition may occur if one worker sends, then proceeds to the second call and sends again; meanwhile, the root is still in the first invocation but receives this second message at the wildcard receive. This results in the entry

```
int myrank, nprocs; double *a, x;

void root() {
  MPI_Status status; int i;
  a = (double*)malloc(nprocs*sizeof(double));
  a[0] = 0.0;
  for (i=1; i<nprocs; i++) {
    MPI_Recv(&x, 1, MPI_DOUBLE, MPI_ANY_SOURCE, 0, MPI_COMM_WORLD, &status);
    a[status.MPI_SOURCE] = x;
  }
#pragma TASS collective assert C true;
  free(a);
}

void worker() {
  x = PID;
  MPI_Send(&x, 1, MPI_DOUBLE, 0, 0, MPI_COMM_WORLD);
#pragma TASS collective assert C x==PROC[0].a[myrank];
}

void main() {
  int argc; char **argv; int i;
  MPI_Init(&argc, &argv);
  MPI_Comm_rank(MPI_COMM_WORLD, &myrank);
  MPI_Comm_size(MPI_COMM_WORLD, &nprocs);
  for (i=0; i<2; i++) if (PID == 0) root(); else worker();
  MPI_Finalize();
}
```

Fig. 6. *Wildcard_gather*: a gather routine that uses a wildcard at root. One number from each non-root process is sent to root, which inserts it into an array. The routine has a race condition revealed by a violation to collective assertion C.

for that process getting set again (in this case, to the same value), while the message from some other process remains unreceived in the first invocation. The array entry for that process will still contain the initial undefined value when the root reaches the collective assertion point and the snapshot is taken, leading to a violation when the assertion expression is evaluated.

If a barrier is placed at the collective assertion point, the race condition disappears: no worker can proceed into the second iteration until the root has received all $n-1$ messages. Hence a system that only checked executions that synchronize at assertion points would fail to detect the race condition.

For 10 processes, the error is detected by TASS after exploring 1011 states. The execution time, which includes the time to write the violating trace to disc, was 0.5 seconds.

Laplace2d. This is the most complex example we studied. It is a numerical solution to the 2d-Laplace equation. The algorithm works on a row-distributed 2d-grid with fixed boundary values. The update formula depends on a cell's upper, lower, right, and left neighbors. Rather than iterate for a fixed number of time steps, as in the diffusion case, the program iterates until a certain convergence criterion is reached (or a bound on the maximum number of iterations is reached, whichever occurs first). The convergence criterion is that the L_2 norm between two consecutive approximate solution falls below a given threshold ϵ. Again, we used TASS to compare a sequential and parallel version. In the parallel version, each process computes the contribution to the error resulting from the rows it owns. These local errors are summed at the end of each iteration to obtain the global error, which is then returned to every process. (This is implemented using a single `MPI_Allgather` collective operation). The joint assertion we formulated claims that at each iteration, the global error in each process in the parallel program agrees with the global error in the sequential program on the corresponding iteration. We successfully verified this assertion for various small configurations. For 6 processes, the dimensions of the grid bounded above by 4×12, and the number of iterations bounded by 3 (inclusive), TASS completed in 18.0 seconds, exploring 49,419 states.

5   Related Work

Composing local snapshots to form a global state of a distributed system is not a new idea. Chandy and Lamport used this notion in their algorithm for computing a globally consistent state [4]. This algorithm has been extended in many directions; see for example [9] and the references cited there. The goal of this line of work is to construct a state that is "close to" an actual global state occurring in the execution, where "close to" preserves some specified class of predicates, such as deadlock or termination. Simmons shows how these notions can be extended to efficiently check a global assertion in a single process by using earlier snapshots, as long as no actions could have taken place in the other processes to impact the evaluation of the global expression [14,15]. Much of the hard work is in figuring out when a process should take its snapshot in order to be consistent with other processes and not affect the property of interest.

Our focus is different: we are not interested in finding a globally consistent set of snapshots or any notion of "close to." Instead, the user decides exactly where the snapshots are to be taken in each process by explicitly placing collective assertion statements at appropriate points. In fact, the selection of these locations is an important part of the specification of the desired behavior. We thus do not have to worry about the many difficult issues that arise in the global assertion approach. (Nor are we concerned with capturing a consistent view of the channel states, a major source of complexity in the earlier work.) Also, for an analysis tool such as TASS, the mechanics of gathering the snapshots is trivial, since TASS itself is not a distributed program.

The basic approach underlying TASS, which combines symbolic execution with a search of the reachable states of a parallel program, was introduced in [6]. There are many other approaches to debugging and verifying parallel programs that may also apply to the kinds of problems discussed here. Kovacs et al. have developed a debugger that can check linear temporal logic formulas on a particular trace as the user guides the execution [8]. The ISP verifier is a dynamic model checker that uses a modified runtime system to explore all relevant behaviors of an MPI program to verify certain safety properties [17]. Both of these approaches, however, only operate on a given concrete input, in contrast to the symbolic execution approach taken by TASS.

There are many other methods for verifying functional equivalence of *sequential* programs; see for example [16] for an approach that can handle complex loop transformations. KLEE is another symbolic execution tool that has been used to check equivalence of sequential programs [3].

6   Conclusion

Collective assertions appear to be a natural way to express many correctness properties of distributed multiprocess programs. We have explored how to verify these assertions in small instances of the programs using TASS, but many questions remain. Can runtime checking of collective assertions be implemented effectively at full scale? To do so would require careful reasoning to determine what part of a process's state is required to evaluate an expression, as sending an entire process snapshot is not feasible for realistic programs.

When multiple collective assertions occur in a program, our semantics requires that each process encounter these assertions in the same order. This may not be the most appropriate choice for all problems. For example, the user might want to specify that two collective assertions are completely independent of each other, and can be encountered in different orders by two processes. A flexible approach would allow the users to specify distinct "communication universes" for this end. Like an MPI *communicator*, each such universe would have associated to it some subset of processes. Each collective assertion would then specify the universe to which it belongs. The assertions within one universe would be required to occur in the same order for every process in that universe's process set. For assertions in two different universes, there would be no such constraint.

We have extended C's expression language to include references to other processes and first-order quantifiers. What other operations would be useful? A sum operator is an obvious candidate, and undoubtedly many array operations could help specify important properties.

The semantics for collective assertions for infinite executions is weak. Would a more useful definition require every entry in a local state queue to eventually be consumed? It would be interesting to see if collective assertions can be applied usefully to reactive programs.

Finally, the general idea of making collective analogs of sequential constructs could have other applications. We have recently begun using TASS to explore "collective loop invariants." In many cases, these enable TASS to verify properties of a parallel program with unbounded loops.

References

1. Baier, C., Katoen, J.-P.: Principles of Model Checking. The MIT Press, Cambridge (2008)
2. Barrett, C., Tinelli, C.: CVC3. In: Damm, W., Hermanns, H. (eds.) CAV 2007. LNCS, vol. 4590, pp. 298–302. Springer, Heidelberg (2007)
3. Cadar, C., Dunbar, D., Engler, D.: KLEE: Unassisted and automatic generation of high-coverage tests for complex systems programs. In: Proc. 8th USENIX Symposium on Operating Systems Design and Implementation (2008)
4. Chandy, K.M., Lamport, L.: Distributed snapshots: Determining global states of distributed systems. ACM Trans. Comput. Syst. 3(1), 63–75 (1985)
5. Godefroid, P. (ed.): Partial-Order Methods for the Verification of Concurrent Systems. LNCS, vol. 1032. Springer, Heidelberg (1996)
6. Khurshid, S., Păsăreanu, C.S., Visser, W.: Generalized symbolic execution for model checking and testing. In: Garavel, H., Hatcliff, J. (eds.) TACAS 2003. LNCS, vol. 2619, pp. 553–568. Springer, Heidelberg (2003)
7. King, J.C.: Symbolic execution and program testing. Comm. ACM 19(7), 385–394 (1976)
8. Kovács, J., Kusper, G., Lovas, R., Schreiner, W.: Integrating temporal assertions into a parallel debugger. In: Monien, B., Feldmann, R.L. (eds.) Euro-Par 2002. LNCS, vol. 2400, pp. 113–120. Springer, Heidelberg (2002)
9. Kshemkalyani, A.D.: Fast and message-efficient global snapshot algorithms for large-scale distributed systems. IEEE Transactions on Parallel and Distributed Systems 21, 1281–1289 (2010)
10. Message Passing Interface Forum: MPI: A Message-Passing Interface Standard, version 2.2, September 4 (2009), http://www.mpi-forum.org/docs/
11. Siegel, S.F., et al.: The Toolkit for Accurate Scientific Software web page (2010), http://vsl.cis.udel.edu/tass
12. Siegel, S.F.: Efficient verification of halting properties for MPI programs with wildcard receives. In: Cousot, R. (ed.) VMCAI 2005. LNCS, vol. 3385, pp. 413–429. Springer, Heidelberg (2005)
13. Siegel, S.F., Mironova, A., Avrunin, G.S., Clarke, L.A.: Combining symbolic execution with model checking to verify parallel numerical programs. ACM TOSEM 17(2), Article 10, 1–34 (2008)
14. Simmons, S., Kearns, P.: A causal assert statement for distributed systems. In: Hamza, M.H. (ed.) Parallel and Distributed Computing and Systems, pp. 495–498. IASTED/ACTA Press (1995)
15. Simmons, S.J.: Causal distributed assert statements. Ph.D. thesis. The College of William and Mary, director-Kearns, Phil (1999)
16. Verdoolaege, S., Janssens, G., Bruynooghe, M.: Equivalence checking of static affine programs using widening to handle recurrences. In: Bouajjani, A., Maler, O. (eds.) CAV 2009. LNCS, vol. 5643, pp. 599–613. Springer, Heidelberg (2009)
17. Vo, A., Vakkalanka, S., DeLisi, M., Gopalakrishnan, G., Kirby, R.M., Thakur, R.: Formal verification of practical MPI programs. In: PPoPP 2009: Proceedings of the 14th ACM SIGPLAN Symposium on Principles and Practice of Parallel Programming, pp. 261–270. ACM, New York (2009)

Sets with Cardinality Constraints in Satisfiability Modulo Theories

Philippe Suter*, Robin Steiger, and Viktor Kuncak

École Polytechnique Fédérale de Lausanne (EPFL), Switzerland
`firstname.lastname@epfl.ch`

Abstract. Boolean Algebra with Presburger Arithmetic (BAPA) is a decidable logic that can express constraints on sets of elements and their cardinalities. Problems from verification of complex properties of software often contain fragments that belong to quantifier-free BAPA (QFBAPA). In contrast to many other NP-complete problems (such as quantifier-free first-order logic or linear arithmetic), the applications of QFBAPA to a broader set of problems has so far been hindered by the lack of an efficient implementation that can be used alongside other efficient decision procedures. We overcome these limitations by extending the efficient SMT solver Z3 with the ability to reason about cardinality (QFBAPA) constraints. Our implementation uses the DPLL(T) mechanism of Z3 to reason about the top-level propositional structure of a QFBAPA formula, improving the efficiency compared to previous implementations. Moreover, we present a new algorithm for automatically decomposing QFBAPA formulas. Our algorithm alleviates the exponential explosion of considering all Venn regions, significantly improving the tractability of formulas with many set variables. Because it is implemented as a theory plugin, our implementation enables Z3 to prove formulas that use QFBAPA constructs with constructs from other theories that Z3 supports, as well as with quantifiers. We have applied our implementation to the verification of functional programs; we show it can automatically prove formulas that no automated approach was reported to be able to prove before.

1 Introduction

Sets naturally arise in software that performs discrete computation, as a built-in data type [2], as container libraries, or inside program specification constructs [11, 20]. An intrinsic part of reasoning about sets is reasoning about sizes of sets, with well-known associated laws such as the inclusion-exclusion principle $|A \cup B| = |A| + |B| - |A \cap B|$. A natural decidable logic that supports set operations (union, intersection, complement) as well as a cardinality operator is a logic we call BAPA, for Boolean Algebra with Presburger Arithmetic [3, 8].

We here consider the quantifier-free fragment of BAPA, denoted QFBAPA. QFBAPA was shown to be NP-complete using a particular encoding into quantifier-free Presburger arithmetic that exploits an integer analogue of Carathéodory

---

* Philippe Suter was supported by the Swiss NSF Grant 200021_120433.

R. Jhala and D. Schmidt (Eds.): VMCAI 2011, LNCS 6538, pp. 403–418, 2011.
© Springer-Verlag Berlin Heidelberg 2011

theorem [10]. We thus think of QFBAPA as a generalization of SAT that is similar to SAT from a high-level complexity-theory point of view. The richness of QFBAPA is reflected in the fact that, being propositionally closed, it subsumes SAT. Moreover, unlike SAT, no encoding is needed to represent integer linear arithmetic in BAPA. Crucially, BAPA supports set operations and cardinality, whose polynomial encoding into SAT is possible but non-trivial [10]. Strikingly, a number of expressive logics can be naturally reduced to QFBAPA [17, 9]. This enables combination of formulas from non-disjoint theory signatures that share set operations, and goes beyond current disjoint theory combinations.

However, although the QFBAPA satisfiability problem is NP-complete, the resulting algorithm has proven difficult for unsatisfiable QFBAPA instances; its improvements have primarily helped dealing with satisfiable instances [10]. This empirical observation is in contrast to the situation for propositional logic, for which the community developed SAT solvers that are effective in showing unsatisfiability for large industrial benchmarks. In this paper we present a QFBAPA implementation that is effective both for satisfiable and unsatisfiable instances.

Our implementation incorporates an important new algorithmic component: a decomposition of constraints based on the hypergraphs of common set variables. This component analyzes the variables occurring in different atomic formulas within a QFBAPA formula and uses the structural property of the formula to avoid generating all Venn regions. Our implementation is integrated into the state-of-the-art SMT solver Z3, whose important feature is efficient support for linear arithmetic [13]. Efficient integration with Z3 was made possible by the recently introduced theory plugin architecture of Z3, as well as by an incremental implementation of our algorithm. In this integration, Z3 processes top level propositional structure of the formula, providing QFBAPA solver with conjunctions of QFBAPA constraints. Our solver generates lemmas in integer linear arithmetic and gives them back to Z3, which incorporates them with other integer constraints. At the same time, Z3 takes care of equality constraints. The net result is (1) dramatic improvement of efficiency compared to previously reported QFBAPA implementations (2) the ability to use QFBAPA cardinality operation alongside all other operations that Z3 supports. We illustrate the usefulness of this approach through experimental results that prove the validity of complex verifications condition arising from the verification of imperative as well as functional programs.

Contributions. In summary, our paper makes the following contributions:

- decomposition theorems and algorithms for efficient handling of QFBAPA cardinality constraints, often avoiding the need for exponentially many Venn regions as in [8], and avoiding complex conditional sums as in [10];
- an incremental algorithm to analyze the structure of QFBAPA formulas and generate the integer constraints following the decomposition theorems;
- an implementation of these algorithms as a theory plugin for the Z3 solver, with support for detecting equalities entailed by QFBAPA constraints and therefore precise combination with other theories supported by Z3;

– encouraging experimental results for benchmarks arising from verification of imperative and functional programs.

2   Example

We next illustrate the expressive power of the SMT prover we obtained by incorporating our QFBAPA decision procedure into Z3. Given a list datatype in a functional programming language, consider the question of proving that the set of elements contained in the list has a cardinality always less than or equal to the length of the list. The set of elements contained in the list and the length of the list are computed using natural recursive functions, specified below in the syntax of the Scala programming language:

```
def content(list: List[Int]) : Set[Int] = list match {
  case Nil ⇒ ∅
  case Cons(x, xs) ⇒ {x} ∪ content(xs)
}
def length(list: List[Int]) : Int = list match {
  case Nil ⇒ 0
  case Cons(x, xs) ⇒ 1 + length(xs)
}
```

Our goal is to prove the property:

$$\forall list : \mathsf{List[Int]} \ . \ |\, \mathsf{content}(list)\,| \leq \mathsf{length}(list)$$

We proceed by unfolding the recursive definitions sufficiently many times to obtain the following verification condition:

$$list \neq \mathsf{Nil} \implies list = \mathsf{Cons}(x, xs)$$
$$\wedge \ \mathsf{length}(\mathsf{Nil}) = 0 \wedge \mathsf{length}(\mathsf{Cons}(x, xs)) = 1 + \mathsf{length}(xs)$$
$$\wedge \ \mathsf{content}(\mathsf{Nil}) = \emptyset \wedge \mathsf{content}(\mathsf{Cons}(x, xs)) = \{x\} \cup \mathsf{content}(xs)$$
$$\wedge \ |\, \mathsf{content}(xs)\,| \leq \mathsf{length}(xs)$$
$$\implies |\, \mathsf{content}(list)\,| \leq \mathsf{length}(list)$$

Note that the formula includes reasoning about function symbols, integers, algebraic data types, sets, and cardinalities of sets. To the best of our knowledge, the implementation we present in this paper is the only one that is complete for proving the validity of formulas with such operators. The proof is found using Z3's DPLL(T) algorithm, which, among others, performs cases analysis on whether *list* is empty. It relies on Z3 to support arithmetic, congruence properties of functions, and algebraic data types. Finally, it crucially relies on invocations of our QFBAPA plugin. In response to currently asserted QFBAPA constraints, our plugin generates integer constraints on Venn regions that are chosen to ensure that the relationships between sets are handled in a complete way. The entire theorem proving process takes negligible time (see Section 5 for experimental results).

3 Decomposition in Solving BAPA Constraints

In this section, we consider formulas over finite sets of uninterpreted elements from a domain $\mathbb{E}$. We show in Section 4 how we combined QFBAPA with other theories to obtain a theory of sets of interpreted elements.

Syntax. Figure 1 presents the syntax of QFBAPA. We use $\mathsf{vars}(\phi)$ to denote the set of free set variables occurring in ϕ.

$$
\begin{aligned}
\phi &::= A \mid \phi_1 \wedge \phi_2 \mid \phi_1 \vee \phi_2 \mid \neg\phi \\
A &::= S_1 = S_2 \mid S_1 \subseteq S_2 \mid T_1 = T_2 \mid T_1 \leq T_2 \\
S &::= s \mid \emptyset \mid \mathcal{U} \mid S_1 \cup S_2 \mid S_1 \cap S_2 \mid S_1 \setminus S_2 \mid S^c \\
T &::= i \mid K \mid T_1 + T_2 \mid K \cdot T \mid |S| \\
K &::= \dots \mid -2 \mid -1 \mid 0 \mid 1 \mid 2 \mid \dots
\end{aligned}
$$

Fig. 1. Quantifier-Free Formulas of Boolean Algebra with Presburger Arithmetic (QFBAPA). S^c denotes the complement of the set S with respect to the universe $\mathcal{U}$, that is, $\mathcal{U} \setminus S$.

Definition 1 (Venn regions). *One central notion throughout the presentation of the theorems and the decision procedure is the notion of* Venn region. *A Venn region of n sets $S = \{S_1, \dots, S_n\}$ is one of the 2^n set expressions described by $\bigcap_{i=1}^{n} S_i^{\alpha_i}$ where $S_i^{\alpha_i}$ is either S_i or S_i^c. By construction, the 2^n regions form a partition of $\mathcal{U}$. We write $\mathsf{venn}(S)$ to denote the set of all Venn regions formed with the sets in S.*

Semantics. An interpretation $\mathcal{M}$ of a QFBAPA formula ϕ is a map from the set variables of ϕ to finite subsets of $\mathbb{E}$ and from the integer variables of ϕ to values in $\mathbb{Z}$. It is a model of ϕ, denoted $\mathcal{M} \models \phi$ if the following conditions are satisfied:

- $\mathcal{U}^{\mathcal{M}}$ is a finite subset of $\mathbb{E}$ and $\emptyset^{\mathcal{M}}$ is the empty set
- for each set variable S of ϕ, $S^{\mathcal{M}} \subseteq \mathcal{U}^{\mathcal{M}}$
- for each integer variable k of ϕ, $k^{\mathcal{M}} \in \mathbb{Z}$
- when $=, \subseteq, \emptyset, \cup, \cap, \setminus$ and the cardinality function $|\cdot|$ are interpreted as expected, ϕ evaluates to true in $\mathcal{M}$

Definition 2. *We define $\sim_V$ to be the equivalence relation on interpretations, parametrized by a set of set variables V, such that:*

$$\mathcal{M}_1 \sim_V \mathcal{M}_2 \iff \forall v \in \mathsf{venn}(V) \ . \ |v^{\mathcal{M}_1}| = |v^{\mathcal{M}_2}|$$

Definition 3. *Let $\mathcal{M}$ be an interpretation and $f : \mathbb{E} \to \mathbb{E}$ a bijection from the interpretation domain to itself (a permutation function). We denote by $f[\mathcal{M}]$ the interpretation such that:*

- $\mathcal{U}^{f[\mathcal{M}]} = \{f(u) \mid u \in \mathcal{U}^{\mathcal{M}}\}$
- for each set variable S interpreted in $\mathcal{M}$, $S^{f[\mathcal{M}]} = \{f(u) \mid u \in S^{\mathcal{M}}\}$
- for each integer variable k interpreted in $\mathcal{M}$, $k^{f[\mathcal{M}]} = k^{\mathcal{M}}$

Theorem 1. *Let ϕ be a QFBAPA formula, $\mathcal{M}$ a model of ϕ and $f : \mathbb{E} \to \mathbb{E}$ a bijection, then $f[\mathcal{M}] \models \phi$.*

Proof. Prove by induction that $t^{f[\mathcal{M}]} = f[t^{\mathcal{M}}]$ for every set algebra term t. By bijectivity of f, $|t^{f[\mathcal{M}]}| = |f[t^{\mathcal{M}}]|$, so the values of all integer-valued terms remain invariant under f. Finally, note that $S_1 \subseteq S_2$ reduces to $|S_1 \setminus S_2| = 0$ whereas $S_1 = S_2$ reduces to $|S_1 \setminus S_2| = 0 \land |S_2 \setminus S_1| = 0$.

3.1 A Simple Decision Procedure for QFBAPA

A simple technique for solving QFBAPA formulas is to reduce the problem to integer linear arithmetic as follows. Introduce a fresh integer variable for each Venn region in $\mathsf{venn}(\mathsf{vars}(\phi))$. Rewrite each constraint of the form $S_1 = S_2$ as $S_1 \subseteq S_2 \land S_2 \subseteq S_1$, and each constraint of the form $S_1 \subseteq S_2$ as $|S_1 \setminus S_2| = 0$. Finally, use sums over the integer variables representing the Venn regions to rewrite the cardinality constraints. This reduction is simple to understand and to implement, but always requires 2^N integer variables, where N is the number of elements in $\mathsf{vars}(\phi)$. In the following, we show how to reduce this number considerably in many cases that arise in practice.

Note that what we describe below is largely orthogonal to the NP procedure in [10]. Our results should in principle apply both to the naive procedure sketched above, and to the sparse encoding procedure in [10]. Note that the NP procedure from [10], although theoretically optimal, has so far been shown to be practically useful only for satisfiable cases. For unsatisfiable cases the sparse encoding generates quantifier-free Presburger arithmetic formulas that are difficult for current SMT solver implementations.

3.2 Decomposing Conjunctions of QFBAPA Formulas

The decision procedure presented in Section 3.1 requires many integer variables because it uses a variable for the intersection of *every* combination of set variables. The intuition behind the following result is that permutations of elements within sets that are not related by a constraint in a formula do not affect the satisfiability of that formula.

Theorem 2. *Let ϕ_1 and ϕ_2 be two QFBAPA formulas. Let V_1 and V_2 denote the sets of set variables appearing in ϕ_1 and ϕ_2, respectively. Let $V_S = V_1 \cap V_2$ be the set of shared variables. Let K_S represent the set of shared integer variables. The QFBAPA formula $\phi \equiv \phi_1 \land \phi_2$ is satisfiable if and only if there exists a model $\mathcal{M}_1$ for ϕ_1 and a model $\mathcal{M}_2$ for ϕ_2 such that, for each integer variable $k \in K_S$, $k^{\mathcal{M}_1} = k^{\mathcal{M}_2}$, and such that $\mathcal{M}_1 \sim_{V_S} \mathcal{M}_2$.*

Proof. We construct a model $\mathcal{M}$ for ϕ by extending $\mathcal{M}_1$ to the variables in $V_2 \backslash V_S$. (The other direction is immediate.) We show that there exists a permutation f on $\mathbb{E}$ such that $f[v^{\mathcal{M}_2}] = v^{\mathcal{M}_1}$ for each Venn region $v \in \mathsf{venn}(V_S)$. In other words, f is a bijection that projects the interpretation in $\mathcal{M}_2$ of all intersections of the shared variables to their interpretation in $\mathcal{M}_1$. We construct f as follows: for each Venn region $v \in \mathsf{venn}(V_S)$, let f_v be a bijection from $v^{\mathcal{M}_2}$ to $v^{\mathcal{M}_1}$. Note that f_v always exists because $v^{\mathcal{M}_1}$ and $v^{\mathcal{M}_2}$ have the same cardinality, by $\sim_{V_S}$. Let $f^\star$ be $\bigcup_{v \in \mathsf{venn}(V_S)} f_v$. Observe that $f^\star$ is a bijection from $\mathcal{U}^{\mathcal{M}_2}$ to $\mathcal{U}^{\mathcal{M}_1}$, because $\mathsf{venn}(V_S)$ forms a partition of $\mathcal{U}$ in both models. To obtain the desired f, we can extend $f^\star$ to the domain and range $\mathbb{E}$ by taking its union with any bijection from $\mathbb{E} \setminus \mathcal{U}^{\mathcal{M}_2}$ to $\mathbb{E} \setminus \mathcal{U}^{\mathcal{M}_1}$. The model $\mathcal{M} = \mathcal{M}_1 \cup f[\mathcal{M}_2]$ is a model of ϕ_1 (trivially) and of ϕ_2 (by Theorem 1), therefore, it is a model of ϕ.

The following result is a generalization of Theorem 2 for a conjunction of arbitrarily many constraints.

Theorem 3. *Let $\phi_1, \ldots, \phi_n$ be n QFBAPA formulas. Let V_i denote $\mathsf{vars}(\phi_i)$ for $i \in \{1, \ldots, n\}$. Let*

$$V_S = \bigcup_{1 \leq i < j \leq n} V_i \cap V_j$$

be the set of all variables that appear in at least two sets V_i and V_j. The formula $\phi_1 \wedge \ldots \wedge \phi_n$ is satisfiable if and only if: 1) there exist models $\mathcal{M}_1, \ldots, \mathcal{M}_n$ such that, for each i, $\mathcal{M}_i \models \phi_i$ and 2) there exists an interpretation $\mathcal{M}$ of the variables V_S such that $\mathcal{M} \sim_{V_S \cap V_i} \mathcal{M}_i$ for each $1 \leq i \leq n$.

(Note that the conditions imply that $|\mathcal{U}^{\mathcal{M}}| = |\mathcal{U}^{\mathcal{M}_i}|$ for each i.) The proof follows the idea of the proof of Theorem 2: it suffices to show that one can extend the model $\mathcal{M}$ to each model $\mathcal{M}_i$ by finding a bijection f_i. Note that f_i is guaranteed to exist because $\mathcal{M} \sim_{V_S \cap V_i} \mathcal{M}_i$.

Remark. It is not sufficient that for each $0 \leq i < j \leq n$, $\mathcal{M}_i \sim_{(V_i \cap V_j)} \mathcal{M}_j$, that is, that there exists bijections between all pairs of models $\mathcal{M}_i$ and $\mathcal{M}_j$. A simple counter-example is given by the (unsatisfiable) constraints:

$$\phi_1 \equiv |A| = 1 \wedge |B| = 1 \wedge |A \cap B| = 1$$
$$\phi_2 \equiv |A| = 1 \wedge |C| = 1 \wedge |A \cap C| = 1$$
$$\phi_3 \equiv |B| = 1 \wedge |C| = 1 \wedge |B \cap C| = 0$$

Although any conjunction $\phi_i \wedge \phi_j$ can be shown satisfiable using Theorem 2, the conjunction $\phi_1 \wedge \phi_2 \wedge \phi_3$ is unsatisfiable, because a common model $\mathcal{M}$ cannot be built from models for each three constraints.

Lemma 1. *Let $\phi_1, \ldots, \phi_n$ be n QFBAPA formulas, and let $V_1, \ldots, V_n, V_S$ be defined as above. Assume there exist $\mathcal{M}, \mathcal{M}_1, \ldots, \mathcal{M}_n$ satisfying the conditions of Theorem 3 and the additional condition that:*

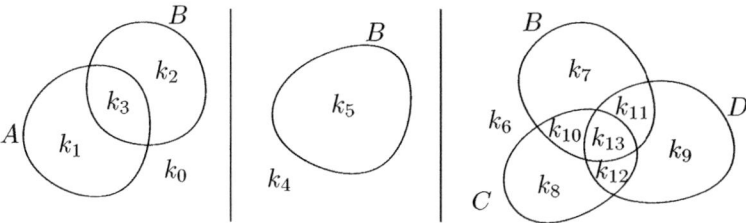

Fig. 2. Independent naming of the Venn regions of set variables $V_1 = \{A, B\}$, $V_S = \{B\}$, and $V_2 = \{B, C, D\}$

$$|\mathcal{U}^\mathcal{M}| \geq |\bigcup_{S \in V_S} S^\mathcal{M}| + \sum_{i=1}^{n} |\bigcup_{S \in V_i \setminus V_S} S^{\mathcal{M}_i}|$$

Then there exists a model $\mathcal{M}_d$ such that, for any two sets $S_i \in V_i \setminus V_S$ and $S_j \in V_j \setminus V_S$ (with $i \neq j$), if (1) $\forall S \in V_S \cap V_i$. $\mathcal{M}_i \models S_i \neq S$ and (2) $\forall S \in V_S \cap V_j$. $\mathcal{M}_j \models S_j \neq S$, and (3) either $\mathcal{M}_i \models S_i \neq \emptyset$ or $\mathcal{M}_j \models S_j \neq \emptyset$, then $\mathcal{M}_d \models S_i \neq S_j$.

Intuitively, Lemma 1 states that for two sets variables that appear in different constraints and that are not shared, if there exists a model in which these sets are not empty and are not equal to some shared set variable, then there exists a model in which the two sets are not equal. The correctness follows from the fact that with $\mathcal{U}^\mathcal{M}$ sufficiently large, it is always possible to find bijections f_i such that for each i the non-shared sets are mapped to a different subset of $\mathcal{U}$. We omit the details of the proof in the interest of space.

Lemma 2. *The additional conditions of Lemma 1 are fulfilled when $\mathbb{E}$ is infinite and $|\mathcal{U}|$ is not constrained in any formula ϕ_i.*

This result is important for the combination of QFBAPA with other theories, as explained in Section 4. The proof follows from the fact that with an infinite domain $\mathbb{E}$ and an unconstrained universe $\mathcal{U}$, if there exists a model, we can extend it to a model $\mathcal{M}$ where $|\mathcal{U}^\mathcal{M}|$ is sufficiently large.

A decision procedure based on decompositions. Theorem 3 yields a decision procedure for the satisfiability of conjunctions of QFBAPA constraints $\phi_1 \wedge \ldots \wedge \phi_n$: independently for ϕ_1 to ϕ_n, introduce integer variables for the regions of $\mathsf{venn}(V_1)$, ..., $\mathsf{venn}(V_n)$, respectively, then introduce fresh variables for the regions of $\mathsf{venn}(V_S)$, where V_S is computed as in the theorem. Finally, constrain the sums of variables representing the same regions to be equal. (This ensures that the bijections f_i can be constructed in the satisfiable case.) As an example, consider the formula

$$|A \setminus B| > |A \cap B| \wedge B \cap C \cap D = \emptyset \wedge |B \setminus D| > |B \setminus C|$$

Let ϕ_1 be the first conjunct and ϕ_2 the other two. We have $V_1 = \{A, B\}$ and $V_2 = \{B, C, D\}$. Using the naming for regions shown in Figure 2, we obtain the integer constraints

$$
\begin{aligned}
&k_1 > k_3 && \text{reduction of } \phi_1 \\
&\wedge\, k_{13} = 0 \wedge k_7 + k_{10} > k_7 + k_{11} && \text{reduction of } \phi_2 \\
&\wedge\, k_4 = k_0 + k_1 = k_6 + k_8 + k_9 + k_{12} && \text{representations of } |\,B^c\,| \\
&\wedge\, k_5 = k_2 + k_3 = k_7 + k_{10} + k_{11} + k_{13} && \text{representations of } |\,B\,|
\end{aligned}
$$

A possible satisfying assignment for the integer variables is $k_4 = 2$, $k_0 = k_1 = k_2 = k_5 = k_8 = k_9 = k_{10} = 1$, and $k_3 = k_6 = k_7 = k_{11} = k_{12} = k_{13} = 0$. From these values, we can build the assignment to set variables

$$
\begin{aligned}
&\mathcal{U}_1 = \{e_1, e_2, e_3\},\, A = \{e_1\},\, B = \{e_2\} && \text{for } \phi_1 \\
&\mathcal{U}_2 = \{e_4, e_5, e_6\},\, B = \{e_4\},\, C = \{e_4, e_5\},\, D = \{e_6\} && \text{for } \phi_2
\end{aligned}
$$

Finally, to build a model for $\phi_1 \wedge \phi_2$, we need to construct two bijections f_1 and f_2 such that $f_1(e_4) = f_2(e_2)$ and $f_1[\{e_5, e_6\}] = f_2[\{e_1, e_3\}]$. This is always possible in this decision procedure, because we constrain the sizes of the Venn regions of shared variables to be equal. Intuitively, the freedom in the construction for this example comes from the fact that when we merge the models, the overlapping between C or D and A is unconstrained: we can choose to map either e_5 or e_6 to the same element as e_1, in which case either C or D will share an element with A. So one possible model for ϕ is $A = \{e_1\}, B = \{e_2\}, C = \{e_1, e_2\}, D = \{e_3\}$. (Here we chose the identity function for f_1.) Note that this model also satisfies the property of models described in Lemma 1, since, in this interpretation, $A \neq C$ and $A \neq D$.

3.3   Hypertree Decompositions

In general, and as in the previous example, the constraints ϕ_i in Theorem 3 can contain top-level conjunctions. It is thus in principle possible to decompose them further. In this section, we introduce a hypergraph representation of constraints from which it is straightforward to apply the decision procedure presented above recursively.

Definition 4 (Hypertree Decomposition). *Let ϕ be a QFBAPA formula and let $V = \mathrm{vars}(\phi)$. Let $\phi_1, \ldots, \phi_n$ be top-level conjuncts of ϕ and $V_1, \ldots, V_n$ the sets of variables appearing in them, respectively. We assume without loss of generality that $V_i \neq V_j$ for $i \neq j$. (If two constraints ϕ_i and ϕ_j have the same set of variables, consider instead the constraint $\phi_i \wedge \phi_j$.) Let $\mathbf{V}$ denote $\{V_1, \ldots, V_n\}$. Let $\mathcal{H} = (\mathbf{V}, \mathbf{E})$ be a hypergraph on the set of sets of variables $\mathbf{V}$ (so $\mathbf{E} \subseteq 2^{\mathbf{V}}$). Let $l : \mathbf{E} \to 2^V$ be a labeling function that associates to each hyperedge a subset of the set variables of ϕ (that subset need not be one of V_i). We call $\mathcal{H}$ a hypertree decomposition of ϕ, if the following properties hold:*

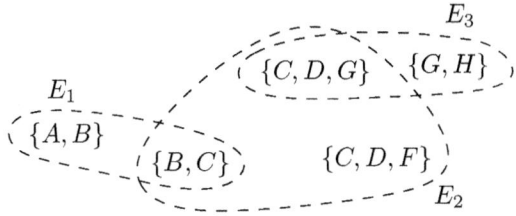

Fig. 3. A hypertree decomposition of (1). The labeling is given by: $l(E_1) = \{B\}$, $l(E_2) = \{C, D\}$, $l(E_3) = \{G\}$.

$(H1)$ $\forall V_i, V_j$. $V_i \cap V_j \neq \emptyset \implies \exists E \in \boldsymbol{E}$. $V_i \in E \wedge V_j \in E \wedge (V_i \cap V_j) \subseteq l(E)$

$(H2)$ $\forall E \in \boldsymbol{E}, \forall V \in \boldsymbol{V}$. $V \in E \iff V \cap l(E) \neq \emptyset$

$(H3)$ $\mathcal{H}$ is acyclic[1]

Property $(H1)$ states that two nodes that share at least one variable must be connected with an hyperedge whose label contains at least their shared variables, and Property $(H2)$ states that a node is contained in a hyperedge if and only if the label of that hyperedge shares at least one set variable with the node. Note that a formula ϕ admits in general many distinct hypertree decompositions. For instance, the hypergraph $\mathcal{H} = (\boldsymbol{V}, \boldsymbol{E})$ with a single hyperedge $E = \boldsymbol{V}$ and $l(E) = \mathsf{vars}(\phi)$ always satisfies Definition 4. To illustrate hypertree decompositions, consider the (unsatisfiable) formula

$$|A \cup B| \leq 3 \wedge C \subseteq B \wedge |(C \cap D) \setminus F| = 2 \wedge |(C \cap G) \setminus D| = 2 \wedge H \subseteq G \quad (1)$$

If we number the conjuncts from 1 to 5, we have $V_1 = \{A, B\}$, $V_2 = \{B, C\}$, $V_3 = \{C, D, F\}$, $V_4 = \{C, D, G\}$, $V_5 = \{G, H\}$. Figure 3 shows a possible hypertree decomposition of (1). The intuition behind hypertree decompositions is that hyperedges represent set of constraints, and that models for these sets need to agree only on the variables they share in their common nodes.

Reduction to integer arithmetic from hypertrees. We show now how to adapt the decision procedure presented at the end of Section 3.2 to hypertree decompositions. We proceed as follows: for each set of set variables V_i (each node in the hypertree), we introduce integer variables for all regions $\mathsf{venn}(V_i)$. Then, for each hyperedge E, we add variables for the regions $\mathsf{venn}(l(E))$. Finally, for each node V_i and each hyperedge E such that $V_i \in l(E)$, we constrain the sums of variables describing the same Venn regions to be equal. For each $v \in \mathsf{venn}(V_i \cap l(E))$, we generate the constraint:

---

[1] We define as a cycle any set of at least two hyperedges such that there exists a node reachable from itself by traversing all hyperedges in the set. This implies in particular that no two hyperedges intersect on more that one node. Note that this is more restrictive than the definition of a hypertree as a hypergraph that admits a tree as a host graph.

$$\sum_{\substack{v_1 \in \mathsf{venn}(V_i) \\ \text{s.t.} v_1 \subseteq v}} k_{V_i}(v_1) = \sum_{\substack{v_2 \in \mathsf{venn}(l(E)) \\ \text{s.t.} v_2 \subseteq v}} k_{l(E)}(v_2)$$

where $k_{V_i}(\cdot)$ and $k_{l(E)}(\cdot)$ denote the integer variable representing a Venn region in the naming scheme for the Venn regions of V_i and $l(E)$, respectively.

This decision procedure has the same worst-time complexity as the one presented in Section 3.1; indeed, it is possible to construct a formula ϕ with a hypertree decomposition that leads to a reduction that uses up to 2^{N+1} integer variables, where N is the number of set variables in ϕ. We have found however that the reduction works well in practice (see Section 5).

4   Integration with Z3

We implemented our new decision procedure for QFBAPA constraints based on the results of Section 3 as an extension to the state-of-the-art SMT solver Z3 [14]. In this extension, sets do not range over uninterpreted elements but over the integers. The resulting prover can thus handle constraints such as

$$(S_1 = \{1, 2, 3, 4\} \wedge S_2 \subseteq S_1 \wedge S_2 \neq \emptyset) \implies |S_2| \in S_1$$

and such as our example from the introduction. Although we are thus in effect performing non-disjoint theory combination, we were able to implement our techniques using only the mechanism of theory plugin extensions to interact with the prover. Because such extensions can add arbitrary axioms (i.e. that are not restricted to theory elements) to the logical context of Z3 at any time, this was indeed not a major limitation. We wrote our extension in Scala and used the Java Native Interface [12] to access the C API of Z3[2]. We did not observe any significant overhead in the forwarding of function calls from and to the Java virtual machine.

Reduction to the integers. We handle constraints on sets with cardinalities by reducing them to integer linear arithmetic using the translation presented in Section 3.3. Assume for now a fixed naming of Venn regions (we describe below how we maintain a hypertree and thus a naming in the presence of incremental reasoning). For each set constraint $S_1 \subseteq S_2$ or $S_1 = S_2$, we add an axiom constraining the integer representation of the set variables in the atom. For instance, using the naming of Venn regions in Figure 2, we would add for the constraint $B \cup C \subseteq D$ the implication $B \cup C \subseteq D \implies k_7 + k_8 + k_{10} = 0$. Similarly, for each cardinality term $|S|$, we add an axiom expressing the cardinality in terms of integer variables. Using the same naming as above, we would for instance add for the term $|C \setminus B|$ the equality $|C \setminus B| = k_8 + k_{12}$. These axioms enforce that whichever boolean value the SMT solver assigns to the set predicate, it will be forced to maintain for the integer variables an assignment that is consistent with the constraints on the sizes of Venn regions.

---

[2] Our Scala interface to Z3 is available at http://lara.epfl.ch/dokuwiki/jniz3

Incremental introduction of Venn regions. Our theory extension receives messages from the core solver whenever a constraint on sets or an application of the cardinality operator is added to the logical context. We maintain at all times a hypertree decomposition $\mathcal{H}$ of the conjunction of all constraints that are on the stack. Whenever a new constraint ϕ_i is pushed to the stack, we apply the following steps:

1. We compute $V_i = \mathsf{vars}(\phi_i)$.
2. If there is a node in $\mathcal{H}$ labeled with V_i, we use the naming of Venn regions in that node to generate the axiom expressing the reduction of ϕ_i and skip the following steps.
3. Else we introduce a new node V_i and we create fresh integer variables for each region of $\mathsf{venn}(V_i)$.
4. For each node V_j in $\mathcal{H}$ such that $V_i \cap V_j \neq \emptyset$, we add a hyperedge $E = \{V_i, V_j\}$ labeled with $l(E) = V_i \cap V_j$.
5. In the new graph, we collapse any introduced cycle as follows: let $E_1, \ldots, E_n$ be the hyperedges that participate in the cycle. We introduce a new hyperedge E labeled with $\bigcup_{i \in \{1,\ldots,n\}} l(E_i)$ and whose content is the union of the contents of $E_1, \ldots, E_n$. We then remove from the graph the edges E_1 to E_n.
6. For each newly created edge E in the obtained, acyclic, hypergraph we introduce fresh integer variables to denote the regions of $\mathsf{venn}(l(E))$.
7. Finally, for each node in the new edge, we constrain the sums of integer variables that denote the same Venn regions to be equal.

Note that all introduced integer variables are additionally constrained to be non-negative. When constraints are popped from the stack:

1. We remove from $\mathcal{H}$ all nodes that were created for these constraints, if any.
2. For each hyperedge E that contained at least one removed variable, we check whether it now contains only one node, in which case we delete it.

Removing such nodes and edges provides two benefits: constraints added in a different search branch may generate a smaller (less connected) hypertree, and Z3 has the opportunity to remove from its clause database reduction axioms that have become useless. We efficiently detect cycles by maintaining equivalence classes between nodes that correspond to the connected components in the hypertree. We can then check, when we introduce a new hyperedge, whether it connects nodes from different equivalence classes, which corresponds to our definition of a cycle. We use a union-find data-structure to maintain the equivalence classes.

Interpreted elements. When considering sets in combination with other theories, it is natural to allow the use of the predicate $e \in S$ denoting that a given set contains a particular (interpreted) element, or constant sets $\{e_1, e_2\}$. For the simplicity of the argument, we assume here that all sets have the same underlying element sort $\mathbb{E}$. We handle interpreted elements such as e, e_1 and e_2 by adding to the logic two connecting functions, $\mathsf{singleton} : \mathbb{E} \to \mathsf{Set}$ and $\mathsf{element} : \mathsf{Set} \to \mathbb{E}$. We create for each interpreted element that appears in a predicate $e \in S$ or in a constant set a singleton set term $\mathsf{singleton}(e)$, and we add the axioms $|\,\mathsf{singleton}(e)\,| = 1$ and $\mathsf{element}(\mathsf{singleton}(e)) = e$. So singleton is interpreted as a constructor that builds a singleton set from an element, and element as a function that for singleton sets computes its element, and that is uninterpreted otherwise. We can thus rewrite $e \in S$ as $\mathsf{singleton}(e) \subseteq S$ and constant sets as unions of singletons. The connecting functions are used to propagate equalities: when two elements are found to be equal in their theory, congruence closure will conclude that their singleton sets (if they exist) need to be equal as well. The other direction is covered in the following paragraph.

Communicating equalities. The reduction to integer linear arithmetic ensures that if two sets must be equal, then the sizes of the Venn regions of their symmetric difference will be constrained to be 0. However, for completeness we also need to detect that if their symmetric difference is forced to be empty by some integer constraints, then the sets must be equal. To enforce this, we could, for each pair of set variables (S_1, S_2) generate an axiom equivalent to

$$(\,|\,S_1 \setminus S_2\,| = \emptyset \wedge |\,S_2 \setminus S_1\,| = \emptyset) \implies S_1 = S_2$$

where the cardinality terms would be rewritten using the naming of set regions for S_1 and S_2. However, because not every pair of set variable appears together in some constraint, our hypertree decomposition does not in general define names for the intersections of any variables S_1 and S_2. Our solution is to generate such axioms for all pairs of variables that appear together in a node of the hypergraph. Additionally, for each set variable we generate the axiom $|\,S\,| = 0 \iff S = \emptyset$. We argue that, for sets that range over an infinite domain (such as the integers), this is sufficient: Consider two set variables S_1 and S_2 that do not appear in a common node. From lemmas 1 and 2, we have that as long as S_1 or S_2 is non-empty or distinct from a shared set variable, there exists a model in which $S_1 \neq S_2$. Both cases are covered by the introduced axioms. Indeed, even if the two variables are equal to a different shared variable, by transitivity of the equality, their equality will be propagated. We thus have the property that any two set variables that are not constrained to be equal can be set to be distinct in a model. This is consistent with the theory combination approach taken in Z3 [13]. When we construct the hypergraph as presented above, we also make sure that all terms representing singleton sets (that is, applications of the $\mathsf{singleton}(\cdot)$ function) share a common hyperedge, even if they don't syntactically appear in a common constraint. This ensures that all equalities between finite sets induced by cardinality constraints will result in equalities between their elements through Z3's congruence closure algorithm, and will be communicated to the proper theory solver.

5   Evaluation

We evaluated our implementation using benchmarks from two verification sources. Figure 4 shows our experimental results[3].

---

[3] All benchmarks and the set of axioms we used are available from
http://lara.epfl.ch/~psuter/vmcai2011/

Benchmark	status	sets	cons.	Venn regs.	prop.	prev. best	our time
CADE07-1	unsat	1	1	2	1.00	< 0.1	< 0.1
CADE07-2	unsat	2	1	4	1.00	< 0.1	< 0.1
CADE07-2a	unsat	6	5	28	0.44	1.8	< 0.1
CADE07-2b	sat	6	5	28	0.44	< 0.1	< 0.1
CADE07-3	unsat	2	1	4	1.00	< 0.1	< 0.1
CADE07-3a	unsat	5	4	16	0.50	0.4	< 0.1
CADE07-3b	sat	5	4	16	0.50	< 0.1	< 0.1
CADE07-4	unsat	5	5	80	2.50	0.5	< 0.1
CADE07-4b	sat	5	5	76	2.38	0.1	< 0.1
CADE07-5	unsat	7	5	168	1.31	13.6	< 0.1
CADE07-5b	sat	7	5	168	1.31	0.4	< 0.1
CADE07-6	unsat	6	6	32	0.50	0.4	< 0.1
CADE07-6a	unsat	16	20	596	0.01	> 100	0.3
CADE07-6b	sat	16	22	1120	0.02	0.8	0.3
CADE07-6c	sat	16	20	596	0.01	0.9	0.4
listContent	sat	3	4	14	1.75		< 0.1
listContent-ax	unsat	4	5	16	1.00		< 0.1
listReverse	sat	6	6	26	0.41		< 0.1
listReverse-ax	unsat	9	11	308	0.60		0.2
setToList	sat	6	8	76	1.19		< 0.1
setToList-ax	unsat	7	9	114	0.89		< 0.1
listConcat	sat	11	19	54	0.03		0.2
listConcat-ax	unsat	28	33	268	< 0.01		0.4
treeContent	sat	4	5	24	1.50		0.1
treeContent-ax	unsat	6	7	28	0.44		0.1
treeMirror	sat	6	6	20	0.31		< 0.1
treeMirror-ax	unsat	11	11	572	0.28		0.3
treeToList	sat	8	10	24	0.09		0.1
treeToList-ax	unsat	29	35	2362	< 0.01		1.7

Fig. 4. Experimental results. The column "sets" is the number of set variables, "cons." is the maximal number of constraints on the stack, "Venn regs." is the maximal number of distinct Venn regions created from the hypertree structure, "prop." is the proportion of created Venn regions compared to the 2^N naive naming scheme and is a measure of the efficiency of our decomposition technique, "prev. best" indicates the previously best solving time, and "time" is the running time with the new implementation. All times are in seconds. The experiment was conducted using a 2.66GHz Quad-core machine, and using Z3 2.11.

Jahob benchmarks. We included all benchmarks from [10] in our evaluation. These formulas express verification conditions generated with the Jahob system [7] for programs manipulating (abstractions of) pointer-based data-structures such as linked lists. In [10], the benchmarks were used to compare the efficiency of the sparse encoding into linear arithmetic with the explicit one (as in Section 3.1). We indicate for these benchmarks the previously best time using either method. It is important to note that it was shown in [10] that the two methods were complementary: the sparse encoding outperformed the explicit one for sat instances and vice-versa. We do not claim that the absolute difference in time is a significant measure of our algorithmic improvements, but rather provide these numbers to illustrate that our new techniques can be used to efficiently handle sat and unsat instances.

Functional programs. We also included new benchmarks consisting of verification conditions for Scala functions without side effects. Additionally to sets and elements, these examples contain constraints on algebraic data types and functions symbols. Each verification condition contains at least one (recursive) function call. We first treated these function symbols as uninterpreted. We then used universally quantified axioms to define the interpretation of the functions and used Z3's pattern-based instantiation mechanism to apply the axioms. Without the axioms, all formulas were invalid (sat), and with the axioms, they were all proved valid.

To the best of our knowledge, the only previous implementation that is complete for QFBAPA and reports performance on benchmarks is [10]. We show significant improvement over the existing benchmarks. While results in [10] were unable to handle unsatisfiable formulas with 16 variables, we report success on formulas with 29 variables, which were automatically generated from verification of functional programs.

6   Related Work

The complexity of QFBAPA was settled in [10] to be NP. The complexity of the quantified case as well as the first quantifier elimination implementation was described in [8]. The decidability of the logic itself dates back at least to [3].

The work of combination of QFBAPA with other decidable theories has so far included implementation as part of the Jahob system [7], which requires manual decomposition steps to be complete [20, 21]. A complete methodology for using QFBAPA as a glue logic for non-disjoint combination was introduced in [17], with additional useful cases introduced in [16, 18], some of which are surveyed in [9]. The combination method we describe is simple, in that it does not require exchanging set constraints between different theories that share sets of objects. In that sense, it corresponds to the multi-sorted combination setup of [19], which introduces a non-deterministic procedure that was, to the best of our knowledge, not implemented. Combinations of theories that have finite domains has been explored in [6]. In this paper we have focused on combinations with integers, but we believe that our approach can be adapted to more general cases.

Our decomposition of formulas was inspired by the algorithms for bounded (hyper)tree width from constraint satisfaction [4], although we do not directly follow any particular decomposition algorithm from the literature. These algorithms are typically used to reduce subclasses of NP-hard constraint satisfaction problems over finite domains to polynomial-time algorithms. To the best of our knowledge, they have not been applied before to satisfiability of sets with cardinality operators. Our results suggest that this approach is very promising and we expect it to extend to richer logics containing QFBAPA, such as [18].

Research in program analysis has used cardinality constraints in abstract domains [5, 15], typically avoiding the need for a full-fledged QFBAPA decision procedure. Thanks to our efficient implementation of QFBAPA, we expect that precise predicate abstraction approaches [1] will now also be able to use QFBAPA constraints.

Acknowledgments. We thank Nikolaj Bjørner and Leonardo de Moura for their help with Z3.

References

1. Beyer, D., Henzinger, T.A., Jhala, R., Majumdar, R.: The software model checker Blast. STTT 9(5-6), 505–525 (2007)
2. Dewar, R.K.: Programming by refinement, as exemplified by the SETL representation sublanguage. ACM TOPLAS (July 1979)
3. Feferman, S., Vaught, R.L.: The first order properties of products of algebraic systems. Fundamenta Mathematicae 47, 57–103 (1959)
4. Gottlob, G., Greco, G., Marnette, B.: HyperConsistency width for constraint satisfaction: Algorithms and complexity results. In: Lipshteyn, M., Levit, V.E., McConnell, R.M. (eds.) Graph Theory, Computational Intelligence and Thought. LNCS, vol. 5420, pp. 87–99. Springer, Heidelberg (2009)
5. Gulwani, S., Lev-Ami, T., Sagiv, M.: A combination framework for tracking partition sizes. In: POPL, pp. 239–251 (2009)
6. Krstić, S., Goel, A., Grundy, J., Tinelli, C.: Combined satisfiability modulo parametric theories. In: Grumberg, O., Huth, M. (eds.) TACAS 2007. LNCS, vol. 4424, pp. 602–617. Springer, Heidelberg (2007)
7. Kuncak, V.: Modular Data Structure Verification. Ph.D. thesis, EECS Department, Massachusetts Institute of Technology (February 2007)
8. Kuncak, V., Nguyen, H.H., Rinard, M.: Deciding Boolean Algebra with Presburger Arithmetic. J. of Automated Reasoning (2006)
9. Kuncak, V., Piskac, R., Suter, P., Wies, T.: Building a calculus of data structures. In: Barthe, G., Hermenegildo, M. (eds.) VMCAI 2010. LNCS, vol. 5944, pp. 26–44. Springer, Heidelberg (2010)
10. Kuncak, V., Rinard, M.: Towards Efficient Satisfiability Checking for Boolean Algebra with Presburger Arithmetic. In: Pfenning, F. (ed.) CADE 2007. LNCS (LNAI), vol. 4603, pp. 215–230. Springer, Heidelberg (2007)
11. Lam, P., Kuncak, V., Rinard, M.: Generalized typestate checking for data structure consistency. In: Cousot, R. (ed.) VMCAI 2005. LNCS, vol. 3385, pp. 430–447. Springer, Heidelberg (2005)
12. Liang, S.: The Java Native Interface: Programmer's Guide and Specification. Addison-Wesley, Reading (1999)
13. de Moura, L., Bjørner, N.: Model-based theory combination. Electronic Notes in Theoretical Computer Science 198(2), 37–49 (2008)
14. de Moura, L., Bjørner, N.: Z3: An efficient SMT solver. In: Ramakrishnan, C.R., Rehof, J. (eds.) TACAS 2008. LNCS, vol. 4963, pp. 337–340. Springer, Heidelberg (2008)
15. Pérez, J.A.N., Rybalchenko, A., Singh, A.: Cardinality abstraction for declarative networking applications. In: Bouajjani, A., Maler, O. (eds.) CAV 2009. LNCS, vol. 5643, pp. 584–598. Springer, Heidelberg (2009)

16. Suter, P., Dotta, M., Kuncak, V.: Decision procedures for algebraic data types with abstractions. In: POPL (2010)
17. Wies, T., Piskac, R., Kuncak, V.: Combining theories with shared set operations. In: Ghilardi, S., Sebastiani, R. (eds.) FroCoS 2009. LNCS, vol. 5749, pp. 366–382. Springer, Heidelberg (2009)
18. Yessenov, K., Kuncak, V., Piskac, R.: Collections, cardinalities, and relations. In: Barthe, G., Hermenegildo, M. (eds.) VMCAI 2010. LNCS, vol. 5944, pp. 380–395. Springer, Heidelberg (2010)
19. Zarba, C.G.: Combining sets with integers. In: Armando, A. (ed.) FroCos 2002. LNCS (LNAI), vol. 2309, pp. 103–116. Springer, Heidelberg (2002)
20. Zee, K., Kuncak, V., Rinard, M.: Full functional verification of linked data structures. In: PLDI, pp. 349–361 (2008)
21. Zee, K., Kuncak, V., Rinard, M.: An integrated proof language for imperative programs. In: PLDI, pp. 338–351 (2009)

Author Index